Positive Behavioral Support

Positive Behavioral Support

*Including People
with Difficult Behavior
in the Community*

edited by

Lynn Kern Koegel, Ph.D.

Robert L. Koegel, Ph.D.

Glen Dunlap, Ph.D.

·P·A·U·L·H·
BROOKES
PUBLISHING CO ®

Baltimore • London • Sydney

·P A U L·H·
BROOKES
PUBLISHING CO ®

Paul H. Brookes Publishing Co.
Post Office Box 10624
Baltimore, Maryland 21285-0624
www.brookespublishing.com

Typeset by Brushwood Graphics, Inc., Baltimore, Maryland.
Manufactured in the United States of America by
The Maple Press Co., York, Pennsylvania.

Fifth printing, April 2006.

Photographs in this book and on the covers are courtesy of Mary Baker, Stephen M. Camarata, Meme Eno-Hieneman, Lise Fox, Lynn Kern Koegel, David Lutz, Cheryl Nickels, Karen Pierce, Smita Shukla, Annette Smith, and James Yerman.

Library of Congress Cataloging-in-Publication Data

Positive behavioral support : including people with difficult behavior in the
   community / edited by Lynn Kern Koegel, Robert L. Koegel, and Glen Dunlap.
     p. cm.
   Includes bibliographical references and index.
   ISBN-13: 978-1-55766-228-6
   ISBN-10: 1-55766-228-2
   1. Problem children—Behavior modification.   2. Mentally handicapped—
   Behavior modification.   3. Problem children—Services for.   4. Mentally
   handicapped—Services for.   I. Koegel, Lynn Kern.   II. Koegel, Robert L.,
   1944–   .   III. Dunlap, Glen.
   HQ773.P67   1996
   362.2—dc20   95-42839
                                                                  CIP

British Library Cataloguing-in-Publication data are available from the British Library.

Contents

Contributors

The Editors

Lynn Kern Koegel, Ph.D., CCC-Speech/Language Pathology, Clinic Director, Autism Research Center, Graduate School of Education, University of California, Santa Barbara, CA 93106-9490

Robert L. Koegel, Ph.D., Director, Autism Research Center, Professor, Educational Psychology and Counseling/Clinical/School Psychology, and Professor, Special Education, Disability, and Risk Studies, Graduate School of Education, University of California, Santa Barbara, CA 93106-9490

Glen Dunlap, Ph.D., Director, Community Development Programs, and Professor, Department of Child and Family Studies, Florida Mental Health Institute, University of South Florida, 13301 Bruce B. Downs Boulevard, Tampa, FL 33612-3899

The Chapter Authors

Richard W. Albin, Ph.D., Specialized Training Program, 1235 University of Oregon, Eugene, OR 97403-1235

Jacki L. Anderson, Ph.D., Department of Educational Psychology, California State University, Hayward, CA 94542

William R. Ard, Jr., Specialized Training Program, 1235 University of Oregon, Eugene, OR 97403-1235

Jon S. Bailey, Ph.D., Department of Psychology, Florida State University, Tallahassee, FL 32306-1051

Wendy Berg, M.A., Division of Developmental Disabilities, University Hospital School, Room 251, Hawkins Drive, University of Iowa, Iowa City, IA 52242

Stephen M. Camarata, Ph.D., Department of Hearing and Speech Sciences, Bill Wilkerson Center, Vanderbilt University, Nashville, TN 37203

Edward G. Carr, Ph.D., Department of Psychology, State University of New York at Stony Brook, Stony Brook, NY 11794-2500

Carol Davis, Ed.D., University of Minnesota, Pattee Hall, 150 Pillsbury Drive S.E., Minneapolis, MN 55455

H. Michael Day, Ph.D., Independent Living Services, 4603 Albion, Boise, ID 83705

Gigi De Vault, M.A., Program Development Services, Box 357925, College of Education, University of Washington, Seattle, WA 98195-7925

K. Mark Derby, Ph.D., Neurobehavior Unit, Department of Behavioral Psychology, Kennedy Krieger Institute, Johns Hopkins University School of Medicine, Baltimore, MD 21205

William L.E. Dussault, J.D., Attorney at Law, 219 E. Galer, Seattle, WA 98102

Kathleen Feeley, M.S., University of Minnesota, Pattee Hall, 150 Pillsbury Drive S.E., University of Minnesota, Minneapolis, MN 55455

K. Brigid Flannery, Ph.D., Specialized Training Program, 1235 University of Oregon, Eugene, OR 97403-1235

Lise Fox, Ph.D., Department of Child and Family Studies, Florida Mental Health Institute, University of South Florida, 13301 N. Bruce B. Downs Boulevard, Tampa, FL 33612-3899

Jay Harding, Ed.S., Division of Developmental Disabilities, University Hospital School, Room 251, Hawkins Drive, University of Iowa, Iowa City, IA 52242

Norris G. Haring, Ph.D., Program Development Services, College of Education, Box 357925, University of Washington, Seattle, WA 98195-7925

Peggy P. Hester, Ph.D., Department of Special Education, George Peabody College, Vanderbilt University, Nashville, TN 37203

Robert H. Horner, Ph.D., Specialized Training Program, 1235 University of Oregon, Eugene, OR 97403-1235

Tiina Itkonen, M.D., Hawaii Department of Education, 3430 Leahi Avenue, Honolulu, HI 96804

Susan Johnston, Ph.D., University of Minnesota, Pattee Hall, 150 Pillsbury Drive S.E., Minneapolis, MN 55455

Ann P. Kaiser, Ph.D., Department of Special Education, George Peabody College, Vanderbilt University, Nashville, TN 37203

Diane Kellegrew, Ph.D., University of Southern California, Department of Occupational Therapy, 1540 Alcazar Street, CHP-133, Los Angeles, CA 90033

Craig H. Kennedy, Ph.D., College of Education, Division of Special Education, 1776 University Avenue, Wist 208, University of Hawaii, Honolulu, HI 96822

Don Kincaid, Ph.D., West Virginia University, UACDD/WVLI, 918 Chestnut Ridge Road, Morgantown, WV 26506

Frank W. Kohler, Ph.D., Allegheny-Singer Research Institute, 320 E. North Avenue, Pittsburgh, PA 15212-4772

Joseph M. Lucyshyn, Ph.D., Specialized Training Program, 1235 University of Oregon, Eugene, OR 97403-1235

Darlene Magito-McLaughlin, M.A., Department of Psychology, State University of New York at Stony Brook, Stony Brook, NY 11794-2500

Mary McEvoy, Ph.D., University of Minnesota, Pattee Hall, 150 Pillsbury Drive S.E., Minneapolis, MN 55455

Gail McGee, Ph.D., Emory Autism Resource Center, Department of Psychiatry and Behavioral Sciences, Emory University School of Medicine, 718 Gatewood Road, Atlanta, GA 30322

Kimberly Mullen, M.A., Department of Psychology, West Virginia University, Morgantown, WV 26506

Cheryl Nickels, 545 North 100 West, Jerome, ID 83338

Stephanie Peck, Ph.D., Department of Special Education, Gonzaga University, Spokane, WA 99258-0001

Karen L. Pierce, M.A., Department of Psychology, University of California, San Diego, CA 92093-0109

Christine E. Reeve, M.A., Department of Psychology, State University of New York at Stony Brook, Stony Brook, NY 11794-2500

Joe Reichle, Ph.D., Department of Communication Disorders, University of Minnesota, 47 Shevlin Hall, 164 Pillsbury Drive S.E., Minneapolis, MN 55455

Todd Risley, Ph.D., Department of Psychology, University of Alaska, 3211 Providence Drive, Anchorage, AK 99508

Elisabeth Rogers, Ph.D., State University of New York, One College Circle, Geneseo, NY 14454-1401

Audrey Russo, M.T.A., Virginia Institute of Developmental Disabilities,Virginia Commonwealth University, Richmond, VA 23284

Wayne Sailor, Ph.D., The University of Kansas, Schiefelbusch Institute for Life Span Studies, 1052 Dole Human Development Center, Lawrence, KS 66045

Laura Schreibman, Ph.D., Department of Psychology, University of California, San Diego, CA 92093-0109

Denise D. Shearer, M.A., Allegheny-Singer Research Institute, Pittsburgh, PA 15212-4772

Aubyn C. Stahmer, Ph.D., Department of Psychology, P.O. Box 200, State University of New York, Cortland, NY 13045

Phillip S. Strain, Ph.D., University of Colorado, School of Education, 1444 Wazee, Denver, CO 32312

Connie C. Taylor, Ph.D., Private Consultant, 9120 Bithlo Lane, Tallahassee, FL 32312

Ann P. Turnbull, Ed.D., Beach Center on Families and Disability, c/o Life Span Institute, 3111 Haworth Hall, University of Kansas, Lawrence, KS 66045

H. Rutherford Turnbull, III, LL.B/J.D., LL.M., Beach Center on Families and Disability, c/o Life Span Institute, 3111 Haworth Hall, University of Kansas, Lawrence, KS 66045

Bobbie J. Vaughn, Ph.D., Department of Child and Family Studies, Florida Mental Health Institute, University of South Florida, 13301 Bruce B. Downs Boulevard, Tampa, FL 33612-3899

David P. Wacker, Ph.D., Division of Developmental Disabilities, University Hospital School, Room 251, Hawkins Drive, University of Iowa, Iowa City, IA 52242

Kathleen Wolff, M.S., University of Minnesota, Pattee Hall, 150 Pillsbury Drive S.E., Minneapolis, MN 55455

Preface

Positive behavioral support refers to the broad enterprise of helping people develop and engage in adaptive, socially desirable behaviors and overcome patterns of destructive and stigmatizing responding. The term typically refers to assistance that is provided for people with developmental, cognitive, or emotional/behavioral disabilities; however, the principles and approaches have much greater generality. Positive behavioral support incorporates a comprehensive set of procedures and support strategies that are selectively employed on the basis of an individual's needs, characteristics, and preferences. These procedures are drawn from the literatures in operant psychology and applied behavior analysis as well as all other disciplines and orientations that offer demonstrable improvements in a person's behavior and manner of living.

Positive behavioral support emerged from the foundation of behavior management in the 1980s and since then has gained converts, credibility, substance, and a growing base of encouraging data (Horner et al., 1990; Meyer & Evans, 1989). It was developed in an effort to help people with disabilities and serious problem behaviors with methods that would be effective in changing undesirable patterns of behavior; respectful of a person's dignity; and successful in promoting a person's capabilities, expanding a person's opportunities, and enhancing the quality of a person's lifestyle. The essential features of positive behavioral support include a grounding in person-centered values; a commitment to outcomes that are meaningful from the perspective of a person's preferred lifestyle; a reliance on individualized, functional assessment; and an appreciation and utilization of multiple interventions and support strategies.

The objectives of a program of support and intervention have a great deal to do with the selection of procedures and the manner with which they are implemented. In the context of positive behavioral support, objectives are geared to improving the way that a person lives, learns, socializes, and participates in community activities. Objectives arise from an appreciation of a person's directions, aspirations, and preferences and of the cultural expectations that are expressed by one's family and social institutions. Objectives always include the establishment of desired repertoires of responding, including those repertoires that are functionally incompatible with occurrences of problem behavior. One of the values that defines positive behavioral support is that interventions should strive to enhance a person's competencies and access to desirable environments, social circumstances, and activities. A value that is equally fundamental is the acknowledgment that all people are to be treated with respect and dignity and that intervention programs must therefore refrain from interactions that are degrading, humiliating, or pain inducing.

The focus on and respect for every person's individuality not only are central values of positive behavioral support but are also indispensable features of assessment and intervention. Functional assessment is a process that produces an understanding of a person's strengths, inclinations, and communication strategies as well as specific knowledge of the stimuli and circumstances that influence problem behavior. The literature documents many categories of support options. A partial list includes 1) the establishment and incorporation of functional communication options; 2) the development of useful and pleasurable recreation skills; 3) revised contingencies of reinforcement and correction; 4) new curricula and activity schedules; 5) the development of self-management skills; 6) training of support personnel; 7) modifications in the delivery of requests and instructions; and 8) health care, exercise, and medical management. In addition, comprehensive behavioral support efforts need to consider significant lifestyle adjustments (e.g., changing jobs, moving to a new residence, entering a new social clique), which can often be the most effective way of altering destructive patterns of responding. A central feature of positive behavioral support is that it offers multiple components to draw upon for individual needs and characteristics.

The perspectives, values, and components that define positive behavioral support are increasingly widespread; however, it is important to recognize that it has not been much more than 10 years since this orientation was first articulated and seriously advanced. Indeed, positive behavioral support remains a dynamic enterprise, with new interventions being defined and incorporated on a regular basis. New demonstrations are being reported, new research is being published, and refined conceptual frameworks are being advanced. These efforts are incorporating more diverse settings and participants, and they are adding important testimony to the generality of the procedures and to the creativity with which procedures can be applied.

There have been many support providers, family members, policy makers, and researchers who have contributed to the development and definition of positive behavioral support. The editors of this volume and many of the contributors are affiliated with one group that has been organized to conduct research and provide training on positive behavioral support since 1987. Funded by the National Institute on Disability and Rehabilitation Research (U.S. Department of Education), the *Research and Training Center on Positive Behavioral Support (RTC-PBS)* operates out of six university locations. The six participating universities are the University of Oregon (Robert H. Horner and Richard W. Albin), the University of California at Santa Barbara (Robert L. Koegel and Lynn Kern Koegel), the University of South Florida (Glen Dunlap), the State University of New York at Stony Brook (Edward G. Carr), the University of Kansas (Wayne Sailor, Doug Guess, and Ann P. Turnbull), and the California State University at Hayward (Jacki L.

Anderson). In addition, numerous other trainers and researchers have collaborated with the project on various investigations, workshops, and conferences.

The RTC-PBS project has contributed over 100 research articles to journals in the areas of developmental disabilities, behavioral disorders, special and general education, psychology, and behavior analysis. Numerous books, book chapters, and monographs have also been published, and project personnel have delivered hundreds of presentations at conferences and conventions. A diverse preservice and in-service training agenda has been pursued, and a major emphasis in training has been invested in the development and support of state training teams (Anderson, Albin, Mesaros, Dunlap, & Morelli-Robbins, 1993), some aspects of which are discussed in Chapter 20 of this volume.

Another major ingredient of the RTC-PBS has been the operation of national conferences focusing on practical and conceptual developments in positive behavioral support. To date, seven conferences have been held nationwide, which have served as an opportunity for thousands of family members and support providers to gain access to the most current information on effective and positive approaches. The conferences have also served as a site for concentrated interactions among some of the leading contributors to practice and research. Speakers at the conference have included RTC-PBS researchers along with numerous experts from other programs who have made important additions to positive behavioral support. The chapters in this volume were solicited from influential authors who have delivered major presentations at one or more of the RTC-PBS national conferences.

The content and organization of this book were selected to depict the expanding and maturing character of positive behavioral support. Some chapters focus exclusively on practical considerations in implementing support programs, while others emphasize new developments in applied research. Some chapters present strategies that apply to young children or to elementary or secondary students, and others present approaches that are most relevant for adults. Some chapters focus on systems issues and the overall design of support programs, and others concentrate on the details of language development or individualized assessment and intervention.

The organization of the book into four sections provides another indication of the comprehensive nature of positive behavioral support. We have chosen four dominant contexts in which positive behavioral support must be provided, and we have identified authors whose work exemplifies important developments in these contexts. Although the sections have a good deal of overlap, they represent distinctive and dynamic arenas of behavioral support activity. Each of the four sections ends with a discussion that establishes a framework within which to reflect on the contributions of the selected chapters.

The first section includes five chapters that address *Family Issues and Family Support*. These chapters include a variety of perspectives and data-based demonstrations that involve effective, practical strategies for helping families address the special challenges of living with serious problem behavior. The second section, *Education Issues*, focuses on support strategies for students who have disabilities and problem behaviors. Included in this section are a discussion of the design of educational systems, a personal description of a mother's efforts to build a desirable educational experience for her son, considerations of training for educational interventionists, and a consideration of legal avenues to appropriate educational supports.

The third section, *Social Inclusion*, presents three chapters and a discussion that address social relationships, social interactions, and the relevance of social inclusion to the subject of behavioral challenges and behavioral support. Social inclusion has come to be regarded as an integral process and outcome consideration in positive behavioral support, and the chapters that make up this section illustrate important perspectives. The final section, *Community Inclusion*, includes contributions that have broad implications for support strategies in diverse community environments. Together, the chapters in this section blend conceptual and methodological advances with practical considerations pertaining to lifestyle arrangements, person-centered planning, and comprehensive training projects.

This book is intended for professionals, students, and all individuals who are concerned with the status of positive behavioral support efforts, its expanding foundation of empirical testimony, and its powerful diversity. We hope that all readers will recognize the features that unite these chapters under the theme of positive behavioral support, including the commitment to person-centered values and comprehensive support alternatives that are individualized and oriented to the development of meaningful outcomes. The essence of positive behavioral support is that it is a human endeavor.

This book is the product of many people. We would like to acknowledge all of the individuals who have worked on the RTC-PBS, all of the students and staff who were involved in the production of the national conferences, and Cindy M. Carter and Josh K. Harrower for their editorial assistance with this book. We are also grateful to all of the chapter authors who shared their expertise at our conferences and who have delivered thoughtful contributions to this volume. And, finally, we are grateful to the parents, researchers, service providers, and administrators who have attended the conferences and who have helped to define current socially meaningful issues of positive behavioral support.

REFERENCES

Anderson, J., Albin, R., Mesaros, R.A., Dunlap, G., & Morelli-Robbins, M. (1993). Issues in providing training to achieve comprehensive behavioral support. In J. Reichle & D. Wacker (Eds.), *Communication and language intervention: Vol. 3. Communicative alternatives to challenging behavior: Integrating functional assessment and intervention strategies* (pp. 363–406). Baltimore: Paul H. Brookes Publishing Co.

Horner, R.H., Dunlap, G., Koegel, R.L., Carr, E.G., Sailor, W., Anderson, J., Albin, R.W., & O'Neill, R.E. (1990). Toward a technology of "nonaversive" behavioral support. *Journal of The Association for Persons with Severe Handicaps, 15,* 125–132.

Meyer, L., & Evans, I.M. (1989). *Nonaversive interventions for behavior problems: A manual for home and community.* Baltimore: Paul H. Brookes Publishing Co.

Positive Behavioral Support

I

Family Issues
and Family Support

1

Parent Education for Prevention and Reduction of Severe Problem Behaviors

Lynn Kern Koegel, Robert L. Koegel,
Diane Kellegrew, and Kimberly Mullen

The literature suggests several systematic avenues for the improvement of interventions for autism and the prevention of the expression of severe problem behaviors through parent involvement. First, including parents as active participants in the delivery of intervention, as opposed to using a solely clinician-provided model, is a time- and cost-efficient means of intervention delivery (Koegel, Glahn, & Nieminen, 1978; Koegel, Schreibman, Britten, Burke, & O'Neill, 1982; Lovaas, Koegel, Simmons, & Long, 1973; Schreibman, Koegel, Mills, & Burke, 1984;

Schreibman, Runco, Mills, & Koegel, 1982). Second, family–professional collaboration and partnerships have been major variables in successful outcomes, and programs that provide families with support, resources, and effective procedures for dealing with the complex difficulties of having a child with a disability can greatly strengthen family functioning (cf. Dunst, Trivette, Starnes, Hamby, & Gordon, 1993). Third, when a gap in communication or collaboration is eliminated, intervention procedures typically have improved service utility and are more likely to prevent or ameliorate problem behaviors and the stressful effects of a disability on the family (cf. Turnbull et al., 1993).

The significance of parent involvement has continued to gain recognition (Peterson & Cooper, 1989; Sloane, Endo, Hawkes, & Jenson, 1991), and the literature has long suggested that only by viewing parents as part of the solution will progress be made in the habilitation process (cf. Schopler, 1971). For children with autism, successful parent education programs have demonstrated increases in efforts to speak and sophistication of speech (Harris, 1986), decreases in inappropriate behaviors (Marcus, Lansing, Andrews, & Schopler, 1978), improved generalization and maintenance of treatment gains (Koegel, Koegel, & Schreibman, 1991; Koegel et al., 1982), and decreases in institutionalization of adolescents with autism (Schopler, Mesibov, De Vellis, & Short, 1981). Such demonstrated benefits of incorporating parents as active participants in the habilitation process have led researchers to focus on the efficiency and effectiveness of parent intervention models. In our clinics, we have focused attention on developing communication and managing behavior through parent education and teacher–parent collaboration for enhancing full-inclusion school programs. This chapter reviews a few programs that have been scientifically documented to promote effective change and reduce or prevent severe problem behaviors from occurring in natural environments such as home and school.

PIVOTAL RESPONDING AND MOTIVATION

One area that may relate to the success of interventions concerns the apparent lack of motivation in children with autism to learn verbal communication (Dunlap, 1984; Dunlap & Koegel, 1980; Koegel & Koegel, 1986). Such lack of motivation is *pivotal* in that it influences large numbers of behaviors. The lack of motivation to communicate may be displayed in mild forms, such as walking away from an individual who attempts to engage the child in a task or interaction, or in more severe forms, such as temper tantrums, aggression, self-injury, or property destruction. Early intervention for individuals with autism focused on punitive procedures to decrease disruptive and interfering behaviors before beginning to teach

The child's selection of items helps to enhance motivation.

target behaviors such as verbal communication. However, the field has shifted toward an emphasis on the interrelationship of these areas (e.g., Crystal, 1987; Koegel, Camarata, & Koegel, 1994; Koegel, Valdez-Menchaca, & Koegel, 1994). Within this perspective, researchers are discussing problems of communication as the primary aspect of autism and other disruptive behaviors as secondary (symptomatic) manifestations. This is demonstrated in functional assessments of disruptive behavior that clearly link a social–communicative function with various disruptive behaviors such as aggression, self-injury, self-stimulatory behavior, and so forth (Carr & Durand, 1985; Durand & Carr, 1987; Durand & Crimmins, 1988; Koegel, Valdez-Menchaca, & Koegel, 1994). Intervention techniques based on functional assessments can dramatically decrease or successfully replace these often severely disruptive behaviors with appropriate communicative behaviors. For example, teaching children to request assistance or attention significantly reduces behaviors such as aggression, tantrums, and self-injury. This reciprocal pattern is also seen when children are taught to request teacher assistance as a functionally equivalent communicative alternative to escape-motivated stereotypic behavior (Durand & Carr, 1987).

These studies and others demonstrate the significance of motivation for verbal communication as a pivotal target behavior. Although typically developing children learn very young that appropriate vocalizations and verbalizations are desirable to a parent and that improved specificity increases the likelihood of reinforcement, children with speech and language impairments may find communication difficult and continue to rely on other patterns of nonverbal communication to get their needs and desires met. At very young ages, these types of nonverbal communicative behaviors are relatively mild (e.g., crying, tantrums); however, they are likely to develop into more serious topographies as the child grows older. Aggression, property destruction, and self-injury are just a few of the more severe problems that evolve if no appropriate equivalent communicative behaviors are learned early.

Rapidly growing databases and professional opinion agree that intervention at a very early age results in more favorable prognoses, and communication is a main target behavior of most successful programs. Logically, early intervention can prevent relatively mild behavior problems from increasing in severity, especially if functional communication is a primary goal. However, one difficulty in teaching speech and language to children with autism is that they often lack adequate motivation to even attempt to learn to communicate. This can be seen at very young ages when the children actively avoid social situations. To overcome this challenge, a number of researchers have successfully targeted motivation as a pivotal behavior to improve communication skills. Some effective techniques include incorporating child choice in relation to stimulus items and conversational topic (Koegel, Dyer, & Bell, 1987), reinforcing attempts rather than using a more narrowly defined shaping contingency under which only strictly defined successive approximations to a target verbalization are reinforced (Koegel, O'Dell, & Dunlap, 1988), interspersing maintenance tasks rather than solely presenting acquisition (new) tasks (Dunlap, 1984), and using naturally reinforcing consequences rather than arbitrary reinforcers. When all these techniques are combined and used in teaching language to children with autism the effects are especially powerful (Koegel, O'Dell, & Koegel, 1987; Laski, Charlop, & Schreibman, 1988).

Table 1 lists the differences between the less effective analog procedures and the natural language paradigm (NLP) (Koegel, O'Dell, & Koegel, 1987). Impressive results also occur when using similar language teaching techniques with other children, such as children with Down syndrome (Hart & Risley, 1980; Warren & Kaiser, 1986; Yoder, Kaiser, & Alpert, 1991), language delays (Camarata & Nelson, 1992), and general developmental disabilities (Cavallero & Bambara, 1982), and with disadvantaged children (Hart & Risley, 1980).

Parents have been shown to be successful at implementing these procedures in the context of their routine interactions in home and commu-

Table 1. Differences between the analog and the natural language paradigm (NLP) procedures

	Analog condition	NLP condition
Stimulus items	a. Chosen by clinician b. Repeated until criterion is met c. Phonologically easy to produce, irrespective of whether they were functional in the natural environment	a. Chosen by child b. Varied every few trials c. Age-appropriate items that can be found in child's natural environment
Prompts	a. Manual (e.g., touch tip of tongue, hold lips together)	a. Clinician repeats item
Interaction	a. Clinician holds up stimulus item; stimulus item not functional within interaction	a. Clinician and child play with stimulus item (i.e., stimulus item is functional within interaction)
Response	a. Correct responses or successive approximations reinforced	a. Looser shaping contingency so that attempts to respond verbally (except self-stimulation) are also reinforced
Consequences	a. Edible reinforcers paired with social reinforcers	a. Natural reinforcer (e.g., opportunity to play with the item) paired with social reinforcers

Adapted from Koegel, O'Dell, and Koegel (1987).

nity settings (Laski et al., 1988). Furthermore, in addition to improving expressive vocabulary and language proficiency, untreated disruptive behavior has been shown to decrease when teaching linguistic skills while incorporating motivational procedures (Koegel, Koegel, & Surratt, 1992). Moreover, when parents are taught to use the paradigm, the serendipitous benefit of reducing parental stress has been demonstrated (Moes, Koegel, & Schreibman, 1994).

Skill Acquisition and Practice Through Daily Routines

One particular feature of the home environment that has a direct impact on the skill acquisition of children is the daily routines of the home (Bronfenbrenner, 1979). Daily routines are the events and rituals that make up everyday life. These may include self-care tasks such as dressing, eating, or bathing. Daily routines may also include rest, exercise, home management, or recreational activities. Daily rituals and routines give purpose and structure to one's life (Clark et al., 1991).

Through the process of daily routines, children are given hundreds of opportunities to practice and develop skills necessary to fully participate in society. These daily opportunities form an efficient method of transmitting the values and practices of the culture in which the child is raised. Precisely because of the dynamic influence of daily routines, these family rituals are important factors in intervention for children with disabilities.

All children benefit from opportunities to practice newly learned skills through the course of daily routines; however, lack of opportunities is a salient issue for children at risk. This may be a particularly serious problem for children with autism who often seem unmotivated to engage in seemingly simple self-help skills. As a result, a cycle may develop in which such children are provided with very few opportunities to engage in self-help skills. Therefore, methods of improving participation in the daily routines that incorporate opportunities are especially important for children with disabilities, as they may need additional learning and reinforcement (cf. Brown et al., 1991).

In contrast to the positive impact of opportunities to perform on skill achievement, lack of opportunities to practice learned skills has been associated with skill decline in children with disabilities. For example, Horner, Williams, and Knobbe (1985) examined the effect of opportunities to perform on the skill maintenance of high school students with severe disabilities. Results indicated that students were more likely to maintain skills targeted by their individualized education program (IEP) for which there were a higher number of opportunities to perform as opposed to those skills with a lower number of opportunities. The authors argue that, when goals and objectives are established, care should be taken that a plan exists for providing regular opportunities to perform a skill once it is learned. In this way, the systematic presentation of opportunities to perform newly learned skills, through the course of daily routines and activities, assists in the maintenance of these skills. Therefore, the types of opportunities available to the child on an everyday basis can be a pivotal factor in the types of skills the child performs and the subsequent maintenance of those skills.

Ecological Variables A number of ecological variables, such as room arrangements, toy availability, and scheduling considerations, can contribute to increased opportunities for children to perform skills. Burnstein (1986) noted that the placement of toys and location of activities in the room affected the child's participation. Many children with disabilities tend to play with toys that are accessible and familiar. Consequently, the physical layout of the room and types of equipment contribute to the opportunities for skill development, thus enhancing learning.

Types of Opportunities Available The child's responsivity has also been related to the types of opportunities for interaction and skill practice offered in the home and other environments. Researchers suggest that the cues given by the child with disabilities are less clear (Dunst, 1983; Yoder, 1987), and as a consequence they may receive fewer opportunities for interaction. For example, Guralnick and Bricker (1987) report that children with Down syndrome do not use materials as effectively during play as do typically developing children, and they fail to use opportunities to involve others in their play. Thus, differences in responsivity displayed by children with disabilities can contribute to decreased opportunities for interaction with both caregivers and peers (Guralnick, 1991; Hupp, 1991; Koegel & Johnson, 1989; Koegel & Koegel, 1987; Schwethelm & Mahoney, 1986).

Involving Parents in Home Interventions

In light of these factors relating to decreased opportunities and the learning potential of daily routines, researchers have begun to systematically address the issue of teaching during daily routines. For example, Stremel et al. (1992) incorporated IEP objectives into the daily routines of children with disabilities. The families determined which daily routines would incorporate an additional therapeutic intervention, such as increasing the child's vocalizations. Frequently, routines involving self-care were chosen because of their daily nature. Specific procedures for accomplishing each step of the targeted intervention were modeled and videotaped by the professional staff. The child's family was encouraged to watch the videotaped example as often as necessary in order to successfully model the technique. Progress toward the goals was monitored on a regular basis by the professional staff.

In another study, Vincent, Salisbury, Laten, and Baumgart (1979) identified potential opportunities in the daily routines and schedule of the home. Intervention priorities were then developed with the family. With this information, parents were guided in considering when and where the child's intervention priorities could be accommodated in the daily schedule. Intervention techniques were modeled and described by the professional staff, but parents also were encouraged to develop and explore their own strategies for achieving the goals. Other members of the family and family support system, such as siblings and child care workers, also were incorporated into the intervention program. Thus, the approach became one of expanding the role of the child's school as a necessary support to the naturally occurring educational opportunities that exist at home.

Although these types of programs have been successful, other such programs have reported limited success. Some areas that seem to limit success may relate to the fact that many programs view the child's development from the perspective of only one point in time (Schafer, Bell, & Spalding, 1987). Furthermore, some programs do not take into account differences in home environments (Handen, Feldman, & Honigman, 1987) or specific parental characteristics that might affect developmental gains, such as parent educational level (Donneley, Doherty, Sheehan, & Whittemore, 1984), cultural variables (e.g., parental beliefs and expectations, religious beliefs, cultural habits and rituals), and child-rearing practices (cf. Weisner, Gallimore, & Jordan, 1993).

Kellegrew (1994) has conducted some preliminary research on families that attempts to address some of these issues. A first study interviewed parents and staff regarding the child's opportunities for and performance of self-care skills in the home. This study indicated that parents' reports corresponded to the staff's reports concerning the child's *ability* to perform these tasks. However, the staff predicted that the children would have fewer *opportunities* to engage in these skills in the home than the parents reported.

A second study attempted to scientifically document, via direct observation, the actual opportunities the children had to perform self-care skills and to see how these observations corresponded with the parental and staff reports. The results of this investigation showed that areas where the child demonstrated greater competency (e.g., self-feeding) were associated with increased opportunities to perform the activities in the home. In contrast, the parents were observed to actually provide fewer opportunities than they reported in areas that were more difficult for their children (e.g., self-dressing).

Based on these findings, parents who provided no opportunities for their child to engage in certain self-care procedures were selected to participate in an intervention program designed to increase the number of opportunities for self-care skills provided to the child. This was accomplished by teaching the parents to self-manage their own behavior related to increasing the number of opportunities they provided to the child to engage in the self-help skill independently. The parents monitored whether the child attempted to perform the skill independently or if the parents assisted the child either verbally or physically. Initially, when self-management forms were given to the parents, intervention consisted of conveying three concepts to the parents. The first related to the importance of self-care, the need to create independence on the part of the child, and the increased likelihood that the child would be more functional in an integrated setting once self-help skills were acquired. The second concept was that the child with the disability was indeed ready to perform the self-help skill and should therefore engage in the activity. The third concept was that the child needed to be provided with the opportunities to practice self-help skills. No direct intervention was provided on skill acquisition; the parent self-management sheets focused only on providing opportunities to engage in the target behavior and monitoring the degree of assistance the parents provided. The majority of the families who participated demonstrated immediate increases in the number of opportunities for self-care provided for their children. In addition, only when the children were provided with such opportunities did they improve in skill ability, eventually being able to complete the self-help skill completely independently.

A final phase in Kellegrew's (1994) study was to explore possible variables relating to how parents construct self-care routines and to why opportunities may not be provided to some children. Three major themes grew out of these assessments. First, many cultural beliefs (e.g., the school should teach the skill; the child has a disability and therefore is less capable) influenced the number of opportunities that parents provided. The second area that limited opportunities concerned ecological limitations (e.g., time constraints). The third area related to the parents' invalid perceptions of their child's skill capabilities (e.g., underestimating the child's ability). The results of this study suggested that many children with disabilities were not provided with opportunities to perform self-care skills for a variety of reasons. However, once parent education programs were implemented that resulted in increases in opportunities, most of the children were actually capable of performing the self-help skills.

These studies, at minimum, suggest the importance of assessing children's opportunities to practice skills before designing elaborate skill development programs. Interviews may be a simple way to assess and normalize the opportunities provided during everyday activities (Bailey & McWilliams, 1990; Winton, 1990). Within a prevention framework, the goals of early intervention are considered in terms of enhancing typical development, thus minimizing developmental delays rather than intervening to remediate delays. With an increased interest in early intervention in terms of prevention (Shonkoff, Hauser-Cram, Krauss, & Upshur, 1988; Simeonsson, 1991), further research into the notion that the child's skill performance can be enhanced by simply supporting the family's participation in more normalized routines is particularly appealing.

Functional Analysis

In addition to teaching general self-care and language skills in the context of parent education, we have studied the feasibility of using a consultation model whereby parents are taught to functionally assess their child's disruptive behavior by identifying setting events, antecedents, and consequences that influence a behavior, and then hypothesizing as to the function the behavior is serving (also see Chapter 3 for home programs using functional analysis). There were several reasons that parents were chosen to perform the functional analysis. First, when significant others in a child's natural environment can be taught to accurately conduct a reliable and valid assessment, there exists the possibility for ongoing, systematic study of behavior (Handleman, Powers, & Harris, 1984). Individuals who interact with a person with developmental disabilities on a regular basis are able to consider the needs of the entire family system (cf. Foster, Berger, & McLean, 1981), and thus, intervention programs may be designed that have a high probability of conforming with individual and idiosyncratic family values (e.g., child-rearing philosophies, family priorities, family members' interrelationships) and circumstances (e.g., economic, cultural, religious). Second, many parents are able to provide "round-the-clock" intervention (Koegel et al., 1982; Koegel et al., 1991), unlike professionals who see the child relatively infrequently. In addition, the potential for more valid data collection exists, as parents have access to the child in natural environments for many more hours than would a professional. Such a comprehensive perspective may be particularly useful in situations that are not straightforward in terms of identifying a single behavior with a single controlling variable, such as when topographically different behaviors are functionally related or when behaviors have multiple maintaining variables. Finally, it is logical that when a parent's input is valued and incorporated into the development of an intervention procedure, the likelihood that the replacement behavior will fit into the family's unique circumstances and thus be taught, reinforced, and maintained is enhanced. Developing intervention programs in isolation, without coordination and cooperation, is not likely to result in a positive difference in the child's life or in the overall quality of family life (Mullen & Frea, 1995; Turnbull et al., 1993).

All of the children who participated in this program were diagnosed with autism, lived in a home with their parents or grandparents, demonstrated aggression and other disruptive behaviors, and resided in a different city (at least 45 minutes away from the clinic). The first phase of the study focused on teaching the parents how to functionally assess the child's problem behavior. The goal of the assessments was to collect ongoing information in home and community settings using a functional analysis (e.g., Frea, Koegel, & Koegel, 1993; O'Neill, Horner, Albin, Storey, & Sprague, 1990). The caregivers met on a weekly basis in the clinic for 1-hour sessions with a staff member. During the initial sessions the parents were familiarized with the data recording sheets (Figure 1). The following five measures were then recorded by the parents in the home and community:

1. The topography of the disruptive behavior (e.g., hit, threw toy, tore book)
2. The date, time, and location of the behavior
3. The antecedent of the behavior
4. The consequence of the behavior
5. The function of the behavior as perceived by the parent

During the 1-hour clinic session, a staff member independently recorded data in an attempt to verify the accuracy of the recording and to provide feedback to the caregiver when necessary.

Following this type of data collection, parents typically are able to identify the function of the behavior quite rapidly (ranging from a few days to several weeks). Once the function of the behavior was identified,

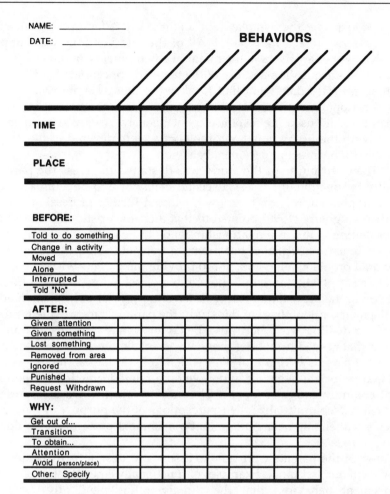

Figure 1. Sample data sheet for functional analysis. This particular data sheet was used by parents to collect data on their children's behaviors in community settings.

parents and staff worked together to identify a behavior to focus on during intervention, based on the perceived function. The target behavior selected was typically the most frequent or the most disruptive to family life. Following selection of a target behavior, the parent–professional team developed an intervention plan. Functionally equivalent communicative utterances were chosen based on the child's linguistic functioning level and the caregivers' determination that a phrase would fit into their daily living routines. For example, one child who lived with his grandmother and who was exhibiting severe aggression in order to obtain her attention was taught to say, "Look, Nana," to gain her attention. Another 3-year-old child who was repeatedly aggressive toward other children when he

wanted to engage them in play was taught to say, "Play" along with a desired activity (e.g., "Play ball"). All of the interventions were implemented by the caregivers in their natural environments. In order to assess
each child's acquisition and use of the targeted appropriate behavior, the
parents recorded data regarding 1) when the child was prompted to use
the functionally equivalent communicative response, and 2) instances
when the child used the response spontaneously. Weekly sessions in the
clinic with the professional and the family were devoted to the child's
practice of the target replacement behavior.

The third phase of the study was designed to assess the parents'
ability to functionally assess a second behavior and develop an intervention plan entirely on their own, without further professional assistance. Dougherty (1990) points out that a characteristic of professional
consultation is that the relationship tends to be collaborative and temporary in nature. A goal of our program was not to simply deal with individual problem behaviors, but to provide the parents with a skill that
could be applied to an indefinite number of behaviors in need of remediation in the present and future. Interestingly, prior to implementation
of the intervention phase of this study, the parents' most frequent procedure for dealing with disruptive behavior was to administer punish-
ments that ranged from brief time-outs to spankings. We wanted to provide the parents with a tool with which to hypothesize the function of
an inappropriate behavior and develop a related functionally equivalent communicative response. Thus, these families were essentially
helped to reconceptualize their perceptions of the purpose of their children's challenging behaviors so that punishment procedures would not
be required.

All of the parents were able to assess and design further interventions without assistance. Examples of functionally equivalent effective replacement behaviors that the caregivers independently designed
included saying, "I'm done," based on the hypothesis that the child was
throwing and spitting food when he or she was finished eating and
wanted the plate removed, and saying, "Can I do something else now?",
based on the hypothesis that disruptive behavior occurred when the child
was bored playing in a particular game or activity.

As a whole, the results of this project demonstrated two major
points. First, it replicated previous research showing that functional assessment could facilitate the design of effective individualized intervention programs (e.g., Carr & Durand, 1985; Cooper, Wacker, Sasso,
Reimers, & Donn, 1990; Mace, Page, Ivancic, & O'Brian, 1986). Second, although parents have been incorporated as adjuncts and intervention
providers in the implementation of functional analysis (Cooper et al.,
1990), this research extended the role of parents, demonstrating that they

can learn to effectively and independently assess their child's behavior and subsequently develop and teach a functionally equivalent replacement behavior.

INDEPENDENT FUNCTIONING

Although the benefits of procedures designed to improve motivation and teach functional communication have had quite a significant effect both on improving language skills and decreasing inappropriate and disruptive behaviors (e.g., Koegel, Koegel, & Surratt, 1992), the need to address the child's independence remains an area warranting attention. Many of the existing parent intervention programs designed to teach communication and other skills to children posit the parent as the primary intervention agent, and the children frequently become overly dependent on their parents, often exhibiting newly learned behaviors only in their presence. To deal with this problem, researchers have concentrated efforts on developing programs to increase independent responding and communication through the use of self-management and child-initiated language-learning strategies.

Child Self-Management

Self-management as a pivotal behavior taught in the context of parent education was developed to reduce the need for constant parental vigilance and to increase the child's independence. Self-management has been shown to be effective with a variety of populations including children without disabilities (Broden, Hall, & Mitts, 1971; Drabman, Spitalnic, & O'Leary, 1973), people with mild to moderate mental retardation (Gardner, Cole, Berry, & Nowinski, 1983; Horner & Brigham, 1979), and children with learning disabilities (Dunlap, Dunlap, Koegel, & Koegel, 1991). For children with autism, preliminary research is suggesting that self-management is an effective tool to promote the use of newly learned behaviors in the absence of a trained interventionist (Koegel & Koegel, 1990; Koegel, Koegel, Hurley, & Frea, 1992).

The general steps in a self-management program include the following:

1. Operationally defining the target behavior(s)
2. Identifying functional reinforcers for the child to earn
3. Designing a self-monitoring method or device
4. Teaching the child to use the self-monitoring device
5. Fading the use of the self-monitoring device
6. Validating whether the child is using the self-monitoring device in natural environments

We have been teaching self-management in the context of parent education so that parents can apply the procedures to any behaviors they want
to teach their children to perform independently. Following are descriptions of a few self-management programs that have been implemented in
the homes of children with autism with their parents' assistance. Although similar conceptually, self-management programs and procedures
for children who lack expressive language skills and have delayed receptive language require a different set of self-management procedures from
those used for children who are more skilled in this area. Research suggests that pictorial self-management may be most effective for nonverbal
children (Pierce & Schreibman, 1994).

We are currently implementing programs in which parents choose
target behaviors they desire their child to use, and intervention is implemented in the context of self-management. The parents attend weekly sessions in which teaching self-management is practiced, and then throughout the week they implement the procedures in the community setting
they have chosen. For example, one family whose 9-year-old child displayed limited verbal skills chose lunch packing as a target goal. In this
particular family, the mother worked in the evenings and felt it would be
helpful if her son packed his own lunch. To accomplish this, we drew several pictures including a lunch box, napkin, sandwich, drink, fruit, and
vegetables. Lunch items were pre-cut and placed in a plastic refrigerator
container. We first showed the child one picture, the lunch box, and taught
him to take it out and open it. Next a second picture was added, such as
the sandwich, and the child was taught to take out a sandwich (from a pre-
made batch in the freezer), place it in a plastic sandwich bag, and then put
it in the lunch box. The number of pictures was systematically increased
until the child was able to put all of the items in his lunch box after he was
given the set of cards. To be sure that he was actually self-monitoring and
not simply learning a rote routine, the order of the cards was frequently
changed. This ensured that the child was actually responding independently by attending to each particular card. Similar programs using pictorial self-management have been successfully implemented with nonverbal
children or children with limited verbal skills to complete dressing in the
morning, setting the table, self-care skills in the evening, and so forth.

For children with verbal skills, some behaviors lend themselves more
readily to *event-monitoring* procedures (such as those described above),
and others are more easily monitored through interval recording, where
the child monitors intervals of time in which the behavior is exhibited.
For example, Koegel, Koegel, Hurley, and Frea (1992) increased verbal responsivity following an adult's question using wrist (golf) counters as a
self-monitoring device for the child to monitor verbal response (events).
Children were selected to participate in the study based on their frequent

failure to attempt to answer questions from others. The children were taught to answer the questions, then to press the wrist counter to earn a point following each successful interaction. The number of verbal responses required by the child to receive a self-chosen reward was gradually increased (beginning with one during the first session and ending with several hundred in later sessions). It appeared that when the children were consistently involved in verbal interactions, the fluency of the overall interaction seemed to make the interchange less difficult for them. The results indicated that, in addition to significantly improving the children's responsivity, the children all demonstrated decreases in untreated disruptive behaviors such as aggression, self-stimulation, and self-injury (apparently used for avoidance or escape purposes from the previously discontinuous and confusing verbal interchanges).

Another study (Koegel & Koegel, 1990) demonstrated the use of an *interval* system to self-manage self-stimulatory behavior. In this study, the children wore a watch (purchased at a sports store) with a countdown alarm function. Children were taught to record intervals with the absence of self-stimulatory behavior when the alarm chimed. Initial intervals were very short to ensure success and then were gradually and systematically increased. Ultimately, the system was implemented throughout most of the child's day (e.g., school, other community settings), and the data indicated that this procedure was effective in reducing or eliminating self-stimulatory behavior without the continual presence of an intervention provider.

It should be noted that the major goal of teaching self-management in the context of parent education is to provide parents with the general procedures to design a program relevant to any behavior that may be conducive to change using such a technique. Following acquisition of the procedures involved, parents can implement programs to teach their children independence through self-managing many types of behavior in a variety of environments, such as school, home, the park, and so on.

Self-Initiated Queries

A second area of focus related to child independence concerns child-initiated strategies to evoke language learning from the environment. Acquisition of lexical items and language learning in typical children is often a result of their own initiations, which become increasingly sophisticated over the years. Many of these self-initiations are in the form of direct queries, such as asking questions. In fact, a common utterance during a child's acquisition of his or her first vocabulary words is "that?" (pronounced "dat?"), which is often used while pointing to items (Miller, 1981). This verbalization and nonverbal cue can be a specific prompt for a parent to label the item for the child (Halliday, 1975). Questions become increasingly more sophisticated and increase in number, so that by 4 years of age the typically developing child is using a variety of questions including forms that begin with "what," "where," "whose," "who," and "why."

In contrast to typical language developers, children with autism rarely, if ever, ask questions. Differences during language activities were analyzed by Wetherby and Prutting (1984), who discovered that in addition to emitting fewer utterances, children with autism use communication almost exclusively for protesting (e.g., "Stop it") and requesting (e.g., "Want cookie"). Unlike their peers who frequently requested information (e.g., "What's that?") and often labeled items (e.g., pointing to a doll's foot and saying "foot"), the children with autism *never* requested information, nor did they label items. Thus, these children are at an extreme disadvantage in terms of their ability to verbally gain access to information. To address this problem, we have begun teaching a series of child-initiated utterances and have also assessed the effects of these utterances on language acquisition.

The first question we chose for the child to learn, and the earliest developmental form learned by typical children, was "What's that?" To accomplish this, the child's parent prompted him or her to ask the question. In order to increase the child's motivation to ask the question, initial questions were prompted by hiding highly desired objects in bags, and when the child queried, "What's that?", with regard to the contents of the bag, the parent labeled and then gave the child the highly desired item. Once the child was asking the target question and repeating the label of the item at a high frequency, other less familiar and less desired items were gradually added, and then the bag was removed. The end result was that the children continued to spontaneously ask questions about a variety of unfamiliar items in their various environments. Acquisition of vocabulary was assessed, and the results showed that the children demonstrated rapid gains in vocabulary following implementation of the self-initiated strategy. Furthermore, untreated disruptive behavior spontaneously decreased during the sessions, suggesting that the increased language ability was replacing disruptive behavior as a form of communication.

A second question we targeted was "Where?" and we assessed the children's acquisition of prepositions. To increase the children's motivation to ask the question, their mothers hid desired items in various locations. For example, one child liked gummy bears so his mother hid them in various locations of a tabletop dollhouse. The children were prompted to ask, "Where is it?", then told the location (e.g., the prepositions *in, on, under, behind*). Prior to receiving the item, the children were required to repeat the preposition. As with the first study, all of the children were successful in learning a variety of prepositions and demonstrated generalized spontaneous use of the target question and prepositions.

Teaching child-initiated queries reduces the need for the adult to initiate language-learning interactions. In this photograph, the child's mother has taught her to ask "What's that?" as a child-initiated strategy to increase her expressive vocabulary.

The next child-initiated strategy we addressed was teaching the child to ask, "Whose is it?" to employ the possessive morpheme (e.g., "Daddy's") and to learn the possessive pronouns *yours* and *mine*. To teach *yours* and *mine*, items that were highly desired by the child were selected. The child was then prompted to ask, "Whose is it?" Before the desired item was given to the child, the parent said, "yours," and the child was taught to respond with "mine." Initially, it was necessary to ensure that all of the child's items ("mine") were highly desirable to the child, while all of the parents' items ("yours") were items belonging to the parents but of low interest to the child. The child also was taught to respond with "yours" when the parent said "mine." The possessive morpheme was taught analogously, using items that were highly desired; however, these items were interspersed with items that the child associated with a specific family member. For example, the mothers brought in items such as toys belonging to one of the child's siblings, or a slipper belonging to the father. Following the question "Whose is it?" the mother responded with "It's Teddy's," or "It's Daddy's." The child was required to repeat the possessive form and then was given the item.

While study relating to child independence is still in its infancy, an accumulating database is suggesting that strategies requiring children to serve as their own intervention providers shift some of the responsibility off of the parents. This may have the additional benefit of reducing some of the stress associated with the increased demands related to raising a child with a disability. In short, the use of child-initiated learning strategies is likely to both accelerate learning and provide for reduced stress levels in the family. As such, this area is expected to gain increased research attention in the future.

HOME–SCHOOL COORDINATION

There appears to be little doubt that cooperative partnerships between the home and the school can dramatically raise educational productivity (Walberg, 1984). Changes in the structure of educational systems make such coordination more important than ever. Now that full inclusion is becoming a reality for many children, the need to develop procedures that guarantee success and reduce the possibility of exclusion, due to behavior challenges and academic delays, is critical. However, research suggests that the effects of parent involvement on school achievement are inconsistent and open to question (Keith et al., 1993). Many of the inconsistencies relate to methods of data collection and disparate definitions of what parent involvement actually comprises.

One area of parent involvement that has been of particular interest to researchers is homework. Interestingly, as suggested earlier in this chapter, a number of variables (e.g., socioeconomic status, ethnicity, television time, motivation, gender, previous achievement) may directly or indirectly affect parent involvement in time spent on homework. Although it has not been clearly documented that higher grades are correlated with amount of time dedicated to homework, there is a tendency for those doing more homework to obtain better grades (Tymms, 1992), and there is an increasing consensus that, when carefully planned and programmed, homework can enhance learning in typical developers.

Logically, researchers have begun efforts to address the practice of homework with children with disabilities. Again, this literature has yielded mixed results, with most students showing improvements and some showing regressions when homework (vs. no homework) is assigned (Cobb, Peach, Craig, & Wilson, 1990). One plausible explanation that may positively or negatively alter effects of homework for children with and without disabilities relates to the fact that many homework activities are simply a method of practicing what has been presented in class. Such practice will have limited success with children who do not fully understand the assignment or with children who present behavior difficulties that inhibit understanding during class activities.

Priming

With these issues in mind, we have begun some research investigating the effects of home–school coordination on academic achievement and disruptive behavior for children with autism. One area of particular concern is that many of the children with autism who participate in full-inclusion environments demonstrate a variety of inappropriate (e.g., self-stimulation) and disruptive (e.g., screaming, throwing tantrums) behaviors that appear to function as escape or avoidance mechanisms during class activities. One research project discussed below (see Wilde, Koegel, & Koegel, 1992) was based on casual observations that children with autism participating in full-inclusion preschools behaved better during circle time when stories were being read with which they were familiar from their homes. We attempted to systematically assess this effect by having preschool teachers send home storybooks the night before they read them during circle time. The data consistently indicated that when the teacher read the stories during circle time to which the children had been previously exposed in a pleasant manner (e.g., reading before bedtime) at home the night before, their behavior improved in school the next day. In contrast, when stories were read in school that were unfamiliar to the child, inappropriate and disruptive behavior was always at higher levels during circle time the following day. Furthermore, listening comprehension was always higher for stories that parents had read the previous night. We have since replicated this procedure with children at a variety of age levels, and on a variety of different academic tasks, and found repeated success in reducing disruptive behavior and increasing appropriate responding.

The success of this procedure may be partially related to variables that have been discussed as important in relation to homework assignments in general. First, it has been reported that conditions surrounding homework assignments should include individualization, teacher evaluation, and family encouragement (cf. Epstein, Polloway, Foley, & Patton, 1993; Paschal, Weinstein, & Walberg, 1984). When assignments are planned, assigned, and implemented in a systematic and coordinated manner, they can serve as a vehicle for additional practice opportunities and provide a further source of learning time (Rosenberg, 1989). Such variables were important components in our studies; assignments were thoroughly coordinated with the teacher, presented as closely as possible to the way they would be presented in class, and introduced in a non-threatening relaxed environment free from distractions (e.g., incorporating the assignment into the routine of reading a story at bedtime) (Wilde et al., 1992).

Such proactive, prevention-oriented approaches that benefit the child both academically and behaviorally are likely to receive increased attention in the future. As teachers encounter more diverse groups of children, the need to strengthen home–school coordination and involve families as partners in the educational process, to understand the unique characteristics each child possesses, and to individualize accordingly has considerable potential to enhance education for all children.

Child and Family Characteristics

Another area of importance regarding prognosis and outcome relates to family characteristics. Data collected in our clinics (Koegel, Schreibman, et al., 1992; Moes, Koegel, Schreibman, & Loos, 1992) show that parents of children with autism, particularly mothers, experience significant stress for themselves, family members, and the family as a whole in caring for the child with autism. In relation to intervention programs, the mothers feel that increased family support and cooperation would be likely to reduce their stress.

Although we have found that substantial and empirically measurable improvements in intervention delivery can typically be documented, there is always a subgroup of children that has not responded favorably. As alluded to throughout this chapter, this difficulty does not universally relate to the effectiveness of a particular intervention, but may also relate to a complex set of issues involving family variables, child characteristics, and the need to individualize the intervention so that suitable intervention techniques can be paired with the families' and children's unique characteristics.

In relation to child characteristics, recent interest in the heterogeneity of autism has supported our substantial database that indicates that considerable variability exists within the diagnosis of autism. It is now well recognized that autism most likely has distinctly different etiologies in different children (Courchesne et al., 1994; Courchesne et al., 1995; Damasio & Maurer, 1978; Gillberg & Gillberg, 1983; Ritvo, Ritvo, & Brothers, 1982; Rosenberger-Debiesse & Coleman, 1986). Relatedly, the behavioral expression of the symptoms of autism varies significantly across children and within the children themselves throughout development (Waterhouse, Fein, Nathe, & Snyder, 1983). Such heterogeneity of behavioral characteristics and variability in the course of the disability make comparison of specific interventions difficult. This suggests the importance of shifting attention to the individualization of intervention techniques to maximize their effectiveness.

An example supporting the argument for individualization of intervention relates to the data collected on self-management discussed earlier. These data suggest that specific quantifiable variables (e.g., IQ over 50) may relate to the effectiveness of the specific type of self-management intervention. That is, children with higher cognitive abilities seem to make more significant gains when parents teach them to use self-management procedures. In contrast, children with lower cognitive skills may need adaptations of generally successful procedures (e.g., pictorial self-management) and may in some areas even demonstrate greater gains when the skills are at least initially taught in the context of a more

Home–school coordination, when carefully planned, enhances learning. For example, when parents read stories that will be presented the following day during circle time, inappropriate behaviors decrease and comprehension improves.

traditional parent-management program (e.g., Baker, Brightman, Heifetz, & Murphy, 1976; Koegel et al., 1989). Such continued individualization is likely to result in improved outcomes for a much larger number of children as well as larger gains for each individual child. In addition, the ability to suggest a prognosis very early on, based on subtyping observable child characteristics in the early years and independent of the special nature of the intervention, might ultimately be possible.

Further literature in the area of parent education suggests that some types of parent training may actually increase the stress parents experience (Benson & Turnbull, 1986; Gallagher, Beckman, & Cross, 1983). This is supported by data from our clinics that suggest that providing certain types of parent training, such as teaching parents procedures that are simple to implement and fit easily into daily routines (e.g., the NLP), actually reduce parental stress (Moes et al., 1994). This is in contrast to methods that require special times set aside to work one-to-one with a particular family member with a disability, which do not seem to reduce parental stress. Other variables that may relate to the effectiveness of parent involvement may be educational level, socioeconomic status, and marital status (Clark & Baker, 1983). In the area of autism, parental stress has been shown to inversely correlate with the amount of progress demonstrated by the child in family-oriented training programs. Specifically, the relative magnitude of stress in the parent–child system, relating to dimensions of parenting stress pertinent to personal adjustment and family functioning (e.g., financial stress, marital stress), is highly correlated with degree of child improvement in a parent intervention program. Such variables relate specifically to intervention effectiveness and should be considered in regard to intervention type (Robbins, Dunlap, & Plienis, 1991).

Directly related to the extreme variablity in child and family characteristics is the implicit need to individualize the intervention based on the particular goals addressed. This is because the specific target behaviors also seem to have an interactive effect with intervention type. For example, a first lexicon responds significantly better when variables known to influence motivation (described above) are incorporated (Koegel, O'Dell, & Koegel, 1987; Schreibman, Charlop, & Koegel, 1982). In contrast, some structures, such as grammatical features that occur infrequently (Camarata & Nelson, 1992), may be enhanced with at least some components of a more structured and traditional individualized target behaviors model. Such individualization, depending on child characteristics (Yoder et al., 1991), family variables, and target behaviors, is likely to result in an individualized prescriptive intervention, enhancing outcomes for all children with disabilities.

CONCLUSIONS

Overall, it is clear that specific gaps exist in the treatment of children with autism relating to the issue of heterogeneity of the symptoms exhibited in autism. Research suggests that specific variables associated with outcomes relate to the complex interactions of child characteristics, family variables, and target behaviors. Specifically, it appears that an individualized intervention that addresses these variables has the potential to ultimately result in a prescriptive approach to parent education, so that implementation of an intervention would result in prevention and reduction of severe problem behaviors and significant skill acquisition across all children.

There is now a growing body of literature documenting effective procedures for parent–professional collaboration in the habilitation process. Many of these procedures have a heavy emphasis on developing communication in children with disabilities. Early communication problems often antedate serious learning and psychosocial problems and are often directly correlated with severe problem behaviors. Therefore, intervention procedures that address communication and language must be central goals for children with disabilities. In summary, parents' active participation in implementing language, communication, and other goals will most likely hasten and facilitate acquisition and generalization in the habilitation process.

REFERENCES

Bailey, D.B., & McWilliam, R.A. (1990). Normalizing early intervention. *Topics in Early Childhood Special Education, 10*(2), 33–47.

Baker, B.L., Brightman, A.J., Heifetz, L.J., & Murphy, D.M. (1976). *Behavior problems.* Champaign, IL: Research Press.

Benson, H.A., & Turnbull, A.P. (1986). Approaching families from an individualized perspective. In R.H. Horner, L.H. Meyer, & H.D. Fredericks (Eds.), *Education of learners with severe handicaps: Exemplary service strategies* (pp. 127–157). Baltimore: Paul H. Brookes Publishing Co.

Broden, M., Hall, R., & Mitts, B. (1971). The effect of self-recording on the classroom behavior of two eighth-grade students. *Journal of Applied Behavior Analysis, 4*(4), 191–199.

Bronfenbrenner, U. (1979). *The ecology of human development: Experiments by nature and human design.* Cambridge, MA: Harvard University Press.

Brown, L., Schwartz, P., Udvari-Solner, A., Kampschroer, E.F., Johnson, F., Jorgensen, J., & Gruenewald, L. (1991). How much time should students with severe intellectual disabilities spend in regular education classrooms and elsewhere? *Journal of The Association for Persons with Severe Handicaps, 16*(1), 39–47.

Burnstein, N.D. (1986). The effects of classroom organization on mainstreamed preschool children. *Exceptional Children, 32*(5), 425–434.

Camarata, S.M. (1993). The application of naturalistic conversation training to speech production in children with speech disabilities. *Journal of Applied Behavior Analysis, 26,* 167–178.

Camarata, S.M., & Nelson, K.E. (1992). Treatment efficiency as a function of target selection in the remediation of child language disorders. *Clinical Linguistics and Phonetics, 6,* 167–178.

Carr, E.G., & Durand, V.M. (1985). Reducing behavior problems through functional communication training. *Journal of Applied Behavior Analysis, 18,* 111–126.

Cavallero, C.C., & Bambara, L.M. (1982). Two strategies for teaching language during free play. *Journal of The Association for the Severely Handicapped, 7,* 80–92.

Clark, D.B., & Baker, B.L. (1983). Predicting outcome in parent training. *Journal of Counseling and Clinical Psychology, 51,* 309–311.

Clark, F.A., Parham, D., Carlson, M.E., Frank, G., Jackson, J., Pierce, D., Wolfe, R.E., & Zemke, R. (1991). Occupational science: Academic innovation in the service of occupational therapy's future. *American Journal of Occupational Therapy, 45*(4), 300–310.

Cobb, S., Peach, W., Craig, K., & Wilson, V. (1990). The effects of homework on academic performance of learning disabled and non handicapped math students. *Journal of Instructional Psychology, 16*(4), 168–171.

Cooper, L.J., Wacker, D.P., Sasso, G.M., Reimers, T.M., & Donn, L.K. (1990). Using parents as therapists to evaluate the appropriate behavior in their children: Application to a tertiary diagnostic clinic. *Journal of Applied Behavior Analysis, 23,* 285–296.

Courchesne, E., Saitoh, O., Townsend, J.P., Yeung-Courchesne, R., Press, G.A., Lincoln, A.J., Haas, R.H., & Schreibman, L. (1995). Two distinctly different cerebellar pathologies in infantile autism: Hypoplasia and hyperplasia. *Lancet, 343,* 63–64.

Courchesne, E., Townsend, J., Akshoomoff, N.A., Saitoh, O., Yeung-Courchesne, R., Lincoln, A.J., James, H.E., Haas, R.H., Schreibman, L., & Lau, L. (1994). Impairment in shifting attention in autistic and cerebellar patients. *Behavioral Neuroscience, 108*(5), 848–865.

Crystal, D. (1987). Towards a bucket theory of language disability: Taking account of interaction between linguistic levels. *Clinical Linguistics and Phonetics, 1,* 7–21.

Damasio, A.R., & Maurer, R.G. (1978). A neurological model for childhood autism. *Archives of Neurology, 35,* 777–786.

Donneley, B., Doherty, J., Sheehan, R., & Whittemore, C. (1984, April). *A comparison of maternal, paternal, and diagnostic evaluation of typical and atypical infants.* Paper presented at the National Conference for the Council for Exceptional Children, Washington, DC.

Dougherty, A.M. (1990). *Consultation: Practice and perspective.* Pacific Grove, CA: Brooks/Cole.

Drabman, R.S., Spitalnic, R., & O'Leary, K.D. (1973). Teaching self-control to disruptive children. *Journal of Abnormal Psychology, 83,* 10–16.

Dunlap, G. (1984). The influence of task-variation and maintenance tasks on the learning and affect of autistic children. *Journal of Experimental Child Psychology, 37,* 41–64.

Dunlap, G., & Koegel, R.L. (1980). Motivating autistic children through stimulus variation. *Journal of Applied Behavior Analysis, 13,* 619–627.

Dunlap, L.K., Dunlap, G., Koegel, L.K., & Koegel, R.L. (1991). Using self-monitoring to increase students' success and independence. *Teaching Exceptional Children, 23,* 17–22.

Dunst, C.J. (1983). Communicative competence and deficits: Effects on early social interactions. In E. McDonald & D. Gallagher (Eds.), *Facilitating social-emotional development in the young multiply handicapped child.* Philadelphia: Home of Merciful Saviour Press.

Dunst, C.J., Trivette, C.M., Starnes, A., Hamby, D.W., & Gordon, N.J. (1993). *Building and evaluating family support initiatives: A national study of programs for persons with developmental disabilities.* Baltimore: Paul H. Brookes Publishing Co.

Durand, V.M., & Carr, E.G. (1987). Social influences on self-stimulatory behavior: Analysis and treatment application. *Journal of Applied Behavior Analysis, 20,* 119–132.

Durand, V.M., & Crimmins, D.B. (1988). Identifying the variables maintaining self-injurious behavior. *Journal of Autism and Developmental Disorders, 18,* 99–117.

Epstein, M.H., Polloway, E.A., Foley, R.M., & Patton, J.R. (1993). Homework: A comparison of teachers' and parents' perceptions of the problems experienced by students identified as having behavioral disorders, learning disabilities, or no disabilities. *Remedial and Special Education, 14*(5), 40–50.

Foster, M., Berger, M., & McLean, M. (1981). Rethinking a good idea: A reassessment of parent involvement. *Topics in Early Childhood Special Education, 1,* 55–65.

Frea, W.D., Koegel, R.L., & Koegel, L.K. (1993). *Understanding why problem behaviors occur: A guide for assisting parents in assessing causes of behavior and designing treatment plans.* Santa Barbara: University of California.

Gallagher, J.J., Beckman, P.J., & Cross, A.H. (1983). Families of handicapped children: Sources of stress and its amelioration. *Exceptional Children, 50*(1), 10–19.

Gardner, W.I., Cole, C.L., Berry, D.L., & Nowinski, J.M. (1983). Reduction of disruptive behaviors in mentally retarded adults: A self-management approach. *Behavior Modification, 7*(1), 76–96.

Gillberg, C., & Gillberg, I.C. (1983). Infantile autism: A total population study of reduced optimality on the pre-, peri-, and neonatal period. *Journal of Autism and Developmental Disorders, 13,* 153–166.

Guralnick, M.J. (1991). The next decade of research on the effectiveness of early intervention. *Exceptional Children, 58*(2), 174–183.

Guralnick, M.J., & Bricker, D. (1987). The effectiveness of early intervention for children with cognitive and general developmental delays. In M.J. Guralnick & F.L. Bennett (Eds.), *The effectiveness of early intervention for at-risk and handicapped children* (pp. 115–173). Orlando, FL: Academic Press.

Halliday, M.A.K. (1975). *Learning how to mean: Explorations in the development of language*. New York: Elsevier–North Holland Publishing Co.

Handen, B., Feldman, R.S., & Honigman, A. (1987). Comparison of parent and teacher assessments of developmentally delayed children's behavior. *Exceptional Children, 54*(2), 137–144.

Handleman, J.S., Powers, M.D., & Harris, S.L. (1984). Teaching of labels: An analysis of concrete and pictorial representations. *American Journal of Mental Deficiency, 88*(6), 625–629.

Harris, S.L. (1986). Families of children with autism: Issues for the behavior therapist. *Behavior Therapist, 6*, 175–177.

Hart, B., & Risley, T.R. (1980). In vivo language intervention: Unanticipated general effects. *Journal of Applied Behavior Analysis, 7*, 243–256.

Horner, R.H., & Brigham, T.A. (1979). The effects of self-management procedures on the study behavior of two retarded children. *Educating and Training of the Mentally Retarded, 14*(1), 18–24.

Horner, R.H., Williams, J.A., & Knobbe, C.A. (1985). The effect of "opportunity to perform" on the maintenance of skills learned by high school students with severe handicaps. *Journal of The Association for Persons with Severe Handicaps, 10*(3), 172–175.

Hupp, S.C. (1991). Promoting cognitive competence in children at risk. *American Behavioral Scientist, 34*(4), 454–467.

Keith, T.Z., Troutman, G.C., Trivette, P.S., Keith, P.B., Bickley, P.G., & Singh, K. (1993). Does parental involvement affect eighth-grade student achievement? Structural analysis of national data. *School Psychology Review, 22*(3), 474–496.

Kellegrew, D.H. (1994). *The impact of daily routines and opportunities on the self-care skill performance of young children with disabilities*. Unpublished dissertation, University of California, Santa Barbara, CA.

Koegel, L.K., Koegel, R.L., Hurley, C., & Frea, W.D. (1992). Improving social skills and disruptive behavior in children with autism through self-management. *Journal of Applied Behavior Analysis, 25*, 341–353.

Koegel, L.K., Valdez-Menchaca, M.C., & Koegel, R.L. (1994). Autism: Social communication difficulties and related behaviors. In M. Hersen & V.B. Van Hasselt (Eds.), *Advanced abnormal psychology* (pp. 165–187). New York: Plenum.

Koegel, R.L., Camarata, S.M., & Koegel, L.K. (1994). Aggression and noncompliance: Behavior modification through naturalistic language remediation. In J.L. Matson (Ed.), *Autism in children and adults: Etiology, assessment, and intervention*. Sycamore, IL: Sycamore Press.

Koegel, R.L., Dyer, K., & Bell, L.K. (1987). The influence of child-preferred activities on autistic children's social behavior. *Journal of Applied Behavior Analysis, 20*, 243–252.

Koegel, R.L., Glahn, T.J., & Nieminen, G.S. (1978). Generalization of parent-training results. *Journal of Applied Behavior Analysis, 11*, 95–109.

Koegel, R.L., & Johnson, J. (1989). Motivating language use in autistic children. In G. Dawson (Ed.), *Autism: New perspectives on diagnosis, nature, and treatment*. New York: Guilford Press.

Koegel, R.L., & Koegel, L.K. (1986). Promoting generalized treatment gains through direct instruction of self-monitoring skills. *Direct Instruction News, 5*, 13–15.

Koegel, R.L., & Koegel, L.K. (1987). Generalization issues in the treatment of autism. *Seminars, 8*, 241–256.

Koegel, R.L., & Koegel, L.K. (1990). Extended reductions in stereotypic behavior of students with autism through a self-management treatment package. *Journal of Applied Behavior Analysis, 23*, 119–127.

Koegel, R.L., Koegel, L.K., & Schreibman, L. (1991). Assessing and training parents in teaching pivotal behaviors. In R. Prinz (Ed.), *Advances in behavioral assessment of children and families*. London: Jessica Kingsley.

Koegel, R.L., Koegel, L.K., & Surratt, A.V. (1992). Language intervention and disruptive behavior in preschool children with autism. *Journal of Autism and Developmental Disorders, 22*, 141–153.

Koegel, R.L., O'Dell, M.C., & Dunlap, G. (1988). Producing speech use in nonverbal autistic children by reinforcing attempts. *Journal of Autism and Developmental Disorders, 18*(2), 187–200.

Koegel, R.L., O'Dell, M.C., & Koegel, L.K. (1987). A natural language paradigm for teaching non-verbal autistic children. *Journal of Autism and Developmental Disorders, 17*, 187–199.

Koegel, R.L., Schreibman, L., Britten, K.R., Burke, J.C., & O'Neill, R.E. (1982). A comparison of parent training to direct child treatment. In R.L. Koegel, A. Rincover, & A.L. Egel (Eds.), *Educating and understanding autistic children*. San Diego, CA: College-Hill Press.

Koegel, R.L., Schreibman, L., Good, A., Cerniglia, L., Murphy, C., & Koegel, L.K. (1989). *How to teach pivotal behaviors to children with autism: A training manual*. Santa Barbara: University of California.

Koegel, R.L., Schreibman, L., Loos, L.M., Dirlich-Wilhelm, H., Dunlap, G., Robbins, F.R., & Plienis, A.J. (1992). Stress profiles for mothers and fathers of children with autism. *Journal of Autism and Developmental Disorders, 22*, 205–216.

Laski, K., Charlop, M.H., & Schreibman, L. (1988). Training parents to use the natural language paradigm to increase their autistic children's speech. *Journal of Applied Behavior Analysis, 21*(4), 391–400.

Lovaas, O.I., Koegel, R.L., Simmons, J.Q., & Long, J.S. (1973). Some generalization and follow-up measures on autistic children in behavior therapy. *Journal of Behavior Analysis, 6*, 131–166.

Mace, F.C., Page, T.J., Ivancic, M.T., & O'Brian, S. (1986). Analysis of environmental determinants of aggression and disruption in mentally retarded children. *Applied Research in Mental Retardation, 7*, 203–221.

Marcus, L.M., Lansing, M.D., Andrews, C.E., & Schopler, E. (1978). Improvement of teaching effectiveness in parents of autistic children. *Journal of the American Academy of Child Psychiatry, 17*, 625–639.

Miller, J. (1981). *Assessing language production in children*. Boston: Allyn & Bacon.

Moes, D., Koegel, R.L., & Schreibman, L. (1994, August). *Behavior therapy paradigms and parenting stress*. Paper presented at the American Psychological Association, Los Angeles.

Moes, D., Koegel, R.L., Schreibman, L., & Loos, L. (1992). Stress profiles for mothers and fathers of children with autism. *Psychological Reports, 71*, 1272–1274.

Mullen, K.B., & Frea, W.D. (1995). A parent–professional consultation model for functional analysis. In R.L. Koegel & L.K. Koegel (Eds.), *Teaching children with autism* (pp. 175–188). Baltimore: Paul H. Brookes Publishing Co.

O'Neill, R.E., Horner, R.H., Albin, R.W., Storey, K., & Sprague, A.L. (1990). *Functional analysis of problem behavior: A practical assessment guide*. Sycamore, IL: Sycamore Press.

Paschal, R.A., Weinstein, T., & Walberg, H.J. (1984). The effects of homework on learning: A quantitative synthesis. *Journal of Educational Research, 78*(2), 97–104.

Peterson, N.L., & Cooper, C.S. (1989). Parent education and involvement in early intervention programs for handicapped children: A different perspective on parent needs and the parent–professional relationship. In M.J. Fine (Ed.), *The second handbook on parent education: Contemporary perspectives. Educational psychology*. San Diego, CA: Academic Press.

Pierce, K.L., & Schreibman, L. (1994). Teaching daily living skills to children with autism in unsupervised settings through pictorial self-management. *Journal of Applied Behavior Analysis, 27*, 471–481.

Ritvo, E.R., Ritvo, E.C., & Brothers, A.M. (1982). Genetic and immunohematologic factors in autism. *Journal of Autism and Developmental Disorders, 12*(2), 109–114.

Robbins, F.R., Dunlap, G., & Plienis, A.J. (1991). Family characteristics, family training, and the progress of young children with autism. *Journal of Early Intervention, 15*(2), 173–184.

Rosenberg, M.S. (1989). The effects of daily homework assignments on the acquisition of basic skills by students with learning disabilities. *Journal of Learning Disabilities, 22*(5), 314–323.

Rosenberger-Debiesse, J., & Coleman, M. (1986). Brief report: Preliminary evidence for multiple etiologies in autism. *Journal of Autism and Developmental Disorders, 16*, 385–392.

Schafer, D.S., Bell, A.P., & Spalding, J.B. (1987). Potential predictors of child progress as measured by the early intervention developmental profile. *Journal of the Division for Early Childhood, 11*(2), 106–117.

Schopler, E. (1971). Parents of psychotic children as scapegoats. *Journal of Contemporary Psychotherapy, 4*, 17–22.

Schopler, E., Mesibov, G., De Vellis, R., & Short, A. (1981). Treatment outcome for autistic children and their families. In D. Mittler (Ed.), *Frontiers of knowledge in mental retardation*. Baltimore: University Park Press.

Schreibman, L., Charlop, M.H., & Koegel, R.L. (1982). Teaching autistic children to use extra stimulus prompts. *Journal of Experimental Child Psychology, 33*, 475–491.

Schreibman, L., Koegel, R.L., Mills, J.I., & Burke, J.C. (1984). Training parent-child interactions. In E. Schopler & G.B. Mesibov (Eds.), *The effects of autism on the family* (pp. 187–205). New York: Plenum.

Schreibman, L., Runco, M.A., Mills, J.I., & Koegel, R.L. (1982). Teacher's judgments of improvements in autistic children in behavior therapy: A social validation. In R.L. Koegel, A. Rincover, & A.L. Egel (Eds.), *Educating and understanding autistic children*. San Diego, CA: College-Hill Press.

Schwethelm, B., & Mahoney, G. (1986). Task persistence among organically impaired mentally retarded children. *American Journal of Mental Deficiency, 90*(4), 432–439.

Shonkoff, J.P., Hauser-Cram, P., Krauss, M.W., & Upshur, C.C. (1988). Early intervention efficacy research: What have we learned and where do we go from here? *Topics in Early Childhood Special Education, 8*(1), 81–93.

Simeonsson, R.J. (1991). Primary, secondary, and tertiary prevention in early intervention. *Journal of Early Intervention, 15*(2), 124–134.

Sloane, H., Endo, G., Hawkes, T., & Jenson, W. (1991). Reducing children's interrupting through self-instructional parent training materials. *Education and Treatment of Children, 14*(1), 38–52.

Stremel, K., Matthews, P., Wilson, R., Molden, R., Yates, C., Busbea, B., & Holston, J. (1992, December). *Facilitating infant/toddler skills in family-child routines*. Paper presented at the Council for Exceptional Children/Division of Early Childhood International Conference on Children with Special Needs, Washington, DC.

Turnbull, A.P., Patterson, J.M., Behr, S.K., Murphy, D.L., Marquis, J.G., & Blue-Banning, M.J. (1993). *Cognitive coping, families, and disability*. Baltimore: Paul H. Brookes Publishing Co.

Tymms, P.B. (1992). The relationship of homework to A-level results. *Educational Research, 34*(1), 3–10.

Vincent, L.J., Salisbury, C., Laten, S., & Baumgart, D. (1979). *Designing home programs for families with handicapped children*. Unpublished manuscript.

Walberg, H.J. (1984, February). Families as partners in educational productivity. *Phi Delta Kappan, 397*–400.

Warren, S.F., & Kaiser, A.P. (1986). Incidental language teaching: A critical review. *Journal of Speech and Hearing Disorders, 51,* 291–299.

Waterhouse, L., Fein, D., Nath, J., & Snyder, D. (1983). Pervasive developmental disorders and schizophrenia occurring in childhood: A review of critical commentary. In G.L. Tischler (Ed.), *Diagnosis and classification in psychiatry: A critical appraisal of DSM-III.* New York: Cambridge University Press.

Weisner, T.S., Gallimore, R., & Jordan, C. (1993). Unpackaging cultural effects on classroom learning: Hawaiian peer assistance and child-generated activity. In R.N. Roberts (Ed.), *Coming home to preschool: Sociocultural context of early education* (pp. 59–90). Norwood, NJ: Ablex.

Wetherby, A.M., & Prutting, C.A. (1984). Profiles of communicative and cognitive-social abilities in autistic children. *Asha, 27,* 364–377.

Wilde, L.D., Koegel, L.K., & Koegel, R.L. (1992). *Increasing success in school through priming: A training manual.* Santa Barbara: University of California.

Winton, P.J. (1990). Promoting a normalizing approach to families: Integrating theory with practice. *Topics in Early Childhood Special Education, 10*(2), 90–103.

Yoder, P.J. (1987). Relationship between degree of infant handicap and clarity of infant cues. *American Journal of Mental Deficiency, 91*(6), 639–641.

Yoder, P.J., Kaiser, A.P., & Alpert, C.L. (1991). An exploratory study of the interaction between language teaching methods and child characteristics. *Journal of Speech and Hearing Research, 34,* 155–167.

2

Early Intervention and Serious Problem Behaviors

A Comprehensive Approach

Glen Dunlap and Lise Fox

E arly intervention is valued by researchers and service providers as
an essential component of the array of supports and services that
assists individuals with developmental disabilities and their fami-

Preparation of this chapter was supported by two projects funded by the U.S. Department of Education: 1) Cooperative Agreement No. H133B2004 from the National Institute
on Disability and Rehabilitation Research, and 2) Early Intervention Model Demonstration
Grant No. H024B30022 from the Office of Special Education Programs. However, the opinions expressed herein are those of the authors, and no official endorsement should be
inferred.

lies. The importance of early intervention is supported by the Education of the Handicapped Act Amendments of 1986 (PL 99-457) and the Individuals with Disabilities Education Act Amendments of 1991 (PL 102-119), two pieces of legislation that provide an entitlement to services; federal funding initiatives (e.g., model demonstration programs, Head Start); and efficacy research. Support of early intervention is based upon the belief that early intervention may make a significant difference in the outcomes expected for children with disabilities and their families (Guralnick, 1991).

In this chapter, the importance of early intervention for young children who have serious problem behaviors is described. The chapter begins with a discussion about current conceptualizations of early intervention and how they have evolved. Following a description of early intervention, the rationale for early intervention with problem behavior is presented with supportive research. The main body of the chapter presents a discussion of three themes that should be considered as principal components in the design of comprehensive intervention for children with serious problem behaviors.

EARLY INTERVENTION: AN ECOLOGICAL PERSPECTIVE

Initial efforts in early intervention were primarily focused on increasing the skill repertoires of young children with disabilities. Dependent measures used to evaluate effectiveness were focused on gains in mental, motor, and communication development (Guralnick, 1991). Over time, early intervention has moved beyond a focus mainly on the child to understanding the importance of providing supports and services to the family. In recent years, researchers have questioned the appropriateness of using global development measures as the test for success and have called for adopting a broader conceptualization of early intervention as an aggregation of supports and services provided to assist families and their children with disabilities (Bailey & Wolery, 1992; Dunst, 1986). This broadened conceptualization stems from the realization that interventions that are narrowly focused on changes in child skill development fail to consider the child as a member of a complex family system whose interdependent and interrelated parts also influence development. A broadened view of the child within a family promotes the acknowledgment that child outcomes are not independent of family functioning, but are dependent on a complex array of factors and relationships within the system.

The recognition that children are influenced by the family and reciprocally affect the family, and that families are embedded within and influenced by neighborhoods and communities, is reflective of an ecological theoretical perspective (Bailey & Wolery, 1992). In an ecological perspective, appropriate practices are ones that consider the whole unit of the child within the family when deciding on the nature of intervention. Early intervention may take the form of teaching children new skills, providing support and information to families, and assisting caregivers in developing the skills needed to support the child and family. An ecological perspective provides a framework for understanding contextual issues that may affect an aspect of early intervention (e.g., reducing problem behavior) as well as offering guidance for approaches in the design of intervention programs.

Early Intervention and Problem Behavior

Viewing early intervention from an ecological perspective provides a foundation for understanding the role of early intervention in supporting young children with serious problem behaviors and their families. The notion that child skill changes should not be the sole focus of intervention efforts is complementary to the idea that behavior interventions must not be solely focused on the reduction of problem behavior, but must also emphasize the ecological context in which the behavior occurs (Horner et al., 1990). A comprehensive approach to positive behavioral support is aimed at altering the lifestyle of the individual who engages in problem behavior. Effective behavioral support programs should result in

1. Changes in the individual's social relationships and daily activity patterns
2. Increases in community inclusion
3. Changes in the individual's health status or need for crisis intervention
4. An expansion of skill repertoires
5. A generalized reduction in problem behavior

An ecological perspective guides the interventionist to look beyond a narrow focus on the problem behavior of the individual and toward an understanding of the individual as a member of his or her immediate environments and settings as well as larger social contexts.

There is encouraging evidence that early intervention is effective for young children with serious problem behaviors. Behavioral research provides support for the conclusion that greater improvements may be expected if intervention is begun when the child is very young. For example, in a retrospective analysis, Fenske, Zalenski, Krantz, and McClannahan (1985) report that children with autism who began an intervention program before age 5 had significantly greater improvements than children who began the same program after age 5. Other researchers have presented findings that support the notion that early intervention can produce impressive improvements in skill development and problem behavior (Anderson, Avery, DiPietro, Edwards, & Christian, 1987; Dunlap, Johnson, & Robbins, 1990; Dunlap, Robbins, Morelli, & Dollman, 1988; Lovaas, 1980, 1987; Rogers & DiLalla, 1991).

Research and experience lead us to believe that the following phenomena explain, in part, the powerful effects of early intervention on problem behavior. First, the early years of development appear to be a critical period for the acquisition of communication skills. This critical period seems to have a relationship to the neurological development that occurs in the infant and toddler years. Researchers agree that the early social–communicative behaviors of the infant and toddler are the foundation for later language development (Bricker, 1993).

The early years of development offer a window of opportunity to affect significantly serious problem behavior. A substantial number of studies document the power of communication-based interventions for problem behavior (Billingsley & Neel, 1985; Bird, Dores, Moniz, & Robinson, 1989; Carr & Durand, 1985; Durand & Carr, 1987; Horner & Budd, 1985). Thus, the early childhood years may be an especially salient period of time for an intervention that is focused on the development of communication skills.

Second, young children have brief learning histories, and their problem behavior is less likely to be associated with a string of varied and complex interventions. In addition, the skill repertoires, relationships with others, and social ecologies of young children are limited and easier to assess. As a consequence, it generally seems easier to interpret the functions of a young child's problem behavior. Observations of children in natural contexts and interviews with caregivers often lead directly to fruitful hypotheses about the functions of the problem behavior.

Third, it is often easier to gain access to and work in partnership with the caregiver of the young child than with the caregiver of an adult. The age of the child requires more vigilance and support from the parent or caregiver. Parents are typically very anxious to intervene appropriately with problem behavior and are eager to collaborate with professionals to develop support strategies. It is also socially normative for parents of young children to seek outside assistance in guiding their child's social development and intervening with problem behavior. As typically developing children grow older, behavior interventions are imposed by other systems (e.g., schools) and may not include a component of facilitating the skill development of caregivers.

Finally, it is often easier to intervene with the problem behavior of young children because of their physical size. For example, a young child who bites, hits, and knocks over materials is much easier to manage physically than an adult who engages in the same behaviors.

The legislative mandate to provide early intervention to young children with developmental delays and disabilities (PL 99-457 and PL 102-

Early intervention, focusing on expanding skill repertoires and building communication with caregivers at home can ameliorate problem behavior and provide an "inoculation" against later reemerging problems. In this photo, a mother encourages communication using her child's favorite book.

119) offers an opportunity to affect significantly the developmental course of a young child with problem behaviors. Early, systematic, and intensive intervention that is communication focused and that builds skill development can ameliorate problem behavior (Dunlap et al., 1988; Robbins, Dunlap, & Plienis, 1991) and provide an "inoculation" against the later reemergence of such problems (Dunlap et al., 1990). In that effort, early interventionists should make use of functional assessment and comprehensive behavior support strategies. Intervention that is focused on the development of skills rather than the reduction of problem behavior and that recognizes that the child is a member of complex social systems holds the most promise of having an impact on the development of the young child.

AN APPROACH TO COMPREHENSIVE SUPPORT

The remainder of this chapter describes the principal characteristics of an approach to comprehensive support for young children with severe challenges in communication and behavioral adjustment (Dunlap & Robbins, 1991, 1993). The approach is based on available data and the accumulated outcomes of families and professionals. It is based, in particular, on our own experiences in collaborating with families and providing early intervention services for children with disabilities.

This approach was designed to be suitable for children with varying abilities and challenges and for families with diverse backgrounds and resources. Accordingly, the approach incorporates a high degree of indi- --

vidualization in all aspects of its structure and implementation. An assumption of the approach is that the specifics of the comprehensive support plan are based on an ongoing process of ecological assessment that is multivariate (e.g., Plienis, Robbins, & Dunlap, 1988) and that relies on the full participation and unfettered guidance of the child's family.

The fundamental objectives of this approach to comprehensive early intervention are to improve the current and future lives of the child and the child's family. This involves helping the child to develop skills, interests, and relationships to the fullest extent possible. It means providing the child with the resources that are most valuable in preventing the occurrence of serious problem behaviors that can plague functioning during early childhood and beyond. It also means helping the child's family to participate in and, as appropriate, orchestrate plans for the child's development and support. As discussed in a later section of this chapter, a central objective of comprehensive intervention is to help the family system to be strong, to employ its resources, and to enjoy the pleasures of inclusive and cohesive family life. The family system is the essential context in which the child lives and grows, and consequently early intervention practices must have a major family focus if they are to be comprehensive and ultimately effective.

The approach outlined in the subsequent pages includes three dominant themes or governing considerations. These components overlap and interrelate, but it is useful to present them as distinguishable points that should be pervasive in the design and implementation of early intervention services. The first theme is to focus intervention efforts on the establishment of new skills that are developmentally appropriate and serve useful functions for the child. It is especially important that these instructional targets enhance the child's abilities and opportunities to communicate and to develop pleasurable and satisfying relationships. The second major theme is to provide support in typical, inclusive environments and to promote opportunities for community exposure and contextually relevant interactions. It is through participation in real circumstances that the most valuable and generalizable learning occurs. The third theme is to provide comprehensive, individualized family support. Family support is being conceptualized now as consisting of much more than traditional training and information services, although these continue to be extremely beneficial for many families. Family support needs to be viewed as a process that must be individualized and that can include a great diversity and combination of support options.

Skill Development

A distinguishing characteristic of approaches that have demonstrated empirical success in early intervention with young children with autism and related disabilities is that they embrace an instructional orientation. That is, they seek to teach competencies that are observable and replicable. In addition, the skills should be effective in helping the child to manage his or her surroundings, and the functions should be appropriate to the child's age and developmental level. Within these parameters, a principal aim of early intervention must be to establish a growing repertoire of meaningful skills that the child can use in the ongoing context of daily interactions.

The chief focus of skill development for children with autism or related disabilities needs to be communication. This is the case for several reasons: 1) communication represents the most pervasive area of developmental delay among this population of children, 2) it is the area of functioning that is most crucial for all aspects of socialization and cognitive development, and 3) it relates centrally to the occurrence of problem behaviors. Instruction in communication is designed to provide children with a generative tool that will serve a broad range of purposes immediately and throughout the child's life.

Many authors have described the important relationship between communication and problem behaviors (Carr et al., 1994; Donnellan, Mirenda, Mesaros, & Fassbender, 1984; Durand, 1990). These authors have pointed out that behaviors such as tantrums and self-injury most frequently have social motivations and can be interpreted as intentional (although not necessarily conscious) acts of communication. This perspective has extremely important implications for the understanding of problem behaviors as well as the focus with which early intervention programs are developed. In particular, an understanding of the purposes (i.e., communicative functions) of a child's problem behaviors should inform interventionists of specific objectives for early instruction in communication.

Functional assessment strategies (e.g., Lennox & Miltenberger, 1989; O'Neill, Horner, Albin, Storey, & Sprague, 1990) can be used to determine the function(s) of a child's problem behaviors. Then, functionally equivalent alternatives can be identified as appropriate targets for instruction (Carr, 1988; Carr & Durand, 1985). The forms that are selected as equivalent alternatives should fit within a more conventional communicative system for the child, be easy to perform, and be effective in producing the desired outcomes. The conceptual and practical details of this instructional strategy, known as *functional communication training*, have been described in a number of valuable articles, manuals, and books (e.g., Carr et al., 1994; Durand, 1990; Durand, Berotti, & Weiner, 1993) (see also Chapter 3).

The important message in this approach to skill development is that problem behaviors are recognized as communicative expressions and that instruction can replace the problem behavior with a more effective, conventional, acceptable, and desirable alternative. In this manner, the violent tantrums of a 4-year-old child might be determined through functional assessment methods to be communicating a request for attention. Instruction for this child would seek to establish a communicative alternative, such as a vocal request (e.g., "Mama") or, if the child was unable to speak, a nonvocal signal such as a picture symbolizing mother–child interaction. As long as the alternative replicated the functions (i.e., obtaining attention) of the tantrums and was established during the times when tantrums would otherwise occur, the alternative should increase in frequency and the tantrums should decline. This pattern, in fact, has been documented in many case studies and research reports (e.g., Bird et al., 1989; Carr & Durand, 1985; Horner & Budd, 1985).

A concerted effort to establish communicative alternatives can produce substantial reductions in problem behaviors as well as help to prevent recurrence of the difficulties as the child matures through childhood and beyond (Dunlap et al., 1990). However, functional communication training is just one component of the more general enterprise of instruction in communication and language. There is also a tremendous need to establish a generative language system that the child can use for the myriad purposes that are served by communication—for example, to issue requests, express desires and feelings, share comments about the environment, receive and transmit information, and develop interpersonal rapport and relationships. The extent to which a useful system of communication is established in a child's early years is likely to have a significant impact on the extent to which the child will be able to handle the challenges of disability (Prizant & Wetherby, 1988).

There are, of course, many other competencies that are necessary as a child grows into an increasingly independent and capable member of the community. These include play, sharing, mobility, self-care (including dressing, toileting, feeding, etc.), independent completion of daily routines, and the general ability to consider and incorporate other people in daily transactions and activities. Although communication skills are dominant priorities in skill development, it is also likely that general increases in competent performance in all of these other areas are conversely associated with the occurrence of problem behaviors.

Inclusion and Socialization

The inclusion of children with problem behaviors in the community should be viewed as an important outcome of comprehensive support and a method for promoting skill development. Young children with serious problem behaviors are at increased risk of being denied access to opportunities for community participation. As a consequence, the child with serious problem behaviors may have limited opportunities to practice social and communication skills and develop supportive relationships with peers.

Inclusion may be described as providing unconditional opportunities for children with diverse abilities to participate actively in natural environments within their communities. For the young child, these environments may include preschool programs, child care centers, parties and outings with peers, shopping centers, parks, restaurants, churches, museums, and friends' houses. Inclusion may be understood as contributing in both a distal and proximal manner to the development of the child with serious problem behaviors. The distal benefits include facilitating and supporting the perspective of the family that their child, regardless of disability and intensity of problem behavior, belongs in the community. The proximal benefits of inclusion include the opportunities for the development of friendships, improved social and communication skills, and participation in a normalized curriculum (Bailey & McWilliam, 1990).

As young children become toddlers and preschoolers, interactions with peers become a relevant context in which social and communication skills are learned and practiced. Young children with serious problem behaviors typically have skill deficits in communication and social competency that are directly related to the nature and persistence of their problem behavior. For example, a toddler with communication delays may use biting and hitting to signal to a peer that he or she wants a turn with a toy. The behavioral support plan for this toddler will include providing the child with a new form of communication for making requests as well as facilitating the development of social interaction and play skills with peers. A toddler who has difficulty interacting with peers without displaying serious problem behaviors is likely to have reduced opportunities for interaction, as other children may avoid him or her as a playmate or the parent may avoid placing the child in situations that result in conflict. In this case, the toddler with problem behaviors will not only need to be instructed in social and communication skills with peers, but also need increased opportunities to practice and generalize those skills.

A primary setting in which inclusion may occur is in community early childhood programs. When children with disabilities are supported in quality programs with children without disabilities, they may be expected to make developmental progress that is similar to children who receive services in specialized, segregated environments (Lamorey & Bricker, 1993; Odom & McEvoy, 1988). It is also important to note that the inclusion of peers with disabilities into early childhood programs does not affect the developmental progress of the other children (Esposito, 1987). An inclusive early education environment offers young children with problem behaviors opportunities to develop friendships with their peers, observe and learn appropriate behavior, and develop desirable patterns of social interaction. In addition, an inclusive environment offers a natural context for the acquisition and generalization of communication skills. When social and communication skills are taught in isolated contexts or with children who do not socialize, the child often has difficulty with skill generalization. Effective, systematic instruction in the natural context of an inclusive program may reduce these problems significantly.

When young children with disabilities are in inclusive programs, they are involved in more social interactions (Beckman & Kohl, 1984; Guralnick & Groom, 1988) and verbal interactions (Devoney, Guralnick, & Rubin, 1974; Paul, 1985). Most researchers agree that positive outcomes from placement in inclusive early education programs are most likely to occur when children are provided with systematic instruction embedded in routine and planned activities (Fox & Hanline, 1993; Goldstein & Kaczmarek, 1992; Odom & Brown, 1993; Ostrosky, Kaiser, & Odom, 1993; Wolery & Fleming, 1993). Systematic instruction that is applied in relevant, natural contexts relies upon the natural cues and reinforcers that exist in those contexts. Although empirical support that is specific to the instruction of young children with serious problem behaviors in inclusive programs is limited, there are many demonstrations of success with young children who have autism and other developmental disabilities. Systematic techniques that may be used to support children with problem behaviors to develop social interaction and play skills include peer-mediated interventions (Hendrickson, Strain, Tremblay, & Shores, 1982; Odom, Chandler, Ostrosky, McConnell, & Reaney, 1992; Strain, Shores, & Timm, 1977), teacher-mediated interventions (Goldstein, Wickstrom, Hoyson, Jamieson, & Odom, 1988; Haring & Lovinger, 1989; McConnell, Sisson, Cort, & Strain, 1991), affection activities (McEvoy et al., 1988; Twardosz, Nordquist, Simon, & Botkin, 1983), incidental teaching (Brown, McEvoy, & Bishop, 1991), and integrated play groups (Wolfberg & Schuler, 1993).

Milieu teaching procedures may be used to support communication and language skill development in natural contexts. Milieu procedures are brief episodes of systematic instruction that follow the child's lead or interest and provide explicit prompts for communication or language production (Kaiser, Yoder, & Keetz, 1992). Milieu strategies that may be applied in inclusive programs to promote communication and language acquisition include incidental teaching (Hart & Risley, 1975, 1980), time delay (Warren & Gazdag, 1990), mand-model (Warren, McQuarter, & Rogers-Warren, 1984), and child-cued modeling (Alpert & Kaiser, 1992).

Community early childhood programs are not the only context to consider when providing community inclusion opportunities. There are other community contexts that are very important to families and present challenges for the young child with problem behaviors. For example, a child may be unable to accompany a parent on grocery shopping trips or a family may have curtailed its participation in church activities because of the child's problem behaviors. When children have difficulty in community environments, the family may restrict activities in those environments, feel a lack of competence to support their child in the community, and become anxious about other people's perceptions of their child. A comprehensive support plan should focus on those environments important to the family as targets for functional assessment and intervention and should consider success in those contexts as meaningful outcomes.

Family Support

The final major element of comprehensive early intervention is family support. This term has gained very wide use since the late 1980s, so it is important that the term be defined. Family support, as it is presented in this chapter, refers to any and all actions that serve to strengthen and sustain the family system, especially as these actions pertain to the family's assimilation and understanding of the child's disability.

In the vast majority of cases, the family provides the indispensable context for and the most powerful influence on a child's development. Given the increasing appreciation for the role of context in a child's development, it is apparent that the well-being of the family system is a prominent factor in the maturation and progress of the child (Robbins et al., 1991). A child spends more waking (and sleeping) hours in a family home ecology, with his or her family members, than in any other environment. In addition, family members, especially parents, represent by far the most enduring resources available for children, and this may be even more pronounced for a child with serious disabilities.

Aside from being an essential resource, families have at least two other characteristics that are important considerations in the delivery of family support. First, families are unique experts when it comes to their members. Family members have a singular and intimate knowledge of a child's history; behavioral tendencies; and idiosyncrasies, preferences, and special abilities. They also have a familiarity with the child's environments that cannot be duplicated by service providers. This unique expertise should be considered carefully in developing early intervention programs, and for this reason it is reasonable and most appropriate for families to participate as partners with professionals in the design of intervention activities.

A second characteristic is that families are highly individual and diverse systems. No two families are exactly alike. Although there may be some similarities, such as the presence of a child with unusual support needs, families also have tremendous differences. They differ with regard to their composition; their cultural and ethnic backgrounds; the personal-

The home, where young children spend most of their waking hours, provides an excellent and enduring context for intervention. In this picture a child is rewarded with opportunities to use the family computer, an activity that is enjoyable for both parent and child.

ities, needs, and strengths of their members; the history and context of the members' interactions; and the values and priorities of the family unit. Optimal family support programs are structured to respond to these individualized characteristics, to build on family strengths, and to ameliorate the challenges (Turnbull, Turnbull, Summers, Brotherson, & Benson, 1986).

The diversity of families suggests that there is a similar diversity in the range of supports that families might require (Barber, Turnbull, Behr, & Kerns, 1988; Powell, Hecimoric, & Christensen, 1993); however, the principal kinds of assistance that are apt to be most beneficial can be categorized and presented as a list of support options. These service options are listed in Table 1 and discussed in the following sections. The list presented in Table 1 is not exhaustive, nor is it offered as an ideal menu of alternatives. It is proposed primarily as a depiction of the variety of supports that can be helpful for families that include a child with a serious disability.

Information   A tremendous need of all families is information. When a child is first identified as having a disability, parents and other family members have an intense need for facts and materials about the disability and about what impact the condition is likely to have on the child's development and on the family's dynamics. Although the specific questions change, the need for information continues throughout a child's lifetime. An ongoing source of meaningful assistance for many families is updated information from the literature about the child's disability, intervention

Table 1.   Service delivery options for individualized family support

Information
    about disabilities, the specific child's disability, legal and procedural rights, services and
    service options, other resources, and so on

Education and training
    in behavioral support strategies, child development and parenting, and advocacy

Planning and assistance
    person-centered planning, transitions, finances, and so on

Service coordination (case management)
    identification of appropriate services, brokering, arranging for transportation, and other
    logistical support

Social and emotional support
    counseling, support groups, Parent-to-Parent, sibling support, friendship

Respite care
    in-home, out-of-home, child care, extended respite, and crisis relief

strategies, and state-of-the-art program options. It is also important for families to have ready access to information about available services, legal and civil rights, the experiences of other families, and the child's progress in school and community environments. Family support programs need to consider explicitly how families are going to gain efficient and expeditious access to these different kinds of information.

Education and Training   Many families, especially families with young children, can benefit from education and training in areas such as child development, behavior management, and advocacy. Parent training is an area of family support that has received a great deal of research attention (see, e.g., Dangel & Polster, 1984), and there is no question that it can be a tremendous benefit for many families (Koegel, Schreibman, Johnson, O'Neill, & Dunlap, 1984). Of particular value can be general approaches and specific techniques for promoting all aspects of development, including communication, within the context of home and community interactions. Instruction on the reduction of serious problem behaviors is also requested by many families (Dunlap, Robbins, & Darrow, 1994). Training in positive parenting and typical child development can be very useful for parents of children with serious disabilities because it can be easy to lose sight of typical variances and expectations. Another key area for parent training involves operating within the system, negotiating for individualized program options, and serving as one's own (and the child's) advocate. Self-advocacy training can be a most crucial element of family support because it promotes the recruitment of necessary resources and because it involves skills that will be of benefit as long as the child and family have any dependence on community-based social services.

Planning and Assistance   Planning and assistance is a broad category of family support that is beginning to be implemented across the country. It is frequently the case that families live day to day with little opportunity to develop careful plans for the future. This can create substantial anxiety and, correspondingly, a deleterious influence on a family's quality of life. Fortunately, an influx of planning strategies is now available in which families gather with supportive professionals and friends to develop visions, outlines, and specific plans for a child's support and development for a period covering several years (see Chapter 19 for a detailed discussion of person-centered planning). The plans can incorporate strategies for mobilizing resources and creating opportunities that might not have been developed without the group planning dynamics. Such planning processes can be pivotal in addressing specific concerns (e.g., transitions, financial responsibilities), but their greatest advantage may be in building a common set of goals and ideals to guide work on behalf of the child with the disability.

Although valuable, planning is not sufficient. There must be distinct assistance that can be made available to implement the plans. Without the commitment of resources and personal effort, the planning process can end up as little more than a vacuous gesture.

Service Coordination (Case Management)   Service coordination can represent valuable support for a family because it can reduce the time, trouble, and frustration involved in locating and procuring services. Ideally, service coordination is structured from a "wrap-around" perspective with the coordinator serving as a broker, making a variety of services available to the child and family. The relief provided by an effective coordinator can preserve crucial energy that can then be directed to other, more direct, parenting functions. A number of authors (e.g., Dunst & Trivette, 1989) have offered perspectives on this form of assistance that directly address issues pertinent to the strengthening of the family system.

Social and Emotional Support   All people have needs for social and emotional support, but these are often difficult to find when one is faced with the unusual circumstances of being the parent of a child with autism or related disability. Parents who are informed that their child has such a disability need to make substantial adjustments. They find that few (perhaps none) of their friends can relate to their experiences, and they may be particularly vulnerable to feelings of isolation, loneliness, and depression. Some family members find that counseling can be very helpful, while others find suitable sustenance in social support groups or from the guidance and encouragement that are available from more experienced parents (and from organizations such as Parent-to-Parent). In some cases, special value can come from support networks that are designed for siblings of children with disabilities.

Some of the most compelling support that can be offered, even by professionals, is described best as friendship. Parents and other family members often have very few contacts who can understand the challenges and stresses associated with unusual disabilities. It is often difficult to find people who can listen sympathetically and nonjudgmentally and who might be able to help with a comment or a suggestion. In support programs with which we have been associated, family members have stated that an extremely valuable feature of the program was the ability to talk openly to people who had a sense of what they were experiencing—their frustrations and challenges as well as their successes and delights. This sense of community and friendship is a critical, and often neglected, part of family support.

Respite Care Respite care is an essential program component for family members who need a recess from the demands of caring for a child with significant needs. Many families can be well supported by efforts that develop or identify quality respite and child care programs that parents can regard as safe and healthy for their child. Depending on their available resources, such as the local presence of close relatives, some families may have needs for brief, occasional respite. Others, however, may have a temporary need for an extended respite in which the family system can regroup, find solutions to crises, and identify means by which the family can overcome challenges and welcome its next experiences.

It is important to remember that families are individual systems with diverse strengths and diverse needs. No two families will benefit optimally from the exact same configuration of services. However, all families can be assisted, and the assistance that is provided can have substantial effects on the lifelong development of a child with disabilities.

CONCLUSIONS

Early intervention for young children with disabilities and serious problem behaviors is an endeavor that has great potential for meaningful outcomes that will be apparent very rapidly and that can last with a child and family throughout the course of the child's development. There is now an accumulation of data and experience that attest to the benefits of early intervention and provide guidelines for the optimal construction of early intervention services. In this chapter, three components have been identified that are crucial for the short- and long-term benefits of young children with disabilities and problem behaviors. The three components are the development of functional communication skills, the provision of inclusive experiences that promote desirable social interactions, and the delivery of individualized family support.

Although these guidelines are offered with conviction, they are fairly general and there is a tremendous amount that is not known about the specific means of service delivery or about the best ways to assess child and family characteristics. Research and demonstration projects have taught interventionists a great deal, and it is readily apparent that additional research can help identify and develop even more effective responses to the enormous challenges that are faced by these children and their families.

REFERENCES

Alpert, C.L., & Kaiser, A.P. (1992). Training parents as milieu language teachers. *Journal of Early Intervention, 16*, 31–52.

Anderson, S.R., Avery, D.L., DiPietro, E.K., Edwards, G.L., & Christian, W.P. (1987). Intensive home-based early intervention with autistic children. *Education and Treatment of Children, 10*, 352–366.

Bailey, D.B., & McWilliam, R.A. (1990). Normalizing early intervention. *Topics in Early Childhood Special Education, 10*, 33–47.

Bailey, D.B., & Wolery, M. (1992). *Teaching infants and preschoolers with disabilities* (2nd ed.). New York: MacMillan.

Barber, P.A., Turnbull, A.P., Behr, S.K., & Kerns, G.M. (1988). A family systems perspective on early childhood special education. In S.L. Odom & M.B. Karnes (Eds.), *Early intervention for infants and children with handicaps: An empirical base* (pp. 179–198). Baltimore: Paul H. Brookes Publishing Co.

Beckman, P., & Kohl, F.L. (1984). The effects of social and isolate toys on the interactions and play of integrated and nonintegrated groups of preschoolers. *Education and Training of the Mentally Retarded, 19*, 169–175.

Billingsley, F.F., & Neel, R.S. (1985). Competing behaviors and their effects on skill generalization and maintenance. *Analysis and Intervention in Developmental Disabilities, 5*, 357–372.

Bird, F., Dores, P.A., Moniz, D., & Robinson, J. (1989). Reducing severe aggressive and self-injurious behaviors with functional communication training. *American Journal on Mental Retardation, 94*, 37–48.

Bricker, D. (1993). Then, now, and the path between: A brief history of language intervention. In A.P. Kaiser & D.B. Gray (Eds.), *Communication and language intervention: Vol. 2. Enhancing children's communication: Research foundations for intervention* (pp. 11–31). Baltimore: Paul H. Brookes Publishing Co.

Brown, W.H., McEvoy, M.A., & Bishop, N. (1991). Incidental teaching of social behavior: A naturalistic approach for promoting young children's peer interactions. *Teaching Exceptional Children, 24*, 35–38.

Carr, E.G. (1988). Functional equivalence as a mechanism for response generalization. In R.H. Horner, G. Dunlap, & R.L. Koegel (Eds.), *Generalization and maintenance: Lifestyle changes in applied settings* (pp. 221–241). Baltimore: Paul H. Brookes Publishing Co.

Carr, E.G., & Durand, V.M. (1985). Reducing behavioral problems through functional communication training. *Journal of Applied Behavior Analysis, 18*, 111–126.

Carr, E.G., Levin, L., McConnachie, G., Carlson, J.I., Kemp, D.C., & Smith, C.E. (1994). *Communication-based intervention for problem behavior: A user's guide for producing positive change*. Baltimore: Paul H. Brookes Publishing Co.

Dangel, R.F., & Polster, R.A. (Eds.). (1984). *Parent training: Foundations of research and practice*. New York: Guilford Press.

Devoney, C., Guralnick, M.J., & Rubin, H. (1974). Integrating handicapped and nonhandicapped preschool children: Effects on social play. *Childhood Education, 50,* 360–364.

Donnellan, A.M., Mirenda, P.L., Mesaros, R.A., & Fassbender, L.L. (1984). Analyzing the communicative functions of aberrant behavior. *Journal of The Association for Persons with Severe Handicaps, 9,* 201–212.

Dunlap, G., Johnson, L.F., & Robbins, F.R. (1990). Preventing serious behavior problems through skill development and early intervention. In A.C. Repp & N.N. Singh (Eds.), *Perspectives on the use of nonaversive and aversive interventions for persons with developmental disabilities* (pp. 273–286). Sycamore, IL: Sycamore Press.

Dunlap, G., & Robbins, F.R. (1991). Current perspectives in service delivery for young children with autism. *Comprehensive Mental Health Care, 1,* 177–194.

Dunlap, G., & Robbins, F.R. (1993). *Individualized support for young children with severe problems in communication and behavior* (Model Demonstration Grant No. H024B30022). Washington, DC: U.S. Department of Education, Office of Special Education Programs.

Dunlap, G., Robbins, F.R., & Darrow, M.A. (1994). Parents' reports of their children's challenging behaviors: Results of a statewide survey. *Mental Retardation, 32,* 206–212.

Dunlap, G., Robbins, F.R., Morelli, M.A., & Dollman, C. (1988). Team training for young children with autism: A regional model for service delivery. *Journal of the Division for Early Childhood, 12,* 147–160.

Dunst, C.J. (1986). Overview of the efficacy of early intervention programs. In L. Bickman & D. Weatherford (Eds.), *Evaluating early intervention programs for severely handicapped children and their families* (pp. 79–147). Austin, TX: PRO-ED.

Dunst, C.J., & Trivette, C.M. (1989). An enablement and empowerment perspective on case management. *Topics in Early Childhood Special Education, 8,* 87–102.

Durand, V.M. (1990). *Functional communication training: An intervention program for severe behavior problems*. New York: Guilford Press.

Durand, V.M., Berotti, D., & Weiner, J.S. (1993). Functional communication training: Factors affecting effectiveness, generalization, and maintenance. In J. Reichle & D.P. Wacker (Eds.), *Communication and language intervention: Vol. 3. Communicative alternatives to challenging behavior: Integrating functional assessment and intervention strategies* (pp. 317–340). Baltimore: Paul H. Brookes Publishing Co.

Durand, V.M., & Carr, E.G. (1987). Social influences on "self stimulatory" behavior: Analysis and treatment application. *Journal of Applied Behavior Analysis, 20,* 119–132.

Education of the Handicapped Act Amendments of 1986, PL 99-457. (October 8, 1986). Title 20, U.S.C. 1400 et seq: *U.S. Statutes at Large, 100,* 1145–1177.

Esposito, B.G. (1987). The effects of preschool integration on the development of nonhandicapped children. *Journal of the Division for Early Childhood, 12,* 31–46.

Fenske, E.C., Zalenski, S., Krantz, P.J., & McClannahan, L.E. (1985). Age at intervention and treatment outcome for autistic children in a comprehensive intervention program. *Analysis and Intervention in Developmental Disabilities, 5,* 49–58.

Fox, L., & Hanline, M.F. (1993). A preliminary evaluation of learning within developmentally appropriate early childhood settings. *Topics in Early Childhood Special Education, 13,* 308–327.

Goldstein, H., & Kaczmarek, L. (1992). Promoting communicative interaction among children in integrated intervention settings. In S.F. Warren & J. Reichle (Eds.), *Communication and language intervention: Vol. 1. Causes and effects in communication and language intervention* (pp. 81–111). Baltimore: Paul H. Brookes Publishing Co.

Goldstein, H., Wickstrom, S., Hoyson, M., Jamieson, B., & Odom, S. (1988). Effects of sociodramatic script training on social and communicative interaction. *Education and Treatment of Children, 11,* 97–111.

Guralnick, M.J. (1991). The next decade of research on the effectiveness of early intervention. *Exceptional Children, 58,* 174–183.

Guralnick, M.J., & Groom, J.M. (1988). Peer interactions in mainstreamed and specialized classrooms: A comparative analysis. *Exceptional Children, 5,* 415–425.

Haring, T.G., & Lovinger, L. (1989). Promoting social interaction through teaching generalized play initiation responses to preschool children with autism. *Journal of The Association for Persons with Severe Handicaps, 14,* 255–262.

Hart, B.M., & Risley, T.R. (1975). Incidental teaching of language in the preschool. *Journal of Applied Behavior Analysis, 7,* 243–256.

Hart, B.M., & Risley, T.R. (1980). In vivo language intervention: Unanticipated general effects. *Journal of Applied Behavior Analysis, 13,* 407–432.

Hendrickson, J.M., Strain, P.S., Tremblay, A., & Shores, R.E. (1982). Functional effects of peer social initiations on the interactions of behaviorally handicapped children. *Behavior Modification, 6,* 323–353.

Horner, R.H., & Budd, C.M. (1985). Teaching manual sign language to a nonverbal student: Generalization of sign use and collateral reduction of maladaptive behavior. *Education and Training of the Mentally Retarded, 20,* 39–47.

Horner, R.H., Dunlap, G., Koegel, R.L., Carr, E.G., Sailor, W., Anderson, J., Albin, R.W., & O'Neill, R.E. (1990). In support of integration for people with severe problem behaviors: A response to four commentaries. *Journal of The Association for Persons with Severe Handicaps, 15,* 145–147.

Individuals with Disabilities Education Act of 1990 (IDEA), PL 101-476. (October 30, 1990). Title 20, U.S.C. 1400 et seq: *U.S. Statutes at Large, 104,* 1103–1151.

Individuals with Disabilities Education Act Amendments of 1991, PL 102-119. (October 7, 1991). Title 20, U.S.C. 1400 et seq: *U.S. Statutes at Large, 105,* 587–608.

Kaiser, A.P., Yoder, P.J., & Keetz, A. (1992). Evaluating milieu teaching. In S.F. Warren & J. Reichle (Eds.), *Communication and language intervention: Vol. 1. Causes and effects in communication and language intervention* (pp. 9–47). Baltimore: Paul H. Brookes Publishing Co.

Koegel, R.L., Schreibman, L., Johnson, J., O'Neill, R.E., & Dunlap, G. (1984). Collateral effects of parent training on families with autistic children. In R.F. Dangel & R.A. Polster (Eds.), *Parent training: Foundations of research and practice* (pp. 359–378). New York: Guilford Press.

Lamorey, S., & Bricker, D. (1993). Integrated programs: Effects on young children and their parents. In C.A. Peck, S.L. Odom, & D.D. Bricker (Eds.), *Integrating young children with disabilities into community programs: Ecological perspectives on research and implementation* (pp. 249–270). Baltimore: Paul H. Brookes Publishing Co.

Lennox, D.B., & Miltenberger, R.G. (1989). Conducting a functional assessment of problem behavior in applied settings. *Journal of The Association for Persons with Severe Handicaps, 14,* 304–311.

Lovaas, O.I. (1980). Behavioral training with young autistic children. In B. Wilcox & A. Thompson (Eds.), *Critical issues in educating autistic children and youth* (pp. 220–233). Washington, DC: U.S. Department of Education.

Lovaas, O.I. (1987). Behavioral treatment and normal educational and intellectual functioning in young autistic children. *Journal of Consulting and Clinical Psychology, 55,* 3–9.

McConnell, S.R., Sisson, L.A., Cort, C.A., & Strain, P.S. (1991). Effects of social skills training and contingency management on reciprocal interaction of preschool children with behavioral handicaps. *Journal of Special Education, 24,* 473–495.

McEvoy, M.A., Nordquist, V.M., Twardosz, S., Heckaman, K., Wehby, J.H., & Denny, R.K. (1988). Promoting autistic children's peer interaction in an integrated early childhood setting using affection activities. *Journal of Applied Behavior Analysis, 21,* 193–200.

Odom, S.L., & Brown, W.H. (1993). Social interaction skills interventions for young children with disabilities in integrated settings. In C.A. Peck, S.L. Odom, & D.D. Bricker (Eds.), *Integrating young children with disabilities into community programs: Ecological perspectives on research and implementation* (pp. 39–64). Baltimore: Paul H. Brookes Publishing Co.

Odom, S.L., Chandler, L., Ostrosky, M., McConnell, S.R., & Reaney, S. (1992). Fading teacher prompts from peer-initiation interventions for young children with disabilities. *Journal of Applied Behavior Analysis, 18,* 307–318.

Odom, S.L., & McEvoy, M.A. (1988). Integration of young children with handicaps and normally developing children. In S.L. Odom & M.B. Karnes (Eds.), *Early intervention for infants and children with handicaps: An empirical base* (pp. 241–267). Baltimore: Paul H. Brookes Publishing Co.

O'Neill, R.E., Horner, R.H., Albin, R.W., Storey, K., & Sprague, J.R. (1990). *Functional analysis of problem behavior: A practical assessment guide.* Sycamore, IL: Sycamore Press.

Ostrosky, M.M., Kaiser, A.P., & Odom, S.L. (1993). Facilitating children's social-communicative interactions through the use of peer-mediated interventions. In A.P. Kaiser & D.B. Gray (Eds.), *Communication and language intervention: Vol. 2. Enhancing children's communication: Research foundations for intervention* (pp. 159–185). Baltimore: Paul H. Brookes Publishing Co.

Paul, L. (1985). Programming peer support for functional language. In S. Warren & A.K. Rogers-Warren (Eds.), *Teaching functional language* (pp. 289–307). Austin, TX: PRO-ED.

Plienis, A.J., Robbins, F.R., & Dunlap, G. (1988). Parent adjustment and family stress on factors in behavioral parent training for young autistic children. *Journal of the Multihandicapped Person, 1,* 31–52.

Powell, T.H., Hecimovic, A., & Christensen, L. (1993). Meeting the unique needs of families. In D.E. Berkell (Ed.), *Autism: Identification, education and treatment* (pp. 187–224). Hillsdale, NJ: Lawrence Erlbaum Associates.

Prizant, B.M., & Wetherby, A.M. (1988). Providing services to children with autism (ages 0 to 2 years) and their families. *Topics in Language Disorders, 9,* 1–23.

Robbins, F.R., Dunlap, G., & Plienis, A.J. (1991). Family characteristics, family training, and the progress of young children with autism. *Journal of Early Intervention, 15,* 173–184.

Rogers, S.J., & DiLalla, D.L. (1991). A comparative study of the effects of a developmentally based instructional model on young children with autism and young children with other disorders of behavior and development. *Topics in Early Childhood Special Education, 11,* 29–47.

Strain, P.S., Shores, R.E., & Timm, M. (1977). Effects of peer social initiations on the behavior of withdrawn preschool children. *Journal of Applied Behavior Analysis, 10,* 289–298.

Turnbull, A.P., & Turnbull, H.R., with Summers, J.A., Brotherson, M.J., & Benson, H.A. (1986). *Families, professionals, and exceptionality: A special partnership.* Columbus, OH: Merrill.

Twardosz, S., Nordquist, V.M., Simon, R., & Botkin, D. (1983). The effects of group affection activities on the interaction of socially isolate children. *Analysis and Intervention in Developmental Disabilities, 3,* 311–338.

Warren, S.F., & Gazdag, G. (1990). Facilitating early language development with milieu intervention procedures. *Journal of Early Intervention, 14*(1), 62–86.

Warren, S.F., McQuarter, R.J., & Rogers-Warren, A.K. (1984). The effects of teacher mands and models on the speech of unresponsive language-delayed children. *Journal of Speech and Hearing Research, 49,* 43–52.

Wolery, M., & Fleming, L.A. (1993). Implementing individualized curricula in integrated settings. In C.A. Peck, S.L. Odom, & D.D. Bricker (Eds.), *Integrating young children with disabilities into community programs: Ecological perspectives on research and implementation* (pp. 109–132). Baltimore: Paul H. Brookes Publishing Co.

Wolfberg, P.J., & Schuler, A.L. (1993). Integrated play groups: A model for promoting the social and cognitive dimensions of play in children with autism. *Journal of Autism and Developmental Disorders, 23,* 467–489.

3

Developing Long-Term Reciprocal Interactions Between Parents and Their Young Children with Problematic Behavior

David P. Wacker, Stephanie Peck,
K. Mark Derby, Wendy Berg, and Jay Harding

This chapter provides a model for increasing the long-term positive interactions that young children with problematic behavior have with their parents. The model is based on research that we are conducting in children's homes (Wacker & Berg, 1992a, 1992b). Some children have been followed for over 3 years, and our focus has been on establishing long-term, reciprocal positive interactions, which we believe are the key to maintaining reductions in problematic behavior. The children in the project range in age from 1 to 5 years, and most have severe developmental disorders as well as severe behavior problems that include self-injury and aggression. Through this research, we have developed a maintenance model to guide our assessment and intervention approaches.

Before describing this model, a few introductory comments are needed. Assessment, specifically functional analysis, is a key component in all intervention activities. We do not believe that appropriate intervention can occur without a functional analysis (Iwata, Dorsey, Slifer, Bauman, & Richman, 1982). The first section of this chapter provides only a limited summary of the assessment methodology because it is described in more depth elsewhere (Wacker, Cooper, Peck, Derby, & Berg, in press). The results of the assessment guide our selection of treatments. When the function of problematic behavior is known, appropriate intervention can be matched to the target behavior (Iwata, Pace, Kalsher, Cowdery, & Cataldo, 1990).

Our preferred intervention is *functional communication training* (FCT) (Carr & Durand, 1985). As we describe in the intervention section, we almost always attempt to teach children to mand (i.e., request) reinforcers and to substitute manding for problematic behavior. However, this substitution can occur only if the function of problematic behavior is identified (Carr, 1988). We are biased toward functional communication training for three basic reasons. First, as described by Durand and Carr (1985), the manding response is often an efficient, immediate way for the child to obtain reinforcement. Identifying the function of problematic behavior and then teaching the child an alternative response for gaining the same reinforcers should lead to a reduction in problematic behavior via *response covariation* (Parrish & Roberts, 1993); as the alternative response increases, challenging behavior should decrease. Furthermore, if the manding response (e.g., a sign) is more efficient and effective than problematic behavior for gaining reinforcement, relatively quick results should occur when the mand is trained. The goal is for the manding response to be independent (unprompted), an outcome that often takes times to achieve. As Wacker and Reichle (1993) discussed, functional communication training is a differential reinforcement procedure, and, like any other reinforcement procedure, the initial training time can be extensive (i.e., several months). In addition, the motivation for problematic behavior must be removed. Thus, extinction or mild punishment is a critical component of our intervention procedures.

Second, functional communication training seldom results in negative side effects. Even when the procedures fail to control problematic behavior, the parents have, at the very least, worked on a socially important skill. The parents who have participated in these projects are volunteers, and all have agreed that functional communication is a valuable skill.

Third, as discussed by Koegel and Koegel (1988), independent manding can be a *pivotal response*; it can facilitate other forms of social interactions. As parents work with their children in our functional communication training programs, both the child and the parent often begin to interact in more positive ways. These "side effects" to intervention are critical for maintenance (see the Response Generalization section of this chapter).

Assuming that the mand replaces problematic behavior and that training results in improved social interactions, a final component of intervention is still needed for maintenance to occur: *stimulus generalization* (DePaepe, Reichle, & O'Neill, 1993). In order for long-term maintenance to occur, the children and parents must generalize their new behaviors across settings, care providers, and activities.

A MODEL FOR MAINTENANCE

The intervention process is complex and includes several steps. Table 1 summarizes these steps and provides a rationale and conceptual basis for each step in intervention. When an operant function for problematic behavior is identified via a functional analysis (Step 1), functional communication training (Step 2) is initiated to replace problematic behavior with

Table 1.   A model for maintenance via functional communication training

Step	Procedure	Purpose	Conceptual mechanism
1	Functional analysis	Identify reinforcers of problematic behavior	Operant function of problematic behavior (Iwata, Dorsey, Bauman, Slifer, & Richman, 1982)
2	Functional communication training	Replace problematic behavior with one or more mands	Functional equivalency (Carr, 1988)
3	Reinforcement of associated social–communicative responses	Increase repertoire of appropriate, reinforced behavior (response generalization)	Induction (Koegel & Koegel, 1988)
4	Differential reinforcement of social–communicative responses	Maintenance	Matching theory (McDowell, 1988)
5	Implement training across situations	Stimulus generalization	Stimulus control (Halle & Holt, 1991; Halle & Spradlin, 1993; Shore et al., 1994)

a mand. When success occurs, it is because the manding response serves the same function as problematic behavior but is more efficient and more effective in gaining reinforcement.

This initial manding response may only be important early in the training process. When the mand is displayed independently by the child, the focus of intervention becomes the other appropriate social–communicative behaviors that are induced (Step 3) through mand training. These other behaviors, through reinforcement, gradually increase in number and in frequency and serve to replace both the problematic behavior *and* the original mands trained (Step 4). They comprise the reciprocal interactions between parent and child. Concurrently, training across stimulus conditions (Step 5) is conducted to promote generalization.

In the following sections, each component is discussed as it pertains to our work with young children in their homes, and actual case examples are briefly described. The model in Table 1 represents our set of working guidelines. A legitimate question, then, is how often does this model work? As of this writing, we have attempted this approach with 13 children for at least 6 months. Thus far, 77% have shown reductions in problematic behavior of at least 90%, and 92% have displayed the anticipated increases in social collateral behavior. Thus, the intervention model is promising, but further refinement is needed.

In-Home Assessment of Problematic Behavior

Researchers have used a variety of direct observation techniques to investigate the variables controlling young children's problematic behavior in the home. A common focus for this type of naturalistic study is the analysis of interactions between children and family members during normal daily routines. These investigations have used either multicode observational systems (Karpowitz & Johnson, 1981; Patterson, 1974; Sanders & Glynn, 1981; Wahl, Johnson, Johansson, & Martin, 1974; Wahler & Dumas, 1986; Wahler, Williams, & Cerezo, 1990) or narrative recording (Pettit & Bates, 1989) as a method for identifying the naturally occurring sequence of antecedent–behavior–consequence (A–B–C) events that produce and maintain behavior. Overall, the results of these descriptive analyses suggest functional relations between ongoing child behavior and parent responses (Mace & Lalli, 1991).

The following is a brief overview of a multiphase assessment method that is used to select and evaluate individualized interventions in home settings (see Table 2). The parents conduct each assessment procedure with our coaching. In Phase 1, a descriptive assessment is conducted that includes a parent interview and parent completion of checklists. In Phase 2, a structural analysis is performed to more precisely identify antecedent

Table 2.   In-home assessment procedures

Method	Purpose
Phase 1: Descriptive	
Scatterplot[a]	Identify times of the day associated with problematic behavior
A-B-C assessment[b]	Identify naturally occurring events associated with behavior
Parent interview	Identify primary behavior concerns and events associated with occurrence of behavior
Activity selection	Categorize toys and activities across structural variables (preference, demand, and attention for use in subsequent assessment activities)
Preference assessment	Identify potential reinforcers
Phase 2: Structural	
Structural analysis[c]	Identify antecedent events that set the occasion for behavior
Phase 3: Functional	
Brief functional analysis[d]	Identify maintaining events for behavior
Phase 4: Follow-up	
Treatment probes	Analyze treatment effects across intervention sessions and generalization conditions
Brief functional analysis	Analyze durability of maintaining events over time
Parent checklist	Assess correspondence of treatment probes to parent reports of child behavior
Treatment acceptability[e]	Assess general acceptability of treatment, parent perceptions of treatment effectiveness, and any negative side effects

[a]From Touchette, MacDonald, & Langer (1985).
[b]From Bijou, Peterson, & Ault (1968).
[c]From Carr & Durand (1985).
[d]From Iwata, Dorsey, Slifer, Bauman, & Richman (1982).
[e]From Reimers & Wacker (1988).

conditions that may set the occasion for problematic behavior to occur. In Phase 3, a functional analysis is conducted to test hypotheses regarding events that maintain problematic behavior. In Phase 4, ongoing intervention outcomes, the durability of initial assessment results, and treatment acceptability are evaluated.

Phase 1. Descriptive Assessment: Identifying Events Associated with Problematic Behavior

Child Behavior Record   Parents are first asked to record their child's behavior for 1 week by indicating the frequency of inappropriate behaviors during 30-minute intervals throughout the day. Based on the scatterplot analysis described by Touchette, MacDonald, and Langer (1985), the parent's record is used to identify the times of day in which problematic behavior typically occurs. Second, parents are asked to write a brief description of the events that precede or occur concurrent with the problematic behavior, the specific behavior they observe, and their response to the child's behavior (A–B–C assessment) (Bijou, Peterson, & Ault, 1968).

Parent Interview Interviews are conducted to facilitate the identification of variables that influence the occurrence of problematic behavior (O'Neill, Horner, Albin, Storey, & Sprague, 1989). The results of the parents' scatterplot and A–B–C assessments are reviewed to clarify parent concerns and develop preliminary hypotheses regarding events that may control child behavior. However, interpretation of this information is treated cautiously because a number of unknown factors may affect the accuracy of parent reporting.

Activity Selection Play activities are typically an important part of a child's day and may have a functional relationship to the occurrence of both appropriate and inappropriate behaviors. Following the descriptive assessment of child behavior, parents complete an activity selection form that provides information on activities and toys available in the home. This assessment is conducted to obtain a selection of activities for use in subsequent analyses and to identify potential reinforcers for appropriate behavior. Parents are instructed to go through the child's toys and categorize them as high or low with respect to child preference, difficulty level, and amount of parent attention that is typically associated with each activity. This is followed by a brief preference assessment in which we observe the child playing. In this procedure, the child is given free access to toys, and data are collected on the percentage of time the child plays with each toy.

Conducting this type of descriptive assessment allows the involvement of parents as active collaborators from the beginning of the assessment process and may provide information that increases the precision and efficiency of subsequent assessments (Lalli & Goh, 1993). However, as noted by Lalli and Goh (1993) and Lerman and Iwata (1993), descriptive data are often difficult to interpret and only suggest functional relationships. This limits their utility in determining what specific intervention will be most effective in treating the problematic behavior (Cooper, Wacker, Sasso, Reimers, & Donn, 1990). Thus, the following experimental analyses are conducted to more directly assess the relationship between the child's behavior and the variables of task difficulty, task preference, and parent attention.

Phase 2. Structural Analysis: Systematic Manipulation of Antecedent Variables that Occasion Problematic Behavior

In Phase 2, a structural analysis (Axelrod, 1987; Carr & Durand, 1985) is conducted to more precisely identify antecedent events that may set the occasion for problematic behavior. In this procedure, information from the descriptive assessment is used to evaluate, as needed, the effects of high and low parent attention, task preference, and task demands on child behavior. This analysis consists of a series of 5- to 10-minute analog conditions conducted within a multielement design. These conditions are repeated across at least 2 days to partially verify the stability of assessment results.

We begin by assessing the variable that we hypothesize, based on the descriptive assessment, to be related to inappropriate behavior. Thus, the effect of one structural variable (e.g., demand) on child behavior is evaluated while the other two variables (e.g., attention, preference) are held constant. For each analysis, the variables held constant are provided noncontingently and in a manner typically associated with appropriate behavior. Thus, if demands are being evaluated, high- and low-demand tasks are varied using preferred tasks and continuous attention from the parent. When a stable pattern of behavior is observed, the next two variables, if necessary, are assessed in a similar manner.

Phase 3. Functional Analysis: Identifying the Variables that Maintain Problematic Behavior

In Phase 3, a functional analysis (Iwata et al., 1982) is conducted to test hypotheses regarding the consequences (reinforcers) that maintain problematic behavior. Maintaining events can be divided into three general categories: 1) *positive reinforcement*, where the behavior enables the child to gain a desired item or activity; 2) *negative reinforcement*, where the behavior results in the child's avoiding or escaping from a nonpreferred activity; and 3) *automatic reinforcement*, where the behavior is maintained by an intrinsic variable (e.g., self-stimulation). The functional analysis consists of a series of brief analog conditions in which the child is provided with reinforcers contingent on the occurrence of problematic behavior. For example, if low levels of attention during the structural analysis are associated with inappropriate behavior, the functional analysis provides brief amounts of parent attention contingent on the occurrence of inappropriate behavior (e.g., "Don't do that; you'll hurt yourself"). This contingent attention condition is then alternated with control conditions (e.g., free play) to identify if attention is, indeed, maintaining problematic behavior.

We begin the functional analysis by conducting a control condition: free play. During free play, the child has unrestricted access to preferred toys and noncontingent parent attention, and no demands are placed on the child. The order and type of subsequent assessment conditions are based on hypotheses generated during the structural and descriptive analyses. Again, a multielement design is used to evaluate the results.

The primary reason to conduct a functional analysis is to match an intervention to the function of problematic behavior (Iwata et al., 1990). Although descriptive and structural analysis procedures provide information regarding variables that influence child behavior, a functional analysis is needed to verify functional relationships.

Phase 4. Follow-Up: Assessment of Treatment Outcomes

In Phase, 4, a combination of assessment procedures is used to evaluate treatment outcomes and the durability of the initial assessment results. Weekly intervention probes are conducted that include both intervention sessions and generalization probes. Intermittent assessment probes using brief functional analyses are conducted to determine if the maintaining variables for problematic behavior persist over time. Parents are asked to complete a simple checklist used by Cooper et al. (1992) that rates the child's behavior during the week. Checklist results are compared to direct observation data to determine the correspondence between our observations and what the parent observes throughout the day. Finally, parents are asked to complete an acceptability checklist: the Treatment Acceptability Rating Form–Revised (Reimers & Wacker, 1988). This form assesses parent perceptions of treatment effectiveness, parent understanding of treatment, and negative side effects of treatment. Information from this form is used to adjust the intervention as needed. Case Study 3.1 is an example of our in-home assessment procedures.

THE ASSESSMENT–INTERVENTION RELATIONSHIP

Intervention strategies for behaviors such as self-injury, aggression, and stereotypy are diverse and include the use of mechanical and physical restraints, psychotropic medications, reinforcement procedures, and punishment. Even with this wide array of treatments, selection of appropriate intervention for any given individual has proven to be complex (Lennox & Miltenberger, 1989). As we discussed in the previous section, experimental analysis is an assessment methodology that permits care providers to select the right type of intervention. The results of an experimental analysis directly influence treatment intervention by specifying 1) which consequences maintain problematic behavior, 2) which antecedent conditions should be removed or selected for intervention, and 3) which reinforcers should be used to increase alternative behavior (Lennox & Miltenberger, 1989).

A positive side effect of experimental analysis is that it leads practitioners to focus on reinforcement-based procedures and to rely less heavily on restrictive, punishment-based procedures (Axelrod, 1987).

Case Study 3.1.   Ben

Ben was a 2-year-old boy who was diagnosed with developmental delay. He was referred for aggressive behaviors (biting and hitting), destructive behaviors (destroying toys or furniture), noncompliance, and temper tantrums. Descriptive assessment results (Phase 1) indicated that problematic behaviors occurred throughout the day across a variety of situations. Although these results documented the occurrence of problematic behavior, the information did not lead to a clear hypothesis regarding the function of Ben's behavior.

A structural analysis (Phase 2) was then conducted to identify relationships between Ben's behavior and parent demands and attention. Structural analysis results showed that problematic behavior was occasioned most often by parent demands and, to a lesser extent, by situations in which Ben received reduced amounts of parent attention. Thus, two hypothesized functions for Ben's behavior were plausible: 1) escape from parent demands and 2) gaining parent attention.

These hypotheses were tested via a brief functional analysis (Phase 3). During contingent attention conditions, Ben was given brief parent attention (reprimands) only when he displayed inappropriate behavior. During contingent escape conditions, Ben was asked to complete a sorting task with his parents, and inappropriate behavior resulted in a brief break from the task. These conditions were compared to a control condition (free play). The results showed that Ben's inappropriate behavior almost never occurred during either free play or contingent attention, but increased substantially during contingent escape conditions. Thus, the functional analysis identified escape to be the major reason for his problematic behavior.

Punishment-based procedures may, at first, be appealing to care providers because decreases in inappropriate behavior are usually observed relatively quickly. However, punishment-based intervention procedures should be used only as a default treatment intervention (Iwata, 1988) or as a small part of a predominantly reinforcement-based intervention package. This latter approach is one we typically use in our own work.

When the function of problematic behavior has been identified, a variety of treatments within functional categories can be selected. One intervention component is to use extinction to stop the reinforcement of problematic behavior. Thus, for children whose problematic behavior is maintained by attention, intervention might involve withholding attention or removing attention (time-out). For children whose behavior is maintained by escape, intervention might involve continuing to deliver task prompts or using guided compliance.

An alternative intervention option is to eliminate, as much as possible, those antecedent events that occasion problematic behavior. Thus, for children whose behavior is maintained by attention, intervention might involve avoiding situations in which attention is diverted from the child. For children whose behavior is maintained by escape, intervention might involve reducing demands. We use a commonsense approach: If problematic situations cannot be avoided, extinction or mild punishment is often incorporated into the intervention package.

The primary intervention component, however, is to teach the child new, more adaptive responses that can be used to obtain the same reinforcement that maintains problematic behavior. The child is taught a new response that is functionally equivalent (Carr, 1988) to the problematic response. The new, adaptive response must result in the same reinforcement that maintains the problematic response. For example, if the behavior is maintained by positive reinforcement, such as access to attention, then the new response must also result in access to attention. Conceptually, this form of intervention should result in decreased aberrant responding because the child now has an alternative way to gain reinforcement. Again, however, problematic behavior must not lead to reinforcement or the problematic behavior, too, will continue to occur.

A variety of alternative responses can be selected to replace aberrant responses. The function of the alternative response selected for intervention is more important than the form of the alternative response. Iwata et al. (1990) referred to the importance of establishing a functional match between assessment and treatment. For example, if self-injury is maintained by escape (negative reinforcement), intervention might involve removing demands contingent on compliance. If self-injury is maintained by attention (positive reinforcement), intervention might involve providing access to increased attention for compliance. Thus, appropriate behavior is reinforced by the same reinforcer identified as maintaining problematic behavior.

Functional Communication Training

Of the reinforcement-based treatments available, one of the most successful is FCT. In FCT, communicative responses such as words, gestures, or signs are used as the replacement responses for problematic behavior to obtain reinforcement. Therefore, the communicative response is functionally equivalent (Carr, 1988) to the problematic behavior. Carr and Durand (1985) applied this procedure with children diagnosed with autism. They taught each child two verbal responses, one to solicit attention and one to decrease demands (e.g., "How am I doing?" to solicit attention; "Help me" to decrease demands). Of special importance was that, in all cases, inappropriate behavior was reduced only when the response that matched the function of the problematic behavior was used. This study provided evidence that the function of behavior is the most relevant variable related to successful communication training. This finding has been supported several times across diverse populations in subsequent research (Durand & Carr, 1985, 1991; Northup et al., 1991; Wacker et al., 1990).

At first, FCT may appear to be a rather simple intervention. However, FCT is best thought of as a multicomponent intervention package that begins with a functional analysis (Durand & Carr, 1985). When the maintaining contingency has been identified, a mand (communicative response) is taught to the child so that he or she can request reinforcement. It makes intuitive sense that a reduction in problematic behavior should occur if 1) the mand results in reinforcement, and 2) the problematic behavior no longer results in reinforcement. In most cases, FCT packages include contingencies for aberrant responding as well as contingencies for appropriate responding. For example, while providing reinforcement contingencies for mand responses, Carr and Durand (1985) also placed all aberrant behavior on extinction, and Steege et al. (1989) provided extinction and redirection contingent on aberrant behavior. The results of these and other studies (Fisher et al., 1993; Wacker et al., 1990) indicate that contingencies for both appropriate and inappropriate responses are necessary for successful FCT interventions. It is for this reason that these procedures are combined into packages when FCT is used in home settings.

When FCT packages are based on the results of functional analysis and contain contingencies for both appropriate and inappropriate behavior, relatively quick initial results can be achieved. For example, Northup et al. (1991) conducted brief functional analyses in an outpatient clinic to identify the variables maintaining aggressive behavior displayed by young adults and adolescents with developmental disabilities. Following the functional analysis, each client received an FCT package that included reinforcement for a mand response (e.g., signs, words) and extinction or mild punishment for aggression. This resulted in a high occurrence of manding and a low occurrence of aggressive behavior within 90 minutes of introducing the intervention.

Applying FCT Packages in Children's Homes We often devote several weeks to assessment in children's homes. This allows us to better understand the children and their families and gives them an opportunity to adjust to our coming into their homes. Case Studies 3.2 and 3.3 summarize the assessment and intervention procedures conducted with Billy, a child whose inappropriate behavior was maintained by positive reinforcement (i.e., attention), and with Nile, a child whose inappropriate behavior was maintained by negative reinforcement (i.e., escape). Billy and Nile were the first two children to enroll in our in-home project.

Incorporating Choice Making into FCT Packages   The results we obtained with Billy and Nile represent the results we have obtained with

---

Case Study 3.2.   Billy

Billy was a 2-year-old boy who was nonverbal and diagnosed with developmental delay. When we first became involved with Billy, his mother told us that she carried him around on her hip for the majority of the day, even when she was engaged in household chores such as washing dishes. If she attempted to set him down, he usually engaged in severe tantrums, during which he would scream, thrust his body back and forth, destroy toys, and bang his head on the floor. Therefore, Billy's mother allowed him to stay on her lap to avoid tantrums and self-injury.

We began our assessment by directly observing Billy's behavior under various structural conditions. Because his inappropriate behavior appeared to be related to the amount of attention his mother provided, we first observed him under varying levels of parent attention (e.g., high vs. low attention). As expected, Billy engaged in the most problematic behavior when his mother ignored him, but he engaged in very little inappropriate behavior when his mother provided him with continuous attention. This was confirmed by our functional analysis.

Conditions in which attention was available continuously were alternated with conditions in which attention was provided contingent on inappropriate behavior (i.e., Billy's mother attempted to take him off her lap, but, if he began to have a tantrum, she allowed him to stay on her lap). Inappropriate behavior occurred only when his mother attempted to remove him from her lap, but decreased immediately when she allowed him to stay on her lap. These results confirmed the hypothesis that parent attention served as a reinforcer for his inappropriate behavior.

(continued)

Case Study 3.2. (*continued*)

Billy's mother then implemented a treatment package that consisted of functional communication training and brief time-out.
Billy was first taught to sign PLEASE to maintain his mother's attention. Initially, his mother prompted him to sign PLEASE throughout
the sessions so that he was able to remain on his mother's lap for
the entire session. Over several weeks, these prompts were faded,
and he was required to sign PLEASE independently to maintain his
mother's attention.

Throughout treatment, Billy's mother provided him with preferred toys in addition to her attention for signing PLEASE. Our hope
was that, by pairing toys with his mother's attention, he would
learn to find toys to be just as reinforcing as his mother's attention.
This would permit his mother to leave him briefly with preferred
toys. Finally, if Billy engaged in inappropriate behavior rather than
signing PLEASE, his mother implemented time-out. During time-out,
his mother left the room. (He was monitored by another adult to
prevent injury.) As soon as he stopped having a tantrum, he was
prompted to sign PLEASE, and his mother immediately returned to
the room to play with him. Within 4 months, Billy played by himself
out of his mother's lap for several minutes, and he signed PLEASE independently to request his mother's attention when she was busy
with other tasks. Self-injury occurred very rarely.

Case Study 3.3.   Nile

Nile was a 3-year-old boy who was nonverbal and had been diagnosed with developmental delay and autism. Whenever family
members attempted to interact with him, he engaged in severe aggression (e.g., biting, pinching, scratching others), self-injury (e.g.,
biting, hitting himself, head banging), and tantrums (e.g., screaming, destroying toys).

As with Billy, we began our assessment by directly observing
Nile's behavior under various antecedent conditions (e.g., high vs.
low attention, high vs. low demand tasks, high vs. low preference
tasks). Although Nile engaged in some inappropriate behavior during all conditions, he consistently exhibited the most problematic

(*continued*)

Case Study 3.3. *(continued)*

behavior when he was required to perform demanding tasks, which for him even included requests to play. This was consistent with his parents' reports to us and led to the hypothesis that Nile's inappropriate behavior was maintained by negative reinforcement.

Next, we conducted a functional analysis to verify that escape from demanding tasks served to increase, or reinforce, Nile's inappropriate behavior. During the functional analysis, we alternated conditions in which no demands were placed on Nile (parallel play with his mom) with conditions in which he was required to complete a demanding task (play a certain way) but was allowed to briefly escape the task contingent on inappropriate behavior. Inappropriate behavior increased during sessions in which he was allowed to escape demanding tasks; however, once the task demands were removed, inappropriate behavior decreased immediately. This confirmed our hypothesis of negative reinforcement.

The functional communication training package involved teaching Nile to request breaks from demanding tasks by signing DONE. The package consisted of three major components: 1) providing breaks from demanding tasks contingent on signing, 2) withholding reinforcement (continuing the activities) contingent on inappropriate behavior, and 3) pairing positive parent attention with access to reinforcement. During treatment, Nile was prompted by his mother (and later by his brother and father) to complete part of a play activity. As soon as he complied with one step of the activity, Nile was prompted to sign DONE. If Nile signed DONE, the task was removed, and he was allowed to take a break. On his breaks, Nile's parents "shadowed" him and played with him, but they did not attempt to direct him to other activities. Our hope was that, over time, social interactions with his family would become reinforcing rather than aversive to him. After his break, Nile was required to complete another step of the task and to sign DONE. If he engaged in inappropriate behavior at any time, he was not allowed to take a break; instead, he was required to continue working on the task.

Over time, we gradually increased the amount of time he stayed on task prior to requesting a break. After approximately 3 months, Nile began to sign DONE independently and even began to verbalize "done." Within 6 months, a marked decrease in inappropriate behavior occurred, and, equally important, he began to play with family members and to verbalize other words.

many children involved in our projects. We have been very pleased with the overall success that has been achieved using intervention packages based on FCT. However, we are continually searching for ways to improve our treatment strategies. For example, for some children, we are attempting to incorporate choice making via matching theory into our FCT intervention packages.

As described previously, a key component of FCT packages is withholding reinforcement for inappropriate behavior. Although this is conceptually simple, in reality it is rarely possible to adhere strictly to this rule. For example, if the problematic behavior is life threatening and is maintained by attention, most care providers will be unable to ignore the behavior or to enforce a time-out. Similarly, if the life-threatening behavior is maintained by escape from nonpreferred tasks, care providers may be unable to continue presenting task demands while blocking self-injury. In both examples, the care provider is not able to withhold reinforcement completely (i.e., some attention is provided or a brief break is allowed). Thus, the child receives some reinforcement. In these situations, the care provider must attempt to minimize the reinforcement for problematic behavior and to maximize reinforcement for the appropriate mand in order to increase the probability that the child will use the mand rather than the aberrant response to seek reinforcement.

In situations where it is not possible for care providers to completely withhold reinforcement, the child essentially has two responses (the appropriate communicative response and the inappropriate response) with which to gain reinforcement. This constitutes a two-choice situation in which the child selects which response to use to obtain reinforcement. The communicative response and the inappropriate response can be viewed as response options that result in their own schedules of reinforcement. If these responses are viewed as choices, Mace and Roberts (1993) suggest that *matching theory* (McDowell, 1988) may provide the best model for intervention.

Matching theory has been derived from basic research on concurrent schedules and the matching law (de Villiers, 1977; Herrnstein, 1961, 1970). The underlying premise of matching theory is that individuals have an array of concurrently available responses and that each response is associated with an independent schedule of reinforcement. The schedule of reinforcement associated with each response affects the individual's choices or the allocation of behavior among these response alternatives. According to matching theory, individuals should exhibit responses that result in the most reinforcement.

Mace and Roberts (1993) suggested that there are four factors that may affect choices or response allocation: 1) rate (schedule) of reinforcement, 2) quality of reinforcement, 3) immediacy of reinforcement, and 4) response effort. In most situations, it is likely that these factors interact. By increasing the rate, quality, or immediacy of reinforcement, or by decreasing the response effort associated with the mand, it is hypothesized that the probability of the individual's "choosing" to mand rather than to engage in the inappropriate response will increase.

In FCT, the probability that children will choose to engage in an appropriate response rather than an aberrant response can be increased by maximizing the amount of reinforcement provided for mand responses and minimizing the amount of reinforcement provided for aberrant responses. This response teaches children that appropriate communication results in the greatest reinforcement. Increasing the communicative response will result in a similar increase in a wide array of other social–communicative behaviors, such as smiling and laughing, because they are associated with reinforcement (Sprague & Horner, 1992). These behaviors become part of an increasingly large prosocial response class, which in turn results in even more reinforcement for the child. As the response class of appropriate behaviors continues to grow, the amount of reinforcement the child receives for appropriate responses continues to increase, and it is likely that the amount of reinforcement received for inappropriate behaviors continues to decrease. Thus, according to matching theory, the child should be more likely to engage in an increasing number of appropriate social responses in his or her repertoire rather than choosing to engage in a very limited number of aberrant responses. The choice options for the child are "biased" in favor of prosocial, communicative responses through FCT. To increase the child's options for appropriate behavior, response generalization is needed.

Response Generalization

For FCT to have long-term effects, the child's repertoire of prosocial responses that result in reinforcement must be expanded. Therefore, in addition to the replacement of problematic behavior with one or more mands (functional equivalence), response generalization also must occur. Response generalization occurs if there are increases in other behaviors when a target behavior is developed or increased via reinforcement (Sulzer-Azaroff & Mayer, 1991). For example, reinforcing a newly trained mand may result in behaviors associated with that mand such as smiling, hugging, and other communicative responses. In essence, the overall manner in which the child interacts with the parent may change. If the parent responds by reinforcing the child for each new behavior, then the parent's behavior also changes. When the behavior of both the parent and the child is modified during interactions, this constitutes changes in reciprocal interactions. Based on this analysis, reinforcing a mand might induce positive changes in other prosocial behaviors of the child and the parent, modifying their overall interactions.

Through the early 1990s, only one published investigation has analyzed response generalization with FCT (Sprague & Horner, 1992). These authors were interested in the changes in behavior that occurred when either 1) the occurrence of an inappropriate behavior within a response class is decreased via punishment, or 2) the occurrence of an alternative, socially acceptable behavior (i.e., asking for help) is increased via FCT. Although both treatments reduced problematic behavior, different types of response generalization occurred for each treatment. When punishment procedures were in place, a *positive contrast effect* (Reynolds, 1961) occurred; that is, a decreased occurrence of one inappropriate behavior was found to covary with an increased occurrence of other inappropriate behaviors within the same response class. It is important to note that this increase in inappropriate behaviors occurred without increasing the reinforcement obtained for these behaviors. Conversely, when a mand was increased via FCT, all inappropriate behaviors emitted within the same response class decreased. In addition, response generalization was demonstrated; that is, a simultaneous increase in other socially acceptable behaviors was observed.

As discussed by Koegel and Koegel (1988), when the initial target response is shown to increase other desired behavior, the initial response can be considered as a *pivotal response*. When the child mands (i.e., appropriately requests attention, a break, or a preferred toy), and the parent responds positively ("Okay, let's play!"; "Yes, you can take a break"; "Here's your toy"), the child is then likely to respond to the parent with other pro-social behaviors such as smiling, showing affection, or playing. When this occurs, we say that manding has induced prosocial behavior. When a response like a mand induces other behavior, such as more positive interactions with others, the mand is called a pivotal response.

If the induced prosocial behaviors also are reinforced by the parent (and parents are likely to do so), then not just manding but an entire class of prosocial behavior is increased. Therefore, when the child wants attention, he or she might, of course, mand. Gradually, however, as other prosocial responses are reinforced, the child might become more likely to smile, show affection, or even use other words ("play") rather than to emit the initial mand. Over time, an entire class of prosocial behaviors is used by the child as an alternative response to problematic behavior. Based on our conceptual model, if inappropriate behavior is replaced with a mand that serves the same function, intervention is successful initially because of functional equivalence (Carr, 1988). The manding response serves as a one-to-one replacement response for inappropriate behavior: The manding response replaces the inappropriate behavior because the mand is reinforced and problematic behavior is not. However, the mand is also associated with a variety of social–communicative behaviors such as smiling and playing; therefore, as manding increases, so do smiling and playing because of response generalization. When multiple behaviors are reinforced, the reinforcement obtained via these appropriate behaviors should exceed the reinforcement obtained for the relatively fewer number of inappropriate behaviors.

Northup et al. (1994) suggested that mands might, indeed, function as pivotal responses. In their study, Northup et al. evaluated the maintenance of FCT in classroom settings during a 17-month period for five students with severe disabilities. For three students whose appropriate behavior was maintained for the entire 17 months, there was a consistent downward trend in their display of the original mand as well as in their inappropriate behavior. This decrease in both manding and inappropriate behavior over time was not anticipated because manding was hypothesized to replace inappropriate behavior.

To further investigate this finding, Fus, Wacker, Grisolano, Berg, and Rogers (1991) conducted a retrospective study of the same students (all sessions had been videotaped) and demonstrated that reinforcement of the original mands induced multiple other appropriate behaviors. This occurred in two steps. During the first year of the investigation, an increased occurrence of the mand covaried with a decreased occurrence of inappropriate behavior, suggesting that the mand was functionally equivalent to the original aberrant behavior (Carr, 1988). In addition, it was observed that the behavior of the teachers changed throughout the year. As the child increased his or her use of the mand and displayed less frequent problematic behavior, the teachers interacted in more positive ways with the child. Thus, in the first year, response generalization occurred with the teachers' behavior. During the second year, the mand was rarely displayed by the children, but instead a relatively large number of other socially appropriate behaviors (e.g., toy play, greetings) occurred with increasingly high frequencies. Fus et al. (1991) hypothesized that these newly induced social behaviors displayed by the students further increased the overall amount of reinforcement that they obtained. This overall increase in social behavior reduced the need for the original mand as well as for the problematic behavior.

To summarize, in the first year, FCT resulted in a more reinforcing situation for the students; as prosocial behaviors were displayed, they were reinforced. By the second year, enough other behaviors had been induced and reinforced that neither the mand nor the problematic behavior occurred. Thus, the mand functioned as a pivotal response that induced changes first in teacher behavior and then in student behavior. Carr, Taylor, and Robinson (1991) also showed that student behavior can affect teacher behavior. In their study, problematic behavior affected the way educational tasks were presented. In the Fus et al. (1991) study, similar changes were noted, but in this case the changes in teacher behavior were related to the mands used by the student.

Using the conceptual model for maintenance described in Table 1 as a guideline, one explanation for Fus et al.'s (1991) results is that the alternative mand served as a pivotal response (Koegel & Koegel, 1988) to induce a class of socially acceptable behaviors. The reason both inappropriate behavior and manding decreased was that these generalized behaviors resulted in more reinforcement than either manding or problematic behavior. Based on matching theory (McDowell, 1988), the social–communicative behaviors may have "overwhelmed" manding as well as for the problematic behaviors.

We used the model in Table 1 as the basis for our initial intervention procedures in children's homes. Our explicit intent was to use FCT to train pivotal mands. We hoped that, initially, the mands would covary with problematic behavior, and, as described in our case studies for Billy and Nile, this result occurred. However, we were convinced that for long-term maintenance to occur, response generalization was needed: The mands needed to serve as pivotal responses, and the parents needed to reinforce the generalized responses. Therefore, we coached parents to train the mand (FCT) and to reinforce all novel behavior (differential reinforcement of other behavior). To better describe these results, we return to a discussion of Billy and Nile (see Case Studies 3.4 and 3.5).

For both Billy and Nile, FCT allowed us to teach an alternative communicative response that effectively replaced inappropriate behavior because the mand served the same function as inappropriate behavior. A beneficial side effect of the intervention was that the communicative response was pivotal: A relatively large number of other appropriate behaviors emerged throughout intervention. This new class of appropriate behaviors resulted in an overall increase in reinforcement (for both parent and child) and served to suppress recurrences of inappropriate behaviors at home. Unfortunately, we have found that neither this increase in prosocial behavior nor the mand automatically generalizes outside the home. Instead, problems persist at church, child care, the store, and in other community settings. When problems of this type occur, we need to evaluate stimulus generalization (Step 5 in Table 1).

Stimulus Generalization

Some children continue to engage in high frequencies of problematic behavior and display little communicative or prosocial behaviors within environments other than the home, even after months of successful home intervention. Although a lack of generalization may have several causes,

Case Study 3.4. Response Generalization for Billy

Before treatment, inappropriate behavior was found to be maintained by positive reinforcement. Billy's treatment posed some interesting concerns. First, his communicative abilities were limited to babbling, screaming, and crying, which he engaged in as soon as his mother removed him from her lap. Second, Billy's repertoire of independent toy play behaviors was virtually nonexistent, which removed any option of diverting his attention away from his mother and toward preferred play activities while his mother was completing household chores.

Given these concerns, we trained Billy to use an appropriate mand (signing PLEASE) to gain his mother's attention. When he signed PLEASE, his mother attended to him, always gave him toys, and always played with him using the toys. Thus, we were increasing toy play via response induction by providing Billy with continuous access to toys while he interacted with his mother. Based on our conceptual model, we hypothesized that new toy play behaviors would occur for two reasons. First, the mand would lead to increased contact with toys and play opportunities along with his mother's attention. Second, because the identified reinforcer (i.e., his mother's attention) was paired with toys, increased toy play would lead to an overall increase in reinforcement.

Again, based on our conceptual model, we hypothesized that three outcomes would occur during the course of treatment. First, manding behavior would initially increase, and, via functional equivalence, this increase would be correlated with a simultaneous decrease in inappropriate behavior. Second, as the mand became a more established part of his behavior, a variety of new social behaviors would emerge, such as increased toy play behaviors. Third, treatment gains would be maintained because he would begin to play more with toys and would not require so much attention from his mother. After 4 months of FCT, inappropriate behavior decreased to near zero occurrence. Equally important, he was now out of his mother's lap most of the time, and he spent more of his time playing than demanding his mother's attention.

When he was now provided with access to toys and his mother's attention was diverted away from him, Billy's inappropriate behavior remained at zero or near zero occurrence for the next 2 years. In addition, he rarely signed PLEASE to request attention but

(continued)

Case Study 3.4. (*continued*)

instead played for several minutes and began using verbal words ("watch"). Overall, a 100% increase in novel play behaviors occurred over the 2-year period.

Case Study 3.5. Response Generalization for Nile

Before treatment, the function of Nile's inappropriate behavior was found to be maintained by escape from any situation that required interaction with his parents or other care providers. For example, during block play, Nile would engage in inappropriate behaviors if his mother handed him blocks, but no inappropriate behavior was observed if he was allowed to play by himself with the blocks. When he was seen in an outpatient clinic, he was fine when left alone in an exam room, but screamed and had a tantrum if any adult even stood in the doorway.

Given that Nile's inappropriate behavior was maintained by escape, we taught him via FCT to request breaks by signing PLEASE. Thus, during tasks like block play or rolling a ball, he could request a break at any time. However, we did not want him to simply remain alone during the break because we wanted to induce better interactions with his parents. Thus, during the break his mother "shadowed" him. She did not place demands on him but instead tried to anticipate what he wanted and gave it to him. If she thought, for example, that he might like a cracker, the following scenario occurred: Nile signed PLEASE and would usually leave the activity immediately. If he headed for the kitchen, she would walk with him, get a cracker, smile, and hand it to him. If he headed for a toy, she would hand the toy to him. In this way, even on break, Nile was interacting with his mom but in ways that were most preferable to him. Over time, his mother gradually increased her verbal and physical interactions with him while he was on break.

We implemented this type of shadowing, combined with FCT, because we wanted to induce appropriate interactions between Nile and his mother. Given this objective, a common one for children whose behavior is maintained by escape from adult contact, we attempted to 1) teach the child to mand for a break and 2) provide

(*continued*)

Case Study 3.5. *(continued)*

> the child with preferred activities delivered by the parent during breaks. For Nile, we provided preferred toys and edibles after he manded for a break appropriately, and we asked his mother to follow him closely to provide access to preferred items. As with Billy, the mand served as a pivotal response because it provided access to preferred items as well as access to breaks from demands or contact with adults.
>
> We followed Nile for a period of 8 months. During the initial months of treatment, an increased occurrence of the targeted mand was observed with a simultaneous decrease in inappropriate behavior. During breaks, and later during demands, his social interactions with his mother improved. He touched her more often, began to verbalize ("ball"), and was more affectionate. In the final months of treatment, we began to observe that Nile sought out his mother when her attention was diverted away from him. We believe that this increase in social initiations is due to induction. Finally, Nile and his mother no longer needed the break sign as he seldom resisted contact with her.

at least three reasons appear to relate directly to the use of FCT as an intervention for aberrant behavior. The first involves the adequacy of assessment. Given that each FCT plan is derived directly from the results of a functional analysis, the intervention package will be only as thorough as the assessment. In some cases, assessment may not adequately identify the various functions for aberrant behavior that occurs across different environments or events. In this case, the mand selected as the alternative response for intervention may not result in desired outcomes for the child in some contexts.

The second set of potential problems relates to the adequacy of the response selected as the mand. The mand selected for training may not be an effective means of obtaining desired outcomes across settings because it is either not recognized or not acceptable (Durand & Carr, 1991) to the care providers in that context.

The final set of problems reflects inadequate stimulus control for the adaptive behavior. The antecedent stimuli that control manding and other social–communicative behavior in the home may not be present or recognized by the child outside the home.

As suggested by Halle and Spradlin (1993), an evaluation of the conditions maintaining problematic behavior and the effects of intervention needs to be extended to identify the antecedent stimuli as well as the consequences controlling the display of behavior within and across contexts. Identification of these antecedent stimuli is essential for developing intervention packages that promote generalization across different contexts. Antecedent stimuli include any object, event, or person that is present immediately before the target response/mand or other behavior or during the display of the target response. Thus, any objects in the house, the activities used with FCT, the parents or siblings, and the types of prompts used by the parent are all antecedent stimuli. When these stimuli control the occurrence of behavior, they become *discriminative stimuli* and are sometimes referred to as *controlling stimuli.*

Adequacy of Assessment As demonstrated by Asmus, Derby, Wacker, Porter, and Ulrich (1993) and Derby et al. (1994), aberrant behavior may serve different functions for the same child depending on the context of the behavior. Asmus et al. (1993) showed that the function of aberrant behavior may vary for a given child depending on the presence or absence of specific antecedent stimuli in the immediate environment. In addition to comparing the effects of different consequence stimuli within a functional analysis, Asmus et al. also compared the effects of the presence or absence of siblings within the assessment conditions. For most children, performance was consistent, meaning that the function of problematic behavior remained the same regardless of the presence of a sibling. However, some children demonstrated different patterns of responding within the functional analysis depending on the presence or absence of their sibling during the assessment session. It is important to note that the parents conducted all conditions, and the sibling did not interact with the child; he or she was simply present. In one case, the presence of the sibling changed the function of aberrant behavior from escaping contact with the parent to seeking attention from the parent.

If relatively subtle changes in setting variables such as the presence or absence of siblings affect the results of assessment, then it is logical that other contextual changes, such as different care providers (e.g., teacher vs. parent), settings (school vs. home), and tasks (types of demands), would have a similar impact on behavior. Unless the effects of different antecedent variables are assessed and, when needed, incorporated into the intervention package, it is unlikely that any one intervention will be effective across all situations. In these cases, generalization will not occur, and maintenance will be problematic.

Derby et al. (1994) showed that different aberrant behaviors may serve different functions for the same child. In this investigation, the authors examined the results of a brief functional analysis for four clients who displayed multiple problematic behaviors (aggression, self-injury, and stereotypy). The results of the analysis were first evaluated with the multiple behaviors recorded as constituting one class of inappropriate behavior. The data were then reanalyzed with each topography of aberrant behavior scored separately. The results of this second analysis demonstrated that different forms of aberrant behavior sometimes served different functions. For example, one client engaged in self-injury to gain social attention and displayed aggression to escape task demands. Again, unless the intervention package addressed the function of each behavior, a reduction of all aberrant behavior across different antecedent conditions (e.g., during demanding times vs. low attention times) would not be expected to occur.

These two investigations highlight the importance of extending functional analyses to identify different functions of aberrant behavior for a given child, either across different contexts (Asmus et al., 1993) or across behaviors (Derby et al., 1994). If aberrant behavior serves multiple functions for a child, then it is imperative for intervention to address each function. In some cases, this can be accomplished by using a single mand that addresses both functions of the behavior (see Case Study 3.6).

For some children, a more generic response (e.g., the PLEASE sign) may serve multiple functions, such as "I want a break, please," and "I want a [specific item], please." In these instances, the parent or teacher must use the context of the behavior to determine the appropriate consequence for the "please" response. We have found that generic responses—ones that can serve multiple functions depending on context—are generalized more often than are highly specific responses.

Adequacy of Selected Response   As discussed by Reichle, York, and Sigafoos (1991), communicative responses vary in their effectiveness as a signal across different contexts. Manual signs may be readily available to the user but may not be understood by the different care providers whom the child encounters. Language boards and microswitches may be readily understood by others but may not be easily transportable. Even vocal communication may be misunderstood if the message is too generic or does not produce the outcome desired by the child. Each limitation affects the usefulness of the manding response across different environments and therefore decreases the likelihood that the response will be maintained across different situations.

To facilitate long-term maintenance of intervention gains, it is necessary to choose a communicative response that will solicit the desired outcome across settings, care providers, and activities. This can best be accomplished by selecting a communicative response that is readily recognized by people with whom the child is likely to interact. Durand and Carr (1991) demonstrated that long-term (2 years) maintenance of intervention gains and generalization across care providers and settings are possible when the communicative response is one that solicits natural maintaining contingencies for the child. In the Durand and Carr (1991)

> **Case Study 3.6.   Lyle**
>
> Lyle was a 4-year-old boy whose behavior had both a gain function (social attention) and an escape function (task demand). He engaged in aggressive behavior (pinching and scratching) and destruction (throwing objects) throughout most of his school day. The results of a functional analysis revealed that both behaviors served either an escape or a social attention function, depending on the context. A treatment plan was implemented in which Lyle learned to press a microswitch to activate the message, "I want to play." Intervention was initiated within a low social situation (attention was diverted from Lyle), and pressing the switch resulted in positive attention from the classroom teacher in the form of praising and talking with Lyle while he played with a toy. Later, the same switch and message were introduced into a demand situation. Pressing the microswitch in this context resulted in the same outcome: The teacher offered Lyle a preferred toy and praised him while he played appropriately. In this case, the message ("I want to play") served two functions for Lyle. It produced positive social attention and offers to play and, by the nature of the interaction, resulted in the temporary termination of task demands.

study, three students who engaged in self-injurious and aggressive behaviors to reduce task demands and, in one case, to gain social attention were taught simple verbal sentences to solicit help and gain attention. The trained responses consisted of "I don't understand" and "Help me" to solicit help, and "Am I doing good work?" to gain positive social attention. All students maintained their use of the mands across a 2-year period and generalized their use of the mands to a novel classroom and a novel teacher during the second year of the investigation. In two of the three cases, the mands resulted in the desired outcome for the students in the new environment without extra training or instruction for the classroom teacher. Therefore, the mand selected for use with any given child is critical for stimulus generalization and maintenance to occur.

Adequacy of Stimulus Control   In some cases, a child may use an effective mand within the context of intervention but may not display the response across other settings, care providers, or activities. In these instances, the child may not display the mand because the stimuli that control the behavior are either not present or not recognized by the child outside the intervention setting. Unless the child has a history of receiving the desired outcome contingent on the mand across multiple examples of care providers, activities, and situations, it is unlikely that the mand will be displayed in the presence of these novel stimuli. Durand and Carr (1991) addressed this problem by using multiple trainers to conduct mand training with the three boys in their investigation. Using multiple trainers ensured that the boys received the desired outcome for using the mand across different people and reduced the likelihood that manding would come under the control of extraneous stimuli that would not be common across different care providers (e.g., specific mannerisms of the trainer).

The importance of promoting generalization across untrained events is exemplified by our experience with Billy (see previous case study examples). After a year of training at home, Billy engaged in no self-injury and routinely displayed multiple communicative responses with family members, but at his preschool, he never displayed his "words," even when prompted by his teacher. Billy's mother was asked to come to school and interact with him for 1 hour. The teacher paired herself with his mother, and, within 1 hour, Billy began to sign independently. Pairing trained conditions (Billy's mother) with untrained conditions (Billy's teacher) can often result in transfer of stimulus control to the new condition. These transition periods are critical and warrant careful planning.

CONCLUSIONS

This chapter reviewed some of the procedures that are needed when working with young children who display problematic behavior in their homes. Collaborating directly with parents makes it possible to identify why problematic behavior occurs and to develop effective interventions. The goal is simple: to develop positive reciprocal interactions that endure over long periods of time. The processes needed for obtaining that goal are, however, quite complex.

When parents understand the function of behavior, they are often able to intervene more effectively. Uncertainty is the variable of concern, and conducting a thorough descriptive and functional analysis provides parents with confidence. FCT has been acceptable to parents and offers an intervention that not only suppresses aberrant behavior but also produces many desirable side effects. It is these side effects—changes in the way parents and children interact—that are the keys to maintenance. Equally important, however, is the systematic incorporation of these changes in behavior across people, settings, and activities. If these variations are not considered, even the most positive changes at home may be disrupted later when the child starts school, changes classrooms or teachers, or experiences other variations in his or her routine.

A number of interventions are possible. We have used FCT almost exclusively in our work because it can produce immediate changes in the interaction between children and their parents. However, it is not "magical" and often requires the concurrent use of other differential reinforcement and mild punishment procedures. Further refinement is still needed, as over 20% of the children with whom we work have not benefited from our intervention, even under the most optimal circumstances. For this reason, we continue to view the procedures that are presented in Table 1 as guidelines and not as a guaranteed formula for success. Too much is claimed too often for too many treatments, resulting in cynicism in both parents and professionals. FCT offers a very desirable set of intervention procedures, and the initial success of this intervention warrants further consideration.

REFERENCES

Asmus, J., Derby, K.M., Wacker, D.P., Porter, J., & Ulrich, S. (1993, May). *The stimulus control effects of siblings during functional analyses conducted in home settings.* Paper presented at Stimulus Control of Problem Behavior, a symposium presented at the annual conference of the Association for Behavior Analysis, Chicago.

Axelrod, S. (1987). Functional and structural analyses of behavior: Approaches leading to reduced use of punishment procedures. *Research in Developmental Disabilities, 8,* 165–178.

Bijou, S.W., Peterson, R.F., & Ault, M.H. (1968). A method to integrate descriptive and experimental field studies at the level of data and empirical concepts. *Journal of Applied Behavior Analysis, 1,* 175–191.

Carr, E.G. (1988). Functional equivalence as a mechanism of response generalization. In R. Horner, R.L. Koegel, & G. Dunlap (Eds.), *Generalization and maintenance: Life-style changes in applied settings* (pp. 221–241). Baltimore: Paul H. Brookes Publishing Co.

Carr, E.G., & Durand, V.M. (1985). Reducing behavior problems through functional communication training. *Journal of Applied Behavior Analysis, 18,* 111–126.

Carr, E.G., Taylor, J., & Robinson, S. (1991). The effects of severe behavior problems in children on the teaching behavior of adults. *Journal of Applied Behavior Analysis, 24,* 523–535.

Cooper, L.J., Wacker, D.P., Sasso, G.M., Reimers, T.M., & Donn, L.K. (1990). Using parents as therapists to evaluate the appropriate behavior of their children: Application to a tertiary diagnostic clinic. *Journal of Applied Behavior Analysis, 23,* 285–296.

Cooper, L.J., Wacker, D.P., Thursby, D., Plagmann, L.A., Harding, J., & Derby, K.M. (1992). Analysis of the role of task preferences, task demands, and adult attention on child behavior in outpatient and classroom settings. *Journal of Applied Behavior Analysis, 25,* 823–840.

DePaepe, P., Reichle, J., & O'Neill, R. (1993). Applying general-case instructional strategies when teaching communicative alternatives to problematic behavior. In J. Reichle & D. Wacker (Eds.), *Communication and language intervention: Vol. 3. Communicative alternatives to challenging behavior: Integrating functional assessment and intervention strategies* (pp. 237–262). Baltimore: Paul H. Brookes Publishing Co.

Derby, K.M., Wacker, D.P., Peck, S., Sasso, G., DeRaad, A., Berg, W., Asmus, J., & Ulrich, S. (1994). Functional analysis of separate topographies of aberrant behavior. *Journal of Applied Behavior Analysis, 27,* 267–278.

deVilliers, P.A. (1977). Choice in concurrent schedules and a qualitative formulation of the law of effect. In W.K. Honig & J.E.R. Studdon (Eds.), *Handbook of operant behavior* (pp. 233–287). Englewood Cliffs, NJ: Prentice Hall.

Durand, V.M., & Carr, E.G. (1985). Self-injurious behavior: Motivating conditions and guidelines for treatment. *School Psychology Review, 14*, 171–176.

Durand, V.M., & Carr, E.G. (1991). Functional communication training to reduce challenging behavior: Maintenance and application in new settings. *Journal of Applied Behavior Analysis, 24*, 251–264.

Fisher, W., Piazza, C., Cataldo, M., Harrell, R., Jefferson, G., & Conner, R. (1993). Functional communication training with and without extinction and punishment. *Journal of Applied Behavior Analysis, 26*, 23–36.

Fus, L., Wacker, D., Grisolano, L., Berg, W., & Rogers, L. (1991, May). *Social collateral behavior as a long-term maintenance factor for treatment of aberrant behaviors for profoundly handicapped students.* Paper presented at Recent Applications of Social Interaction Interventions Across Populations, a symposium presented at the annual conference of the Association for Behavior Analysis, Atlanta.

Halle, J.W., & Holt, B. (1991). Assessing stimulus control in natural settings: An analysis of stimuli that acquire control during training. *Journal of Applied Behavior Analysis, 24*, 579–589.

Halle, J.W., & Spradlin, J.E. (1993). Identifying stimulus control of challenging behavior. In J. Reichle & D. Wacker (Eds.), *Communication and language intervention: Vol. 3. Communicative alternatives to challenging behavior: Integrating functional assessment and intervention strategies* (pp. 83–109). Baltimore: Paul H. Brookes Publishing Co.

Herrnstein, R.J. (1961). Relative and absolute strength of response as a function of frequency of reinforcement. *Journal of the Experimental Analysis of Behavior, 4*, 267–272.

Herrnstein, R.J. (1970). On the law of effect. *Journal of the Experimental Analysis of Behavior, 13*, 243–266.

Iwata, B.A. (1988). The development and adoption of controversial default technologies. *The Behavior Analyst, 11*, 149–157.

Iwata, B.A., Dorsey, M.F., Slifer, K.J., Bauman, K.D., & Richman, G.S. (1982). Toward a functional analysis of self-injury. *Analysis and Intervention in Developmental Disabilities, 2*, 3–20.

Iwata, B.A., Pace, G.M., Kalsher, M.J., Cowdery, G.E., & Cataldo, M.F. (1990). Experimental analysis of self-injurious escape behavior. *Journal of Applied Behavior Analysis, 23*, 11–27.

Karpowitz, D.H., & Johnson, S.M. (1981). Stimulus control in child-family interaction. *Behavioral Assessment, 3*, 161–171.

Koegel, R.L., & Koegel, L.K. (1988). Generalized responsivity and pivotal behaviors. In R. Horner, G. Dunlap, & R. Koegel (Eds.), *Generalization and maintenance: Life-style changes in applied settings* (pp. 41–66). Baltimore: Paul H. Brookes Publishing Co.

Lalli, J.S., & Goh, H. (1993). Naturalistic observations in community settings. In J. Reichle & D. Wacker (Eds.), *Communication and language intervention: Vol. 3. Communicative alternatives to challenging behavior: Integrating functional assessment and intervention strategies* (pp. 11–39). Baltimore: Paul H. Brookes Publishing Co.

Lennox, D.B., & Miltenberger, R.G. (1989). Conducting a functional assessment of problem behavior in applied settings. *Journal of The Association for Persons with Severe Handicaps, 14*, 304–311.

Lerman, D.C., & Iwata, B.A. (1993). Descriptive and experimental analyses of variables maintaining self-injurious behavior. *Journal of Applied Behavior Analysis, 26*, 293–319.

Mace, F.C., & Lalli, J.S. (1991). Linking descriptive and experimental analyses in the treatment of bizarre speech. *Journal of Applied Behavior Analysis, 24*, 553–562.

Mace, F.C., & Roberts, M.L. (1993). Factors affecting selection of behavioral interventions. In J. Reichle & D. Wacker (Eds.), *Communication and language intervention: Vol. 3. Communicative alternatives to challenging behavior: Integrating functional assessment and intervention strategies* (pp. 113–133). Baltimore: Paul H. Brookes Publishing Co.

McDowell, J.J. (1988). Matching theory in natural human environments. *The Behavior Analyst, 11*, 95–109.

Northup, J., Wacker, D.P., Berg, W.K., Kelly, L., Sasso, G., & DeRaad, A. (1994). The treatment of severe behavior problems in school settings using a technical assistance model. *Journal of Applied Behavior Analysis, 27*, 33–47.

Northup, J., Wacker, D., Sasso, G., Steege, M., Cigrand, K., Cook, J., & DeRaad, A. (1991). A brief functional analysis of aggressive and alternative behavior in an outclinic setting. *Journal of Applied Behavior Analysis, 24*, 509–522.

O'Neill, R.E., Horner, R.H., Albin, R.W., Storey, K., & Sprague, J.R. (1989). The functional analysis interview. In R.H. Horner, J.L. Anderson, E.G. Carr, G. Dunlap, R.L. Koegel, & W. Sailor (Eds.), *Functional analysis of problem behavior: A practical assessment guide* (pp. 10–23). Eugene: University of Oregon Press.

Parrish, J.M., & Roberts, M.L. (1993). Interventions based on covariation of desired and inappropriate behavior. In J. Reichle & D. Wacker (Eds.), *Communication and language intervention: Vol. 3. Communicative alternatives to challenging behavior: Integrating functional assessment and intervention strategies* (pp. 135–173). Baltimore: Paul H. Brookes Publishing Co.

Patterson, G.R. (1974). A basis for identifying stimuli which control behaviors in natural settings. *Child Development, 45*, 900–911.

Pettit, G.S., & Bates, J.E. (1989). Family interaction patterns and children's behavior problems from infancy to 4 years. *Developmental Psychology, 25*, 413–420.

Reichle, J., York, J., & Sigafoos, J. (1991). *Implementing augmentative and alternative communication: Strategies for learners with severe disabilities.* Baltimore: Paul H. Brookes Publishing Co.

Reimers, T., & Wacker, D. (1988). Parents' ratings of the acceptability of behavioral treatment recommendations made in an outpatient clinic: A preliminary analysis of the influence of treatment effectiveness. *Behavioral Disorders, 14*, 7–15.

Reynolds, G.S. (1961). Behavioral contrast. *Journal of the Experimental Analysis of Behavior, 4*, 53–59.

Sanders, M.R., & Glynn, T. (1981). Training parents in behavioral self-management: An analysis of generalization and maintenance. *Journal of Applied Behavior Analysis, 14*, 223–237.

Sprague, J.R., & Horner, R.H. (1992). Covariation within functional response classes: Implications for treatment of severe problem behavior. *Journal of Applied Behavior Analysis, 25*, 735–745.

Steege, M.W., Wacker, D.P., Berg, W.K., Cigrand, K.K., & Cooper, L.J. (1989). The use of behavioral assessment to prescribe and evaluate treatments for severely handicapped children. *Journal of Applied Behavior Analysis, 22*, 23–33.

Sulzer-Azaroff, B., & Mayer, G.R. (1991). *Behavior analysis for lasting change.* Chicago: Holt, Rinehart & Winston.

Touchette, P.E., MacDonald, R.F., & Langer, S.N. (1985). A scatter plot for identifying stimulus control of problem behavior. *Journal of Applied Behavior Analysis, 18*, 343–351.

Wacker, D.P., & Berg, W.K. (1992a). *Functional analysis of feeding and interaction disorders with young children who are profoundly disabled*. Washington, DC: U.S. Department of Education, National Institute on Disability and Rehabilitation Research.

Wacker, D.P., & Berg, W.K. (1992b). *Inducing reciprocal parent/child interactions.* Washington, DC: Department of Health and Human Services, National Institute of Child Health and Human Development.

Wacker, D.P., Cooper, L.J., Peck, S., Derby, K.M., & Berg, W.K. (in press). Community-based functional assessment. In A.C. Repp & R.H. Horner (Eds.), *Functional analysis of problem behavior: From effective assessment to effective support*. Pacific Grove, CA: Brooks/Cole.

Wacker, D.P., & Reichle, J. (1993). Functional communication training as an intervention for problem behavior: An overview and introduction to our edited volume. In J. Reichle & D. Wacker (Eds.), *Communication and language intervention: Vol. 3. Communicative alternatives to challenging behavior: Integrating functional assessment and intervention strategies* (pp. 1–8). Baltimore: Paul H. Brookes Publishing Co.

Wacker, D.P., Steege, M.W., Northup, J., Sasso, G., Berg, W., Reimers, T., Cooper, L., Cigrand, K., & Donn, L. (1990). A component analysis of functional communication training across three topographies of severe behavior problems. *Journal of Applied Behavior Analysis, 23*, 417–429.

Wahl, G., Johnson, S.M., Johansson, S., & Martin, S. (1974). An operant analysis of child–family interaction. *Behavior Therapy, 5*, 64–78.

Wahler, R.G., & Dumas, J.E. (1986). Maintenance factors in coercive mother–child interactions: The compliance and predictability hypotheses. *Journal of Applied Behavior Analysis, 19*, 13–22.

Wahler, R.G., Williams, A.J., & Cerezo, A. (1990). The compliance and predictability hypotheses: Sequential and correlational analyses of coercive mother–child interactions. *Behavioral Assessment, 12*, 391–407.

4

Contextual Fit for Behavioral Support Plans

A Model for "Goodness of Fit"

Richard W. Albin, Joseph M. Lucyshyn,
Robert H. Horner, and K. Brigid Flannery

Preparation of this chapter was supported in part by U.S. Department of Education Grant Nos. H133C20114 and H133B20004. However, the opinions expressed herein do not necessarily reflect the position or policy of the U.S. Department of Education, and no official endorsement by the Department should be inferred.

The authors extend appreciation to Drs. Glen Dunlap, Jacqui Lichtenstein, Charles D. Nixon, Robert E. O'Neill, and Ann P. Turnbull and to Ms. Roz Slovic for their comments and input in the development of this chapter.

The criteria by which behavioral support plans for persons with challenging problem behaviors are evaluated are changing. It is no longer enough simply to create behavioral intervention strategies that are technically sound in their application of behavioral principles. Although it remains essential that behavioral support plans be well grounded technically, such plans also must fit well with the people and environments where implementation occurs. The concept of *contextual fit* is proposed in this chapter to describe the congruence between behavioral support plan features and a set of variables that seriously affects the development and implementation, and therefore the effectiveness, of those plans. This chapter 1) defines the concept of contextual fit and describes the authors' development and understanding of the concept, 2) presents a rationale for attending to the contextual fit of behavioral support plans, 3) identifies and describes variables that contribute to contextual fit, and 4) presents one approach for designing behavioral support plans that are a good fit for families of children with challenging problem behaviors along with a form for evaluating the *goodness of fit* of the plans.

CONTEXTUAL FIT AND BEHAVIORAL SUPPORT PLANS

Contextual fit refers to the congruence or compatibility that exists between specific features and components of a behavioral support plan and a variety of relevant variables relating to individuals and environments. These variables fall into three general classes:

1. Characteristics of the person for whom the plan is designed
2. Variables related to the people who will implement the plan
3. Features of the environments and systems within which the plan will be implemented

Our approach to contextual fit follows from the goodness-of-fit framework used by Bailey and colleagues (1990) to guide their family-focused, early intervention approach. Bailey et al. used the goodness-of-fit concept to describe the suitability of the match between early intervention support and the unique characteristics of children and their families. In our experience, the idea of creating good contextual fit is relevant, not only in working with families, but also in providing behavioral support within schools, supported living and work contexts, and other community environments.

When contextual fit is high or good, a support plan and its components are consistent with or highly compatible with the values and skills of key stakeholders and plan implementors; readily sustainable given the resources and constraints of the environments, conditions, and systems where the plan is implemented; and suitable to the unique needs of the person with problem behaviors. Put simply, the support plan works well for (i.e., makes a good fit for) the people and environments where it is being implemented. People who are key stakeholders in the plan's implementation (e.g., the person with challenging behaviors, family members and friends, teachers and other direct support givers) 1) are comfortable with the goals driving the plan and with the strategies included in the plan, 2) perceive those strategies as things for which they have the skills and resources to perform, and 3) view the plan as having a high likelihood of success.

A support plan may be theoretically well designed and solidly grounded in both behavior theory and documented practice, and yet still not be a good fit for the people and environments involved. A plan lacking good contextual fit may be inconsistent with strongly held values and beliefs or may be incompatible with existing routines and everyday patterns of living in the environment. It may include features that are not sustainable for long periods of time, or for which resources are inadequate. A plan may not be a good fit for its implementors because it includes strategies that have proved ineffective in the past, that are viewed as likely to be ineffective, or that have previously been rejected for logistical reasons. Or, the plan may fail to meet important needs of key stakeholders beyond the person with difficult behaviors (e.g., parents, teachers).

For example, if a parent considers it inappropriate to use verbal reprimands with his or her child, the use of reprimands within a support plan for that child represents a poor contextual fit. Reprimands should not be a part of the support plan, even if there is reason to believe that reprimands would be an effective intervention component. Similarly, a teacher who is adamantly opposed to a particular approach to support (e.g., the use of time-out, the use of food reinforcers) is likely to find a support plan containing that approach unacceptable. A plan that fails to address sources of stress in a family (e.g., a need for respite) or includes strategies that may be effective but whose implementation also increases stress in support providers (e.g., by adding large costs to already strained financial resources) lacks good contextual fit. In any case in which a support plan, or any of its components, is not a good contextual fit, effective implementation of that plan is seriously jeopardized. Unfortunately, the absence of good contextual fit may not be made explicit by people responsible for plan implementation and may be discovered only when the plan is poorly implemented or fails.

The concept of the contextual fit of a support plan is a natural outgrowth and logical extension of current emphasis on the application of positive behavioral support approaches. Positive approaches emphasize the design of comprehensive, multicomponent support plans that attend to many features of support environments including 1) manipulation of ecological variables and setting events; 2) manipulation of immediate antecedent variables; 3) response and skill interventions, including teaching new responses; 4) manipulation of consequences; and 5) crisis intervention (Horner, Albin, & O'Neill, 1991; Horner et al., 1990; Horner, O'Neill, & Flannery, 1993; Lucyshyn & Albin, 1993). The assumption is that there always will be multiple options and combinations of component strategies that could make up an effective support plan. It is highly unlikely that there would be a set of circumstances in which only one set of support strategies, one single intervention plan, would be successful. The challenge is to choose among the potential options to develop a comprehensive support plan that is technically sound in its application of the principles of applied behavior analysis, is compatible with the values and skills of its implementors, and is consistent with important features of the environments where it will be implemented.

Emphasis on the contextual fit of a support plan acknowledges that patterns of problem behavior cannot be understood and addressed without attending to the broader environmental contexts within which they occur (e.g., homes, classrooms, activity settings) (Horner, 1994). Support plans and intervention strategies must fit into, as well as build from, those contexts. The concept of contextual fit also acknowledges the important role played by all stakeholders in the design, implementation, and evaluation of support plans. The goals of key stakeholders, their levels of knowledge and skills, and the resources available to them must be reflected in the plan to promote successful implementation.

Emphasis on creating good contextual fit also is consistent with the idea of embedding support interventions within the overall context of everyday environments and routines, both to facilitate implementation and to increase generalization and maintenance of intervention effects (Martens & Witt, 1988; O'Donnell & Tharp, 1990). O'Donnell and Tharp (1990) argue that activity settings, rather than individual persons, must be the basic unit of analysis in behavioral intervention. Only then are the rich interactions and patterns of reciprocal participation that occur within activity settings considered in the process of planning and implementation for changing patterns of behavior. Attention to the goodness of fit of a support plan requires consideration of the full range of person and environment variables present within any activity setting.

Rationale for Attention to Contextual Fit

Many clinicians and consultants have had the experience of designing very elegant and technically sound behavior programs that 1) are poorly or inconsistently implemented, 2) are implemented but not maintained across significant periods of time, or 3) simply collect dust in desk drawers without ever being utilized. Poor contextual fit is one likely contributor to this phenomenon. Our clinical experience suggests that the biggest impact accruing from good contextual fit for a behavioral support plan lies in the implementation of the plan (Horner et al., 1996; Lucyshyn, Olson, & Horner, 1995).

A support plan that has good contextual fit is responsive to the values and goals of plan implementors; utilizes the experience, knowledge, and skills these people bring to implementation environments; and is compatible with the typical routines and daily activities that characterize implementation environments and contribute to their uniqueness. Such characteristics cannot help but promote increased fidelity of implementation of support plan strategies as well as increased maintenance or sustainability of support plan implementation. People with severe problem behaviors often require long-term, comprehensive support plans that are implemented with fidelity across periods of time ranging into many years (Lucyshyn et al., 1995). Support plans with good contextual fit can meet this requirement, increasing their likelihood of long-term success.

In addition, support plans with good contextual fit are likely to generate increased satisfaction among those consumers of the plan who are involved in development and implementation (e.g., family members, direct support providers). Increased consumer satisfaction may not only enhance implementation fidelity and sustainability, but also may reduce the barriers or impediments to support plan success that grow out of divergent goals, disagreement, or dissatisfaction among support team members.

Variables Contributing to Contextual Fit

Designing a behavioral support plan with good contextual fit requires attention to each of three elements that converge within any support plan: 1) variables and issues related to the person with problem behaviors and his or her patterns of behavior, 2) variables and issues related to the people involved in developing and implementing the support plan, and 3) variables and issues related to the environments where the plan will be implemented and the systems in place in those environments.

Person with Problem Behaviors Any behavioral support plan, to be effective, must have as its foundation a set of intervention strategies that is logically linked to the information and hypotheses identified from a comprehensive functional assessment process (Carr, Robinson, & Palumbo, 1990; Horner et al., 1993; Iwata, Volmer, & Zarcone, 1990; O'Neill, Horner, Albin, Storey, & Sprague, 1990). If a plan is not technically sound, the concept of good contextual fit becomes meaningless. One key element in achieving a plan that is both technically sound and a good contextual fit is reaching consensus among plan developers and implementors regarding the hypotheses about predictors and maintaining consequences for problem behaviors. Failure to reach agreement, particularly on functions of problem behaviors, so seriously hampers plan implementation that plan design and implementation should not move forward until agreement is reached. Good contextual fit is unlikely when key stakeholders disagree on why problem behaviors are occurring.

An additional consideration for goodness of contextual fit related to the person for whom the plan is designed is that the plan's features build on and incorporate the person's existing strengths and capabilities. Although this consideration may seem obvious, too often situations occur in which plans fail to capitalize on existing strengths (e.g., idiosyncratic communication strategies, interest in community activities or other preferences) or, in some cases, even program against existing interests or long-established routines (e.g., eliminating or withholding preferred activities until problem behaviors are "controlled").

Finally, comprehensive support plans should, to the greatest extent possible, address all areas of need, for the person with problem behaviors. Plans that fail to address all areas of need, because they are incomplete, may not result in significant reduction in problem behaviors or in significant improvements in quality of life. This may lead to increased resistance from the person with problem behaviors, who experiences people tinkering with his or her life but does not experience positive outcomes associated with a successful support plan. Also, barriers to implementation may be created by the failure to address some areas of need. Unaddressed areas of need may limit options for intervention strategies or may negatively influence implementation of proposed strategies. For example, failure to address the need for an adequate crisis response procedure(s) may result in an unwillingness on the part of plan implementors to provide access to highly preferred community activities, which may be a key element for overall support plan success. Also, if unaddressed needs result in a lack of behavior change or success in some environments or situations, plan implementation may be influenced in other contexts.

Plan Implementors and Other Key Stakeholders Typically, behavioral support plans are viewed as being designed to change the problem behaviors of the focus individual. However, support plans are actually a prescription, or set of directions, for those people involved in implementing the plan. Support plan components identify how plan implementors should behave, interact, and respond in order to effect and support changes in an individual's patterns of problem behavior. Plan components also direct setting modifications or other ecological developments designed to create supportive environmental features. Clearly, a set of person variables related to support plan implementors will have a substantial impact on the contextual fit of a support plan.

Two important person-related variables affecting contextual fit are the values and skills that plan implementors bring to the behavioral support process. Every family has a characteristic style, a way of doing things, that is shaped, in large part, by the values, perspectives, and skills of parents or primary caregivers within the home. In working with families it is important that support plan features take into consideration the family's views and approaches regarding parenting and what "being a family" means and entails. Similarly, schools and community support programs have their own unique cultures that reflect, in large part, the values, experiences, and skills of their support personnel. There are likely to be fairly well established "ways that things are done around here." Support plan components that are inconsistent with people's values or that exceed current levels of knowledge, skills, and experience are not likely to be implemented with any consistency or fidelity. However, if implementors have experience using a particular procedure and have had success with the procedure, there is a substantial increase in the likelihood that the plan will be implemented with fidelity (Reimers, Wacker, & Koeppl, 1987; Sprague & Horner, 1991). Whether working with families, schools, or support agencies, it is important that support plan features draw on and emphasize existing family, school, or agency strengths.

A third critical person-related variable is the extent to which the goals of a support plan are consistent with the goals of plan implementors. Unfortunately, in developing behavioral support plans, it is not unusual to encounter situations in which the explicit goals identified in, and presumably driving, the plan are not shared by all of the plan's implementors. For example, a plan may be developed with the identified goal of maintaining a student with severe problem behaviors in a particular classroom or school, but key staff members actually may desire to have the student moved into another classroom or setting. In such a case, effective support is seriously compromised. Discrepancies in goals among key stakeholders also may translate into disagreement over support plan procedures and features as well as disagreement over plan goals and objectives. If congruence regarding goals is not readily achieved, goals should be negotiated until a consensus is reached.

Finally, in addressing variables related to plan implementors, it is important to consider stressors that are experienced by plan implementors. This includes not only stressors related to problem behaviors (e.g., anxiety or fears related to the occurrence of very severe or out-of-control behaviors, need for respite or time away from a person who is very challenging), but also stressors, such as those frequently experienced by many families, that are unrelated to a child or adult with problem behaviors (e.g., financial worries, job dissatisfaction or other job-related stress, marital problems, health problems). Obviously, good support plans should be designed so as not to create stressors. Support plans with good contextual fit also should look to address or eliminate sources of stress that may interfere with plan implementation.

Environments and Systems Contextual fit is likely to be affected by variables related to the structural and programmatic features of the environments where a support plan is implemented. The physical layout of the environment, the number of different people in the environment, typical routines and activities in the environment (especially in a home), schedules of events or activities (especially in schools or job sites), and curriculum characteristics and demands all work, alone and in combinations, to influence how behavioral support plans should be constructed. One way to promote good contextual fit is to ensure that support plan strategies are embedded into the relevant routines and activities of everyday life in the home, school, and community (Lucyshyn & Albin, 1993; O'Donnell & Tharp, 1990).

In general, the plan should look to alter existing routines, performance goals, and the structure of daily life as little as possible. Rather, it should take advantage of naturally occurring routines, activities, reinforcers, and social support structures. Support plans that fit well into existing routines can be sustained for extended periods of time. Support plans that require significant change in typical routines or activities and/or significant alteration of environmental or programmatic features, or that depend on extraordinary efforts or extensive outside resources, are likely to be poorly implemented and unsustainable over time.

When current activities, routines, or features within environments are incompatible with requirements for a technically sound behavioral support plan, or when it is desirable to construct new routines or new patterns of activities, key stakeholders should engage in a collaborative process to negotiate these changes. The goals of this collaboration are to produce competent environments and patterns of activities that 1) are conducive to effective behavioral support, 2) reflect key stakeholders' values and visions for a high-quality lifestyle for the person with problem behaviors, and 3) are logistically sustainable. This has important implications, particularly when working with families in their homes. Changes in activities, routines, and home features of families cannot be dictated by outside professionals (Walker & Singer, 1993). As in establishing a common set of goals, it is important that all key stakeholders in the plan work together to achieve consensus around what can and should be done in structuring or restructuring environments to promote good contextual fit (Bailey, 1987; Lucyshyn & Albin, 1994).

Contextual fit is also influenced by several resource and support system variables, including time, effort, and dollars needed for support plan implementation; training and support needs of plan implementors (including family members and paid support staff); administrative and structural support systems (both formal and informal) available; and existing policies within schools and other support agencies. Resource variables may also include the costs for equipment (e.g., augmentative communication devices) and the initial monetary and human costs associated with putting a behavioral support plan into place.

Program initiation costs are of particular importance because they represent a significant potential barrier to plan implementation. Comprehensive support plans may include initial personnel training strategies, the development of support systems such as augmentative communication systems or self-management systems, and the purchasing of materials needed to create more competent environments and to promote desired new activities. The ongoing implementation of such strategies may involve only modest costs in dollars and human effort over time, but the cost and effort to get them established initially may be substantial. Care must be taken when designing a support plan to account for initial implementation costs as well as for the ongoing cost and effort needed to maintain the support plan.

Support plans with good contextual fit will tap into existing resources, including both formal and informal sources of instrumental and social support. This helps to ensure long-term maintenance of plan implementation. An important aspect of contextual fit is the extent to which the support plan ensures that plan implementors receive the support that they need. For families this may mean linking them with formal support networks or assisting them in gaining access to or developing informal sources of support. In schools or support agencies, plans should utilize existing systems. Where such systems do not exist or are inadequate, key stakeholders may need to work on creating effective systems. Systems variables such as existing policies and procedures and the level of administrative support for behavioral programming also will greatly influence contextual fit.

DEVELOPING SUPPORT PLANS WITH GOOD CONTEXTUAL FIT

If a behavioral support plan is to be both technically sound and contextually appropriate, it must be constructed by people with technical competence in behavior analysis *and* people with in-depth knowledge of the values and structure of the implementation environments. This requirement serves to reinforce current efforts to define and emphasize the use of team approaches to building behavioral support plans (Anderson, Albin, Mesaros, Dunlap, & Morelli-Robbins, 1993; Colvin, Kameenui, & Sugai, in press). A collaborative process involving key stakeholders such as family members, school staff, and other direct support professionals and paraprofessionals is essential for good contextual fit (Bailey, 1987; Lucyshyn & Albin, 1993). These are the people who know the person with problem behaviors, who know the environments and the people in them, who are familiar with local resources and systems, and who will be called on to implement and maintain the support plan. A plan developed by a single specialist or consultant may lack important elements or considerations, particularly when that person is working with only minimal information about implementation environments and key plan stakeholders. Those people most directly affected by a behavioral support plan *must* have input and voices in its development.

Much of our initial conceptualization and development of contextual fit has grown out of clinical consultations and research with families of children with developmental disabilities and severe problem behaviors (Lucyshyn & Albin, 1993, 1994; Lucyshyn, Nixon, Glang, & Cooley, 1996). Families are unique in terms of the things they value, the ways that they structure daily living activities and routines, the adaptations and accommodations they have made in response to both a child's strengths and problem behaviors, the barriers and sources of stress they face in providing support to a child with problem behaviors, and the vision they share for what a valued family lifestyle would look like. Creating a behavioral support plan without considering the family culture, values, strengths and weaknesses, resources, and overall needs is a serious mistake that could doom any support plan, regardless of its technical elegance.

Our basic approach to providing behavioral intervention support to families has been described in detail by Lucyshyn and Albin (1993). Lucyshyn and Albin detail a process that begins with an initial referral or problem identification process and then follows these basic steps:

1. Comprehensive functional assessment leading to the development of hypotheses regarding the functions of problem behaviors
2. Preliminary plan design by the team or a behavior specialist to identify potential intervention strategies
3. Team meeting process to finalize both a comprehensive support program and a plan for its implementation
4. Implementation support to the family, including written materials, behavioral rehearsal and coaching, home meetings, assistance in materials development, and support in constructing or restructuring home routines and activities
5. Plan evaluation and follow-up support

The primary objective of the process is to make behavioral support to families a collaborative, family-friendly process that results in significant change in problem behaviors and significant change in the quality of life of both the family and the child involved. Examples of how this process is carried out with a family are presented in Lucyshyn and Albin (1993) and Lucyshyn et al. (1996).

Assessing and Responding to the Family's Ecology and Needs

Attention to contextual fit begins from the very start of our behavioral support process with families. It begins by ensuring that parents and other family members are active collaborators in all aspects of support plan development and implementation processes. Next, specific efforts and activities to address goodness of contextual fit occur throughout the process. During the initial assessment procedures, attention to contextual fit involves the inclusion of family-focused assessment activities, in addition to functional assessment of problem behaviors. A *family ecology* assessment is conducted, aimed at identifying and understanding family characteristics, family values and goals, and the ways in which the family has constructed its home life (Gallimore, Weisner, Kaufman, & Bernheimer, 1989). The primary means of accomplishing this is through interviews and discussions with family members. Figure 1 presents an example of a protocol that we have used in collecting information from families. Just as the information collected in the functional assessment serves as the foundation for behavioral intervention strategies, the information on family characteristics and ecology provides the foundation for good contextual fit.

Throughout the assessment and preliminary support plan development processes, family members' ideas and reactions regarding hypotheses as to the function(s) of problem behaviors, potential support strategies, and issues for implementation and contextual fit are actively solicited. Attention is paid both to the current ways in which the family has structured its daily living patterns and routines, including successful strategies and accommodations to address problem behaviors, and to the family's desires and visions for the future. In addition, sources of stress for the family are identified and discussed.

The family takes the lead in identifying routines and activities (e.g., getting up and off to school, dinner time, getting ready and going to bed, leaving child care to go home) that currently are most problematic or disruptive, and in prioritizing where, or in what sequence, intervention should be implemented to best enhance family life within the home. The family also is encouraged to identify new routines or activities, or ones that have been avoided in the past, that will contribute to an improved family lifestyle as well as improved quality of life for the child with problem behaviors (e.g., going out to eat with the child, shopping with the child, entertaining at home, family visits to friends or relatives). Ideally, a behavioral support plan with good contextual fit will strengthen the family as a unit, with the inclusion of family-focused intervention strategies as needed within the comprehensive support plan (Dunst, Trivette, & Deal, 1988; Lucyshyn & Albin, 1993; Turnbull, 1988). A support plan that

INTERVIEW PROTOCOL

Family Characteristics

1. What would you characterize as the strengths of your family?
2. What are sources of stress in your family?
   a. What is the effect of your child's problem behaviors on you as a parent?
   b. What is the effect of your child's problem behaviors on the family as a whole?
   c. What are other sources of stress in the family?
3. What formal or informal resources have you used to help improve the situation (e.g., respite care, participation in a parent support group, help with child care and household chores by other family members)?
4. What are your sources of social support (i.e., someone with whom you discuss problems and find solutions; someone with whom you do leisure activities; someone who validates your worth as a person)?
5. What are your goals for your child and for your family?

Family Social Construction of Child Activity Settings

1. Description of child activity settings (home routines and community activities) selected for support and intervention:
   a. Who is present?
   b. What resources do you use (or are available)?
   c. What are the tasks to be performed? How are they organized?
   d. What are family goals, values, or beliefs that may inform this routine (activity)? Why is the routine (activity) done in the way you describe? Why is this routine (activity) part of your family's or child's life?
   e. What are common themes that occur during routine (activity) (e.g., common scripts of communication, common patterns of interaction)?
   f. What accommodations have you made that you feel are fairly successful (e.g., sustainable over time; consistent with child characteristics; consonant with family values, goals, or beliefs)?

Family Vision of Successful Activity Settings

1. For the home routine and community activity in which you would like to improve first, how would a successful routine (activity) look?
   a. Who would be there?
   b. What available resources would you use?
   c. What would participants be doing? How would you reorganize tasks or introduce other tasks to enhance the routine (activity)?
   d. What family goals, values, or beliefs would clearly be part of the routine (activity)? What child goals would be part of the routine (activity)?
   e. What themes or scripts would be associated with this enhanced routine (activity)?
   f. What accommodations would enhance the likelihood that the routine (activity) would continue to be successful over a long period of time?

Figure 1. Family assessment interview: Understanding the family ecology.

includes only child-focused strategies, but fails to address needs of the family as a whole, is likely not to be a good contextual fit for the family.

The routines and activities identified by the family become the contexts within which the support plan is implemented, and within which family members are taught, coached, and supported, as needed, to use the plan's intervention strategies. When family goals or priorities for routines and activities are at odds with a technically sound support plan, or when they create logistical or other problems for implementation of the plan, negotiation occurs to achieve an agreeable solution that maintains a balance between technical integrity and contextual fit. In our team approach to support plan development, a behavior specialist or consultant may act as a facilitator in the negotiation process, particularly when there is a lack of agreement among key groups of stakeholders (e.g., family members and school personnel).

Finalizing the components of the comprehensive support program, as well as a plan for its implementation, depends on reaching a consensus among all (or at least a substantial majority of) support team members. This is an essential element for achieving good contextual fit. All stakeholders in the support program are encouraged to participate in the support team meetings in which the features of the support and implementation plans are finalized. As many meetings as needed to reach consensus are held. However, a thorough job of both functional assessment and family assessment, coupled with active collaboration in identifying and discussing potential plan components and strategies, can minimize the difficulties faced and time needed to reach consensus on a final support program and a plan for its implementation.

Attention to Contextual Fit Throughout Plan Implementation

Once implementation of the support plan is under way, attention to contextual fit continues. One key aspect of this attention involves working with family members to provide necessary training and support for successful plan implementation within the routines and activities that the family has identified and targeted. Close collaboration as a team continues throughout the problem-solving and troubleshooting processes that characterize the initial stages of support plan implementation. Our process calls for regular and, particularly during the early stages of support plan implementation, frequent opportunities to discuss and provide feedback related to plan effects as well as the implementation process. Team meetings occur at least weekly. Ongoing monitoring and discussion as a team provide the information that drives decisions regarding the modifications and adjustments in plan features and implementation strategies that are often required to ensure successful and effective support.

Because contextual fit is important to us, we also assess specifically for goodness of fit using a survey form that was developed for use with families. Figure 2 presents the current survey form. This survey is first completed by individual family members once the support plan is finalized. The survey is then completed periodically as the plan is implemented to ensure that good contextual fit is maintained. If contextual fit is slipping, adjustments are made accordingly. It is important to note that, as a support plan is implemented, the family's goals or visions may change, routines and activities may change, and requirements and responsibilities related to implementing plan strategies may change. Goodness of contextual fit must be evaluated on a continuing basis. Thus, the survey serves as a guide, reminding all team members and plan implementors of key considerations for maintaining good contextual fit.

Our experience in using the goodness-of-fit survey with several families has been overwhelmingly positive. Family members have appreciated both the opportunity and format to provide feedback on how the behavioral support process is working for them. To date, our use of the survey has been descriptive, aimed at confirming the goodness of fit of our support plans (Lucyshyn & Albin, 1994). In this regard, the survey has proven to be a useful clinical tool. However, we also foresee the usefulness of the survey as a research measure in studies addressing the relationship between goodness of contextual fit and variables such as the fidelity of implementation of support plan procedures or maintenance of implementation of a behavioral support plan. Such research is needed to provide a data-based foundation confirming the importance of contextual fit as a variable to emphasize in developing effective behavioral support plans.

CONCLUSIONS

This chapter has emphasized the importance of considering the contextual fit of a behavioral support plan, in addition to its technical soundness. We recognize that adding a variable (or set of variables) to consider in developing and implementing behavioral support plans may appear to create added work in an already complex process. However, we see good contextual fit as occurring almost naturally when support plans are developed using a collaborative team approach that involves all of the key stakeholders in the support process. Attending directly to contextual fit, by questioning key stakeholders throughout the support process or by using a form such as the goodness-of-fit survey for families, should further facilitate the development of support plans with high levels of contextual fit. Our clinical experience tells us that failure to address contextual fit variables has such a negative impact on the behavioral support process that working to create good fit is well worth the time and effort.

GOODNESS-OF-FIT SURVEY

Name of family:

Family member(s) completing checklist:

Date:

Introduction: This survey is for use by families working with consultants to improve the behavior and lifestyle of their son or daughter. The survey is based on our experience that the success of a support plan depends a great deal on whether the plan fits with the values and lifestyle of the family. Your responses will help us a) improve the quality of the plan, and b) understand better how to build support plans that are most helpful. Below are 20 questions about the plan and its prospects for success. Please answer each question by rating the number that most closely matches your current view. The ratings read: 1) not at all, 2) not much, 3) can't tell, 4) well (or much), and 5) very well (or very much).

	Not at all	Not much	Can't tell	Well (much)	Very well (very much)
1. Do you believe the support team understands the needs your child has for support across the hours of each day and in each important setting in which he or she participates?	1	2	3	4	5
2. Do you believe the plan takes into account your understanding of your child (e.g., reasons for problem behaviors, strategies that promote positive behavior, child preferences)?	1	2	3	4	5
3. Does the plan really address your highest priority goals for your child and family?	1	2	3	4	5
4. Do you understand what you are expected to do as part of this plan?	1	2	3	4	5
5. Are you comfortable with what you are expected to do?	1	2	3	4	5
6. Do you understand what others (e.g., consultant, teacher, other family members) are expected to do as part of this plan?	1	2	3	4	5
7. Are you comfortable with what others are expected to do?	1	2	3	4	5
8. Does the plan recognize and support your needs as a mother or father?	1	2	3	4	5
9. Does the plan recognize and support the needs of other family members living at home (e.g., other children, grandparents)?	1	2	3	4	5

(continued)

Figure 2.   Goodness-of-fit survey for behavioral support plans used by families.

Figure 2. (*continued*)

	Not at all	Not much	Can't tell	Well (much)	Very well (very much)
10. Overall, how well does the support plan fit with the daily routines of your family (e.g., meals, shopping, social events, bedtime)?	1	2	3	4	5
11. Overall, how well does the plan fit with your values and beliefs about raising your child with a disability and creating a meaningful family life together?	1	2	3	4	5
12. Does the plan include successful strategies you have used during family routines in the home or community?	1	2	3	4	5
13. Will the plan, in the long run, disrupt family routines in the home or community to a point that stress and hardship will be created?	1	2	3	4	5
14. Does the plan recognize and build on your family's strengths?	1	2	3	4	5
15. Does the plan recognize and build on positive contributions your child has made to the family?	1	2	3	4	5
16. Does the plan make use of resources (e.g., help from spouse, respite care, parent support group) available to you and your family?	1	2	3	4	5
17. Does the plan include needs you may have for long-term social-emotional support (e.g., someone with whom you discuss problems, someone with whom you do enjoyable activities)?	1	2	3	4	5
18. All things considered, how difficult will it be for you to use this support plan (e.g., time involved, coordination, tasks)?	1	2	3	4	5
19. Do you believe the support plan will be effective?	1	2	3	4	5
20. If the plan is effective, do you believe you can keep using the support strategies for a long time (e.g., over 1 year) even though other members of the support team will not be available as much (e.g., little to no contact from the consultant, consultative assistance by telephone, less contact with school personnel)?	1	2	3	4	5

General Comments:

REFERENCES

Anderson, J.L., Albin, R.W., Mesaros, R.A., Dunlap, G., & Morelli-Robbins, M. (1993). Issues in providing training to achieve comprehensive behavioral support. In J. Reichle & D.P. Wacker (Eds.), *Communication and language intervention: Vol. 3. Communicative alternatives to challenging behavior: Integrating functional assessment and intervention strategies* (pp. 363–406). Baltimore: Paul H. Brookes Publishing Co.

Bailey, D.B. (1987). Collaborative goal-setting with families: Resolving differences in values and priorities for services. *Topics in Early Childhood Special Education, 7,* 59–71.

Bailey, D.B., Simeonsson, R.J., Winton, P.J., Huntington, G.S., Comfort, M., Isbell, P., O'Donnell, K.J., & Helm, J.M. (1990). Family-focused intervention: A functional model for planning, implementing, and evaluating individualized family services in early intervention. *Journal of the Division for Early Childhood, 10,* 156–171.

Carr, E.G., Robinson, S., & Palumbo, L.W. (1990). The wrong issue: Aversive vs. nonaversive treatment. The right issue: Functional vs. nonfunctional treatment. In A.C. Repp & N.N. Singh (Eds.), *Perspectives on the use of nonaversive and aversive interventions for persons with developmental disabilities* (pp. 361–379). Pacific Grove, CA: Brooks/Cole.

Colvin, G., Kameenui, E., & Sugai, G. (in press). Reconceptualizing behavior management and school-wide discipline in general education. *Education and Treatment of Children.*

Dunst, C.J., Trivette, C.M., & Deal, A.G. (1988). *Enabling and empowering families: Principles and guidelines for practice.* Cambridge, MA: Brookline Books.

Gallimore, R., Weisner, T.S., Kaufman, S.Z., & Bernheimer, L.P. (1989). The social construction of ecocultural niches: Family accommodation of developmentally delayed children. *American Journal on Mental Retardation, 94,* 216–230.

Horner, R.H. (1994). Functional assessment: Contributions and future directions. *Journal of Applied Behavior Analysis, 27,* 401–404.

Horner, R.H., Albin, R.W., & O'Neill, R.E. (1991). Supporting students with severe intellectual disabilities and severe challenging behaviors. In G. Stoner, M.R. Shinn, & H.M. Walker (Eds.), *Interventions for achievement and behavioral problems* (pp. 269–287). Washington, DC: National Association of School Psychologists.

Horner, R.H., Close, D.W., Fredericks, H.D., O'Neill, R.E., Albin, R.W., Sprague, J.R., Kennedy, C.H., Flannery, K.B., & Heathfield, L.T. (1996). Supported living for people with severe problem behaviors: A demonstration. In D.H. Lehr & F. Brown (Eds.), *People with disabilities who challenge the system.* (pp. 209–240). Baltimore: Paul H. Brookes Publishing Co.

Horner, R.H., Dunlap, G., Koegel, R.L., Carr, E.G., Sailor, W., Anderson, J., Albin, R.W., & O'Neill, R.E. (1990). Toward a technology of "non-aversive" behavioral support. *Journal of The Association for Persons with Severe Handicaps, 15,* 125–132.

Horner, R.H., O'Neill, R.E., & Flannery, K.B. (1993). Effective behavior support plans from functional assessment information. In M. Snell (Ed.), *Systematic instruction of persons with severe handicaps* (4th ed., pp. 184–214). Columbus, OH: Charles E. Merrill.

Iwata, B.A., Volmer, T.R., & Zarcone, J.R. (1990). The experimental (functional) analysis of behavior disorders: Methodology, applications, and limitations. In A.C. Repp & N.N. Singh (Eds.), *Perspectives on the use of nonaversive and aversive interventions for persons with developmental disabilities* (pp. 301–330). Pacific Grove, CA: Brooks/Cole.

Lucyshyn, J.M., & Albin, R.W. (1993). Comprehensive support to families of children with disabilities and behavior problems: Keeping it "friendly." In G.H.S. Singer & L.E. Powers (Eds.), *Families, disability, and empowerment: Active coping skills and strategies for family interventions* (pp. 365–407). Baltimore: Paul H. Brookes Publishing Co.

Lucyshyn, J.M., & Albin, R.W. (1994, December). *An experimental and descriptive analysis of positive behavioral support with a family of a child with severe disabilities and problem behaviors.* Paper presented at The Association for Persons with Severe Handicaps Conference, Atlanta, GA.

Lucyshyn, J.M., Nixon, C., Glang, A., & Cooley, E. (1996). Comprehensive family support for behavior change in children with ABI. In G.H.S. Singer, A. Glang, & J. Williams (Eds.), *Children with acquired brain injury: Educating and supporting families* (pp. 99–136). Baltimore: Paul H. Brookes Publishing Co.

Lucyshyn, J.M., Olson, D., & Horner, R.H. (1995). Building an ecology of support: A case study of one young woman with severe problem behaviors living in the community. *Journal of The Association for Persons with Severe Handicaps, 20,* 16–30.

Martens, B.K., & Witt, J.C. (1988). Ecological behavior analysis. In M. Hersen, R.M. Eisler, & P.M. Miller (Eds.), *Progress in behavior modification* (Vol. 22) (pp. 115–140). Newbury Park, CA: Sage Publications.

O'Donnell, C.R., & Tharp, R.G. (1990). Community intervention guided by theoretical development. In A.S. Bellack, M. Hersen, & A.E. Kazdin (Eds.), *International handbook of behavior modification and therapy* (2nd ed., pp. 251–266). New York: Plenum Press.

O'Neill, R.E., Horner, R.H., Albin, R.W., Storey, K., & Sprague, J.R. (1990). *Functional analysis of problem behavior: A practical assessment guide.* Pacific Grove, CA: Brooks/Cole.

Reimers, T., Wacker, D., & Koeppl, G. (1987). Acceptability of behavioral interventions: A review of the literature. *School Psychology Review, 16,* 212–227.

Sprague, J.R., & Horner, R.H. (1991). Determining the acceptability of behavior support plans. In M. Wang, H. Walberg, & M. Reynolds (Eds.), *Handbook of special education* (pp. 125–142). Oxford, London: Pergamon Press.

Turnbull, A.P. (1988). The challenge of providing comprehensive support to families. *Education and Training in Mental Retardation, 23,* 261–272.

Walker, B., & Singer, G.H.S. (1993). Improving collaborative communication between professionals and parents. In G.H.S. Singer & L.E. Powers (Eds.), *Families, disability, and empowerment: Active coping skills and strategies for family interventions* (pp. 285–315). Baltimore: Paul H. Brookes Publishing Co.

5

Group Action Planning as a Strategy for Providing Comprehensive Family Support

Ann P. Turnbull and H. Rutherford Turnbull, III

As parents of a 26-year-old man, JT, who has encountered behavioral challenges, the authors are painfully aware of the need for relevant information and especially for a comprehensive network of formal and informal supports to create inclusive, state-of-the-art lifestyle options. This chapter blends both our personal and our professional research perspectives in addressing the following high-priority topics for the field of positive behavioral support:

1. The family's extensive need for comprehensive positive behavioral support
2. Criteria for measuring *lifestyle* change as contrasted to *behavioral* change
3. Group Action Planning as a strategy for providing comprehensive family support

FAMILY NEED FOR COMPREHENSIVE POSITIVE BEHAVIORAL SUPPORT

The Family Connection staff at the Beach Center on Families and Disability, where the authors conduct their research and training, completed a qualitative study that involved in-depth interviews with 17 families of individuals with problem behavior (Turnbull, Ruef, & Reeves, 1994). The study revealed two pervasive themes:

1. Many families are going to extraordinary lengths to try to create a reasonable lifestyle for their son or daughter, but most services and supports are provided in segregated settings.
2. The system has continually failed to provide even limited, much less comprehensive, support to families.

Figure 1 graphically portrays the extent of overwhelming family responsibility as a mosaic composed of the various elements (Mirenda, 1993) characterizing the lifestyles of individuals with challenging behavior. The family's extensive responsibility is depicted by the overwhelmingly prominent "tile" representing families' responsibilities and the very small tiles representing the services and supports that families receive. For example, in the Turnbull et al. (1994) qualitative inquiry, fewer than one third of the individuals with challenging behavior had even one friendship, and, of the four adults in the study, none were gainfully employed.

Some of the comments about friendships related in the interviews included

- "Danny has no relationships outside his family."
- "Josh does not have companions or friends that he plays with."
- "Jessie has no friends at school . . . she has only been there 1 1/2 years."
- "Patrick walks home from school with a paid friend." (Turnbull et al., 1994, p. 23)

In terms of employment, one family described the day program that their adult-age son attended as follows: "We have gone there three or four times and every time he is just sitting down not doing anything. He is just playing with blocks" (p. 43).

The majority of services reported were provided in segregated settings. Families described the unrelenting obligation to advocate for services and support with and from extended family, teachers, administrators, employment agencies, churches, physicians, neighbors, community citizens, and a host of others. The family responsibility of never-ending service advocacy and coordination is the "grout" in the social mosaic. It is an extremely demanding task that often limits the visions and resilience of many families. In fact, families described much more frustration in dealing with the resistance and inflexibility of the service system than in dealing with their son's or daughter's challenging behavior.

The mosaic in Figure 1 resonates deeply, given our own experience. When our son JT, along with every other student with a disability in our local community, transitioned from the high school to the *only* adult agency in town and to its segregated employment, segregated housing, segregated transportation, and segregated recreation. We have characterized that lifestyle as reflecting the "herd mentality" because adults with disabilities always move from one setting to the next in large groups, often without regard to their individual preferences.

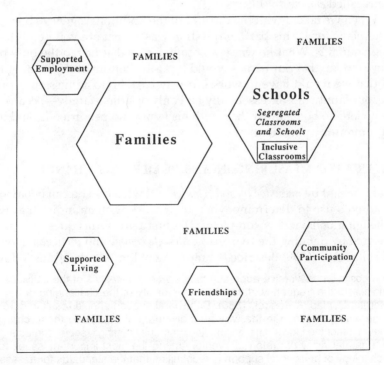

Figure 1.   Mosaic of *typical* supports and services for lifestyles of individuals with problem behavior.

Within just a few months, JT experienced profound frustration and alienation as his life became increasingly segregated and his activities increasingly herdlike. He started hitting, choking, pulling hair, and refusing to get up in the morning. His behavior was saying loudly and clearly what he was not able to articulate: "I'm lonely. I'm afraid. I don't feel valued and respected. I feel like a second-class citizen. I'm not getting the support that I need to do the best that I can do."

After 5 months of intensive advocacy and attempts to work with and improve the adult agency, we faced the inevitable. We withdrew JT from the program just as its administrators were ready to expel him. We made this decision with two commitments in mind. First, we committed to never again subject JT to mediocrity in services. Second, we committed to developing for JT and others with disabilities a service model that is characterized by interdependence (friendships), inclusion (through supported education, supported employment, and supported living), and contribution (community participation). Underlying these two commitments was this general one: We would do all that is necessary to help JT get what he wants in life; after all, it is his life, and he has a well-developed sense of what he wants. Today, this "whatever it takes to get what he wants" attitude is called *empowerment*.

When we talked with the director of the traditional agency about our future plans for JT, his parting question was "What are you going to do when you fail?" What he was really saying was that he ran the only program in town, that our names would be at the bottom of the waiting list, and that we would have to work our way back up to admission. At that time, our family mosaic essentially had only one tile—family—because JT had no job, no home other than with his family, no peer friends, and limited community participation.

CRITERIA FOR MEASURING INCLUSIVE LIFESTYLE CHANGE

What is meant by *inclusive lifestyle change* and what criteria can behavioral consultants use to determine when their work with an individual with challenging behaviors is complete? The first part of this question can be answered by defining the two terms: *lifestyle change* and *inclusion*. Horner and colleagues (1990) describe the meaning of lifestyle change as follows:

> The positive/nonaversive approach focuses on the lifestyle of the individual, in addition to the frequency, duration, and intensity of the challenging behaviors (Horner, Dunlap, & Koegel, 1988). Behavioral support should result in durable, generalized changes in the way an individual behaves, and these changes should affect the individual's access to community settings, social contacts, and to a greater array of preferred events. Among the most important issues for a technology of behavioral support is recognition that the standards for assessing "success" are changing. (p. 127)

This definition of lifestyle change properly calls for a technology (positive behavioral support) that produces desired outcomes—namely, changes in behavior that increase individuals' access to community environments, social contacts, and a greater array of preferred events. *Inclusive lifestyle change* may be further defined by reference to interdependence (friendships and other social contacts), inclusion (supported education, supported employment, and supported living), and contribution (community participation and productivity), all as enabled by the element of *choice*, which comes alive through empowering contexts and personalized supports.

It can easily be overwhelming for families and professionals to breathe life into such a protean definition. Many professionals tend to specialize in only one life-span stage and in a relatively narrow range of issues. For example, there are behavioral consultants who typically focus on school problems, others who focus on employment, and still others who specialize in communication or social relationships. If families are fortunate enough to have a consultant at all, the consultant often concentrates on only one tile of the family mosaic and does not take into account the family's compelling need for comprehensive support across all lifestyle mosaic tiles.

Although in the field of positive behavioral support professionals are beginning to "talk the talk" of lifestyle change, there is still a way to go to "walk the walk." We are still learning how to make desirable changes for inclusive experiences, changes that are rooted in the principles of positive behavioral support, that pervade every waking and sleeping hour of the individual's life, and that cause and then reflect changes in professional systems.

For example, current professional literature makes it clear that the "standards for assessing success" (Horner et al., 1990, p. 127) have not changed very much at all during the last decade. Studies often describe one or two intervention techniques implemented in a single environment. The question is this: Does that kind of intervention represent and ensure *inclusive lifestyle change?* In fact, long-term follow-up is often characterized by going back to the family to see how things are 3–6 months following intervention. Consider how much time would have been needed to consult with us as a family to achieve an inclusive lifestyle for JT.

It took us 6 years to put into place the lifestyle changes that balance the elements of family, friendship, community participation, supported living, and supported employment—depicted in Figure 2—despite the fact that we have six degrees between us, are immersed in the disability field, have ready access to university faculty and students, and have financial resources with which to purchase services. If it took us that long, how long will behavioral consultants need to work with typical parents,

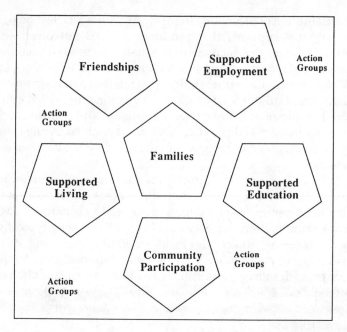

Figure 2. Mosaic of *comprehensive* supports and services for lifestyles of individuals with problem behavior.

and how much support will typical families really need to make lifestyle changes—yes, profound, new paradigm-breaking lifestyle changes—that go significantly beyond mere behavioral changes?

Most professionals have not fully come to grips with the enormity of this task, the scope of time, and the financial resources it will take to provide genuine comprehensive support to achieve inclusive lifestyle change. The next section briefly highlights the mosaic of JT's life today and the process we have used to accomplish these profound lifestyle changes.

GROUP ACTION PLANNING AS A STRATEGY FOR PROVIDING COMPREHENSIVE FAMILY SUPPORT

After being asked the question, "What are you going to do when you fail?", we set out on a task where failure was absolutely unacceptable. We started out very informally, but over the years our efforts evolved into a process that we now call Group Action Planning. The two fundamental characteristics of Action Groups are that they 1) create a context for social connectedness and interdependent caring, and 2) through the social connectedness, engage in dynamic and creative problem solving and action.

The idea is to build a network with people who are passionately committed to the individual with a disability. These people include the individual with a disability, family members, friends, community citizens, and professionals. The network comes together on a regular basis to envision and create a lifestyle that is consistent with the preferences of the individual with a disability. Rather than being agency or professionally directed, Action Groups are first and foremost directed by the preferences of the individual with a disability and his or her family. Action Group members boldly view the world from the individual's perspective and ask: Why not?

Outcomes

The following have been important outcomes of Group Action Planning for JT.

Supported Employment JT works 30 hours a week at The University of Kansas as a clerical aide. As faculty members, we were able to help him get this position; however, this is not unlike the strategy that many people without disabilities use. Many people get jobs through a network of family and friends. JT makes more in a month than he would have made in a sheltered workshop in a year; has had only one incident of challenging behavior at work in the last 6 years; and works within a caring network of co-workers who like him, believe in him, and help him advance his skills.

Supported Living As of this writing, JT has lived in his own home for 5 years—a home that he is helping to buy with his own salary. He shares his three-bedroom home with two university students. In exchange for rent and utilities, his roommates each provide him with about 12–15 hours a week of personal support, helping him to learn new skills, coordinate his schedule, and experience enjoyable and emotionally connected companionship.

Use of Public Transportation Rather than riding the disability-only van, JT walks down to the corner of the block and catches the city bus, which takes him to campus. Once he gets to campus, he walks a complicated route through a couple of different buildings and down a steep hill in order to get to his job. Never in our wildest dreams did we think he would be able to do this by himself, particularly after he had experienced a 12-month period when someone always had to accompany him because of the unpredictability of his aggressive behavior.

Friendships The most exciting aspect of JT's life is that he is surrounded by caring and enjoyable friends. Each week, he hangs out with approximately a dozen different people during different times of the week. For a young man who never had a friend his own age until he was 21 years old, he is substantially making up for lost time.

Community Participation One of JT's first introductions to inclusion was through getting involved with a university fraternity about 5 years ago. From that beginning of having a place to hang out, with opportunities to attend parties and special activities, JT has branched out into the community in many ways. He has many "Cheers"-like connections— places he can go where everyone knows his name—including a popular bakery, two jazz clubs, restaurants (especially ones with live music), church, a neighborhood grocery store, and a fitness center. A key aspect of JT's life is that he goes around the community as an individual rather than as a member of a herd. We continue to be awed and inspired by the number of ordinary community citizens who are invested in his success and who look out for his interests when he needs some extra support.

Group Action Planning Components

Group Action Planning components that we put into place to create the inclusive lifestyle changes described above are explained in the following sections and include:

- Inviting support
- Creating connections
- Envisioning great expectations
- Solving problems
- Celebrating success

Inviting Support   One of the key aspects of Action Groups is that they are composed of individuals representing each of the necessary tiles of the lifestyle mosaic. For JT, we started with his family, including both parents and his sisters, Amy and Kate; family friends; and guys JT was beginning to get to know from the fraternity. It was two of his fraternity brothers who initiated the idea of JT moving out of our home and being their roommate, and it was family friends who initiated and helped secure his job at the university. After he began to interact in these two new environments—employment and a home of his own—his job coach, some co-workers, and his roommates became additional Action Group members. Because JT deeply enjoys music, we included a university faculty member who teaches music therapy and who, in turn, has brought dozens of musicians into JT's life. Next, we looked for strategic community leaders who are natural "matchmakers" with inclusive community opportunities. Thus, we reached out to someone from our church, who also happens to work at the local bakery, knows almost everyone in town, and has keen communication skills, to act as a group facilitator.

The point is that Action Groups are composed of people across every single lifestyle tile because lifestyle change requires that significant supports and services be provided in each of these settings. By having significant representatives from each lifestyle tile, the supports and skill development can be coordinated, and thus JT's learning and inclusion can be far more effective. For example, everyone in his network is prompting his conversation skills using similar approaches, as contrasted to that happening in only one or two of his environments previously. Not only is the rate of his learning accelerated, but generalization is as well.

We had lived in Lawrence for 8 years before we actively invited support. It has been amazing to us what natural and potent resources we were surrounded by all of those years that were dormant because we had not invited them to be part of our lives.

Families with a member with a disability have been conditioned to assume almost sole responsibility for their family member, not to impose on others or expect their help, and generally to live on the fringe of community life. Action Groups have the major challenge and opportunity to expand support from just a sole focus on one lifestyle tile (the family) to the orchestration of all tiles (work, living, and other community environments) and from just a few professionals and parents to the rich and extensive arena of family, friends, and community citizens.

Creating Connections At many individualized education program (IEP) and individualized transition plan (ITP) meetings, there often tends to be a routinized agenda characterized by somberness, anxiety, tension, and distance. As contrasted to the typical individualized team meetings, a teacher who attended an Action Group for a junior high student in our community commented that he could not decide if he was going to a meeting or a party. It is highly unlikely that anyone ever mistook a typical IEP or ITP meeting for a party.

Group Action Planning places strong emphasis on creating social and emotional connectedness among all group members, especially with the individual with the disability. It is typically the case that almost everyone in the group—professionals, friends, community citizens, and family—is tired and overextended from multiple responsibilities. Thus, a key in Group Action Planning is to create a context in which people can enjoy themselves, feel a sense of renewal and rejuvenation, and obtain personal gratification and validation that they are making a difference in someone's life. There have to be enough personal rewards created for each person that it is worth their valuable and limited time and energy to invest in this process, one which usually takes place outside of their typical workdays. In terms of creating social connectedness within the Action Group, key considerations include the following:

- Holding meetings in people's homes rather than in professional settings
- Telling stories about the person's past and hopes for the future rather than relying on test scores or formal reports
- Providing food and opportunities for socializing before and after meetings
- Looking for ways to enhance benefits for everyone in terms of self-esteem, gratification in making a difference, professional benefits, and responding to each member's personal needs

- Embracing crisis as a time for group solidarity in sharing both the pain of problems and the triumph of overcoming them

In addition to creating *social* connectedness, it is also critical to enhance a sense of *emotional* connectedness—not only to the individual with the disability and the family but to all group members. In terms of the individual with the disability, group members can be supported to learn how to

- Best interact with the individual so that the relationship moves beyond a superficial level to a more intimate level of emotional connectedness
- Acknowledge the individual's preferences and strengths so that those can be the basis for relationships and for transitional planning
- Encourage the individual to express positive and negative feelings and to carry on reciprocal conversations to the extent possible

For example, we found that as family members we know certain techniques that work with JT to help him feel especially connected to others. Rather than asking each new member to figure out these techniques by trial and error, we easily share examples with the Action Group so that new members can observe and quickly pick up on them. Also, many meetings start with each group member stating something positive about JT that he or she particularly appreciates. This helps everyone get to know his strengths so that they can build on those, and it is a powerful experience for JT to hear so much positive feedback.

Most of the emphasis in the field of developmental disabilities has been focused on the quantity of social relationships that people experience. It is one thing for a person with a severe disability to have someone with whom to go to a movie on a Saturday night, but it is another thing to attempt to guarantee that relationship outcomes such as emotional support and companionship are derived from the interaction. Certainly, spending time together is a necessary prerequisite; however, professionals must learn to not only focus on the social connectedness of the relationship, but also learn to facilitate and document relationships that have meaningful outcomes.

We also found that JT needed to enhance the relationships he was developing—to ensure reciprocity—by expressing interest in others and responding to their instrumental and emotional needs. For example, he has expanded his conversational skills by learning information that is relevant to each of his group members, such as the names of their pets or their hobbies. It is important for him to acknowledge the happy and sad events in their lives, do thoughtful favors, and inquire about and respond to their preferences (especially when there is a conflict of interest with his own). There has not been nearly enough attention paid to relationship enhancement for people with disabilities, yet it is an essential component of an inclusive adult lifestyle.

Envisioning Great Expectations It is essential in Group Action Planning for there to be at least some great expectations for what the future might hold. In fact, from our experience it appears that Action Groups work far more effectively when the expectations tend to be high. The challenge of reaching goals that many people foresee to be unreachable can provide motivation for group members to beat the odds.

Increasingly, there is a great deal being written about the importance of visions in future planning (see, e.g., Senge, 1990). In our own Group Action Planning, we found that great expectations grow in ever-increasing circles. It would have been absolutely impossible for us to have envisioned 7 years ago how really good life is for JT today. In fact, gradually, as one goal was reached our expectations for others became possible.

With regard to great expectations, in JT's group we found that it was essential to involve people who tended to see the cup as half-full rather than half-empty. In inviting support, it is important not to surround yourself with nay-sayers, but rather to invite people who are willing to work hard to achieve what many people might think impossible.

Solving Problems A key attribute of Action Groups is that they focus on creative problem solving. As contrasted to traditional team meetings where many decisions have actually been made in advance of the meeting and the discussion at meetings tends toward a review of these already established decisions, Action Groups are absolutely open in terms of assuming that any solution to a problem is possible. The group facilitator may be a professional, friend, or family member, but he or she must have excellent communication skills, as the group facilitator has a critical role in leading the group through steps of problem solving, including

1. Analyzing preferences, strengths, and needs
2. Brainstorming a wide range of options
3. Carefully evaluating each option
4. Selecting the preferred option in developing a detailed action plan
5. Implementing the plan
6. Evaluating plan outcomes

It is essential to create a problem-solving atmosphere in which everyone is open to full inquiry into all options, all group members have equal opportunities for participation, and there is a commitment to create win/win outcomes.

When there is diverse membership—especially when there are friends and community citizens participating—a whole new pool of diverse resources and options is available for solving problems, as contrasted to those available in traditional team meetings. Consideration is given to how each person can complement the efforts of others so that as many different bases as possible are covered.

In JT's Action Group, we have dealt with very large problems that require systemic change as well as smaller challenges that primarily involve learning new skills (e.g., learning to shave, learning to ride the city bus, finding new roommates). In terms of the larger systemic issues, JT went through a period after he started his job and moved into his new home where he once again started engaging in some aggressive behavior.

As we made progress in a variety of lifestyle tiles, we began to recognize that we had a proliferation of behavior management programs. JT had one behavior program that involved getting up in the morning on his own initiative, another behavior program for work motivation, and a series of fairly inconsistent attempts to encourage his appropriate behavior in afternoon and evening friendship and recreational experiences. We realized that essentially every lifestyle tile had at least one behavior program and that we were tinkering with repairing broken tiles rather than creating a mosaic.

At one Action Group meeting in the spring of 1989, one year after we had started working on the lifestyle mosaic, we squarely acknowledged as a group the grim reality that we were failing to grasp the full significance of inclusive lifestyle support. JT's roommates were instrumental in designing a comprehensive behavior support program and getting implementation under way. They made an extraordinary difference in JT's life and ours, and they supported us in grasping the magnitude of the task with which we were faced:

1. Implementing a behavior management plan that clearly specified JT's responsibilities and the rewards that he would get from the time that he got up each morning to the time he went to bed at night as he interacted in every lifestyle tile
2. Communicating among roommates, family, job coach, and friends so that *all* of the people in his life would implement the behavior management plan in a consistent manner
3. Distinguishing the unique roles of friends by seeking to incorporate only the essential aspects of behavioral programming into the relationship and avoiding the use of friends as peer tutors
4. Expanding the number of people in JT's social network and encouraging his emotional connectedness with every network member
5. Providing JT with consistent notice of schedule changes and a back-up system of activities to put into place when these changes occurred
6. Training JT and group members how to handle change with confidence rather than anxiety

7. Encouraging JT to learn to express his preferences verbally and to assert himself when other people are not honoring his preferences while also encouraging members of his social network to listen, reinforce, and respond

8. Training JT to appropriately express negative emotions such as worry, frustration, anger, and fear and training his support network to listen, reinforce, and respond

9. Desensitizing JT to long, black ponytails, which he tended to pull when he experienced intense feelings of worry, frustration, anger, and fear

10. Training all group members on warning signals of JT's aggressive outbursts, how to respond to warning signals, and what to do if an outburst occurred

11. Supporting group members in envisioning great expectations and learning not to be so worried about the dangerous behavior that might happen, focusing instead on success and strengths

Attending to all of these tasks amounted to more than three full-time jobs, yet everyone in JT's Action Group had multiple other responsibilities. Unfortunately, many families feel so overwhelmed by what needs to be done that they give up on doing much of it at all.

A highly supportive aspect of JT's Action Group was that, as parents, we did not have to initiate, plan, and implement all of these interventions ourselves. With two jobs where we each typically work more than 40 hours a week and with two other children to care for besides JT, not to mention our other roles and responsibilities, it would have been extremely difficult for us to have created JT's inclusive adult lifestyle on our own. Rather, working over about a 3-year period with the help and contribution of every single Action Group member, significant progress has been made with all of the proposed tasks; however, eternal vigilance is still required for continued skill development, monitoring, and revision. What we have essentially learned is that few things last forever, but positive behavioral support is surely an ongoing process. Expanding and enhancing an inclusive adult lifestyle is a lifelong commitment, one that must continue even after the individual's parents are no longer living.

One of the best aspects of Action Groups in terms of problem solving is that the critical people are there across all of the different environments in which the person participates. Thus, there can be coordination, sharing of responsibility, and a sense of support that everyone's needs will be considered. At the end of every meeting, it is critical to write out a clear Action Plan with specific, assigned tasks to execute before the next meeting. If every member of the Action Group leaves with one task to accomplish, there can be approximately 10–14 different goals achieved without anyone feeling overwhelmed, with people helping each other, with peer support and review as a quality assurance technique, and with JT's inclusion being enhanced in all of his domains.

Celebrating Success One of the unfortunate aspects of many traditional team meetings is that there is rarely an opportunity for celebration. The atmosphere typically tends to be somber and serious. In contrast, a key aspect of Action Groups is to take every occasion for celebration in terms of affirming progress, allowing and encouraging gratitude, and setting aside time to "party" rather than to always problem solve.

One way to celebrate is actually to have parties, something that we have done frequently over the last 6 years. There have been opportunities for birthday parties, potluck dinners, holiday parties, and just times to have fun together. A typical approach is for JT to dictate the invitation, so that it is clear that it comes from him and that he has an opportunity to be the host. This, in turn, creates social and emotional connections by enhancing his reciprocity.

Another way to celebrate is occasionally to take time at meetings to affirm the power and contributions of the group. At one of our recent Action Group meetings, we gave everyone a candle and began the celebration by lighting only the candles of family members and showing the limited amount of light that could be generated if it was only the family light that was burning for JT. Then by going around the circle and having everyone light their candles, the vibrant blaze signified the light that could be created for JT's life by collaborating in a synergistic way. The meeting ended with JT singing "This Little Light of Mine" as a way of celebrating the progress that everyone had made by working together.

IMPLICATIONS

One of the most successful aspects of JT's Action Group has been a consistent feeling of group synergy—a powerful sense that the whole is truly greater than the sum of its parts and that the group's energy and creativity outshine what any individual could generate alone. The concept of synergy is hard to put into words. It means being with a group of people in which any individual ability to create change becomes part of a movement or wave that is unstoppable. The resulting rush of possibility and empowerment is a renewing experience, one that truly transforms great expectations from visions into lifestyle options.

Returning to an earlier question, when would a behavioral consultant know that an inclusive adult lifestyle had been accomplished for the individual with whom he or she is consulting? As Dick Schiefelbusch, our mentor at The University of Kansas, is fond of saying, "Progress is a new set of problems." For example, as soon as JT learned to ride a taxi to get to work—a task that was no small accomplishment—it occurred to us that he might be able to ride the city bus. As soon as he went through the training procedures to ride the bus to work, he then needed to learn to ride the bus from work to home—a task that involved a different set of skills in figuring out which bus to take, getting off at a different place in his neighborhood, and learning to walk a different route to his house. Similarly, as soon as JT acclimates to one roommate situation and all of the kinks are worked out, it is time to start thinking about when that roommate is going to leave, locating the next one, and beginning to reestablish these supports.

The point is that comprehensive family support in creating an inclusive lifestyle mosaic does not mean implementing procedures to handle two or even 10 behaviors within only one or two tiles. Rather, it means working cohesively and coherently, embracing complexity through the whole broad ecology of every single tile in the lifestyle mosaic over decades.

Essentially, what are the new criteria for "assessing success" (Horner et al., 1990, p. 127) of lifestyle interventions? The answer to that question is that positive behavioral support for people with challenging behavior is, indeed, a lifelong intervention. We are just beginning to encounter a new era in our Action Group where increasing amounts of responsibility are being initiated by community citizens who have gotten to know JT in casual ways as he has expanded his "Cheers"-like connections. Waitpersons in restaurants provide additional support when he seems anxious, bus drivers know how to get him home safely if he gets on the wrong bus, and people in his neighborhood watch to make sure that he gets on the bus in the morning. No one has ever asked these people to take on this role, but increasingly the community is coming forward and initiating support. Perhaps behavioral consultants will know that they have finished with creating inclusive lifestyles when the individual with challenging behavior has a reliable alliance of ordinary community citizens within each lifestyle tile. That is the next naturalistic observation we will be making as our family's mosaic continues to evolve.

Our experience with Action Groups has taught us many things, but nothing more important than what anthropologist Margaret Mead said many years ago: "Never doubt that a small group of thoughtful, committed citizens can change the world; indeed it's the only thing that ever has."

REFERENCES

Horner, R.H., Dunlap, G., & Koegel, R.L. (Eds.). (1988). *Generalization and maintenance: Life-style changes in applied settings*. Baltimore: Paul H. Brookes Publishing Co.

Horner, R.H., Dunlap, G., Koegel, R.L., Carr, E.G., Sailor, W., Anderson, J., Albin, R.W., & O'Neill, R.E. (1990). Toward a technology of "nonaversive" behavioral support. *Journal of The Association for Persons with Severe Handicaps, 15*(3), 125–132.

Mirenda, P. (1993). AAC: Bonding the uncertain mosaic. *AAC Augmentative and Alternative Communication, 9,* 3–9.

Senge, P.M. (1990). *The fifth discipline: The art and practice of the learning organization.* New York: Doubleday.

Turnbull, A.P., Ruef, M., & Reeves, C. (1994). *Family perspectives on lifestyle issues for individuals with problem behavior* (Monograph No. P-11). Lawrence: University of Kansas, Beach Center on Families and Disability.

Discussion

Norris G. Haring and Gigi De Vault

As early as 1905, during the free education reform movement in England, Joseph Lancaster developed a system that was based primarily upon positive reinforcement, token reinforcement, and peer monitors. Moving forward at a breathtaking pace in the 1950s, Skinner's establishment of basic behavioral principles came to be applied to education with phenomenal success. As early attempts at using applied behavior analysis are reexamined, the procedures employed then seem stiff and awkward by today's standards. Using tokens and M & M candies was so contrived that it is incredible that behavior analysts experienced such successful results. It is important to recognize, however, that throughout the same period the competing strategies for changing behavior (i.e., psychotherapy and counseling) were relatively ineffective.

During the 1970s and 1980s, significant refinements in the strategies and procedures for implementing behavioral interventions occurred. These advances have been due largely to the fact that interventionists adhered strictly to basic behavioral principles and technologies. In addition, interventionists have accumulated a large database of strategies effective for a wide variety of settings and conditions. The importance of functional assessment is now acknowledged as the touchstone of behavioral interventions.

This volume explains advances in the literature of applied behavior analysis and offers a powerful comprehensive approach designed to demonstrate several successful applications of positive behavioral support within the community and the family and to support efforts directed toward restructuring education. Moreover, the editors have selected distinguished authors who are currently involved in research and demonstration of positive behavioral support. Positive behavioral support embraces several vital concepts that have been included in the literature; however, this excellent collection of writings articulates these procedures with outstanding clarity and with much greater applicability for parents and educators. As defined in Section I, Family Issues and Family Support, positive behavioral support means

- Interventions that consider the contexts within which the behavior occurs
- Interventions that address the functionality of the problem behavior
- Interventions that can be justified by the outcomes
- Outcomes that are acceptable to the individual, the family, and the supportive community

Two fundamental attributes of positive behavioral support extend the approach beyond earlier approximations that emphasized disruptive behavior as the target of intervention. These attributes are a focus on 1) functionally equivalent behaviors and 2) appropriate communication, both within the framework of a comprehensive behavioral support plan. When this comprehensive plan is carried out, it strengthens the dignity of each individual involved. The issue of dignity for individuals who display a high frequency of disruptive behavior continues to be important, particularly in response to the controversy surrounding the use of aversive consequences. Presently, the most significant value of positive behavioral support is the effectiveness of the approach in achieving positive behavior change without resorting to aversive consequences.

Koegel, Koegel, Kellegrew, and Mullen open Section I by presenting a research base for asserting that increasing communication with children who display autistic behaviors dramatically decreases the frequency of those behaviors; furthermore, the authors assert that involving parents in the collaborative relationship with professionals strengthens the establishment and maintenance of communication. The idea that a lack of appropriate vocalization in young children can lead to inappropriate nonverbal behavioral patterns through which they express their desires is an extremely important finding. This perspective provides a vital shift from the traditional notion that the lack of verbalization and vocalization is simply another characteristic of children with autism. In other words, the lack of communication in early childhood results in crying and screaming, which accelerates to aggression and destructive behavior in later childhood. It is crucial, then, that positive behavioral support intervention be initiated at a very early age because it does increase the probability of success; moreover, building communication skills should be the primary target for intervention. Teaching and supporting parents to use functional assessment procedures is an important strategy for effective intervention of their child's disruptive behavior. Parents, in the Koegel et al. research, learn to use functional assessment in order to identify more precisely the setting events, antecedents, and consequences directly associated with their child's behavior.

Dunlap and Fox present an ecological approach to early intervention for young children with serious problem behaviors in Chapter 2. A major theme throughout this chapter is that of grounding intervention for problem behavior within the broader perspectives of families, neighborhoods, and communities. This ecological approach underscores the influence of a complex array of contextual factors on intervention outcomes for a child. The emphasis is on the development of strong family systems able to identify and obtain needed supports and to function within inclusive communities. Dunlap and Fox remind the reader that attending to the support and resource needs of families sets the occasion for effective early intervention. Impressive outcomes may result from early intervention, especially in the areas of communication and problem behavior, and particularly when the complex social systems of which the child is a member are also a focus of the intervention plan. Here, as in Chapter 1, skill development is viewed as an important attribute of early intervention for young children with serious problem behavior. A key consideration in a skill development approach to problem behaviors is the potential for "inoculation" to help prevent recurrence of the behavior over time. Perhaps this is particularly true when communicative alternatives for problem behavior are established. The reader is reminded of the importance of the match between an intervention selected from the range of possible and appropriate strategies and the context in which the intervention is anticipated to be employed.

Wacker, Peck, Derby, Berg, and Harding in Chapter 3 add another dimension to the consideration of context when addressing problem behavior— that of maintaining positive outcomes over the long term. Their chapter provides a maintenance model that guides both assessment and intervention. Parents are clearly partners in the implementation of this model as well. Assessment and technical assistance may be carried out directly in the home of the child, resulting in a collaborative effort that achieves benefit for children and families while simultaneously making demands on the collaborators. The parity of the parent-implementors in this collaborative relationship with professionals is enhanced by providing parents with frameworks through which they may better understand problem behavior and with effective strategies for bringing about behavior change. It is in this chapter that the complexities of context become apparent, as the authors elucidate the importance of a systematic approach to dealing with variation across people, settings, and tasks.

In Chapter 4, Albin, Lucyshyn, Horner, and Flannery, present a very strong argument for persons involved in any implementation plan to consider carefully the factors present within the context of the larger environment. They emphasize the strength of positive behavioral support, particularly when this approach is combined within a comprehensive, multicomponent plan involving as many of the people in the child's environment for as much of the child's day as possible. The authors make a convincing argument for interventionists to consider the fact that challenging behavior can be more precisely comprehended if that behavior is determined through cue analysis of the total context within which it occurs.

As consultants, the authors of this discussion have had similar experiences with weak intervention plans, and we were impressed with Albin et al.'s identification of problems that they commonly encounter as they assist others to develop and implement interventions. They have observed elegant plans that follow all of the principles and procedures embraced by positive behavioral support, yet fail to be as effective as they can or should be. The authors provide four main reasons why implementation plans result in poor outcomes. Such plans are

1. Poorly or inconsistently implemented
2. Implemented but not maintained across significant periods of time
3. Never fully implemented
4. Not sensitive to the importance of *contextual fit*

The essential elements of plans with a high probability of success according to Albin and colleagues are plans that are

1. Considerate of the context in which the behaviors occur
2. Conducive to effective behavioral support
3. Reflective of the key stakeholders' values and visions for a high-quality lifestyle
4. Logistically sustainable
5. Fully implemented and maintained

Turnbull and Turnbull conclude Section I with a strategy for providing comprehensive family support. This strategy represents an excellent blending of family concerns, group action planning, and positive behavioral support. Among many attributes of the chapter is the Turnbulls' ability to draw clear-cut, believable examples from actual experiences with their own son, JT, who has a disability. They stress the importance of parents having a skill such as positive behavioral support, which will enhance the positive characteristics of their child to increase his or her inclusion in community settings. Also included in this chapter are the procedures of problem solving used by the Action Group. While the creative problem solving referred to is reminiscent of the Osborn and Parnes

Creative Problem Solving strategy, the authors describe a different set of steps that they have found to be more suitable to their application.

We continue to admire the Turnbulls in the way they have developed positive solutions for parents, in part built on their own successful experience with rearing their son JT from infancy to adulthood. Over the years, they have provided many substantial contributions to the literature for parents and professionals. Their writings are truly an affirmation of the strength of "celebrating successes." Certainly the collaboration of parents and professionals exemplified by today's successful intervention practices is diametrically opposed to Bettelheim's (1967) recommended separation of the child from his or her parents.

Each of the chapters in this section presents technically sound and comprehensive strategies for supporting positive behavior change in children who exhibit problem behavior. Embedded within the approaches presented in Section I is an emphasis on identifying the functions that a child's problem behavior achieves and collaboratively generating acceptable, functionally equivalent alternatives. A common thread throughout the chapters is the importance of developing intervention procedures that may be implemented in a manner that is sensitive to immediate context and, at the same time, addresses the dynamic nature of context. A good match between an intervention and the context or environment in which it is implemented takes on particular significance in light of the fact that an important outcome of behavioral support is increased participation in inclusive environments. The authors have thoughtfully detailed strategies for developing the skills of children with problem behavior as well as the skills of family and community members for addressing problem behavior. Although these strategies are based on research and also, in some instances, stem partly from conventional wisdom, they are of immediate utility to families.

The framework in which approaches to intervention are presented in this section is one that emphasizes skill development, family support, and quality of life for children with problem behavior and their families. The authors present an enthusiastic balance of technically precise intervention strategies within a pervasive humanism that asserts the dignity of individuals with disabilities and families who are challenged by problem behavior. Features that distinguish Section I are the thoughtful manner in which the authors have acknowledged the complexity of the influence of interventions on problem behavior and their sensitive insistence on the benefits of understanding these interactions as part of larger systems. This section has much to offer families, and it will certainly promote the development of insightful and effective practice for those who desire to support families with members who engage in challenging behavior.

REFERENCE

Bettelheim, B. (1967). *The empty fortress*. New York: Free Press.

II

Education Issues

A Gift from Alex—The Art of Belonging

Strategies for Academic and Social Inclusion

Cheryl Nickels

This chapter is somewhat different from most of the other chapters in this book. There are no impressive initials behind the author's name, nor are there tables and charts or findings and conclusions based on research and scientific method. Several years ago my husband, Alf, became aware of my sense of inadequacy and intimidation about presenting at a professional conference due to the lack of important initials behind my name. One day, shortly before the conference, he presented to me an overhead transparency with the recommendation that I use it to introduce my upcoming presentation. On the transparency, I found my name followed by what appeared to be three very impressive initials. The initials were M.O.S. While the initials looked terrific behind my name, I realized I did not know what they stood for. When I asked for an explanation, my husband proudly replied that the initials stood for *Mother of Six*. Furthermore, he said the letters represented a fine qualification for giving a presentation because, if you added the ages of our six children together, the initials represented 65 years of experience in parenting. I suddenly felt very tired! As of this writing, that total number of years has increased to 122 years. And so, in lieu of research and scientific method, I offer a perspective and understanding that comes from my heart after many years of parenting children.

My hope is that, by the end of this chapter, readers may have a clearer idea of the human dimension behind the concept of inclusion, the hopes and dreams, the reasons and the benefits, as a parent sees them. I would like to share a story about lessons learned, gifts given and gifts received, and a miracle created by a little boy named Alex, now grown into a young man.

In November 1985, my husband and I received an evaluation with program recommendations from Dr. H. Michael Day, an educational consultant from Boise, Idaho. Dr. Day had agreed to help us advocate with a reluctant school system as we attempted to achieve the first mainstream placement for a child with a serious disability in our rural Idaho school district. We sought that placement for our then–6-year-old son, Alex, who has autism. The following are a few lines from Dr. Day's cover letter regarding our impending journey into uncharted territory.

> There is always a gap between research or best practice and the widespread use of that practice. It has been said that it may take as much as 10 to 15 years for research to be incorporated into widespread usage. Change seems all too slow when it comes to these matters. However, take heart in the fact that the impetus for change is usually well-informed consumers like yourselves. The program you desire for Alex will be something bordering on, if not exceeding, "state-of-the-art" practices. This does not make it wrong or unrealistic, only a challenge for all involved, and with all challenge comes growth. This just may be Alex's gift to others. (H. Michael Day, personal communication, November 5, 1985)

The gift from Alex to others could not be clearly known or appreciated in November 1985. However, 10 years later, we fully know of Alex's gift, for I and many others have received his gift over and over again. What I would most like to see our schools, churches, and communities do is learn the strategies and techniques that allow people with disabilities to belong and participate in general classrooms, scout troops, church meetings, and all community activities where typical people are found. Only then will society be privileged to receive the gifts that are given by Alex and others like him. My greatest hope is that the day will come when families can gain such placements for their children without the tremendous difficulties and barriers they now encounter. There are still many who doubt that this type of integration can be successfully achieved. Our experience as a family is that they can be achieved and that, when integration is provided, many of the difficulties of disability subside without further intervention.

Several years ago, I sat in a meeting for scout leaders and listened to a speaker tell a story that captured my attention. I have since forgotten who the speaker was or the point he was making with his story. But for me the story took on a particular meaning and left a strong impression on my mind. The story was of a man who had been named Outstanding Blind Golfer of the Year. We were given to understand that in blind golfing a beeper is placed in the ball and in the hole and that, by listening to the beeps, the person golfs. The award was presented at a banquet. During the presentation of the award, the presenter challenged the recipient to a round of golf. The challenge was accepted. Thinking to perhaps even the odds between the seeing and nonseeing golfers, the presenter generously offered to allow the award recipient to set the time and place for the round of golf. After careful consideration, the award recipient named the golf course of choice and set the time for 12:00 midnight.

Perhaps because I have a son with a disability, this story was significant to me and from it I drew two important lessons. First, a slight change of conditions can alter greatly our perception of who has a disability. And second, given some adaptive tools, people with disabilities can "play" on the same "course" with the rest of us. The story reminds us that perhaps we need to reframe how we think about people who have disabilities, where they can be, and what they can do. Perhaps we need to learn how to provide the adaptive tools that allow children with disabilities to participate and belong in our general school classrooms and community activities. It is important that children with disabilities be allowed to play on the same "field," but they will need some different tools if they are to be successful there. For too long it has been said that they could play on the same field, but only if they could do so using the same tools as everyone else. If they could not succeed using the same tools, they were sent away. We must invite these children to play on the same fields—that is, in general classrooms—by providing them with some additional tools that can enable them to succeed there.

The needs of children with disabilities extend beyond the functional and academic curricula of the sheltered and protected environments of self-contained classrooms. Emotions and feelings and living in the real world must be part of the equation. These children and their families feel the rejection and isolation of the segregated system. It has been said that the greatest pain on earth is not the pain of poverty and hunger, but the feeling of isolation. People with disabilities have known the pain of this isolation. The purpose of inclusion is to end this feeling of isolation, rejection, and stigmatization.

The greatest pain I felt when my son was diagnosed with a severe disability was not that he might have trouble learning to read or add or have difficulty relating socially or that there was going to be a new set of responsibilities on my shoulders. No, my greatest fear and pain came from what I knew society would do to him because he had a disability. In the recesses of my mind was the memory of the morning in sixth grade when my friend had come to school crying, not rejoicing, because her baby sister had been born early that morning, born with a handicap she called "mongoloidism." Throughout my lifetime, I had carried with me the haunting awareness that, through all the years of growing up with my friend, I never saw her baby sister. I remembered also the young woman who attended our church. Always she was with only her mother, always at the perimeter, never drawn in or included with other young people. Society had taught me early, while still a child, that people with disabilities were difficult "things" that were hidden behind closed doors and in silent places. And now one of those hidden children was mine.

During those early months of dealing with the reality of my son's condition, I quietly observed the lot of children with disabilities in our local schools and community, hoping that I would find that conditions had improved. What I found was that children with disabilities were drawn away into separate classes that were housed in the basement or in the annex at the back of the school. At lunch they sat at their own table, did not mingle with typical children at recess, and seemed to exist in a glass bubble through which they did not exit and through which typical children did not enter. As they grew older, it seemed they became more bizarre and weird, stigmatized and isolated, and often the target of ridicule and rejection by their peers. Also in my mind was the pain in the eyes of Alex's 14-year-old brother when he came home from junior high one afternoon after observing the treatment of young people with disabilities at his school and asked, with tears running down his face, "Mom, is that what kids are going to do to Alex when he grows up?"

If people are really interested in helping, the greatest gifts they can give families are inclusive placements for their children. When we as a family see Alex belonging and participating, accepted and supported by his peers, and surrounded by a group of children who are his friends, our pain is diminished and we rejoice in the life of our son.

STEPS TO INCLUSION

Gaining an inclusive educational placement for Alex in a school system unaccustomed to such placements required an intensive commitment on the part of his family. The development and implementation of Alex's program became a team effort between his teachers and myself. Building inclusive programs continues to be a joint effort between educators and parents. As I have worked closely with educators in Alex's program since the mid-1980s, I have identified five basic steps that are useful in developing an inclusive placement. These steps are the following:

1. Know what inclusion means.
2. Know why inclusion is important.
3. Know what the goals are.
4. Know how to build a program in typical environments.
5. Know how to help children make friends.

The first three steps constitute basic elements that are essential components to the process of building inclusive programs. Some find them to be too elementary for consideration, but experience with both parents and professionals shows that they are usually overlooked. And because these basic elements are overlooked, inclusive programs often fail. These elements are vital to understanding why families seek inclusive programs. They are precursors to Steps 4 and 5, the actual nuts and bolts of creating an inclusive program. These first three steps are the philosophical ingredients we use to make the building blocks, the foundation on which we build our commitment.

Step 1: Know What Inclusion Means

It is important to the integrity of the program to define, as a team, just what inclusion means. Inclusion means more than the child being present for recess and opening exercises, for music and P.E. Children in those placements are just part-time visitors; they do not really belong. Inclusion means that children will have the opportunity to go to school with their brothers and sisters and attend class with children from the neighborhood. They will spend their day sitting beside, eating with, playing with, and learning beside typical children. They will belong to a group of children, not a group of children with disabilities. Until the ideas of part-time and token inclusion are discarded, we will not build successful inclusive programs.

Step 2: Know Why Inclusion Is Important

Inclusion offers several outcomes that are difficult, if not impossible, to achieve in segregated placements. How do children learn appropriate responses and behaviors if they are restricted from being with the typical children who model them? From whom do they learn how to play, share, and get along with other children, if not from typical children who can show them how? Inclusion provides the places where friendships are built, where children belong, participate, and develop a sense of worth and self-esteem.

Children in inclusive environments are exposed to the myriad bits and pieces that make up the world around them. Their awareness of the world is increased and their horizons of daily life broadened. And indeed, contrary to popular opinion, children with a disability can learn letters, numbers, sounds, language, how to cut, color, write, read, attend, and finish a task in the typical classroom.

In addition, it is important not to overlook the significance of inclusion to typical children. The learning and opportunities of typical children are enlarged, not limited, when a child with a disability is present. When children with disabilities are included, the attitudes of society are altered. Typical children who have grown up with Alex have a new perspective on what people with disabilities are all about. When a person with a disability presents himself or herself at the workplace or church or in the family of one of these children who have grown up with Alex, these children will know that this is a person of worth, talent, and ability, not a mysterious unknown quantity to be feared and ignored. When children with disabilities are drawn in, loved, appreciated, accepted, and found worthy, *all* children can begin to sense and know that, in spite of their limitations, they too are acceptable, lovable, and worthy.

Step 3: Know What the Goals Are

During the first few years of Alex's mainstream placement, it became obvious to me that the issue that most impeded the process was an inability of school personnel to catch the vision of why Alex was there. This lack of vision continues to be a major obstacle. School personnel look at a fifth-grade curriculum and a child who has first-grade skills and say, "I'm supposed to write goals that are relevant to this child using these materials?" I discovered early that the thinking of educators was based mainly on issues of cognitive functioning and self-help skills. We, as parents, however, were considering additional issues that we felt needed to be addressed so that Alex might learn to escape the parameters autism had imposed on him and be able to function in real-world places and situations.

When developing goals for children in general classrooms, the many things they will learn there that go beyond cognitive or self-help skills must be considered. Issues such as being aware and accepting of the real world; participating in part of an activity or project; taking directions and paying attention in large-group environments; learning to overcome and tolerate the distractions that such environments impose; learning to listen, follow along, finish a task, and take appropriate instructions from a peer helper or teacher and discriminate and respond on command; and learning to develop appropriate social responses and behaviors, to be a friend, and to spontaneously follow the natural rhythms and routines of normal life must be incorporated into the goals. These are the purposes of inclusive environments—the important skills and abilities that can be taught in general classrooms. These are the outcomes Alex needed for his future that could not be attained in segregated environments. When properly designed, a general classroom setting should and can provide opportunities for good instructional techniques and for mastery teaching of cognitive and self-care skills that reflect the child's individual needs. However, in considering goals for children with severe disabilities, educators must also begin to look further to those issues that allow children to become full citizens in the community of their peers now and in the future. Educators will not be looking only at academic mastery. Rather they will be using the letters and numbers and concepts of the general classroom curriculum to teach a child to become responsive to the natural environment so that he or she will learn to function in such a way that the natural environment will become hospitable to the child. Educators struggle to know how to write such goals for the individualized education program (IEP) that reflect this philosophy. I share now how we have learned to do this over the course of Alex's education.

The first part of Alex's IEP reflects traditional cognitive and self-help goals such as letter and sound recognition, reading, math facts, tying shoes, and so forth. These goals are carried out during a pull-back session of about 1-hour duration during which Alex receives one-to-one tutoring. The remainder of his IEP reflects goals that are to be met through general classroom participation. Based on a knowledge of Alex's disability and an evaluation of his behaviors, we knew that in order to function in the world as an adult, both in the workplace and socially, Alex was going to have to develop certain skills. Those needed skills fell into four basic categories. First, Alex needed to learn to *attend*, to pay attention to what was going on around him. Second, Alex needed to learn to *participate* in what was going on around him. Third, Alex needed to learn how to *respond* appropriately to directives given to him by those in charge. And fourth, Alex needed to learn how to have *friends* and how to be a friend. Over the years, we learned how to write goals based on Alex's need to attend, participate, comply, and be a friend. Table 1 presents a few examples taken from Alex's eighth-grade IEP.

All of the essential goals presented in Table 1 can be carried out in typical classrooms using grade-level curriculum. Developing goals that

Table 1. Alex's eighth-grade IEP

CLASSROOM GOALS: Utilizing the materials and curricula of the eighth-grade classes (English, Math, Science, Social Studies, Exploratory, and Enrichment classes), Alex will participate in typical classroom activities.

I. Alex will ATTEND to classroom activities, discussions, and presentations.
   A. Alex will look at the page in the book, at the board, chart, or screen.
   B. Alex will use follow-along materials and strategies.
      1. Alex will keep his finger on the place in the book or on the paper where the class is working.
      2. Alex will circle the number of the question being discussed.
      3. Alex will place an answer label in the blank to answer the question being discussed.
   C. Alex will pay attention when requested to do so.

II. Alex will PARTICIPATE in classroom activities, presentations, and discussions.
   A. Alex will respond without protest to simple directives given by the classroom teacher or peer helper.
      1. Alex will take out his book.
      2. Alex will find the page number.
      3. Alex will transition from one task to another without resistance.
      4. Alex will direct his attention to certain items when asked.
   B. Alex will respond to two simple questions asked by the teacher during class sessions such as:
      1. Alex, what is 3 plus 2?
      2. Alex, what is the answer to the flashcard problem?
      3. Alex, what is in the picture?
      4. Alex, what is this word?
   C. Alex will raise his hand to answer questions that he has prepared in advance.
   D. Alex will present a special report on a concept from each unit using visual materials.
   E. Alex will master at least four concepts from each unit by completing adapted, modified, and/or pretaught materials and by completing a test on these concepts.
   F. Alex will accept feedback from teachers and peers and will correct work when asked.
   G. Alex will manage his materials in an appropriate manner (locker management, organizing book bag, bringing supplies to class, arranging materials on desk, etc.).

III. Alex will PARTICIPATE in social activities.
   A. Alex will initiate conversation and interactions with other children at school.
   B. Alex will converse at appropriate times in the classroom.
   C. Alex will demonstrate appropriate turn taking.
   D. Alex will greet unknown adults in an appropriate manner (shaking hands).
   E. Alex will address teachers and peers using appropriate names.
   F. Alex will participate in social extracurricular activities as planned by a peer circle.

From Koegel, R.L., O'Dell, M.C., & Koegel, L.K. (1987). A natural language paradigm for teaching non-verbal autistic children. *Journal of Autism and Developmental Disorders, 17,* 187–199; reprinted by permission.

Classmates provide support and assistance to Alex in the classroom.

are based on skills and behaviors rather than on subject, allows parents and educators to understand the purpose of the child's placement in the typical classroom and how his or her other needs can be met there. General education teachers are given a better sense of their role in the child's education and what they can expect the child to do. Once a strong foundation has been built based on the three steps discussed thus far, parents and educators can go on to develop a successful inclusive program by implementing two more steps as follows.

Step 4: Know How to Build a Program in Typical Environments

The first step in building an inclusive program should be an in-service meeting that involves everyone who will be part of the program from principal to parent. This in-service meeting should be presented by an individual or individuals who can explain what the program looks like, why the child is there, what the goals are, how the child will participate, the roles of each person involved, and basic behavior management and reinforcement techniques that will be needed to obtain the student's cooperation. The in-service presenter may be a consultant hired by the district to assist in the development of an inclusive program, district personnel who have implemented the program in previous years, or a parent who may be closely involved in the program.

Next, the schedule and program for a typical classroom day is observed and evaluated. A careful analysis is made to identify those parts of the school day that appear to be least hospitable to the child's participation. Those times are used for the *pull-back* program. During this time, the child can be pulled to the back of the classroom or to a small desk in the hall for one-to-one tutoring in individual cognitive and self-help goals. Care should be taken that this time does not exceed 1–2 hours per day. The rest of the day will be spent in typical classroom activities.

Then, based on the day's activities, the kind of support needed for the child to succeed is determined. It is likely, depending on the nature and severity of the child's disability, that a teacher's assistant may be needed in the classroom when the child is initially placed. The child may require a great deal of direction and assistance at first. For example, the child may need help in understanding what he or she should do, in paying attention to the relevant information, in managing papers and materials, and in staying on-task. The teacher's assistant serves to guide the child through each activity and project, reflecting the teacher's instructions and directions. Some children may need to be physically prompted to follow directions as to when to stand up, when and where to move in the classroom, how to pledge allegiance to the flag, and so forth. This intensive assistance will be faded over time. Initially, the goal will be to develop in the child the ability to be responsive and comfortable in the classroom under the direction of the teacher's assistant.

Next, the assistant will begin to direct the child's attention to the teacher, prompting the child to look at and listen to the teacher. The assistant might also teach the class for a period of time each day. During this period, the general classroom teacher will spend one-to-one time with the child, developing a rapport and learning and practicing techniques needed to give instruction and gain compliance. Then the teacher begins to implement those techniques in the full classroom setting and the instruction of the child gradually begins to transfer from the assistant to the teacher. The assistant begins to withdraw from the child, moving on to help other students but keeping a close eye on the child should he or she falter or get off-task. The assistant returns to provide aid and support as needed. Eventually, the assistant may be completely faded out.

In addition to support from the teacher's assistant, the classroom programs and activities should be examined to see how the child will be able to participate. Each project, activity, or worksheet needs to be considered to determine which part of it the child can do and how other parts can be modified so that the child can do them. In some cases, educators may decide to use material that is essentially different from what the typical children are doing. However, in many cases the same materials can be used if they are modified and adapted to suit the child's abilities and needs. Several guidelines can assist in this process. First, identify which part the child can do; then find a way to simplify the rest of the task. Simplifying the task may be done by 1) making the activity more concrete, 2) identifying and limiting the concept the child is to learn, 3) using orientation cues, 4) adapting the material to the child's skill level, 5) making the material more relevant, 6) using tape recordings to extend written information and provide directions to the child, and 7) preteaching material to the child prior to the child doing it in class. (See Figures 1–7 at the end of the chapter for adapted worksheet samples.)

Placement in typical classrooms does not have to be synonymous with "dumping." It should and can be a carefully planned and designed program. The program should be monitored, data should be kept, and follow-up should be maintained. It is a combined effort of the special education staff and the general education teachers. Special educators develop the program and the materials and general education teachers implement it. When given adequate information, experience, and support, administrators and teachers who may have been unsure and even hostile about Alex's presence became his advocates and supporters. They came to claim ownership of the program they once feared and take pride in its success. And when their time with Alex ended, they spoke of lessons learned, of genuine affection for their unique student, and of gratitude for the experience.

The beauty of these kinds of strategies is that they work across the board, year after year, and they can be adapted to various levels of ability. An added bonus is that these techniques of adaptation and partial participation can provide the means to draw the child into church classes and activities, scout troops, and other community programs. The focus changes from how many concepts can be stuffed into the child's brain, or how many skills he or she can acquire, to how the mainstream environment can be used to ensure that the child learns to function in natural environments and spends his or her life in them instead of behind the closed doors and in the silent places I had learned to fear as a child. Through inclusive education, the natural environment becomes a hospitable place to the child, and the world becomes a place in which he or she can find friendship, acceptance, support, and mutual gift giving.

Step 5: Know How to Help Children Make Friends

Friendship is an area that is often neglected for children with disabilities. In our experience with Alex, we found that friendships do not just happen because the child is with his or her peers. Building friendship requires the same careful attention and structured programming as do other areas of skill development. The basic premise in this area is that most of the work will be done by the typical children. They are the best teachers and therapists that families could possibly employ. The task of adults will simply be to give typical children open and frank information about disabilities and serve to facilitate the interactions of the children. Children need to be given opportunities to express their fears and ask questions about differences they are not familiar with, they need to be helped to see how people with disabilities are more like them than different, and they may need to be given help on how to develop interactions with children who have disabilities. Educators and parents should not be afraid to invite typical children to assist in the process of drawing children with disabilities into their activities.

A week or two after a child has been placed in a typical classroom, an open and frank conversation should be held with the typical children. This conversation could be carried out by the child's parent or a staff person from the school. I like to start by presenting some very concrete, visual materials that illustrate several important concepts and then draw the children to conclusions about how these concepts apply to people. And we try to have fun in the process. For example, I often start with a story about a place called the "Land of Shapes," where the rule was that all the shapes had to stay with their own kind and could not get mixed up with shapes that were different than themselves. The story is told using a variety of shapes placed on a board. In time, the shapes discovered that their rule was holding them back and that if they were to get mixed up with each other, wonderful things could happen. While moving the shapes around on the board, I explain that the shapes decided to get all mixed up and turn themselves into something special. As they watch, the children discover that the shapes are turning themselves into a wonderful train.

Next, I present a cracker box that has been emptied of crackers and filled with cookies. I also present a tin can on which the label has been changed to show that there is fruit in the can instead of green beans. On opening the containers, the children are surprised as the contents do not reflect the outside label. I also tell the story of an imaginary community where all people have dark brown hair and dark brown eyes. I ask the class to imagine what happens when a boy with blond hair and blue eyes comes to the town and school and how people would react to him because he is so "weird." I explain how, over time, the community gets used to his "weirdness" and learns to accept the boy and value him because of who he is—his blond hair becomes irrelevant. From these stories and visual aids, the children are led to identify several important lessons, which are written on the board:

1. It's okay to be different.
2. When you put things that are different together, something wonderful can happen.
3. You can't tell by looking on the outside what's on the inside.
4. Weird isn't weird anymore when you get used to it.

We discuss how these concepts or lessons apply to people, including people with disabilities. Then we talk about the specific child, about the nature of child's disability, about the particular challenges the child faces because of the disability, and about how the child is different and yet just the same as all other children. The children are given the opportunity to express their feelings, concerns, questions, and fears. This is an important part of the process. It seems that as children express their fears and concerns, and they are dealt with in a calm and responsive manner by an adult, those fears dissipate and the barriers that have been erected come down. I invite the children to help their fellow student overcome the disability. Specific ideas are shared about what they can do. Children volunteer and assignments are given and accepted. As I have watched children go through this process, my heart has been deeply touched by the warmth and strength of their response.

A GIFT FROM ALEX

Alex's regular classroom placement began during the second semester of first grade. By the end of the school year he had made significant growth in many areas, but it was evident to me that the social progress I had so hoped for was not occurring. Alex maintained his aloof distance from others. In September of the next fall, we implemented the program I described above. I visited Alex's classroom and, in time, all the classrooms in his school. We discussed this strange little person who was in their school, and we talked about autism. I acknowledged, to the obvious relief of the children, that Alex was indeed "weird." They seemed to feel better knowing that even his mother knew he was weird. And maybe if she knew it and she thought it was okay, maybe it actually was okay that he was weird! We decided that he was different, but somehow it didn't seem to matter much now that we all understood why. We decided together that one of the most important things Alex needed to learn was how to be a friend. We identified three specific things the children could do, and I left the school with the children responding to my invitation to help.

Every few weeks I returned to school and watched as the children in Alex's class tried to draw him in by touching his shoulder as they passed, peering closely into his face and saying "hi," and entreating him to join them in their play. I marveled at their persistence as I watched for 3 months while they maintained a relentless onslaught in the face of Alex's total retreat, resistance, and anger at their effort. As I observed Alex's negative response over many weeks, I confided to my husband with a sinking heart that perhaps the experts were right, perhaps Alex would never have a friend. I feared that the children would soon weaken in their efforts to

Friends join Alex for after-school activities such as a trip to the game arcade.

reach him. But they did not give up! Week after week, they persisted in their mission, reassuring me on my visits that they would "get" him.

One day just before Christmas vacation, I made my usual visit and was treated to a beautiful gift. As I watched, I noticed that occasionally Alex responded and did not retreat from a child's advance. His wall was beginning to crumble! In the late spring, at track and field day, my heart was warmed and a few tears dropped from my eyes as I watched my son sitting in the middle of a crush of children, tugging and pushing as children do and, from time to time, reaching out and gathering another child up in his embrace. The work of the children and Alex's progress have continued. The children have performed a miracle, a miracle that has continued to grow through the years. As of this writing Alex is a student in tenth grade and continues to be challenged by autism. But no longer does it inhibit him from living a full, interesting, happy, and satisfying life in the society of others. No longer does he wait in the shadows, fearful and unsure, unable to enjoy the warmth and love of family and friends. Today he walks in the bright sunshine of daily life, catching the bus to school with his sister; making his way unattended through the bustle of crowded halls in the morning; going to his locker and preparing for the day; sharing a high five or a headlock with a buddy; musing over a comic book or airplane magazine with a friend; whispering to a classmate when he shouldn't; passing the sacrament at his church; attending an ordinary, regular Boy Scout camp; inviting his friends to a birthday party and overnighter; and going with the guys to the game arcade and fast-food joint for lunch.

And what of the wonderful children who, through these many years, have stood by his side, loyal, accepting, tolerant, supportive, and giving? Have they not also been recipients of great gifts from their strange friend with autism? They have learned compassion, tolerance, the beauty of diversity, and the sense of camaraderie as they have climbed to the top of the mountain with Alex and have known the rush of pride for having helped make the miracle happen.

The challenge that lies ahead is to learn the "art of belonging." As we learn that art, as we create ways for children to belong, we all become the givers and the receivers of a beautiful gift. I like to think of it as "Alex's gift."

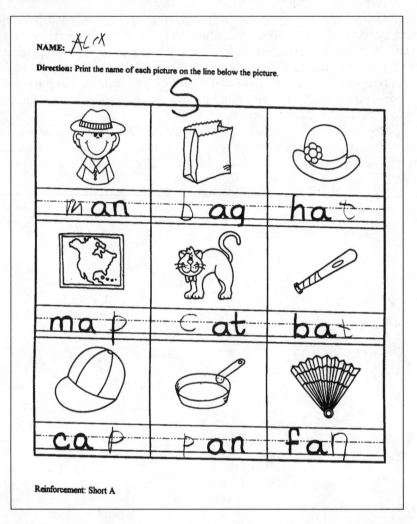

Figure 1.   If the child is unable to complete the entire task, find a way he can participate partially. In this exercise, typical children were to write the entire word with emphasis on the vowel sound. At the time the class did this worksheet, Alex was learning beginning and ending sounds. Therefore this worksheet was adapted to reinforce that concept. On this worksheet, the teacher filled in most of the letters for each word, leaving only one beginning or ending letter for Alex to fill in.

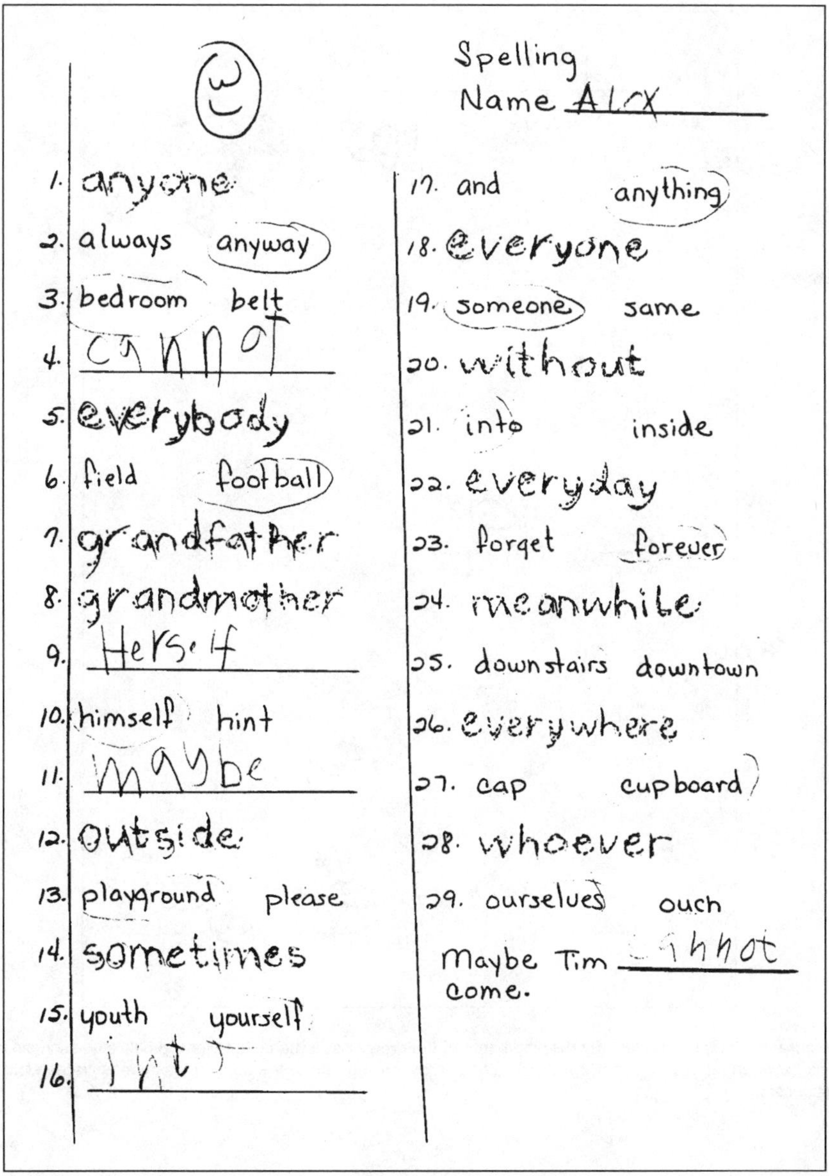

☺ (3)

Spelling
Name _Alex_

1. anyone
2. always (anyway)
3. bedroom belt
4. _cannot_
5. everybody
6. field (football)
7. grandfather
8. grandmother
9. _Herself_
10. himself hint
11. _maybe_
12. outside
13. playground please
14. sometimes
15. youth yourself
16. _int_

17. and (anything)
18. everyone
19. (someone) same
20. without
21. into inside
22. everyday
23. forget (forever)
24. meanwhile
25. downstairs downtown
26. everywhere
27. cap (cupboard)
28. whoever
29. ourselves ouch

Maybe Tim _cannot_ come.

Figure 2.   If the child cannot learn all the words for a spelling test, present some words in dotted form for the child to trace. Other words can be presented in multiple choice form, allowing the child to circle the correct word. For words the child has learned to spell, leave the space open so the child can write the word.

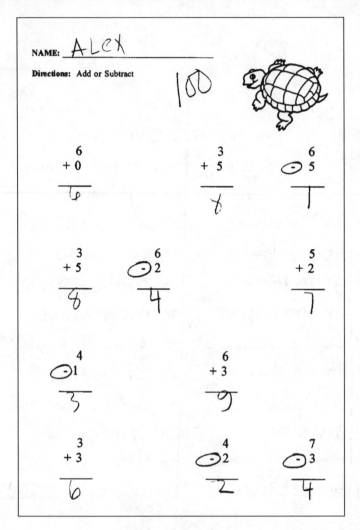

Figure 3. Simplify the task by deleting some of the problems. If the child is having difficulty discriminating between the signs, orient the child's attention by circling one of the signs, thus increasing the child's success.

NAME: ALeX

Directions: Identify the pre-fixes *re* or *un* and choose the correct meaning.

88%

re -----→ again

un -----→ not

1. The rules were **unfair**.
   a. fair again.
   b. not fair.
   c. fair.

2. Dad **repainted** the fence.
   a. not painted.
   b. painted
   c. painted again.

3. Mom **recooked** the food.
   a. not cooked.
   b. cooked.
   c. cooked again.

4. The boy's words were **unkind**.
   a. not kind.
   b. kind.
   c. very kind.

5. I had to **redo** the work.
   a. do it.
   b. do it again.
   c. don't do it.

6. Mom made me **rebrush** my teeth.
   a. brush again.
   b. not brush.
   c. brush.

7. He was **unlucky**.
   a. lucky.
   b. not lucky.
   c. very lucky

8. The room was **unchanged**.
   a. changed again.
   b. changed.
   c. not changed.

Figure 4.   Make the task more concrete by adding an information key at the top for the child's referral. Provide orientation cues by circling the prefixes to help the child attend to the relevant features.

142

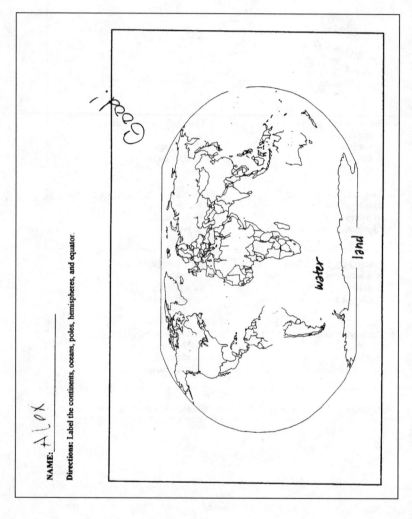

NAME: Alex

Directions: Label the continents, oceans, poles, hemispheres, and equator.

[handwritten labels on map: God; water; land]

Figure 5. Identify and limit the concepts the child will learn. While typical children were directed to identify the poles, hemispheres and equator and to name the continents and oceans on this worksheet, Alex was learning which parts on the map represented land and water. He was provided with sticky labels marked "land" and "water" that he was to place correctly on the map.

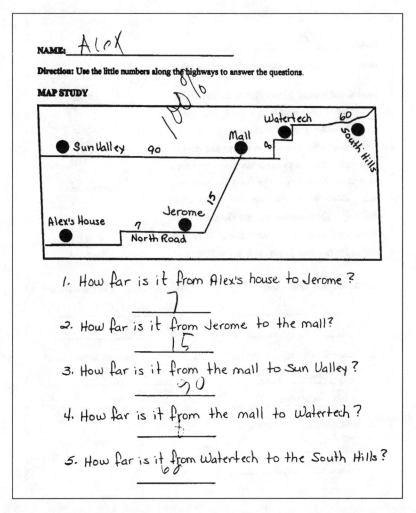

NAME: Alex

Direction: Use the little numbers along the highways to answer the questions.

MAP STUDY

1. How far is it from Alex's house to Jerome?

7

2. How far is it from Jerome to the mall?

15

3. How far is it from the mall to Sun Valley?

90

4. How far is it from the mall to Watertech?

5. How far is it from Watertech to the South Hills?

60

Figure 6. Simplify the material and make it more relevant to the child. The original worksheet presented a complex map of New York City. While Alex did the same task as the other children, the map was replaced by a much simpler map that contained places of importance to him.

NAME: A L /X

Direction: Read the story and answer the questions below:

Jacob's dad worked in an office in the city. Jacob was going to go to work with his dad. Dad picked up his briefcase and told Jacob to get into the car. Dad drove to the train station and parked the car. Dad and Jacob ran to catch the train. The train took them downtown. The buildings were very tall. Jacob walked with his Dad to the office building. They stepped into the elevator. Jacob pushed the button to the 23rd floor. When they got to Dad's office, Jacob sat at his dad's desk.

1. Where was Jacob going?
   ⓐ farm
   ⓑ city

2. Where did Dad drive in the car?
   ⓐ church
   ⓑ train station

3. How did Jacob get downtown?
   ⓐ train
   ⓑ walk

4. What did Jacob do in the elevator?
   ⓐ sat down
   ⓑ pushed button

5. Where did Jacob sit in the office?
   ⓐ dad's desk
   ⓑ floor

Figure 7. Adapt the work to the child's ability level. This story was recorded in a simplified form on an audiotape with special emphasis on the main ideas. While other children wrote their answers in the blanks, multiple choice options were provided on Alex's worksheet. The questions and possible answers were also recorded along with instructions. Alex followed along with the tape recording to complete the worksheet.

7

How Everyday Environments Support Children's Communication

Ann P. Kaiser and Peggy P. Hester

As a postdoctoral student in 1975, I (the first author) spent a year dividing my time between taking classes in linguistics and observing adolescents with mental retardation who were living in an institution. As an observer for several hours each morning, I recorded, or at least attempted to record, the communicative behaviors of a group of

An earlier version of this chapter was presented at the Fifth Annual National Institute on Disability and Rehabilitation Research and Training Center Conference on Non-Aversive Behavior Management, September 1992, Nashville, Tennessee. Conduct of this research was supported in part by Grant No. G008730528 from the Office of Special Education Programs and by Grant Nos. HD15051 and HD27583 from the National Institute of Child Health and Human Development.

young men as they lived their lives in a residential treatment facility. In 1975, an institution—even one with well-intentioned staff and university affiliations—was a very restrictive environment. Programs to teach language and fundamental self-help skills had just been initiated. Residents spent large portions of their time in the "cottage areas"—large empty rooms, sparsely furnished, with few materials and even fewer conversational partners. Most of the participants in my observational study had few language and social skills. Their most likely communication partners were staff and service providers—who for the most part were rarely available to them. It was required that one staff member be present with residents at all times. Two staff were assigned to the unit, but rarely were there two staff on the unit at the same time. By some intriguing orchestration, one staff member was always leaving (to put away laundry, to finish charts, to do some errand) just as the other was returning. The young men sat by themselves, quietly, sometimes engaging in self-stimulating behavior, often dozing in what appeared to be an overmedicated state. There were occasional incidents when a resident began engaging in behavior judged to be inappropriate, which, when it was noticed by a staff member, resulted in interventions such as time-out.

Not surprisingly, my analysis of the content of the young men's utterances (an analysis heavily influenced by my concurrent enrollment in linguistics courses) revealed very little of interest—mostly one word utterances and unintelligibles. "No" was the word most frequently used. My analysis of the environment examined the opportunities for communication and the frequency of social–communicative responses and initiations. The summary of these counts was interesting; there were few opportunities to talk (e.g., few instances of talk addressed to the residents), and interactions were brief and often related to instructions for behavior. At the time, the data were not very interesting, but the effect on me of observing day after day the quality of the environment was profound. I quickly concluded that I could not work in that setting; that children did not belong in institutions; and that early intervention, especially early language intervention, was essential for children with mental retardation. At the end of the data collection, I left the institution. I started a preschool and began research on early language intervention.

Almost exactly 20 years later, many of the same issues about the social–communicative environments provided for children with disabilities are of interest to me and my research group (the Milieu Teaching Group at Vanderbilt University). We continue to seek to understand how children can be supported to learn and use new functional language in everyday conversations. Although there have been many positive changes in intervention and educational services for children with disabilities, comprehensive, effective communication interventions have continued to challenge both researchers and practitioners. The conceptual and practical movement from dyadic-oriented language instruction on a one-to-one basis to more naturalistic approaches that support functional use and generalization across relevant partners and contexts has affected instructional models for language intervention (Warren & Reichle, 1992). This shift has focused the field's efforts to support children's communication development on the naturally occurring opportunities for language use and learning.

As language interventionists develop models of naturalistic teaching for implementation by teachers, parents, and significant others, it is important that the settings in which children will be expected to use their newly learned language be systematically examined. The framework of generalization across settings that has been a guiding concept for determining the effects of language instruction on children's use of language outside the training environment (cf. Costello, 1983; Warren & Rogers-Warren, 1985) may be insufficient for understanding and facilitating the functional use of language. This framework, derived from behavior-analytic perspectives, places the onus for language use almost exclusively on the learner. It is his or her task to generalize or transfer skills from the training context to another environment with other people. What is lacking in this framework is both a conceptual model of and an empirically based understanding of the environments in which children with limited language must use their newly learned skills. It is not that the understanding of generalization is incorrect, but that the current understanding of environments for young children with disabilities is incomplete.

This chapter offers a view of one type of environment in which young children with disabilities frequently find themselves—the preschool classroom. Based on an informal review of three studies that included assessments of generalization and modified ethnographies of preschool classrooms, we offer some principles of environmental effects on language use and some suggestions for modifications of these environments to support communication by young children with disabilities. The report offered here is not intended to present a complete description of the studies; the intent is only to use these observations as illustrations of environmental principles for supporting communication.

PRESCHOOL CLASSROOMS AS COMMUNICATIVE ENVIRONMENTS

For the past 4 years, we have been conducting studies of naturalistic language interventions in preschool classrooms (cf. Kaiser & Hester, 1994; Kaiser, Hester, Harris-Solomon, Delaney, & Keetz, 1995; Kaiser, Hester, Harris–Solomon, & Keetz, 1994). In the course of these interventions, we have conducted a series of single subject studies investigating the effects

of *enhanced milieu teaching* (EMT) when applied with conversational partners (language interventionists, teachers, and peers) in children's classrooms. In addition, we have examined children's language environments
using both single-subject observational methods to assess generalization
to new settings (classroom snack times, small-group times, play with peer
partners, and time at home with parents) and modified ethnographic
methods to examine the classroom from a more holistic perspective. We
have videotaped hundreds of hours of children interacting with various
conversational partners in the course of these studies. The classrooms
which we have observed are by no means a random or representative
sample. Thus, any conclusions that might be drawn from them must be
limited only to these classrooms. We tracked only 12 children extensively
in these studies. Table 1 presents the characteristics of the children,
the conversational partners, and the strategies for assessing peer-
directed talk.

The children participating in these studies were selected because of
their similarity in language skills. They were between 37 and 81 months
of age, with a mean age of 58 months. They had language skills that were
tested to be in the 16–36 months range (as measured by the Sequenced Inventory of Communication Development (SICD) (Hedrick, Prather, & Tobin, 1975). Each child used oral language as his or her mode of communication and was verbally imitative. Their average mean length of utterance
(MLU) in morphemes was 1.5 (range 1.1–2.8).

The classrooms in which these children were enrolled were all public
school classrooms. Although the children enrolled in these classrooms
varied in level of overall functioning and language skill, the classrooms
were self-contained and enrolled only children with disabilities. Each
classroom had at least two adults in the room on a full-time basis, usually
one lead teacher and one or two assistant teachers. In four of the five
classrooms, children were included with typically developing peers for
some part of the day, usually gym, music, lunch, or outdoor play. An average of eight children were in each classroom.

The primary purpose of these studies was to examine the effects of
EMT on children's language use and development. In two of the three
studies, we trained the children's classroom teachers to provide the EMT
intervention. In each study, we examined children's generalized use of
newly learned language to conversations in the classroom and, in one
case, at home. This chapter does not report all the procedures and results
of these studies. Instead, the chapter focuses on what we learned about
the environments in which we assessed generalization and in which we
expected children to use their newly learned skills.

EMT is a hybrid, naturalistic language intervention that combines
environmental arrangement, variants of incidental teaching, and respon-

Table 1. Child participants, conversational partners, and strategies for assessment

| | Children | | | | | | | |
| | Gender | | Age (Mo) | | SICD-E[a] (Mo) | | Conversational partners | Strategy for assessing peer-directed talk |
	Boys	Girls	Mean	Range	Mean	Range		
Study 1	5	1	53.8	37–81	29	16–36	Interventionist[b] Teacher Parent Peer	Direct observation of generalization
Study 2	4	0	61.5	57–71	24	24–24	Interventionist[b] Teacher[b] Peer[b]	Direct observation of generalization to peers Modified ethnography in classroom
Study 3	2	0	60	55	16	20	Teacher[b] Peer	Modified ethnography in classroom

[a]Language skill level as assessed by the *Sequenced Inventory of Communication Development, Expressive Scale* (Hedrick et al., 1975).
[b]Indicates this partner was included in intervention.

sive interaction strategies. The basic components of EMT are summarized in Table 2. A more complete description of EMT and the research supporting its development may be found in Kaiser (1993).

Study 1: Generalized Effects of EMT

In the first study (Kaiser & Hester, 1994), we examined the effects of EMT with six preschool children. Their use of language was assessed with three different conversational partners during three sessions before, and three sessions after, the intervention was implemented by a trained interventionist in an area within or immediately adjacent to the children's classrooms. The conversational partners were their parents at home during a play activity, their primary teacher in a naturally occurring small-group activity in the classroom, and their peers who had slightly more advanced language abilities during a free play activity. Although some

Table 2.   Components of enhanced milieu teaching

I. Environmental Arrangement[a]	
Selecting materials of interest	Facilitates: 1) child interest in the environment,
Arranging materials to promote requests	2) sustained attention to the environment, 3) verbal and nonverbal communicative
Mediating the environment	initiations including requests and comments,
Engaging in activities with the child	4) engagement between the child and adult
II. Responsive Interaction Strategies[b]	
Following the child's lead	Facilitates: 1) engagement between the child
Balancing turns	and adult, 2) turn taking, 3) sustained
Maintaining child's topic	interactions, 4) topic continuation,
Modeling linguistically and topically appropriate language that maps adult and child actions	5) comprehension of language spoken 6) spontaneous communicative imitations to the adult
Matching child's complexity level (talk at the target level)	
Expanding and repeating child utterances	
Responding communicatively to child's verbal and nonverbal communication	
III. Milieu Teaching Techniques[c]	
Child-cued modeling	Facilitates: 1) responsiveness to adult requests
Mand modeling	for communication, 2) generalized imitation
Time delay	skills, 3) requesting behavior, 4) production
Incidental teaching	of elaborated lexical and syntactic skills (and targets), 5) turn-taking skills, 6) topic continuation skills, 7) communicative initiations to the adult, 8) improved conversational skills

[a]Detailed descriptions of these procedures may be found in Ostrosky and Kaiser (1991).

[b]Detailed descriptions of these procedures may be found in Hemmeter and Kaiser (1994) and Weiss (1981).

[c]Detailed descriptions of these procedures may be found in Alpert and Kaiser (1992).

generalization from the intervention was observed on at least one measure of the four measures of child language use (number of utterances, MLU, diversity of vocabulary, and use of targets) for each child with each partner, the level of generalization varied by partners.

The children showed the most consistent generalization to interactions with their parents, the second most consistent with teachers, and the least consistent with their peer partners. The level of generalization and, more importantly, the amount and complexity of their talk at *both the pre- and postgeneralization assessment* were significantly correlated with two specific partner behaviors: 1) the number of questions (mands) and 2) total partner talk. These findings suggested that the amount of support partners provide for children's language learning has a dependable effect on child communication. When children learn new skills, levels of partner support will be at least one factor in determining the extent of generalized use of the new skills. When partners provided more support, more generalization was observed. When they provided little support for child performance, as was the case in the peer-to-peer interactions, children showed only modest changes in the frequency of talk and the complexity of talk after intervention. In the one-to-one parent–child sessions, children showed marked improvements in frequency and complexity of their talk. The teachers in the small-group context were particularly interesting because the lesser amount of support provided by teachers was, at least in part, a function of teachers distributing their attention among the three children present. Thus, although teachers were skillful in asking questions and talking to the target children, the relatively lesser amounts of talk to the target children were still associated with lower levels of generalization.

These results, although not surprising, suggest that language-learning children in classrooms where there are two teachers and 8–10 children, and where the children do not have many language skills, may experience limited support for using their new language. The extent to which they demonstrate generalization will depend on the amount of talk and specific invitations to talk (e.g., questions, mands) provided by teachers and peers. Environmental conditions, such as scheduling, the size of small groups, composition of groups, and teacher emphasis on conversational interactions, may directly affect how much support for communication is available to children. The amount of actual support the child receives may vary across children within the same classroom based on the child's specific skills for engaging teachers and peers and the child's perceived language abilities, as we describe in Studies 2 and 3 below.

Concurrent with this first study, we observed two of the six children's classrooms across the school day. Our informal observations suggested that the level of teacher–child talk that occurred in the teacher generalization probes was not typical. That is, most activities throughout the day provided few opportunities for prolonged teacher engagement, even within a small group of children. Teachers rarely talked to an individual child for more than a few seconds (one or two utterances). Most teacher talk to children was instructional or corrective rather than conversational. Very little child-to-child talk was observed. In sum, the kinds of support that we had determined were associated with child generalization were not frequent in the classroom. The target children, not surprisingly, used little of their newly learned language in their classroom.

From this study we derived two principles about environments that support language learning:

1. How much partners talk and how often they elicit responses with questions affect how much children talk.
2. Environments that support frequent child talk will also support generalization of newly learned skills.

Study 2: An Analysis of EMT Applications by Interventionists and Classroom Teachers

In the second study (Kaiser et al., 1994), we conducted a three-part intervention in which each of the four children was provided EMT by a trained language interventionist, by one of his or her teachers (whom we trained), and by a peer partner during a play interaction. The design was a multiple baseline design across conversational partners (trainer, teacher, peer) and replicated across children. Prior to the beginning of baseline, we observed and videotaped each child in the classroom for 2 complete school days. We repeated these observations at the end of the study for a total of 16 classroom days. Because we had been in the classroom on a daily basis for more than a month before the study began, the observations and videotaping were relatively nondisruptive to the children and the teachers.

As in the previous study, implementation of EMT by the trained language interventionist resulted in systematic changes in children's use of target words and intentional communicative exchanges with the trainer. The single-subject design of the study allowed us to monitor generalization across partners as part of the multiple baseline design. In addition, we probed generalization by children across teachers and peers not involved in the training. Some modest child generalization was observed during trainer implementation of EMT to the children's baseline interactions with their teachers. No generalization was observed in the peer baselines even after more than 20 sessions of trainer and teacher implementation of EMT had occurred. By the end of the intervention portion of the study, children talked more frequently and with more complexity with all three partners. They used their targets (e.g., agent and action combinations such as "boy eat") and learned new language targets (e.g., action and object combinations such as "blow bubbles") rapidly in both the trainer and teacher implementations of EMT. They talked more with peers and showed other positive changes in frequency and duration of peer social interaction in the teacher-mediated peer intervention. At the end of the study, children demonstrated modest levels of generalization to other (nontrained) teachers and variables and very modest generalization to other (nontrained) peers.

The notes from classroom observations and videotapes were transcribed in their entirety to provide almost verbatim transcripts of talk by the children and talk to the children across the classroom day. Field notes describing the context of the teacher and child communications were prepared on site by three research assistants, and these notes were included in the final set of descriptive data. These classroom data provided an overview of the types of interactions that children had in the classroom before and after training, as well as provided a basis for comparing the children's performance across intervention and naturally occurring settings.

The data set resulting from these observations is considerable; to date we have focused our analysis on developing a case study description for one child, Casey, a 5-year-old boy with language skills tested to be in the 24- to 28-month range both receptively and productively. Several aspects of Casey's communication opportunities in the classroom were striking. First, Casey was a soft-spoken child, with moderate articulation difficulties, who was often not heard or understood when he spoke. During the 4 days of ethnographic data, a significant portion of his utterances, about 25%–30%, received no response because either no one heard him or the listener did not understand what he said.

Second, Casey had distinct preferences for conversational partners. He spent most of his choice time with one teacher with whom he had a close, affectionate relationship. Casey's relationship with Ms. Karen was described during interviews with all three teachers in the room as long-term, "special," and important to him. Our observations corroborated their reports and also suggested some communicative reasons why Ms. Karen was an important conversational partner. More than any other teacher, she persisted in resolving communication breakdowns with Casey; she was skilled in scaffolding questions to ascertain Casey's meanings when his articulation was unclear or he did not have precise language for describing his intentions or needs. She frequently initiated conversations with him, and she sustained her attention to him. Unlike the other two teachers who rarely sat with Casey, Ms. Karen would join him in activities; ask him simple questions requiring one or two word responses; and make comments to him in a friendly, engaging manner. Possibly because she engaged him more frequently than the other teachers and because he sought her out, she was knowledgeable about his preferences and interests, and she appeared to have less difficulty determining his meanings when his speech was unclear. She used a gentle questioning strategy and offered choices to resolve unclear communication episodes.

In contrast, the other two teachers were more likely to use long, complex questions; explicit prompts; and a relatively more direct style in their attempts to determine Casey's meanings. For Casey, who was a quiet and somewhat withdrawn child, these direct approaches were rarely successful. He frequently withdrew from the questioning and put his thumb in his mouth. These teachers concluded, "he talks when he wants to; he can be very stubborn about talking." Their approach, although well intentioned and effective with other children, was rarely successful in supporting Casey's communication.

The contrasts we observed in Casey's willingness to talk in the classroom and in the three intervention settings were marked. In each of the intervention settings, Casey gradually became a willing conversational partner. In the two adult interventions, Casey's behavior changed in about 10 sessions. Change was slow to emerge in the peer-to-peer intervention, although changes were observed here as well. All three teachers reported changes in Casey's responsiveness in the classroom; however, our ethnographic observations suggested that these changes were less clear than those observed in the training setting, and the change was most evident with his preferred communication partner. No changes in peer-directed communication were apparent in the classroom, even though Casey showed modest generalization to peers in a small-group probe setting.

As in the first study, we perceived that the differences in communicative support for child talk in the classroom and in the intervention settings were a result of both the implementation of the EMT intervention in the experimental settings and the general environmental context of the classroom. In the experimental settings, a conversational partner was continuously available, focused on the child's interests, and attentive to the child's communication attempts. Our experimental data included sufficiently long baselines to safely conclude that simply making partners available and encouraging them to engage with Casey would not have been enough to increase his language use and new learning. However, the baseline conditions were more supportive of child communication than the typical conditions we observed in the classroom. If Casey was unable to talk readily in the baseline, where the partners were available and listening to him, it is not surprising that he did not talk in the classroom where he spent most of his time alone and where his communication attempts were often missed or misunderstood by his teachers. When more supportive conditions were available (as with his preferred conversational partner, Ms. Karen), Casey's communication was markedly more frequent and more easily understood.

From these observations, two additional principles emerged:

1. *Ongoing positive relationships between teachers and children provide specific support for communication.* Ongoing relationships provide more frequent contact between partners, thus increasing the adult's specific knowledge of the child's communication skills and strategies and the adult's opportunities to determine what specific strategies work to elicit talk and to repair breakdowns in communication. The child's motivation to engage and persist in communication may also be increased when he or she has an ongoing positive relationship with a particular teacher.

2. *Children's use of communication skills is discriminated across partners, again, largely on the basis of differences in partner behavior.* Partner behavior, especially those responsive and incidental teaching behaviors associated with the EMT intervention, systematically influenced child performance. Our primary data and the ethnographic data showed that children could appear very skilled with one partner and, concurrently, less skilled with another partner.

Study 3: Social Effects of Naturalistic Language Intervention on Peer-Directed Communication

In the third study, we conducted an in-class teacher implementation of EMT (Kaiser et al., 1995). We proposed that training teachers in the context of ongoing classroom activities would have a greater impact on the children's everyday communicative environment than the previous outcomes associated with interventions conducted outside the regular activities of the classroom. Four teachers (one lead teacher, two paraprofessionals, and a graduate student assisting in the classroom) were trained with two children. The design was a multiple baseline across two teacher conversational partners, replicated across children. All training and implementation took place in the classroom during free play time. As in the previous study, we videotaped each teacher and child for 2 days before and after the intervention for a total of 20 days of classroom data. Videotapes were transcribed and coded using protocols similar to those used in the primary portion of the study. Field notes describing the contexts of teacher and child communication were prepared.

The results of the teacher training portion of the study showed that all four teachers learned to use EMT at near criterion levels in their interactions with their target child in the classroom. The two children showed marked increases in total talk, use of targets, and diversity of vocabulary during the intervention with both of their partners.

The ethnographic data on this classroom were summarized using both qualitative and quantitative methods. The quantitative analysis is the focus of this discussion. In this classroom, two of the teachers had relatively high rates of verbal contact with the eight children enrolled. As shown in Figure 1, prior to intervention, Teacher A was observed to make 1,731 utterances to children during 6 hours (2 classroom days) of observation. Teacher C made 935 utterances. Teacher B made 397 child-directed utterances. After the intervention, all three teachers talked to children between 1,000 and 1,150 times in 6 hours.

Figure 2 shows teacher mands, models, and corrective feedback before and after the intervention. Figure 3 shows teacher expansions of child utterances. Teacher expansions are responses to child utterances that repeat the child's utterance, but add syntactic or semantic information. Again, Teacher A showed the highest levels of mands and expansions before the intervention, Teacher C showed a medium level, and Teacher B showed a lower level. After intervention, all three teachers provided a similar frequency of expansions. Teachers A and C reduced their numbers of mands, models, and corrective feedback, while teacher B markedly increased her frequency of these behaviors.

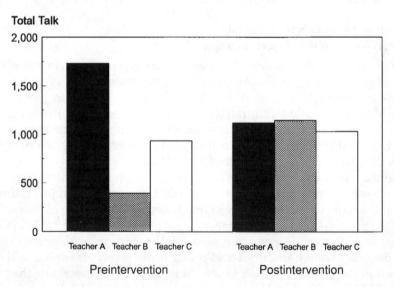

Figure 1. Number of utterances to children by Teachers A, B, and C during pre- and postintervention observations in the classroom.

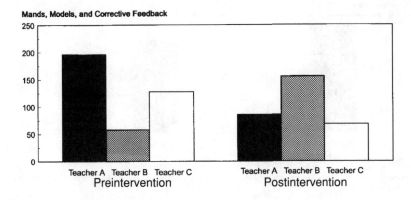

Mands, Models, and Corrective Feedback

Figure 2. Number of mands, models, and corrective feedback provided to the children by Teachers A, B, and C during pre- and postintervention.

It is difficult to make judgments about the "goodness" of these specific levels of behavior. What is of interest is the patterns across teachers. In this classroom, Teacher A was a masters-level prepared lead teacher. She assumed most of the responsibility for teaching lessons and leading groups. Teachers B and C were experienced paraprofessionals. Teacher C routinely led the play activities and conversed with children in a playful manner. Teacher B took responsibility for tasks such as collecting lunch money, toileting, changing diapers, getting snacks ready, and transitioning children through activities. Although she spent as much time in the classroom and in physical proximity to the children as the other teachers, she talked much less to them. One of the effects of the intervention in the classroom was a shift toward more equal teacher engagement in conversation with the children. Teacher A talked less (much of her training in EMT had included feedback about listening and waiting for kids to respond); Teacher B talked more and used more of the two key components (i.e., responsive interaction strategies and milieu teaching techniques) of the EMT intervention. Teacher C, who had a warm, engaging style and moderately paced rate of talking with children, changed only slightly. Other changes in teacher talk included a more equitable distribution of talk by all teachers across all children and a closer match of complexity of teacher talk to individual children's language skills. For example, prior to the intervention, Teacher B had talked to one of the target children only five times (1% of her child-directed talk) in 6 hours, while Teachers A and C talked 305 (18%) and 204 (22%) times to the same target child. After the intervention, Teacher B talked to this target child 264 times (23% of her child-directed talk), while Teacher A talked to him 176 times (16%) and Teacher C, 226 times (20%).

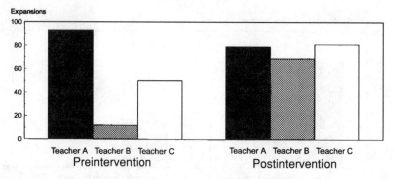

Figure 3. Number of expansions provided to the children by Teachers A, B, and C during pre- and postintervention.

From these observations and our involvement in this classroom, we saw further evidence of how classroom organization, in this case assignment of teachers to tasks and their evolving roles in the classroom, may have affected how much teachers talked and the content of their talk. The differences in teacher style, skill, and child-contact patterns were sufficiently different among these three teachers to highlight the need to consider individual adult conversational partners rather than simply the environment or teachers in the aggregate. The presence of multiple teachers in this classroom provided a richness in the linguistic environment (lots of talk, lots of questions and expansions) and opportunities to engage with adults that would have not been possible in a classroom with one adult and eight children.

Our observations in Study 3 suggested two further principles:

1. *The communication environment will be influenced by both the skills of individual teachers and the ways in which the classroom is organized.* Teacher roles and responsibilities provide a context in which conversational talk with children occurs. For teachers who define their primary role as *teachers*, much of their talk will be instructional and questioning. Talking rather than listening may define teachers' interactions. Conversely, adults who provide functional assistance in the classroom may not see their role as a communication partner as a primary part of their interactions with children.

2. *More is not always better.* In baseline observations of teachers in interactions with children and in the classroom observations, we often saw teachers talking too much. The data showed many instances of teachers not allowing children time to talk or to answer and of teachers overriding children's interests and talking about their own topics. Although the general principle articulated earlier regarding the importance of sufficient talk to children still applies, we posit that there

are parameters of amount and content that modify this principle. Teacher A in Study 3 was an example of an adult partner who did too much of a good thing. She asked lots of questions (many of them "test" questions to which she already had an answer), and she talked almost nonstop when she interacted with children. The frequency and directiveness of her conversational style limited children's opportunities to initiate.

HOW COMMUNICATION ENVIRONMENTS FOR CHILDREN WITH DISABILITIES HAVE CHANGED

The six classrooms we observed contrasted sharply with the cottages in the state institution for children with mental retardation observed by the first author almost 20 years before. The children were younger, the schedule was filled with age-appropriate activities, the setting was a public school, the lead teachers had specific training in special education, and speech-language therapists were assigned to each school. Contemporary preschool classrooms appear to be richer and more supportive settings. Given the improved characteristics of these environments, it would be reasonable to expect that the support for social and language behavior of preschoolers would also be greatly improved.

The data derived from classroom observations associated with these three studies suggest, however, that the specific support for language use and learning in these preschool classrooms was still variable and sometimes more limited than a global assessment of these settings would have indicated. When we observed and recorded the talk directed to children and the opportunities for them to engage in language use and learning, we sometimes found that there was limited specific support for communication. Outside the contexts in which we trained teachers to use EMT, we observed little incidental teaching of language skills except in speech therapy sessions in the classroom.

Based on these observations, we conclude that the availability of a conversational partner to engage with the child, the focused attention of that partner as a basis for understanding the child's communication attempts, the partner's active engagement with the child as indicated by coparticipation in child activity and talk directed to the child, and the partner's use of questions to elicit child talk are important aspects of the social–communicative environment that supports language use. The classroom observations suggest that there may be qualitative aspects of conversational partner behavior that will also influence the support provided to the child. These include a responsive style of interaction in which child comments and other communication attempts are acknowledged, adjustment of the style of the partner's verbal interaction to fit the child's style (e.g., if the child is quiet, using a soft voice and gentle prompts), and the conversational partner's ongoing relationship with the child.

Relationship is an illusive and unfamiliar concept to language interventionists, yet our observations suggest that children in classrooms have very specific, well-defined relationships with various adults and children in their environment. When children had a favorite teacher or friend, verbal and nonverbal communication was relatively more frequent between the children and this partner. When children were not anyone's favorite, or were actively disliked by one or more adults, the content of communication was different and conversation (prolonged engagement around a topic of mutual interest) was rare. One of the children we observed in Study 1 was regarded by his teachers as a "behavior problem." In our anecdotal observations, we noted that almost all teacher utterances directed to this child were instructions for behavior. Clearly both teachers and children contribute to the development of relationships that support or discourage communication, but the consequences of less positive relationships may be to further inhibit the child's opportunities to develop the social–communicative skills he or she needs.

IMPLICATIONS FOR CLASSROOM INTERVENTIONS: SOME SIMPLE SOLUTIONS

Although we continue to advocate for the usefulness of complex naturalistic interventions such as EMT, applying the environmental principles we derived from our observations might constitute a relatively simple intervention to improve the communicative environments of young children with disabilities. These principles are summarized in Table 3.

In addition to these suggestions for improving classroom environments, there is a more general set of principles about communicative environments that might inform our understanding of how communication develops and how it can be supported. Unlike the simple suggestions for improving environments outlined in Table 3, this second set of related but more complex principles requires an ecosystem-level analysis. Table 4 offers these environmental systems principles as a conceptual bridge toward such analyses.

CONCLUSIONS

This chapter reported some informal observations about preschool classrooms for children with disabilities and the characteristics of these

Table 3. Environmental principles to create supportive social–communicative environments

1. **Talk to children.** Engage in conversation and make yourself available to the child as a communication partner.

2. **Ask questions.** Eliciting new information (not testing the child's knowledge) at a moderate rate encourages child talk.

3. **Follow the child's lead.** Talk about what the child is interested in and what the child is doing in order to make language more functional for the child. Child talk will be more easily understood when the adult is engaged with the child in an activity.

4. **Talk at a moderate rate and take turns.** Give the child a chance to talk, to initiate, and to respond in conversations.

5. **Build positive relationships with children.** Ongoing relationships encourage talk and provide a basis for knowing children's interests and understanding children's idiosyncratic or unclear communication patterns.

6. **Organize the schedule, the setting, and teacher roles to include conversations.** Adults provide a unique context and set of supports for child talk. It is important that all adults, regardless of background, training, or role, be willing participants in conversations with children.

classrooms that may support or inhibit communication. There is an impressive array of studies available describing the effects of environmental and instructional interventions on the language of young children with disabilities. However, there are few observationally based analyses of the contexts in which these children are expected to use newly learned language and even fewer functional analyses of how environment specifically affects these children's communication and acquisition of new

Table 4. Environmental systems principles

1. Communication and behavior occur in the context of ongoing relationships; thus, relationships are a critical aspect of environments. Positive relationships create a context where both participants are motivated to communicate about shared knowledge and interests.

2. Environments have an affective valence "created" by standing patterns of interaction, contingencies, and content of interactions. Environments may be experienced as positive when teachers smile at, laugh with, and encourage children.

3. Relationships, positive affective interactions, and responsiveness support the development of shared meaning and communication.

4. The same characteristics of environment that support communication support other positive social behavior.

5. The characteristics of the physical and temporal environment (macro-level variables) affect relationships, affective valence, and specific interpersonal behaviors (micro-level variables). Scheduling, classroom management strategies, and practical manifestations of developmentally appropriate practice provide support for positive teacher–child interactions and conversations.

6. Learning and development are facilitated when the macro- and micro-levels of the environment are supportive.

language skills. Systematic research in this area might yield both a better understanding of environments and of the skills children need to be successful communicators and learners in classroom settings.

REFERENCES

Alpert, C.L., & Kaiser, A.P. (1992). Training parents as milieu language teachers. *Journal of Early Intervention, 16*(1), 31–52.

Costello, J.M. (1983). Generalization across settings: Language intervention with children. In J. Miller, D.E. Yoder, & R.L. Schiefelbusch (Eds.), *Contemporary issues in language intervention*. Rockville, MD: American Speech-Language-Hearing Association.

Hedrick, D.L., Prather, E.M., & Tobin, A.R. (1975). *Sequenced inventory of communication development*. Seattle: University of Washington Press.

Hemmeter, M.L., & Kaiser, A.P. (1994). Enhanced milieu teaching: Effects of parent-implemented language intervention. *Journal of Early Intervention, 18*(3), 269–289.

Kaiser, A.P. (1993). Parent-implemented language intervention: An environmental system perspective. In A.P. Kaiser & D.B. Gray (Eds.), *Communication and language intervention: Vol. 1. Enhancing children's communication: Research foundations for intervention* (pp. 63–84). Baltimore: Paul H. Brookes Publishing Co.

Kaiser, A.P., & Hester, P.P. (1994). Generalized effects of enhanced milieu teaching. *Journal of Speech and Hearing Research, 37*(6), 1320–1340.

Kaiser, A.P., Hester, P.P., Harris-Solomon, A., Delaney, E., & Keetz, A.F. (1995, March). *The social effects of naturalistic language intervention on peer-directed communication*. Paper presented at the 28th Annual Gatlinburg Conference on Research and Theory in Mental Retardation and Developmental Disabilities, Gatlinburg, TN.

Kaiser, A.P., Hester, P.P., Harris-Solomon, A.C., & Keetz, A. (1994, May). *Enhanced milieu teaching: An analysis of applications by interventionists and classroom teachers*. Paper presented at the 118th Annual Meeting of the American Association on Mental Retardation, Boston.

Ostrosky, M.M., & Kaiser, A.P. (1991). Preschool classroom environments to promote communication. *Teaching Exceptional Children, 23*(4), 6–10.

Warren, S.F., & Reichle, J. (1992). The emerging field of communication and language intervention. In S.F. Warren & J. Reichle (Eds.), *Communication and language intervention: Vol. 1. Causes and effects in communication and language intervention* (pp. 1–8). Baltimore: Paul H. Brookes Publishing Co.

Warren, S.F., & Rogers-Warren, A.K. (1985). *Teaching functional language*. Austin, TX: PRO-ED.

Weiss, R.S. (1981). INREAL intervention for language handicapped and bilingual children. *Journal of the Division for Early Childhood, 4*(1), 40–52.

8

New Structures and Systems Change for Comprehensive Positive Behavioral Support

Wayne Sailor

The focus of this chapter is positive behavioral support for persons with severe behavior disorders in inclusive settings. I argue here that the task of including children, youth, and adults who have severe behavior disorders into the everyday settings of school, community, and work, even given the extensive technology of positive behavioral support that has emerged in just the past few years, and which is largely reviewed elsewhere in this book, is daunting indeed. I argue further that, beyond isolated examples and demonstrations, widespread inclusionary practices with this population are unlikely to occur unless positive behavioral supports are fully identified with, and are an integral part of, the systems transformation processes described here. The proverb "it takes a whole village to raise a child" was never truer than when applied to a child who has severe behavior disorders. The chapter begins with a look at some brief, historical benchmarks in the history of managing difficult behavior and then moves to a discussion of paradigmatic issues in philosophy that arguably inform current directions in both inclusion and behavior management practices. The remainder of this chapter is about the processes under which "villages" are reinventing the way they respond to the special support needs of children and families so that inclusion can become a reality for all.

Prior to 1985, the rubric for affecting change in the contextual circumstances of people with severe behavior disorders was *deinstitutionalization*. The present rubric is *inclusion*. There are still institutions, however, and behavioral scientists who argue for a continued need for aversives in behavior management (Mulick, 1994); yet the trend in the bulk of scientific endeavor on this issue has clearly shifted to a broader-based analysis appropriate to a more complex set of social circumstances (see, e.g., Carr et al., 1994; Horner, Sprague, & Flannery, 1993; Schroeder, Oldenquist, & Rojahn, 1990).

In an earlier paper (Sailor, Goetz, Anderson, Hunt, & Gee, 1988), I and my colleagues argued a case for research and development in a broader, more community- and lifestyle-focused arena for the teaching of new adaptive and generalizable skills to persons with severe intellectual and behavior disorders. Developing a framework we called *context relevance theory*, we suggested that outcomes for such students, clients, and so on could be referenced against a set of criteria that had application in a wider social context. The criteria are the following:

1. **Utility:** Do the outcomes produce something useful to the person?
2. **Desirability:** Are the outcomes those the person would likely choose for himself/herself from an array of choices?
3. **Social:** Are the outcomes the product of interactions with persons other than paid support staff?
4. **Situational:** Are the outcomes developed in the context in which they have applicability (versus simulated contexts)?
5. **Practicality:** Are the outcomes likely to be practiced by the person in real situations?

6. **Appropriateness:** Are the outcomes age appropriate and likely to enhance the person's emergence into less dependent and more integrated circumstances?
7. **Adaptability:** Do the outcomes have a problem-solving component that allows the person to extend beyond the specific "topographical" configurations under which learning occurred? (Sailor et al., 1988, pp. 68–69)

In a similar vein, Schroeder et al. (1990) concluded a review of considerations in determining the effectiveness and humaneness of behavioral interventions in the broader social context by endorsing the 13 principles put forward by Horner et al. (1990) for development of a "community-referenced behavioral technology." These (in title only) are "Ethical Behavioral Procedures; Effective Technology; Marriage of Values and Technology; High Methodological Rigor; Address the Most Severe Behavior Problems; Community-Focused; Comprehensive Technology; Practical Procedures; National Consensus; Focus on Student Lifestyle; Interdisciplinary Collaboration; Consumer Involvement; and Social Ecological Adaptation" (Horner et al. as cited in Schroeder et al., 1990, pp. 114–115).

Schroeder et al. (1990) added a thirteenth consideration to the list that helps to illustrate the process of integration of values into a changing context of scientific endeavor. The thirteenth principle, Social Ecological Adaptation, states that "behavioral techniques should reflect the social ecology of a particular community in terms of accessibility, continuity, resource networking, cultural and ethnic specificity, and respect for religious, racial and social values" (Schroeder et al., 1990, p. 115).

Much has been written on the topic of aversive versus nonaversive behavioral intervention methods (e.g., Repp & Singh, 1990). In retrospect, the year 1990 seems now to serve as a temporal landmark for a change of focus as regards a significant historical problem in psychology—the humane and ethical treatment of severe behavior disorder. As Carr, Robinson, and Palumbo (1990) reason, circumstances of social context now dictate that a move is in order away from a technology of crisis management and toward a broader analysis of functional treatments that can avert crises before the need for intrusive interventions arises.

CONTEXTUALISM IN POSITIVE BEHAVIORAL SUPPORT

Schroeder et al. (1990) argue that systems of behavioral interventions are greatly dependent upon the *environmental context* in which they are performed. These authors, building upon a framework for community-referenced behavioral technology (Horner et al., 1990), conclude that a changing context for applications of intervention technologies dictates a joining of ethical and scientific sources of knowledge in the application of interventions. Furthermore, Carr et al. (1990), Carr and Sailor (1994), and Sailor and Carr (1994) argue that the question of aversives versus non-aversives, in light of present contextual circumstances affecting people with severe behavior disorders, is indeed the wrong question. The right question in the light of present demands for new, applicable knowledge from behavioral/social scientists is—what are the requirements for a technology of behavioral support in the context of a reasonable lifestyle (Horner et al., 1993)?

In retrospect it should surprise no one that a technology for the management of severe behavior disorders emerged prior to 1985 that was heavily intrusive at best and strongly aversive at its worst. The social context for the scientific bases for behavior management was for the most part isolated and self-contained. There were usually more clients in need of behavioral support (or management) than there were staff deemed qualified to provide treatment, and the result was a technology of crisis management (Carr et al., 1990).

As is so often the case in the history of academic controversies, the lens has shifted focus from a micro-analysis (aversives, such as the use of punishers, vs. nonaversive technologies, such as interventions growing out of functional assessments) to a more macro-picture (lifestyle in community settings, curriculum in school settings, etc.). Viewed in the broader context, the earlier controversy seems trite and irrelevant, yet the change in focus, to belabor the lens metaphor a bit more, could not have occurred without the passage of time and the corresponding changes in social circumstances affecting people with behavior disorders, such as the agendas for inclusion (Sailor & Skrtic, 1995), full citizenship (Turnbull & Turnbull, 1990), and supported living that have occurred just since the mid-1980s (e.g., see Kaiser, Chapter 7).

It is probably safe now to conclude that a general consensus has been reached on the need to concentrate resources and effort on the development of a community-referenced technology of behavioral support geared to participation in a broad social context and to lifestyle changes in scope and applicability. The emphasis on inclusion alone is sufficient to tax the bulk of available resource development systems. Horner, Diemer, and Brazeau (1992), for example, reported that the single most common technical assistance request from teachers and adult services personnel is increasingly for "managing problem behaviors." But while there is a growing consensus on the social and contextual demands for an emergent technology of behavioral support, there is no consensus whatever on the best approach for the development of this technology (or whether it should even be considered a technology at all).

FUNCTIONALISM VERSUS INTERPRETIVISM

While it is becoming increasingly unfashionable (and unnecessary) to challenge behavioral psychologists on the issue of aversives (Carr et al., 1990; Carr & Sailor, 1994), there now appears to be a corresponding shift of focus (the lens metaphor again) to challenges to the very premise of psychology as a science in general (Evans, 1993; Hoshmand & Polking-horne, 1992; Meyer & Evans, 1993). Meyer and Evans (1993) mount the "postmodern" perspective on community-referenced, positive behavioral support by arguing that "human behavior does not necessarily follow the same law-like relationships that were believed to be universally evident in the physical world" (p. 232). They cite the contributions of the philosopher Habermas (Ewert, 1991) to argue the case for *constructivism* (i.e., "qualitative research" methods) as the appropriate process of science in addressing the social needs of persons requiring special supports. Meyer and Evans (1993) argue that nothing less than a "major paradigm crisis" (p. 224) is under way in the social sciences and that the direction is away from functionalism (or *positivism*, as an outgrowth of British associationistic philosophy) and toward interpretivism (or *constructivism*, as an outgrowth of the German philosophical tradition).

Although not particularly explicit in the article, the general tone of the Meyer and Evans piece seems to equate the development of aversive technologies in behavioral science with the broader shortcomings of functionalistic (e.g., Neutonian, linear) science. The reader is left with the impression that, because of their outdated, "modern," functionalist paradigm, behavioral scientists evolved draconian methods with which to control the behavior of persons with disabilities. By this reasoning, a new paradigm, the "postmodern" agenda, is emerging with interpretivistic methods of science at the cutting edge. This paradigm, say Meyer and Evans, is not only more humanistic but much better suited to the study of human problems in general (e.g., Ewert, 1991). So having resolved (to a large degree) one controversy we are mired in a new one, and at a significantly more "macro" level of analysis.

The Meyer and Evans (1993) piece drew immediate response (see Baer, 1993; Ferguson & Ferguson, 1993; Kaiser, 1993; Morris, 1993). Of the various rebuttals, two are relevant to the present discussion. First, Ferguson and Ferguson (1993) point to the need to distinguish between methods and paradigms. Qualitative research methods, for example, need not be exclusively identified with interpretivism and can, in fact, be incorporated into positivistic (functionalist) strategies of scientific investigation (e.g., Lucyshyn & Albin, 1993). While Ferguson and Ferguson (1993) would prefer to retain a clear distinction between functionalist and interpretivist paradigms, they point out that Meyer and Evans have mis-interpreted Skrtic's (1991a, 1991b) perspective as one of support for an in-terpretivist paradigm in science. Skrtic (1991a, 1991b) argues that the postmodernist agenda is, in fact, antiparadigmatic, in that all paradigms are grounded in certain assumptions that can always be challenged. Post-modernism offers the possibility of a science of constructivism wherein scientists/practitioners proceed on the basis of building a foundation of knowledge from a premise of pragmatism (Dewey, 1982; Rorty, 1991a, 1991b), or *what works* in the service of humanity (Sailor & Skrtic, 1995).

The second rebuttal to Meyer and Evans (1993) of interest here is that by Morris (1993). Morris equates postmodernism with poststructuralism (Day, 1988; Dougher, 1993), or the shift from mechanism to contextualism (Goerner, 1994; Pepper, 1946). Morris (1993) argues that there is indeed such a thing as postmodern applied behavior analysis and that its values are at least as humanistic as those that characterize interpretivistic science (see also, Fawcett, 1991).

In short, it would appear that there really are not good guys or bad guys in this debate, but simply a changing ethos characterized by more complexity and requiring more dynamic and systematic (less mechanis-tic) levels of analysis and intervention. It is the thesis of this chapter that we are indeed entering an era of postmodern thought and that the metaphorical lens is beginning to turn yet again, bringing into focus an even more complex agenda for those concerned with positive behavioral support, namely the agenda for comprehensive systems change at all levels of school and community services for those who require special assistance in order to be fully included.

POSTMODERNISM: COLLABORATION
AND VOICE AS HALLMARKS OF PARADIGMATIC CHANGE

Tom Skrtic and I argue elsewhere (Sailor & Skrtic, 1995) that present transformations in public policy affecting schools and school–community partnerships can best be understood in terms of their linkages to broader-based transformations affecting virtually all human endeavors and contemporary bases for knowledge (Derrida, 1976; Searle, 1983). If this analysis has merit, then the implications for scientists and practitioners advancing an agenda for positive behavioral support in inclusive circum-stances call for very large-scale, systems-analytic levels of analysis indeed. At the very least, scientists/practitioners must consider the rela-tionships among systems change processes occurring in schools and those occurring across community-based service systems for clients with severe behavior disorders. This relationship is examined in a later section under the rubric *New Community School*.

Space limitations of this chapter do not permit an adequate discussion of the philosophical issues that surround the concept of postmodernism. Readers interested in pursuing this broader topic in some depth, particularly in its implications for social sciences and education, should see Goerner (1994), Paul, Yang, Adiegbola and Morse (1995), Rhodes, Danforth, and Smith (1995), Skrtic (1991a, 1991b), and Sailor and Skrtic (1995).

Postmodernism in essence rejects the cognitive-rational basis for knowledge. Against this philosophical backdrop, what then is there to guide epistemology, the basis for scientific investigations? One very suitable answer can be found in pragmatism (Dewey, 1982, 1990; James, 1948). In pragmatism, the basis for knowledge shifts from discovering facts to problem solving (Rowland, in press; Sailor & Skrtic, 1995). Ideas approach the status of truths to the extent that they serve purposes in the interests of humanity. The use of interpretivistic research methods advances this process by helping investigators to understand how participants in evolving complex systems contextualize their social reality (make sense of circumstances). Interventionists, operating with systems-analytic models can then facilitate recontextualization (help to frame alternative understandings) as a means to effect change (Kelly & Maynard-Moody, 1993).

Kuhn (1970), in his now classic piece on the structures of paradigm-level changes in science and their effects, noted that when paradigms change, whole definitions of "reality" change. Sailor and Skrtic (1995) note that the major transformational processes that can be identified in school restructuring and in health and social services reform have their counterpart processes in such diverse areas as women's studies (Riger, 1992), rhetoric (Rowland, in press), psychology (Sampson, 1993), and education (Rhodes et al., 1995). Two processes that can be readily identified across reform efforts in all of these fields, and which are uniquely postmodern and can be viewed as hallmarks of a paradigmatic shift, are those described variously as *collaboration* and *voice*.

If pragmatic, social constructivism through discourse is the means for a new foundational basis for knowledge under postmodernism, then voice, the progenitor of discourse, is at the heart of the process and provides a means for social change. Voice, for example, in the case of women's issues refers to legitimization of a socially constructed body of knowledge that is reflected in the discourse of the women who advance a reform agenda. This is in contradistinction to the response of modern social systems, arguably male dominated, in reacting to newly emerging concerns of women within the boundaries of existing categorical, social structures and their traditional mechanisms of support.

An interesting example of voice from the field of disability can be found in a novel person-centered planning approach called Group Action

Planning (GAP) (Turnbull, Turnbull, Shank, & Leal, 1995). A problem-solving group forms under this method to address the issue of fully including a student with severe behavior disorders in the life of a high school. Family members and professionals may be included in the group, but for the most part, membership consists of the person with the disability and his or her peers at the school. Through discourse, the student with disabilities comes to be better able to express his or her preferences and make choices from among alternatives. The course of the plan for the inclusion and education of the student is thus guided by a process that empowers the student with disabilities to structure his or her support through group participation and discourse.

The related issue of collaboration has to do with recognition of interdependency in social constructivism. Collaborative processes can be observed, for example, in education when challenges presented by voice issues in policy reform, such as inclusion, are responded to by a shift in decision authority away from traditional (modern) hierarchical structures (i.e., principal, school psychologist, special education administrator) and toward transdisciplinary, team-governed processes. When empowerment becomes legitimate, then authority tends to shift toward veridicality, or a more "truthful" representation arising from mutuality. Voice and collaboration are thus interdependent processes that emerge in a postmodern transformational agenda.

One can view these interdependent processes as well from the reverse direction. Again using the emergent issue of inclusion as a case in point, collaboration can be viewed as a force propelling the social policy reform process along. Parents, diverse professionals, and other staff come together at the school site in problem-solving team arrangements (what Skrtic, 1991a, refers to as *adhocratic* as opposed to *bureaucratic* structures) to facilitate inclusive education. The basis for the collaboration is voice or the legitimization of perspective of each of the participants independent of his or her preassigned structural role (e.g., parent versus professional) or his or her categorical identity (e.g., paraprofessional versus speech therapist). The product of these processes of collaboration and voice is a socially constructed basis for the conduct of inclusive education. Without collaboration and voice it is doubtful that such a rigid and complex system could adapt to the demands posed by so radical a change as inclusive education.

The modern alternative processes to collaboration and voice can be viewed as *cooperation* and *hierarchical decision making*. Rather than problem solving as a basis for discourse, the focus is upon exploring ways to adapt existing fragmented, piecemeal, and rigidly categorical structures to accommodate to radical change of venue in the context of hierarchical authority. The family is viewed as a stressor to which the system must adapt or respond with adversity. No one "worker bee" (i.e., teacher) wants to be perceived as an element in a process of failure should things go wrong because of the demands of hierarchical authority. As a result, school personnel may, from the positions of their respective categorical identities, agree to cooperate in the interests of attempting inclusion, but the effort is likely to be tentative; as low risk as possible; and piecemeal rather than tied to substantive, systemic change. If one of the children to be included happens to be characterized by a severe behavior disorder, the process is likely to turn to adversity as an alternative to systems change.

Thus far, I have argued that the earlier debate in the literature of behavioral support on aversives versus nonaversives was a micro-focused discourse reflecting the response of modern structures to demands for significant social change implicit in outcomes of deinstitutionalization and integration processes. Furthermore, I suggested that debate at present is more reflective of the large-scale, epistemological implications growing out of the recognition that transformations requiring a technology of positive behavioral support are occurring at broad-based levels of systems change across all human services structures. Finally, I reasoned that these changes may be viewed as parts of a much broader and more significant set of transformational processes that cut across all aspects of human endeavor. These latter processes, referred to as the emergence of the postmodern world view, have elements in common that may be useful to scientists/practitioners with an interest in positive behavioral support. Two of these interdependent processes, collaboration and voice, afford a useful context in which to view potential points of intervention of a systems change nature, to accomplish positive behavioral support in the service of inclusion. These two processes are discussed in the following section in terms of school reform.

NEW COMMUNITY SCHOOL

The term *New Community School* is used as a rubric, not as the title for any particular approach to school reform. We use the term to describe schools that are full participants in and directly affected by three different, but highly interdependent, processes of public policy reform affecting children and families (Sailor, 1994a, 1994b; Sailor, Kleinhammer-Tramill, Skrtic, & Oas, 1996; Sailor & Skrtic, 1995). The term, as I describe in the pages to follow, encompasses more than a school but reaches beyond, and describes policy changes that affect services to children and families in the community of which the school is a part.

The New Community School rubric encompasses three public policy transformation processes at present: 1) special education reform, as a special case of school reform; 2) general education reform; and 3) community-based human assistance program reform, including school–community partnership arrangements. Transformational processes operating at the level of community human assistance programs can be referred to generically as *school-linked, services integration* efforts (Kagan & Neville, 1993). Much of the impetus for this reform effort, which began in the early 1970s and has only now begun to swing into full force, arose from the observations of educators and other human services professionals that if children whose basic needs for shelter; for love and family or caregiver support; for nutrition, health care, and so on, are not met, those children cannot realize their learning potential from public education and indeed, in many cases, cannot benefit from school at all. Our *modern* systems of public assistance and support are not working because conditions of children are worsening, and the support service systems are growing prohibitively expensive and cannot continue to be maintained in the absence of encouraging outcomes. Children with disabilities are included in this group, but the circumstances described here extend beyond that population, to children of poverty and those affected by other adverse circumstances.

The fragmentation and disconnectedness that characterizes community human resource service systems also characterize modern schools. When the *school excellence* movement of the 1980s produced positive gains for high-achieving students but largely ignored those at risk for a variety of academic and social ills (Elmore, 1988), a second wave of school reform, generically called *school restructuring*, emerged as a kind of "bottom-up," grass roots initiative, with outcomes geared to *all* children and with full participation by families.

Finally, the term *inclusive education* is emerging as the generic descriptor for policy reform in federal, categorical programs such as special education, limited English proficiency, Chapter programs (e.g., Title I), and so on. While these reform processes are operating in all categorical, educational support programs to varying extents, special education is presently the most strongly affected (National Association of State Boards of Education [NASBE], 1992). Recognizing that schools have become analogous to apartment houses with the individual apartments divided against themselves, many educators are increasingly viewing inclusive education as one strategem with which to begin a process of reunification of public education (Sage & Burrello, 1994; Sailor & Skrtic, 1995).

Each of these policy reform efforts taken alone will facilitate an agenda for the inclusion of students with severe behavior disorders with appropriate, positive supports. However, there is increasing evidence that none of the three reform processes can complete an agenda for transformation in the absence of progress in the other two (Sailor et al., 1996). In other words, the processes are *interdependent*. In my view, the processes are interdependent because much of the variance in their common loci of change is referenced to much larger change processes, described earlier in this chapter as the shift from modern to postmodern structures (Sailor & Skrtic, 1995; see also, Paul & Rosselli, 1995; Rhodes et al., 1995).

If the concepts of *voice* and *collaboration* are indeed characteristics of postmodern human assistance structures, then evidence for the interdependence of the three policy reform processes can be gleaned from a closer examination of each of the three processes in evolution. Voice and collaboration characterize forms representing each process at some stage in its evolution.

Consider educational reform. The core of the present school restructuring agenda is site management, a team-driven governance process that roughly parallels the reforms described as *total quality management* (TQM) when viewed from the standpoint of business and industry. In business, the voice of the workers finds expression in management through group, participatory decision making. In schools, school site councils or teams, often including parents, manage schools at the building level, a process that stands in sharp distinction to traditional, modern school structures as rigid bureaucracies run according to the dictates of the central district office (Skrtic, 1991a, 1991b).

Similarly, processes that include more integrated curriculum and decentralized instruction promote and encourage more active student involvement in the learning process, including the selection and determination from among options, that which will be taught. Giving voice to students empowers them in the active process of their education. Similar processes are at work in school reform efforts to involve parents more effectively in public education and to present them with active choices in teaching their children.

The second hallmark of postmodern human services systems, collaboration, can also be found at the heart of all three reform processes. Team-driven processes that respect professional competence yet de-emphasize specific disciplinary authority and turf issues; that promote and value diversity; and that enhance role release and participation in group rather than in isolated, professionally determined ways can be detected in each reform process. Cooperative group processes are modern because they retain differential, categorical role differentiations; separate budgets; and so forth and evolve into collaborative processes. They are postmodern because each participant is regarded as an equal contributor, and funds respective to each "department" are pooled in a common problem-solving agenda when human services transformations are in full swing (Kagan & Neville, 1993).

SCHOOL-LINKED SERVICES INTEGRATION

Services Integration History

The history of efforts to integrate human assistance service programs dates all the way back to the 18th century in America, yet implementation strategies have always fallen victim to strong forces in the American capitalist economic structure toward concentration of resources in the hands of a few. Pluralistic management of public redistributive resources has not enjoyed public support until very recently (Crowson & Boyd, 1993; Kagan & Neville, 1993). Although the current "wave" of services integration initiatives can be traced to federal planning and development efforts in the 1960s (Kagan & Neville, 1993), current activities, such as the Healthy Start initiative in California and the administrative mechanism for consolidated state plans for services in Indiana and West Virginia, are being touted as novel approaches to providing services in a cost-effective manner.

Local (community-level) efforts to capture control of human assistance resources certainly have roots in the rapid escalation of service need costs and in the intensity of community problems, such as the plight of children's health care, the escalating rise in numbers of poor families with no health insurance, and the rising tide of violence in American schools and neighborhoods. The recent failure of the federal government to enact comprehensive health care reform in the face of a growing crisis in health management is helping to drive the process by concentrating efforts at solutions at the state and city levels. State legislatures are increasingly casting about for examples of local solutions that may have implications for state human services transformation policy ("Strategic Partnership," 1994). "Managed care," for example, is one forum of health care resource management at the local level that is getting a lot of scrutiny by reform-minded states. Where efforts are under way to improve the delivery of health, education, and social welfare services to children and families through local-council–driven services integration arrangements that include family services plans of one sort or another, the concept of health care management as a part of the process becomes viable. The problems of equitability across all consumers and the nature of the "gatekeeping" systems, will, of course, continue to present formidable challenges.

Those wishing to acquire further knowledge of the complex processes of transformation that make up the services integration movement would do well to examine at least Kagan and Neville (1993), Melaville and Blank (1991), and Packard Foundation (1992). Taken together, these three works present a remarkably coherent view of one of the largest and most significant policy transformation agendas in the history of the United States.

The services integration movement began in earnest as a *prevention* agenda, aimed at services reforms affecting the lives of children and their families. More recently, however, the focus has shifted beyond childhood and is finding affinity with broad-based, neighborhood revitalization programs such as those embodied in the Clinton administration's "empowerment zone" legislation (e.g., "Strategic partnership for urban revitalization," 1994). While services integration is primarily a reform agenda targeted to community health and social welfare support programs, its early linkages with schools emerged out of the recognition that these systems needed first to become more responsive to the needs and concerns of children and families. For this to occur, revitalization of health and social services delivery systems is necessary, if not at school sites, then at least in close proximity to and in conjunction with individual schools (Kirst, 1992).

By linking with schools (and ultimately with school reform processes), the services integration movement affords a mechanism to more effectively address the factors that place children at risk for educational failure and chronic dependency upon human assistance programs, namely, hunger, poverty, abuse, neglect, physical and emotional disorders, and so forth. It accomplishes this by effecting a single point of contact for the consumer of services, that is, the family (in whatever form). These *family resource centers*, as they are coming to be known, are often located on school campuses (Sailor, 1994a) or are located in neighborhoods served by the school and usually in close proximity to the school (Crowson & Boyd, 1993; Kirst, 1992). Table 1 presents key components of school-linked, integrated services models described in this section.

Need for Integration of Services

Services integration at this point in U.S. history is rapidly becoming imperative rather than simply desirable. First, the condition of children as a

Table 1. Key components of school-linked, integrated services models

- Family-focused, consumer-driven social/health/education service provision
- Coordinated service provision through the Community Service Coordination Council
- Eligible clients identified through school screening and referral processes
- "Case management" through school-based service coordinators responsible to the Community Service Coordination Council
- All agency funding for identified clients administered through Community Service Coordination Council
- Flexible funding for problem-solving approaches as alternative to expensive services that may be unnecessary
- Service coordinators members of school site resource management team

From Sailor, W. (1994). New community schools: Issues for families in three streams of reform. *Coalition Quarterly, 11*(3), 11–13; reprinted by permission.

class in the United States is worsening (Morrill & Gerry, 1990). The situation is aggravated by factors such as lack of education, cultural isolation, poverty, non–English-speaking status, and so forth, that prevent many families from even using services to which they have an entitlement ("New beginnings," 1990). Second, statistics on child abuse, housing, income supports, and so on, are continuing to indicate that levels of support for children are actually declining at the same time that costs of the supports are rising (Kirst, 1989, 1992). Because the human assistance service system structure is rigidly categorical, many children and families fail to qualify, under eligibility requirements, for services they desperately need (Morrill & Gerry, 1990).

Families that are in poverty find themselves led by the social welfare system into a pattern of "learned helplessness" (Seligman, 1975), wherein needed assistance is provided only when the family exhibits the pattern of pathology required to be eligible for the service. Overworked "case managers" further demean self-respect with attitudes of blame and impatience, often following long periods of waiting, and so on. Families of children with disabilities, such as severe behavior disorders, feel these patterns of service adversity acutely (Turnbull, Ruef, & Reeves, 1993). Their children are unwelcome almost anywhere. Simply finding a dentist who will look after their child's dental needs may consume an inordinate amount of time and resources.

Because human services support systems are separate, categorical, and almost always noncooperating, even within a single community, families with multiple support needs (e.g., poverty and disability) often find themselves confronting multiple case managers. Because each service has its own confidentiality requirements and database, these services do not share information on clients with one another. Families as a result fill out endless forms for each service and undergo time-consuming, if not demeaning, interviews at different physical locations within the same community. Frequently, the attainment of eligibility for one service results in a determination of ineligibility for another service, even though both are needed. For example, a single parent's sole income is from cleaning houses across town while her youngest children are cared for under a respite eligibility. When the local bus company eliminates the route across town, the woman loses both her income and her eligibility for respite care. Finally, families often find themselves with a need for special assistance in an area where there is no pertinent service.

"Wrap-Around" Services: A Fully Integrated Services Arrangement

The school-linked, services integration agenda affords a ready solution to these kinds of problems. The available human support services systems in a community are brought together in a fully integrated arrangement, and their individual services and supports are "wrapped around" the client through a single-point-of-contact mechanism. Under this arrangement such systems as public education, community health, mental health, employment development, business/industry, social welfare, parks and recreation, the judicial authority, housing supports, the clergy, early childhood programs, gerontological programs, and so on, are fitted to the needs of individual families, often through the auspices of a family resource center at or near a school (see Case Study 8.1).

Taking services to the client rather than requesting the client to come to each agency requires an extraordinary transformation in the way that most bureaucratically organized categorical service systems typically operate. When services integration mechanisms are at an advanced phase of the transformation process, funding for services becomes tailored to actual need, rather than geared to categorical eligibility, and flexible funding becomes possible in order to address needs for which no service exists (Melaville & Blank, 1991). Under these arrangements, there is no wasteful duplication of services (e.g., vocational education in school, vocational training through developmental disabilities services after school) on the one hand, and no children "fall through the cracks" because of a lack of needed services in a particular community, on the other.

Services integration mechanisms replace the older "case management" models with a single *service coordinator* (sometimes called a *family advocate*). The task of the family advocate is to assist the family, through the provision of information as well as analysis of need, to select those services that they need from an array of choices. Services are then provided on or near the contact site in accordance with the specifications in a *family services plan* to which the family member(s) actively contribute through their participation.

Such school-linked, services integration mechanisms are *prevention* focused, rather than crisis oriented, and begin at the level of neonatology and extend through the period of transition from school to work and adult status. Increasingly, such programs are geared for support throughout the person's life span. The emphasis in such arrangements is on the delivery of needed services with actual support recipient outcomes as evaluative indicators of progress and success, rather than on the dictates of the categorical service delivery system and its eligibility "gatekeeping" functions. Such service transformations are simultaneously geared to the culture and makeup of the community in the process of becoming a source of strength and assistance to the community (Gerry & Certo, 1992). When flexible funding becomes possible under such arrangements, the service systems become problem-solving focused rather than wholly concerned with categorical definitions of needs. When human assistance needs are met through collaborative, problem-solving "adhocracies" (Skrtic, 1991a), then the process of *reinventing government* (Sailor & Skrtic, 1995) at the local level begins to get under way. For example, pilot projects in New Jersey and New York have reportedly turned up examples of up to 29% of all assistance support dollars in a community spent under flexible funding arrangements rather than in accordance with existing categorical services.

As one might expect, such a radical transformation process is not easy to accomplish. In the modern period, when categorical services and their bureaucracies were at their zenith, say 1975, such sweeping changes would have been almost impossible. Pooled or flexible funding, use of which is partly at the discretion of the consumer family itself, would have been nearly unthinkable. But with the beginning of the advent of the postmodern era, collaboration and voice, the processes that help to drive fully integrated services arrangements, are increasingly in evidence. In California, for example, SB820, the Healthy Start initiative, required local community councils, empowered and funded under the legislation, to begin the transformation to services integration arrangements to comprise equal numbers of agency service provider representatives and consumers. Consumer empowerment in California is a critical part of the legislated transformation agenda. Healthy Start proceeds as if the state of California has offered its human services bureaucracies a vote of no confidence and was instead suggesting to people in circumstances of poverty, disability, poor health, non–English-speaking newcomers, and so on, "Here, take the money, and by forming partnerships with rank and file service providers in your community, invent something at the local level that will work for you."

Case Study 8.1. Ricky

Ricky is a sociable, dark-haired 9-year-old, one of four children born to a Spanish-speaking, migrant farm worker's family in California. Ricky was born prematurely and sustained serious complications following birth. He has developmental disabilities (described as severe mental retardation) and serious behavior disorders, including episodes of self-destructive behavior and violence toward property and other children. Most of the time, however, Ricky is pleasant, sociable, and attentive. Ricky's family has now lived for 1 year in a northern California community that operates New Community School–type programs at the elementary and middle school levels.

(continued)

Case Study 8.1. Ricky *(continued)*

Prior to moving to their new community, Ricky's family lived in a town in the San Joaquin Valley in central California. There, Ricky was placed by the County Office of Education in a separate school for children with severe disabilities called a "Development Center for the Handicapped." It was there that Ricky "developed" some of the more extreme forms of his aberrant behavior patterns.

Services available to Ricky's family in the central California town were few and inadequate. The school offered no after-school programs and no advice to the family on how to look after Ricky at home and in the community. Because of Ricky's worsening condition, one regional caseworker from the developmental disabilities service agency recommended an evaluation for institutional placement, an option that Ricky's mother would not consider. When the same agency responded to its own budget problems by withdrawing respite care support for Ricky's family, the family made the decision to relocate.

Things are very different for Ricky's family in their new community. When Ricky's mother went to the County Office of Education to register Ricky for school, she was told that she would be contacted by a family advocate from the neighborhood school where two of her other children were to enroll. In the previous community, the local school had refused to even evaluate Ricky for placement. The family advocate visited Ricky and his family at home and explained that Ricky could not only attend the neighborhood school if that was what his family wished, but that he would have a regular third-grade placement.

During Ricky's school evaluation, his mother was invited to attend a family support group session at the school's family resource center. This session, which was conducted in Spanish by the school psychologist and a public health nurse, included seeking advice from Ricky's parents on ways that the school could support them for in-home care needs.

As a result of Ricky's evaluation and his mother's involvement at the school, Ricky had an individualized education program (IEP) designed for him that called for a positive behavioral support program that operated under a cooperative arrangement among the school staff, the community parks and recreation department, and the family at home. Ricky's IEP was embedded in a more compre-

(continued)

Case Study 8.1. Ricky *(continued)*

hensive family services plan (FSP), approved by the Community Integrated Services Coordination Council, that provided assistance to Ricky's family from a variety of community support services including services available through the school. The FSP was, furthermore, a product of problem-solving sessions that included school staff in addition to the family advocate. The family was able to select resources to meet their needs from an array of support service choices.

Program evaluation data from Ricky's family 1 year after relocation to the new community are suggestive of a significant improvement in the family members' perceptions of the adequacy of the community support services. Ricky's behavior disorders abated over the course of 1 year to the extent that he was able to sustain general classroom participation for up to 80% of the school day. Ricky made friends among his peers without disabilities, was taught a picture booklet-assisted communication aid that enabled him to interact socially with his peers, and was fully included in all school activities. Ricky's mother was so taken with the overall program that she eventually enrolled in a training program so that she herself could become a family advocate.

Exploring the Outcomes of School-Linked Services Integration

What made the critical differences in these two communities in response to Ricky and his family (Case Study 8.1)? Both communities had large, Spanish-speaking populations, yet service providers in the first community never attempted to communicate with Ricky's mother in her native language. Economic considerations cannot account for the differences because, if anything, the northern California county had a lower tax base and fewer resources overall than the central county. Finally, Ricky's family's total income declined upon relocating in the north.

The differences experienced by Ricky and his family are attributable to the outcomes of a series of very substantive transformations that the northern California community has undergone in just the past few years in its human assistance services support structure. The northern community, with start-up assistance from a state Healthy Start grant, had developed a school-linked, integrated services model that included a school–community partnership arrangement, restructured school processes, and a family resource center at the school. Inclusive education was embedded in the school restructuring agenda, so that it was not an isolated attempt at reform within special education, but was part of a broad school unification process that was comprehensive across the entire school (and now progressing districtwide).

One outcome of this transformation is that the school hums with teamwork. Governance at the school is effected with an interactive arrangement that includes the principal and a site management team (called a *site resource management team*) consisting of teachers (both general education and support program), school staff (whoever was willing to put in the time), allied health support personnel (e.g., therapists), and family members of children with and without disabilities. The role of the team is to allocate and distribute resources to the school (see later section, Site-Based Management, for more information). Family advocates on the site team are fully familiar with the specialized resource supports to individual students for whom they broker and arrange services within the community. It is this process of within school and school–community services coordination and integration that leads to the possibility of a comprehensive FSP. This plan allows all supports needed by Ricky and his family to "wrap around" the family, rather than requiring the family to seek out each agency. Only one set of forms is filled out, and the family only interacts with one person (the family advocate) for all aspects of the FSP development. Most of the actual supports, including health care, are delivered through the family resource center at the school.

Overcoming Barriers to Services Integration

In order for the northern California community to evolve such a unique, flexible, and efficient system of human assistance supports it had to overcome some very formidable obstacles. Other communities in California and elsewhere have yet to assume the challenges that this community did in developing school-linked integrated services, but increasingly there are incentives to do so, and more communities are coming on-line each year.

Some of the more formidable barriers to services integration include the following:

- *Discrete, categorical service programs:* Congress addresses problems by authorizing a program and seeking an appropriation with which to start it up. These programs are usually geared to specific social problems (e.g., teen pregnancy, drug abuse) and address no other problems. Each such program has its discreet eligibility requirements, forms, place of access, caseworkers, and so forth. Various other closely related programs do not coordinate with or share databases with one another.
- *Confidentiality:* Authorizations are administered through agency bureaucracies (e.g., U.S. Department of Health and Human Services). Each subagency has its own confidentiality guidelines and maintains a separate database on its consumers. Because each has a policy of

nonsharing with other agencies (in the interests of "consumer protection"), it is nearly impossible to coordinate services to a single family (or client) across several agencies. Each agency will have "case managers" who will treat clients as cases who need to be managed. These do not correspond or communicate with one another. None of the case managers can inform clients, in most situations, about programs operating outside of their agency for which the client may be eligible.

- *Funding restrictions:* Because there are no mechanisms for flexible funding to solve human support problems, and because a particular client need for support may not be able to be met by the existing agency programs in a particular area, certain family assistance needs may go unaddressed and lead to problems becoming much more severe and expensive to solve later on.
- *Eligibility:* Each agency responsible for an authorization program will set its own standards for eligibility for assistance. Sometimes various "safety net" programs will effectively cancel each other out because of eligibility issues. For example, a client goes on Medicaid and Aid to Families with Dependent Children (AFDC) after a period of extended unemployment. Another community job development support program results in a part-time placement in a low-paying job. Job placement results in cancellation of the client's AFDC and Medicaid, but health care costs alone lead to the necessity of quitting work to get back on welfare.
- *Turf:* The biggest barrier to integrated services transformations is allegiance to agencies. Shrinking budgets and lack of information work against cooperation and lead directly to agency self-protectionism.

These and other barriers are difficult to overcome, but there are examples of successful transformations of this type all over the country, for example, the Alaska Youth Initiative (AYI), Healthy Start (California), Community Vision Now (Kansas), and New Community School (Kansas, California). Under these kinds of arrangements, children and families (however defined) become the focus of the support service systems, rather than the agencies that deliver the service. The process is usually begun as an investment in children and families, a *prevention* effort to head off more significant problems later on.

Agency supports under these arrangements are decentralized through use of a community planning council that is represented by all of the community's human services support systems. If any services are left out (e.g., religious supports, parks/recreation, judicial), the program will be less successful. It really does take the whole village to raise the child who has need of special services and supports.

States and communities vary as to the extent of true consumer empowerment in school-linked services integration arrangements. The Healthy Start initiative in California, for example, mandates significant consumer participation on the implementation councils at the local, community level. Some models rely solely on agency membership with representation on the implementation councils at the local, community level. Other models rely solely on agency membership with representation from business and industry interests, but with little consumer input. While all of these models lack comparative, evaluative data with which to judge adequacy, anecdotal information seems to suggest that the greater the involvement of consumers in the governance and implementation team arrangements, the more positive and significant the outcomes.

The phrase "reinventing government" begins to come into play when various school-linked services integration models evolve from a status of cooperation among various agencies represented on the local council, together with recognition of the role of consumers, to a status of collaboration among council members characterized by voice as a mechanism for empowering consumers through direct participation in choices among implementation alternatives, planning for new and reconfigured systems, and governance (Kagan & Neville, 1993; Sailor & Skrtic, 1995; Sailor et al., in press). Only when the stage of collaboration is reached can *flexible funding* mechanisms be brought into play. The process seems to require trust and mutual respect to a degree that permits cost-sharing and reinventive processes to occur (Kagan & Neville, 1993).

SCHOOL RESTRUCTURING AND INCLUSIVE EDUCATION

Harnessing community support systems to provide an integrated, seamless web of services through a coordinated, brokered plan to support child and family needs in the community is but one part of the process. The next two sections address the part of the process that comes under the term *school linked*. These processes can be examined as considerations involved with general education reform, called *school restructuring*, and then under reform processes in categorical school support systems such as special education. The latter is often described under the rubric *inclusive education*. The question to be addressed in the next two sections is, what must occur in schools in order for them to become effective support systems within school-linked integrated services arrangements? Finally, how can such system transformation arrangements significantly increase the likelihood of positive lifestyle changes and outcomes for persons with severe behavior disorders requiring positive behavioral supports in the school and community?

School Restructuring

For reasons that Skrtic (1991a, 1991b) analyzed in some detail, schools organized in a time-honored, modern, traditional fashion simply do not lend themselves to the *postmodern* processes represented in either school–community partnerships (services integration) or in the kinds of arrangements needed to impart inclusive education (Sage & Burrello, 1994; Sailor & Skrtic, 1995). To respond to and effectively participate in community service transformation processes, schools must themselves transform from *organizational bureaucracies* to *participatory adhocracies* (Skrtic, 1991a, 1991b).

Schools are traditionally organized the same way many large corporations were structured before the advent of TQM. The central district office dictates school operation, often to a significant degree of micro management, by holding a single manager (the school principal) responsible for operations. Line workers (teachers and others) are expected to carry out their missions in accordance with board policy as dictated by the district office and communicated through the principal, who has absolute authority.

School–community partnership processes require much greater flexibility and permeability. Parents, for example, to feel not only welcomed at a school but actively invited to participate in school processes (e.g., study hall, homework support sessions) must feel that their ideas are welcomed as well. Otherwise, their status as "outsider" carries too high a level of discomfort. Even more so, the family advocate in school-linked, services integration models must be welcomed as a participating member of the school site council as well as provide the school's link to the consumer and services community. Such processes require teamwork and team structures. When teams involving teachers, staff, and parents gain decision-making authority with respect to how school resources are organized and utilized, the organizational system transforms from a bureaucracy to an adhocracy. Where the former is a pyramidal management structure, the latter is a veridical, problem-solving system. The former is organized to maintain a preexisting structure. The latter is organized to adapt to changing demands on the structure. When circumstances change the nature of the marketplace demand for a system's product (i.e., child learning), then the system must adapt or suffer a loss of confidence in (and demand for) the product (i.e., "white flight to private schools"). "Marketplace" changes in American communities are impelling the transformations of schools from modern bureaucracies to postmodern adhocracies (Skrtic, 1991a, 1991b). When these processes are geared to a broader citywide or state-level initiative, they are referred to as school restructuring processes.

Trends in School Reform   Recent school reform processes have their origins in a sweeping effort that was launched by Congress and the Department of Education in the early 1980s in response to publication of the report *A Nation at Risk* (National Commission on Excellence in Education, 1983). This first wave of significant school reform came to be termed the *school excellence* model (Darling-Hammond & Berry, 1988; Firestone, Fuhrman, & Kirst, 1989).

The states responded to these initiatives at the federal level (some 700 laws passed between 1983–1985) (Darling-Hammond & Berry, 1988) by enacting reforms such as increases in academic content, graduation requirements, teacher certification requirements, standardized student assessment guidelines, longer instructional time, and so forth, but ignored school organization (Firestone et al., 1989). According to Bell (1993) these "top-down" kinds of initiatives failed to meet the expectations of policy makers because they failed to directly involve those responsible for the *implementation* of change processes in the decision-making structure under which the changes were to be implemented. It became clear by the mid-1980s that the school excellence reforms were positively affecting students who were already achieving at acceptable levels of expectation, but the same reforms were missing the low-achieving students portrayed in *A Nation at Risk* (Hallinger, Murphy, & Hausman, 1992).

The early excellence movement in school reform was strongly geared to holding teachers to a higher standard of productivity as reflected in student performance on standardized tests. The primary focus of educators was in curriculum improvement during this period. Students whose performance was in jeopardy from a number of risk factors, including disability, were offered a "dumbed down" curriculum (Honig, 1987) that focused largely on basic skills such as arithmetic computation and remedial reading. There was little concern with the application of schooling to real-life situations. Facts were to be learned by rote memory and fed back on standardized tests. For many students, the rote learning tedium rewarded by grades (often deficient) seemed irrelevant and unlikely to lead in the end to anything useful.

Toward the end of the 1980s, educators realized that excellence can only exist to the extent that it is coupled with equity (Murphy, 1993). The discrepancy between "have" and "have not" schools had grown to staggering proportions. The rhetoric of the excellence in education movement could not begin to be matched by student successes unless the low-achieving students in the poorer schools began to show progress.

Where the excellence movement was largely a top-down effort to improve curriculum; introduce new instructional practices (Slavin, 1990); and, most of all, hold schools accountable for student performance, the restructuring movement (the second wave in educational reform) showed characteristics of being a grass roots or bottom-up set of initiatives. As less affluent schools reacted to the pressures of "schoolwide report cards" and "quality indicator checklists," it became increasingly obvious that more *systemic* changes than better teaching practices and upgraded curriculum would be needed to improve educational performance (Hallinger, Murphy, & Hausman, 1992). Beginning about 1989, several significant new reform processes began to emerge, first in less affluent school districts but then spreading more widely through the mechanism of statewide school restructuring initiatives. The hallmarks of the school restructuring agenda, which continues at present, include the following:

1. Student-centered and individualized approaches to learning
2. Outcomes-based assessment and curricular adaptations
3. Participatory and site- (rather than district-) level management
4. School unification practices that serve to harness the categorical programs' resources in the interests of improving the performance of *all* of the students at the school
5. Strong incentives for greater parent involvement in the learning process through strengthening school linkages with other community agencies and groups

The Council of Chief State School Officers (CCSSO) adopted a position that explicitly called for equity in processes that restructured curriculum and instructional guidelines (CCSSO, 1989). In this position paper, the school chiefs signaled an end to the watered-down approach to students with disabilities and those at risk for learning problems, and ordered into effect processes that were geared to facilitating learning styles of a demographically diverse population. For example, the chiefs adopted a position in favor of placing stress on higher-order thinking skills and abstract reasoning processes over the rote learning processes that characterized most mathematics instruction. The shift in philosophy, from the idea that disadvantaged students should get "what they can" from education, to a philosophy that required each student to perform at the highest level of expectation and capability, was quite dramatic (Boyer, 1990).

School restructuring, according to Murphy and Hallinger (1993), represented nothing less than a shift in "the core technology of schooling" (p. 12). The decentralized instructional methods, that is, research-based teaching methodologies, that had been introduced in the mid-1980s through "effective schools" finally began to emerge in earnest. The use of cooperative learning strategies (Johnson & Johnson, 1990; Schlechty, 1989; Slavin & Madden, 1989), peer instructional methods (Clark, 1989), and other small-group instructional arrangements that occurred throughout the school day (Boyer, 1990) were increasingly coming, through systematic research, to be associated with positive outcomes for all students, including those with high-risk factors and disabilities (CCSSO, 1989).

Whereas traditional instructional practices and grouping arrangements tended to further segregate students with disabilities from the general classroom because of the need to reflect higher performance through increases in standardized class and schoolwide achievement tests, the school restructuring agenda began to have the opposite effect (Sailor & Skrtic, 1995). Small-grouping instructional arrangements are conducive to the inclusion of students with more diversity in learning styles and capabilities, and promote the school unification agenda by bringing more educators into the process through the direct inclusion of children in categorical programs.

Site-Based Management   One very significant difference between the first and second waves of reform has to do with how schools are governed, that is, how decisions are made to distribute school resources and manage the schoolwide budget (Sage & Burrello, 1994). Where the school excellence reforms subordinated the accountability of schools to authority of the central district office, the school restructuring movement is shifting the authority for day-to-day school management increasingly to the school site. Under site management processes, a school site council, sometimes called a site resource management team (Sailor et al., 1989), is empowered to carry out a school unification agenda. As described earlier, these site teams are made up of both general and categorical teachers, other school personnel, sometimes parents of children who attend the school, and occasionally students. Among the responsibilities of the team are planning for the means with which to meet the needs of students at the school who require special supports.

Under site-based management processes, governance works in a combination of arrangements that balance the site manager's authority (the school principal) with that of the site council through shared decision making (Darling-Hammond, 1990). The principal acts as the chief negotiator for the school with the central district office in governing the resources needed to implement the site resource management plan designed by the site council (Sailor et al., 1989). Principals under this arrangement assume authority for the management of the budgets and resources of all of the categorical programs, such as Chapter 1 (or Title I), English as a second language (ESL), special education, vocational education, gifted and talented programs, and other programs. Often waiver processes must be put into effect at the school site to enable coordinated and consolidated site budgeting to occur.

Empowering Teachers   School restructuring processes are proving to be tremendously empowering for teachers (Bell, 1993). Rather than struggling to "teach to the test scores," teachers in restructured schools can be

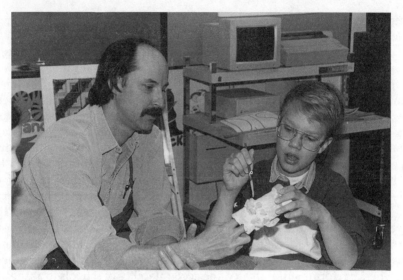

A teacher provides art instruction for a student in a small group setting.

more creative and test some of their own ideas within a broader instructional framework (Skrtic, 1988). For example, according to Tyack (1993)

> A key way to improve schooling is to start with the classroom and to attend to the teachers who do that steady work. By moving from the inside out, and not from the top down, one may gain a better sense of how to improve instruction. (p. 25)

Teachers, under these arrangements, move from a status of mere technicians in imparting a uniform curriculum, to true professionals who have the responsibility for structuring, to a degree, what is to be taught and in what manner to which groups of students. In this sense, a teacher becomes the person who "orchestrates" the instructional design and guides the expertise of others, including students, in the teaching process.

The Council on School Performance Standards (1989; also cited in Sailor et al., 1996) developed a list of standards for teachers in restructured schools. Among these standards, note the following:

- Teachers need to be able to manage a number of learning groups of different sizes, all operating at the same time.
- Teachers need to manage flexible time schedules, a wide variety of learning resources, and the effective use of space.
- Teachers need to master assessment of what students have learned and make judgments about a student's most profitable next learning experience.

- Teachers need to evaluate and record student progress in basic and higher-order/problem-solving skills, personal and social attributes, and the ability to learn new things on their own.
- Teachers need to be able to identify and use community resources from service agencies, government, and business and industry as additional learning resources.
- Teachers need to possess the skills to use computers and other technology appropriately as tools for learning and sources of information.
- Teachers of middle school, high school, and vocational school need to serve on interdisciplinary teaching teams to plan, implement, and evaluate instruction as a group—no longer with only one or two academic or technical fields of study in a single classroom.

The essential components of voice and collaboration come through in these recommendations. Different educational practices, such as the inclusion of students with severe behavior disorders and other disabilities in general classroom processes, become more possible when the tactics to accomplish the practices are generated through collaborative team arrangements. Under these arrangements a general education teacher does not have to feel burdened, for example, by having a student with disabilities placed in his or her classroom because the pattern of supports and responsibilities has been a group, if not a schoolwide, process (Sailor, 1991).

School Unification   Where site-based management practices provide the mechanism under school restructuring for the equitable distribution of school resources, the school unification agenda provides the mechanism for the procurement and coordination of what is to be distributed (McLaughlin & Warren, 1992). According to Sage and Burrello (1994), many restructured schools assume dominion over all of the categorical resources available to the school site. These resources are then coordinated through team processes so that they benefit not only their respective, categorically identified students (i.e., special education students with IEPs), but in such a manner that, in combination, they can benefit *all* of the students at the school. This school site agenda is nearly the reverse of the agenda under the school excellence movement. Under school excellence, students who did not achieve at higher rates of performance on standardized assessment indicators were frequently tagged for one of a variety of special, categorical assistance programs that would remove them, for at least some portion of the day, from the educational mainstream. Lipsky and Gartner (1989) actually cited some research that indicated that "the residue" (i.e., the students left in the classroom when all categorical resources had been utilized to the maximum extent allowable) was presenting more challenges for instruction than those challenges that characterized the categorically identified students!

Under the school restructuring agenda, by contrast, the central issue is schoolwide improvement. Special resources available through Chapter 1, special education, and so on (e.g., some California schools at one time had up to 32 distinct categorical resource programs operating at the sites [Sailor, 1991]), are harnessed, integrated, and coordinated in such a manner that the collective expertise, equipment, and other resources can be put into play in the service of better educational outcomes for all of the students. Such a process is not easy to achieve and can require new training for teachers, principals, and others to be successful (Sage & Burrello, 1994). Furthermore, particular care must be exercised to operate categorical programs in a manner that respects compliance with their various statutory and regulatory requirements (Sailor, 1991). However, school unification can be accomplished under the present legal and regulatory structures, and examples of success under school restructuring abound in the literature (e.g., McLaughlin & Warren, 1992).

Burrello and Lashley (1992) reported 11 key considerations that provide a basis for carrying out a school unification agenda. Table 2 presents these restructuring outcomes.

Outcomes-Based Education Of all of the principle reforms of the school restructuring movement, none has met greater resistance from var-

Table 2. Key considerations for carrying out a school unification agenda

- Everyone in the school is responsible for the education of each student residing in the school's attendance area, regardless of his or her learning needs.
- Everyone in the school should be focused on meeting the needs of all students in a unified system of education. Labeling and segregation of students are counterproductive to educational excellence.
- All educators have skills and knowledge that should be used to support the efforts of all other teachers.
- All students benefit from participation in inclusive classrooms and schools. Students themselves are the best teachers and role models for individuals with significant learning needs.
- The prevention of learning problems is the proper province of special education.
- Assessment of students' needs is a regular part of curricular and instructional planning for all teachers and related services personnel.
- Special education and related services personnel should serve as full members of teacher teams under the leadership of the school principal.
- Special education and related services personnel should provide services to students within the context of the general school program.
- Funding and budgeting should allow for the provision of services to students with special needs in the home school and local community.
- Community-based human services for children should be coordinated at the school.
- Evaluation of the effectiveness of a school's program should include consideration of the post-school adjustment of students with special needs.

From Burrello, L.C., & Lashley, L.A. (1992). On organizing for the future: The destiny of special education. In K.A. Waldron, A.E. Reister, & J.H. Moore (Eds.), *Special education: The challenge of the future* (pp. 64–95). San Francisco: Mellen Research University Press; reprinted by permission.

ious community (and national) constituencies as outcomes-based education (OBE). For example, some fundamentalist groups, through their national radio network, almost daily deride the essentials of the outcomes-based movement. Such organized resistance can be hard to interpret and understand, and often seems to be grounded in misinformation. The effort, for example, to shift away from rote learning to higher-order thinking skills can be effectively driven by outcomes-based evaluation practices (Ysseldyke, Thurlow, & Shriner, 1992). The vigor of the religious group opposition seems to be attributable to some early examples of identified educational outcomes such as those that tended to shade away from exclusively academic areas and into values issues. The Kansas State Board of Education, for example, responding to verbal attacks from members of the state legislature on the Board's new outcomes-driven school accreditation standards, deleted a set of outcomes that corresponded to a broad goal of good citizenship and ethical behavior on the part of Kansas students. The goal drew fire from these legislators for perceived encroachment by a public agency (education) on the traditional prerogatives of the family (i.e., values).

The goals of OBE are to define, design, deliver, and document educational processes by what is *gained from learning* rather than simply by *what is learned*. The concern represents a shift of focus to what a student can accomplish with what she learns, an outcome of her learning processes. *Portfolio assessments,* for example, that provide samples of students' written work, computations, applications of concepts, lists of books read independently, and so on, first supplement and later replace performances measured by standardized tests (Ysseldyke et al., 1992). Educational processes thus shift away from acquisition of predetermined content (e.g., every second grade teacher will teach all sight words from the basal reader) to emphasis on the measurable results of instruction (e.g., elementary students will, every 2 weeks, read and discuss a choice from among works of children's literature) (Sailor et al., in press). Through the process of shifting to OBE, education starts to become more *individualized* for all students, including those with diverse learning styles and a need for specialized instructional resources and supports.

School Restructuring and the Postmodern Era The previous section examined the processes that are emerging under the rubric school-linked, integrated services. In these processes, voice and collaboration, the hallmarks of postmodernism in human services transformations, emerge as cornerstones of the movement. The coordination of service systems to effectively and efficiently meet the needs of a child and family with special assistance needs at the community level requires a *services coordinator,* sometimes called a *family advocate,* who enables the process of "wrap-around" by providing a single point of contact for the family. How would such a transformational process link with the traditionally organized school? The answer is, it cannot. For the school to be an effective participant in the integrated services, collaborative process, it must itself mirror that process internally (Sailor & Skrtic, 1995). For the services coordinator to effectively link the services plan for the child *in school* to the services plan for the child and family *in the community*, the services coordinator must be a member of the school site resource management team. If the school is not site-based managed, then such participation and linkages become difficult at best, and most likely impossible.

The processes involved in the transformation of schools as reflected in the school restructuring agenda and those involved in the transformation of all human assistance and support systems at the community (and ultimately the state) level are *interdependent*: one set of transformations cannot fully occur without the other (Sailor & Skrtic, 1995). That these transformations are occurring in concert with each other in many states and communities is evidence that they are part of broader-based changes reflective of our passage from the modern to the postmodern era (Sailor & Skrtic, 1995; Rhodes et al., 1995).

What remains is to examine one further set of transformational processes that will return us to the central question of this chapter—how can we effectively include a student who has severe behavior disorders in the mainstream of educational practices and life in the community? If it can be said that the principal direction of reform in public policy that characterizes the federal, categorical programs in the schools is best described under the rubric inclusion, and there is mounting evidence that it is (e.g., see McLaughlin & Warren, 1992; Sage & Burrello, 1994), then the transformations that characterize inclusive education within the field of special education offer an important piece of the change agenda.

Inclusive Education

There are two kinds of processes that are described under the rubric inclusion. The first, the one with which most readers of this chapter will be familiar, is use of the term *inclusion*, or *full inclusion*, to describe the trend toward the placement of students with severe disabilities in general education classrooms (Stainback & Stainback, 1984). The second, and the one I would like to examine in some detail here, is a broader-based concept that describes processes necessary to achieve *school unification*. The term *inclusive education* then, is used in the remainder of this chaper to describe the processes of transformation by which specialized school support programs, funded under federal (and sometimes state and local) categorical programs, come to be fully integrated and coordinated with the general education program at the school site under a school-site unification program (Sailor et al., 1996). Thus, where full inclusion refers to student placement and participation issues, inclusive education refers to the organization and utilization of school support services. The placement of students with disabilities in general groupings is implicit in the concept of inclusive education as one cannot successfully integrate special education (or other categorical) services unless one integrates (includes) the students identified for specialized supports, those with IEPs.

This section presents special education as a representative case of how the process of inclusive education proceeds from a separate, parallel educational program, geared to a circumspect, identified "class" of students, to a fully integrated program, coordinated with the total school curriculum and instructional system. The same, or very similar transformational processes occur with Chapter 1, ESL, gifted, and other programs as well (Sage & Burrello, 1994). Inclusive education as the principal reform agenda of the categorical school support programs exhibits the same postmodern transformational hallmarks as described in the previous sections for general education (restructuring) and community human assistance services (school-linked services integration). The processes of voice and collaboration are in evidence here, too, as inclusive educational practices come to be structured through team arrangements that focus the talents and creativity of a variety of professionals, staff, and parents on the support needs of individual children in noncategorical arrangements (York, 1994).

Special Education Policy Reform The field of special education has undergone significant reform processes over the past 15 years that have paralleled the reforms affecting general education and only in very recent years have the two reforms begun to merge (McLaughlin & Warren, 1992; Sage & Burrello, 1994). The principal landmark of this reform movement is represented by the initiative of then Assistant Secretary for Special Education and Rehabilitative Services, Madeleine Will's, "Regular Education Initiative (REI)" (Will, 1986).

In this initiative, Will relied substantively on the research of Margaret Wang and her colleagues (Wang, Reynolds, & Walberg, 1988) in proposing to bring to an end the practices of pull-out, resource rooms and other categorically segregating programs and to merge the resources of special education, Chapter 1 (Title I), and bilingual (including migrant) education into a systemically unified educational structure. It is to put it mildly to point out that the Wang et al. proposals in support of Will's merger agenda generated significant opposition from within the special education academic community. An entire issue of the *Journal of Learning Disabilities* (1987, 20[5]) was dedicated to a rebuttal of this position. The gist of the rebuttal was in part a series of criticisms of methodology used by Wang and her associates in their published reports, but to a much greater degree reflected a genuine anxiety concerning the future of special education in its categorical form. Wang et al.'s position was interpreted by the editors of the *Journal of Learning Disabilities* as an effort to return responsibility for children with mild/moderate learning disabilities to the purview of general education and eventually thus eliminate the category of learning disabilities from the special education amendments to the Education for All Handicapped Children Act of 1975 (PL 94-142).

While the REI was primarily concerned with integration of students with less significant disabilities (i.e., "learning disabilities") into general education contexts for their special supports, a second, related reform process concerned with students with more significant disabilities (i.e., "severe and profound disabilities") was also under way (Sailor et al., 1989). This process, referred to as *integration*, gained national attention particularly within general education, with the publication of Gartner and Lipsky's (1987) and Skrtic's (1991a, 1991b) critiques of special education systems. The integration portion of special education reform has also come under strong opposition from special educators and, interestingly, from some of the same professionals who "led the charge" against REI (i.e., Fuchs & Fuchs, 1994; Kauffman, 1989; Semmel, Gerber, & MacMillan, 1994; Vergason & Anderegg, 1989). While much of the national media attention has focused on the full inclusion agenda, the combined reform processes of special education (REI, integration) have come together most recently in combination with school restructuring reforms in general education under the rubric inclusive education (McLaughlin & Warren, 1992; NASBE, 1992; Sage & Burrello, 1994; Sailor, 1991; Sailor et al., 1996; Snell, 1991; York, 1994).

To understand the goals of inclusive education as distinct from the earlier reform processes, one has to consider the shift of focus away from exclusively matching special categorical resources to categorically identified students. Under inclusive education, the focus becomes supporting students with special needs in a manner that allows all students at the school to benefit from all of the services. The accomplishment of this school unification (McLaughlin & Warren, 1992) reform agenda requires at least the following transformations to occur in the manner in which special education sources are imparted at the school (Sailor, Gerry, & Wilson, 1993):

- All students with disabilities attend the school they would attend if they did not have disabilities, as a matter of family choice.
- Students with disabilities are included in general education contexts in natural proportion to their incidence in the school district (or community) at large.

- All grouping arrangements at the school (and in the community, as school activities) are heterogeneous and respective of the natural proportion.
- All students with disabilities are placed in and are regular members of general education classrooms appropriate to their chronological ages.
- The school employs site-based management and coordination of school resources as systemic practices.
- The school employs decentralized instructional practices in accordance with a schoolwide restructuring plan.

The hallmark of inclusive education is the full integration and participation of students with special support needs at the school. Unified schools, that is, schools that are restructured to include the practices of inclusive education, do not, for example, operate special, categorical classrooms. Students are not grouped, in fact, in any arrangement at the school or in the community on the basis of their categorical "label" or even on the basis of banning special support needs. In special education children still need to be counted, for federal reporting purposes, as "learning disabled (LD)," "seriously emotionally disturbed (SED)," and so on, but these stigmatizing (Sage & Burrello, 1994) and nonprescriptive labels are not used at the school site and are unknown to most staff, children, and families associated with the school.

Under inclusive educational arrangements the nature of special education supports is determined through team processes (York, 1994) that include family members in the decision process. If the decision is made to add paraprofessional support to a general education classroom, the aide is never encouraged to be the primary support person for the student with disabilities who is included. Rather, it is to support the student *as a member of the class* in a manner that fosters social relationships with regular class members and facilitates the total classroom programs. The processes of decentralized instruction (Slavin, 1990) enhance this process by facilitating common learning outcomes for typical students and those who require special supports and assistance. Peer supports and adapted curriculum become fluid processes under methods of decentralized instruction (York, 1994).

Under the way special education services have been traditionally organized, a student with severe behavior disorders would likely receive, after extensive (and expensive!) assessments have been performed, a label such as SED, autism, or behavior disorders (BD) and be referred for placement to a special class (or even school) where such students are categorically grouped. It is logical to question whether the practice of grouping students with severe problems of socialization together for their education is likely to remediate their difficulties. Such grouping arrange-

An educator provides support for a student with special needs.

ments are clearly to the benefit of the service provision agencies (i.e., school special education services) rather than for the student with disabilities. For students to learn appropriate patterns of behavior and to become socialized, they must interact on a regular and sustained basis with peers who model such patterns. The question is not and has really never been whether students with severe behavior disorders should be grouped together (Schroeder et al., 1990). The question of greater relevance has been how to meet the challenges of supporting such students in the mainstream.

Students with Behavior Disorders   Under inclusive educational practices the "management" of students with severe behavior disorders is a schoolwide issue, rather than the exclusive purview of a particular service system. A plan for the positive management of severe behavior disorders may be developed under such an arrangement, that includes input from and participation by

- A multidisciplinary team at the school
- Students at the school
- Teaching staff at the school, both general and categorically identified
- Parents of the child as well as other parents at the school
- Members of the community served by the school

Such a positive behavioral support plan (Carr, 1988) becomes a part of the student's IEP. If full-time, general class participation is a goal of the plan, the student's placement and membership in the target classroom is given at the outset of the plan. The amount of time the student actually spends in the classroom or in any general education instructional grouping may be dependent upon a phased-in schedule of participation geared to increased socialization outcomes consistent with the objectives of the plan. When not in the general classroom, the student may be instructed elsewhere in the school or in the community, but never in segregated or categorically grouped circumstances. Such an arrangement can greatly tax the resources of a school in the initial stages of implementation, but over time can have very beneficial consequences in helping a school come together to meet the needs of all students who present socialization challenges (Turnbull et al., 1993).

Goals 2000: The Present Agenda in Educational Reform The Clinton administration introduced a package of educational reform programs to Congress in 1993 called Goals 2000, the Educate America Act (PL 103-227). This act, chartered as S.1150 in the Senate, is directly linked to the Americans with Disabilities Act (ADA) (PL 101-336) and both Section 504 of the Rehabilitation Act of 1973 (PL 93-112) and the 1990 amendments to the Education of the Handicapped Act (the Individuals with Disabilities Education Act [IDEA], PL 101-476). The Senate report that accompanies the Goals 2000 Act (Senate Report 103-85) addresses the issue of inclusive education directly. Guidance to educators on the issue of inclusive education in the Senate report takes three forms. First, it directs the National Center on Educational Outcomes at the University of Minnesota to increase the likelihood, through its assessment system–development practices, of making such assessments applicable to all students with disabilities, in a nondiscriminating manner. The net effect of this recommendation is to shift the emphasis on the identification of outcomes of education that apply to students with disabilities away from identifying separate indicators (i.e., a "functional curriculum") and toward progress indicators of some form on the general education curriculum (i.e., an "adapted curriculum").

Second, the report explicitly requires that such assessment systems actively encourage the placement of students with disabilities in the regular classroom and in the general education program. Finally, the report directs the National Education Goals Panel to review standards and assessment data relevant to the national goals of Goals 2000 to ensure that they apply to students with disabilities.

The Minnesota Center responded to the challenge of the Senate report in recent publications (Shriner, Ysseldyke, & Thurlow, 1994; Shriner, Ysseldyke, Thurlow, & Honetschlager, 1994) in which it calls for school districts to

1. Include all students in schoolwide systems of accountability for student performance.

2. Make reasonable accommodations in schoolwide assessment systems to promote inclusion of all students.
3. Promote wide latitude in scaling performance outcomes so that partial performances of students with disabilities can be reflected on the same scales.
4. Build such efforts on the basis of existing assessment and data collection practices whenever possible.

The Minnesota Center cites the Kentucky School Reform Act (1990) as one example of an outcomes-based educational effort that includes all students and measures performance of students with disabilities on the same curricular areas (e.g., science classes) that reflect performances by general education students.

INCLUSIVE EDUCATION; SCHOOL RESTRUCTURING; AND SCHOOL-LINKED, INTEGRATED SERVICES: INTERDEPENDENT, POSTMODERN PROCESSES

The three processes of reform in human services discussed in this chapter thus far have been presented as part of a broader set of transformations described as postmodern and interdependent, as none of the three can be fully realized without corresponding changes in the structure and systems represented in the other two. Examples of these processes in operation at particular school sites, in conjunction with school–community partnership arrangements (Sailor, 1994a, 1994b), have been discussed illustrating these interdependent linkages under the rubric New Community School.

The basic premise of New Community School is interdependence. In the modern era, we have tried to address human assistance needs categorically, that is, in isolation, as if each identifiable problem could be solved with a specific serial program. In postmodern structures, human problems are viewed more systemically. There is recognition that interconnectedness exists across all aspects of human endeavor, and that forces affecting behavior can be complex and extend across numerous environments and relationships.

The interdependence that can be observed in social reform processes can be traced in part to economics. It simply becomes increasingly expensive to address human support needs as if their associated "problems" existed in a state of isolation from other aspects of life. Because the factors that contribute to the need for supports are complex, attempts to address needs in isolation mean fewer and fewer tangible returns for increased expenditures. For example, schools in many parts of America have special programs to combat drug abuse. Funding for these programs has increased, reflecting corresponding increases in the magnitude of the drug abuse problem. But schools are only one place where social problems affected by drug abuse are manifest. Positive outcome data from expenditures addressed to that discreet problem are linked to much broader school–community factors than can be addressed solely in a schools-based program.

Special education offers a case in point. Addressing the learning support needs of people with disabilities *in isolation*, without attention to interdependent factors affecting their socialization, that is, their ability to work independently and exist in mainstream community life, has led to an increasing "backlash" concerning the rising costs of special education relative to the outcomes gained (Shapiro, Loeb, & Bowermaster, 1993).

In New Community Schools, inclusion is not an end in itself. The question of whether or even how to include, for example, a child with severe behavior disorders in a general classroom must go well beyond the specific and isolated concerns of special educators to come into better compliance with the *least restrictive environment* (LRE) precept of the IDEA. The adjustments necessary to successfully include such students are necessarily schoolwide and linked to support structures in the community as well. Inclusion under this concept is but one factor in a much larger framework of system restructuring that is geared to more effective utilization of all supports to increase educational outcomes for all students.

To recapitulate briefly, the key ingredients of public policy transformations that make up the New Community School concept are

1. *School-linked services integration:* A school–community partnership arrangement that addresses human support needs in a broader social context and that is consumer rather than agency empowering
2. *School restructuring:* General education reform processes that utilize the collective strengths of school staff through collaborative planning and governance structures, to better address the needs of all students
3. *Inclusive education:* Reform processes in special education that apply the specialized supports and technology of that discipline in an integrated context that enhances the education of all students at the school while supporting specific students in the mainstream of general education.

Efforts to effect the inclusion of students with disabilities, particularly those with severe behavior disorders, are unlikely to succeed beyond isolated demonstrations in a few places, if such efforts are driven by special education and are not perceived as having value for broader objectives of the total school program. Where such efforts, however, are consistent with a schoolwide program of restructuring and school–community partnership arrangements, then the process is likely to advance, particularly if the support needs of the student are viewed as a problem for the *school* to solve, not just special education.

New Community Schools exemplify these processes. First, they are unified schools. Special education as well as the other categorical supports are fully integrated and coordinated so that each program can support its identified students while meeting the total support needs of the school at the same time. Second, such schools are governed by collaborative team arrangements that empower teachers as well as parents at the same time as they draw upon their expertise and creative energy. The services within the school are harnessed and "wrapped around" the students with need for special assistance while the needs of the child and family in the community are similarly addressed through services coordination and use of a single point of contact. A child who needs a program of positive behavioral support both at school and in the community can have a single, focused effort applied under this arrangement with the incorporation of the IEP within the broader family services support plan under the integrated services arrangement.

New Community Schools are thus postmodern. The processes of voice and collaboration are in evidence at these schools. New Community Schools form one component of a comprehensive, integrated services arrangement that places the family at the hub of the wheel. The school performs its particular functions in combination with health, social, and other human assistance services within the community, thus helping to empower families to better manage their resources and to enjoy a higher quality of life in a postmodern society.

REFERENCES

Americans with Disabilities Act of 1990 (ADA), PL 101-336. (July 26, 1990). Title 42, U.S.C. 12101 et seq: *U.S. Statutes at Large, 104*, 327–378.

Baer, D.M. (1993). To disagree with Meyer and Evans is to debate a cost-benefit ratio. *Journal of The Association for Persons with Severe Handicaps, 18*(4), 235–236.

Bell, T.H. (1993). Reflections one decade after "A Nation at Risk." *Phi Delta Kappan, 74*, 592–604.

Boyer, E. (1990). *The basic school.* New York: Harper & Row.

Burrello, L.C., & Lashley, C.A. (1992). On organizing for the future: The destiny of special education. In K.A. Waldron, A.E. Riester, & J.H. Moore (Eds.), *Special education: The challenge of the future* (pp. 64–95). San Francisco: Mellen Research University Press.

Carr, E.G. (1988). Functional equivalence as a means of response generalization. In R.H. Horner, G. Dunlap, & R.L. Koegel (Eds.), *Generalization and maintenance: Life-style changes in applied settings* (pp. 221–241). Baltimore: Paul H. Brookes Publishing Co.

Carr, E.G., Levin, L., McConnachie, G., Carlson, J.I., Kemp, D.C., & Smith, C.E. (1994). *Communication-based intervention for problem behavior: A user's guide for producing positive change.* Baltimore: Paul H. Brookes Publishing Co.

Carr, E.G., Robinson, S., & Palumbo, L.W. (1990). The wrong issue: Aversive versus nonaversive treatment. The right issue: Functional versus nonfunctional treatment. In A. Repp & N. Singh (Eds.), *Perspectives on the use of nonaversive and aversive interventions for persons with developmental disabilities* (pp. 361–379). DeKalb, IL: Sycamore.

Carr, E.G., & Sailor, W. (1994). Should only positive methods be used by professionals who work with children and youth? [Response to Birnbrauer]. In M. Mason & E. Gambrill (Eds.), *Debating children's lives: Current controversies on children and adolescents* (pp. 250–254). Thousand Oaks, CA: Sage Publications.

Clark, R.M. (1989). *The role of parents in assuring education success in restructuring efforts.* Washington, DC: Council of Chief State School Officers.

Council of Chief State School Officers (CCSSO). (1989). *Success for all in a new century: A report by the Council of Chief State School Officers on restructuring education.* Washington, DC: Author.

Council on School Performance Standards. (1989). *Preparing Kentucky youth for the next century: What students should know and be able to do and how learning should be assessed.* Report of the Council on School Performance Standards, Frankfort, KY, presented to Governor Wallace G. Wilkinson, the Kentucky General Assembly, the Superintendent of Public Instruction, and the State Board for Elementary and Secondary Education.

Crowson, R.L., & Boyd, W.L. (1993). Coordinated services for children: Designing arks for storms and seas unknown. *American Journal of Education, 101,* 140–170.

Darling-Hammond, L. (1990). Teachers and teaching: Signs of a changing profession. In R. Houston, M. Haberman, & J. Sikula (Eds.), *Handbook of research on teacher education* (pp. 267–290). New York: Macmillan.

Darling-Hammond, L., & Berry, B. (1988). *The evolution of teacher policy.* Santa Monica, CA: RAND.

Day, W.F. (1988). Hermeneutics and behaviorism. *American Psychologist, 43,* 129.

Derrida, J. (1976). *Of grammatology.* Baltimore: Johns Hopkins University Press.

Dewey, J. (1982). The development of American pragmatism. In H.S. Thayer (Ed.), *Pragmatism: The classic readings* (pp. 253–336). Indianapolis, IN: Hackett.

Dewey, J. (1990). *The school and society and the child and the curriculum.* Chicago: University of Chicago Press.

Dougher, M.J. (1993). Interpretive and hermeneutic research methods in the contextualistic analysis of verbal behavior. In S.C. Hayes, L.J. Hayes, H.W. Reese, & T.R. Sarbin (Eds.), *Varieties of scientific contextualism* (pp. 211–221). Reno, NV: Context Press.

Education for All Handicapped Children Act of 1975, PL 94-142. (August 23, 1975). Title 20, U.S.C. 1401 et seq: *U.S. Statutes at Large, 89,* 773–796.

Elmore, R.F. (1988). *Early experience in restructuring schools: Voices from the field.* Washington, DC: National Governors' Association.

Evans, I.M. (1993). Constructional perspectives in clinical assessment. *Psychological Assessment, 5,* 264–272.

Ewert, G.D. (1991). Habermas and education: A comprehensive overview of the influence of Habermas in educational literature. *Review of Educational Research, 61,* 345–378.

Fawcett, S.B. (1991). Some values guiding community research and action. *Journal of Applied Behavior Analysis, 24,* 621–636.

Ferguson, D.L., & Ferguson, P.M. (1993). Postmodern vexations: A reply to Meyer and Evans. *Journal of The Association for Persons with Severe Handicaps, 18*(4), 237–239.

Firestone, W.A., Fuhrman, S.H., & Kirst, M.W. (1989). *The progress of reform: An appraisal of state education initiatives.* New Brunswick, NJ: Center for Policy Research in Education.

Fuchs, D., & Fuchs, L.S. (1994). Inclusive schools movement and the radicalization of special education reform. *Exceptional Children, 60*(4), 294–309.

Gartner, A., & Lipsky, D.K. (1987). Beyond special education: Toward a quality system for all students. *Harvard Educational Review, 57,* 367–395.

Gerry, M.H., & Certo, N.J. (1992). Current activity at the federal level and the need for service integration. *The Future of Children, 2*(1), 118–126.

Goals 2000: Educate America Act of 1994, PL 103-227. (March 1994). Title 20, U.S.C. 5801: *U.S. Statutes at Large, 108,* 125–280.

Goerner, S.J. (Ed.). (1994). *Chaos and the evolving ecological universe.* Langhorne, PA: Gordon and Breach.

Hallinger, P., Murphy, J., & Hausman, C. (1992). Restructuring schools: Principals' perceptions of fundamental educational reform. *Educational Administration Quarterly, 28*(3), 330–349.

Honig, W. (1987, April). *Honig Advisory Committee Meeting.* Sacramento, CA.

Horner, R.H., Diemer, S.M., & Brazeau, K.C. (1992). Educational support for students with severe problem behaviors in Oregon: A descriptive analysis from the 1987–1988 school year. *Journal of The Association for Persons with Severe Handicaps, 17*(3), 154–169.

Horner, R.H., Dunlap, G., Koegel, R.L., Carr, E.G., Sailor, W., Anderson, J., Albin, R.W., & O'Neill, R.E. (1990). Toward a technology of "nonaversive" behavioral support. *Journal of The Association for Persons with Severe Handicaps, 15*(3), 125–132.

Horner, R.H., Sprague, J.R., & Flannery, K.B. (1993). Building functional curricula for students with severe intellectual disabilities and severe problem behaviors. In R. Van Houten & S. Axelrod (Eds.), *Behavior analysis and treatment* (pp. 47–71). New York: Plenum Press.

Hoshmand, L.T., & Polkinghorne, D.E. (1992). Redefining the science-practice relationship and professional training. *American Psychologist, 47*(1), 55–66.

Individuals with Disabilities Education Act of 1990 (IDEA), PL 101-476. (October 30, 1990). Title 20, U.S.C. 1400 et seq: *U.S. Statutes at Large, 104,* 1103–1151.

James, W. (1948). Pragmatism's conception of truth. In A. Castell (Ed.), *Essays in Pragmatism.* New York: Hafner.

Johnson, D.W., & Johnson, R.T. (1990). Social skills for successful group work. *Educational Leadership, 47*(4), 29–33.

Kagan, S.L., & Neville, P.R. (1993). *Integrating human services: Understanding the past to shape the future.* New Haven, CT: Yale University Press.

Kaiser, A.P. (1993). Understanding human behavior: Problems of science and practice. *Journal of The Association for Persons with Severe Handicaps, 18*(4), 240–242.

Kauffman, J.M. (1989). The Regular Education Initiative as Reagan-Bush education policy: A trickle-down theory of education of the hard-to-teach. *Journal of Special Education, 23*(3), 256–278.

Kelly, M., & Maynard-Moody, S. (1993). Policy analysis in the post-positivist era: Engaging stakeholders in evaluating the Economic Development Districts program. *Public Administration Review, 53*(2), 135–142.

Kentucky School Reform Act. (1990). House Bill 940. *Kentucky Revised Statutes.*

Kirst, M.W. (1989). *The progress of reform: An appraisal of state education initiatives.* New Brunswick, NJ: Center for Policy Research in Education.

Kirst, M.W. (1992). *Financing school-linked services* (Policy Brief #7). Los Angeles: Center for Research in Education Finance, University of Southern California.

Kuhn, T. (1970). *The structure of scientific revolutions* (2nd ed.). Chicago: University of Chicago Press.

Lipsky, D.K., & Gartner, A. (Eds.). (1989). *Beyond separate education: Quality education for all.* Baltimore: Paul H. Brookes Publishing Co.

Lucyshyn, J.M., & Albin, R.W. (1993). Comprehensive support to families of children with disabilities and behavior problems. In G.H.S. Singer & L.E. Powers (Eds.), *Families, disability, and empowerment: Active coping skills and strategies for family intervention* (pp. 365–407). Baltimore: Paul H. Brookes Publishing Co.

McLaughlin, M.J., & Warren, S.H. (1992). *Issues & options in restructuring schools and special education programs.* Reston, VA: Council for Exceptional Children.

Melaville, A.I., & Blank, M.J. (1991). *What it takes: Structuring interagency partnerships to connect children and families with comprehensive services.* Washington, DC: Education & Human Services Consortium.

Meyer, L.H., & Evans, I.M. (1993). Science and practice in behavioral intervention: Meaningful outcomes, research validity, and usable knowledge. *Journal of The Association for Persons with Severe Handicaps, 18*(4), 224–234.

Morrill, W.A., & Gerry, M.H. (1990, February). *Integrating the delivery of services to school-aged children at risk: Toward a description of American experience and experimentation.* Washington, DC: U.S. Department of Education.

Morris, E.K. (1993). Revise and resubmit. *Journal of The Association for Persons with Severe Handicaps, 18*(4), 243–248.

Mulick, J.A. (1994). Should only positive methods be used by professionals who work with children and youth? No. In M.A. Mason & E. Gambrill (Eds.), *Debating children's lives: Current controversies on children and adolescents* (pp. 228–236). Thousand Oaks, CA: Sage Publications.

Murphy, J. (1993). Restructuring: In search of a movement. In J. Murphy & P. Hallinger (Eds.), *Restructuring schooling: Learning from ongoing efforts* (pp. 1–31). Newbury Park, CA: Corwin Press.

Murphy, J., & Hallinger, P. (1993). *Restructuring schooling: Learning from ongoing efforts.* Newbury Park, CA: Corwin Press.

National Association of State Boards of Education. (1992). *Winners all: A call for inclusive schools.* Washington, DC: NASBE Study Group on Special Education.

National Commission on Excellence in Education. (1983). *A nation at risk: The imperative for educational reform.* Washington, DC: U.S. Government Printing Office.

New Beginnings: A feasibility study of integrated services for children and families. (1990). San Diego: City of San Diego Public Schools.

Packard Foundation. (1992). *The future of children. Vol. 2: School-linked services.* Los Altos, CA: Center for the Future of Children.

Paul, J., & Rosselli, H. (1995). Integrating the parallel reforms in general and special education. In J.L. Paul, H. Rosselli, & D. Evans (Eds.), *Integrating school restructuring and special education reform* (pp. 188–213). Ft. Worth, TX: Harcourt Brace Jovanovich.

Paul, J., Yang, A., Adiegbola, M., & Morse, W. (1995). Rethinking the mission and methods: Philosophies for educating children and the teachers who teach them. In J.L. Paul, H. Rosselli, & D. Evans (Eds.), *Integrating school restructuring and special education reform* (pp. 9–29). Ft. Worth, TX: Harcourt Brace Jovanovich.

Pepper, S. (1946). *World hypotheses: Prolegomena to systematic philosophy and a complete survey of metaphysics.* Berkeley: University of California Press.

Rehabilitation Act of 1973, PL 93-112. (September 26, 1973). Title 29, U.S.C. 701 et seq: *U.S. Statutes at Large, 87*, 355–394.

Repp, A., & Singh, N. (Eds.). (1990). *Perspectives on the use of nonaversive and aversive interventions for persons with developmental disabilities.* Sycamore, IL: Sycamore.

Rhodes, W., Danforth, S., & Smith, T. (1995). Inventing the future: Paradigmatic, programmatic and political challenges in restructuring education. In J.L. Paul, H. Rosselli, & D. Evans (Eds.), *Integrating school restructuring and special education reform* (pp. 214–236). Ft. Worth, TX: Harcourt Brace Jovanovich.

Riger, S. (1992). Epistemological debates, feminist voices: Science, social values, and the study of women. *American Psychologist, 47*, 730–740.

Rorty, R. (1991a). *Objectivity, relativism, and truth: Philosophical papers* (Vol. 1). Cambridge, England: Cambridge University Press.

Rorty, R. (1991b). Inquiry as recontextualization: An anti-dualist account of interpretation. In D. Hiley, J. Bohman, & R. Shusterman (Eds.), *The interpretive turn: Philosophy, science, culture* (pp. 59–80). Ithaca, NY: Cornell University Press.

Rowland, R.C. (in press). In defense of rational argument: A pragmatic justification of argumentation theory and response to the postmodern critique. *Philosophy and Rhetoric, 28*(4).

Sage, D.D., & Burrello, L.C. (1994). *Leadership in educational reform: An administrator's guide to changes in special education.* Baltimore: Paul H. Brookes Publishing Co.

Sailor, W. (1991). Special education in the restructured school. *Remedial and Special Education, 12*(6), 8–22.

Sailor, W. (1994a). New community schools: Issues for families in three streams of reform. *Coalition Quarterly, 11*(3), 4–7.

Sailor, W. (1994b). Services integration: Parent empowerment through school/community partnerships. *Coalition Quarterly, 11*(3), 11–13.

Sailor, W., Anderson, J., Halvorsen, A., Doering, K.F., Filler, J., & Goetz, L. (1989). *The comprehensive local school: Regular education for all students with disabilities.* Baltimore: Paul H. Brookes Publishing Co.

Sailor, W., & Carr, E.G. (1994). Should only positive methods be used by professionals who work with children and youth? Yes. In M. Mason & E. Gambrill (Eds.), *Debating children's lives: Current controversies on children and adolescents* (pp. 225–227). Thousand Oaks, CA: Sage Publications.

Sailor, W., Gerry, M., & Wilson, W.C. (1993). Disability and school integration. In T. Husen & T.N. Postlethwaite (Eds.), *International encyclopedia of education: Research and studies* (2nd suppl., pp. 175–195). New York: Pergamon Press.

Sailor, W., Goetz, L., Anderson, J., Hunt, P., & Gee, K. (1988). Research on community intensive instruction as a model for building functional, generalized skills. In R.H. Horner, G. Dunlap, & R.L. Koegel (Eds.), *Generalization and maintenance: Life-style changes in applied settings* (pp. 67–98). Baltimore: Paul H. Brookes Publishing Co.

Sailor, W., Kleinhammer-Tramill, J., Skrtic, T., & Oas, B. (1996). Family participation in New Community Schools. In G.H.S. Singer, L.E. Powers, & A.L. Olson (Eds.), *Redefining family support: Innovations in public–private partnerships* (pp. 313–332). Baltimore: Paul H. Brookes Publishing Co.

Sailor, W., & Skrtic, T. (1995). American education in the postmodern era. In J.L. Paul, H. Rosselli, & D. Evans (Eds.), *Integrating school restructuring and special education reform* (pp. 418–432). Ft. Worth, TX: Harcourt Brace Jovanovich.

Sampson, E.E. (1993). Identity politics: Challenges to psychology's understanding. *American Psychologist, 48*(12), 1219–1230.

Schlechty, P. (1989). *Creating the infrastructure for reform.* Washington, DC: Council of Chief State School Officers.

Schroeder, S.R., Oldenquist, A., & Rojahn, J. (1990). A conceptual framework for judging the humaneness and effectiveness of behavioral treatment. In A. Repp & N. Singh (Eds.), *Perspectives on the use of nonaversive and aversive interventions for persons with developmental disabilities* (pp. 103–118). Sycamore, IL: Sycamore.

Searle, J. (1983, October 27). The world turned upside down. *New York Times Book Review,* 74–79.

Seligman, M. (1975). *Helplessness: On depression, development, and death.* San Francisco: W.H. Freeman.

Semmel, M.I., Gerber, M.M., & MacMillan, D.L. (1994). Twenty-five years after Dunn's article: A legacy of policy analysis research in special education. *Journal of Special Education, 27*(4), 481–495.

Shapiro, J.P., Loeb, P., & Bowermaster, D. (1993). Separate and unequal. *U.S. News & World Report, V*(23), 46–60.

Shriner, J.G., Ysseldyke, J.E., & Thurlow, M.L. (1994). Standards for all American students. *Focus on Exceptional Children, 26*(5).

Shriner, J.G., Ysseldyke, J.E., Thurlow, M.L., & Honetschlager, D. (1994). "All" means "all." *Educational Leadership, 51*(6), 38–43.

Skrtic, T. (1988). The organizational context of special education. In E. Meyen & T. Skrtic (Eds.), *Exceptional children and youth: An introduction* (3rd ed., pp. 479–517). Denver, CO: Love.

Skrtic, T.M. (1991a). *Behind special education: A critical analysis of professional culture and school organization.* Denver: Love.

Skrtic, T.M. (1991b). The special education paradox: Equity as the way to excellence. *Harvard Educational Review, 61*(2), 148–206.

Slavin, R.E. (1990). General education under the regular education initiative: How must it change? *Remedial and Special Education, 11*(3), 40–50.

Slavin, R.E., & Madden, N.A. (1989). What works for students at risk: A research synthesis. *Educational Leadership, 46*, 14–20.

Snell, M.E. (1991). Schools care for all kids: The importance of integration for students with severe disabilities and their peers. In J.W. Lloyd, A.C. Rapp, & N.N. Singh (Eds.), *The Regular Education Initiative: Alternative perspectives on concepts, issues and models.* Sycamore, IL: Sycamore.

Stainback, W., & Stainback, S. (1984). A rationale for the merger of special and regular education. *Exceptional Children, 51*, 102–111.

Strategic partnership for urban revitalization (SPUR): Austin's nomination and strategic plan for an empowerment zone (1994). Proposal presented to the City of Austin and Travis County, Texas.

Turnbull, A.P., Ruef, M., & Reeves, C. (1993). *Family perspectives on life style issues for individuals, a problem behavior.* Unpublished manuscript, Beach Center on Families and Disability, University of Kansas, Lawrence.

Turnbull, A.P., & Turnbull, H.R. (1990). A tale about lifestyle changes: Comment on "Toward a technology of 'nonaversive' behavioral support." *Journal of The Association for Persons with Severe Handicaps, 15*(3), 142–144.

Turnbull, A.P., Turnbull, H.R., Shank, M., & Leal, D. (1995). *Exceptional lives: Special education in today's schools.* Englewood Cliffs, NJ: Merrill/Prentice Hall.

Tyack, D. (1993). School governance in the United States: Historical puzzles and anomalies. In J. Hannaway & M. Carnoy (Eds.), *Decentralization and school improvement: Can we fulfill the promise?* San Francisco: Jossey-Bass.

Vergason, G.A., & Anderegg, M.L. (1989). An answer to The Regular Education Initiative: A force for change in general and special education. *Education and Training in Mental Retardation, 24*(1), 100–101.

Wang, M.C., Reynolds, M., & Walberg, H. (1988, November). Integrating the children of the second system. *Phi Delta Kappan, 44*(1), 26–31.

Will, M.C. (1986). Educating students with learning problems: A shared responsibility. *Exceptional Children, 42*, 411–415.

York, J. (1994). A shared agenda for educational change. *TASH Newsletter, 20*(2), 10–11.

Ysseldyke, J., Thurlow, M., & Shriner, J. (1992). Outcomes are for special educators too. *Teaching Exceptional Children, 25*(1), 36–50.

9

Reducing Corporal Punishment with Elementary School Students Using Behavioral Diagnostic Procedures

Connie C. Taylor and Jon S. Bailey

Corporal punishment has a long and controversial history, with foundations in religious, historical, and legal perspectives. The early colonists in America often quoted the Bible as the justification for paddling children. The familiar phrase, "spare the rod and spoil the child," is only one of many scripture verses endorsing the use of

The authors thank the faculty and staff of the elementary school for their participation and cooperation throughout the study. They gratefully acknowledge the efforts of everyone who assisted in data collection including Jodi Butler, Karie Gabik, Tami Knott, Allan McConnell, Ken Wagner, Anja Wulf, Frances Beck, Paulette Kunz, Felix Munoz, and Carrie Pierce.

physical punishment (Cryan, 1987; Wilson, 1982). These beliefs appeared to set the tone for early American educational practices. Corporal punishment was commonly accepted and freely dispensed. A list of consequences implemented in the late 1800s stated: "For boys and girls playing together, four lashes; for failing to bow at the entrance of strangers, three lashes; for blotting copy book, two lashes; for scuffling, four lashes; for calling each other names, three lashes" (Cryan, 1987).

With its roots in English law, the concept of *in loco parentis* ("in place of parents") gave responsibility to teachers to act as parents in their absence (Cryan, 1987; Wilson, 1982). Although the court struck down the concept of *in loco parentis*, which would have limited paddling in schools (*Glaser v. Marietta*, 1972), subsequent cases reaffirmed the states' right to use corporal punishment as a means of maintaining control in the classroom (Cryan, 1987). In contemporary America, a significant number of parents strongly disapprove of the use of corporal punishment, and many school districts are restricting or prohibiting its use altogether.

Behavior analysis methodology, which has evolved over the past 25 years, can provide an alternative to the use of corporal punishment to deal with challenging behavior. Research in the treatment of severe challenging behavior has emphasized the use of extensive behavioral assessments to determine the factors that appear to produce the challenging behavior. Functional assessments (Iwata, Dorsey, Slifer, Bauman, & Richman, 1982) involve the presentation of specially designed analog sessions in which it can be determined if any given challenging behavior is maintained by attention, escape or avoidance, automatic stimulation, or other contingencies of reinforcement (Carr & Durand, 1985; Day, Rea, Schussler, Larsen, & Johnson, 1988; Repp, Felce, & Barton, 1988). In addition to these experimental methods of determining factors controlling behavior, descriptive analyses (Bijou, Peterson, & Ault, 1968) are becoming more widely used (Touchette, MacDonald, & Langer, 1985; Wahler & Fox, 1981). A major limitation of an experimental functional analysis is the degree of control necessary to discover the maintaining variables. Also, an experimental analysis does not determine the degree of generalization to natural conditions under which the behavior occurs (Sasso et al., 1992). Descriptive analyses provide only correlational data but offer the advantage of being more easily conducted in natural environments by nonexperimental personnel (e.g., teachers). Sasso et al. (1992) determined with precise comparative data that descriptive analyses yielded the same conclusions as the more rigorous functional analysis.

Variables that produce behavior are generally conceptualized as falling into two types: 1) reinforcement contingencies, and 2) setting events. Interventions based on contingencies have a long tradition (Hall, Lund, & Jackson, 1968; Porterfield, Herbert-Jackson, & Risley, 1976) and constitute the standard method of behavior change in behavior analysis. The analysis of setting events and the development of appropriate setting event interventions are more recent innovations (Kennedy & Itkonen, 1993). Setting events are those activities or occurrences that may increase the likelihood of a specific behavior occurring (Baer, Wolf, & Risley, 1987). Setting events include *preceding* and *concurrent* variables (Gerwirtz, 1972). Preceding variables include such variables as whether the student had a good night's sleep, ate breakfast before coming to school, or was involved in an altercation on the bus. Concurrent variables include such things as the way an instructional task is presented to a child or whether the student has a comfortable desk and curriculum materials geared to his or her academic level. Bailey and Pyles (1989) have referred to the analysis of both setting events and the effects of contingencies of reinforcement as *behavioral diagnostics* and recommend a thorough search for any and all variables that may affect behavior. (For a detailed explanation of the relationship between setting events and problem behavior, see Chapter 16.) The research to date comparing and evaluating descriptive and functional analyses has been conducted exclusively with individuals with conditions such as autism (Sasso et al., 1992), retardation (Kennedy & Itkonen, 1993; Lalli, Browder, Mace, & Brown, 1993), and severe emotional disturbance/schizophrenia/attention deficit disorder (Dunlap, Kern-Dunlap, Clarke, & Robbins, 1991).

This chapter describes a method developed by the authors of extending the assessment and intervention technology to typically developing elementary school students who present challenges of sufficient frequency or magnitude that they are repeatedly sent to the principal's office for paddling. An extensive descriptive analysis was conducted for each child in the study, and individualized interventions combining setting events and contingencies were implemented. These diagnostic-based interventions were evaluated in general education classrooms in an attempt to reduce behaviors that resulted in corporal punishment.

THE SCHOOL ENVIRONMENT
AND PARTICIPANT SELECTION PROCESS

The first author, while serving as a school psychologist at a rural elementary school in north Florida, was asked by the principal to explore "alternatives" to the use of corporal punishment. Initial possibilities the principal suggested included the use of a time-out room, picking up trash from the school grounds, or physical exercise. The school served approximately 600 students in kindergarten through fifth grade. Approximately 80% of the students were Caucasian and 20% were African American. The principal was a Caucasian male who had served in that position for the previous 15 years.

Teachers sent children to the principal's office, at the teachers' discretion, for disruptive and aggressive behaviors. The principal determined and administered the disciplinary action for each student. Pilot data collected during the 1990–1991 school year indicated that corporal punishment (paddling on the buttocks) was the most frequent disciplinary action taken by school administrators (52%) followed by stern lectures about the inappropriateness of the behavior (41%) and severe warnings about the possible use of paddling (36%). (Lectures and warnings were often delivered simultaneously.) Seventy-six percent of the students who were paddled were Caucasian and 24% were African American. Eighty-nine percent of the students receiving corporal punishment were male and 11% were female.

The participant selection process included a variety of measures to identify children who frequently exhibited disruptive and maladaptive behaviors in the classroom. Initially, all students who had been previously paddled by school officials were identified from student discipline records maintained by the school principal. Next, the teachers of those students completed the Child Behavior Checklist (CBCL) (Achenbach & Edelbrock, 1983), which resulted in standardized ratings of each child's classroom behavior. Finally, brief observations were conducted on each of these students to assess rates of occurrence of various kinds of behaviors. Seven children who 1) had been paddled one or more times during the present school year, 2) scored above the 90th percentile (near or within the clinical range) on three or more scales of the CBCL, and 3) displayed frequent disruptive and maladaptive behaviors during informal observations were chosen as participants for the intervention.

The format of the study was explained to the students in a manner they could understand. In addition, the students and their parents were asked to sign an assent form agreeing to participate in the activities according to the rules presented. The current chapter presents three students, Bob, Joe, and Alex, as representative samples from the study.

Three Students with Challenging Behaviors

Bob was a 7-year-old African American student in the second grade. He was described as immature, fidgety, disliked, and disobedient. According to his teacher, he often engaged in fights with peers, made noises in class, had trouble finishing his work, and demanded frequent attention. Discipline records from the 1990–1991 school year indicate Bob was sent to the office on four occasions. He was lectured once, his mother was contacted once, and he was paddled twice. Bob's teacher was female and in her early 40s. She had 21 years of teaching experience.

Joe was an 8-year-old Caucasian student in the second grade. He was described as destructive, impulsive, aggressive, and fidgety. He talked out of turn, disturbed others, had difficulty concentrating, and frequently failed to finish his work. Joe was sent to the office on five occasions during the 1990–1991 school year. He was lectured twice and paddled three times. Joe's teacher was female and in her early 40s. She had 20 years of teaching experience.

Alex was a 6-year-old Caucasian student in the first grade. He was described as immature, hyperactive, argumentative, and disobedient. Reportedly, he had trouble concentrating, talked out of turn, disturbed others, and engaged in many fights. Discipline records indicate Alex was sent to the office six times during the 1990–1991 school year. He was lectured twice and paddled four times. His teacher was female and approximately 45 years old. She had 21 years of teaching experience.

DIAGNOSTIC METHOD

Behavioral diagnostics (Bailey & Pyles, 1989; Pyles & Bailey, 1990, 1991) is an assessment approach that stresses the importance of determining antecedent, setting event, and consequence factors that may "cause" a target behavior. In an attempt to determine the factors likely to produce the targeted behaviors, several measures were completed before any treatments were begun. Initially, the first author interviewed the teacher of each student for approximately 45 minutes and asked a series of basic diagnostic questions, which addressed factors including situational variables, setting events, physiological variables, and operant variables (see Figure 1). The teachers were asked to document major disruptive events by completing antecedent and consequent checklists (see Figure 2). They also completed daily checklists indicating the presence or absence of minor disruptive behaviors across different class periods. This information was used to compile pattern analyses for each participant that were visually inspected to identify patterns of inappropriate behavior. This overall strategy is illustrated in Figure 3, where a variety of methods of gaining important diagnostic information is compiled and results in a multifaceted treatment approach.

Baseline Observations

Prior to any treatment, formal direct observations were conducted in the classroom on each of the target children. Observation sessions were 25–30 minutes in length. An observation code was utilized to accurately record rates of occurrence of disruptive student behavior. Data were collected by trained undergraduate students. Observers and teachers were blind to the purpose and stages of the study. The observers were trained in the use of the coding system by the first author by studying videotapes filmed in the actual school settings of interest. Eleven 2-hour training sessions were held over a 1-month period. Data collection began once observers demonstrated a minimum occurrence reliability rate of 85% for three consecutive sessions.

Behavioral Diagnosis and Treatment: School Version

Student_____ Target Behavior_____

1. Situational Variables

❑ Is there any circumstance under which the behavior does NOT occur?
❑ Is there any circumstance under which the behavior ALWAYS occurs?
❑ Does it occur at certain times of the day?
❑ Does the behavior occur only with certain people?

━━━━━━ Recommendations ━━━━━━

2. Operant Variables

❑ Does the student engage in the behavior to gain attention? Is it peers or teacher?
❑ Does the student engage in the behavior to escape the learning situation?
❑ Does the student engage in the behavior out of boredom or lack of challenging activities or materials?
❑ Does the behavior occur antecedent to or collateral with any other behavior?
❑ Could it be related to any social or academic skills deficit?

━━━━━━ Recommendations ━━━━━━

3. Physiological Variables

❑ Does the behavior occur during certain seasons of the year?
❑ Could the client be signalling some emotional problem?
❑ Could the behavior be a side-effect of medication (e.g. tired, unsteady, upset stomach, headache, etc.)?
❑ Does the student engage in the behavior as a self-stimulation activity?

━━━━━━ Recommendations ━━━━━━

4. Other Considerations

❑ Is the behavior dangerous?
❑ Does it prevent the student from learning?
❑ Does it disrupt other students?

━━━━━━ Recommendations ━━━━━━

COMMENTS: _____

_____

INSTRUCTIONS: Review all questions prior to the development of a treatment plan. Possible antecedent factors affecting performance should be isolated in special sessions before they are implemented in the treatment plan.

Figure 1. Behavioral diagnostic questions asked during teacher interviews. (Adapted from Bailey & Pyles, 1989).

Behavioral Diagnostics for School Settings

Checklist of Antecedent and Consequent Conditions

Student: _____

Date: _____

School: _____

Teacher: _____

Person completing this form: _____

1. Describe the problem behavior: _____

   _____

2. Did the behavior result in injury? If yes, describe: _____

3. Time and duration of the behavior. Start time _____   End time _____

4. Where did the behavior occur?
   ☐ Classroom. Which one? _____   ☐ Special Area: Which one? _____
   ☐ Office area   ☐ Dining Room
   ☐ Playground   ☐ Bus
   ☐ Hallway   ☐ Other: _____

5. Which staff were present? _____

6. Name of staff(s) or student(s) the behavior was directed toward if any.
   ☐ N/A
      Staff: _____
      Student(s): _____

7. Could other students easily see or hear the event?

   ☐ No
   ☐ Yes, see what happened. About how many? _____
   ☐ Yes, hear what happened. About how many? _____

8. What type of instruction (if any) was the student receiving just prior to the event?

   ☐ None   ☐ Small group instruction
   ☐ 1:1 instruction   ☐ Small group project
   ☐ Seatwork   ☐ AV presentation
   ☐ Large group lecture   ☐ Test/Quiz
   ☐ Large group discussion   ☐ Other: _____

9. What type of activity was occurring at the time of the event?

   ☐ Math   ☐ PE
   ☐ Reading   ☐ After school program
   ☐ Social Studies   ☐ Before school program
   ☐ Language Arts   ☐ Free time
   ☐ Science   ☐ Meal time
   ☐ History   ☐ Other: _____

(continued)

Figure 2. Checklist of antecedent and consequent conditions. Adapted from Behavioral Diagnostics—Behavior Management Consultants, Inc. Schools version dated 10/1/91

Figure 2. *(continued)*

10. Did the student make any type of complaint within the hour before the behavior occurred?
    ☐ N/A
    ☐ Yes, _____

11. Did another student do or say something that might have set off the event?
    ☐ N/A
    ☐ Yes, _____

12. Did the student have any extra assignments or responsibility to meet on this day?
    ☐ N/A
    ☐ Yes, _____

13. Had the student been consequated (loss of points, corrective feedback, name on the board, etc.) for some other problem within a few minutes of the event?
    ☐ N/A
    ☐ Yes, _____

14. Was the student interrupted from doing/completing another activity?
    ☐ N/A
    ☐ Yes, _____

15. Was a request made to the student to stop doing something just before the event?
    ☐ N/A
    ☐ Yes, _____

16. Was a request made to the student to start to do something just before the event?
    ☐ N/A
    ☐ Yes, _____

17. How was the student's behavior consequated? If more than one used , indicate sequence by placing a number in each relevent box in the order that things took place.

    ☐ Ignored   ☐ Loss of privilege
    ☐ Calm, neutral discussion   ☐ Name on board
    ☐ Interrupt, redirect   ☐ Sent to another classroom
    ☐ Reprimand   ☐ Go to office
    ☐ Sit and watch   ☐ Called parent
    ☐ Time-out chair   ☐ Sent home
    ☐ Time-out room   ☐ Other: _____

18. Do you think the student's behavior resulted in a "payoff"?

    ☐ Received attention   ☐ Received help
    ☐ Avoided work or tasks   ☐ Other _____
    ☐ Self-stimulation
    ☐ Obtained desired object/activity

19. Please comment on anything else that you think is relevent to the problem:
    _____
    _____
    _____
    _____
    _____

1. Basic Diagnostic Questions

2. Antecedent & Consequent Checklist

3. Daily Checklist of Minor Disruptives

4. Pattern Analysis

5. Direct Observation with Trained Observers

Hypothesized Likely Causes

Multifaceted Treatment
taking into account:

•Stimulus control & environmental variables

•Appropriateness of academic material

•Current contingencies of reinforcement, escape & avoidance

•Skills and skill deficits of student

•Physical characteristics of student

•Peer-mediated reinforcement

Figure 3. Schematic diagram of the behavioral diagnostic approach used to reduce corporal punishment.

Individualized Treatment

The treatment chosen for each student was determined by the results of the behavioral diagnostic procedure and implemented as appropriate on an individual basis. Several factors were considered when developing the treatments. First, individual programs were designed to focus on positive behavior with the least intrusive procedures necessary. For example, consequence variables were not manipulated in cases where environmental changes alone might result in improved behavior. Second, treatments were designed to be efficient, cost-effective, and endorsed by the teachers. The various treatments were intended to be easy for the teachers to understand and should have required little time to set up and implement in any school environment. They did not require extra supplies, additional personnel, or large quantities of tangible reinforcers. The following sections describe diagnostic information and classroom treatments for each of the three students.

Bob: Diagnostic Information and Classroom Treatment During the diagnostic interview, Bob's teacher said that Bob was frequently off task, had difficulty sitting still, and liked to show off. She stated he always had difficulty during less structured activities and seemed to engage in inappropriate behavior to gain attention from peers. In addition, Bob was often successful at escaping the learning situation, as he was often sent out of the room when his behavior became inappropriate. A pattern analysis of Bob's behavior across 1 week, completed by his teacher, revealed no particular pattern. Bob's teacher completed two antecedent and consequent checklists documenting major disruptive events. During both events, many peers were present, he received attention, and he avoided work. Informal observations revealed that Bob often received teacher and peer attention when he engaged in disruptive behavior. However, he received little attention for appropriate behavior.

Before the treatment began, the experimenter told Bob he would earn stickers to be placed on his special sticker sheet when he engaged in appropriate behaviors such as listening to teacher instructions and working on assigned activities. However, he would not receive stickers when he engaged in disruptive behaviors such as making noises or rocking back in his chair.

At the beginning of each observation session, a timer was set to provide an audible signal at 5-minute intervals. Each time the signal sounded, Bob was quickly observed to determine if he was engaged in the assigned activity. If he was doing what he was supposed to be doing at the moment the signal sounded, the experimenter gave him specific praise and placed a sticker in the correct box. If Bob was not engaged in the assigned activity at the moment the alarm went off, the experimenter marked an "X" in the box, explained in a neutral tone why he did not receive a sticker, and encouraged him to work for a sticker in the next interval. The stickers and Xs were recorded on a card taped to Bob's desk to provide him with immediate feedback on his behavior. If Bob met his goal at the end of the observation session, he was allowed to select a small prize from a treasure box containing a variety of items such as pencils, erasers, and stamps. Bob could earn approximately 12 stickers in an average session, with this number decreasing to 6 stickers as the intervals became longer. He was required to earn 80% of the total number of possible stickers in order to meet his goal. Near the end of the treatment, the intervals were increased from 5 to 10 minutes.

In addition, a group contingency was implemented to decrease the amount of peer attention Bob received for disruptive behavior. The experimenter explained to the class that Bob would earn each student 5 extra minutes of free time if he met his goal for that day. His peers were encouraged not to distract him while he was working or laugh at him when he did something inappropriate.

Joe: Diagnostic Information and Classroom Treatment During the diagnostic interview, Joe's teacher described him as aggressive, off task, and

Individualized programs, implemented in the classroom, can greatly reduce punishers administered by school personnel. In this photograph, the school psychologist developed a reward system based on timed intervals to increase the child's on-task behavior and decrease disruption in the class.

fidgety. She said he usually had difficulty during less structured activities such as transitions (e.g., walking to physical education class, returning to the classroom after lunch) and special area classes. Joe's teacher related that he might have engaged in disruptive behavior to get attention from peers. She also said that his inability to do his work caused much of his inappropriate behavior.

A pattern analysis of Joe's behavior across 4 weeks, completed by his teacher, indicates that he was consistently disruptive during transitions. She did not complete any antecedent and consequent checklists. Informal observations revealed that Joe frequently received teacher and peer attention when he engaged in disruptive behavior. However, he generally did not receive attention when he was engaging in appropriate behavior.

Before the treatment began, Joe's chair was moved so that he no longer sat next to the peer who consistently reinforced his inappropriate behavior. Next, the teacher modified academic assignments for Joe. She often provided activities that were more appropriate to his abilities and reduced the number of problems he was expected to complete.

During the observation sessions, Joe earned stickers and contingent positive attention (as was described for Bob) every 15 minutes. In an attempt to further reduce the frequency of disruptive behaviors, the schedule of contingent positive attention was changed to 5-minute intervals in

Session 45. Initially, Joe could earn 4 stickers in an average session. This number increased to 12 stickers once the intervals became more frequent. If Joe earned 80% of the total number of possible stickers, he was allowed to select a small prize from the experimenter's treasure box. In addition, the same group contingency implemented for Bob was used to decrease the amount of peer attention Joe received for disruptive behavior.

Finally, Joe was required to demonstrate appropriate behavior during transitions. If he did not break in line, run down the hall, or aggress against others while moving from one area in the school to another, he was allowed to spend 5 minutes working at a table in the back of the classroom making a paper airplane (previously determined to be a reinforcer for him).

Alex: Diagnostic Information and Classroom Treatment   In response to the diagnostic interview questions, Alex's teacher described him as impulsive, hyperactive, aggressive, and off task. He talked out of turn, rocked back and forth in his chair, and was frequently out of his seat. According to his teacher, Alex was usually disruptive all day and had the most trouble during large-group activities. Although Alex was placed on Ritalin in baseline Session 19 to help to manage his behavior, he continued to engage in disruptive and off-task behaviors.

Despite several prompts, Alex's teacher did not complete any pattern analyses or antecedent and consequent checklists. Informal observations revealed that Alex frequently received attention from the teacher for engaging in inappropriate behavior; therefore, the same teacher contingency plan described for Bob was used with Alex.

During the observation sessions, Alex earned stickers and contingent positive attention as was described for Bob. He was required to earn 80% of the total number of possible stickers in order to select a small prize from the experimenter's treasure box. Alex could earn approximately 12 stickers in an average session.

EXPERIMENTAL DESIGN

A multiple-baseline-across-students design (Baer, Wolf, & Risley, 1968; Bailey & Bostow, 1979; Hersen & Barlow, 1978) was used to demonstrate that the treatments were in fact effective. Treatments varied from one student to the next depending on the outcome of the individual diagnostic information.

Data Collection

Baseline Data on Child Behaviors   Data were collected in the classroom at the same time each afternoon. These particular times were chosen because the diagnostic assessments indicated it was during these periods that the students typically engaged in high rates of disruptive behavior. A

10-second partial interval time-sampling procedure was used to record the occurrence of disruptive behavior. Observers unobtrusively listened to a cueing tape through an earphone and recorded all behaviors that occurred during the 10-second interval by circling the appropriate symbol on the data sheet. Treatment sessions were approximately 60 minutes in length. However, because of variations in class activities and school schedules, observation sessions ranged from 25 to 30 minutes in length.

Disruptive behavior occurring during all or part of the 10-second interval was denoted by circling "Dis." This category included

1. Noises such as singing, humming, whistling, barking, growling, burping, or laughing for more than 2 seconds
2. Talking when it is not allowed by the teacher, interruptions, call outs, yelling across the room
3. Active, nonverbal behaviors such as tapping or pounding the desk with hands or objects, snapping fingers, scraping furniture on the floor, leaning back on two legs in the chair, kicking furniture, throwing objects across the room, swinging body or objects, destroying property, knocking things over, touching others' bodies in a nonaggressive way (e.g., touching a peer's head or arm while walking past his or her desk)

Baseline Incidents of Corporal Punishment Student discipline records were maintained by the school principal throughout the year and indicated each time a target child was paddled. This information was recorded on 4×6 cards and stated the date of the offense, a brief description of the offense, the location of the offense, and the number of times the child was struck on the buttocks. Corporal punishment was usually administered by the principal. However, during the study, teachers paddled Bob and Joe one time. State law required that an adult witness be present any time any child was paddled. The presence of a witness was verified on records maintained by the school principal.

Treatment Data on Child Behaviors and Corporal Punishment During treatment, data collection continued as described in baseline until the end of the school year. Data were collected on the occurrence of disruptive child behaviors as well as the incidents of corporal punishment.

Number of Reinforcers Earned per Student Data were also collected on the number of reinforcers earned by each student as per the individual treatment programs. Analysis of the contingent attention sticker sheets for Bob and Alex indicated these students earned a special prize on 100% of the treatment days. Joe earned a special prize and the airplane reinforcer on 86% of the treatment days.

Reliability of Direct Observations Reliability of direct observations was assessed by two observers observing independently on 45% of baseline observations and on 40% of treatment observations. Each 10-second interval on the coding sheet was scored for agreements and disagreements. Separate reliability figures assessing occurrence (both observers agree the behavior did occur during the interval) and nonoccurrence (both observers agree the behavior did not occur during the interval) were calculated for each observation category (Bailey & Bostow, 1979). Percentage of agreement among independent observers was determined by dividing the total number of agreements by the total number of agreements plus disagreements and multiplying by 100. The mean occurrence reliability for disruptive behavior was 88% with a range of 0%–100%. The mean nonoccurrence reliability was 97.8% with a range of 90%–100%.

Treatment Outcomes

The results of the direct observations assessing changes in targeted disruptive behaviors are presented first. Next, baseline rates of corporal punishment are compared to treatment rates.

Changes in Student Behavior   The number of intervals in which at least one disruptive behavior occurred during baseline and treatment conditions is presented for Bob, Joe, and Alex in Figure 4. Every participant demonstrated decreases in disruptive behaviors following implementation of the diagnostic-based treatment.

Bob engaged in a mean of 35.5 intervals scored disruptive during baseline. His data varied, ranging from 6 to 102, and showed a downward trend. Once the treatment package was introduced, he exhibited a generally stable reduction in intervals scored disruptive, and the mean decreased to 7.2 intervals scored disruptive.

Joe engaged in a mean of 36.0 intervals scored disruptive during baseline with the data ranging from 9 to 95. The mean decreased to 11.1 intervals scored disruptive during the treatment condition.

Alex's data during baseline were highly variable, resulting in a mean of 49.2 intervals scored disruptive. During the treatment condition, the mean decreased to a stable level of 5.0 intervals scored disruptive.

Reductions in Corporal Punishment   The frequency of corporal punishment per week for all participants is presented in the top of Figure 5. The overall rate of corporal punishment in baseline was .53 incidents per week. The rate decreased to zero incidents per week during treatment. In total, there were 17 paddlings before and zero paddlings after treatment was implemented (see bottom of Figure 5 for individual rates). In every case, the rate per week was reduced.

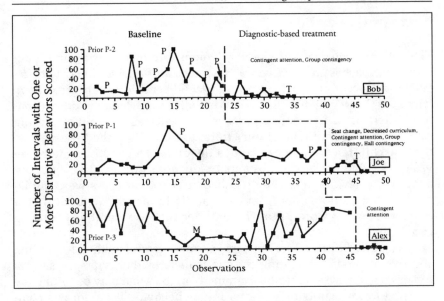

Figure 4. Frequency of intervals scored with disruptive behavior for all participants across baseline and treatment conditions. (P = corporal punishment administered; T = change in contingent attention schedule; M = first day of Ritalin.)

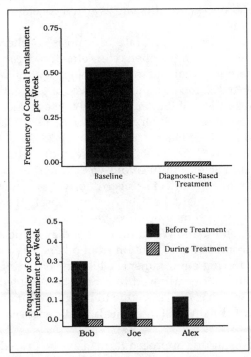

Figure 5. The top figure is the frequency of corporal punishment per week for all participants across baseline and treatment conditions. The bottom figure is the individual rates of corporal punishment per week before and during treatment. (Black bar represents rates before treatment, striped bar represents data during treatment.)

CONCLUSIONS

The data presented in this chapter demonstrate that a behavioral diagnostic approach is an effective way to determine variables likely to be related to the occurrence of inappropriate child behaviors in the classroom. Although the principal of the school initially suggested the authors analyze "alternatives to corporal punishment," such as time-out or picking up trash, we chose to direct our efforts to preventing the behaviors so that the children were never sent to the office. Direct observations revealed the children made substantial reductions in disruptive and maladaptive behaviors once the diagnostic-based treatments were implemented. In addition, data from student discipline records indicate the frequency of corporal punishment declined substantially during treatment.

A diagnostic procedure appears to be a successful method for finding effective methods for treating chronic challenging behaviors for several reasons. First, it systematically examines variables that may be setting the occasion for or maintaining inappropriate behavior. Behavior is a complex combination of many factors that cannot be overlooked. In a diagnostic approach, environmental stimuli, situational events, physiological conditions, and operant contingencies are all considered in an attempt to pinpoint relevant variables.

Second, following an accurate "diagnosis" of the variables eliciting or maintaining challenging behavior, effective treatments can be designed. In the traditional classroom management literature, procedures have often been designed for the entire class, and identical consequences are applied regardless of the cause underlying a particular behavior (see, e.g., Barrish, Saunders, & Wolf, 1969; Christy, 1975; Dietz & Repp, 1973; Foxx & Shapiro, 1978; Harris & Sherman, 1973; Marholin & Steinman, 1977; Pfiffner & O'Leary, 1987). Whereas one student may have a tantrum to gain attention or avoid work, another may engage in the same behavior due to hunger or sleep deprivation. However, typical programs would consequate the behavior in precisely the same manner. Although this approach may be effective on some occasions, it is likely to be ineffective on others. When utilizing a diagnostic approach, a child who has tantrums to gain attention from others may be removed briefly from the reinforcing environment, while one engaging in an avoidance response would not be allowed to escape task-related demands. Likewise, a child who has tantrums due to hunger or fatigue would be most appropriately treated with larger meals, additional snacks, or opportunities for rest.

Third, a diagnostic approach formalizes the procedure by which the variables that might affect behavior are identified. Behavioral diagnostics is based on the analysis of several forms of data by an experienced behavior analyst. When information is systematically gathered and examined, diagnostic conclusions and treatment choices become more credible and easier to evaluate.

Finally, utilizing behavioral diagnostics should be cost-efficient because the resulting analysis suggests where and how to intervene most effectively. Although a diagnostic approach requires skilled observers to spend some time in the classroom, their presence is usually not disruptive to teachers or students. Diagnoses are more likely to be correct because a broad spectrum of factors is analyzed to determine the nature of the causal variables. Therefore, time and effort are not wasted by applying treatments arbitrarily. Given the substantial amount of time that teachers spend on discipline, a diagnostic procedure for coping with challenging behavior appears to be efficacious.

The use of a diagnostic procedure to treat recurrent challenging school-related behaviors appears to have worthwhile clinical applications. Significant decreases in inappropriate behavior could result in the elimination of the use of corporal punishment in school environments. Before the present study began, participants engaged in high levels of disruptive and maladaptive behavior and were frequently sent to the principal's office to be punished. Although they were often lectured or warned, they received corporal punishment on several occasions.

Data from the present study suggest that corporal punishment does not result in long-term improvements in classroom behavior. If it did, there would be no need for students to be paddled numerous times. Direct observations made on those occasions when corporal punishment was applied directly prior to data collection revealed that corporal punishment resulted in, at best, a reduction in inappropriate behavior only on the day it was administered. Subsequent to this study the principal adopted the methodology employed and encouraged the teachers to explore classroom-based treatments that would preclude students being sent to the office.

REFERENCES

Achenbach, T.M., & Edelbrock, C. (1983). *Manual for the Child Behavior Checklist and Revised Child Behavior Profile*. Burlington: University of Vermont, Department of Psychiatry.

Baer, D.M., Wolf, M.M., & Risley, T.R. (1968). Some current dimensions of applied behavior analysis. *Journal of Applied Behavior Analysis, 1*(1), 91–97.

Baer, D.M., Wolf, M.M., & Risley, T.R. (1987). Some still-current dimensions of applied behavior analysis. *Journal of Applied Behavior Analysis, 20*(4), 313–327.

Bailey, J.S., & Bostow, D.E. (1979). *Research methods in applied behavior analysis*. Tallahassee, FL: Copygrafix.

Bailey, J.S., & Pyles, D.A.M. (1989). Behavioral diagnostics. In E. Cipani (Ed.), *The treatment of severe behavior disorders: Behavior analysis approaches* (pp. 85–107). Washington, DC: American Association on Mental Retardation.

Barrish, H.H., Saunders, M., & Wolf, M.M. (1969). Good behavior game: Effects of individual contingencies for group consequences on disruptive behavior in a classroom. *Journal of Applied Behavior Analysis, 2*(2), 119–124.

Bijou, S.W., Peterson, R.F., & Ault, M.H. (1968). A method to integrate descriptive and experimental field studies at the level of data and empirical concepts. *Journal of Applied Behavior Analysis, 1*(2), 175–191.

Carr, E.G., & Durand, V.M. (1985). Reducing behavior problems through functional communication training. *Journal of Applied Behavior Analysis, 18*(2), 111–126.

Christy, P.R. (1975). Does the use of tangible rewards with individual children affect peer observers? *Journal of Applied Behavior Analysis, 8*(2), 187–196.

Cryan, J.R. (1987). The banning of corporal punishment: In child care, school and other educational settings in the United States. *Childhood Education, 63*(3), 146–153.

Day, R.M., Rea, J.A., Schussler, N.G., Larsen, S.E., & Johnson, W.L. (1988). A functionally based approach to the treatment of self-injurious behavior. *Behavior Modification, 12*, 565–589.

Dietz, S.M., & Repp, A.C. (1973). Decreasing classroom misbehavior through the use of DRL schedules of reinforcement. *Journal of Applied Behavior Analysis, 6*(3), 457–463.

Dunlap, G., Kern-Dunlap, L., Clarke, S., & Robbins, F.R. (1991). Functional assessment, curricular revision, and severe behavior problems. *Journal of Applied Behavior Analysis, 24*(2), 387–397.

Foxx, R.M., & Shapiro, S.T. (1978). The timeout ribbon: A nonexclusionary timeout procedure. *Journal of Applied Behavior Analysis, 11*(1), 125–136.

Gerwitz, J.L. (1972). Some contextual determinants of stimulus potency. In R.D. Parke (Ed.), *Recent developments in social learning theory* (pp. 7–33). New York: Academic Press.

Glaser v. Marietta, 35 1 F. Supp. 555 (W.D. PA. 1972) S.4.3.

Hall, R.V., Lund, D., & Jackson, D. (1968). Effects of teacher attention on student behavior. *Journal of Applied Behavior Analysis, 1*(1), 1–12.

Harris, V.M., & Sherman, J.A. (1973). Use and analysis of the "good behavior game" to reduce disruptive classroom behavior. *Journal of Applied Behavior Analysis, 6*(3), 405–417.

Hersen, M., & Barlow, D.H. (1978). *Single-case experimental designs: Strategies for studying behavior change.* New York: Pergamon Press.

Iwata, B., Dorsey, M., Slifer, K., Bauman, K., & Richman, G. (1982). Toward a functional analysis of self-injury. *Analysis and Intervention in Developmental Disabilities, 2*, 3–20.

Kennedy, C.H., & Itkonen, T. (1993). Effects of setting events on the problem behavior of students with severe disabilities. *Journal of Applied Behavior Analysis, 26*(3), 321–327.

Lalli, J.S., Browder, D.M., Mace, F.C., & Brown, D.K. (1993). Teacher use of descriptive analysis data to implement interventions to decrease students' problem behaviors. *Journal of Applied Behavior Analysis, 26*(2), 227–238.

Marholin, D., & Steinman, W.M. (1977). Stimulus control in the classroom as a function of the behavior reinforced. *Journal of Applied Behavior Analysis, 10*(3), 465–478.

Pfiffner, L.J., & O'Leary, S.G. (1987). The efficacy of all-positive management as a function of the prior use of negative consequences. *Journal of Applied Behavior Analysis, 20*(3), 265–271.

Porterfield, J.K., Herbert-Jackson, E., & Risley, T.R. (1976). Contingent observation: An effective and acceptable procedure for reducing disruptive behavior of young children in a group setting. *Journal of Applied Behavior Analysis, 9*(1), 55–64.

Pyles, D.A.M., & Bailey, J.S. (1990). Diagnosing severe behavior problems. In A. Repp & N. Singh (Eds.), *Perspectives on the use of nonaversive and aversive interventions for persons with developmental disabilities*. Sycamore, IL: Sycamore Press.

Pyles, D.A.M., & Bailey, J.S. (1991). Behavioral diagnostic interventions. In J. Luiselli, J. Matson, & N. Singh (Eds.), *Comprehensive handbook of self-injury*. New York: Springer-Verlag.

Repp, A.C., Felce, D., & Barton, L.E. (1988). Basing the treatment of stereotypic and self-injurious behaviors on hypotheses of their causes. *Journal of Applied Behavior Analysis, 21*(3), 281–289.

Sasso, G.M., Reimers, T.M., Cooper, L.J., Wacker, D., Berg, W., Steege, M., Kelly, L., & Allaire, A. (1992). Use of descriptive and experimental analyses to identify the functional properties of aberrant behavior in school settings. *Journal of Applied Behavior Analysis, 25*(4), 809–821.

Touchette, P.E., MacDonald, R.F., & Langer, S.N. (1985). A scatter plot for identifying stimulus control of problem behavior. *Journal of Applied Behavior Analysis, 18*(4), 343–351.

Wahler, R.G., & Fox, J.J. (1981). Setting events in applied behavior analysis: Toward a conceptual and methodological expansion. *Journal of Applied Behavior Analysis, 14*(3), 327–338.

Wilson, F.C. (1982). A look at corporal punishment and some implications of its use. *Child Abuse and Neglect, 6*(2), 155–164.

10

Coordinating Preservice and In-Service Training of Early Interventionists to Serve Preschoolers Who Engage in Challenging Behavior

Joe Reichle, Mary McEvoy, Carol Davis, Elisabeth Rogers, Kathleen Feeley, Susan Johnston, and Kathleen Wolff

This chapter was supported in part by Grant No. H024P10017, Developing and Evaluating a Model of Inservice and Technical Assistance to Prevent Challenging Behavior in Preschoolers, from the U.S. Department of Education to the University of Minnesota, Institute on Community Integration, a University Affiliated Program.

This chapter focuses on the need to coordinate and improve preservice and in-service training (including technical assistance) for professionals who serve individuals and family members who live or work with young children who engage in challenging behavior. The chapter establishes that the number of young children who engage in challenging behavior is increasing and that current preservice and in-service activities have not kept pace with strides in instructional technology and more progressive service delivery strategies. After identifying needs in current preservice and in-service training regimens, practices are suggested that represent some of the steps needed to create a more coordinated approach to preservice and in-service training.

CHALLENGING BEHAVIOR AMONG YOUNG SCHOOL-AGE CHILDREN: A SIGNIFICANT AND GROWING PROBLEM

Challenging behavior (i.e., problem behavior, excess behavior, and behavior disorder) has been defined as "behavior emitted by an individual that results in self-injury, injury to others, causes damage to the physical environment, interferes with the acquisition of new skills or isolates the learner" (Doss & Reichle, 1991, p. 215). Retrospective analyses suggest that a significant proportion of individuals with severe challenging behaviors had onset in early childhood (Green, 1967; Schroeder, Mulick, & Rojahn, 1980); these numbers appear to be increasing in both urban and rural areas. For example, Brandenberg, Friedman, and Silver (1990) have reported that 14%–20% of typically developing and at-risk children exhibit behavioral and emotional difficulties, while other investigations have estimated that 13%–31% of young children with identified developmental disabilities have severe behavior disorders (Chess & Hassibi, 1971; Donahue & Abbas, 1971; Eaton & Menolascino, 1982). Timm (1993) has noted that families of young children described as having moderate to severe behavioral disorders have constituted the largest group of referrals to regional intervention programs across the United States. In addition, a recent Government Accounting Office (GAO) report ("Briefing," 1994) noted that unprecedented numbers of low-income children are collecting disability benefits for behavior problems. In fact, the report notes that the number of children receiving SSI (Supplemental Security Income) benefits more than doubled in 4 years from 296,300 in 1989 to 770,500 in 1993.

Unfortunately, among many who serve preschoolers who engage in challenging behavior, there is a tendency to believe that children may "outgrow" challenging behavior. This, in turn, fosters a benign ignoring of low-level repertoires of self-injury, aggression, and stereotypic behavior. Actually, there is evidence to suggest that behavior problems emitted

by preschoolers are *not* outgrown and, in fact, have a propensity to worsen over time (Green, 1967; Schroeder et al., 1980; Smeets, 1971).

CHILDREN WITH CHALLENGING BEHAVIOR ARE AT RISK FOR NOT RECEIVING A QUALITY EDUCATIONAL EXPERIENCE

Will (1984) observed that children with behavior problems do not benefit maximally from their educational placements. Among general education elementary school teachers serving children with disabilities in typical educational settings, the reason most frequently cited for returning children to a more restrictive educational placement is the emergence or persistence of a repertoire of socially motivated challenging behavior. Although there is a strong consensus that providing educational services in inclusive educational and home environments is critical, children with challenging behavior are often not included in child care and inclusive public school programs involving peers who are typically developing (Danforth & Drabman, 1989; Giangreco & Putnam, 1992; Walker & Rankin, 1983). Teachers and related services personnel report that they are faced with an overwhelming array of behavior problems that must be addressed quickly and efficiently in order to create effective and long-term inclusion opportunities. Schloss, Miller, Sedlacek, and White (1983) reported that general educators tend to have a limited tolerance for children who engage in challenging behavior. In part, this limited tolerance may account for teachers' propensity to rely more on reactive strategies (time-out, overcorrection, response cost, verbal threats, and reprimands) rather than on more proactive strategies that manipulate conditions *prior* to the individual's engagement in challenging behavior. Social workers report repertoires of challenging behavior as one of the greatest stumbling blocks in providing home-based services to preschoolers (Reichle,

1993). In fact, Carta et al. (1994) reported that challenging behaviors are the number one reason given by teachers for referring young children to special education programs.

INCREASED NEED FOR TRAINING OF EARLY INTERVENTIONISTS WHO SERVE CHILDREN WHO ENGAGE IN CHALLENGING BEHAVIOR

The educational dilemma is striking. Educators have a propensity to terminate typical educational placements for children with challenging behavior, presumably assuming that the children would be better served by professionals who have the expertise to address their needs. Unfortunately, available data suggest that professionals who serve preschoolers may also have limited expertise and confidence in implementing strategies to proactively address repertoires of challenging behavior emitted by young children. With the increasing demands for progressive educational services come critical needs for professionals to receive assistance in learning how to implement proactive assessment and intervention strategies with young children who engage in challenging behavior.

Wolff (1993) conducted a survey to examine the in-service and technical assistance needs of educators serving preschoolers in Minnesota. The 464 professionals surveyed (including special education leaders, early childhood teachers, speech-language pathologists, and school psychologists) were asked to rank areas for which additional training was needed. In order of priority, educators specified the greatest need for additional training in 1) functional communication intervention, and 2) antecedent-based intervention strategies to address challenging behavior.

In addition to the critical need for in-service training, recognition of significant preservice training needs in the area of best educational and family support practices was highlighted in a national working conference on positive approaches to the management of challenging behavior sponsored by the National Institute on Disability and Rehabilitation Research (Reichle, 1991). Among the most critical priorities identified was the prevention of emerging repertoires of challenging behaviors through improving the quality and availability of preservice and in-service training.

At first glance, one might view that we have identified a need for enhanced in-service and technical assistance. This need could be explained logically as emanating from rapid scientific advances that have led to the development of more effective assessment and intervention strategies. To some extent, this is the case. Since the mid-1970s, a technology of assessment and intervention that increasingly relies on preventive intervention strategies rather than reactive intervention strategies has emerged. At the same time the instructional technology was expanding, there were increased demands on special educators to transmit this information to general educators in the process of creating more inclusive educational environments. Lack of success in adequately transmitting information regarding this new technology has resulted in the failure to develop quality inclusive educational placements for children who engage in challenging behavior.

However, to place responsibility for the challenges that we have identified solely on the need for updating the skills of professionals would be a gross oversimplification of the real problem. The basic staff needs that we have observed suggest that a significant proportion of public school professionals are not being adequately trained at the preservice level. Gaps of knowledge and implementation skills required to work with persons who engage in challenging behavior go far beyond the need for fine tuning an existing repertoire of established professional competencies. Many of the challenges to preservice training programs involve more carefully attending to the tasks that professionals will be required to perform when they have completed their degrees.

Challenges Facing Preservice Personnel Preparation Programs

Improved preservice training addressing proactive approaches to managing challenging behavior has been forthcoming but limited at the university level (U.S. Department of Education, 1993). A principal reason for this is that preservice training programs in special education and related disciplines (e.g., speech-pathology, occupational and physical therapy, psychology) are often isolated from one another, and participants are cut off from involvement with their colleagues working in public schools.

Preservice students in education and related therapy disciplines rarely interact in courses or in practicum experiences (Rainforth, 1985), even though each of these groups of professionals must share a common base of information regarding communication, behavior management, positioning and handling, and a host of other areas. Because it is very difficult for one person to be an expert in all areas, there is a tremendous need for professionals serving young children with disabilities and their families to engage actively in a joint transdisciplinary effort in decision making and program implementation. Despite this need, Locke and Reichle (1989) reported that public school professionals often report that they work in isolation. Additionally, Courtnage and Smith-Davis (1987) reported that of the 360 higher education institutions that participated in their investigation, 48% offered no training in team collaboration. Among the most frequently cited stumbling blocks to the implementation of a collaborative model of personnel preparation are 1) confusions regarding responsibilities, 2) the absence of administrative support and structure, and 3) "turfism" regarding the ownership of courses within departments. A further reason for a lack of collaboration is the isolation of preservice training programs mentioned earlier.

Baumgart and Ferguson (1991) have emphasized the importance of refocusing university preservice instruction to place greater emphasis on team collaboration and the use of on-site team problem solving. In placing greater emphasis on applied experiences, they have suggested that it will be necessary to ensure that practica are not simply "practicing labs" but collaborative instructional settings in which the practicum student is given sufficient support to approximate a more errorless (vs. trial and error) learning environment. If this is to occur, there must be clear advantages for practicing professionals to provide this arrangement, and there must be an active collaborative interaction between university faculty and public school professionals. Inadequate training in collaboration in preservice preparation represents a critical factor in the lack of collaboration among professionals serving children in public schools (Campbell, 1987; Wolery & Dyk, 1984). Rainforth, York, and Macdonald (1992) summarized a number of benefits of a collaborative service delivery model that include 1) increased instructional time for children with disabilities (Albano, 1983; McCormick, Cooper, & Goldman, 1979), 2) improved skill acquisition (Campbell, McInerney, & Cooper, 1984; Giangreco, 1986), 3) decreased passive caregiving in general educational environments (McCormick et al., 1979), and 4) reduced conflicts among team members (York & Rainforth, 1987).

One significant stumbling block to the implementation of preservice training programs that focus on collaboration with university professionals in other disciplines and with local service providers in serving young children with challenging behavior is the manner in which U.S. Department of Education personnel preparation funding priorities are constructed. Currently within personnel preparation, there are separate grant competitions for in-service training projects (model in-service) and preservice training (master's degree personnel preparation). Within preservice training competition, an additional distinction is made between special education training programs and related services. The separation in these competitions makes it particularly challenging to fund a well-coordinated training program that seeks to commingle preservice and in-service training activities. A modification to funding priorities is warranted to more thoughtfully encourage collaboration across disciplines and across preservice and in-service activities.

In summary, university training programs in the aggregate have not done a particularly good job in developing interdisciplinary and transdisciplinary training across university departments responsible for preparing general and special educators, speech-language pathologists, physical and occupational therapists, school psychologists, and a host of other related disciplines. Additionally, the development of collaborations between universities and public schools has been very modest to date. To some extent, federal funding policy and university bureaucracies contribute to the existing problem.

Challenges Facing Effective Provision of In-Service Training and Technical Assistance

Traditionally, school districts have relied on external consultants to work with educators to design effective interventions for children with moderate and severe disabilities (including those who engage in challenging behavior). This consultation often includes a combination of limited in-service and direct aperiodic consultation after a brief amount of direct observation of the child by the consultant. Typically, consultants to a school program only become involved after a behavior problem has reached a crisis level (Reichle, 1993). At this point, technical assistance often focuses on reactive intervention strategies designed to quickly interrupt the child from damaging her- or himself or others. Unfortunately, even when more crisis-driven procedures are successful in interrupting challenging behavior, often they do not include procedures for teaching positive replacement behaviors or provisions for fading more intrusive interventions. Many times this unfortunate cycle is repeated with crisis-focused reactive procedures becoming progressively more intrusive (Nord, 1994). Consequently, the social motivation that led to the child's emission of the challenging behavior may never be addressed adequately. Because educators are only taught how to address the crisis, it is likely that, at some future point, the antecedents and consequences that led to the crisis will again occur because they may have been easily overlooked in developing the crisis intervention procedure. A more progressive model must provide on-site technical assistance to work with teachers and parents to develop a compendium of proactive strategies focused on preventing the need for crisis intervention.

The general components of in-service delivery strategies that might best meet the collaborative agenda of both preservice training programs and public school service providers have been addressed by Bailey (1989) and Campbell (1990). They concluded that the most immediate short-term in-service personnel needs are likely to be met through a continuum of in-service mechanisms that range from intensive didactic provision of information to longitudinal on-site technical assistance. There appears to be a growing consensus that longitudinal on-site technical assistance represents a critical component of any exemplary in-service training model (Fredericks & Templeman, 1990). Campbell (1990) suggested that a comprehensive package of in-service and technical assistance requires 1) the delineation of specific training needs, 2) incentives for personnel to participate, 3) clear identification of expected outcomes, and 4) supervised application of information with ongoing feedback.

OVERVIEW OF A MODEL FOR PRESERVICE AND IN-SERVICE PREPARATION OF THOSE WHO SERVE PRESCHOOLERS WITH BEHAVIOR DISORDERS

The Minnesota Early Childhood Behavior Support Project (MECBSP) is based on the premises that a core transdisciplinary group of universities and school districts can do the following:

1. Improve services in least restrictive environments for young children with emotional–behavioral problems
2. Become expert deliverers of longitudinal technical assistance and can participate in preservice instruction
3. Design and implement in-service coursework delivered to other professionals and paraprofessionals in intensive workshops that are coordinated with professional advancement
4. Implement intensive workshops and on-site training that serve both preservice and in-service students (McEvoy, Davis, & Reichle, 1993)

Furthermore, in order to be effective, the model must include incentives for participation, a clear delineation of outcomes, and the active involvement of parents.

ESTABLISHING COLLABORATIVE RELATIONSHIPS BETWEEN UNIVERSITIES AND PUBLIC SCHOOLS

The following sections discuss the efforts of the MECBSP in establishing collaborative relationships between universities and public schools in order to create strong service delivery systems for young children with challenging behavior.

Identifying Needs and Resources

The first step in generating a collaboration between any two entities is determining that the collaboration is mutually beneficial. Consequently, university personnel preparation programs must work carefully with public school professionals, administrators, and parents to identify complementary preservice and in-service needs. This initial activity requires a discussion with school district administrators and a sampling of relevant professionals and parents within the district. At this discussion, the scope and magnitude of challenging behavior along with the model of preservice, in-service, and technical assistance collaboration that might be possible between a university and a public school system are discussed openly. If there is widespread support among discussion participants for the future identification of the need, Minnesota project staff conduct a survey of school district personnel to verify that managing repertoires of challenging behavior constitutes a significant and ongoing in-service and technical assistance need.

Once evidence is accumulated that supports significant in-service and technical assistance needs and shows that a cooperative program could be mutually beneficial, the university preservice program offers to work with the school district to plan a collaborative project that can continue minimally for a 2- to 3-year period (with yearly joint reviews by the participating parties). School district administration must be willing to create adequate release time or financial compensation to establish a transdisciplinary team. Eventually, this team will assume responsibility for providing on-site technical assistance in the home and school. Additionally, team members will develop and implement a plan of longitudinal inservice for district staff in topics pertaining to developing proactive behavioral support plans for young children who engage in challenging behavior.

To create the time resources required to engage in these activities, MECBSP has encouraged participating school districts to release up to .25–.33 full-time equivalent (FTE; .20 = 1 day per week) of each of three or four public school professionals' time to participate. The university, in turn, commits the equivalent of approximately .5 FTE of a highly skilled professional (postdoctoral associate or advanced doctoral candidate) during the period of the project to provide mentoring and to work collaboratively with the team to meet its objectives. The resulting advantage for participating school districts is a decreased need for expensive external consultants whose information is often not well coordinated and difficult for practitioners to implement and troubleshoot. The advantage for the participating university program is the establishment of high-quality training sites that better support practica, applied research, and model demonstration activities.

Implementing Joint Preservice and In-Service Coursework

Rather than quickly moving to select a team of individuals who may not fully understand the scope of effort required from their involvement, participating university faculty work with school district administrators to organize an on-site, two-credit 10-week course addressing proactive approaches to managing challenging behavior. This course is open to all district staff. Staff may take the course for academic credit (at their own expense) or they may participate at no cost if they do not desire university credit. If participants take this course at their own expense, they can apply the credit toward incremental salary advancements. Additionally, this course is available to preservice students at the University of Minnesota.

Preservice graduate students can be served by community-based coursework at two levels. First, graduate students who will be candidates for practicum experience can work collaboratively with prospective public school practicum mentors and gain from the experience and knowledge that these professionals bring to the class. Second, advanced leadership graduate students can participate in the delivery of course information. Table 1 lists the competencies that students will have acquired as a result of successfully completing this course. A syllabus for this course is included in the appendix to this chapter. Although instruction in a variety of areas is of great importance, information in three areas is particularly critical to the impact of preservice and in-service coursework in developing positive behavioral support plans for young children who engage in challenging behavior. These areas are 1) recognizing that challenging behavior may serve social functions, 2) being familiar with assessment activities that can be used to determine the function of challenging behav-

Table 1. Competencies acquired as a result of successfully completing a 10-week course addressing proactive approaches to managing challenging behavior

- Students will gain an understanding of socially motivated and nonsocially motivated challenging behavior.
- Students will become familiar with a variety of medical and biological factors associated with challenging behavior.
- Students will gain an understanding of the relationship between communication and challenging behavior and will be able to identify the communicative functions served by challenging behaviors.
- Students will be able to implement the range of assessment strategies that may be used to determine the function of challenging behavior (including review of existing documents, the interview process, direct observations, and environmental manipulations).
- Students will become familiar with a series of intervention strategies for individuals who have severe communication deficits.
- Students will become familiar with the implementation of environmental rearrangements and social interaction interventions used to address challenging behaviors.
- Students will be able to implement interventions that address communicative alternatives to escape-motivated challenging behavior (request to take leave, rejecting response, request for assistance, request for attention, etc.).
- Students will be able to implement interventions that address communicative alternatives to obtain access-motivated challenging behavior (request for attention, request for assistance, request for desired items and events, etc.).
- Students will be able to implement interventions that address escape-motivated challenging behavior that cannot be honored (high-probability request sequence, tolerance for delay of reinforcement, collaboration, preferred item as distractor, etc.).
- Students will gain an understanding of a variety of prompting strategies used for each of the interventions introduced.
- Students will gain experience evaluating and troubleshooting interventions.

ior, and 3) identifying intervention options available to address socially motivated challenging behavior. Each of these is discussed briefly below.

Recognizing that Challenging Behavior May Serve Social Functions Challenging behavior may be either *socially* or *nonsocially* motivated. Behaviors that require the mediation of others in order to be consequated are referred to as socially motivated. Examples of socially motivated challenging behaviors include screaming in order to draw the attention of the teacher or throwing objects to escape a task that has become too difficult or boring. Even though each of the preceding behaviors is associated with a different social function, both require the mediation of another person in the environment in order to be consequated. Thus, both are examples of socially motivated challenging behaviors. Behaviors that do not require the mediation of others in order to be consequated are referred to as nonsocially motivated. Examples of nonsocially motivated challenging behaviors include rocking to obtain sensory stimulation and hitting oneself on the side of the head in response to an earache.

Some challenging behavior may originate as nonsocially motivated behavior but across instances become socially motivated. For example, a child might poke his fingers into his eyes because of the sensory stimulation that it provides (nonsocially motivated). However, across instances of eye poking, a history of receiving comforting attention immediately after each instance may develop. If the child enjoys the attention that he is receiving, he may learn to poke his eyes as a means of obtaining attention. Consequently, a behavior that originally served a nonsocial function may through reinforcement history come to serve a social function. Understanding that challenging behaviors are displayed in order to serve a variety of functions is important in that it enables the educator to consider the range of functionally equivalent, socially acceptable forms of behavior that serve the same purpose as an existing repertoire of challenging behavior. Recognizing that challenging behavior may be a functional response to antecedents that are biologically or medically related or socially or nonsocially related is important if professionals are to generate viable hypotheses to test during assessment. Generating viable hypotheses addressing the cause of challenging behavior will allow the most comprehensive scrutiny of antecedents and consequences that may need to be manipulated in order to effect a deceleration of challenging behavior.

In interviewing 20 professionals who work with children who engage in challenging behavior, Reichle (1993) observed that 70% were unable to describe the possible functions served by the challenging behavior emitted by the children. For example, it is quite common for staff to report that challenging behavior is emitted because a child is angry or upset. Although accurate, this level of analysis will not result in sufficiently operationalized functions of behavior to develop viable intervention strategies. Being able to identify the function(s) served by challenging behavior is vital if interventionists are to match intervention strategies that involve replacing challenging behavior with functional and socially acceptable alternatives.

Being Familiar with Assessment Activities   A variety of assessment strategies have been described that assist the interventionist in developing and confirming a hypothesis regarding the social function of a challenging behavior. Generally, assessment strategies include 1) interviews, 2) direct observations, and 3) environmental manipulations.

As the name implies, an interview usually comprises a series of questions or checklists that must be completed by an individual who is familiar with the child and the challenging behaviors that the child emits. The goal of the interview is to 1) describe the challenging behavior(s), 2) identify when the challenging behavior is most likely to occur, and 3) identify the possible functions of the challenging behavior. Although beneficial in providing a quick and relatively easy way to begin to identify factors that may contribute to the emission of a challenging behavior, interviews are only as reliable as the observations of the informant.

Directly observing children in situations in which challenging behaviors occur and do not occur (e.g., home, preschool environments) provides the interventionist with an opportunity to corroborate information provided in interview assessment. During direct observation, information is typically obtained regarding 1) the frequency of the behavior, 2) the antecedents that may influence the behavior (e.g., time of day, people present), 3) the place or setting in which the behavior occurs, and 4) the consequences of the behavior. Reichle (1993), in delivering a workshop to 100 early childhood educators, asked how many participants regularly utilized antecedent–behavior–consequence (A–B–C) analysis (or scatterplots) in assessing the children with challenging behavior whom they served. Less than 25% of the participants responded affirmatively. When asked how many knew what these analyses were, only 50% of the participants responded affirmatively. It appears that many interventionists depend on interview and more speculative forms of data gathering to direct the process of selecting intervention strategies. Although this strategy may seem very efficient, in the long run it may result in the delivery of very inefficient and inadequate intervention.

Upon completion of interviews and direct observations, the function of a particular challenging behavior may still be unclear because specific variables that may provoke the behavior have not been sufficiently associated with it. Environmental manipulations are a helpful means of testing the hypothesis that could not adequately be tested due to confounding conditions present in the milieu of the child's regular routine. Implementing environmental manipulations involves altering particular antecedents or consequences believed to be associated with a child's emission of challenging behavior and then observing how these changes affect the behavior. For example, direct observation results may suggest that a child darts from organized activities. Although it has been documented that this outcome is quite predictable, it could occur for one of several reasons. It is possible that the child is attempting to avoid an undesired activity. Alternatively, the child may not mind participating but attempts to escape when he or she arrives at a particularly difficult step. Finally, the child's behavior may represent an overture to recruit attention from the teacher who usually chases him or her when he or she runs from the table.

In the context of the preceding example, the teacher could compare systematically the influence that task difficulty or providing attention during the tasks had on the child's emission of challenging behavior. In another comparison, the interventionist could compare what happens when the child is given periodic breaks compared to no breaks in activities that he or she typically attempts to escape. By systematically altering and comparing hypothesized factors that contribute to challenging behavior, an interventionist may be able to better match an intervention strategy to the specific motivation behind the inappropriate behavior. Unless the function(s) of challenging behavior is identified accurately, it will be impossible to design an individualized intervention program to establish functional alternatives that can compete successfully with the challenging repertoire.

Identifying Available Intervention Options Because emissions of challenging behavior often represent the product of and interaction between the child and his or her environment (Carr, Taylor, & Robinson, 1991), interventions can be directed at the child, the environment, or both (including the behavior of the persons with whom the child interacts). Given socially motivated challenging behavior, the initial decision that an interventionist must make is whether the function served by an individual's challenging behavior can be honored. For example, a child begins to throw task materials across the room as soon as they are offered (i.e., engages in escape-motivated challenging behavior). The interventionist must decide whether he or she can allow the child to escape the task (honor the function of the challenging behavior). An affirmative answer to this question suggests that it may be feasible to teach a behavior that is functionally equivalent but socially more acceptable than the existing challenging behavior (Carr, 1977; Carr & Durand, 1985). In some instances, the answer to this question will be no. That is, the function of the behavior cannot be honored. For example, a child cannot escape getting on the school bus to go home. In this case, the interventionist must consider intervention strategies that establish 1) better self-regulatory skills for the child or 2) greater tolerance or understanding from others in the child's environment.

Interventions that Establish Functionally Equivalent Responses   If the function of the behavior can be honored, it is important to find a more socially acceptable response that is functionally equivalent. That is, if the child is attempting to avoid the activity, teaching a response to request escape from the activity would serve the same function for the child as throwing the task materials. Another child may not mind initiating the task but may attempt to escape when he or she arrives at a particularly difficult step. Teaching the child to request assistance would be a more socially appropriate and functionally equivalent form of the behavior. Finally, the child's challenging behavior may be the most effective way to recruit attention. In this instance, teaching a more socially acceptable attention-getting response may represent the most appropriate replacement behavior.

If a functionally equivalent replacement behavior is indicated, it is important that it be maximally efficient from the child's perspective. Mace and Roberts (1993) have elegantly articulated four factors that may significantly influence the efficiency of any particular child response in achieving a socially motivated outcome. Responses are most efficient when they 1) result in the immediate delivery of reinforcement, 2) require reasonable response effort, 3) require a low rate of responding to achieve the desired outcome, and 4) result in qualitatively good outcomes. Developing responses that are both functionally equivalent and efficient requires precise understanding of the variables that influence the emission of challenging behavior.

In most instances, when the function served by the challenging behavior can be reinforced contingent on the emission of a more socially acceptable form of behavior, communication intervention is warranted. Although there is a rich and growing literature emphasizing the importance of selecting the most efficient communicative alternative to challenging behavior, evidence suggests that educational professionals have virtually no experience in implementing strategies with which to choose and subsequently implement effective teaching procedures (Reichle & McEvoy, 1994). Table 2 provides examples of intervention strategies that might be implemented to establish a communicative alternative to escape- or avoidance-motivated challenging behavior.

Interventions that Promote Self-Regulation   Unfortunately, in some instances the function served by the child's challenging behavior cannot be honored. For example, administration of medication that helps prevent life-threatening medical emergencies cannot be escaped. In such situations, the interventionist's task is to better enable the child to engage in sufficient self-regulation that will allow at least partial participation in the

Table 2. Examples of intervention strategies for establishing communicative alternatives to escape-motivated challenging behavior

Communicative alternative	Case example
Request to take leave	A young girl who will participate in a structured activity for a brief amount of time, but begins to engage in aggressive behaviors toward her peers upon becoming bored, is taught to request a break by saying, "Break, please."
Rejecting response	A young boy who has tantrums each time he is presented with food items that he dislikes is taught to point to a card with the word "stop" printed on it.
Request assistance	A learner who engages in challenging behavior (e.g., begins to yell and throw materials) upon reaching a step in an activity that he finds difficult is taught to sign HELP.
Request attention	A learner who engages in challenging behaviors while performing an undesirable task in order to procure staff's attention (and as a result is not required to engage in the activity at hand) is taught to point to a graphic symbol containing the message, "Please visit with me."

absence of challenging behavior. Teaching self-regulatory skills to cope with situations where social functions (i.e., escape, avoidance, or obtaining attention or goods and services) cannot be honored also requires an exacting understanding of the variables that surround the challenging behavior. Descriptions of a number of interventions designed to enhance a child's propensity to continue to engage in an important but less preferred activity include environmental arrangement (reorganizing home or classroom to diminish provoking stimuli without creating disruptions or inconveniences for others) (Nordquist, Twardosz, & McEvoy, 1991), high-probability request sequences (Davis, Brady, Williams, & Hamilton, 1992), tolerance for delay of reinforcement (Davis, Reichle, & Light-Shriner, 1995), collaboration, and preferred item as a distractor. Table 3 provides several examples of these interventions that have been validated or partially validated for use when challenging behavior cannot be honored.

Recruiting and Training Technical Assistance Team Members

At the conclusion of the preservice and in-service course, individuals who wish to apply to become members of their school district's technical assistance team are recruited. Having had the significant course information described above (i.e., functional assessment activities and intervention options), potential members of the technical assistance team have obtained a very clear idea of the orientation of and related activities that they would be expected to develop. Applications are submitted to a designated school district administrator. With the permission of the appli-

Table 3. Examples of interventions addressing escape-motivated challenging behavior that cannot be honored

Intervention	Description of implementation
High-probability request sequences	In a high-probability request sequence, the interventionist delivers three to five requests to which a child typically complies (i.e., *high-probability requests*) immediately prior to delivering a request to which a child *does not* typically comply (i.e., a *low-probability request*). Compliance to the high-probability request increases the likelihood that the child will comply with the low-probability request.
Tolerance for delay of reinforcement	Teaching tolerance for delay of reinforcement is a strategy that uses two different cues: a *delay cue* and a *safety signal*. The delay cue is used to signal to the individual the wait period is beginning, and the safety signal is used to signal a release to reinforcement. The purpose of the procedure is to increase the amount of time a learner will continue to participate in an activity without engaging in challenging behavior.
Collaboration	A collaboration intervention program entails sharing with the learner the responsibility of performing an undesirable task. Prior to requesting the learner to engage in the task, the interventionist offers collaboration. In the initial stages of intervention, the interventionist may complete a large percentage of the task (e.g., the interventionist puts 75% of the toys away, the child the remaining 25%). The amount of collaboration may be decreased across opportunities (e.g., the interventionist puts 50% of the toys away, then 25%, etc.).
Preferred item as a distractor	When implementing a preferred item as a distractor intervention program, the interventionist identifies an object or activity that is preferred by the learner. This object or activity is then presented to the learner just prior to requesting him or her to engage in an activity that is likely to elicit challenging behavior. For example, a young child who dislikes riding on the bus is provided with a cassette player for distraction from this activity.

cants, course instructors provide feedback to the administrator with respect to the applicants' grasp of course content, level of participation, and diligence in the course. To date, technical assistance teams have comprised a minimum of three disciplines, including speech-language pathologists, special educators, early childhood educators, paraprofessionals, school psychologists, and occupational or physical therapists.

Once the technical assistance team has mastered the information contained in the initial coursework, a more sophisticated regimen of training is implemented that involves weekly 3-hour sessions over a period of approximately 20 weeks conducted on site at schools within the participating school district. The purpose of these sessions is for technical assistance team members to systematically apply the course information to actual cases using a case study format similar in scope and sequence to case example-focused training described by Anderson, Albin, Mesaros, Dunlap, and Morelli-Robbins (1993). This method is used to elaborate on information regarding curriculum content and best practice instructional strategies. The bulk of instruction that occurs during extended training focuses on identifying members of the child's IEP team who are in need of technical assistance.

The technical assistance team works collaboratively with university faculty and graduate students to systematically apply acquired knowledge and to expand the knowledge base of technical assistance team members. At this level of technical assistance, experienced doctoral students participate actively in the training. These students work side by side with team members in visiting classrooms, accumulating assessment data, formulating and troubleshooting intervention plans, and presenting short in-services to eventual recipients of technical assistance. The close level of collaboration among technical assistance team members and advanced graduate students provides an opportunity to establish mutual respect and colleagueship that serves to create an excellent future training environment for less experienced preservice students. Over time, trainees play an increasingly greater role in the delivery of longitudinal on-site technical assistance. A chronology of extended training topics and brief descriptions of training activities are described in Table 4.

Fiscal Commitment Significant time is required to establish an efficiently operating team of professionals to deliver on-site longitudinal technical assistance to a school district in addition to creating and implementing a systematic plan of coursework and continuing in-service. Consequently, for a school district to develop comprehensive in-service and technical assistance capability requires a significant fiscal commitment. In preparing a technical assistance team, the authors have spent approximately 360 hours in training. Approximately 260 of these hours represent the direct involvement of highly trained doctoral students from disciplines that include early childhood education, special education, and speech-language pathology. The remainder of the effort represents the involvement of regular university faculty.

The cost of the project for the participating university is approximately $15,000 in the initial year, close to $7,500 in the second year, and about $5,000 in the third year. Enabling each member of the technical

Table 4. Chronology of extended training topics and a description of training activities for technical assistance team members

Extended training topics	Training activities
I. Working Collaboratively within an Interdisciplinary Team	• Team members participate in a number of exercises to build their teaming skills. For example, the team members engage in role-playing exercises, working through hypothetical situations that they may encounter while working within a team model (e.g., conflicts between members, challenges presented by professionals outside of the team). • Team members are introduced to the importance of identifying roles and independently assign roles to individual team members. • Team members assess their teaming skills on an ongoing basis by evaluating their performance at team meetings.
II. Development of Operating Procedures	• Provided with guidance from university staff, team members develop a set of operating procedures to ensure that technical assistance activities are conducted in an organized manner that is consistent with district policy. For example, procedures and corresponding forms are developed and approved by district administrators that address the referral process and parental notification and consent, including videotape permission.
III. Introduction of Program Tracking Procedures	• Procedures for implementation of technical assistance activities are established and are presented to the technical assistance team members. Each task to be performed by the technical assistance team (e.g., interview process, direct observation, presenting assessment information to team members and so on) is broken down into a step-by-step format and presented in chronological order to the team members.
IV. Introduction of Technical Assistance Recipient Monitoring Procedures	• In addition to monitoring learner change, the technical assistance team members are responsible for monitoring the extent to which each technical assistance recipient participates in the technical assistance process. Team members are introduced to a number of dependent variables, which are carefully monitored throughout the technical assistance process. The team members then develop a means of collecting information directly related to these variables. For example, a rating scale may be developed and used to evaluate the technical assistance recipient's ability to generalize information and troubleshoot interventions and his or her willingness to follow

(continued)

Table 4. *(continued)*

Extended training topics	Training activities
	through with requests and carefully document learner performance.
V. Participation in Assessment and Intervention Activities Associated with Case Studies	• Each team member identifies a learner who exhibits challenging behavior and whose IEP team desires technical assistance.
	• One team member at a time works through all of the operating procedures, program tracking procedures, and technical assistance recipient monitoring procedures, with university personnel providing support throughout each case study.

assistance team to fully participate in team activity has required participating school districts to offer a minimum of .25 FTE salary for each of a minimum of three professionals who serve on the team. Initially, the costs incurred in implementing this program are shared by the participating university and the participating school district.

Creating a Continuum of In-Service Training within a School District

In order to maximize the technical assistance team's effectiveness, creating a comprehensive plan of in-service for schools to supplement on-site technical assistance is critical. This plan must address 1) staff attrition that will result in new staff who typically have limited experience in proactive approaches to serving children with challenging behavior, as well as 2) highly skilled staff who wish to refine their skills so that they will rarely need a consultation with a technical assistance team member. Strategies for developing a continuum of in-service training are discussed below.

Providing a Menu of In-Service Options Developing a comprehensive in-service plan requires a range of information dissemination options. Regardless of the level of in-service, adequate incentives must be offered so that staff see in-service and/or on-site technical assistance as an opportunity rather than an obligation. Consequently, a continuum of in-service activities that include university course credit, half- to whole-day procedural in-services, site-specific informal in-services, and districtwide task forces must be planned. Table 5 defines each of these levels and delineates involvement of and benefit to both the university and the public school community along with incentives for individual participants.

University Course Credit Earlier this chapter described the course as a prerequisite for applying to be a member of the technical assistance team. However, this course also serves additional important integral functions in the technical assistance operation. Many professionals working in educational settings have had minimal coursework that directly

Table 5. Continuum of in-service activities

In-service activities	Description	Benefits to individuals involved
University credit courses	Team members offer a course addressing proactive strategies for managing challenging behavior that can be taken for university credit.	Provides prospective technical assistance team members with a means of elaborating on a number of topics (including assessment and intervention strategies). Professionals within the district are offered an opportunity to acquire credit to be used for professional advancement or toward a graduate degree program.
Half- to whole-day procedural in-services	A significant amount of time is dedicated to elaborating upon a specific content area. The content area is chosen based upon the individual needs of the site. For example, three preschool teachers and their staff are interested in rearranging their classrooms in order to prevent the occurrence of challenging behaviors. Lectures, discussions, and interactive computer software are then used to convey this information.	Enables the technical assistance team to target needs within a district and to disseminate information in a thorough manner. The professionals within the district are provided with an in-depth presentation of information that directly meets their needs.
Site-specific informal services	A brief overview of topics is provided, including specific content areas (e.g., importance of conducting functional assessments, environ- mental arrangements, communicative re- placement) and the technical assistance process and how to communicate with the team members. Examples of specific learners' programs (including assessment, intervention, and troubleshooting strategies) are presented.	Allows the technical assistance team members to introduce topic areas in an efficient and precise manner. Provides district staff with an overview of available information and services, upon which they may pursue more elaborate technical assistance. Enables the technical assistance team members to share with their colleagues the success of the technical assistance team. It provides professionals

(continued)

Table 5. (continued)

In-service activities	Description	Benefits to individuals involved
		in the district with an example of activities and outcomes that the technical assistance team members can help to facilitate with their individual students.
Districtwide task forces	Task forces are developed in order to meet specific needs of district personnel. District administrators, team members, and professionals from the district come together to determine areas that warrant a task force. For example, if an inclusion program is just being initiated in the school district, the team members can be of service throughout the district in order to help facilitate the students' and staffs' transition.	Enables the technical assistance team members to focus their energy upon a specific area of need within their district. Professionals within the district are provided with resources and support to help them meet the challenges within a specific content area (e.g., inclusion, home intervention, developing appropriate IEP goals).

addresses proactive approaches to managing challenging behavior. It is far more likely that persons who received their professional degree prior to 1985 received assessment information that focused on establishing information referenced to the *form* of challenging behavior rather than its *function*. Furthermore, it is probable that intervention training focused on implementing procedures to suppress challenging behavior (i.e., time-out, overcorrection, response cost). Participation in a comprehensive course makes it far easier for recipients to obtain future technical assistance more efficiently in that significant time need not be spent providing the logic and description of the content being suggested by a technical assistance provider. Instead, a recipient with background knowledge can focus on fine tuning and troubleshooting the implementation of the procedure.

Of course, for a staff member to choose to participate, there must be an incentive. The powerful incentive of becoming a more competent professional may be jeopardized by the abundance of personal responsibilities that may compete for the time required to participate in coursework. In Minnesota, there are two additional incentives to engage in in-service coursework. First, 120 clock hours of coursework per 5-year period are required to maintain state licensure. Second, while the hours do not have to be degree bearing, additional coursework can also lead to increased salary levels based on seniority and level of education.

Half- to Whole-Day Procedural In-Services Unfortunately, the incentives just described may not be sufficient to garner the participation of all (or even the majority) of professionals. An alternative is to parse the information contained in an in-service course into a number of training modules. With these individuals it may be necessary to use regularly scheduled in-service days to present relevant information.

The technical assistance team is responsible for developing a series of 1- or 2-hour in-services that focus on actual assessment and intervention methods that have been validated or partially validated with children who engage in repertoires of challenging behavior. The authors' experiences suggest that many public school early childhood programs have a monthly staff meeting. Often, these meetings are several hours in length and are somewhat equally divided between logistical business and staff development activities.

Building/Site-Specific Informal In-Services Often, professionals are reluctant to seek individualized technical assistance in the area of challenging behavior. Informal retrospective surveys of technical assistance recipients suggest that professionals may see a request for technical assistance as an admission of competence deficiency. Data suggest that professionals are more likely to seek technical assistance regarding challenging behavior emitted by specific children if technical assistance providers are familiar with the professional and his or her classroom prior to the request (Reichle & Doss, 1994).

MECBSP works with the special education coordinator and school building principal to establish brief episodic "within building" training sessions. The purpose of these sessions is to expand on the information provided in more general districtwide in-services by applying training content to specific situations that arise in classrooms. It is particularly helpful if prior to or concurrent with these meetings, the technical assistance provider is allowed to visit the classrooms served by staff who plan on attending the meeting. This results in increased familiarity between the assistance provider and professionals. It also allows the provider to individualize examples applying assessment and intervention techniques to actual situations that arise.

In implementing site-specific longitudinal meetings, it is important that participation be voluntary. If this style of in-service is to be effective, participation should increase as a result of the favorable evaluations offered by participants to their colleagues in nonparticipating schools. MECBSP data suggest that establishing more informal in-services at the school building level is very appealing to staff. It seems to be particularly helpful in generating momentum for change when several staff within a building are anxious to improve educational services at a buildingwide level.

Districtwide Task Forces Within several school districts participating in a comprehensive plan of in-service and technical assistance, task forces have been developed to focus on the development of a product addressing an identified need or issue that the district's identified technical assistance may not have sufficient resources to comprehensively address. These task force members may include a variety of individuals including speech-language pathologists, school psychologists, general educators, special educators, early educators, social workers, parents, paraprofessionals, physical and occupational therapists, and university graduate students. Task force meetings may occur several times a month throughout the school year. Examples of task force activities include generating instructions for requesting third-party payments for augmentative communication devices and working with school administrators on behavior conduct policies.

Establishing Input from Parent Advisory Groups

Families of children with disabilities have extremely diverse needs (Bailey & Simeonsson, 1984; Benson & Turnbull, 1986; Turnbull & Turnbull, 1986). A particular challenge is to ensure that the array of available services and resources adequately addresses a wide range of home ecologies. For example, in some instances, parents may see themselves as separate from the actual implementation of educational services. In other instances, parents may enthusiastically embrace their role as an active agent in the implementation of educational services. However, these parents may become frustrated at their inability to devote what they perceive as a desired level of involvement because of issues external to the actual delivery of service. For example, their efforts to obtain mental health or respite services, medically necessary equipment, or in-home nursing care may be consuming an inordinate amount of their time and energy. Technical assistance teams need to be aware of probable areas of need that parents have that, at first glance, appear to fall outside the realm of educational services or challenging behavior. An effective technical assistance service is willing to reasonably assist families in finding resources that address problems that may be hindering the family's ability to participate more actively in their child's education. This issue is most critically important in the area of home-based early childhood services where the parent is most apt to be placed in the role of the primary interventionist.

Providing Longitudinal On-Site Technical Assistance

Although in-services such as those just described represent important activities for a technical assistance team, they are not sufficient. Many in-service recipients require careful on-site shaping of their assessment and intervention skills to effect child change. Doss and Reichle (1989) examined the outcome of technical assistance in which assessment and intervention strategies were discussed at regularly occurring meetings outside of the actual site of implementation with participants who were licensed as skilled behavior analysts in the state of Minnesota. Assessment and intervention decisions were based on data brought to the meetings by staff. Meetings were held once every 2 weeks. Approximately 40% of the children who were the focus of the consultations made progress, as demonstrated by dependent measures on challenging behavior deceleration as well as data on replacement skill acquisition. As the in-service project progressed, an increasing portion of technical assistance requests was directed at serving children who were improving while progressively less time was spent on children with whom the program was not successful. When asked to spend a greater proportion of meeting time discussing children who were less successful, interventionists often reported that the behavior of the child in question was no longer really a problem. Throughout the delivery of technical assistance, observers were regularly on site to observe the implementation of intervention procedures and social interactions between staff and clients. As a result of the summary of these data, it became clear that children with whom interventionists made the least progress were those who 1) interventionists spent the least discretionary time with prior to the initiation of technical assistance, 2) made no immediate progress when technical assistance programs were implemented, and/or 3) exhibited more severe aggression directed at staff.

Subsequently, technical assistance was delivered on site twice weekly. During these sessions, the technical assistance provider worked directly with staff to coach them in implementing intervention procedures. Over approximately a 6-month period, staff participation was shaped. Without the capability of presenting direct and regular on-site feedback, it is doubtful that many of the professionals with whom the technical assistance team worked would have reliably implemented intervention strategies.

Evaluating and Troubleshooting Problematic Technical Assistance Strategies

At the crux of delivering effective technical assistance are dependent measures that allow careful scrutiny and revision of problematic technical assistance strategies. Traditionally, technical assistance activities have been evaluated modestly for two reasons. First, if effective troubleshooting activities are to be put in place when a desired educational or social outcome is not being achieved, technical assistance providers must be prepared to analyze the intervention systematically. Second, a technical assistance team must be placed in a position to demonstrate the value of its services to justify expenses associated with maintaining a technical assistance team as a recurring budget item.

The most probable evaluation component consists of a consumer satisfaction of professionals receiving technical assistance. Unfortunately, the results from these surveys may not be strongly correlated with a recipient's knowledge gained or ability to implement information provided. More objective data often used to evaluate technical assistance activities focus on learner change data. These data often emphasize decreases in the rate, intensity, or duration of the challenging behavior. Although decelerations of any problem behavior are desirable, these data are less impressive unless, at the same time, engagement in desired social or educational activities is improving. Consequently, dependent measures need to focus at minimum on two sets of behaviors: 1) challenging behavior, and 2) socially acceptable behavior that competes with challenging behavior.

Since the early 1980s, investigators have turned to issues of social validity. That is, even though child change can be demonstrated empirically, it will have little overall impact if those who spend significant time around the child cannot notice significant changes in behavior. Consequently, individuals who regularly come in contact with children/professionals being served through technical assistance need to provide their perception of the child's ability to function in the environments that are the focus of intervention activities.

One aspect of child change data that is frequently overlooked involves measures of procedural reliability. That is, if an interventionist has assisted in designing an intervention plan, can he or she implement it reliably? Without longitudinal and direct contact with the individual implementing technical assistance, procedural reliability is rarely scrutinized. Considering the reliability of the implementation assessment and intervention procedures seems particularly important given recent empirical results suggesting that procedures to establish instructional objectives are often either not implemented or implemented incorrectly (Reichle & Doss, 1994). Procedural reliability examined in the presence of a technical assistance provider may offer little insight into the rigor or regularity with which an intervention strategy is actually implemented in the absence of the technical assistance provider. That is, the interventionist may diligently implement a procedure recommended by a technical assistance provider during visits, but in the absence of the technical assistance provider, there may be sparse implementation.

Sometimes procedural reliability might be better viewed in a larger context of actually consulting with those who interact with an individual who engages in challenging behavior, as in some instances, the challenging behavior may be provoked by the behavior of those who interact with the child. For example, a child may attempt to escape task demands requiring immediate compliance that are offered in the absence of any choices. If the interventionist could alter his or her style of delivering choices, allowing the child to control the order in which he or she completes tasks and allowing a slightly larger window of time, the challenging behavior might diminish significantly. In this instance, one can listen to feedback from observers and role play regarding more fruitful interaction strategies to be implemented with the child for which procedural reliability must be obtained. However, in reality, the recipient of technical assistance (i.e., the staff member receiving technical assistance) is the primary target for behavior change. Procedural reliability then actually represents the primary dependent measure of interest.

The authors' experience suggests that some interventionists may not be willing to implement an intervention procedure that permits a child to escape an undesired activity contingent on the emission of a more socially acceptable communicative alternative. For example, teachers may not be willing to allow a child to terminate an activity after the child touches a graphic symbol that requests task termination. Other staff may not be willing to shorten the length of the activity that would allow a history to develop where the child can be taught to participate without challenging behavior and be released after good rather than challenging behavior. In each of these instances, the interventionist simply may not accept the loss of instructional control inherent in each strategy. Technical assistance providers must therefore take great care to work collaboratively with the team serving the child to lay the necessary rationale for any intervention strategies offered. All team members must feel comfortable implementing intervention strategies before they are put in place. However, frequently this strategy is not considered as a viable option for increasing the participation in the intervention process among recipients of technical assistance.

As discussed earlier, offering menus of intervention options significantly increases the probability that interventions better match the teaching and interactional skills of interventionists. The key to establishing reliable and fluent implementation of instructional programs requires that the technical assistance provider 1) determine that intervention strategies recommended are commensurate with the teaching style and beliefs of the implementers and the child's family, and 2) ensure that the technical assistance recipients are willing to implement strategies with necessary rigor and fluency. Evaluation of technical assistance must include dependent measures that focus on the participation of recipients as well as on the child's emission of challenging behavior and his or her emission of proactive alternatives. It is also important to have some measure of the social validity of the effects of technical assistance implementation. These measures may include the perception of those familiar with the interventionist's and child's pre- and posttechnical assistance activities. Finally, the perception of value of technical assistance from the recipients represents important data that bear directly on the user friendliness and clarity of technical assistance provided.

Future Directions for Establishing Collaboration Between Public Schools and Universities

There is a propensity for university tradition and administrative bureaucracy to either limit or discourage greater collaborative coordination of preservice and in-service training. To combat this propensity, there are a number of strategies that universities could pursue to take advantage of collaborative relationships that have been established during the implementation of a rigorous plan of in-service and technical assistance. Some of these activities are discussed briefly below.

Cost-Sharing Practicum Supervision   To a significant extent, university training programs follow one of two strategies to supervise graduate and undergraduate trainees in student teaching and practicum activities. In one model, the university depends almost exclusively on the goodwill of professionals in the field to accept student trainees. This model requires significant volunteerism on the part of the receiving professional. Even when the professional is diligent and highly motivated, there is no mechanism to ensure the integration of preservice coursework with practicum activities because the supervising professional may not have matriculated through the preservice student's training program. Correspondingly, there may be limited incentive for the supervising professional to participate in preservice coursework to ensure that there is a common background across supervisor and trainee.

In an alternative model, the university training program provides the practicum supervision via a university staff member. In an applied setting, this option has the potential advantage of providing feedback continuity across preservice coursework and implementation of that information in practicum settings. However, this model presents a very inefficient and potentially awkward method of supervision. It places the practicum student in a position to receive feedback from on-site staff as well as from the university supervisor. When feedback is inconsistent across these two sources, all parties are placed in an awkward situation. Additionally, this model of supervision is very duplicative in terms of resource deployment by assigning both a community-based and a university-based supervisor to any given practicum student. It should be possible to provide adequate incentives to public school professionals to ensure that they have a base of information that is consistent with the students whom they supervise as well as to ensure more intensive coparticipation by public school professionals in the mentoring of graduate-level preservice students.

One strategy to create an incentive for better coordination between universities and public schools involves the two working directly to coordinate state Department of Education continuing education requirements with local service providers' criteria for merit salary increases. For example, the state of Minnesota requires that all educational professionals take continuing education courses in order to maintain their teaching licensure. In addition, professionals (teachers, psychologists, speech-language pathologists, etc.) working in public schools can use university credits in a field related to their professional degree for a salary "bump." However, in order to accrue this credit, the professional must pay for the university credit rather than the service provider for whom they work. One viable option for university training programs is to offer tuition vouchers to supervising professionals. Although an empirical question, this strategy should result in sufficient incentive to ensure that supervisors share common content information with students whom they might be called upon to supervise.

Sharing a common content base is important but represents only an initial step in truly collaborative in-service/preservice coordination. To continue collaboration, participating public school professionals must assume a mentoring role to bridge preservice course information with practicum experiences. However, this must be a shared responsibility between school professionals and university personnel. This means that university personnel who teach method-related coursework should spend a significant portion of their effort at community training sites. Time spent should encompass the provision of technical assistance and collegial support to establish commonality between methods taught in coursework and those practiced in practicum settings. Furthermore, selected public school professionals who collaborate in preservice training activities should serve as reimbursed consultants to the preservice training program. It is unrealistic to assume that participation in training activities that go significantly beyond regular employment requirements should represent a totally voluntary activity. Potential recurring funding mechanisms to pay for public school professionals' work as consultants and provide them with tuition stipends include 1) redistributing monies currently allocated to practicum supervision, and 2) creating focused continuing education activities that generate income.

Money currently allocated within a university for practicum supervision could be reallocated to designated public school mentors. For example, the university might cost share positions with a school district in return for the school district guaranteeing a specified amount of supervision. In addition to reallocating existing monies used for practicum supervision, supplemental income to support collaboration between universities and public schools can be generated via university coursework. To this point in the chapter, community-based coursework has been discussed in terms of its educational value. However, an additional outcome of this activity could be the generation of recurring funds to provide a financial incentive for community mentors by utilizing funds derived through the development of continuing education course offerings. For example, at the University of Minnesota, over 50% of the enrollment fee of extension coursework offered is returned directly to the sponsoring department. Offering a plan of applied coursework aimed at both preservice and practicing professionals could generate a substantial income to provide financial incentives to school districts or professionals within school districts who wish to collaborate with universities in preservice training activities. For university faculty, creating a funding mechanism for key public school collaboration seems highly desirable in a climate of shrinking federal dollars to support educational research and training.

Creating a Curriculum Advisory Board Preservice training programs must address their personnel preparation activities to the criteria of the needs of consumers and service agencies that will employ graduates. The university, through coursework and collaboration, has an opportunity to influence those criteria. Equally important is the opportunity for university preservice programs to be influenced by the experience and views of service providers and families. Establishing a curriculum advisory board represents an opportunity to obtain this information in a regular and systematically organized fashion. Parents and consumers represent a critical validating component in designing any educational activity. Planned educational activities should have a significant positive impact on consumers and their families. Therefore professionals must seek out the collaboration of those whom they serve and work jointly to improve service delivery.

The inclusive service delivery in which professionals are mandated to work and to which parents entrust their children represents a vastly different educational environment from that available in the 1980s and earlier. In spite of tremendous advances, many teachers and related personnel openly voice concern about their ability to serve children with challenging behavior. Ironically, a significant methodological expertise exists to serve these children. Furthermore, methodological advances will be compromised unless educators can benefit from them by infusing them into the service delivery system. This infusion will require a major and joint effort by researchers, personnel preparers, public school professionals, and parents.

CONCLUSIONS

Anderson et al. (1993) concluded that "inservice training by itself is not sufficient to ensure accomplishing all of the outcomes desired for effective education and support systems for people with developmental disabilities . . ." (p. 363). The current authors share their orientation that comprehensive training must be useful to a wide variety of professionals and families. Furthermore, it is impossible to divorce in-service training needs from preservice training needs. Unattended preservice needs later become in-service and technical assistance needs.

Coordinating efforts to improve preservice and in-service training involves a number of levels of partnerships. Public school administrators and university personnel must become partners in planning the system that will support coordinated training. University professionals must develop mutually beneficial collaborations with public school professionals and parents. Finally, university preservice students must develop collaborative relationships with university faculty and public school mentors. When preservice students and public school professionals are well trained and actively collaborate with families, they will have a far greater probability of positively affecting the lives of the persons with challenging behavior whom they serve.

REFERENCES

Albano, M.L. (1983). *Transdisciplinary teaming in special education: A case study.* Urbana: University of Illinois-Urbana/Champaign.

Anderson, J.L., Albin, R.W., Mesaros, R.A., Dunlap, G., & Morelli-Robbins, M. (1993). Issues in providing training to achieve comprehensive behavioral support. In J. Reichle & D. Wacker (Eds.), *Communication and language intervention: Vol. 3. Communicative alternatives to challenging behavior: Integrating functional assessment and intervention strategies* (pp. 363–406). Baltimore: Paul H. Brookes Publishing Co.

Bailey, D.B. (1989). Issues and directions in preparing professionals to work with young handicapped children and their families. In J.J. Gallagher, P.L. Trohanis, & R.M. Clifford (Eds.), *Planning for young children with special needs* (pp. 97–132). Baltimore: Paul H. Brookes Publishing Co.

Bailey, D.B., & Simeonsson, R.J. (1984). Critical issues research and intervention with families of young handicapped children. *Journal for Division of Exceptional Children, 9*(1), 38–48.

Baumgart, D., & Ferguson, D.L. (1991). Personnel preparation: Directions for the next decade. In L.H. Meyer, C.A. Peck, & L. Brown (Eds.), *Critical issues in the lives of people with severe disabilities* (pp. 313–352). Baltimore: Paul H. Brookes Publishing Co.

Benson, H.A., & Turnbull, A.P. (1986). Approaching families from an individualized perspective. In R.H. Horner, L.H. Meyer, & H.B. Fredericks (Eds.), *Education of learners with severe handicaps: Exemplary service strategies* (pp. 127–157). Baltimore: Paul H. Brookes Publishing Co.

Brandenberg, N.A., Friedman, R.M., & Silver, S.E. (1990). The epidemiology of childhood psychiatric disorders: Prevalence findings from recent studies. *Journal of the American Academy of Child & Adolescent Psychiatry, 29*(1), 76–83.

Briefing: Behavior problems pay off big. (1994, September 14). *St. Paul Pioneer Press*, p. 3A.

Campbell, P. (1987). The integrated programming team: An approach for coordinating professionals of various disciplines in programs for students with severe and multiple handicaps. *Journal of The Association for Persons with Severe Handicaps, 12*(2), 107–117.

Campbell, P. (1990). Meeting personnel needs in early intervention. In A. Kaiser & C. McWhorter (Eds.), *Preparing personnel to work with persons with severe disabilities* (pp. 111–134). Baltimore: Paul H. Brookes Publishing Co.

Campbell, P.H., McInerney, W.F., & Cooper, M.A. (1984). Therapeutic programming for students with severe handicaps. *American Journal of Occupational Therapy, 38*(9), 594–602.

Carr, E.G. (1977). The motivation of self-injurious behavior: A review of some hypotheses. *Psychological Bulletin, 84*, 800–816.

Carr, E.G., & Durand, V.M. (1985). Reducing behavior problems through functional communication training. *Journal of Applied Behavior Analysis, 18*, 111–126.

Carr, E.G., Taylor, J.C., & Robinson, S. (1991). The effects of severe behavioral problems in children on the teaching behavior of adults. *Journal of Applied Behavior Analysis, 24*, 523–535.

Carta, J.J., Sideridis, G., Rinkel, P., Guimaraes, S., Greenwood, C., Baggett, K., Peterson, P., Atwater, J., McEvoy, M., & McConnell, S. (1994). Behavioral outcomes of young children prenatally exposed to illicit drugs: Review and analysis of experimental literature. *Topics in Early Childhood Special Education, 14*(2), 184–216.

Chess, S., & Hassibi, S. (1970). Behavior deviations in mentally retarded children. *Journal of the American Academy of Child Psychiatry, 9*, 282–297.

Courtnage, L., & Smith-Davis, J. (1987). Interdisciplinary team training: A national survey of special education teacher training programs. *Exceptional Children, 53*(5), 451–458.

Danforth, J.S., & Drabman, R.S. (1989). In E. Cipani (Ed.), *The treatment of severe behavior disorders behavior analysis approaches* (pp. 111–127). Washington, DC: American Association on Mental Retardation.

Davis, C.A., Brady, M.P., Williams, R.E., & Hamilton, R. (1992). Effects of high-probability requests on the acquisition and generalization of responses to requests in young children with severe disabilities. *Journal of Applied Behavior Analysis, 25*, 906–916.

Davis, C.A., Reichle, J., & Light-Shriner, C. (1995). *Teaching a tolerance for a delay in reinforcement: An intervention to reduce challenging behavior of individuals with severe disabilities*. Manuscript submitted for publication.

Donahue, E.D., & Abbas, K.A. (1971). Unstable behavior in severely subnormal children. *Developmental Medicine and Child Neurology, 13*, 512–519.

Doss, S., & Reichle, J. (1989). Establishing communicative alternatives to the emission of socially motivated excess behavior: A review. *Journal of The Association for Severely Handicapped, 14*, 101–112.

Doss, L., & Reichle, J. (1991). Replacing excess behavior with an initial communicative repertoire. In J. Reichle, J. York, & J. Sigafoos, *Implementing augmentative and alternative communication: Strategies for learners with severe disabilities* (pp. 215–237). Baltimore: Paul H. Brookes Publishing Co.

Eaton, L.F., & Menolascino, F.J. (1982). Psychiatric disorders in the mentally retarded: Types, problems, and challenges. *American Journal of Psychiatry, 10*, 139.

Fredericks, H.D., & Templeman, T.P. (1990). A generic in-service training model. In A.P. Kaiser & C.M. McWhorter (Eds.), *Preparing personnel to work with persons with severe disabilities* (pp. 301–317). Baltimore: Paul H. Brookes Publishing Co.

Giangreco, M.F. (1986). Effects of integrated therapy: A pilot study. *Journal of The Association for Persons with Severe Handicaps, 11*, 205–209.

Giangreco, M.F., & Putnam, J.W. (1992). Supporting the education of students with severe disabilities in regular education environments. In L.H. Meyer, C.A. Peck, & L. Brown (Eds.), *Critical issues in the lives of people with severe disabilities* (pp. 245–270). Baltimore: Paul H. Brookes Publishing Co.

Green, A.H. (1967). Self-mutilation in schizophrenic children. *Archives of General Psychiatry, 17*, 234–244.

Locke, P., & Reichle, J. (1989). *A survey of speech-language pathologists.* Unpublished manuscript, University of Minnesota, Minneapolis.

Mace, F.C., & Roberts, M.L. (1993). Factors affecting selection of behavioral interventions. In J. Reichle, J. York, & J. Sigafoos, *Implementing augmentative and alternative communication: Strategies for learners with severe disabilities* (pp. 113–133). Baltimore: Paul H. Brookes Publishing Co.

McEvoy, M., Davis, C., & Reichle, J. (1993). Districtwide technical assistance teams: Designing intervention strategies for young children with challenging behaviors. *Behavioral Disorders, 19*, 27–34.

McCormick, L., Cooper, M., & Goldman, R. (1979). Training teachers to maximize instruction time provided to severely and profoundly handicapped children. *AAESPH Review, 4*(3), 301–310.

Nord, J. (1994). *Reducing escape motivated challenging behavior in an individual with developmental disabilities.* Unpublished manuscript, Institute on Community Integration, University of Minnesota, Minneapolis.

Nordquist, V.M., Twardosz, S., & McEvoy, M.A. (1991). Effects of environmental reorganization in classrooms for children with autism. *Journal of Early Intervention, 15*, 135–152.

Rainforth, B. (1985). *Preparation of physical therapists and teachers of students with severe handicaps.* Unpublished doctoral dissertation, University of Illinois at Urbana-Champaign.

Rainforth, B., York, J., & Macdonald, C. (1992). *Collaborative teams for students with severe disabilities: Integrating therapy and educational services.* Baltimore: Paul H. Brookes Publishing Co.

Reichle, J. (1991). *Determining the needs of professionals who serve preschoolers with disabilities.* Unpublished manuscript, University of Minnesota, Minneapolis.

Reichle, J. (1993, April). *Procedures used in establishing an initial augmentative communication program.* Paper presented at the annual meeting of Wisconsin Speech, Language, and Hearing Association, Stevens Point.

Reichle, J., & Doss, S. (1994). *Variables influencing the delivery of technical assistance.* Unpublished manuscript, University of Minnesota, Minneapolis.

Reichle, J., & McEvoy, M. (1994). *Delineating technical assistance needs for professionals who engage in challenging behavior.* Unpublished manuscript, University of Minnesota, Minneapolis.

Schloss, J., Miller, S.R., Sedlacek, R.A., & White, M. (1983). Social performance expectations of professionals for behaviorally disordered youth. *Exceptional Children, 50*, 70–72.

Schroeder, S.R., Mulick, J.A., & Rojahn, J. (1980). The definition, taxonomy, epidemiology, and ecology of self-injurious behavior. *Journal of Autism and Developmental Disorders, 10*, 417–432.

Smeets, P.M. (1971). Some characteristics of mental defectives displaying self-mutilative behaviors. *Training School Bulletin, 68*, 131–135.

Timm, M. (1993). The regional intervention program: Family treatment by family members. *Behavior Disorders, 19*, 34–43.

Turnbull, A.P., & Turnbull, H.R. (1986). *Families and professionals: Creating an exceptional partnership.* Columbus, OH: Charles E. Merrill.

U.S. Department of Education. (1993). *Fifteenth annual report to Congress on the implementation of the Individuals with Disabilities Act.* Washington, DC: Author.

Walker, H., & Rankin, R. (1983). Assessing the behavior expectations and demands of less restrictive settings. *School Psychology Review, 12*, 274–284.

Will, M.C. (1984). Educating children with learning problems: A shared responsibility. *Exceptional Children, 52*, 411–415.

Wolery, M., & Dyk, P.A. (1984). Arena assessment: Description and preliminary social validity data. *Journal of The Association for the Severely Handicapped, 3*, 231–235.

Wolff, K. (1993). *A survey of preschool educators' priorities for inservice training.* Unpublished manuscript, University of Minnesota, Minneapolis.

York, J., & Rainforth, B. (1987). Developing instructional adaptations. In F.P. Orelove & D. Sobsey, *Educating children with multiple disabilities: A transdisciplinary approach* (pp. 193–217). Baltimore: Paul H. Brookes Publishing Co.

Appendix: Example of Sample Course Syllabus

EPSY 5900: Proactive Approaches to Managing Challenging Behaviors in Young Children

Instructors:

Kathleen Feeley, MS
Doctoral Candidate
Educational Psychology
Phone: 624-2380

Susan Johnston, PhD,
SLP-CCC
Communication Disorders
Phone: 624-2380

Purpose of the Course: The purpose of this course is to discuss positive intervention alternatives for individuals who engage in challenging behavior. A large segment of the course will address 1) intervention strategies aimed at replacing challenging behavior with communicative alternatives, and 2) organizing classrooms to decrease the probability of the occurrence of challenging behaviors while at the same time facilitating social interactions.

Format of the Course: Each week approximately 60 minutes will be devoted to the presentation of assessment and intervention strategies. The remaining 45 minutes will be spent actively applying the information in group activities.

Course Objectives:
1. To familiarize students with the range of assessment strategies that may be used to determine the function of challenging behavior
2. To familiarize students with the range of positive intervention strategies for individuals who engage in challenging behavior (e.g., behav-

ioral momentum, communicative replacement, environmental rearrangement)
3. To familiarize students with ways to modify intervention strategies for individuals who have severe communication deficits

Student Responsibilities in this Course:

Required Readings: Readings will be assigned relative to each topic. Students should complete the readings prior to the class session in which they will be discussed. The text (Durand, 1990) is available at the University of Minnesota Bookstore (Williamson Hall). All additional readings will be distributed in class.

Functional Assessment: Students will be required to complete a functional assessment of behaviors and summarize the results of this assessment. Interview, Direct Observation, and Summary forms will be provided.

Intervention Plan: An intervention plan based on the results of the functional assessment of behaviors will be developed. This plan will draw from the intervention methods presented in class. Forms for completing the intervention plan will be provided.

Grades: Each assignment is worth a total of 10 points. Ten points will be awarded if the assignment is satisfactorily completed and handed in on time.

Assigned Readings:

Durand, V.M. (1990). *Severe behavior problems: A functional communication training approach.* New York: The Guilford Press.

Excerpts from O'Neill, R.E., Horner, R.H., Albin, R.W., Storey, K., & Sprague, J. (1990). *Functional analysis: A practical assessment guide.* Sycamore, IL: Sycamore Press.

Excerpts from McEvoy, M. (Ed.). (1990). Organizing caregiving environments for young children with handicaps. *Education and Treatment of Young Children,* 13(4).

Reichle, J., & Johnston, S. (1993). Replacing challenging behavior: The role of communication intervention. *Topics in Language Disorders,* 13(30), 61–77.

Excerpts from Reichle et al. (in prep). *Intervention module.* Developing and Evaluating a Model of Inservice and Technical Assistance to Prevent Challenging Behavior in Preschoolers (Grant # H024P10017).

Outline of Topics to Be Addressed in this Course:

Week	Date	Course Outline
1	2/3	**Topic:** Introduction

1. Pretest
2. Overview of the Course
3. Socially Motivated and Nonsocially Motivated Challenging Behavior
4. Relationship Between Communication and Challenging Behavior
5. Communicative Functions of Challenging Behavior

Activity: Group discussion of videotape examples
Assigned Reading: Reichle, J., & Johnston, S. (1993) and Chapter 1 and Chapter 2 (Durand, 1990)
Instructors: Feeley & Johnston

2	2/10	**Topics:** Functional Assessment of Challenging Behavior

1. Purpose of Assessment
2. Functional Assessment Strategies
3. Relative Strengths and Weaknesses of Specific Strategies

Activity: Collecting and summarizing information from direct observations
Assignment: Assessment of student (due week 4)
Assigned Reading: Chapter 1 and Chapter 3 (Durand, 1990)
Instructor: Johnston

3	2/17	**Topic:** Functional Assessment of Challenging Behavior (cont.)

Activity: Collecting and summarizing information from direct observations
Assigned Reading: Chapter 3 (Durand, 1990)
Instructors: Feeley & Johnston

4	3/3	**Topic:** Environmental Arrangements

1. Schedules
2. Environmental Rearrangement
   - Rationale for Rearranging the Environment
   - Classroom Arrangement

• Selecting and Arranging Materials

Activity: Small group brainstorming
Assignment: Assessment of student due at beginning of class
Assigned Reading: Reichle et al. (in prep) and McEvoy, M. (1990)
Instructor: Feeley

5   3/10   **Topic:** Interventions that Do Not Honor the Communicative Function of the Challenging Behavior

1. Choice Making
2. Prespecify the Reinforcer
3. Preferred Item as a Distractor

Activity: Small group brainstorming
Assignment: Intervention program for student (due week 8)
Assigned reading: None
Instructor: Johnston

6   3/17   **Topic:** Interventions that Do Not Honor the Communicative Function of the Challenging Behavior (cont.)

4. High Probability Request Sequence
5. Tolerance for Delay
6. Collaboration

Activity: Evaluating an intervention program and data and troubleshooting the intervention program
Assigned Reading: Reichle et al. (in prep)
Instructor: Feeley

7   3/24   **Topic:** Modifications to Intervention Strategies for Individuals Who Have Severe Communication Deficits; Intervention Strategies that Honor the Communicative Function of the Challenging Behavior

1. Communicative Replacements for Challenging Behaviors that Serve the Function of Escape/Avoid

Activity: None
Assignment: Intervention program for student due at beginning of class

Assigned Reading: Chapter 4 and Chapter 5
(Durand, 1990)
Instructors: Feeley & Johnston

8   3/31   **Topic:** Intervention Strategies that Honor the Com-
municative Function of the Challenging
Behavior (cont.)
3. Communicative Replacements for Challenging
Behaviors that Serve the Function of Obtain
Access
4. Additional Considerations
• Functional Considerations
• Response Efficiency

Activity: None
Assignment: Intervention program for student due
at beginning of class
Assigned Reading: Chapter 4 and Chapter 5
(Durand, 1990)
Instructors: Feeley & Johnston

9   4/7   **Topic:** Prompting Strategies; Learner Progress
Monitoring

Activity: None
Assigned Reading: Handouts
Instructor: Feeley

10   4/14   **Topic:** Case Study; Model of Inservice Training and
Technical Assistance; Posttest; Course
Evaluations

Activity: Bringing It All Together
Assigned Reading: Technical Assistance Model
Overview
Instructors: Feeley & Johnston

11

Avoiding Due Process Hearings

Developing an Open Relationship Between Parents and School Districts

William L.E. Dussault

The term *due process hearings*, as used in the context of special educa-tion, refers to the legal forum in which formal conflicts are re-solved between parents of children with disabilities and school districts. Hearings are held before administrative law judges (ALJs) in a very structured legal proceeding. Just as in a trial court, testimony of wit-nesses and evidence are presented, witnesses are cross-examined, and the ALJ makes a written decision. The ALJ decides the facts and applies state and federal law to those facts to determine the case outcome.

Experience is demonstrating that due process hearings are not leading to comfortable or even reasonable resolutions of conflict over the appropriateness of the evaluation, program, or placement of a student with
a disability. Hearings are expensive and extremely time consuming. They
often result in decisions that satisfy neither party. A cursory review of due
process hearing decisions across the United States discloses that issues
are often not properly selected or fully presented by parents or school districts. As a result, students are becoming the victims of parent–district
conflict, the students' needs are not being met, and there are valid claims
by both the parents and the districts that are unresolved.

Decisions are often based upon what is generally acceptable for
many students with disabilities rather than what is individually appropriate for a particular student. District personnel often feel too con-
strained to express the same opinions in a hearing that they offer to
parents in private for fear of losing their jobs. Furthermore, qualified
attorneys are not readily available to all parents. Inexperienced attorneys
need to charge excessive retainers to meet ongoing costs while they learn
the basic law and cases, all at the parents' or school districts' expense.

Most important, the due process hearing itself fosters conflict and disagreement rather than conciliation with a positive attitude for all participants. Although criticism of PL 94-142 (the Education for All Handicapped
Children Act of 1975), its regulations, and their implementation has been
widespread, this author remains firmly convinced of the law's basic
strength and inherent value. A radical, perhaps even revolutionary, new
approach to education has been established, in which educational programs are to be individualized for each child, and parents have the right to
legally challenge adverse decisions. It would be tragically naive to assume
that the course of implementation would be smooth or rapid. No law is
self-enforcing or self-regulating. Certainly, PL 94-142 and its reauthoriza-
tion, the Individuals with Disabilities Education Act of 1990 (PL 101-476),
are not exceptions. Notwithstanding their alleged shortcomings in implementation, they provide parents with a procedural mechanism to resolve
problems in a way that can guarantee effective and appropriate individualized education for each student who has a disability.

Since the early 1980s, I have been involved in hundreds of special education problem situations. Most often I work for or on behalf of a parent
of a special education student or on behalf of the student individually.
Occasionally I have represented school districts. Although some situations have required formal due process appeals, and a few have even required appeals to court, the vast majority of cases have been resolved by
careful preparation, negotiation, and compromise. A good faith effort on
the part of the parents, student, school district personnel, outside professionals, and attorneys is an absolute necessity. A review of the processes

used in our cases may help both school districts and parents find alternative means of defining and resolving their differences without resorting to formal conflict proceedings.

AVOIDING FORMAL CONFLICT PROCEEDINGS

Conflict between the parent—on behalf of a student with disabilities—and a school district can arise in a multitude of situations: if, for example, a student faces excessive or inappropriate discipline, suspension, or expulsion from district programs, or a student is placed in a program that does not provide him or her with meaningful contact with children without disabilities. The district may lack the capacity to provide a program that meets the student's individual needs, and therefore the parent seeks payment from the district for the student's private school placement. Other examples of conflict include insufficient therapy, recreational programming, or counseling services.

By the time parents come to an attorney for assistance, it is frequently the case that a significant special education problem is already evident. The relationship between the parents and the district may have broken down completely. Conflicts in personality may have taken precedence over the primary issue of the appropriateness of the student's education program, the need for related services, the need for a more complete evaluation, and so on. The parents and the district are at odds, with both sides being anxious to "win" at any price. Unfortunately, the price to be paid is often more than just the cost to the parents for attorney's fees and the cost to the district for the hearing examiner. The real cost to be paid is the loss or delay of appropriate educational programming for the child while the competing parties battle.

Such a situation need not occur. Several steps can be taken by both the parents and the district to avoid the frustrating, time-consuming, and expensive involvement of outsiders in what should be an open, honest, and equal give-and-take relationship between the parent, who should be given equal professional credence in this process, and the educator.

Sharing Information

School districts should ensure that all parents of children with disabilities within the district are advised of their basic rights under the law in language that is understandable to them. Moreover, the rights should be verbally explained in a meaningful way, rather than by a photocopied page of "fine print" with no discussion whatsoever with the parents. Many states have now drafted parent information handbooks written in easily understandable language, sometimes in question-and-answer form, which explain options available to the parents and student under the law.

In providing this information to parents and explaining it simply, the school district gains several important advantages:

1. The district establishes an atmosphere of cooperation and trust by disclosing information that the parents have a right to know. If the parents are forced to obtain this information from an outside source, the school district has suffered a drastic loss in credibility from the outset.
2. By providing a simple and understandable explanation of the laws, the school district will not only educate the parents, but it will educate its own employees, thus lessening confusion and minimizing the chances that employees will inadvertently be party to activities that will place the district in conflict with the regulations.
3. The district sets easily understandable ground rules by which both parties can "play" the game.

In the event that the district does not provide basic information on rights to parents, the parents will have to obtain it another way. Several options are available. The state education agency should have copies of both the federal and state special education laws and regulations available for distribution upon request. Parents should request any state agency-sponsored bulletins or pamphlets describing special education and the law. Copies of the federal regulations may also be obtained from the local offices of the U.S. Department of Education or the offices of congresspersons or senators. A copy of the state's current plan for providing special education in compliance with the federal laws could also provide valuable information. The plan is a public document and is obtainable either from the state education office or from the Office of Special Education and Rehabilitative Services (OSERS) of the U.S. Department of Education.

Gathering a Support Base

Long before the parents are placed in the situation of needing to be advocates on a problem-by-problem basis, it would be wise for them to become members of one of the many community organizations established on behalf of persons with disabilities. Such organizations might include The Arc (formerly the Association for Retarded Citizens); the United Cerebral Palsy Association, Inc.; the Autism Society of America; organizations for those with orthopedic, neurological, and behavioral impairments; the Council for Exceptional Children; and many others. The cost of such memberships is usually minimal. Many of the organizations provide memberships even without dues requirements. Valuable information is disseminated through monthly meetings and newsletters. Political trends, advice on state and local budget issues, program ideas, and information about availability of new service options and alternatives are often discussed. The other parents involved can provide mutual help and support and, in doing so, form a necessary grass roots force to effect the overall system change that is often necessary.

But perhaps the most important reason for such an association, when one is faced with a problem that may require action on behalf of one's own child, is the availability of information from other members in the group concerning the basic attitudes of the school district involved. An understanding of the overall philosophy and attitudes of the people providing the program in the school district is absolutely essential to the proper preparation and presentation of a position on behalf of the child. If one is able to determine that the district's special education director is strongly committed to the provision of appropriate, inclusive, and high-quality special education programs and services and has the power to implement such programs, it can be reasonably assumed that a positive, straightforward, well-prepared approach has a reasonable chance at success. If, on the other hand, one is dealing with a school district in which the special education director has no authority, or equally important, has no commitment to appropriate programming, the approach must be totally different. The presentation will then need to emphasize compliance with regulations and strict adherence to time lines. A cooperative effort toward resolution is less likely in this case. Full written documentation of all procedural steps must be obtained, including written confirmation of subjects discussed and recommendations made or received in any personal conferences or telephone conversations. Recourse to experienced advocates and attorneys may be necessary in order to force unwilling compliance from the district and, equally important, to monitor program implementation for continued compliance. A competent independent education expert is invaluable in such situations.

It is critical to know whether the district is failing to provide programs because of a perceived lack of financial resources, lack of appropriate qualified staff, philosophical disagreement with a particular proposed program, or simply a basic personality clash between parents and one or more district personnel. Other parents who belong to the organizations described previously may have had difficulties with the same district in the past. They can provide valuable insights into the attitudes and personalities involved. In attempting to discover reasons other than those that might originate in personality concerns, it might be advisable to simply ask someone in the district, "What are the problems you have in giving my child a program I think is appropriate?" If the question is asked in an open and honest way to a school district representative who has provided good information to parents in the past, it is likely the parents will again obtain a straight answer. Although this information should not necessarily change the goal, it may radically change the type of approach one will have to make to the district. Some problems the parents and district may simply have to live with; however, many of the district's problems, although real and pressing, do *not* justify a denial of appropriate programs for all students with disabilities.

Early Preparation

Avoidance of due process actually commences long before a conflict or problem arises between the parents and the school district. One of the most important qualities of competent parent participation is preparation. Preparation should start prior to the first individualized education program (IEP) conference and, quite probably, prior even to the evaluation of the child. From the time the child is enrolled in school, parents should maintain a complete copy of the student's school records. Active involvement through parent conferences should take place on an ongoing basis.

Children who have severe disabilities have obvious needs for assistance. Advocacy for their programs should start at birth. Children who have mild difficulties are often not classified as "disabled" for purposes of the law until later in their educational programs. A collection of papers they have completed, art projects they have done, report cards they have received, tests they have taken, and other school records can be valuable in documenting the need for special programs. If the parents have failed to maintain such a record, the school district will usually provide copies of the school records upon reasonable request by the parents. Although the school district is obligated to provide any information in the school records to the parents, it may charge a reasonable copying expense for providing the documents.

Assessing a Child's Evaluation by the School District

When a child is evaluated for placement by his or her school district, parents and professionals should consider the following questions to be sure that the child has been evaluated and placed correctly.

What Tests Can I Trust? When a child is referred for special education evaluation, the district is required to comply with certain evaluation procedures. Any tests or evaluation materials must be provided and administered in the child's native language or through another appropriate mode of communication. It is important to remember that many of the so-called "standardized" IQ tests have not been validated for use with children who experience disabilities. They are particularly subject to question when used with children with either perceptual impairments or physical disabilities, especially if the tests require timed answers or answers completed only with pencil and paper. Any tests given must have been validated for the specific purpose and population for which they are used.

Thus, if a vocational evaluation is being given, tests validated to predict vocational ability or outcome should be used. Likewise, evaluation materials must be tailored to assess the specific areas of educational need.

A particular note of caution to parents and professionals concerned with children with learning disabilities, hearing impairments, or both: Be wary of tests that stress verbal performance. The perceptual difficulties of these children make them particularly susceptible to unduly deflated scores in these areas. We are also noting with increasing frequency the importance of complete neurological evaluations, including neuropsychological testing, as our awareness of the incidence of undiagnosed and previously unsuspected neurological dysfunction and seizure disorders is growing.

Tests that result in a simple IQ score are often used by a district for placement purposes, but have little diagnostic value unless coupled with additional tests that review actual needs. No single procedure should be used as the sole criterion for determining the appropriate education program for a child. Reliance on averaged scores, rather than close scrutiny of subtest areas by qualified professionals, often leaves a district with a highly inaccurate picture of the child's ability.

How Does the Multidisciplinary Team Influence the Evaluation? The district is required to evaluate the child through the efforts of a multidisciplinary team or group of persons, including at least one teacher or other specialist with knowledge in the area of the suspected disability. All of the areas of the child's suspected disabilities should be evaluated, including, where appropriate, health and vision screening, social and emotional status, general intelligence, academic performance, communicative ability, motor function, and even complete medical and neurological evaluations. The district may utilize prior outside evaluations or may even request new evaluations at its own expense when indicated. Both the parent and the district must realize that the purpose of the evaluation is not simply to qualify the student for special education services so that the student generates money for the district, but rather to determine the actual functional ability and disability of the student and to provide a prescriptive program based upon those factors. If the only purpose of the evaluation is to generate a general category label or qualification for state funding purposes, and sufficient information is not provided to allow for competent individualized planning for the student, then the evaluation is inappropriate and inadequate and serves no useful function for the district, the parent, or the student. The program must flow from and be directly related to the evaluation.

What Classification Is Appropriate? Many parents and districts are still being sidetracked into arguments as to which classification is appropriate for the particular student. A district may have classified a student as having mental retardation when the parents believe the student is more appropriately classified as having learning disabilities. These arguments often occur in states where local school districts generate state and federal dollars for children based upon the number of children in particular categories. The issue of category is one that is properly argued only between the local education agency and the state. The key issue between the parents and the school district relates to the appropriateness of the program proposed for the student, not the funding label the student bears. Unfortunately, many school districts around the country still determine education placements or student:teacher ratios based upon the classification of the child. In this respect, an argument about classification may seem pertinent, but it must be remembered that the key legal argument is one that relates principally to the appropriateness of the child's IEP to his or her unique needs. One could facetiously say that, insofar as the student is concerned, any label could be used *as long as* the program provided to the child is appropriate to his or her individually demonstrated needs. Obviously, a competent evaluation clearly defining those needs is critical to the design of the ultimate appropriate program.

When Is an Outside Independent Evaluation Appropriate? The federal regulations provide that a parent may request the district to pay for an outside independent educational evaluation in the event that the parents do not think that the district's evaluation is appropriate. In order to determine whether an outside evaluation should be requested, the parents should obtain copies of all test summaries and test results completed in the district's evaluation. The parents should review these test results. If there are any questions—about the kind of test given, the test results, the qualifications of the person giving the test, or the applicability of the test to the particular child's disability—the parents should request a conference with the school district personnel responsible for giving the tests. In such a conference, the parents should be especially concerned about ensuring that the tests given bear a direct relationship to the child's particular disability. Parents should insist on an explanation from the school district personnel in language that is understandable to them, free from psychological jargon. If the parents are left with the instinctive feeling that the tests are not appropriate to the student or that the results do not accurately reflect the student's capacity or needs, then the parents should either request additional tests from the district or should seriously consider requesting outside assistance.

In the vast majority of cases, parents will not be aware of the specific tests given, how the tests are applied, and what the tests are designed to measure. The yardstick for the parents in measuring the appropriateness of the tests is how well the tests describe what the student can and cannot actually do. The parents have a wealth of experience from their daily relationship with the child with which to assess the evaluations. If questions persist after in-district explanations are received, it would be well advised to seek the assistance of an experienced advocate.

If it is decided that an outside evaluation is necessary, parents have the freedom to choose who will do the evaluation. Although recommendations from the school district should be considered, so should all recommendations from any advocacy agencies with which the parents are involved. The outside evaluation should consist of all appropriate tests necessary to assess the child's abilities properly. An important component of the final report of the outside evaluation should be the specific recommendations made concerning program design for the child.

The parents might also keep in mind when choosing a facility for an outside evaluation that it might become necessary for a representative of that outside facility to provide testimony as to the appropriateness of both the district evaluation and the outside evaluation. The district does have the option, under the federal regulations, of requesting a hearing for the purpose of demonstrating that its in-house evaluation is appropriate. Should this hearing be called, the outside facility will no doubt be required to provide testimony to support its own viewpoint.

Even if the parents choose to obtain an outside evaluation without requesting that the school district pay for it, the school district must, and should want to, consider the results of that assessment in preparing the IEP. Because the outside independent facilities are not generally tied to a state funding system that rewards placement of a child in a particular category, outside assessments are often more helpful in providing prescriptions directly related to the child's individual program needs. The school district may even want to suggest an outside evaluation to support its own testing results and further establish its credibility with the parents.

In the event that the school district does choose to request a hearing to avoid the cost of the outside independent educational evaluation, it may be a good idea to suggest delaying that hearing until assessments by both the school district and the outside professional can be compared. Additionally, once the outside assessment is received, discussions concerning the program can commence immediately. If there is to be an argument over the program as well as who should be responsible for paying for the assessment, it can be accomplished in one hearing, thus minimizing the cost and time involved. The alternative is to have a due process hearing to discuss the issue of payment for the outside evaluation, complete that hearing, obtain the outside evaluation, and then have a second hearing to discuss program elements. Obviously, the cost and delay would be substantial in the latter situation. It is far more reasonable to determine whether there will be an argument over program elements before establishing who will take the economic responsibility for the outside evaluation. If there is no argument over program elements, it may be worthwhile to compromise the issue of payment of the outside evaluation in order to continue cooperative relationships between the district and the parents.

IEP CONFERENCE

The single most important contact between the school district and the parents occurs at the IEP conference. Generally, it is the school district's prerogative to schedule this conference. The regulations do provide that the conference should be scheduled at a time that is mutually agreeable to the parents and the school district; therefore, the convenience of both parties must be considered in choosing that time. Both the school district and the parents should be fully prepared for the conference. The school district's preparation may seem obvious. The district should have completed an evaluation of the child that considers the child's actual day-to-day program needs. Based upon the child's evaluation, the school district should have suggestions available both as to the nature of the specially designed instruction that the child is to receive and as to all related services needed by the child. The district must remember that it has an obligation to provide programs for the child on an individually designed basis and not solely based upon the programs the school district currently has available. The program elements of the IEP, including the statement of ability and disability, goals, objectives, and relative time spent in general versus special education classes and related services (or in a full-time inclusive general education classroom), must be decided before a placement decision can be made. Program elements direct the placement decisions, not the other way around. If the district proposes a specific student placement before clearly articulating the program elements of the IEP, the district is in violation of the federal statute and rules. The district should be prepared to discuss its program proposals and placement recommendations completely, knowing they are fully subject to amendment or rejection by the parents who are equal partners in the IEP conference.

The parents should prepare for the IEP conference by carefully, thoughtfully, and completely reviewing the child's education records and the parents' own experiences concerning 1) what methods work and do not work with the child, 2) what the child now knows, and 3) what the parents want the child to learn in the forthcoming year. Parents cannot expect to be treated as "professionals" with professional knowledge about the child unless they prepare in a fully competent and professional manner. A typed summary should be prepared describing the child's strengths and weaknesses. Prior interventions at home and at school that have been tried successfully or unsuccessfully should be listed and fully discussed. The parents' goals for the child should be included with a focus on how those goals will be meaningful to the child's day-to-day living needs. Sufficient copies should be made to allow distribution to all school personnel present at the conference.

The parents need not have a precise idea of what specific teaching program should be applied to meet the child's particular individual needs, but the parents should keep in mind what the general focus of education is for the child. Special education services for children with more severe disabilities should serve one primary purpose above all others: the development of sufficient independent living skills so that, at the end of the child's education career, the child will have moved toward living independently as a self-supporting member of the community in a typical work, living, and social environment. Although total independence might not be seen to be an appropriate goal for every child, reduction of dependency on others should be. For most students with disabilities, normal educational progress—grade level to grade level—should be assumed to be their basic right.

It is possible that the parents may feel intimidated in the IEP conference. This is often the case, particularly when school districts load their side of the table with two, three, four, or even more professionals who speak in a language that is totally unfamiliar to the parents. The best way to overcome that kind of intimidation is for both sides of the IEP team to ground the subject of the conference firmly in the particular child to be addressed. Each time a professional statement is made, it should be directly related to and explained in the context of the child involved. The parents should feel free to ask questions such as the following: How does that apply to my child? How will that work in the classroom on a day-to-day basis? How will that move my child toward independence? If the parents do feel intimidated at an IEP conference, a final proposed IEP probably should not be signed at that time. The parents should request a copy and take it home to study in a less pressured environment. School districts can offer a smaller follow-up conference with only key personnel present. At that point, the parents may contact other parents who have worked with the program or an outside advocate to ensure understanding of the district's proposed program components.

The federal regulations provide that the IEP should contain objective criteria, evaluation procedures, and schedules to determine whether the short-term instructional objectives established in the IEP are being met. This requires that the objectives be established in language that allows for measurement of the child's progress over time. The IEP is not a contract guaranteeing that progress will be made in the child's program; however, it is the basic planning tool for evaluation of whether the program is successful. If progress under the IEP is evaluated on an annual basis only, much time could be lost if the child is not able to benefit from the program designed in the IEP. The lack of the child's progress may not be the school district's "fault." It may simply mean that the program chosen is not the appropriate one for the child. The important factor here is not that the school district admit fault or legal responsibility for the lack of progress, but rather that the program be changed as quickly as possible to become appropriate for the student. Thus, provision for monitoring a student's progress within the program at short intervals (even biweekly) is critical. This provision should be requested by the parent and should be specifically included in the IEP. The goal must be to keep the IEP relevant to the child's needs.

Many parents become extremely concerned about the actual physical location where the program is to be provided. The federal law and regulations emphasize that the program is to take place in the *least restrictive environment*, often defined as the *mainstream*. Current professional language uses the terms *integration* or *inclusion*. The underlying legal requirement simply states that all children should be educated in the class they would attend if they did not have a disability. By definition, the more geographically removed the child's program is from the school in which the child would have been placed but for his or her disability, the more *restrictive* that program is. Neither the school district nor the parent is allowed to move the child from that typical environment until the district can demonstrate that the child cannot receive an appropriate education there, even with the use of supplementary aids and services. The child may then be placed in a more restrictive program, moving from the typical classroom only so far as is necessary to provide a program that is appropriate. Segregated and isolated classrooms, school wings, or school buildings are not the preferred option of the law.

If the discussion in the IEP conference has been open and cooperative, the district has made suggestions for the child's program that appear directly related to his or her needs, and the child's progress toward the goals and objectives can be measured in an objective way, the parent may wish to sign the IEP immediately and commence the program as quickly as possible. However, the parents certainly have a right to take a copy of the district's proposal home, consider it, and obtain whatever outside assistance is appropriate before making their decision.

IEP Follow-Up

The cooperative effort is not completed when the IEP is signed and the program commenced. Progress toward the short-term objectives and the annual goals should be monitored. Ongoing contact between the parent and special education teachers, any therapists, and any general education teachers involved in an inclusive program is critical. The short-term objectives in the IEP should not be cast in concrete, and both sides should be amenable to changes based upon the child's experience and progress in the program. The parents should expect, and the school district should provide, training for the parents and at-home programs that will strengthen the child's school program. It should be evident to all parties involved that the program for the child must be consistently applied, both at school and at home, in order to be effective. If the two areas of the child's life are working at cross purposes, confusion will result and progress may be extremely limited.

The parents are faced with a much more difficult situation when it is felt that the school district is not being responsive to the child's needs or that the appropriate program for the child is simply not being made available. If the parents have the feeling, either at the IEP conference or immediately thereafter, that the district is not willing to provide an appropriate program for their child, the parents should take several preliminary steps before deciding to make a due process appeal. These steps are discussed in the next section.

Decisions Regarding a Due Process Appeal

First, the parents must review their educational goals for the child in light of the school district's evaluation material. The parents must decide if the goals can be realistically obtained and evaluate whether their position is essential to an appropriate program for the child and is not about an extraneous issue, such as categorization or dollars available. Second, they must attempt to identify the areas of disagreement with the school district and determine in each area of disagreement their specific desires for the child's program. If the parents are not able to say what is required to provide an appropriate program for the child in that area, it may be necessary to seek outside assistance. In attempting to clarify the problem areas, it might be advisable for them to talk with the direct staff who have been working with the child. Last year's teacher, therapist, or classroom aide may be able to provide information that will assist in clarifying this year's program needs.

If a conflict does exist between the parents and the district on a program element important to an appropriate education, several alternative methods of approaching the district are possible. If one is dealing with a cooperative district and is involved in a disagreement as to a program component, where both sides express their views openly and honestly, but sincerely differ about the child's needs, it may be best to use an outside professional for an independent opinion. All parties should welcome such an opportunity to avoid the potential for a hearing. It might be extremely advantageous to the parents and child to suggest that they and their expert meet the district representatives in an attempt to resolve conflicts before they resort to due process. Careful scrutiny of the district is required in this situation to ensure that the district truly does have a good faith program disagreement and is not simply stalling to gain time. If a personality conflict appears to be confusing the education issues, it might be useful to ask the district representative to invite a separate, uninvolved administrator from that district, or even from a separate district, the regional education service district, the state education agency, or a local college or university, to act as a mediator. Such sessions should be "off the record" to allow for a full and frank airing of both personality and program disputes. Once the air is cleared and both sides have vented their frustration, negotiation and compromise might be possible.

CONCLUSIONS

Avoidance of due process requires effort, preparation, commitment, and willingness to sacrifice *self* for the educational benefit of the student. Both sides must work in good faith. They must acknowledge what they are able to do and admit what they cannot do. There is little to be gained and much to be lost in standing on principle alone, trying to win at any cost to prevent damage to ego or establishment of precedent. The whole focus must be on the best interests and best educational program for the child. Winning no longer matters if it means sacrifice of the student's progress toward independence as an adult.

REFERENCES

Education for All Handicapped Children Act of 1975, PL 94-142. (August 23, 1977). Title 20, U.S.C. 1401 et seq: *U.S. Statutes at Large, 89,* 773–796.
Individuals with Disabilities Education Act of 1990 (IDEA), PL 101-476. (October 30, 1990). Title 20, U.S.C. 1400 et seq: *U.S. Statutes at Large, 104,* 1103–1151.

Discussion

Lynn Kern Koegel and Robert L. Koegel

E ducation will always be in a continuous process of evolution. Now, possibly more than ever, as the civil rights of increasingly greater numbers of individuals with disabilities are being realized, changes are taking place that can simultaneously benefit children both with and without disabilities. Present research and practice are moving in the direction of a highly productive merger of special and general education. As society moves toward diversity and deinstitutionalization in our communities, this merger is quite timely, as those involved in the education of children with disabilities realize that the need to teach functional academic and social skills and nurture the development of friendships needs to begin at birth and continue throughout life. Only with careful planning and implementation will a child with a disability grow to become a contributing member of society. And only with this same careful planning will children without disabilities learn to appreciate the contributions that all children can make to the quality of life for everyone. The chapters in this section represent the thoughts, research, and experience of people involved in the lives of individuals with disabilities through a variety of perspectives: parental, legal, research, and practitioner. This discussion reviews several important themes that emerge as vitally important to the successful inclusion of children with disabilities in general education classrooms and then summarizes some practical procedures important for achieving such success.

GENERAL IMPORTANT THEMES

Several general important themes appear to be mandatory for successful inclusionary programs. First, success involves careful *planning and prepa-*

ration in the general education classroom. Practitioners, families, researchers, and others well document the fact that, without planning and preparation, the educational process too often ends up as a reactive system in which the child is not experiencing the advantages of inclusion, but is "dumped" in an educational program that depends on punishment as a corrective strategy, as Taylor and Bailey discuss in Chapter 9. In contrast, programs that provide planning can instate the appropriate staff; provide in-services to teachers, families, and other school personnel; and set up the system well in advance are much more likely to implement proactive strategies so that problems are minimized and the reliance on punishment can be avoided.

Second, also related to the above theme of preparation, is the fact that *prevention* of severe secondary behavior problems is a critical goal for children with disabilities, and its importance cannot be minimized. There is now a consensus that, without intervention, academic, social, and linguistic difficulties do not improve with age—they typically worsen. Furthermore, scientific studies document the interrelationships between deficit areas and the negative effect one area can have on others. For instance, early communication problems are likely to be associated with challenging problem behaviors and social difficulties. The onset of challenging problem behaviors often begins in early childhood. Thus, identifying precursors and establishing intervention programs at the earliest possible point in a child's life appears to be critical. Kaiser and Hester (Chapter 7) point out that many language-learning children experience limited support for using new language skills, even in classrooms with a 4:1 adult: child ratio. Because the extent to which children demonstrate generalization largely depends on specific invitations provided by others, enhancing conversational patterns is essential for improving communication. Kaiser and Hester note several strategies to create supportive social communicative environments.

A third theme relates to the fact that *proactive strategies that offer positive behavioral support* need to be regularly implemented throughout the educational process for all children. Functional analyses can be very helpful in determining simple ecological manipulations and treatment plans to reduce many escape, avoidance, and attention-seeking functions that are often the reason for disruptive behaviors. Furthermore, a proactive approach can help determine setting events, previously successful intervention programs, areas of ability and disability, and dislikes and desires of each individual child in order to promote success and reduce the likelihood for reactive and punitive measures. There is now a wealth of information related to nonaversive intervention strategies, many discussed in this book, that greatly reduce or eliminate the need for the regular and common use of punishment procedures in the schools.

Fourth, *coordination and collaboration* appear to be more than worth the effort, and without these two ingredients a successful program is unlikely to emerge. Without coordination and collaboration, gains will be minimal and a child may even be confused by different expectations in various environments. As Dussault (Chapter 11) points out, the lack of coordination and collaboration really hurts the child, and no one will be completely satisfied without a harmonious relationship. Coordination and collaboration involves give and take among the various agencies and individuals (including parents) responsible for a particular child, and efforts to do this are well rewarded.

Fifth, *monitoring* and *evaluation* need to be ongoing processes with continual adjustments to achieve effective educational planning for all children. *Gains* need to be monitored to proceed through *goals* in a timely fashion, but reevaluation and adjusting of goals that are not attained are equally important. This process should not occur at annual IEP meetings, but continue in the classroom throughout the year. Additional monitoring and evaluation of *procedural implementation* also need to be ongoing. Feedback and assistance from co-workers, consultants, parents, and others can help ensure quality of implementation of treatment procedures.

Finally, it is important to remember throughout the educational process that progress toward *socially valid life-span needs* are of the utmost importance. When long- and short-term goals are developed, planners need to consider longitudinal needs and identify factors that will lead to the children's independence as adults. Gains need to be able to be objectively documented to provide socially meaningful behavioral changes and outcomes that can be systematically built upon over the life span of the individual with disabilities. This results in a meaningful accumulation of skills and behaviors that lead to greater self-sufficiency and autonomy in adulthood.

PROCEDURAL IMPLEMENTATION

The authors of the preceding chapters have provided the readers with several practical procedures for promoting educational inclusion. The following procedures have been scientifically documented to result in effective behavior change. First, *functional analysis* needs to be an integral part of *every* child's program. It is no longer sufficient to rely on response consequences alone. As Reichle et al. (Chapter 10) point out, observations need to be made to 1) document the frequency of target behaviors, 2) determine the antecedents that may influence behaviors, 3) identify the setting in which the behavior occurs, and 4) identify the natural consequences of the behavior. Assessing when problem behaviors are present and absent helps to identify the function as well as the factors that relate to the cause of the problem. Then, appropriate functionally equivalent replacement behaviors can be taught. To be specific, environmental rearrangements, ecological manipulations, communicative alternatives, and curricular revisions can be made accordingly.

Second, as Sailor (Chapter 8) notes, *special education services need to be implemented within the context of the general education program.* Special education goals need to be developed within the academic and social context of inclusionary classrooms. Many school districts have assumed an "itinerant" special education classroom where children who were once segregated in a special class are now included in general education classes throughout all or most of the day, while the special education teacher and aides serve as support staff within the general education classrooms that have included children with severe disabilities. Other parents and community volunteers, and cross- and same-age peers can be helpful with the inclusion of these students, maximizing social benefits and minimizing the costs for the district. And, as time passes, the significant gains that these children make when a well-structured program is implemented greatly decreases and can eliminate the need for specialized services in later years of life.

Implementing special education goals within the context of general education necessitates the *adaptation of curriculum.* This can be accomplished via several means. Nickels (Chapter 6) demonstrates the use of *partial participation.* This method incorporates individual goals within exactly the same assignments that peers without disabilities perform. As such, assignments will be age appropriate but geared to the individual's own level of functioning. Coordinating a functional analysis discussed above with curricular goals can result in some *curricular revisions,* such as adjusting the length, difficulty, and demand for fine or gross motor skills; including meaningful and functional tasks with the same goals; and allowing the child some choice-making options (Dunlap & Kern, 1993).

Some other successful procedures worthy of mentioning are discussed in other chapters in this volume, and we have also found them effective in our own research in full inclusion settings. One such procedure is the use of parent–professional collaboration to implement procedures such as academic *priming* so that the child with a disability can be prepared in advance, in a relaxed and informal manner at home, for the following day's lesson. This is an efficient and cost-effective method of treatment delivery and can foster productive relationships between teachers and families. Another tool is *self-management,* wherein a program is set up with gradually increasing autonomous responses required. Self-management has been proven to promote independence and can be nicely tied into the classes' reward systems; furthermore, some studies have shown positive classwide changes when all the children in a classroom evaluate their own behavior.

Finally, social development and friendships are areas too often overlooked (Hurley-Geffner, 1995). Since many children are being regularly exposed to peers with disabilities beginning in the preschool years, they are often much more tolerant and understanding of diversity. However, building friendships is usually tied into careful planning, *working with peers as well as direct work with the child with a disability*. Nickels (Chapter 6) describes an effective program used for younger children to assist with their understanding of diversity. Haring and Breen (1992) have also shown that recruiting an entire peer clique can be successful with older children in the secondary years. Some current work we are implementing in our clinic suggests that relationships can be improved when functional analysis and functionally equivalent responses are incorporated into play situations, along with the development of specialized games that provide inherently natural consequences for the child with disabilities. Families can be recruited to assist with the development of friendships after school and on weekends. Planning activities that are mutually rewarding to both the child with the disability and the peer is essential to positive relationships.

In summary, these chapters have pointed out both philosophical reasons for and practical guides to inclusive education. Although many of the procedures discussed in the chapters were originally developed for children with disabilities, the implementation of the techniques positively affect not only the child with disabilities, but *all* children. As teachers and other school personnel become more adept at techniques such as functional analysis, curricular adaptation and revision, individualization, and so forth, all the children in the classroom are likely to benefit from this progress. Finally, as Nickels points out, over the years the children without disabilities benefit greatly by learning compassion, tolerance, the beauty of diversity, and the sense of camaraderie when inclusionary programs are implemented carefully and properly. These values will endure throughout a person's life and cannot be gained without an inclusionary model wherein adults' examples illustrate the acceptance and inclusion of all children regardless of ability level.

REFERENCES

Dunlap, G., & Kern, L. (1993). Assessment and intervention for children within the instructional curriculum. In J. Reichle, & D.P. Wacker (Eds.), *Communication and language intervention: Vol. 3. Communicative alternatives to challenging behavior: Integrating functional assessment and intervention strategies* (pp. 177–204). Baltimore: Paul H. Brookes Publishing Co.

Haring, T.G., & Breen, C.G. (1992). A peer-mediated social network interventioin to enhance the social integration of persons with moderated and severe disabilities. *Journal of Applied Behavior Analysis, 24,* 337–347.

Hurley-Geffner, C. (1995). Friendships between children with and without developmental disabilities. In R.L. Koegel & L.K. Koegel (Eds.), *Teaching children with autism: Strategies for initiating positive interactions and improving learning opportunities.* (pp. 105–125). Baltimore: Paul H. Brookes Publishing Co.

III

Social Inclusion

12

Social Relationships, Influential Variables, and Change Across the Life Span

Craig H. Kennedy and Tiina Itkonen

It is no overstatement to say that without the existence of social relationships, human beings (as we know ourselves and our cultures) would not exist (Gewirtz & Petrovich, 1983; Mead, 1912). From birth throughout adulthood, the social relationships we engage in influence what we do, how we communicate, with whom we interact, where we interact, the friendships we develop, and the various roles we take in society. In essence, our relationships define who we are as individuals. From a more sociological perspective, interpersonal relationships provide the fundamental basis for how a society and its practices are shaped and evolve over time (Baldwin, 1986; Harris, 1977; Skinner, 1981).

At the most basic level, social relationships are based upon substantive interactions among two or more people that occur repeatedly over time. The benefits that accrue from interpersonal interactions at the individual level include companionship, emotional support, material aid, access to information, help with decision making, and opportunities to meet new people (Gottlieb, 1988). These benefits provide both the physical assistance needed to accomplish many of life's daily tasks as well as the psychological support required to lead satisfactory lives. Unfortunately, not all people have frequent access to social relationships and their attendant benefits. One group in particular, those people characterized as having severe disabilities, conspicuously lacks the benefits of frequent and long-term relationships (Kennedy, Horner, & Newton, 1989).

Increasingly, the focus of policy and research initiatives has been to ameliorate problems occasioned by the paucity of social relationships between people with and without severe disabilities (e.g., Haring, 1991; Kohler & Strain, 1992; Sailor, 1991). In many respects, the social inclusion of people with severe disabilities into the mainstream of society (and the social connections that may result) has become the defining outcome of efforts in this field (Winzer, 1993). Lasting social relationships are an outcome that is clearly valued, fervently sought after, and vexingly elusive (Strain, 1990).

The purpose of this chapter is to survey the current research literature on social relationships, with an emphasis on relationships between people with and without severe disabilities. The chapter asks what investigators have gained in their understanding of social connections and, more specifically, how that knowledge can be used to improve the ability of support environments to develop and maintain these connections. By gaining a better understanding of what the field has learned from past research endeavors, it is hoped that some insight will be gained into how to improve current efforts to provide effective behavioral supports that maximize an individual's social inclusion with other members of society.

A necessary first step in developing an understanding of interpersonal relationships is to distinguish between determinants of social behavior (i.e., *basic behavioral functions*) and parameters mitigating their availability (i.e., *support environments*). This distinction is an important one, and it provides the basis from which the existing literature is analyzed in this chapter. Although this distinction may be implicit in how investigators attempt to arrange behavioral supports for people with severe disabilities, a clearer explication of the distinction may prove useful in improving practices based upon the current research knowledge base.

Basic behavioral functions refer to the variables that determine how, and in what manner, individuals interact with one another; because of this, basic behavioral functions are important and influential variables. Support environments refer to settings that mediate the availability of basic behavioral functions vis-à-vis their physical and social arrangements. Because support environments can facilitate or constrain the occurrence of basic behavioral functions, they too warrant close scrutiny. One result of this disentanglement of functions and support environment arrangements should be a clearer understanding of the basic behavioral functions that influence social relationships. Such an understanding is one goal of this chapter.

A second goal of the chapter is to discuss how support environments are arranged at various points across the life span. If support environments are construed as facilitating (or constraining) influential relationship variables, a more explicit discussion of the forms social settings take seems warranted. Once a knowledge of the variables that influence social behavior is developed, an important question to consider is as follows: How do support environments for people with severe disabilities inhibit or optimize the potential for influential variables to function?

Once it is better understood how environments shape and maintain social behavior, this knowledge can be used to build more effective support environments. Distinguishing between behavioral functions and the arrangement of support environments provides an important basis for understanding social relationships. In making this distinction, this chapter asks the following questions:

1. What are the invariant functional relations that influence relationships?
2. What are the characteristics of current support environments?
3. How can social environments be changed to make more effective use of current data in this field?

INFLUENTIAL VARIABLES AFFECTING SOCIAL RELATIONSHIPS

The psychological contact between individuals provides the basis for understanding variables that influence the development of social relationships. It is this ongoing stream of interaction between individuals and the analysis of variables that influence the development and maintenance of relationships that help discern what variables are indeed influential. Consider an example: Two youths (one with and one without severe disabilities) are sitting next to each other at a table in a classroom used to edit the high school newspaper. Their task for the class period is to crop photographs to include in a story for an upcoming issue. One student comes across a picture of a person skiing and shows it to the other student. The students then begin an interaction with each other regarding the topic of skiing based upon the picture in front of them. This interaction continues for several minutes with both youths agreeing to interact again regarding the topic and perhaps pursue their interests together outside of class.

What variables influenced the occurrence of this social interaction? How might such an interaction lead to other interactions, perhaps in other settings (e.g., eating lunch together, going hiking)? These are important questions because without a basic understanding of why people interact, practitioners can only rely on intuition to guide their efforts. Given the positive effects that empirical research has had on the quality of life for people with severe disabilities, analysis and extension of intuitive knowledge appears a necessary and desirable step. Fortunately, the research literature provides some assistance in identifying several influential variables.

Proximity

One variable related to the development of social relationships is proximity. Proximity refers not only to the physical closeness of two people, but also to technologies that allow two individuals to interact (e.g., telephones, computers). For an interaction to occur, two individuals need to be able to mediate each other's behavior (Chadsey-Rusch & Rusch, 1988; Storey, 1993). For example, gaining a potential interactant's attention is a critical first step in initiating an interaction, yet the lack of proximity between two individuals can make this operation impossible. It is important to note that proximity alone as an influential variable is necessary but not sufficient to establish the interactions upon which relationships are based.

Mutually Reinforcing Events

In addition to proximity, there needs to be some reason for people to interact. Such reasons can be conceptualized most parsimoniously in terms of basic behavioral functions (Catania, 1992; Skinner, 1953; Thompson & Zeiler, 1986). Of primary importance in regard to behavioral functions are the consequences occasioned by social behavior (Skinner, 1981). If the collaboration of two individuals is necessary to obtain a particular outcome (e.g., going skiing, having a conversation, viewing a movie), the individuals will interact to the extent that the outcome(s) functions as a reinforcer. The interactive nature of social relationships is based upon individuals obtaining and/or avoiding particular consequences (Kimmel, 1979; Scanzoni, 1979).

Access to mutually reinforcing events is one such consequential function. For example, two people may attend a baseball game to see their favorite team compete or attend a movie while the carpet in their house is being cleaned. In each case, the individual's interactions result in a mutually reinforcing event. Such arrangements provide the basis for many of the social interactions in which people engage. At a place of employment such interactions may be based on completing a work-related task by a particular deadline or recruiting other co-workers to participate in a softball game. At school, students may work together to stage a musical performance or study together to complete a class assignment. At home, roommates might plan and cook a meal together or engage in spring cleaning.

These examples point to two important dimensions of mutually reinforcing events that appear important in determining the effectiveness of the reinforcers. First, the event(s) needs to function as a reinforcer for each person involved (e.g., Chandler, Fowler, & Lubeck, 1992; Haring & Breen, 1992). If planning and cooking a meal is only positively reinforcing to one person, the event may function as a negative reinforcer for the others involved (e.g., they may leave the house to eat at a restaurant). In this case the reinforcing function of events would actually work counter to the goal of occasioning a social interaction. A second dimension contributing to the influence of mutually reinforcing events is the presence of a *cooperative contingency* for obtaining reinforcement. Cooperative contingencies exist when the coordinated responding of two (or more) individuals is necessary for obtaining reinforcement (Hake & Olvera, 1978; Hake & Vukelich, 1972). For example, if two people are going to attend a baseball game, one person might purchase the tickets and the other could provide transportation and refreshments at the stadium. In this case, the behavior of both individuals is necessary to occasion the reinforcers associated with attending a baseball game. Such cooperative arrangements typically occasion more frequent interactions between individuals than when cooperative contingencies are not in place (Azrin & Lindsley, 1956; Cohen, 1972; Hyten & Burns, 1986). This makes the occurrence of mutually reinforcing and cooperative contingencies a variable of primary importance in maintaining social relationships—two people tend to interact repeatedly when the results are mutually reinforcing.

Reciprocity

A related and important variable for understanding why relationships develop and maintain is reciprocity. Reciprocity can be defined as the exchange of reinforcers between two people (Berndt, 1986; Strain, Odom, & McConnell, 1984). The essence of reciprocity is that each of two individuals contributes in some manner to an interaction or series of interactions (and its maintaining reinforcers). For example, after receiving a birthday present from a friend, the recipient of the gift acknowledges the friend's

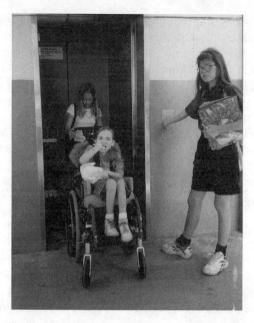

Providing, as well as receiving, social support is an important component in relationship development and maintenance.

efforts and sends him or her a "thank-you" card. Such a reciprocal exchange could be furthered by the birthday gift recipient giving the other friend a gift on his or her birthday, and so on. The central importance of reciprocity is exemplified in an article by Hallinan (1978/1979) focusing on children's social networks. This author assessed the influence of reciprocity on the formation and development of interpersonal relationships for a group of elementary school students across 1 school year. She found that when a high degree of reciprocity between particular individuals existed, relationships typically maintained over time; however, in reverse circumstances they did not typically maintain (see also Strain, Shores, & Timm, 1977).

Similar concerns regarding reciprocity and relationship durability have been noted by Kennedy et al. (1989) regarding interactions between adults with and without severe disabilities. Kennedy et al. hypothesized that it was a general lack of reciprocity between individuals that accounted for the dissolution of some relationships. That is, peers without disabilities were typically responsible for the majority of roles and functions within a relationship. For instance, viewed from the context of participating in activities (e.g., going to the movies, hiking, eating at a restaurant), the person without disabilities was responsible for the majority of tasks relating to interactions (e.g., initiating activities, scheduling activities, providing transportation, paying). For many individuals without disabilities, responsibilities entailed by interacting with people with severe disabilities may be too unidirectional in nature to maintain continued interactions. Thus, reciprocity between two people appears to be a critical variable in understanding relationship development.

Choice

One means of understanding the effects of an individual's contributions to a social relationship (i.e., the reinforcers he or she obtains or avoids in relation to the other person) is to conceptualize such events as choice situations regarding with whom a person spends time. Choices can involve with whom one interacts, when one interacts, where interactions occur, and in what activities one engages. From the perspective of the experimental analysis of behavior, choice is typically studied in terms of *concurrent operants* (Catania, 1966; de Villiers, 1977; Herrnstein, 1970, 1990; Horner & Day, 1991). For the purposes of this chapter, the concept of concurrent operants offers a basis for studying how people choose among available social situations.

The stream of behavior, in which each of us participates, constantly presents an individual with numerous opportunities to select among potential interactants and activities. A primary finding of research on concurrent operants is that four variables are closely associated with choice:

1. *Frequency* of reinforcement (e.g., the number of times a social interaction provides access to a preferred activity or person)
2. *Magnitude* of reinforcement (e.g., the amount of time two people interact in the preferred activity, how reinforcing it is to interact with a particular person)
3. *Delay* of reinforcement (e.g., how immediately accessible the person or preferred activity is)
4. *Effort* involved in occasioning reinforcement (e.g., the amount of work necessary to arrange an interaction or activity)

Of particular interest is how these four variables interact. For instance, the greater the frequency or magnitude of reinforcement, the greater the amount of time spent with that person; however, the greater the delay or effort, the less the amount of time spent with that person (relative to others). Consider a high school lunch period in which a student named Kate can spend time interacting with Joey or Allyssa. If interacting with Joey takes a greater amount of effort (e.g., locating him at one of several disparate locations on campus) and interacting with Allyssa is associated with a greater magnitude of reinforcement (e.g., more time to interact socially), then, on average, Kate will interact more often at lunch with Allyssa than with Joey. This may be the case even though, all other variables being equal, Kate would typically choose to spend more time with Joey. Ideally, practitioners want to maximize an individual's opportunity for interactions associated with frequent and large magnitude reinforcers and minimize delays in reinforcement and the effort required. Potentially, these variables are keys to understanding the interrelations between choice, reciprocity, and how social relationships evolve over time.

External Reinforcers

A final influential variable to discuss is the provision of external reinforcers to support a social relationship. One strategy used is to provide additional reinforcers for one or both individuals to engage in interactions. Monetary incentives (for adults), course credit (for students), and the approbations of teachers (for young children) are typical examples of external reinforcers. If the reinforcers available for engaging in interactions in terms of the variables previously discussed are insufficient to maintain interactions, additional incentives can increase the available reinforcers. For example, one strategy employed in adult support agencies has been to provide financial remuneration for a person without disabilities (and possibly his or her acquaintances) to engage in activities with people with severe disabilities (e.g., Newton & Horner, 1993). Another strategy typically used with preschoolers has been to provide teacher attention and praise for facilitating peers to initiate interactions (e.g., Kohler & Fowler, 1985; Odom & Strain, 1986). The overall goal when using external reinforcers is to "trap" individuals into previously unknown communities of social reinforcers (Baer & Wolf, 1970; McConnell, 1987). That is, external reinforcers can be used as initial incentives to induce people to interact, but optimally, it is the *natural* reinforcers available from social interactions that serve to maintain relationships. In this sense, external reinforcers are employed as a means of providing people with an incentive to get to know one another and then enjoy the resulting benefits.

Stability of Influential Variables

The influential variables just discussed provide a number of indices with which to assess how effectively support environments facilitate or constrain social interactions. However, before beginning a discussion of support environments and their influence on social relationships, it is important to note particular invariancies and changes that exist among variables. It is particularly important to note that the influential variables just outlined do not vary across a person's life span (with the exception of very early development) (Benson, Messer, & Gross, 1992; Sherman, 1982). That is, such variables underlie interactions from early childhood through adulthood and are basic building blocks for social interactions. However, the support environments that people with severe disabilities encounter across their lives do vary enormously in the degree to which the settings facilitate or inhibit the operation of these variables. This is of significant interest at this point in time because practitioners in this field are in the midst of a substantive and pervasive restructuring of supports for people with disabilities (Kohler & Strain, 1992; Sailor, 1991; Skrtic, 1991). Because variables influencing interpersonal relationships change little across an individual's life span and the physical and social arrangements accompanying different environments vary considerably, the next section explores how support environments affect influential variables.

FACILITATING INFLUENTIAL VARIABLES ACROSS THE LIFE SPAN

As more is learned about the behavioral principles underlying social relationships, applying that knowledge to structure the settings that people inhabit will be critical in achieving the valued outcomes the field is seeking. Currently, however, support environments for people with severe disabilities comprise a diverse array of arrangements. Some of these arrangements facilitate the availability of influential variables, while others constrain their availability. This heterogeneity of support environments is based upon such dimensions as 1) the manner in which people with severe disabilities are grouped/clustered, 2) the people who are contacted, 3) the availability of specific types of activities, 4) the emphasis and support available for social relationships, and 5) the physical proximity to typical community settings. Each of these dimensions can either facilitate or inhibit influential variables. When viewed from a life span perspective, support environments vary both across an individual's life span and within any group of people of a particular age. The focus of this discussion is to assay what optimizes influential variables and, conversely, what hinders their availability. Such information should provide a prescriptive understanding of the strengths and weaknesses of current support environments for people with severe disabilities.

Variation in Support Environments

Perhaps the best means of discriminating among the facilitative versus constraining dimensions of environments is to consider two end points along a broad continuum. First, consider an extreme case of an environment designed to inhibit the development of relationships between people with and without severe disabilities. A system producing such an environment would place people with severe disabilities in remote geographical areas; cluster large numbers of these individuals in dense groupings; eliminate access to typical community settings and interactions with community members; restrict the types of activities a person can do; and place little, if any, emphasis on developing and supporting social relationships.

Unfortunately, such constraining environments still exist. In fact, historically, they have been the primary means by which society has arranged environments for people with severe disabilities (e.g., institutionalization). The effect of such an environment on social relationships is quite predictable and undesirable (e.g., Bruininks, Meyers, Sigford, & Lakin, 1981).

Such an environment negates the opportunity for people with disabilities to make contact with others because of basic and pervasive restrictions in influential variables. As noted previously, proximity is a necessary component of social relationships. By removing an individual from typical settings, people, and activities, society restricts his or her opportunities to engage with others. For example, in many regions it is still common for school-age individuals to attend a "cluster" school only serving students with severe disabilities (where individuals are brought in from various communities). Importantly, even if proximity is overcome, such environments constrain other variables necessary to develop and maintain relationships (e.g., mutually reinforcing events, reciprocity, choice).

At the other extreme, consider a support environment designed to develop and maintain social relationships. Such an environment would have people with severe disabilities living in naturally occurring proportions within local communities, doing activities in which other individuals their age engage, choosing interactions in which they would like to engage, and interacting with a diversity of people from their community. This type of support environment actively encourages interactions among peers and sets the occasion for influential variables to act on behavior and their effects to be emphasized.

Current moves toward restructuring schools to be more inclusive environments for students (e.g., Stainback & Stainback, 1992) appear consistent with facilitating the effects of influential variables. Over time, practitioners have realized that such arrangements are more viable options for developing interpersonal relationships. It has been a gradual process in which a great deal has been learned from observing the consequences that result from efforts to help develop and maintain interactions. Whether researchers and practitioners have been cognizant of it, the implicit effects of influential variables have gradually shaped how support environments are structured. Fortunately, practitioners have been sensitive to the consequences of their efforts and are continuing to learn. For instance, as more is learned about the importance of ongoing proximity, the availability of mutually reinforcing events, and reciprocity, practitioners have consistently adjusted what are considered best practices to facilitate those influential variables (e.g., Nisbet, 1992; Odom, McConnell, & McEvoy, 1992; Putnam, 1991; Strain, 1991).

Perhaps because of the perceived effects of this latter approach, inclusive environments are receiving increasing emphasis and experimen-

Being in school with students without disabilities provides for numerous opportunities to interact. Those opportunities provide an initial occasion for developing social relationships.

tal study across the life span. In the area of early childhood education, there is substantive movement toward delivering supports in inclusive settings (Noonan & McCormick, 1993; Strain, 1990). For school-age students, current efforts are focusing on inclusion of support services into general education settings (Sailor, 1991; Salisbury, Palombaro, & Hollowood, 1993). Similarly, support services for adults are focusing on employment in the general work force and residing in typical community settings (Newton & Horner, 1993; Rusch, 1992). Each of these arrangements constructs an environment in such a manner as to negate proximity as an issue and emphasize common activities, cooperation, and choice among peers—conditions that appear consistent with developing knowledge of how relationships emerge and are sustained.

Generally, the move toward more inclusive environments appears to be the way in which service delivery is being restructured; however, environments in any age range still vary considerably. A continuum of services still exists for school-age students ranging from inclusion in general education settings to placement in self-contained classrooms. Each of these approaches to educating students has a very different effect on influential variables. Data from our research indicate that these differences in influential variables have a clear effect on a student's social life (Fryxell & Kennedy, in press; Kennedy & Itkonen, 1994). For example, those students served in inclusive environments have much more contact with and develop more friendships among peers than those in more traditional arrangements (e.g., self-contained classrooms).

Making the Transition from One Environment to Another

Similar concerns are encountered as students make the transition from one support environment to another. For instance, it is becoming increasingly frequent for a student to have been educated in general education settings from preschool through elementary school, only to encounter significant changes when making the transition to secondary school programs. Examples of changes may include 1) moving from a neighborhood school to a "cluster" (or self-contained) school, 2) changing from general education participation to solely special education services, and 3) experiencing an overall decrease (and de-emphasis) in efforts to develop new contacts with peers and maintain preestablished contacts. Changes such as these disrupt previously established social relationships and place students in a new environment not designed to effectively arrange influential variables to support their social lives.

As the field focuses more on the strategies needed for effective transitions to occur from one setting to another, it is becoming clear that the quality and consistency of support environments across the life span are a priority. It is inimical to our goals to arrange environments at one point in a person's life to facilitate influential variables and then to transfer that individual to environments that inhibit and disrupt relationships. Such practices are not acceptable. However, at each point across the life span there are exemplars of how to arrange environments to facilitate and support social interactions. Reducing the heterogeneity of support environments within and across age groups to emphasize influential variables, while continuing to extend the knowledge base of how to facilitate such variables from research and practice, is crucial for optimizing relationship outcomes.

Status of Current Support Environments

Although a great deal has been learned about facilitating versus constraining variables related to social behavior, variability in service delivery quality still exists. However, this heterogeneity in support environments appears to be decreasing over time (Winzer, 1993). As researchers and practitioners work together to restructure settings with social relationships as a primary goal, we continue to learn how to improve our efforts in attaining this outcome. The current status of how environments are arranged to facilitate influential variables across the life span is both encouraging and discouraging. The encouraging news is that there are now excellent examples of how to optimize support environments; such environments can be identified as the current best practices. These environments need to be widely replicated and improved upon. The discouraging news is that less than optimal environments still exist within and across all age ranges. A proliferation of the former type of environment will necessarily reduce the frequency of the latter type. Making the most valued outcomes the central focus as we attempt to synthesize research and practice will be a key means of maximizing the quality of support environments that are developed (Kaiser, 1993).

FUTURE DIRECTIONS FOR RESEARCH

Historically, the lack of meaningful social relationships has been among one of the most often cited concerns of people with severe disabilities. In the absence of active efforts to arrange environments to facilitate influential variables, relationships have developed intermittently and have not been maintained over time (Kennedy et al., 1989). Although a great deal has been learned about influential variables, practitioners still need to improve their ability to develop and maintain social relationships. This chapter attempted to summarize the current understanding of variables that influence relationships and interrelate that evolving knowledge with the field's current range of support environments.

Current efforts to restructure support environments throughout the life span will provide practitioners with a rich source of new learning opportunities. These opportunities present the dual benefits of improving the quality of life of people with severe disabilities through enriching and supporting a stable social life while furthering investigators' understanding of how social relationships develop and are maintained. As support environments are restructured to better achieve these sought after outcomes, researchers and practitioners need to work closely together to ensure that the results from those efforts are replicable and valid strategies. The following are a few areas researchers and practitioners may want to consider as focal points to extend and refine efforts to improve students' social lives.

Behavioral Technologies

One area for further study is how to develop socially meaningful and usable behavioral technologies (Horner, 1991; Lindsley, 1991). The environmental engineering that takes place regarding relationships may, necessarily, need to differ somewhat from previous behavior-analytic technologies. The basic principles of behavior will not differ (they will only need to be replicated and extended), but how practitioners arrange support environments must reflect the nature of the phenomenon under study (Baer, Wolf, & Risley, 1987; Schwartz & Baer, 1991). The complementary relationship between research and practice, along with the frequent and extensive input and direction from consumers, will be a necessary component for improving people's social lives.

Social Relationship Patterns

A second area in need of development is a better understanding of the social relationship patterns that occur between people with and without severe disabilities. Currently, a paucity of information exists regarding the conditions under which people meet, what they do together, how frequently they engage in various activities, and how those patterns of contact extend over time. As more is learned about how successful (and unsuccessful) relationships evolve, practitioners will be in a more advantageous position to provide behavioral supports at the times most critical for relationships to come to fruition. One distinction emerging from our research (e.g., Kennedy & Itkonen, 1994) is differentiating between the *initiation* or *initial development* of social relationships (i.e., how people meet and begin to extend interactions across times and settings) and the *ongoing needs* or *maintenance* of relationships (i.e., relationships with stable patterns of long-term interactions). Both of these aspects of relationships may lead to distinct technologies being developed for supporting various phases through which a relationship naturally evolves. Such a distinction may allow practitioners to better understand the needs that exist for individuals within evolving relationships and how best to provide support to increase the probability of successful outcomes.

Current Methodologies

Each of the areas of research mentioned above are predicated on investigators' abilities to extend current methodologies in at least three ways. First, a larger array of dependent variables related to social relationships needs to be developed. The construct of a social relationship is a complex entity that does not lend itself to easy classification along only a single dimension. In light of this observation, the development and validation of a diverse array of measures should allow for better manipulation of the variety of characteristics associated with this phenomenon. Second, these dependent variables need to be made as user friendly as possible to facilitate their adoption by practitioners. Doing this not only provides tools for practitioners to better assess their efforts at social inclusion, but also strengthens the vital linkage between hands-on efforts to instigate change in local communities and the need to build replicable and valid means of transporting that change across settings and individuals. Finally, the time frame of analyses needs to be extended to encompass more prolonged periods of time. If the goal is to gain a better understanding of how social relationships develop, maintain, and sometimes end, then the duration of investigators' analyses will need, necessarily, to be defined by the phenomenon under study. This may require extending analyses from a few months to several years as investigators seek to document and analyze relationship patterns. Attending to each of these suggestions may enable investigators to better understand the basic relations maintaining interpersonal connections and how to construct support environments more effectively.

CONCLUSIONS

As researchers and practitioners, we stand to gain a great deal as we further our scientific understanding of social relationships; the consumers with whom we are in a long-term partnership stand to gain a great deal more. As was noted in the beginning of this chapter, there are numerous benefits derived from relationships that all members of society should experience in a regular and ongoing manner. Improvements in support technologies to develop and maintain social relationships will serve an important function in supporting people with severe disabilities to achieve the benefits of a satisfying and stable social life.

REFERENCES

Azrin, N.H., & Lindsley, O.R. (1956). The reinforcement of cooperation between children. *Journal of Abnormal and Social Psychology, 52*, 100–102.

Baer, D.M., & Wolf, M.M. (1970). The entry into natural communities of reinforcement. In R. Ulrich, H.H. Sachnik, & J. Mabry (Eds.), *Control of human behavior* (pp. 319–324). Glenville, IL: Scott, Foresman.

Baer, D.M., Wolf, M.M., & Risley, T.R. (1987). Some still-current dimensions of applied behavior analysis. *Journal of Applied Behavior Analysis, 20*, 313–328.

Baldwin, J.D. (1986). *George Herbert Mead*. Beverly Hills, CA: Sage Publications.

Benson, P.A., Messer, S.C., & Gross, A.M. (1992). Learning theories. In V.B. Van Hasselt & M. Hersen (Eds.), *Handbook of social development: A lifespan perspective* (pp. 81–112). New York: Plenum Press.

Berndt, T.J. (1986). Sharing between friends: Contexts and consequences. In E.C. Mueller & C.R. Cooper (Eds.), *Process and outcome in peer relationships* (pp. 105–127). New York: Academic Press.

Bruininks, R.H., Meyers, C.E., Sigford, B.B., & Lakin, K.C. (1981). *Deinstitutionalization and community adjustment of mentally retarded people* (Monograph No. 4). Washington, DC: American Association on Mental Deficiency.

Catania, A.C. (1966). Concurrent operants. In W.K. Honig (Ed.), *Operant behavior: Areas of research and application* (pp. 213–270). Englewood Cliffs, NJ: Prentice Hall.

Catania, A.C. (1992). *Learning* (3rd ed.). Englewood Cliffs, NJ: Prentice Hall.

Chadsey-Rusch, J., & Rusch, F.R. (1988). Ecology of the workplace. In R. Gaylord-Ross (Ed.), *Vocational education for persons with handicaps* (pp. 234–256). Mountain View, CA: Mayfield.

Chandler, L.K., Fowler, S.A., & Lubeck, R.C. (1992). An analysis of the effects of multiple setting events on the social behavior of preschool children with special needs. *Journal of Applied Behavior Analysis, 25*, 249–264.

Cohen, D.J. (1972). Justin and his peers: An experimental analysis of a child's social world. In R. Ulrich & P. Mountjoy (Eds.), *The experimental analysis of social behavior* (pp. 23–44). New York: Appleton-Century-Crofts.

de Villiers, P. (1977). Choice in concurrent schedules and a quantitative formulation of the law of effect. In W.K. Honig & J.E.R. Staddon (Eds.), *Handbook of operant behavior* (pp. 233–287). Englewood Cliffs, NJ: Prentice Hall.

Fryxell, D., & Kennedy, C.H. (in press). Placement along the continuum of services and its impact on students' social relationships. *Journal of The Association for Persons with Severe Handicaps.*

Gewirtz, J.L., & Petrovich, S.B. (1983). Early social and attachment learning in the frame of organic and cultural evolution. In T.M. Field, A. Houston, H.C. Quay, L. Troll, & G.E. Finley (Eds.), *Review of human development* (pp. 3–19). New York: John Wiley & Sons.

Gottlieb, B.H. (1988). *Marshalling social support: Formats, processes, and effects.* Newbury Park: Sage.

Hake, D.F., & Olvera, D. (1978). Cooperation, competition, and related social phenomena. In A.C. Catania & T.A. Brigham (Eds.), *Handbook of applied behavior analysis* (pp. 208–245). New York: Irvington.

Hake, D.F., & Vukelich, R. (1972). A classification and review of cooperation procedures. *Journal of the Experimental Analysis of Behavior, 18,* 333–343.

Hallinan, M.T. (1978/1979). The process of friendship formation. *Social Networks, 1,* 193–210.

Haring, T.G. (1991). Social relationships. In L.H. Meyer, C.A. Peck, & L. Brown (Eds.), *Critical issues in the lives of people with severe disabilities* (pp. 195–217). Baltimore: Paul H. Brookes Publishing Co.

Haring, T.G., & Breen, C.G. (1992). A peer-mediated social network intervention to enhance the social integration of persons with moderate and severe disabilities. *Journal of Applied Behavior Analysis, 25,* 319–334.

Harris, M. (1977). *Cannibals and kings: The origins of cultures.* New York: Vintage Books.

Herrnstein, R.J. (1970). On the law of effect. *Journal of the Experimental Analysis of Behavior, 13,* 243–266.

Herrnstein, R.J. (1990). Behavior, reinforcement, and utility. *Psychological Science, 1,* 217–233.

Horner, R.H. (1991). The future of applied behavior analysis for people with severe disabilities: Commentary I. In L.H. Meyer, C.A. Peck, & L. Brown (Eds.), *Critical issues in the lives of people with severe disabilities* (pp. 607–613). Baltimore: Paul H. Brookes Publishing Co.

Horner, R.H., & Day, H.M. (1991). The effects of response efficiency on functionally equivalent competing behaviors. *Journal of Applied Behavior Analysis, 24,* 719–732.

Hyten, C., & Burns, R. (1986). Social relations and social behavior. In H.W. Reese & L.J. Parrott (Eds.), *Behavior science: Philosophical, methodological, and empirical advances* (pp. 163–183). Hillsdale, NJ: Lawrence Erlbaum Associates.

Kaiser, A.P. (1993). Understanding human behavior: Problems of science and practice. *Journal of The Association for Persons with Severe Handicaps, 18,* 240–242.

Kennedy, C.H., Horner, R.H., & Newton, J.S. (1989). Social contacts of adults with severe disabilities living in the community: A descriptive analysis of relationship patterns. *Journal of The Association for Persons with Severe Handicaps, 14,* 190–196.

Kennedy, C.H., & Itkonen, T. (1994). Some effects of regular class participation on the social contacts and social networks of high school students with severe disabilities. *Journal of The Association for Persons with Severe Handicaps, 19,* 1–10.

Kimmel, D.C. (1979). Relationship initiation and development: A life-span developmental approach. In R.L. Burgess & T.L. Huston (Eds.), *Social exchange in developing relationships* (pp. 351–377). New York: Academic Press.

Kohler, F.W., & Fowler, S.A. (1985). Training prosocial behaviors to young children: An analysis of reciprocity with untrained peers. *Journal of Applied Behavior Analysis, 18,* 187–200.

Kohler, F.W., & Strain, P.S. (1992). Applied behavior analysis and the movement to restructure schools: Compatibilities and opportunities for collaboration. *Journal of Behavioral Education, 2,* 367–390.

Lindsley, O.R. (1991). From technical jargon to plain English for application. *Journal of Applied Behavioral Analysis, 24,* 449–458.

McConnell, S.R. (1987). Entrapment effects and the generalization and maintenance of social skills training for elementary school students with behavior disorders. *Behavior Disorders, 12,* 252–263.

Mead, G.H. (1912). The mechanism of social consciousness. *Journal of Philosophy, Psychology, and Scientific Methods, 9,* 401–406.

Newton, J.S., & Horner, R.H. (1993). Using a social guide to improve social relationships of people with severe disabilities. *Journal of The Association for Persons with Severe Handicaps, 18,* 36–45.

Nisbet, J. (Ed.). (1992). *Natural supports in school, at work, and in the community for people with severe disabilities.* Baltimore: Paul H. Brookes Publishing Co.

Noonan, M.J., & McCormick, L. (1993). *Early intervention in natural environments: Methods and procedures.* Pacific Grove, CA: Brooks/Cole.

Odom, S.L., McConnell, S.R., & McEvoy, M.A. (Eds.). (1992). *Social competence of young children with disabilities: Issues and strategies for intervention.* Baltimore: Paul H. Brookes Publishing Co.

Odom, S.L., & Strain, P.S. (1986). A comparison of peer-initiation and teacher-antecedent interventions for promoting reciprocal social interaction of autistic preschoolers. *Journal of Applied Behavior Analysis, 19,* 59–71.

Putnam, J.W. (Ed.). (1991). *Cooperative learning and strategies for inclusion: Celebrating diversity in the classroom.* Baltimore: Paul H. Brookes Publishing Co.

Rusch, F.R. (1992). *Supported employment: Models, methods, and issues.* Sycamore, IL: Sycamore Press.

Sailor, W. (1991). Special education in restructured schools. *Remedial and Special Education, 12,* 8–22.

Salisbury, C.L., Palombaro, M.M., & Hollowood, T.M. (1993). On the nature and change of an inclusive elementary school. *Journal of The Association for Persons with Severe Handicaps, 18,* 75–84.

Scanzoni, J. (1979). Social exchange and behavioral interdependence. In R.L. Burgess & T.L. Huston (Eds.), *Social exchange in developing relationships* (pp. 61–98). New York: Academic Press.

Schwartz, I.S., & Baer, D.M. (1991). Social validity assessments: Is current practice state of the art? *Journal of Applied Behavior Analysis, 24,* 189–205.

Sherman, J.A. (1982). Behavioral approaches to children's learning. In T.M. Field, A. Huston, H.C. Quay, L. Troll, & G.E. Finley (Eds.), *Review of human development* (pp. 242–252). New York: John Wiley & Sons.

Skinner, B.F. (1953). *Science and human behavior.* New York: MacMillan.

Skinner, B.F. (1981). Selection by consequences. *Science, 213,* 501–504.

Skrtic, T.M. (1991). The special education paradox: Equity as a way to excellence. *Harvard Educational Review, 61,* 148–206.

Stainback, S., & Stainback, W. (1992). Schools as inclusive communities. In S. Stainback & W. Stainback (Eds.), *Controversial issues confronting special education: Divergent perspectives* (pp. 29–44). Needham, MA: Allyn & Bacon.

Storey, K. (1993). A proposal for assessing integration. *Education and Training of the Mentally Retarded, 28,* 279–287.

Strain, P.S. (1977). Effects of peers social initiations on withdrawn children: Some training and generalization effects. *Journal of Abnormal Child Psychology, 5,* 445–455.

Strain, P.S. (1990). LRE for preschool children with handicaps: What we know, what we should be doing. *Journal of Early Intervention, 14,* 291–296.

Strain, P.S. (1991, October). *Future directions for research on social skills training.* Paper presented at the Robert Gaylord-Ross Memorial Symposium on Social Skills Training for Persons with Disabilities, Nashville, TN.

Strain, P.S., Odom, S.L., & McConnell, W.C. (1984). Promoting social reciprocity of exceptional children: Identification, target behavior, selection and intervention. *Remedial and Special Education, 5,* 21–28.

Strain, P.S., Shores, R.E., & Timm, M.A. (1977). Effects of peer social initiations on the behavior of withdrawn preschool children. *Journal of Applied Behavior Analysis, 10,* 289–298.

Thompson, T., & Zeiler, M.D. (1986). *Analysis and integration of behavioral units.* Hillsdale, NJ: Lawrence Erlbaum Associates.

Winzer, M.A. (1993). *The history of special education: From isolation to integration.* Washington, DC: Gallaudet University Press.

13

Examining Levels of Social Inclusion within an Integrated Preschool for Children with Autism

Frank W. Kohler, Phillip S. Strain, and Denise D. Shearer

Preparation of this chapter was supported by National Institute of Mental Health Grant Nos. MH47847-02 to Allegheny-Singer Research Institute and MH37110-12 to the Early Learning Institute.

Rather remarkable progress has been seen since the mid-1980s toward providing inclusive opportunities for young children with severe disabilities. Palpable outcomes can be seen in legislation, advocacy, program planning, intervention research, and a growing professional consensus supportive of inclusive service delivery (Strain & Smith, 1993). In spite of obvious progress, however, the existence of inclusive options for individual children, and particularly for children with autism, is often dependent upon the heroic efforts of families to obtain inclusive services. Frequently and understandably, the central theme surrounding individual struggles is one of *access* to a particular setting or program. It should not be surprising, then, that inclusive placements or administrative arrangements have evolved as the primary focus of concern for many constituents interested in inclusive education (Smith & Rose, 1993). Yet it is becoming increasingly evident that sharing the same physical space and the same administrative arrangement does not lead automatically to developmentally relevant levels of social and instructional inclusion (Guralnick, 1990). Indeed, for children with many learning needs and social skill deficits, active exclusion can dominate their day-to-day experience within inclusive administrative arrangements (McGee, Paradis, & Feldman, 1993). This de facto exclusion within inclusive environments may be particularly evident for children with autism, who are often viewed as needing tutorial-like services from adults to acquire needed competencies (Lovaas, 1987).

The essential challenge that has emerged is one of understanding the complex nature of inclusion and achieving the outcomes that most constituents deeply desire from such arrangements. In a beginning effort to understand the complex nature of social inclusion, not simply placement in a typical setting, the authors have developed a direct observational protocol to assess inclusion at various depths or levels of analysis for preschool-age children. This chapter discusses four levels of social inclusion that apply to children's participation within integrated preschools. The first two levels are ecological in nature, as they address the types of instructional experiences that children have throughout the day and the peer group structure for these activities. A third level specifies teachers' levels of direction, support, and general involvement in children's ongoing play and participation. Finally, the last level indicates the discrete form of children's responses as well as the social context for their actions. An observational code is described that addresses each of these individual levels of inclusion. The range of variables in this code is a widely recognized indicator of high-quality preschool integration.

The primary purpose of this chapter is to discuss and illustrate a variety of code variables that pertain to these four different levels of social inclusion at the preschool stage. This objective is addressed by illustrating data that were collected from two preschoolers with autism and two typically developing youngsters at the LEAP Preschool. The chapter's last section presents conclusions and implications for intervention that can be drawn from these data.

THE FOUR LEVELS OF SOCIAL
INCLUSION IN THE PRESCHOOL ENVIRONMENT

At a most basic level of analysis, it is possible to assess whether children with special needs (autism in the examples that follow herein) share the same social contexts in preschools as do typical children (i.e., Do children with special needs participate in the same range of preschool activities?). Simply put, this first level of analysis examines group differences, individual child variations across days, specially designed intervention procedures to increase participation in all activities, and the stability of routines as imposed by intervention agents.

The second level of analysis asks the question: What is the group size and composition for children's participation? This question looks at with whom the children with special needs interact when they share the same routines as their peers and engage in socially sanctioned behavior during those routines. For many preschool routines, one might argue that being in groups with other children, especially if the groups include some typically developing children, is potentially beneficial.

The third level of analysis shifts the focus of observation to adult behavior. While specific behaviors of adults may be analyzed, an overall *level of effort* perspective is particularly germane to social as well as instructional inclusion. That is, one may consider the question: What level and type of teacher effort is necessary to achieve a certain level of social and instructional inclusion?

At the most detailed fourth level of analysis, one may ask: What is the form and social context for children's participation in preschool activities? This question examines the degree to which children with special needs engage in behavior topographies that resemble those of typical peers engaged in common activities and routines. This level of analysis acknowledges the possibility that all children may follow the same routines, but what they *do* in those contexts (e.g., snack, free play) can look very different. For example, a young child with autism may always participate in free play, but, if her sole interactive behavior is rolling a ball to another child, one might assert the need for intervention to better utilize the developmental and learning potential of free play times.

LEAP PROGRAM (LEARNING EXPERIENCES . . .
AN ALTERNATIVE PROGRAM FOR PRESCHOOLERS AND PARENTS)

In order to portray how these levels of analysis can be addressed, the following sections present illustrative data from both typical children and children with autism who attend the LEAP Preschool. Under the direction of the second author, the LEAP Preschool began in 1982 as a federally funded (i.e., Handicapped Children's Early Education Program) model demonstration program serving young children with autism and typical children ages 3–5 years. At the time of its inception, the LEAP program was one of the few early childhood programs in the country that was committed to inclusive practices for young children with autism and their families.

The LEAP program consists of four main program components: 1) the integrated preschool, 2) a behavioral skills training program and other services for parents, 3) national outreach training activities, and 4) ongoing research on instructional practices. The first program component, the integrated preschool, consists of three classrooms, each serving 13 children (10 typical children and 3 children with autism) ages 3–5 years. The preschool program operates 3 hours a day, 5 days a week, for 12 months of the year. The preschool is cosponsored by the Fox Chapel area school district and is located within a local early childhood center. Staff:child ratio for each classroom is 3 adults to 13 children, with each classroom staffed by two teachers and a classroom assistant. A full-time speech-language specialist provides services to children with disabilities and their families within the classroom and home environments.

In addition to the classroom program, families of children with and without disabilities may participate in a skills training program designed to teach parents the basic principles of behavior management and effective strategies for teaching young children. The program is designed to reflect a family-centered approach, with activities being individualized for each family based upon desired outcomes for training. Additional services available to families include a monthly parent support group, referral services to various community agencies, and transition planning and follow-up activities. Two family service coordinators are available to work with parents who participate in these activities.

The third program component includes national outreach training activities. LEAP Preschool is currently in its seventh year of funding (Early Education Program for Children with Disabilities) as a National Outreach Training project. Training activities focus on seven key areas: 1) child assessment activities, 2) developing individualized education plans, 3) instructional programming for the integrated classroom, 4) behavior management, 5) social skills training, 6) transition planning, and

7) working effectively with families. To date, 20 early childhood programs from 10 states have participated in outreach training conducted by the staff of LEAP Preschool.

The final program component includes ongoing research to uncover new and more effective instructional practices. LEAP has housed over three dozen studies to examine teaching tactics to improve children's social, communicative, and engagement skills.

Guiding principles that have shaped program development efforts since the early 1980s at LEAP Preschool have included the following beliefs:

1. All children (i.e., both children with and without disabilities) can benefit from integrated early childhood environments.
2. Young children with autism benefit most from early intervention when intervention efforts are conducted across school, home, and community environments.
3. Young children with autism make the greatest gains from early intervention when parents and professionals work together as partners.
4. Young children with autism can learn many important skills (e.g., social skills, language skills, appropriate behavior) from typical same-age peers.
5. Young children with autism benefit most from early intervention when intervention efforts are planned, systematic, and individualized.
6. Children with and without disabilities benefit from curricular activities that reflect developmentally appropriate practices.

Preschool Participation Code

This section describes an observational code that is used to examine the four levels of social inclusion described in the first section. The Preschool Participation Code was developed in 1992 as part of an effort to promote children's participation within integrated preschool activities. All of the work with this instrument has been conducted at LEAP.

The Preschool Participation Code is an adaptation of the many observational instruments that have been developed for early childhood programs since the 1980s (Carta, Greenwood, & Atwater, 1985; Parsons, McWilliams, & Buysse, 1989). The code contains six units that apply to children's participation within integrated preschools. The first three units include a range of ecological variables that indicate the structure for children's learning, such as the types of *activities* and the *grouping* and *composition* arrangements (Carta, Sainato, & Greenwood, 1988). The fourth unit includes a variety of *teacher* variables. These variables are important to examine, as certain behaviors might represent functional stimuli for children's appropriate participation and interaction. The last two units concern several *child* variables that address the discrete nature of responses, such as active and passive behavior, as well as the *social context* for engagement (McWilliam, 1991). Although additional variables are pertinent to the assessment of preschool classrooms, this chapter focuses on these units because of their relevance to the four levels of social inclusion described earlier.

The Preschool Participation Code contains 44 different subcodes, which are listed in Table 1. A total of 11 activities indicates the focal child's proximity and participation. Various grouping and composition arrangements note other children's involvement in the same activity with the focal child. Nine subcodes represent the teacher's behavior relative to the focal child. Three general categories of child behavior can be coded, including seven subcodes of active responding. Thus, a child's active engagement can occur in a solitary fashion or may involve a teacher, peer, or both; the child may be attending to another individual; or the child may exhibit none of the engagement behaviors.

Observational staff utilize a 6-second momentary time-sampling system to record the ecology, teacher, and child behavior variables. The activity, grouping, and composition units are coded at the beginning of each 1-minute block. The next six 6-second intervals are devoted to coding the teacher and child variables in an alternating fashion. The various subcodes for each unit are mutually exclusive. That is, only one subcode of teacher and child behavior is coded per 6-second interval. Copies of the Preschool Participation coding manual complete with definitions and scoring procedures are available from the first author.

Code Training and Interrater Agreement Procedures

Eight individuals have learned to conduct observations with the code over the past 2.5 years. Observer training activities are generally conducted for 3–4 hours a day over the course of 3–4 weeks. The training activities occur in three phases. Phase 1 lasts 1 week and entails memorization of the various code definitions and scoring procedures. Trainees finish this phase by completing a quiz that ascertains their mastery of the primary code definitions.

Observer trainees begin using the code during Phase 2. A range of skills is acquired, including structuring observations around a 6-second partial interval system and recording variables within the correct block on a designated sheet. Trainees practice observations with an experienced partner, who provides continual monitoring and coaching. This phase of training is generally completed within 6–12 hours.

Phase 3 entails the establishment of interrater agreement. The trainee continues to conduct daily observations with an experienced partner. Initially, the pair may code independently for only 1 minute (six intervals)

Table 1. Primary units and subcategories of the Preschool Participation Code

Ecological variables	Description	Specific codes
Activity	The learning experience or focus of instruction being provided to the observed child. Activities are either structured and coordinated by the teacher or various options are available for students to make independent choices.	Preacademics/class business (PA/Cl) Language programming (LP) Gross motor/dance (GD) Music/recitation (MR) Self-care (SC) Clean up (CU) Story (St) Fine motor (FM) Play (Pl) Transition (Tr) Time-out (TO)
Grouping	The number of students who are engaged in the same designated activity and in the same vicinity as the observed child.	One teacher/one student (1:1) Small group (Sm) Solitary (0) Large group (Lg)
Composition	The mix of students with disabilities and typically developing children who are within the group. A child is regarded as having a disability if he or she exhibits a delay of at least 1 year in one or more areas of development as indicated by a standardized assessment instrument.	All with disabilities (D) Majority with disabilities (>) Equal proportion (=) Minority with disabilities (<) All typically developing (T) Alone (Al)
Teacher variables		
Teacher behavior	The behavior being used by the teacher in relation to the observed child or the group in which the child is a part (such as circle or group game activities).	Active: Question/discussion (QD) Physical guidance (Ph) Disapproval (Dp) Monitor: None: Modeling (Md) Verbal prompt (Vb) Approval (Ap) Read aloud/sing (RS) Monitor (Mt) None (No)
Student variables		
Engagement behavior	The child's active engagement in an activity.	Active: Pretending (Pr) Communication (Cm) Music/recitation (MR) Attend: None: Preacademic (Ac) Manipulating (Mn) Gross motor/dance (GD) Self-care (SC) Attention (At) None (No)
Social context	The child's engagement that involves direct interaction or associative participation with another person. If the child behavior is Attention, use code None (N) for the engagement context.	Peer (P) Both peer and teacher (B) None (N) Teacher (T) Solitary (S)

before comparing records and discussing discrepancies. As their observations maintain high agreement, however, the team members gradually increase the duration of their independent coding until the trainee is scoring all units independently for an entire 20–30 minute period. At this point, the pair begins the formal calculation of interrater agreement.

Occurrence reliability is calculated by dividing the total number of agreements regarding a specific behavior by the total number of agreements plus disagreements and multiplying by 100. Agreement about occurrence is calculated for each of the primary code units and their subcodes. Average coefficients of interrater agreement range from 96% to 100% for the activity, grouping, and composition variables. Mean agreement on the occurrence of teacher behaviors usually ranges from 93% to 98% for the active, monitor, and none categories. Interrater reliability on the primary child behavior codes of active and attend averages 91%–95%, while coefficients range from 85% to 92% across the five social context codes.

DATA PROFILES ILLUSTRATING
FOUR LEVELS OF SOCIAL INCLUSION

The Preschool Participation Code is used to conduct full-day observations of all children at LEAP on various occasions each year. This section presents data profiles from two children with autism and two typically developing youngsters. It is important to note that these data are not intended to enable conclusions to be drawn about the nature of children's participation at LEAP. For one, the presentation represents a limited sample from only 1 day, whereas assessments from 3–4 different days would be necessary to make conclusions about the structure of LEAP. Furthermore, the authors selected profiles of only 4 children from a larger pool of 25 because they best portray the four levels of social inclusion that are pertinent to this discussion. Given the small and selected nature of this sample, these data are only designed to illustrate the kinds of social inclusion that can be addressed within integrated preschools.

The four children selected for this data profile show considerable variability with regard to developmental needs and abilities. All four youngsters had attended the LEAP program for 1–4 months prior to their observation. Two children were selected from Classroom 1. Neil was a 4-year, 6-month-old boy who had been diagnosed with autism. Although he exhibited many appropriate language and play skills, Neil avoided interacting with other children in unstructured play situations. Katie was a 3-year, 9-month-old typically developing girl who exhibited age-appropriate skills in all developmental areas. Two boys were also selected from Classroom 2. Henry was a 3-year, 4-month-old boy with autism who exhibited very little verbal language and few appropriate play skills.

Finally, Bob was a 3-year, 2-month-old typically developing boy who exhibited age-appropriate skills in all areas. The next section provides the observational profiles for these four children.

Social Inclusion Level 1: Degree to Which Children Are Exposed to the Same Range of Preschool Activities

Many preschool programs place children with disabilities and typically developing youngsters within the same classroom. Their enrollment in the same class and close proximity to one another do not preclude highly idiosyncratic patterns of participation in atypical or unique activities, however. For example, one or more children may be excluded from a circle activity because of limited attending or group participation skills. Furthermore, children may select different activities during free time because of varying interests or developmental skills. The first level of social inclusion addresses the degree to which children with diverse abilities are exposed to the same range of learning activities or opportunities.

Table 2 shows the range and sequence of primary activity periods at LEAP. These periods address a wide variety of skill domains and comprise differing degrees of structure. Opening circle, story, and gross motor activities all entail a great deal of teacher direction or structure. Conversely, children select preferred areas and materials during discovery and centers time, and teachers respond to rather than direct their interests and participation. Table 2 shows that the focal and typical children in both classrooms participated in the same activities on their designated observation day. In addition, children's length of participation in each activity is very similar within each classroom.

Figure 1 illustrates the four children's selected activities during discovery. As noted earlier, children are free to make choices about their preferred areas and materials during this unstructured time. The two children in Classroom 1 both played in the fine motor and sociodramatic areas during most of their period. Interestingly, Henry's and Bob's data bear a striking resemblance during the Classroom 2 discovery period, as both boys spent equivalent time in fine motor, gross dance, sociodramatic play, and transition.

Figure 2 illustrates children's activity selections during centers. Unlike the discovery period, Katie and Neil participated in dissimilar activities, spending 100% of their time in fine motor and sociodramatic play, respectively. The two boys in Classroom 2 also showed significant differences. The majority of Henry's play occurred in gross dance, while Bob preferred the sociodramatic play area.

The data presented thus far illustrate cases of social inclusion as well as examples of individualization. At the general curriculum level, children with autism participated in the same range of learning experiences as their

Table 2. Description of daily class schedule and observed child participation at LEAP Preschool

		Time spent on tasks (min)			
Class schedule	Definition	Focal Child 1	Typical Child 1	Focal Child 2	Typical Child 2
Table time	The children participate in preset individual manipulative or preacademic activities arranged at tables. After completing at least one structured task, each child is free to select from other tasks that are arranged at the tables.	6	6	13	13
Opening circle	The entire class gathers in a semicircle to discuss the calendar, weather, academic, and current topics. A high degree of teacher structure is provided.	17	13	18	15
Discovery	Areas include gross motor, sociodramatic, care of class pets, story, manipulatives, sensory tables, computer, and so on. Each child is free to choose and play in one or all of the activities available.	36	31	29	33
Snack	The children seat themselves and eat. After children finish eating they go to the book area to read. A high degree of teacher structure is provided.	11	13	8	7
Story	Children return to the circle area to listen to a story read by one of the teachers. A high degree of teacher structure is provided.	N/A	N/A	4	8
Gross motor	The entire class participates in an organized gross motor activity such as dancing, red rover, balancing activities, and so on. A high degree of teacher structure is provided.	8	7	9	9
Centers	Children rotate through an organized art activity and preacademic folders and then select from one of many alternative classroom areas. Although the teacher structures the primary activity, children are free to choose and play in all other available activities.	20	17	22	29

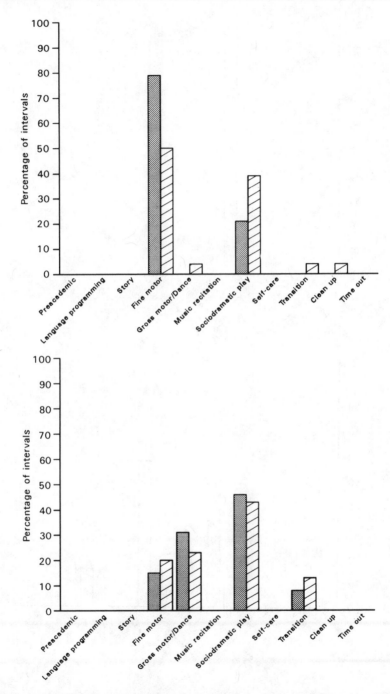

Figure 1. Percentage of coded intervals spent in each activity during the discovery period by two children in Classroom 1 (upper panel) and two in Classroom 2 (lower panel). (Upper panel: shaded bar = Neil, striped bar = Katie. Lower panel: shaded bar = Henry, striped bar = Bob.)

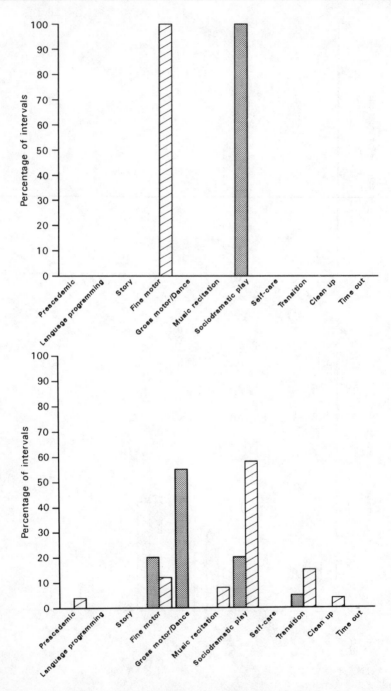

Figure 2.   Percentage of coded intervals spent in each activity during the centers period by two children in Classroom 1 (upper panel) and two in Classroom 2 (lower panel). (Upper panel: shaded bar = Neil, striped bar = Katie. Lower panel: shaded bar = Henry, striped bar = Bob.)

typically developing peers. No youngster was excluded from any activities on the basis of special needs or abilities. The data also reveal periods of individualization, however, as children did seek out divergent experiences when they were given the freedom to do so. Discrepancies in children's choices could be attributed to their differing developmental skills, interests, or even changes in the structure of activities across days.

The optimal model of preschool integration might well contain cases of both inclusion and individualization. On the one hand, some degree of mutual activity exposure is certainly needed to maintain the intent and spirit of preschool integration. In fact, providing individual children with atypical activities throughout their entire day represents social exclusion. On the other hand, specialization may well mean that children participate in some atypical or unique activities during selected periods. In any case, two additional points are warranted. First, this initial level of inclusion is clearly a program variable, as preschool administrators and teachers make decisions about the range and sequence of curriculum for individual children. Second, children's activity experiences have important implications for their development and learning and thus represent a viable index of quality for integrated preschool programs.

Social Inclusion Level 2:
Group Size and Composition of
Children's Participation in Preschool Activities

Student tracking has been a predominant practice within elementary education since the 1980s (Brandt, 1992). An underlying premise of this approach is that teaching can occur most effectively and efficiently when children are placed in homogeneous ability groups. However, a growing amount of research has challenged the assumptions of this approach (Wheelock, 1992). The second level of inclusion pertains to de facto tracking by inquiring about the structure of children's participation in preschool activities. Two dimensions of structure are relevant. First, children can participate in groups of various sizes, including being alone, working one-to-one with the teacher, or being in small and large groups of peers. Second, children's groups can take a variety of forms, including all peers with disabilities, an equal proportion of peers with disabilities and typically developing playmates, all typical peers, and so on.

Figure 3 reveals the group size and composition of children in Classroom 1 during three select activities. The data in the top portion of the figure illustrate a similar balance of small and large group structures during table time. Some contrast is evident during discovery time, however. Neil spent 21% of his time alone or one-to-one with the teacher, whereas Katie was in small or large groups during 100% of observed intervals. Finally, both children participated in the large group for the entirety of their gross motor activity.

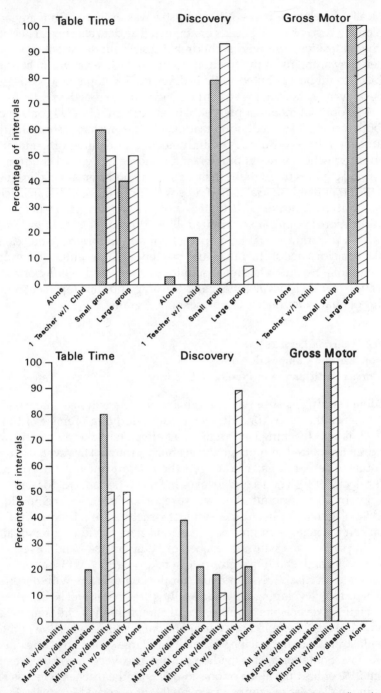

Figure 3. Percentage of coded intervals for each group structure (upper panel) and composition (lower panel) for two children in Classroom 1 during three select activities. (Both panels: shaded bar = Neil, striped bar = Katie.)

The lower portion of Figure 3 illustrates the composition of children's participation in these activities. Although Katie and Neil both participated in small and large groups during table time, the composition of their groups differed. Neil participated with an equal balance of peers with and without disabilities during 20% of his intervals and in groups containing fewer children with disabilities 80% of the time. Conversely, Katie participated in groups composed of all children without disabilities during 50% of her intervals. Similar patterns occur during discovery. Neil participated in groups that included more children with autism during 39% of his intervals and an equal proportion of children with and without autism 21% of the time. In contrast, Katie played in groups composed of all typical peers for 89% of her intervals. Finally, the two children participated in identical compositions during gross motor.

Figure 4 reveals the group size and composition profiles for Classroom 2. Henry and Bob participated in the same structures during table time, although Henry spent a larger proportion of time alone. Similarities also occur during discovery, although Bob was one-to-one with the teacher during 16% of his intervals. Lastly, the two boys show identical profiles in gross motor. The group composition data are shown in the lower portion of this figure. Divergent structures occurred during table time, with Henry spending greater time in groups of more children with disabilities, equal proportions of children with and without disabilities, and alone. Bob played with all typical peers during 40% of discovery intervals, whereas Henry spent more time alone and in groups of equal proportions. As did the two children in Classroom 1, Henry and Bob show identical patterns during gross motor.

Like the activity participation data, the group size and composition records reveal cases of social inclusion as well as time spent alone but still participating. Gross motor provides the highest degree of integration, as all four children participated in this activity with all of their classmates. In contrast, the table and discovery data are more variable. For example, Henry participated in three different group sizes and four compositions during his 13-minute table time activity. Some of Henry's table time data represents social inclusion, as he participated in small and large groups with fewer peers without disabilities or an equal proportion of children with and without disabilities (see Figures 3 and 4). On the other hand, Henry also spent 42% of his time alone, which represents a nonexample of social inclusion. Similar variability is apparent with Bob and Neil during their table time and discovery activities.

Once again, the data suggest that a balance might be most realistic and optimal for this level of inclusion. Some degree of solitary or individual participation is appropriate for children ages 2–5 with disabilities as well as typical youngsters. However, teachers cannot expect to promote

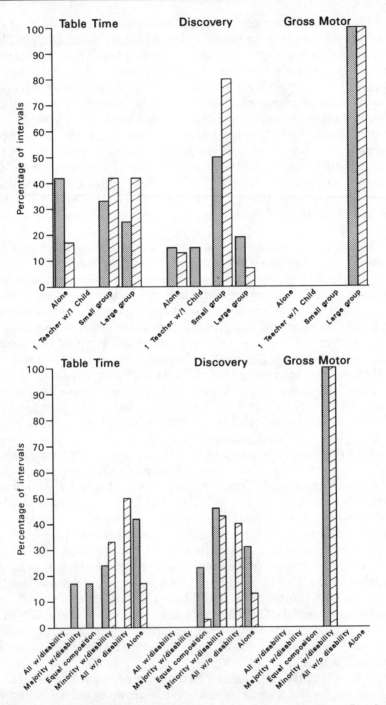

Figure 4. Percentage of coded intervals for each group structure (upper panel) and composition (lower panel) for two children in Classroom 2 during three select activities. (Both panels: shaded bar = Henry, striped bar = Bob.)

peer imitation, social interaction, or mutual play unless children participate in small and large groups with youngsters who display the desired skills. Like the first level of analysis, this second level of social inclusion has significant implications for children's development and thus represents a viable index of program quality. Furthermore, it seems clear that this level of social inclusion is under the control of preschool teachers and administrators (Odom & McEvoy, 1988).

Social Inclusion Level 3:
Degree of Teachers' Participation
in Children's Preschool Activities

Although the relationship between teacher and child behavior is far from being certain, the existing research indicates that teachers' actions may have a variety of significant functions. For example, experimental studies have found that teacher behaviors can facilitate children's active engagement (Strain, Danko, & Kohler, 1995), social interaction with peers (Strain & Odom, 1986), use of language (Hart & Risley, 1975), and a wide range of preacademic skills (Wolery & Brookfield-Norman, 1988). At the same time, research also indicates that teacher behaviors can produce unintended or even undesired effects on children's responses. For example, excessive levels of teachers' prompts and directing statements can *decrease* children's task-related participation or engagement (Hamilton & Gordon, 1978). Similarly, Shores, Hester, and Strain (1976) found that teachers' conversational behaviors can prohibit or interfere with preschool children's exchanges with peers. Regardless of specific function, then, teacher behavior can exert a significant impact on children's responding and is important to examine. Therefore, the third level of social inclusion examines teachers' active participation in children's various preschool activities.

Figure 5 reveals the percentage of intervals wherein teachers directed an active behavior to the four children during select activities. As shown in Table 1, the Preschool Participation Code includes a range of seven active teacher subcodes, including questions, physical guidance, verbal prompts, approval, and so forth. Because story time occurred only in Classroom 2, data for Neil and Katie on this activity are not included. Teachers in Classroom 1 (upper portion of figure) showed significant disparities during the discovery period. Neil was the subject of active teacher behavior and monitoring (close observation) during 20% and 64% of intervals, respectively (total of 84%). In contrast, teachers provided less direction for Katie's play, with active and monitoring behaviors accumulating to only 31% of observed intervals. Teachers directed similar levels of active and monitoring behaviors during Neil's and Katie's snack activities.

The lower portion of Figure 5 indicates that teachers directed active behaviors toward Henry during 24% of his discovery intervals and monitored him 66% of the time (total of 90%). Conversely, teachers directed

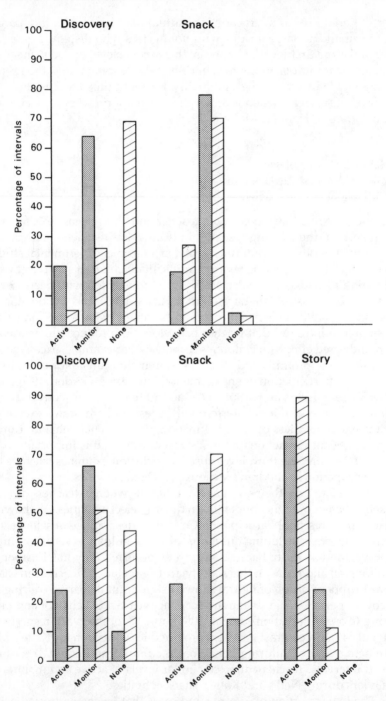

Figure 5. Percentage of coded intervals of active teacher behaviors directed to children in Classroom 1 (upper panel) and Classroom 2 (lower panel) during select activities. (Upper panel: shaded bar = Neil, striped bar = Katie. Lower panel: shaded bar = Henry, striped bar = Bob.)

active and monitoring behaviors to Bob during only 5% and 51% of his discovery time, respectively (total of 56%). The mean percentage of active behaviors directed toward Henry was 26% during snack time, while Bob did not receive any teacher direction. Finally, teachers directed active behaviors toward Henry and Bob during 76% and 89% of their story intervals, respectively.

The data in Figure 5 suggest that teachers' active participation is not uniform or consistent, but varies across individual classroom situations and children. Although the specific child and setting variables that influence teacher behaviors are largely unknown, it is clear that adult inquiries and comments represent the likely infrastructure for activities like circle and story. The incidence of teacher behavior may be less conspicuous during discovery and related unstructured periods, but still exert a potential impact on many important child responses, such as selection of activities and materials, type of thematic play, and quality of language or social interaction. In essence, it is difficult to imagine any situation where teacher monitoring, approval, and guidance should not represent a pivotal component of the preschool milieu.

It is also likely that some variation or balance of teacher behavior is appropriate for preschool-age children. Regardless of their developmental skills, all youngsters can benefit from periods of intensive, moderate, and minimal levels of direction from adults (Wolery, Strain, & Bailey, 1992). The data presented here indicate that teachers can vary their involvement in accordance with individual activities and children. Thus, the assessment of teachers' participation represents a significant and viable measure of children's social inclusion in integrated preschools.

Social Inclusion Level 4:
Form and Social Context of
Children's Participation in Preschool Activities

The preceding levels of social inclusion addressed the range of activities for children's participation, the structure of accompanying peer group sizes and compositions, and the degree of teachers' participation. The discrete form and context of children's responses represent the final dimension of social inclusion. Engagement has been defined as the amount of time that children spend interacting appropriately with their environments (McWilliam, 1991). In essence, research has shown that active responses such as manipulating materials, asking and answering questions, counting objects, and enacting thematic roles contribute directly to young children's learning and mastery of developmental skills (McWilliam & Bailey, 1992). Studies have also noted whether children's active responses involve only materials or occur *with* other youngsters or adults (McWilliam, 1991). Therefore, the final dimension of social inclusion addresses the form and social context of children's participation in preschool activities. As shown in Table 1, the Preschool Participation Code distinguishes between children's active engagement and attending. In addition, all intervals of active responding are coded as occurring in a solitary fashion or involving a peer, a teacher, or both a teacher and peer simultaneously.

Figure 6 shows Neil's and Katie's percentage of active engagement and social context in three select activities. Both youngsters exhibited high levels of active engagement during table time. However, the social context for their responding varied dramatically. The vast majority (95%) of Neil's engagement occurred in a solitary manner, while the other 5% involved only the teacher. Conversely, only 43% of Katie's responding was coded as solitary, and 38% involved peers. As Figure 6 indicates, both children exhibited very little engagement during circle, and the highest proportion of these responses involved both the teacher and peers. Finally, Neil and Katie displayed high levels of active responding in centers and the majority of their engagement occurred in a solitary fashion.

Figure 7 reveals these same profiles for the children in Classroom 2. Henry and Bob show equal levels of engagement during table time, and the vast proportion of their responses is solitary in nature. Like their counterparts in Classroom 1, both boys exhibit very little engagement during circle. In accordance with the structure for this activity, less than 50% of each boy's responses occurs in a solitary manner. Finally, Henry's and Bob's responses increase during centers, with the majority of engagement being solitary in nature.

The data in Figures 6 and 7 reveal three types of variability. First, significant differences in active engagement were observed across the various activities. Overall, the four children exhibited a mean of 71% engagement during table time, 16% in circle, 71% during centers, and 7% for story (Classroom 2 only and not included in Figure 7). This interactivity variability was observed with all four children. Second, a high level of cross-activity variation was observed in the social context data. For example, Katie exhibited a high proportion of her active responses with peers and alone during table time (38% and 43%, respectively). In contrast, the highest proportion of her engagement involved *both* the teacher and peers during circle. Finally, the most responses involved the teacher or occurred in a solitary fashion during centers (18% and 75%, respectively). Like engagement, the social context data showed considerable variation across the different activities. Third, considerable variability can be observed in the social context data for individual children. Very few of Neil's and Henry's responses involved other children (see Figures 6 and 7). In contrast, 8%–23% of Bob's responses involved peers, and Katie's percentage of peer-related engagement ranged from 3% in centers to 38% in table time.

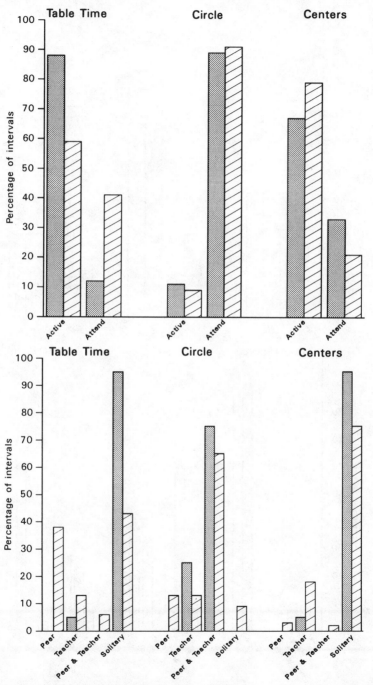

Figure 6. Percentage of coded intervals of active engagement for children in Classroom 1 (upper panel) and social context for these responses (lower panel) during three select activities. (Both panels: shaded bar = Neil, striped bar = Katie.)

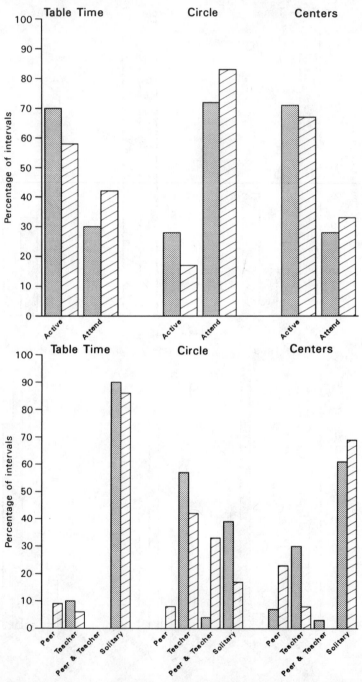

Figure 7. Percentage of coded intervals of active engagement for two children in Classroom 2 (upper panel) and the social context for their responses (lower panel) during three select activities. (Both panels: shaded bar = Henry, striped bar = Bob.)

In essence, then, the sample data suggest that engagement and social context are appropriate indices of children's inclusion in integrated preschool settings. Both measures showed considerable variation across activities that differed in organization and degree of teacher involvement. Furthermore, the social context measure revealed considerable variability across the four selected children.

CONCLUSIONS AND IMPLICATIONS

Three primary conclusions arise from this limited and select observational sample: 1) all four children's profiles revealed examples and nonexamples of each level of social inclusion; 2) the four levels of social inclusion address variables that interrelate in a variety of different ways; and 3) the four levels of inclusion have important implications for early childhood intervention. These primary conclusions are discussed throughout the remainder of this chapter.

Summary of Children's Observational Profiles

All four children's profiles revealed both examples and nonexamples of each level of social inclusion. For example, Neil and Katie participated in the same range of instructional periods within the first LEAP classroom (Level 1). Despite their mutual involvement, however, these children selected divergent areas and activities during a centers period that entailed minimal teacher direction. The Preschool Participation Code also indicated variation in the size and composition of both children's peer groups (Level 2). For example, Neil's and Katie's table time data indicated an equal proportion of small- and large-group structures. Conversely, the majority of discovery time was coded as small group (with some one-to-one teacher time for Neil), while all of gross motor time encompassed a large-group size. The structure of these groups also differed, as observers coded four and two different compositions for Neil and Katie, respectively, across their three select activities.

Examination of the third and fourth levels of social inclusion indicated similar variations. For example, teachers' active behavior and monitoring accumulated to 85% during Neil's discovery activity, compared with only 30% for Katie. However, both children experienced equivalent levels of adult participation in their snack period. Finally, the two children in Classroom 1 showed similar levels of engagement across their select activities. Neil's and Katie's responses often occurred in a solitary manner, but also involved the teacher; peers (Katie only); and both the teacher and peers during segments of table time, circle, and centers.

Observations in Classroom 2 revealed comparable examples and nonexamples of inclusion. Although they participated in the same general periods, Henry and Bob selected differing activities during centers (Level 1). Both boys also participated in various peer group structures throughout the day (Level 2). For example, three to four different group sizes were observed during table time, discovery, and gross motor. Henry also participated in four compositions, including alone, with fewer peers with disabilities, an equal proportion, and more peers with disabilities, while Bob participated in three different group structures. The boys also showed disparities in the third and fourth levels of social inclusion. For example, Henry and Bob received relatively low levels of teacher direction during discovery and snack, compared with 75% or more in story. Finally, children's active engagement fluctuated from an overall mean of 23% in circle to 68% in centers, whereas the social context for their responses included solitary time and time with teacher, peers, and both teacher and peers. In summary, all four children's data reveal examples and nonexamples of each level of social inclusion.

Relationship Between the Four Levels of Social Inclusion

The four levels of social inclusion address variables that imply a variety of different relationships. First, the initial levels of inclusion appear to serve as necessary or prerequisite conditions for the latter levels. For example, preschool staff may direct an individual child to play independently with puzzles while all other children and teachers in the class participate in circle. Besides representing a nonexample of Level 1, this situation necessarily produces nonexamples for all remaining levels of inclusion, as the designated child is alone in the puzzle area (Level 2), engages in very few, if any, interactions with the teacher (Level 3), and exhibits any and all active responses in a solitary fashion (Level 4). Similarly, certain group size and composition variables at Level 2 represent necessary conditions for the fourth type of inclusion. For example, the occurrence of active engagement with a teacher, peers, or both teacher and peers requires the proximity of these individuals in the same activity with the child under consideration. In conclusion, then, it appears that the first two levels of inclusion are *necessary* or *prerequisite* conditions for children's participation to be social in nature.

Despite the necessity of these first levels, however, the data indicate that Levels 1 and 2 are not sufficient conditions to produce Level 4 inclusion. For example, Neil participated in his entire 6-minute table time activity in small or large groups of typically developing youngsters who exhibited age-appropriate social interaction, play, and language skills. Although Neil exhibited active engagement during 88% of his intervals, *none* of these responses involved other children. A similar pattern occurred in Henry's 13-minute table time activity. He spent 58% of his time in small and large groups that included typically developing peers and exhibited active responding during 70% of observed intervals. Despite the presence of other children at the table, however, *none* of Henry's responses involved these youngsters. Thus, the data suggest that the first two levels of social inclusion are necessary but not sufficient conditions for the final level. Worded another way, the presence and availability of typical youngsters do not ensure social interaction and peer-related participation from preschoolers with autism. This finding supports prior research indicating that mere physical integration does not promote peer imitation and interaction from preschool children with disabilities (Cooke, Ruskus, Apolloni, & Peck, 1981; Odom & McEvoy, 1988).

The relationship of teacher behavior (Level 3) to the other levels of social inclusion also warrants discussion. Teachers' directions for children's participation are likely to be affected by several of the variables, including the type of activity (Level 1), size and composition of group participants (Level 2), and the nature and context of children's responses (Level 4). At the same time, certain types of teacher behaviors can also *influence* children's choices to play in a particular area (Level 1) as well as the nature and social context of their participation (Level 4). Although both types of relationships are possible, the data presented in this chapter are far too limited and preliminary to warrant any conclusions. For the present, however, teacher behavior can be surmised to serve as a determinant for children's responses and can also be influenced by the ecological and child behavior variables represented in our model of social inclusion. Future studies should continue to examine the functional relationship between these two variables.

Implications for Early Childhood Intervention

The information presented in this chapter has several important implications for early childhood intervention. First, the highly idiosyncratic data obtained for the four illustrative cases demonstrate the necessity for an individual child focus to evaluating the efficacy of inclusion programs. Although such a statement borders on the patently obvious, it is nonetheless true that a preponderance of inclusion research at the preschool level has obscured, not highlighted, individual child performance (see Guralnick, 1990). The data presented here show that the experience of inclusion may be quite different from child to child and quite different across activities for one child.

A second important implication to be drawn from this multilevel analysis of inclusion is that contextual variables (i.e., activity type) play a significant role in defining the range and type of skills needed within specific inclusive situations. At the individual child level, it may be prudent to consider the systematic arrangement of inclusive contexts that vary in their skill demands, thus affording children with inclusive opportunities within and at the boundary of their developmental abilities.

Finally, the data presented in this chapter suggest that the availability and proximity of typically developing children do not ensure social interaction and peer-related participation from preschoolers with autism. What may contribute to this outcome? All of the authors' experiences indicate that promoting high-quality and sustained interaction between preschoolers with autism and their peers is not something that teachers find natural or easy to accomplish. First, when given a choice, typically developing youngsters generally prefer to interact with classmates who exhibit age-appropriate language and play skills (Kohler & Strain, in press). Second, children with autism often resist teachers' efforts to facilitate their interaction with peers. Given these challenges, it should not be surprising that comprehensive and long-term intervention approaches, especially those based upon peer-mediated tactics, are both a necessary and sufficient condition to promote children's social exchanges (Kohler, Strain, & Shearer, 1992; Strain, Goldstein, & Kohler, in press).

In conclusion, this chapter has described four levels of social inclusion that pertain to children's participation within integrated preschools. Each level was illustrated with sample observational data collected from four youngsters enrolled at LEAP Preschool, an integrated program for children with autism. The data suggested that the four levels address meaningful, interrelated, and intervention-relevant dimensions of children's inclusion. Although this discussion has focused on preschool inclusion for children with autism, the authors believe that the four levels of inclusion also pertain to programs that accommodate youngsters with other developmental needs. Finally, it is important to highlight that all four levels of inclusion can be influenced by early childhood administrators and practitioners who bear responsibility for providing access *and* high-quality outcomes for young children with disabilities and their peers.

REFERENCES

Brandt, R. (Ed.). (1992). Untracking for equity. *Educational Leadership, 50*.

Carta, J., Greenwood, C.R., & Atwater, J. (1985). *ESCAPE: Ecobehavioral system for complex assessment of preschool environments*. Kansas City: Juniper Gardens Children's Project, Bureau of Child Research, University of Kansas.

Carta, J.J., Sainato, D.S., & Greenwood, C.R. (1988). Advances in the ecological assessment of classroom instruction for young children with handicaps. In S.L. Odom & M.B. Karnes (Eds.), *Early intervention for infants and children with handicaps: An empirical analysis* (pp. 217–239). Baltimore: Paul H. Brookes Publishing Co.

Cooke, T.P., Ruskus, J.A., Apolloni, T., & Peck, C.A. (1981). Handicapped preschool children in the mainstream: Background, outcomes, and clinical suggestions. *Topics in Early Childhood Special Education, 1*, 73–83.

Guralnick, M.J. (1990). Major accomplishments and future directions in early childhood mainstreaming. *Topics in Early Childhood Special Education, 10*, 1–17.

Hamilton, V.J., & Gordon, D.A. (1978). Teacher-child interactions in preschool and task persistence. *American Educational Research Journal, 15*, 459–466.

Hart, B., & Risley, T.R. (1975). Incidental teaching of language in the preschool. *Journal of Applied Behavior Analysis, 8*, 411–420.

Kohler, F.W., & Strain, P.S. (in press). The social interactions between preschoolers with disabilities and their peers: Methods for assessment, intervention, and analysis. In E. Cipani and N. Singh (Eds.), *Practical approaches to the treatment of severe behavior disorders*. DeKalb, IL: Sycamore Press.

Kohler, F.W., Strain, P.S., & Shearer, D.D. (1992). The overtures of preschool social skill intervention agents: Differential rates, forms, and functions. *Behavior Modification, 16*, 525–542.

Lovaas, O.I. (1987). Behavioral treatment and normal educational and intellectual functioning of young autistic children. *Journal of Consulting and Clinical Psychology, 55*, 3–9.

McGee, G.G., Paradis, T., & Feldman, R.S. (1993). Free effects of integration on levels of autistic behavior. *Topics in Early Childhood Special Education, 13*, 57–67.

McWilliam, R.A. (1991). Targeting teaching at children's use of time: Perspectives on preschoolers' engagement. *Teaching Exceptional Children, 23*, 42–43.

McWilliam, R.A., & Bailey, D.B. (1992). Promoting engagement and mastery. In D.B. Bailey & M. Wolery (Eds.), *Teaching infants and preschoolers with disabilities* (2nd ed., pp. 229–256). New York: Macmillan.

Odom, S.L., & McEvoy, M.A. (1988). Integration of young children with handicaps and normally developing children. In S.L. Odom & M.B. Karnes (Eds.), *Early intervention for infants and children with handicaps: An empirical analysis* (pp. 241–268). Baltimore: Paul H. Brookes Publishing Co.

Parsons, A.C., McWilliam, R.A., & Buysse, V. (1989). *A procedural manual for coding engagement in early childhood programs*. Chapel Hill: Frank Porter Graham Child Development Center, University of North Carolina at Chapel Hill.

Shores, R.E., Hester, P., & Strain, P.S. (1976). The effects of amount and type of teacher-child interaction on child–child interaction. *Psychology in the Schools, 13*, 171–175.

Smith, B.J., & Rose, D.F. (1993). *Administrators policy handbook for preschool mainstreaming*. Cambridge, MA: Brookline.

Strain, P.S., Danko, C.D., & Kohler, F.W. (1995). Activity engagement and social interaction development in young children with autism: An examination of "free" intervention effects. *Journal of Emotional and Behavioral Disorders, 3*, 108–123.

Strain, P.S., Goldstein, H., & Kohler, F.W. (in press). Peer-mediated interventions for young children with autism. In E. Hibbs and P. Jenson (Eds.), *Psychosocial treatment research with children and adolescents*. Washington, DC: American Psychological Association.

Strain, P.S., & Odom, S.L. (1986). Peer-social initiations: Effective intervention for social skills development of exceptional children. *Exceptional Children, 52*, 543–552.

Strain, P.S., & Smith, B.J. (1993). Comprehensive educational, social, and policy forces that affect preschool integration. In C.A. Peck, S.L. Odom, & D.D. Bricker (Eds.), *Integrating young children with disabilities into community programs: Ecological perspectives on research and implementation* (pp. 209–222). Baltimore: Paul H. Brookes Publishing Co.

Wheelock, A. (1992). The case for untracking. *Educational Leadership, 50*, 6–10.

Wolery, M., & Brookfield-Norman, J. (1988). (Pre)Academic instruction for handicapped preschool children. In S.L. Odom & M.B. Karnes (Eds.), *Early intervention for infants and children with handicaps: An empirical analysis* (pp. 109–128). Baltimore: Paul H. Brookes Publishing Co.

Wolery, M., Strain, P.S., & Bailey, D.B. (1992). Reaching the potentials of children with special needs. In S. Bredekamp & T. Rosegrant (Eds.), *Reaching potentials: Appropriate curriculum and assessment for young children* (pp. 92–111). Washington, DC: National Association for the Education of Young Children.

14

On the Importance of Integrating Naturalistic Language, Social Intervention, and Speech-Intelligibility Training

Stephen M. Camarata

The theoretical origins of *social referencing* (the ability to use social cues to learn new information) include the shift from specific abilities training conducted in pull-out settings to teaching conducted within everyday settings that focuses on functionally appropriate goals (e.g., Carr, 1994; Koegel, O'Dell, & Koegel, 1987). However, there are a number of factors within the social context that directly or indirectly have an impact on the success of the intervention (Carr, 1994). One aspect of *naturalistic language* (the ability to exchange information within social contexts) that is a key to successful communication is the *intelligibility levels* of the messages (Camarata, 1995; Kent, 1993). *Intelligibility* refers to a listener's ability to decode a message accurately. Interestingly, however, this fundamental aspect of communication and social referencing has remained largely the domain of speech-language pathologists who often complete intervention using pull-out service delivery (Bernthal & Bankson, 1993; Camarata, 1995). However, there is preliminary evidence that speech-intelligibility training can be successfully completed using naturalistic intervention (Camarata, 1993, 1995; Edwards, 1992). To date, the theoretical argument has been focused simply on updating intervention for speech intelligibility using naturalistic procedures (e.g., Camarata, 1995; Hoffman, 1992). However, integrating speech-intelligibility training into more general naturalistic language intervention may streamline teaching while providing effective and rapidly generalized improvements in speech intelligibility as well as in overall language and communication skills.

The purpose of this chapter is threefold. First, a number of the fundamental assumptions pertaining to speech-intelligibility training are examined because these assumptions are part of the theoretical underpinnings for completing speech-intelligibility teaching using traditional practice and drill activities within pull-out settings. Second, a case for reexamining intervention procedures in terms of naturalistic language intervention is provided, and a rationale and a preliminary model for inclusion-based delivery of speech-intelligibility training that is fully integrated into the language program are offered. Finally, a rationale is provided for expanding the scope of practice to include individuals with severe disabilities who traditionally have been excluded from speech-intelligibility services. These individuals are likely to benefit from the integrated naturalistic intervention described in the chapter, as intelligible communication is an important behavior for gaining access to self-determination; expanding personal choices; and reducing the frustration associated with disruptive behavior, aggression, and self-injury (Carr, 1992; Dattilo & Camarata, 1991).

SPEECH INTELLIGIBILITY VERSUS ARTICULATION AND PHONOLOGY

Interventions designed to improve the speech production skills of children with unintelligible or partially intelligible speech have been presented under a number of cover terms, including *logopaedics, articulation,* and *phonology.* Although each of these terms refers to problems children have with learning and producing the speech sounds of a language, each term reflects different assumptions about how speech is acquired and mastered. Articulation and logopaedics emphasize training the motor gestures associated with speech production whereas phonology includes, in addition to the motor component, a recognition of a cognitive–linguistic component within the speech production intervention (Bernthal & Bankson, 1993; Camarata, in press). However, as Camarata (1995) argues, these cover terms focus on underlying specific abilities thought to contribute to overall intelligibility rather than on the end product of intervention: an increase in the intelligibility of the child's speech (see also Kent, 1993). Although such semantic analysis may appear unimportant, one could argue that the characteristics of intervention often arise from the philosophies that underpin the cover terminology (Camarata, 1995). As discussed below, there has long been an imitation and drill orientation for improving speech in children with disabilities. Camarata (1995) has argued that a shift in terminology from *articulation* to *phonology* to *speech intelligibility* would both focus intervention on the actual goal of the teaching and also expand intervention perspectives beyond traditional approaches. The term *speech intelligibility* is used throughout this chapter.

SPEECH INTELLIGIBILITY AS AN INTEGRATED PART OF LANGUAGE

Researchers have traditionally subdivided the study of language (and language disorders) into autonomous parts (cf. Bloomfield, 1933; Crystal, 1987). For example, Crystal divides language into morphology (word endings), phonology (speech), semantics (meaning), and syntax (word order and word sequencing). Similarly, Camarata (1991, 1995, in press) defines language along morphological, phonological, pragmatic (social use), semantic, and syntactic dimensions. Historically, language researchers have attempted to isolate and study in detail these individual components of language (e.g., Bloomfield, 1933). Not surprisingly, remediation programs have often been focused on one or more of these domains in an analog manner (cf. Fey, 1986). Although such an analog view may be useful to further some aspects of research and implement some types of intervention, there are crucial advantages to studying and remediating these language dimensions simultaneously. For example, Jakobson (1980) argues that

it is important to approach language and its disruption in the framework of a given level [dimension], while remembering at the same time that any level [dimension] is what the Germans call *das Teilganze* and that the totality and the interrelation between the different parts of the totality have to be taken into account. (pp. 94–95)

Contrary to this idea, the study of speech acquisition (articulating phonology) and the treatment of speech-intelligibility disorders have been conducted primarily in isolation from the other aspects of language (see the review and arguments in Crystal, 1987).

However, preliminary attempts to examine the interrelation among language dimensions have revealed important integration effects between speech and the other dimensions of language. Such studies have indicated that each of the other language dimensions can be interrelated with regard to children with speech and language disabilities. For example, Panagos and his colleagues (Panagos, 1982; Panagos & Prelock, 1982; Panagos, Quine & Klich, 1979), Paul and Shriberg (1982), and Schwartz, Leonard, Folger, and Wilcox (1980) have all reported that changes in syntactic (sentence) complexity can result in changes in speech production accuracy. That is, increased syntactic complexity is often associated with an increase in the number of speech errors. Bock (1982) provided a detailed model to account for this apparent trade-off in complexity among these linguistic domains, suggesting that processing constraints in the child's linguistic system result in a decay in speech production.

Similarly, Camarata and his colleagues (Camarata & Leonard, 1986; Camarata & Schwartz, 1985) conducted a series of studies that revealed the interrelation between semantics (word use) and speech. In this case, greater semantic complexity (object words as compared to action words) was associated with a decrease in speech production accuracy (lower percentage of consonants produced correctly). Note that these latter studies included a high degree of control of potentially confounding factors (e.g., diversity of morphological markers [word endings/suffixes], frequency of presentation, and phonological structure of the lexemes [words] within each class), suggesting once again that processing limitations may result in trade-offs among language domains. Finally, work by Camarata (1990), Camarata and Erwin (1988), and Camarata and Gandour (1985) suggested a relationship between morphology (grammatical morphemes, or suffixes) and speech. These authors reported that difficulty in producing grammatical markers (e.g., plural usage) can lead to shifts in the patterns used to signal the grammatical change (e.g., use of variations in duration; intensity; or fundamental frequency [F_0], the basic frequency of the vocal chord during speech).

Speech-Intelligibility Disabilities as a "Bottleneck" to Successful Communication

As noted previously, the remarkable shift in language intervention procedures in the past decade to include procedures that parallel natural language acquisition more closely has not generally included speech-intelligibility training (Camarata, 1993, 1995). However, an integrated view of communication and social intervention requires, at a basic level, a foundation of intelligibility to be successful (Carr, 1992, 1994). There are a number of reasons for this relationship between speech intelligibility, language, and more general social skills. The literature review cited earlier reveals that speech-intelligibility skills can interact with other domains of language to produce interesting and important covariance, including linguistically related academic skills (Catts, 1989, 1993; Ham, 1958; Hodson, Nomura, & Zappia, 1989). In addition, there is direct evidence to suggest that speech competence plays a more fundamental role in language acquisition and in the remediation of language learning disabilities.

For example, Miller et al. (1990) reported that speech capability was the most predictive factor in the remediation of language disorders in children with Down syndrome. Similarly, Leonard et al. (1982) reported that children actually avoided production of word forms containing sounds that were difficult to produce. Schwartz and Leonard (1982) replicated this finding, reporting that children were much more likely to acquire words that contained phonemes (speech sounds) that were in their sound repertoires prior to learning new words. Also, Camarata (1990) reported that early acquisition of alveolar fricatives (production of the sounds "s" and "z") in word final position can lead to very rapid (and precocious) acquisition of the grammatical markers that require these phonemes (e.g., plural words). Thus, speech difficulties can serve as a "choke point" or "flow restrictor" for the other aspects of language; children with language learning disabilities must be proficient in the form (speech production) of language in order to be successful in overall language and communication skills. From this perspective, the ultimate success of any language intervention is predicated upon at least minimal speech-intelligibility skills. This is especially true for those interventions designed to establish or enhance the child's ability to access or activate teaching responses from parents, teachers, and peers—these communication partners require intelligible input from the child with language learning disabilities in order to respond appropriately (see Yoder & Davies, 1992).

Speech-intelligibility skills also can have an impact on more general social skills as well. The key role of language and language disabilities in the development of social skills has been increasingly recognized (see the review in Carr, 1994). At a fundamental level, difficulty in expressing one's wants, needs, thoughts, and ideas can lead to communication breakdowns in the classroom and to frustration in students with language disabilities.

Building upon this foundation, it has become increasingly clear that preschool students with language disabilities often later develop associated behavior problems (Aram, Ekelman, & Nation, 1984; Cantwell & Baker, 1985; Carr & Durand, 1985). More important, there have been an increasing number of studies demonstrating a link between disruptive behaviors and speech impairments and low levels of speech intelligibility (see the review in Koegel, Camarata, & Koegel, 1994). For example, Carr (1992) reported that relatively low levels of disruptive behaviors were noted when persons with severe disabilities interacted with family and staff members who were familiar with their idiosyncratic (generally low intelligibility) speech productions. However, disruptive behaviors increased dramatically when the persons with disabilities interacted with staff or members of the general public who could not understand their unusual, unintelligible patterns. Carr suggested that staff and other individuals be taught how to understand the unusual production patterns in order to reduce the disruptive behavior, but such an approach may be less efficient than improving overall speech intelligibility (and speech production skills) because 1) *any* staff member, family member, or community member could communicate more efficiently with the individual with severe disabilities, and 2) the individual would have access to a much greater number of opportunities for communication and interaction in mainstream environments. The above studies reveal that persistent speech-intelligibility disabilities can have a negative impact on social skills and act as a barrier to social development.

Traditional Assumptions Concerning Speech-Intelligibility Intervention

There are a number of basic assumptions concerning the ways that children with speech disabilities should be taught. First is the widely held view that speech is primarily a motor behavior that is best addressed using a series of drill activities designed to improve motor function (Bernthal & Bankson, 1981, 1988; Elbert, Powell, & Swartzlander, 1991). Indeed, children with speech-intelligibility difficulties are often referred to as "articulation disordered" (see Bernthal & Bankson, 1981). This emphasis on articulation, defined as "the production of any speech sound [involving] the adjustment of the tongue, with relation to the palate, at the place where the tongue has, for that sound, its maximum elevation" (Webster's Dictionary of the English Language, 1989), is based upon the assumption that improvements in these tongue movements will result in an improvement in intelligibility—an assumption that has had a venerable history in the literature (e.g., Swift, 1918; Van Riper, 1939). Note that an emphasis on articulation may be direct or indirect in the sense that some interventions may train actual tongue movements whereas others may teach these indirectly by requiring the child to imitate individual speech sounds while providing instruction on correct tongue placement.

The term *articulation* could be applied to any speech-intelligibility intervention that initiates training using imitation and drill activities, regardless of whether the description of the intervention includes "linguistic" elements. For example, widely used *phonological process* approaches

(Hodson & Paden, 1981, 1983; Ingram, 1976) or *maximal contrast* approaches (Gierut, 1989) that incorporate direct imitation of individual speech sounds could be classified as basing intervention, in part, on the assumption that articulation training is a fundamental keystone characteristic of intervention. For example, Elbert et al. (1991) argued that "an important aspect of phonological treatment [speech-intelligibility training] is the attainment of easy, automatic production skills. These skills necessarily precede generalization" (p. 86). Note that Elbert et al. were evaluating the effects of a "language-based" approach to phonological treatment that included training designed to highlight the meaningful differences in speech sounds (*minimal contrast* treatment), but retained an imitation and drill component designed to ensure repeated articulatory training of the targeted speech sounds. Thus, imitation and drill approaches to improving speech-intelligibility difficulties have long been prominent in the literature and remain an integral part of current practice (see the review in Bernthal & Bankson, 1993; Swift, 1918).

There are several related aspects of this assumption that should be examined in more detail. First, although none can deny that the ultimate output of the speech signal is a series of motor acts, it has become increasingly clear that there is an absence of evidence of motor disabilities in a large proportion of children with speech-intelligibility disabilities (Shriberg, Kwiatkowski, Best, Hengst, & Terselie-Weber, 1986). Although these children may in fact have some form of motor disability that is not detectible using current medical and neurological evaluation methodologies (Folkins & Bleile, 1990), it is also possible that a portion of these disabilities may actually be associated with language deficits (Camarata, 1995; Folkins & Bleile, 1990; Shriberg et al., 1986). Note that researchers have long discussed the dual linguistic and motor nature of speech intelligibility (e.g., Bloomfield, 1933; Folkins & Bleile, 1990; Ingram, 1976; Stampe, 1969), and a number of intervention procedures have been developed that focus, at least in part, on the language component of speech-intelligibility disabilities (e.g., Gierut, 1989; Hodson, 1980; Ingram, 1981; Williams, 1991). However, as noted earlier, many of these language-based approaches may retain, to a large extent, imitation and drill procedures that resemble traditional articulation approaches in many ways (see the discussion in Camarata, 1995).

A second assumption associated with imitation and drill-based intervention is that individual speech sounds (phonemes) must be treated to improve overall intelligibility. Intelligible speech is hypothesized to consist of a compilation or blending of individual speech sounds (Kent, 1993), and a lack of intelligibility is believed to arise from inaccurate speech–motor gestures or from inaccurate production of individual speech sounds (as in Elbert et al., 1991). Remediation is thus focused on the improved production of individual sounds with the ultimate goal of increasing overall intelligibility. Interestingly, the focus of this intervention has traditionally been on consonant production (see the reviews in Bernthal & Bankson, 1993; Elbert et al., 1991; Hodson, 1994). However, basic research on speech perception reveals that the acoustic properties of vowels provide a much larger contribution to intelligibility than do consonants (Ohde & Sharf, 1992). However, there has been little research on vowel errors in children with speech-intelligibility disabilities and similarly little research on the effects of remediation of vowel production on overall intelligibility (Bernthal & Bankson, 1993; Camarata, 1995).

Again, although the assumption that improved consonant production (produced using imitation and drill) will relate to improved spontaneous speech intelligibility has a high degree of theoretical plausibility, there are surprisingly little data available to directly evaluate the assumption's validity. Elbert, Dinnsen, Swartzlander, and Chin (1990) reported that consonants treated using a combination of speech–motor (imitation and drill) and cognitive–linguistic (minimal pair) approaches resulted in generalization to spontaneous speech for many consonants; however, the authors did not directly test whether this generalization was associated with improved *overall* speech intelligibility. Relatedly, and perhaps most important, is the basic assumption that imitation and drill activities, whether to improve speech–motor control or to improve speech sound production, will ultimately result in production of the speech targets in the child's spontaneous speech. Furthermore, it is thought that such training will result in significant changes in overall intelligibility. These assumptions should be tested more directly if this model of intervention is to be retained, particularly in light of basic shifts away from analog training in pull-out settings toward inclusion models employing naturalistic intervention procedures in other aspects of language and social skills programs.

To summarize, traditional approaches to remediating speech-intelligibility disabilities have been founded upon a motor perspective that includes, to a large extent, imitation and drill activities as a core intervention. This traditional practice has, in turn, been founded upon a series of assumptions regarding the nature of speech-intelligibility disabilities and the procedures and goals that are required to remediate these disabilities. As is discussed in the following section, these assumptions have also had consequences with regard to the ways that speech-intelligibility intervention has not been included in recent shifts in language intervention procedures and in shifts in teaching practices such as inclusion.

Shifts in Language Intervention Procedures

There has been a shift in language intervention practices since the 1980s to include more naturalistic procedures (Camarata, Nelson, & Camarata, 1994; Fey, 1986; Koegel, O'Dell, & Koegel, 1987). However, if one reviews

Example of typical setting for analog treatment: Note the materials and proximity of teacher and child. Teacher provides a high degree of control over stimuli.

the literature prior to this shift, it is clear that language intervention, like speech-intelligibility intervention currently, was primarily completed in pull-out settings using imitation and drill procedures (see the reviews in Fey, 1986; Mowrer, 1984). Interestingly, these earlier language intervention models included theoretical rationales similar to those underpinning traditional approaches to speech intelligibility—specifically, a core element of imitation within highly controlled contexts to ensure productivity (McReynolds & Bennett, 1972). These language intervention models were replaced by more naturalistic interventions, in part because of several limitations in imitation and drill activities in pull-out settings. Specifically, difficulties in generalization (Siegel & Spradlin, 1985; Stokes & Baer, 1977) and related limitations in social validity (Wolf, 1978) have been problematic in approaches that rely upon extensive imitation and drill activities. In addition, research including children with severe disabilities has indicated that such children are often uncooperative within intervention settings that employ imitation and drill activities (e.g., Koegel, Dyer, & Bell, 1987; Koegel, Koegel, & Surratt, 1992).

A parallel to this shift to more naturalistic intervention procedures has been a shift in the environments in which children with disabilities are served. Segregated special education services have often been replaced by mainstream and inclusive service delivery for a wide range of services, including language intervention. Although improved access to mainstream and inclusive services has been firmly rooted in civil rights for children with disabilities, this shift has also resulted in improved service delivery as well (cf. Bricker, 1993; Cirrin & Penner, 1995). However, because speech-intelligibility work has been based upon imitation and drill activities, services have not been delivered extensively in mainstream or inclusive environments (see the discussions in Camarata, 1995; Koegel, Camarata, & Koegel, 1994). Also, because many children with severe disabilities do not cooperate in imitation and drill activities, they are unlikely to have access to speech-intelligibility services, even though intelligible communication is an important skill for achieving self-determination (Dattilo & Camarata, 1991). The following section presents a description of naturalistic language intervention and a discussion of related procedures.

DEFINING NATURALISTIC LANGUAGE INTERVENTION

The word *naturalistic* is defined as being "of or in accordance with nature," whereas *language* is defined as "any means of expressing thoughts or feelings," and *intervention* is defined as "an intervening in any event or affair so as to affect its course" (Barnhart, 1983). Taken together, these words refer to methods employed to impact the course of communication development that resemble the kinds of learning that are observed in the ambient (naturalistic) environment. That is, by definition, naturalistic language intervention is designed to parallel, as much as possible, features observed in typical language development. However, it is clear that the key element in this definition is what one considers to be the "natural" environment and which features in the ambient language learning context are most important for learning. The following pages examine several different theoretical positions on what constitutes the most important aspects of the naturalistic langugage learning context.

An interesting aspect of advances in naturalistic language intervention is strikingly different procedures that are viewed as "naturalistic" (e.g., whole language, Norris, 1992; conversational recast training, Camarata, Nelson, & Camarata, 1994; natural language paradigm, Koegel, O'Dell, & Koegel, 1987). For example, the focus in *whole language* is often on pragmatic (social interaction) aspects of instruction rather than on specific language structures. Conversely, *conversational recast* intervention includes morphological (suffixes and function words) and syntactic (sentence structures) models that are delivered to the children in social contexts thought to induce learning in typically functioning children. In the *natural language paradigm*, specific targets are taught in a variety of social settings using natural reinforcers—that is, continual interaction with a communication partner or access to desired objects rather than using token or food reinforcers. Finally, *incidental teaching* (e.g., Guess, Keogh, &

Sailor, 1978) has been viewed as naturalistic because the teaching, which includes imitative prompts and overt reinforcers, is completed in classroom settings. A common aspect of these procedures is the emphasis on applying interaction procedures observed in interactions with typically functioning children (see the discussion in Nelson, 1989).

Additionally, there has been an ongoing debate over what "language" consists of. Although the focus of this debate has been primarily on establishing criteria for determining whether primates in fact have language (Savage-Rumbagh, Murphy, Sevcik, & Brakke, 1993), there are competing models of human language as well. For example, a number of theoreticians focus on *content, form,* and *use* (Bloom & Lahey, 1978; Lahey, 1988), whereas many psychologists and linguists define language as consisting of *morphology, syntax, semantics, pragmatics,* and *phonology* (see Camarata, 1991). Note that both these models include aspects of speech intelligibility (a part of form and phonology) as an integral part of language (see also the discussion in Crystal, 1987).

Finally, it is also important to note that differences in the definition of intervention may also result in different views on naturalistic language intervention. Although perhaps a less common source of divergent theoretical perspectives, what one considers to be intervention would certainly have a profound effect on the nature of naturalistic language intervention. For example, if one adopts the position that language learning disabilities arise from internal conflicts in the Freudian tradition (cf. Wyatt, 1969) or from a lack of a supportive communicative and emotional environment on the part of the parents, then intervention would be defined as operating on these aspects of the families' psychological status rather than on the contextual variables within the naturalistic language environment thought to enhance language acquisition in typically functioning children (e.g., structural characteristics of the parental input, attention, motivation, language cues, parent–child response variables) (Camarata et al., 1994; Carr, 1994; Moerk, 1992). However, a common aspect of empirical approaches to intervention (whether naturalistic or not) has been the focus on measuring change in the target behaviors (McReynolds & Kearns, 1983).

Taken together, then, naturalistic language intervention can be operationally defined as procedures paralleling those employed to teach typically functioning children that produce measurable (and socially valid) change in the morphological, syntactic, semantic, pragmatic, and speech-intelligibility aspects of the linguistic system of children with disabilities. Note that this definition specifically includes speech intelligibility as a potential language goal within this naturalistic training (see the discussion in Camarata, 1993). This definition also implies that teaching will be completed in the least restrictive environment. Thus, the initial phases of nat-

Example of naturalistic treatment setting: Note the materials and proximity of the teacher and child as they interact. Child is included in the control of stimuli.

uralistic intervention are in fact the direct inverse of those used in imitation and drill activities in pull-out settings.

Implications of Naturalistic Speech-Intelligibility Training

The initial phases of traditional speech-intelligibility training have typically been designed to gain control of the production of the targeted speech sounds. The training is decontextualized to minimize distractions, and the goal of training is to generate accurate imitation of the targets (see Fey, 1986). After production is established under these controlled conditions, teaching shifts to transferring production to the more naturalistic generalization setting wherein imitative prompts and overt reinforcers are faded. Thus, training proceeds from a high degree of support to one of less support and, from a naturalistic perspective, from a low degree of naturalness to a higher degree. In contrast, the naturalistic teaching procedures are initiated with a higher degree of overlap with typical language acquisition, often including natural reinforcers—models delivered in a naturalistic manner—and training is completed in naturalistic settings. From this perspective, one could argue that the goal of intervention is to provide teaching that matches as closely as possible the natural learning environment.

Thus, the model of naturalistic speech-intelligibility intervention is the inverse of traditional approaches: The starting point for intervention is the "generalization phase" of traditional procedures, and additional "production support" is added only when the child demonstrates a lack of progress within the naturalistic intervention. In contrast, analog training is initiated using sound production in isolation, followed by syllable, word, phrase, and sentence level productions. This is followed by procedures designed to fade the prompts and reinforcers and induce generalization. In naturalistic intervention, the initial phase of teaching would be completed within a play or inclusion teaching context and production models at the phrase or sentence level would be delivered without prompts or reinforcers (see Camarata, 1993, 1995, for a detailed description of these procedures). Imitative prompts would be delivered at the phrase level only if the child has demonstrated a lack of progress within unprompted training. From a theoretical perspective, an inverse sequence (relative to traditional procedures) would be employed: Phrase, word, syllable, sound would be initiated only if learning were not demonstrated at higher levels. The latter levels, syllable and sound, would be strictly a *last resort* as these represent decontextualized, nonlinguistic, *unnatural* productions. This naturalistic intervention model is summarized in Figure 1. Figure 2 represents the progression of stimuli and contexts for training that is often employed during speech intervention. Note that this is in direct contrast to the proposed model (Figure 1).

Potential Model for Implementing
Speech-Intelligibility Training in Inclusive Environments

This section includes a potential model for implementing speech-intelligibility training within an inclusive environment. It should be

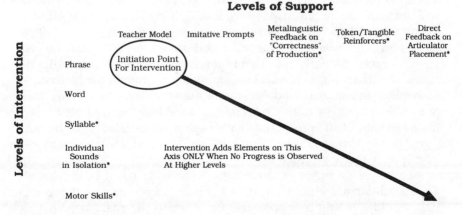

Figure 1. Schematic of naturalistic language intervention. (* indicates that these elements are not included in the initial phases of intervention and represent a transition to motor training when a lack of progress is observed in the naturalistic intervention.)

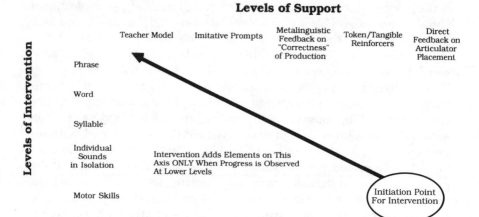

Figure 2. Schematic of analog intervention.

noted that this is a theoretical model generated from preliminary data indicating that naturalistic speech-intelligibility training can be effective (Camarata, 1993) and from a high degree of success for naturalistic teaching on a wide range of language and social skills (see the reviews in Fey, Windsor, & Warren, 1995; Warren & Reichle, 1992). Therefore, the model requires continuing validation from researchers as well as evaluation by teachers, special educators, and speech–language pathologists.

As noted earlier, the most naturalistic intervention in school settings for speech-intelligibility training would be an inclusive setting, wherein speech goals are integrated into the regular classroom activities. Because a number of studies have indicated that general language intervention will not incidentally improve speech intelligibility (Fey et al., 1994), it is important that a specific focus of the inclusion activity be speech intelligibility. This could potentially include recast procedures on consonant and vowel targets, partially intelligible utterances, or even unintelligible strings. Alternatively, as noted above, more direct prompts for production of words or imitation of models could be delivered if needed. Production of isolated sounds or multiple imitations would be required only when the more naturalistic procedures have been demonstrated to be ineffective. The key aspect of this training is the focus on intelligibility rather than speech–motor production.

There are a number of models that potentially could be employed. The speech-language pathologist, as a primary expert on speech production, would typically be responsible for selecting the goal, coordinating the intervention, and monitoring progress. Additionally, the speech pathologist may complete activities in the classroom using lesson plans designed by the teacher but adapted by the speech pathologist to fit the individual needs of the child with speech-intelligibility disabilities. Alternatively, the teacher or special educator or both could integrate speech-intelligibility goals into their regular classroom activities for those children requiring speech-intelligibility intervention (see Cirrin & Penner, 1995, for a description of general inclusion methods). Preliminary results suggest that teachers and special educators are capable of delivering models with a broad intelligibility focus (e.g., instructing students to repeat partially intelligible productions), but are less successful in delivering models that focus on specific speech sounds (Camarata, Koegel, & Koegel, 1993).

CONCLUSIONS

Because traditional analog interventions have dominated speech-intelligibility intervention, the inclusion model presented herein is just beginning to be implemented, and many of the methodological details are now being experimentally validated. In a way, the instructional technology is currently at a similar stage as naturalistic language and social intervention were in the early 1980s. However, this naturalistic, integrated intervention for speech-intelligibility disabilities, like these earlier models for language and social intervention, appears to hold great potential for improving and updating speech-intelligibility training and, if successful, for unlocking even greater improvements in language and social skills for children with disabilities.

REFERENCES

Aram, D.M., Ekelman, B.G., & Nation, J.E. (1984). Preschoolers with language disorders: 10 years later. *Journal of Speech and Hearing Research, 27*(2), 232–244.

Barnhart, C.L. (1983). *The World Book dictionary.* Chicago: World Book.

Bernthal, J., & Bankson, N. (1981). *Articulation disorders.* Englewood Cliffs, NJ: Prentice Hall.

Bernthal, J., & Bankson, N. (1988). *Articulation disorders* (2nd ed.). Englewood Cliffs, NJ: Prentice Hall.

Bernthal, J., & Bankson, N. (1993). *Articulation disorders.* (3rd ed.). Englewood Cliffs, NJ: Prentice Hall.

Bloom, L., & Lahey, M. (1978). *Language development and language disorders.* New York: John Wiley & Sons.

Bloomfield, L. (1933). *Language.* New York: Holt, Rinehart & Winston.

Bock, K. (1982). Toward a cognitive psychology of syntax: Information processing contributions to sentence processing. *Psychological Review, 89,* 1–47.

Bricker, D. (1993). A rose by any other name, or is it? *Journal of Early Intervention, 17*(2), 89–96.

Camarata, S. (1990). Semantic iconicity in plural acquisition: Extending the argument to normal children. *Clinical Linguistics and Phonetics, 4,* 319–325.

Camarata, S. (1991). Assessment of oral language. In S. Salvia & J. Ysseldyke (Eds.), *Assessment in special and remedial education* (5th ed., pp. 263–301). Boston: Houghton Mifflin.

Camarata, S. (1993). The application of naturalistic conversation training to speech production in children with speech disabilities. *Journal of Applied Behavior Analysis, 26,* 176–182.

Camarata, S. (1995). A rationale for naturalistic speech intelligibility intervention. In M. Fey, J. Windsor, & S. Warren (Eds.), *Language intervention: Preschool through the early school years* (pp. 63–84). Baltimore: Paul H. Brookes Publishing Co.

Camarata, S. (in press). Assessment of oral language. In J. Salvia & J. Ysseldyke (Eds.), *Assessment in special and remedial education* (6th ed.). Boston: Houghton Mifflin.

Camarata, S., & Erwin, L. (1988). Rule invention in the acquisition of morphology revisited: A case of transparent semantic mapping. *Journal of Speech and Hearing Research, 31,* 425–431.

Camarata, S., & Gandour, J. (1985). Rule invention in the acquisition of morphology. *Journal of Speech and Hearing Disorders, 50,* 40–45.

Camarata, S., Koegel, R., & Koegel, L. (1993, November). *Naturalistic treatment for disruptive behavior and speech intelligibility in autism and other disabilities.* Paper presented at the American Speech-Language-Hearing Association Conference, Anaheim, CA.

Camarata, S., & Leonard, L. (1986). Young children pronounce object words more accurately than action words. *Journal of Child Language, 13,* 51–65.

Camarata, S., Nelson, K.E., & Camarata, M. (1994). A comparison of conversation based to imitation based procedures for training grammatical structures in specifically language impaired children. *Journal of Speech and Hearing Research, 37,* 1414–1423.

Camarata, S., & Schwartz, R. (1985). Production of object words and action words: Evidence for a relationship between phonology and semantics. *Journal of Speech and Hearing Research, 28,* 323–330.

Cantwell, D., & Baker, L. (1985). Psychiatric and learning disorders in children with speech and language disorders: A descriptive analysis. *Advances in Learning & Behavioral Disabilities, 4,* 29–47.

Carr, E. (1992, September). *Mood, menses, and meaning: Complex determinants of severe problem behavior.* Paper presented at the Fifth Annual NIDRR Research and Training Center Conference on Nonaversive Behavior Management, Nashville, TN.

Carr, E.G. (1994). Emerging themes in the functional analysis of problem behavior. *Journal of Applied Behavior Analysis, 27,* 393–399.

Carr, E.G., & Durand, M. (1985). Reducing behavior problems through functional communication training. *Journal of Applied Behavior Analysis, 18*(2), 111–126.

Catts, H. (1989). Speech production deficits in developmental dyslexia. *Journal of Speech and Hearing Disorders, 54,* 422–428.

Catts, H. (1993). The relationship between speech-language impairments and reading disabilities. *Journal of Speech and Hearing Research, 36,* 948–958.

Cirrin, F., & Penner, S. (1995). Classroom based and consultative service delivery models for language intervention. In M.E. Fey, J. Windsor, and S.F. Warren (Eds.), *Language intervention: Preschool through the elementary years* (pp. 333–362). Baltimore: Paul H. Brookes Publishing Co.

Crystal, D. (1987). Towards a bucket theory of language disability: Taking account of interaction between linguistic levels. *Clinical Linguistics and Phonetics, 1,* 7–21.

Dattilo, J., & Camarata, S. (1991). Facilitating conversation through self-initiated augmentative communication treatment. *Journal of Applied Behavior Analysis, 24,* 369–378.

Edwards, M. (1992). In support of phonological processes. *Language, Speech, and Hearing Services in Schools, 23,* 233–240.

Elbert, M., Dinnsen, D.A., Swartzlander, P., & Chin, S.B. (1990). Generalization to conversational speech. *Journal of Speech and Hearing Disorders, 55*(4), 694–699.

Elbert, M., Powell, T., & Swartzlander, P. (1991). Toward a technology of generalization: How many exemplars are sufficient? *Journal of Speech and Hearing Research, 34,* 81–87.

Fey, M.E. (1986). *Language intervention with young children.* San Diego: College-Hill Press.

Fey, M.E., Cleave, P., Ravida, A., Long, S., Dejmal, A., & Easton, D. (1994). The effects of grammar facilitation on the phonological performance of children with speech and language impairments. *Journal of Speech and Hearing Research, 37,* 594–607.

Fey, M.E., Windsor, J., & Warren, S.F. (Eds.). (1995). *Language intervention: Preschool through the elementary years.* Baltimore: Paul H. Brookes Publishing Co.

Folkins, J., & Bleile, K. (1990). Taxonomies in biology: Phonetics, phonology, and speech motor control. *Journal of Speech and Hearing Disorders, 55,* 596–611.

Gierut, J. (1989). Maximal opposition approach to phonological treatment. *Journal of Speech and Hearing Disorders, 54,* 9–19.

Guess, D., Keogh, W., & Sailor, W. (1978). Generalization of speech and language behavior. In R. Schiefelbusch (Ed.), *Bases of language intervention* (pp. 373–395). Baltimore: University Park Press.

Ham, R. (1958). Relationship between misspelling and misarticulation. *Journal of Speech and Hearing Disorders, 23,* 294–297.

Hodson, B. (1980). *The assessment of phonological processes.* Danville, IL: Interstate Printers & Publishers.

Hodson, B. (1994). Helping individuals become intelligible, literate, and articulate: The role of phonology. *Topics in Language Disorders, 14*(2), 1–16.

Hodson, B., Nomura, C., & Zappia, M. (1989). Phonological disorders: Impact on academic performance? *Seminars in Speech and Language, 10,* 252–259.

Hodson, B., & Paden, E. (1981). Phonological processes which characterize unintelligible and intelligible speech in early childhood. *Journal of Speech and Hearing Disorders, 46,* 369–373.

Hodson, B., & Paden, E. (1983). *Targeting intelligible speech.* San Diego: College-Hill Press.

Hoffman, P. (1992). Synergistic development of phonetic skill. *Language, Speech, and Hearing Services in Schools, 23,* 254–260.

Ingram, D. (1976). *Phonological disability in children.* New York: Elsevier.

Ingram, D. (1981). *Procedures for the phonological analysis of children's language.* Baltimore: University Park Press.

Jakobson, R. (1980). *The framework of language.* Ann Arbor, MI: University of Michigan Press.

Kent, R. (1993). Speech intelligibility and communicative competence in children. In A. Kaiser and D. Gray (Eds.), *Enhancing children's communication: Research foundations for intervention* (pp. 223–237). Baltimore: Paul H. Brookes Publishing Co.

Koegel, R., Camarata, S., & Koegel, L. (1994). Aggression and noncompliance: Behavior modification through naturalistic language remediation. In J. Matson (Ed.), *Autism in children and adults: Etiology, assessment, and intervention* (pp. 165–180). Sycamore, IL: Sycamore Press.

Koegel, R., Dyer, K., & Bell, L. (1987). The influence of child-preferred activities on autistic children's social behavior. *Journal of Applied Behavior Analysis, 20,* 243–252.

Koegel, R., Koegel, L., & Surratt, A. (1992). Language intervention and disruptive behavior in preschool children with autism. *Journal of Autism and Developmental Disorders, 22,* 141–153.

Koegel, R., O'Dell, M., & Koegel, L. (1987). A natural language teaching paradigm. *Journal of Autism and Developmental Disabilities, 17,* 187–199.

Lahey, M. (1988). *Language disorders and language development.* New York: Macmillan.

Leonard, L., Camarata, S., Schwartz, R., Chapman, K., & Messick, C. (1985). Homonymy and the voiced-voiceless distinction in the speech of children with specific language impairment. *Journal of Speech and Hearing Research, 28,* 215–224.

Leonard, L., Schwartz, R., Chapman, K., Rowan, L., Prelock, P., Terrell, B., Weiss, A., & Messick, C. (1982). Early lexical acquisition in children with specific language impairment. *Journal of Speech and Hearing Research, 25,* 554–559.

McReynolds, L., & Bennett, S. (1972). Distinctive feature generalization in articulation training. *Journal of Speech and Hearing Disorders, 37,* 462–470.

McReynolds, L.V., & Kearns, K. (1983). *Single-subject experimental strategies in communicative disorders.* Baltimore: University Park Press.

Miller, J., Miolo, G. Murray-Branch, J., Pierce, K. Rosin, M., Sedey, A., & Swift, E. (1990, November). *Facilitating speech and language development in children with Down syndrome.* Paper presented at the annual conference of the American Speech-Language-Hearing Association, Seattle, WA.

Moerk, E.L. (1992). *A first language taught and learned.* Baltimore: Paul H. Brookes Publishing Co.

Mowrer, D. (1984). Behavioural approaches to treating language disorders. In D. Muller (Ed.), *Remediating children's language: Behavioural and naturalistic approaches* (pp. 18–54). San Diego, CA: College-Hill Press.

Nelson, K. (1989). Strategies for first language teaching. In M. Rice & R. Schiefelbusch (Eds.), *The teachability of language* (pp. 263–310). Baltimore: Paul H. Brookes Publishing Co.

Norris, J. (1990). Whole language in theory and practice: Implications for language intervention. *Language, Speech, & Hearing Services in Schools, 21,* 212–220.

Ohde, R., & Sharf, D. (1992). *Phonetic analysis of normal and abnormal speech.* New York: Macmillan.

Panagos, J. (1982). The case against the autonomy of phonological disorders in children. *Seminars in Speech, Language, and Hearing, 3,* 172–182.

Panagos, J., & Prelock, P. (1982). Phonological constraints on the sentence productions of language disorderd children. *Journal of Speech and Hearing Research, 25,* 171–177.

Panagos, J., Quine, M., & Klich, R. (1979). Syntactic and phonological influences on children's articulation. *Journal of Speech and Hearing Research, 22,* 841–848.

Paul, R., & Shriberg, L. (1982). Associations between phonology and syntax in speech delayed children. *Journal of Speech and Hearing Research, 25,* 536–547.

Savage-Rumbaugh, S.E., Murphy, J., Sevcik, R.A., & Brakke, K.E. (1993). Language comprehension in ape and child. *Monographs of the Society for Research in Child Development, 58*(3–4), 221.

Schwartz, R., & Leonard, L. (1982). Do children pick and choose? Phonological selection and avoidance in early lexical acquisition. *Journal of Child Language, 9,* 319–336.

Schwartz, R., Leonard, L., Folger, M., & Wilcox, M. (1980). Evidence for a synergistic view of linguistic disorders: Early phonological behavior in normal and language disordered children. *Journal of Speech and Hearing Disorders, 45*, 357–377.

Shriberg, L., Kwiatkowski, J., Best, S., Hengst, J., & Terselie-Weber, B. (1986). Characteristics of children with phonological disorders of unknown origin. *Journal of Speech and Hearing Disorders, 51*, 140–160.

Siegel, G., & Spradlin, J. (1985). Therapy and research. *Journal of Speech and Hearing Disorders, 50*, 226–230.

Stampe, D. (1969). The acquisition of phonetic representation. *Papers from the Fifth Regional Meeting of the Chicago Linguistic Society* (pp. 433–444). Chicago, IL: Chicago Linguistic Society.

Stokes, T., & Baer, D. (1977). An implicit technology of generalization. *Journal of Applied Behavior Analysis, 10*, 349–367.

Swift, W. (1918). *Speech defects in school children.* Cambridge, MA: Riverside Press.

Van Riper, C. (1939). *Speech correction.* Englewood Cliffs, NJ: Prentice Hall.

Webster's Dictionary of the English Language (2nd ed.). (1989). Springfield, MA: Merriam-Webster.

Warren, S., & Reichle, J. (Eds.). (1992). *Communication and language intervention series: Vol 1. Causes and effects in communication and language intervention.* Baltimore: Paul H. Brookes Publishing Co.

Williams, L.A. (1991). Generalization patterns associated with training least phonological knowledge. *Journal of Speech and Hearing Research, 34*(4), 722–733.

Wolf, M.M. (1978). Social validity: The case for subjective measurement or how applied behavior analysis is finding its heart. *Journal of Applied Behavior Analysis, 11*, 203–214.

Wyatt, G.L. (1969). *Language learning and communication disorders in children.* New York: Free Press.

Yoder, P., & Davies, B. (1992). Greater intelligibility in verbal routines with young children with developmental delays. *Applied Psychologistics, 13*, 77–91.

15

Alternative Applications
of Pivotal Response Training

*Teaching Symbolic Play
and Social Interaction Skills*

Laura Schreibman, Aubyn C. Stahmer, and Karen L. Pierce

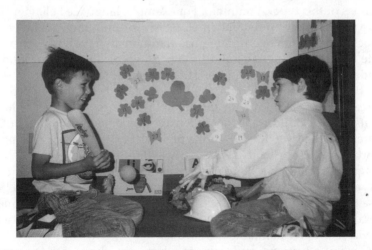

One of the most significant advances in intervention for children with autism has been the change of focus from training individual target behaviors to training in *pivotal responses*. This change in focus reflects the results of systematic, programmatic research that indicated that the initial and substantial improvements found in children who had received behavioral instruction did not show the generality that would make the intervention as effective as hoped. This limitation led to further research aimed at developing improved strategies that would have more widespread and durable effects. One result of this research trend was the identification of *pivotal behaviors*—that is, behaviors that, when changed, were associated with widespread effects on other behaviors. The focus on pivotal behaviors, which at first was utilized primarily to teach verbal behaviors, has not only led to improvements in generality of intervention effects but also provided a set of procedures that has been useful in building other behavioral repertoires. This chapter describes pivotal response training and elaborates and describes alternative applications of this technology, specifically with regard to symbolic play and social interaction.

PIVOTAL RESPONSE TRAINING

Historically, behavioral intervention for children with autism has involved focusing on individual behaviors targeted for change. Essentially such treatment involves the identification of a specific behavior to be changed followed by the systematic application of behavioral principles with the goal of affecting behavioral change in the desired direction (see Schreibman, 1988; Schreibman & Koegel, 1981, for more complete descriptions of this type of training). For example, language behaviors have been a major area of intervention emphasis for individuals with autism, and behavioral language training has traditionally involved focusing on single aspects of language at a time (e.g., vocal imitation of modeled sounds, identification of colors, use of pronouns). Intervention based upon this model comprised the foundation of the behavioral approach to the treatment of children with autism and was empirically determined to be effective for building rather extensive response repertoires in these children (see Schreibman, 1988, for a review). However, as promising and important as these advances were, early enthusiasm was tempered by the subsequent finding that there were some rather significant limitations to intervention effectiveness (Lovaas, Koegel, Simmons, & Long, 1973). These limitations consisted of failures of the intervention outcomes to generalize to nonintervention environments, to generalize to nontreated behaviors, or to be maintained over time.

Our investigations, and those of other researchers, into the generalization limitations of this work implicated deficits in *motivation* (e.g., Koegel & Mentis, 1985) and *responsivity to simultaneous multiple cues* (e.g., Lovaas, Koegel, & Schreibman, 1979) as important variables. Difficulties with motivation are well documented concerning children with autism and are noted when the children fail to exhibit learned behaviors in new situations or to initiate spontaneous behaviors such as social interactions.

Problems with responsivity to simultaneous multiple cues, or *stimulus overselectivity*, are evident when the children's breadth of attention is too narrow to allow for learning of new behaviors (Schreibman & Koegel, in press). We hypothesized that these deficits in motivation and responsivity might indeed contribute substantially to the generalization problems noted in past behavioral interventions and that a promising new form of intervention might be one in which the intervention focuses not on individual target behaviors but rather on increasing motivation and re-sponsivity directly (Schreibman & Koegel, in press). It was reasoned that by increasing these pivotal target behaviors, interventionists might indi-rectly affect a large number of individual behaviors. Such an intervention promised to be not only more efficient in terms of the time and effort re-quired of the child and clinician but also more effective in terms of pro-moting generalized gains.

Our results, and those of other investigators (e.g., Hart & Risley, 1980; McGee, Krantz, & McClannahan, 1985; Neef, Walters, & Egel, 1984), suggest that intervention for children with autism that focuses on increas-ing pivotal behaviors does indeed lead to more generalized intervention gains (e.g., Schreibman & Koegel, in press). For example, utilization of procedures known to increase responsivity to simultaneous multiple cues in children with autism has been shown to have generalized effects in ac-quisition of behaviors using prompting techniques (Schreibman, Charlop, & Koegel, 1982) and increases in incidental learning and social respon-siveness (Burke & Koegel, 1982). Similarly, procedures known to increase motivation in children with autism have been associated with increased generalization of language use (Koegel, Dyer, & Bell, 1987; Koegel, O'Dell, & Dunlap, 1988; Koegel, O'Dell, & Koegel, 1987; Laski, Charlop, & Schreibman, 1988) and more positive affect (emotional response) in the child (Koegel & Egel, 1979) and the parents (Schreibman, Kaneko, & Koegel, 1991).

Procedures to Enhance Motivation

The specific procedures used in pivotal response training (PRT) are de-rived directly from prior research identifying the effectiveness of the method for increasing motivation and enhancing learning in children with autism. The following procedures are described in detail in a train-ing manual by Koegel et al. (1989).

Clear Instructions and Questions The interventionist must be careful to present instructions or questions in a clear, unambiguous manner and to present instructions that are relevant and appropriate to the task. Care is also taken to be certain the child is attending to the interventionist and to the training materials (e.g., Schreibman & Koegel, 1981). For example, an interventionist is working with a child and trying to teach him to get dressed. The child, however, is looking at the ceiling and ignoring the interventionist. The interventionist taps the child lightly on the shoulder, calls his name, and ensures eye contact. After the child is looking at the interventionist, she says, "Put on your shirt." Notice that in this example the interventionist ensures that the child is paying attention by touching him and making eye contact. The instruction was brief, to the point, and clear.

Interspersal of Maintenance Tasks Motivation is enhanced if the child's overall level of success is high (thus maintaining high rates of reinforcement). This is accomplished by frequently interspersing previously mastered tasks among more difficult acquisition tasks (Dunlap, 1984).

Child Choice To maximize the child's interest in the learning situation, he or she is allowed to have a great deal of input in determining the specific stimuli and the nature of the learning interaction (Koegel, Dyer, & Bell, 1987). This is in contrast to previous methods wherein the interventionist determined the learning task, the learning materials, and the reinforcers. With child choice, the child is presented with a variety of materials (e.g., toys, games, snacks) and allowed to select an activity or object about which the learning activity will take place. The interventionist is alert to changes in the child's interest and allows the child to change to another preferred activity. It should be noted that child choice is not absolute in that inappropriate, compulsive, or potentially harmful activities are not allowed.

Direct Reinforcement Direct reinforcers are those consequences directly related to the response they follow. Thus, a direct reinforcer for the verbal response "ball" might be the opportunity to roll a ball as opposed to obtaining a bite of food or a token reinforcer (traditional reinforcement methods). Access to a ball is a direct and natural consequence of saying "ball," whereas food or a token is not. Utilization of direct reinforcers is associated with enhanced learning and generalization, likely because this is the type of reinforcement available in the natural (generalization) environment (Koegel & Williams, 1980).

Reinforcement of Reasonable Attempts To maximize reinforcement and therefore enhance the child's motivation, interventionists reinforce all reasonable attempts made by the child to respond (Koegel, O'Dell, & Dunlap, 1988). Thus, reinforcers are contingent upon attempts that may not be completely correct and may not be quite as good as previous attempts, but are within a broader range of correct responses. This is in contrast to earlier training programs that used shaping and required a response at least as good as prior responses in order to merit reinforcement. Essentially, the child is reinforced for "trying," so that efforts to continue in the learning situation are increased. However, to be reinforced a response has to be "reasonable" in terms of being directed at the interventionist or training materials and being within the broader class of correct responses. Thus, a child who has demonstrated the ability to say "ball" clearly will not receive reinforcement for a muffled "ba" sound on a later occasion because it is not a reasonable attempt.

An example of a reasonable attempt would be as follows: An interventionist is working with a child and trying to teach her animal names. The interventionist picks up a plastic elephant and bear from the child's play zoo set and asks, "Do you want the elephant or the bear?" The child attempts to grab the elephant. The interventionist pulls the toys away from the child and repeats the prompt. The child responds "ell-ee." The interventionist says "good" as she hands the child the elephant. Notice in this example that the interventionist accepts the reasonable response "ell-ee" and lets the child have the elephant. By reinforcing this attempt, the interventionist is ensuring that the child is successful and that she will be motivated to continue to work on the task in the future. Also notice that when the child said nothing, her behavior was not reinforced (i.e., she was not given the elephant).

Turn Taking Activities are arranged such that the child and the interventionist alternate responding. This serves to allow the child to become accustomed to the normal "give-and-take" of social interaction. It also provides the opportunity for the interventionist to frequently model appropriate responses for the child. The child is thus exposed to multiple exemplars of appropriate stimuli and correct responding, which should serve to enhance the generalization of intervention effects.

Increasing Responsivity to Multiple Cues

As noted earlier, prior research has identified and described an attentional deficit, stimulus overselectivity, characterizing many children with autism (see Schreibman, 1988, for a review). Briefly, this pattern of deviant attention is characterized by the failure to respond to simultaneous multiple cues such as those that occur in a learning situation. This attentional deficit has been implicated in a wide range of behavioral deficits in autism including failure to generalize (e.g., Lovaas et al., 1979; Schreibman, 1988). However, research has demonstrated that, for many of these children, overselectivity may be substantially reduced or remediated with special training that focuses on teaching the child a series of *conditional discriminations* (Koegel & Schreibman, 1977; Schreibman et al., 1982). This research has demonstrated that children who initially respond to multiple-component discriminations on the basis of only one of the components learn a generalized strategy to respond to these discriminations after such training. A conditional discrimination is one that *requires* responding on the basis of multiple cues. To illustrate, asking a child to get her white shoes is requiring the child to make a conditional discrimination. Assuming the child has other shoes (of other colors) and has other white items of clothing (not shoes), the child must respond to both object (shoes) and color (white) in order to respond correctly.

In our training, the interventionist is encouraged to provide the child with learning tasks that require responding to multiple cues. This means that the interventionist, whenever possible and appropriate, will choose tasks that encourage or require the child to respond on the basis of multiple cues. Based upon our previous findings, we reason that as the children learn to respond on the basis of multiple stimuli in their environment, their attention will be more normalized, allowing more cues in their environment to become functional. This should broaden the stimulus control of their behavior leading to enhanced learning and generalization.

SYMBOLIC AND SOCIODRAMATIC PLAY SKILLS AND AUTISM

Although PRT has most often been used to increase language skills in children with autism, other behaviors have been targeted using this technique. Specifically, difficult types of play skills that involve symbolic representation and social skills have been successfully targeted (Pierce & Schreibman, in press; Stahmer, 1993, 1995; Thorp, Stahmer, & Schreibman, 1995). These specific types of play were targeted because of the severe deficits seen in children with autism in these areas (see Jarrold, Boucher, & Smith, 1993, for review).

Individuals with autism, by definition, have extreme difficulty in social situations (e.g., Schreibman, 1988). For young children, opportunities for social interaction occur most frequently in play situations. Children with autism, however, often do not exhibit appropriate play skills (e.g., Schreibman, 1988). These children may engage in repetitive actions with toys or become obsessive with them. They may even use them in stereotyped ways such as acting out a scene from a favorite movie. Children with autism rarely perform the types of creative, spontaneous play activities exhibited by typical children. In addition, there is a striking lack of symbolism in the play of children with autism (Baron-Cohen, 1987; Mundy, Sigman, Ungerer, & Sherman, 1987; Wulff, 1985). Because of these difficulties in play, it is important that researchers, teachers, and parents teach play to these children in a way that promotes symbolism, creativity, and spontaneity.

Two of the most difficult forms of play in which young children engage are symbolic play and sociodramatic play (e.g., Bretherton, 1989; McCune-Nicolich, 1981). These are difficult because they require the child to use symbolism. Symbolic play is play in which a child

(1) is using one object as if it were another object (e.g., a banana is a telephone), and/or (2) the subject is attributing properties to an object which it does not have (e.g., a toy stove is "hot"), and/or (3) the subject is referring to absent objects as if they were present (e.g., pantomime). (Baron-Cohen, 1987, p. 140)

Additionally, the child must be able to perform complex play actions—that is, link symbolic actions together to form a complete story with the toys. Sociodramatic play is an advanced form of symbolic play in which groups of children plan and carry out cooperative dramatizations centered about a familiar theme. Fully developed sociodramatic play contains five elements: 1) role playing, such as pretending to be the ice cream vendor; 2) make-believe transformations, such as pretending a block is a car; 3) social interaction; 4) verbal communication; and 5) persistence, or the ability to carry out a play theme from beginning to end (Smilansky, 1968). Existing literature suggests that symbolic play emerges between 12 and 24 months of age (e.g., McCune-Nicolich, 1981) and sociodramatic play develops in the third or early fourth year of life (Fein, 1981; Forys & McCune-Nicolich, 1984).

Play behavior, symbolic forms in particular, may be very important in the treatment of autism because of the relationship between play and language and communication skills. Vygotsky (1978) believed that play was the primary medium through which language developed. Research with typical children indicates that pretend play may be indicative of the representational skills necessary for verbal communication (Perlmutter & Pelligrini, 1987). There is strong evidence for at least a correlational relationship between symbolic forms of play and more complex language abilities as well as social interaction (e.g., Bates, Benigni, Bretherton, Camaioni, & Volterra, 1979; Rubin, 1986). Some researchers have also found a relationship between pretending and receptive language in children with autism (Ungerer & Sigman, 1987). Thus, symbolic and sociodramatic play skills may be very important for language development in children with autism, and teaching these play skills might even facilitate language skills (Stahmer, 1993).

Although there is some indication of a correlation between language and play in children with autism, these children seem to have a symbolic play deficit that exceeds their language deficit. In other words, they exhibit far fewer symbolic play actions and less complex play than typical children or children with mental retardation who have been matched for language ability (e.g., Baron-Cohen, 1987; Riquet, Taylor, Benaroya, & Klein, 1981; Stahmer, 1995). Children with other types of developmental disabilities also exhibit delays in symbolic and sociodramatic play; however, they usually engage in play that would be typical for their mental age (Beeghly, Weiss-Perry, & Cicchetti, 1989; Hill & McCune-Nicolich, 1981). All children progress through the same stages, although those with mental retardation have a delay. Children with autism, however, seem to show an absence of spontaneous symbolic play regardless of their mental age, indicating some type of play deficit that goes beyond mental retardation in general (Baron-Cohen, 1987).

Research has overwhelmingly indicated that children with autism show deficits in spontaneous symbolic play (e.g. Baron-Cohen, 1987; Lewis & Boucher, 1988; Ungerer & Sigman, 1981; Wing, Gould, Yeates, & Brierly, 1977). However, research suggests that they can engage in simple symbolic play actions if the actions are prompted either verbally or through direct modeling. For example, Lewis and Boucher (1988) examined a group of children with autism during structured play with specific objects appropriate for symbolic play. The children with autism did not engage in any spontaneous symbolic play with the toys. When symbolic play was elicited verbally they performed symbolic actions at levels similar to those of typical controls. This research suggests that these children have the potential to perform symbolic play at levels similar to those of language-matched peers. In addition, as is discussed in more detail below, our research indicates that with specific play training, children with autism can learn spontaneous, complex symbolic play (Stahmer, 1995).

There has been very little research examining the nature of sociodramatic play in children with autism. However, there is research to support deficits in areas such as symbolic play (e.g., Baron-Cohen, 1987; Stahmer, 1995), play complexity (Baron-Cohen, 1987; Stahmer, 1995), assuming another's role (Baron-Cohen, 1987; Rutter, 1974), and social-interactive skills (Rutter, 1978; Schreibman, 1988), all prerequisites for sociodramatic play. In addition, our research indicates that children with autism have great difficulty with sociodramatic play before specific training (Thorp et al., 1995).

Because of the level of difficulty of these types of play, some prerequisite behaviors should be present before this training is attempted. In other words, the child with autism should be developmentally ready to learn symbolic play skills. The child should play appropriately with more simple toys, such as manipulative toys, and some functional toys such as a toy car or play food. In addition, some language is necessary for learning these skills. We suggest that children have a vocabulary at the 2-year-old level before attempting to teach symbolic play skills and at least the 3-year-old level for sociodramatic play skills. In addition, if a child does not engage in symbolic play, such play should be taught prior to teaching the more difficult skills required for sociodramatic play.

In the current literature, there have been very few attempts to teach these advanced levels of play to children with autism. Most research has looked at training simpler types of play, usually involving object manipulation, ball tossing, and so forth. This play training has been shown to reduce off-task behavior and increase play behavior (e.g., Quinn & Rubin, 1984; Stahmer & Schreibman, 1992). However, teaching symbolic and sociodramatic play has been more complicated because the "rules" are constantly changing and evolving as the children interact. One investigation involved training children with autism to perform three specific sociodramatic play scripts with some success (Goldstein & Cisar, 1992). However, according to the authors, training specific scripts sometimes resulted in stereotypic routines and boredom in the children. The task, then, becomes one of teaching difficult play skills in such a way that the children learn to generate creative, complex play themes in a spontaneous, natural manner.

Teaching Symbolic and Sociodramatic Play Skills Using PRT

Pivotal response training has provided interventionists with a naturalistic training method that has proven structured enough to help the children learn these complex skills, while still being flexible enough to allow the children to remain creative in their play. In order to assess the use of PRT in teaching these types of skills, we adapted the steps described earlier to emphasize symbolic or sociodramatic play skills. The adapted procedures are described in detail below.

Clear Instructions and Questions   The task at hand is made clear to the child. For example, the interventionist might ask the child what could be done with a particular toy. Modeling and the use of maintenance tasks should both be used to clarify the tasks early in training. Of course, the child should be attending to the interventionist and the training materials (e.g., Schreibman & Koegel, 1981).

Interspersal of Maintenance Tasks   It is important to intersperse play at simpler levels while training symbolic and sociodramatic play skills. When typical children play, they do not use one type of play at the exclusion of another (e.g., they do not use only substitute objects) but instead tend to use a mixture of play levels at any one time. Therefore, it is important that children with autism learn to combine different types of play behavior. In addition, interspersing easier types of play that the child has already mastered increases success and thereby motivation.

Child Choice   Allowing the child to choose the specific toy set to be used in training will enhance motivation and performance. In our research, we found that the children will typically change toys at a rate similar to that of typical children once they have mastered the play skills (Stahmer, 1993). A variety of toys that support the type of play being taught should be available during each training session. Again, child choice only works to a point. If a child begins to wander from toy to toy with no direction or begins to act inappropriately, the interventionist may prompt the child to play appropriately with a specific toy.

Direct Reinforcement   In our play training, we have used the child's choice of toys as the reinforcer for more advanced levels of play. For example, if a child chooses to play with a car and driver the child might be required to perform a symbolic action with the toy before being given free access to it. A symbolic action might be pretending to wash the car, pretending to put gas in the car, pretending to feed the driver, and so forth.

A mother teaches her child with autism how to use a block as a telephone via symbolic play PRT.

After the performance of the symbolic action, the child may then play freely with the toys. As the child progresses in ability, more complex play is required before free access is allowed. Typically, the children will become accustomed to performing these symbolic actions and will incorporate them into their play with little or no prompting from the interventionist.

Reinforcement of Reasonable Attempts   Attempts at correct responding are reinforced as well. For example, if a child is pretending to be a firefighter and wants to use a hose, it would be appropriate to make "water" noises and point the hose toward the imaginary fire. If the child makes the appropriate motions but fails to use the appropriate sound effects, this might be reinforced as an attempt at sociodramatic play.

Turn Taking   The interventionist takes turns performing appropriate play actions to provide examples as well as to promote social interaction skills.

Examples of Symbolic and Sociodramatic Play Training

An example of a symbolic play interaction might be as follows: A child may choose to play with a playhouse and dolls. The child is then given a block and a doll seated at a table in the playhouse and instructed, "Show me what you can do with these toys." The child would be expected to "feed" the block to the doll as she or he would a cookie or other food item. If the child does not respond, the interventionist feeds the block to the doll and makes eating sounds (e.g., "yum, yum") and then returns the block to the child. If the child still does not respond a new toy is chosen. When the child does respond, the entire playhouse and the dolls are given to the child to play with. If the child makes an attempt at symbolic play, for example, she or he makes a "yum, yum" noise and uses the block as food for her- or himself but not the doll, the child receives reinforcement (access to the toy) for the attempt.

As the child improves at symbolic play, she or he would be expected to engage in more complex play. For example, with the playhouse and dolls the child might be prompted to wake the dolls up from sleep, use a substitute object to brush their teeth, sit them down to breakfast and use a substitute object as food, and have the dolls clean up the meal before being allowed free access to the toys. By this point in training, children typically perform several related play actions spontaneously.

An illustration of sociodramatic play training might be as follows. If the child expresses an interest in playing with a tool set, he or she would be encouraged to 1) develop a play theme related to these toys (e.g., building a house), 2) adopt a role appropriate to this theme (e.g., construction worker), and 3) assign a complementary role to the interventionist (e.g., homeowner, another worker, or boss). Ensuing sociodramatic play would be interactive and would develop these roles in the chosen play theme. The interventionist would prompt the child to assume the presence of an imaginary character or to involve a doll in the play.

Outcomes of Symbolic and Sociodramatic Play Training

Our research indicates that children with autism with the appropriate language ability can learn to engage in spontaneous, creative symbolic and sociodramatic play with another adult at levels similar to those of language-age matched typical peers (Stahmer, 1995; Thorp et al., 1995). In addition, social behaviors, such as positive responding, increase after play training as does the amount of language used during play. Generalization to new toys and new adults is also impressive, and these improved play behaviors maintain over time. When rated by naive observers for creativity, spontaneity, and "typical" play, children with autism improved significantly after play training; however, their play was still qualitatively distinguishable from the play of the typical children (Stahmer, Schreibman, & Palardy, 1994). One area of difficulty for the children, even after play training, was play with another peer. Although their play skills had increased, interacting with another child did not improve. It seems that specific interaction training is needed to increase play with peers. Future research will focus on having peers themselves teach these play skills as well as further increasing the quality of the children's play.

SOCIAL COMPETENCE AND AUTISM

Children with autism are characterized by their profound deficits in the area of social competence (Rutter, 1978). Examples of this deficit include a failure to maintain eye contact, initiate conversation, engage in appropriate affect, and label emotions in themselves and others; thus there are myriad variables to consider when attempting to define (or teach) the abstract concept of social competency. Although this concept is multidimensional, there is overall agreement that the essence of social behavior consists of the ability to relate to others in a mutually reinforcing and reciprocal fashion and to adapt social skills to the varying demands of interpersonal contexts (Howlin, 1986). Also central to the definition of social competence is the ability to communicate effectively with another person. Children with autism are typically late beginning to speak, and approximately half never develop meaningful speech (Rutter, 1978). Of those who do speak, their speech is often qualitatively different than the speech of typical children (e.g., Baltaxe, 1984), thus making acquisition of effective social skills even more challenging.

The ability to coordinate one's attention between an object and interactant (i.e., joint attention) is also an important social skill and has been shown to be impaired in children with autism (Mundy & Sigman, 1989). In addition, research suggests that coordination between interactants is an important forum for language and social development (Bakeman & Adamson, 1986), but this skill is rarely taught or assessed in traditional social skills interventions.

Failure to learn (and subsequently engage in) complex social behaviors in children with autism may be related to motivation deficits. That is, the children may not engage in social behaviors not only because they lack the behavioral repertoire per se, but also because they are not motivated to do so. As mentioned earlier, PRT has been shown to increase the motivation of children with autism and thus may be an effective technique for increasing social skills (Pierce & Schreibman, 1995).

Increasing Social Competence Through Peer-Implemented PRT

The use of chronologically age-matched peer trainers not only may be a viable option for social skills training in terms of practicality (i.e., peers are readily available in school environments), but may have developmental implications as well. Contemporary researchers suggest that peer relations are extremely important in the normal social development of children. For example, Hartup (1983) suggests that peer relations serve functional purposes such as 1) aiding in learning language and other cognitive skills, 2) providing companionship and bolstering feelings of self-worth, and 3) providing a staging area for the transmission of social norms. Therefore, utilizing peers as trainers may have benefits extending beyond the immediately apparent benefits associated with increased social competency (e.g., increased play skills).

In addition to the strategies described earlier, PRT adapted to increase social competency includes the following strategies.

1. *Encourage and Extend Conversation:* In order to increase verbal interaction, peers are instructed to encourage the target child to request whatever he or she wants to play with. If the target child is motivated to interact with a particular toy, he or she must emit a verbalization in order to obtain it. Once the target child emits a verbalization relating to the preferred object, the peer extends the conversation by commenting and asking questions relating to the target child's statements. To illustrate, suppose the target child chooses to play with a ball. After requesting to play ball, the peer would extend the conversation by saying something like, "I like to bounce the ball high. Do you like to bounce the ball or throw it?" After some time the peer may attempt to further extend the conversation by saying, "I like to play ball outside with my brother. Where do you like to play ball?" Because the target child chose to interact with the ball, he or she may be more willing to talk about ideas relating to that particular toy.

2. *Exaggerate Positive Affect:* Peers are instructed to act in a highly animated fashion both verbally, by utilizing "happy" words such as "wow," and nonverbally, by smiling. Implementing positive affect is especially important when peers are delivering verbal reinforcement. For example, consider a peer who tells a target child "Good throw [target child's name]!" Exaggerated positive affect may serve to increase the salience of the interaction and express very clearly to the target child the parameters of the interaction.

3. *Model Social Statements:* Peers are also instructed to engage in friendly or social verbal behavior. For example, peers might say, "I like playing with you," or "This game is fun!" This allows the peer to provide appropriate social statements for the target child to imitate. In addition, after emitting a positive social statement, such as "I'm having fun," the peer would then ask the target child, "Are you having fun?"

4. *Ignore and Redirect Inappropriate Behavior:* Because of inappropriate behaviors often associated with autism, such as echolalia (i.e., repetition of words), self-stimulatory behaviors (e.g., hand flapping), and other inappropriate behaviors (e.g., yelling), which have been shown to interfere with learning, peers are instructed to ignore inappropriate behavior. During instances where the target child is not engaging in inappropriate behavior, the peer would then redirect the target child to engage in more appropriate behaviors such as playing a game or choosing another activity.

Teaching Peers to Implement Strategies   An effective method for teaching peers to implement PRT strategies consists of didactic instruction with a PRT manual (which has been adapted to include the strategies mentioned earlier and is appropriate for young children; see Pierce, 1993), role playing, and contingent feedback of performance. During the initial stages of peer training, peers are given a PRT social skills manual with the strategies depicted in both pictorial and written form. An adult then verbally explains each of the strategies followed by modeled examples. Next, the peers are instructed to verbally explain each of the techniques to the adult and then demonstrate understanding by providing examples of each. Later steps of training consist of having the peer role-play each of the strategies with another typical peer. During the final stage, the peer is instructed to implement all strategies with a schoolmate with autism followed by contingent feedback from a trained interventionist.

Although research shows that children with autism can be taught to respond to initiations, complex social behaviors such as initiating play and conversation typically remain low. For example, Odom, Hoyson, Jamieson, and Strain (1985) taught peers of children with autism to engage in a variety of approach strategies (e.g., persistence) to increase the social behaviors of their schoolmates with autism. Results of this research indicated that, over time, these children can be taught to respond to and play with their peers. However, the overall level of complex social behaviors (e.g., initiations) in which the children with autism engaged remained relatively unchanged.

Results from peer-implemented PRT research indicate that not only is this technique effective for teaching children with autism to respond to initiations, but it also holds promise for increasing more complex social behaviors such as initiations (Pierce & Schreibman, 1995). In the Pierce and Schreibman study, two 10-year-old boys with autism, poor social skills, and nonverbal IQ scores of 40 and 65 were taught to engage in social interactions via peer-implemented PRT. Prior to intervention, the target children engaged in low levels of interaction and no initiations with a typical peer during a 10-minute play session. After several weeks of training, however, both target children maintained interactions over 75% of the time, and their initiations increased to levels ranging from 0% to 35% per session. Initiations made by the target child were either based on play activities (e.g., "I want to play ball") or conversation (e.g., "How are you?").

Collateral Changes in Nontargeted Behaviors   Research in this area also suggests that, as a result of peer-implemented training, collateral changes in other behaviors such as joint attention (the ability to shift attention from interactant to activity) become evident (Pierce & Schreibman, 1995).

During baseline, the target child engaged in little, if any, joint attention. That is, the child typically stared into space or exhibited no attentional focus at all. During later phases of training, the target child's attentional focus was related to the peer or the play objects. These results are important because, even though training did not specifically target attention behaviors, the target child's attentional focus came to resemble patterns of typical attention (i.e., engagement in joint attention).

It is a reliable finding that the general procedures of PRT are effective at increasing the language skills of children with autism (Koegel, O'Dell, & Koegel, 1987; Laski, Charlop, & Schreibman, 1988). Importantly, effects of peer-implemented PRT suggest that peers are also effective at increasing the language skills of their schoolmates with autism (Oke, 1993; Pierce & Schreibman, 1995). Specifically, children with autism who were taught social skills via PRT by their peers verbalized more frequently and spoke with longer sentence length after training.

Practical Considerations

Two factors are critical to consider when implementing PRT with peers: 1) peer trainer characteristics and 2) target child characteristics.

Peer Trainer Characteristics Several characteristics are important when choosing a peer trainer. First, a peer trainer should be chosen who has consistent school attendance, thus ensuring continuity and consistency of intervention application. Second, peer trainers who are friendly and outgoing and have high social skills should be chosen to participate. Selection of competent peer trainers is important because these individuals are acting as models for the target child. Also, the literature suggests that these children may be more persistent with, and accepting of, their schoolmates with disabilities. Information regarding peer characteristics can most easily be obtained from the peer's teacher and observation during instances of high social interaction (e.g., recess).

Target Child Characteristics Because of the highly verbal nature of most social interactions, target children with some verbal skills are better suited for peer training than their nonverbal cohorts. Selection of target children with some verbal skills is also important because peer trainers may become discouraged or fail to maintain interactions if the target child does not verbally respond to the peer's initiations.

SUMMARY AND CONCLUSIONS

The emphasis on training pivotal behaviors has allowed for the promising evolution of intervention for children with autism and similar disorders. It is hoped that the work summarized in this chapter provides a convincing and compelling argument for the inclusion of PRT and its subsequent variants in the overall intervention plan of such children. The basis for PRT lies in the results of programmatic and systematic research emphasizing the importance of focusing on pivotal behaviors such as motivation and responsivity for enhancing generalization of intervention outcomes. Continued research has demonstrated that adapted variants of PRT can be effective in teaching a wide variety of important skills to children with autism, including advanced forms of symbolic play and social interactions. It should be emphasized that the PRT variants presented in this chapter represent only some of the first few extensions of PRT technology. Research focusing on the pivotal behavior of self-management has also led to the development of important teaching strategies (e.g., Koegel & Koegel, 1990; Pierce & Schreibman, 1994; Schreibman & Koegel, in press). There are undoubtedly many other variants of the technique that will be developed in the future to allow for the acquisition of other advanced behavioral repertoires. In essence, one may expect the future to hold exciting advances in this area.

REFERENCES

Bakeman, R., & Adamson, L. (1986). Infants' conventionalized acts: Gestures and words with mothers and peers. *Infant Behavior and Development, 9*, 215–230.

Baltaxe, L.A.M. (1984). Use of contrastive stress in normal, aphasic, and autistic children. *Journal of Speech and Hearing Research, 27*, 97–105.

Baron-Cohen, S. (1987). Autism and symbolic play. *British Journal of Developmental Psychology, 5*, 139–148.

Bates, E., Benigni, L., Bretherton, I., Camaioni, L., & Volterra, V. (1979). *The emergence of symbols: Cognition and communication in infancy.* New York: Academic Press.

Beeghly, M., Weiss-Perry, B., & Cicchetti, D. (1989). Beyond sensorimotor functioning: Early communicative and play development of children with Down syndrome. In D. Cicchetti & M. Beeghly (Eds.), *Children with Down syndrome: A developmental perspective* (pp. 329–368). New York: Cambridge University Press.

Bretherton, I. (1989). Pretense: The form and function of make-believe play. *Developmental Review, 9*, 383–401.

Burke, J.C., & Koegel, R.L. (1982, May). *The relationship of stimulus overselectivity to autistic children's responsiveness and incidental learning.* Paper presented at the Association of Behavior Analysis, Milwaukee, WI.

Dunlap, G. (1984). The influence of task variation and maintenance tasks on the learning and affect of autistic children. *Journal of Experimental Child Psychology, 37*, 41–64.

Fein, G. (1981). Pretend play in childhood: An integrative review. *Child Development, 52*, 1095–1118.

Forys, S., & McCune-Nicolich, L. (1984). Shared pretend: Sociodramatic play at 3 years of age. In I. Bretherton (Ed.), *Symbolic play: The development of social understanding* (pp. 159–191). New York: Academic Press.

Goldstein, H., & Cisar, C. (1992). Promoting interaction during sociodramatic play: Teaching scripts to typical preschoolers and classmates with disabilities. *Journal of Applied Behavior Analysis, 25*, 265–280.

Hart, B., & Risley, T.R. (1980). In vivo language intervention: Unanticipated general effects. *Journal of Applied Behavior Analysis, 13*, 407–432.

Hartup, W.W. (1983). Peer relationships. In E.M. Hetherington (Ed.) & P.H. Mussen (Series Ed.), *Handbook of clinical psychology: Vol. 4. Socialization, personality and social development* (pp. 103–196). New York: John Wiley & Sons.

Hill, P.M., & McCune-Nicolich, L. (1981). Pretend play and patterns of cognition in Down syndrome children. *Child Development, 52*, 611–617.

Howlin, P. (1986). An overview of social behavior in autism. In E. Schopler & G.B. Mesibov (Eds.), *Social behavior in autism* (pp. 101–131). New York: Plenum Press.

Jarrold, C., Boucher, J., & Smith, P. (1993). Symbolic play in autism: A review. *Journal of Autism and Developmental Disorders, 23*, 281–307.

Koegel, R.L., Dyer, K., & Bell, L.K. (1987). The influence of child preferred activities on autistic children's social behavior. *Journal of Applied Behavior Analysis, 20*, 243–252.

Koegel, R.L., & Egel, A.L. (1979). Motivating autistic children. *Journal of Abnormal Psychology, 88*, 418–426.

Koegel, R.L., & Koegel, L.K. (1990). Extended reductions in stereotypic behavior through self-management in multiple community settings. *Journal of Applied Behavior Analysis, 23*, 119–127.

Koegel, R.L., & Mentis, M. (1985). Motivation in childhood autism: Can they or won't they? *Journal of Child Psychology and Psychiatry, 26*, 185–191.

Koegel, R.L., O'Dell, M.C., & Dunlap, G. (1988). Producing speech use in nonverbal autistic children by reinforcing attempts. *Journal of Autism and Developmental Disorders, 18*, 525–538.

Koegel, R.L., O'Dell, M.C., & Koegel, L.K. (1987). A natural language teaching paradigm for nonverbal autistic children. *Journal of Autism and Developmental Disorders, 17*, 187–200.

Koegel, R.L., & Schreibman, L. (1977). Teaching autistic children to respond to simultaneous multiple cues. *Journal of Experimental Child Psychology, 24*, 299–311.

Koegel, R.L., Schreibman, L., Good, A., Cerniglia, L., Murphy, C., & Koegel, L. (1989). *How to teach pivotal behaviors to children with autism: A training manual.* Santa Barbara: University of California.

Koegel, R.L., & Williams, J. (1980). Direct vs. indirect response-reinforcer relationships in teaching autistic children. *Journal of Abnormal Child Psychology, 4*, 536–547.

Laski, K.E., Charlop, M.H., & Schreibman, L. (1988). Teaching parents to use the natural language paradigm to increase their autistic children's speech. *Journal of Applied Behavior Analysis, 21*, 391–400.

Lewis, V., & Boucher, J. (1988). Spontaneous, instructed and elicited play in relatively able autistic children. *British Journal of Developmental Psychology, 6*, 325–339.

Lovaas, O.I., Koegel, R.L., & Schreibman, L. (1979). Stimulus overselectivity in autism: A review of research. *Psychological Bulletin, 86*, 1236–1254.

Lovaas, O.I., Koegel, R.L., Simmons, J.Q., & Long, J.S. (1973). Some generalization and follow-up measures on autistic children in behavior therapy. *Journal of Applied Behavior Analysis, 6*, 131–166.

McCune-Nicolich, L. (1981). Toward symbolic functioning: Structure of early pretend games and potential parallels with language. *Child Development, 52*, 785–797.

McGee, G.G., Krantz, P.J., & McClannahan, L.E.S. (1985). The facilitative effects of incidental teaching on preposition use by autistic children. *Journal of Applied Behavior Analysis, 18*, 17–31.

Mundy, P., & Sigman, M. (1989). The theoretical implications of joint-attention deficits in autism. *Development and Psychopathology, 1*, 173–183.

Mundy, P., Sigman, M., Ungerer, J., & Sherman, T. (1987). Nonverbal communication and play correlates of language development in autistic children. *Journal of Autism and Developmental Disorders, 17*, 349–364.

Neef, N.A., Walters, J., & Egel, A.L. (1984). Establishing generative yes/no responses in developmentally disabled children. *Journal of Applied Behavior Analysis, 17*, 453–460.

Odom, S.L., Hoyson, M., Jamieson, B., & Strain, P. (1985). Increasing handicapped preschoolers social interactions: Cross-setting and component analysis. *Journal of Applied Behavior Analysis, 18*, 3–16.

Oke, N.J. (1993). *A group training program for siblings of children with autism: Acquisition of language training procedures and related behavior change.* Unpublished doctoral dissertation, University of California, San Diego.

Perlmutter, J., & Pelligrini, A. (1987). Children's verbal fantasy play with parents and peers. *Educational Psychology, 7*, 269–280.

Pierce, K. (1993). *Strategies for increasing social behavior in children with autism: A manual.* Unpublished manuscript, University of California, San Diego.

Pierce, K.L., & Schreibman, L. (1994). Teaching daily living skills to children with autism in unsupervised settings through pictorial self-management. *Journal of Applied Behavior Analysis, 27*, 471–481.

Pierce, K., & Schreibman, L. (1995). Increasing complex social behavior in children with autism: Effects of peer-implemented pivotal response training. *Journal of Applied Behavior Analysis, 28*, 285–295.

Quinn, J.M., & Rubin, K.H. (1984). The play of handicapped children. In T. Yawkey & D. Pelligrini (Eds.), *Child's play: Developmental and applied* (pp. 63–79). Hillsdale, NJ: Lawrence Erlbaum Associates.

Riquet, C.B., Taylor, N.D., Benaroya, S., & Klein, L.S. (1981). Symbolic play in autistic, Down's and normal children of equivalent mental age. *Journal of Autism and Developmental Disorders, 11*, 439–448.

Rubin, K.H. (1986). Play, peer interaction, and social development, In A.W. Gottfreid & C.C. Brown (Eds.), *Play interactions: Contributions of play materials and parental involvement to children's development* (pp. 163–174). Washington, DC: Lexington Books.

Rutter, M. (1974). The development of infantile autism. *Psychological Medicine, 4*, 147–163.

Rutter, M. (1978). Diagnosis and definition of childhood autism. *Journal of Autism and Childhood Schizophrenia, 8*, 139–161.

Schreibman, L. (1988). *Autism.* Newbury Park, CA: Sage Publications.

Schreibman, L., Charlop, M.H., & Koegel, R.L. (1982). Teaching autistic children to use extra stimulus prompts. *Journal of Experimental Child Psychology, 33*, 475–491.

Schreibman, L., Kaneko, W.M., & Koegel, R.L. (1991). Positive affect of parents of autistic children: A comparison across two teaching techniques. *Behavior Therapy, 22*, 479–490.

Schreibman, L., & Koegel, R.L. (1981). A guideline for planning behavior modification programs for autistic children. In S.M. Turner, K.S. Calhoun, & H.E. Adams (Eds.), *Handbook of clinical behavior therapy* (pp. 500–526). New York: John Wiley & Sons.

Schreibman, L., & Koegel, R.L. (in press). Training for parents of children with autism: Pivotal responses and generalization. In P.S. Jensen & E.D. Hibbs (Eds.), *Psychosocial treatment research with children and adolescents.* Washington, DC: American Psychological Association.

Smilansky, S. (1968). *The effects of sociodramatic play on disadvantaged preschool children*. New York: John Wiley & Sons.

Stahmer, A.C. (1993). *Teaching symbolic play to children with autism using pivotal response training: Effects on play, language and interaction*. Unpublished doctoral dissertation, University of California, San Diego.

Stahmer, A.C. (1995). Teaching symbolic play skills to children with autism. *Journal of Autism and Developmental Disorders, 25*, 123–141.

Stahmer, A.C., & Schreibman, L. (1992). Teaching children with autism appropriate play in unsupervised environments using a self-management treatment package. *Journal of Applied Behavior Analysis, 25*, 447–459.

Stahmer, A.C., Schreibman, L., & Palardy, N. (1994, May). *Social validation of symbolic play training for children with autism*. Paper presented at the meeting of the Association for Behavior Analysis, Atlanta.

Thorp, D.M., Stahmer, A.C., & Schreibman, L. (1995). The effects of sociodramatic play training on children with autism. *Journal of Autism and Developmental Disorders, 25*, 263–281.

Ungerer, J.A., & Sigman, M. (1981). Symbolic play and language comprehension in autistic children. *Journal of the American Academy of Child Psychiatry, 20*, 318–337.

Ungerer, J.A., & Sigman, M. (1987). Categorization skills and receptive language development in autistic children. *Journal of Autism and Developmental Disorders, 17*, 3–16.

Vygotsky, L.S. (1978). *Mind in society: The development of higher psychological processes*. Cambridge, MA: Harvard University Press.

Wing, L., Gould, J., Yeates, S.R., & Brierly, L.M. (1977). Symbolic play in severely mentally retarded and autistic children. *Journal of Child Psychology and Psychiatry, 18*, 167–178.

Wulff, B. (1985). The symbolic and object play of children with autism: A review. *Journal of Autism and Developmental Disorders, 15*, 139–148.

Discussion

Glen Dunlap

There is nothing that defines our lives as completely as our social relationships. Our relationships control our psychological, cognitive, and emotional development from infancy through adulthood, and they constitute the fullest proportion of our life experiences. Many authors have observed that social connectedness is the essential feature of being human and that social context is the factor that brings meaning to one's activities and accomplishments. It is hard to conceive of our existence without a diversity of social relationships, ranging from intricate and enduring attachments (e.g., family, friends) through momentary, albeit indispensable, interactions (e.g., with a clerk who mediates a necessary transaction). The types of relationships that compose our social lives form a ubiquitous, multilayered network, and the competence and comfort with which we navigate our respective networks may be the most crucial feature of our fulfillment. Indeed, we frequently assess our happiness and satisfaction with life in terms of the status of our personal partnerships and the adequacy of our social contacts and social support.

Given the fundamental role of relationships in the lives of human beings, it can be argued that relationships should assume a primary position in programs of support for people with disabilities, especially for people who have lacked the opportunity and the preparation for productive and reciprocal interactions (Newton, Horner, Ard, LeBaron, & Sappington, 1994; Odom, McConnell, & McEvoy, 1992). The inclusion movement, in fact, is based largely on the premise that social relationships are important for all people and that they cannot be expected to flourish in segregated, static environments. If typical interactions are to occur, and if relationships are to develop, then natural opportunities for social contact and shared experiences must be pervasive. Regular presence and participation in inclusive environments is necessary for people to experience meaningful social lives.

Social relationships, in and of themselves, are an overriding concern, but it is valuable to recognize also that they are functionally related to the occurrence of problem behaviors. Problem behaviors are, for the most part, governed by social interactions. Problem behaviors communicate messages in a social environment and may be described as functionally equivalent to alternative social–communicative acts (Carr et al., 1994). Problem behaviors can therefore be interpreted as undesirable forms of social interaction. From the same perspective, it is reasonable to view problem behaviors as signals that a person is disturbed or provoked by the circumstances in the prevailing social environment. An implication of this vantage point is that enhancements in one's social milieu, and in one's interpersonal effectiveness, can ameliorate one's grievances and thus diminish the occurrence of problem behaviors (e.g., Koegel, Dyer, & Bell, 1987; Turnbull & Turnbull, 1990). Simply stated, improvements in one's social interactions and relationships can result in an enhanced, more stimulating, and more pleasurable lifestyle (Newton & Horner, 1993), with corresponding reductions in problem behaviors.

It is gratifying that a general trend in intervention programs has been to emphasize meaningful outcomes (Meyer & Evans, 1993), including the promotion of social relationships. A vital step is to provide the opportunity for social contact by ensuring that activities are conducted in inclusive contexts and that participation in those contexts is optimized. However, as numerous authors have observed (including several authors in this volume), even though physical integration is a necessary condition, it is often insufficient to precipitate social interaction. Myriad other elements may need to be considered.

Social interactions and social relationships are extraordinarily complex phenomena. There are an array of ecological, intrapersonal, and interpersonal variables that affect the initiation and continuation of interactions, and there are limitless paths through which interactions can form various kinds of elaborated relationships. There is a parallel immensity in the number of issues that confront researchers and support personnel seeking to comprehend, organize, and deploy optimal strategies for enhancing relationships. A few of the pressing questions include the following:

- What circumstances in the environment are most conducive to the initiation and maintenance of social interactions?
- What specific behavioral characteristics should support personnel seek to establish in the repertoires of people with disabilities?

- How can support personnel best match types of social assistance with the idiosyncratic strengths and weaknesses of each person with disabilities?
- What combinations of social contexts, group dynamics, and interpersonal characteristics are most favorable for the development of relationships?
- What are the attributes of people *without* significant disabilities that contribute to an inclination to form lasting friendships with people who *do* have significant disabilities?
- How can support personnel best identify an individual's particular needs for social support, what kinds of social support are most needed, and how can an appropriate support network be developed and maintained without the ongoing need for artificial intervention?

Although these are a very small sampling of the important questions in social support, they are sufficient to reveal the need for multiple research strategies, including experimental, descriptive, and interpretive methodologies. They also suggest that researchers and support personnel need to use considerable acumen and sensitivity in their selection of these intervention strategies.

The four chapters in this section reflect important analyses of issues pertaining to social relationships, social inclusion, and the occurrence of problem behaviors. Each chapter comes from a research team that has employed exemplary science to address significant topics in the domain of social interactions and inclusion for people with disabilities.

Kennedy and Itkonen (Chapter 12) offer some timely and well-sorted ideas about variables that affect social interactions: those that govern social behavior and those that influence environmental opportunities for social behavior. Their review summarizes factors that are recognized as being influential in each of these two categories. Kennedy and Itkonen also highlight issues of social support that pertain across the life span and across diverse environments. This latter focus represents a special contribution because very few authors have adopted this broad perspective, even though it is imperative if we are to establish comprehensive community supports that produce generalized benefits in the form of adaptive performance and enhanced social relationships.

Kohler, Strain, and Shearer (Chapter 13) focus on methodological aspects of their seminal work at the LEAP Preschool. The research and demonstration projects conducted by Strain and his colleagues at LEAP have been among the most influential and inspirational in the field of early childhood inclusion, and they have had a major influence on social inclusion in general. The data collection scheme that is illustrated in this chapter offers a valuable assessment tool, and the data underscore the importance of an individualized child focus. In addition, the analyses highlight underappreciated conceptual distinctions among levels of social inclusion. These distinctions are crucial for further developing inclusive environments and for advancing our knowledge of social development in inclusive educational settings.

Camarata (Chapter 14) addresses issues in language development and the intelligibility of communicative utterances. Communication is integral to social interactions, and it is evident that the more efficient the communicative transaction, the greater the potential for interactional depth and the development of meaningful relationships. Camarata's discussion of inadequate intelligibility as a "bottleneck" that can restrict elaborated social contact raises important points about communicative proficiency and social competence. This chapter also contributes a rationale for providing intelligibility training within an inclusive and natural context of interaction. This argument has significant implications for social development because extensive pull-out programs, including traditional speech therapy approaches, serve to separate children and limit opportunities for interactions and shared experiences.

Schriebman, Stahmer, and Pierce (Chapter 15) summarize a series of noteworthy advances in providing intervention for children with autism. These authors discuss the benefits of focusing intervention on two major barriers associated with autism—poor motivation and impaired responsivity—and they describe exciting applications directed at the social inclusion of these children. Play is the principal context through which children acquire friends and many social routines, so reports of interventions capable of equipping children with elevated levels of play skills are extremely encouraging.

Several other chapters in this volume discuss social relationships, and that is altogether appropriate because social inclusion is a concept that transcends family, school, and community ecologies. Indeed, social relationships and the concept of social inclusion are so pervasive that attempts at analysis can seem daunting. However, the present writings offer impressive testimony that data and understanding are accumulating and, most important, people with disabilities are gaining support and opportunities for enhanced social relationships in the context of typical community activities.

REFERENCES

Carr, E.G., Levin, L., McConnachie, G., Carlson, J.I., Kemp, D.C., & Smith, C.E. (1994). *Communication-based intervention for problem behavior: A user's guide for producing positive change.* Baltimore: Paul H. Brookes Publishing Co.

Koegel, R., Dyer, K., & Bell, L. (1987). The influence of child-preferred activities on autistic children's social behavior. *Journal of Applied Behavior Analysis, 20,* 243–252.

Meyer, L.H., & Evans, I.M. (1993). Meaningful outcomes in behavioral approaches to the remediation of challenging behaviors. In J. Reichle & D. Wacker (Eds.), *Communicative alternatives: Integrating functional assessment and intervention strategies* (pp. 407–428). Baltimore: Paul H. Brookes Publishing Co.

Newton, J.S., & Horner, R.H. (1993). Using a social guide to improve social relationships of people with severe disabilities. *Journal of The Association for Persons with Severe Handicaps, 18,* 36–45.

Newton, J.S., Horner, R.H., Ard, W.R., LeBaron, N., & Sappington, G. (1994). A conceptual model for improving the social life of individuals with mental retardation. *Mental Retardation, 32,* 393–402.

Odom, S.L., McConnell, S.R., & McEvoy, M.A. (1992). Peer-related social competence and its significance for young children with disabilities. In S.L. Odom, S.R. McConnell, & M.A. McEvoy (Eds.), *Social competence of young children with disabilities: Issues and strategies for intervention* (pp. 3–35). Baltimore: Paul H. Brookes Publishing Co.

Turnbull, A.P., & Turnbull, H.R. (1990). Reader response. A tale of lifestyle changes: Comments on "Toward a Technology of 'Nonaversive' Behavioral Support." *Journal of The Association for Persons with Severe Handicaps, 15,* 142–144.

IV

Community Inclusion

16

The Relationship Between Setting Events and Problem Behavior

Expanding Our Understanding of Behavioral Support

Robert H. Horner, Bobbie J. Vaughn,
H. Michael Day, and William R. Ard, Jr.

The activity that is the subject of this chapter was supported in whole or in part by the U.S. Department of Education, Grant No. H133B2004. However, the opinions expressed herein do not necessarily reflect the position or policy of the U.S. Department of Education, and no official endorsement by the department should be inferred.

Natural events in our daily lives function as reinforcers and punishers for our behavior. It is seldom acknowledged, however, that the momentary value of these events as reinforcers or punishers is continually in flux. The reinforcing value of food rises and falls depending on circadian cycles and when we ate our last meal. The reinforcing value of social contact changes depending on the amount and type of contact recently experienced. The reinforcing value of escaping from an unpleasant task can rise or fall depending on whether one has a headache. To date, behavior analysts have been prone to describe behavior (and build models of behavior) with the assumption that the value of reinforcers and punishers is stable. A key feature in expanding our understanding of human behavior is that the value of available consequences is forever increasing and decreasing. This has tremendous implications for assessing problem behaviors and designing effective behavioral support.

Events that change the momentary value of reinforcers and punishers have been labeled *setting events* (Bijou & Baer, 1961; Gardner, Cole, Davidson, & Karan, 1986; Kantor, 1959; Wahler & Graves, 1983) or *establishing operations* (Catania, 1992; Kennedy & Itkonen, 1993; Michael, 1988, 1993; Vollmer & Iwata, 1991). Although these concepts do not overlap completely, they intersect on the key idea that events at one point in time may change the likelihood of a targeted behavior at a later point in time by momentarily altering the value of consequences. Drinking liquid now may change the value of liquid in an hour. Spending the day alone may change the value of social contact this evening. Being in love may change the degree to which criticism from a co-worker is punishing. Being deprived of one's regular exercise routine for a few days may increase the value of engaging in exercise tomorrow. For the purposes of this chapter, the term *setting events* is used to indicate events that alter the likelihood of a behavior by momentarily altering the value of reinforcers or punishers. The term itself is less important than two key messages. First, events that happen at one point in time (either just before or long before a response) can alter the likelihood of a targeted response. Second, the mechanism by which this occurs is that the setting event alters the momentary value of available consequences.

The implications of setting events for an increased understanding of human behavior have been long recognized (Kantor, 1959). The concept has renewed importance now, as researchers struggle to build a technology of behavioral assessment and support that meets the challenges of applied settings (Carr et al., 1994). Schools, homes, workplaces, and communities are complex environments. In order to understand and influence behavior in these contexts, researchers need to look at more than just the events that happen immediately before and immediately after a target behavior. A functional technology of behavioral support requires that assessment of problem behaviors includes assessment of possible setting events (Carr et al., 1994; Dadson & Horner, 1993; Durand, 1990). Similarly, behavioral support strategies must include procedures for altering the effects of setting events.

This chapter provides 1) a model for integrating setting events into a greater understanding of problem behaviors, 2) research documenting a relationship between setting events and problem behaviors, and 3) a model for manipulating setting event variables to influence problem behaviors.

UNDERSTANDING HOW SETTING EVENTS INFLUENCE PROBLEM BEHAVIOR

Figure 1 provides a conceptual model for how setting events influence problem behaviors through the following case example. Consider a situation in which a teacher gathers her fifth grade class together after a recess

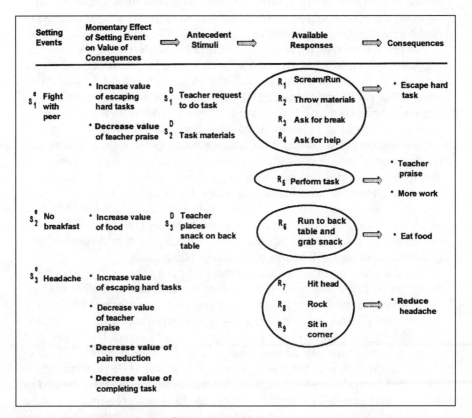

Figure 1.   Effects of setting events on Eric's problem behavior.

and presents the materials for the next class assignment. One of the students, Eric, has severe disabilities and very limited communication skills. He does well working on his adapted curriculum on most days, but on some days he screams, destroys his materials, and runs around the room. In fact, the list of problem behaviors goes on and on. Some days Eric is wonderful, and some days he is a very difficult child to be around.

The top of Figure 1 lists the general sequence of events on the day in question:

Setting Events → Antecedent Stimuli → Response → Consequences

Several setting events occurred prior to the teacher's presentation of the next task. These setting events alter the value of reinforcers typically present in the classroom (e.g., teacher praise). Eric's behavior when the task is presented is predicted by understanding the comparative *value* of the different consequences that are available at that point in time.

The purpose of this example is to demonstrate the complex ways in which events interact to produce a particular behavior. Consider for a moment the complexity of Eric's situation. Sometime before the class period began three setting events occurred: 1) Eric had a physical fight with a peer just before the end of recess (S_1^e), and he reentered the class breathing hard, with a fast heart rate, and with a sore left shoulder (where he was hit); 2) he did not have breakfast this morning due to a variety of scheduling problems at home (S_2^e); and 3) he has a headache due to an emerging head cold (S_3^e). These events do not in and of themselves set the occasion for problem behavior. What they do is change the value of different reinforcers at the moment the teacher presents the task. For example, teacher praise (which typically is a powerful reinforcer for Eric) momentarily decreased in value as a result of the setting events. Hard tasks became more aversive, and hence behaviors that result in escape from hard tasks become more likely. Food will be more reinforcing for Eric than it is on most days because he did not eat breakfast, and anything that decreases the throbbing of his head (e.g., rocking back and forth, sitting quietly in a corner) will be more reinforcing than usual.

The teacher is unaware of the brief playground fight, the absence of breakfast, or Eric's headache. She presents the task, just as she has the previous several days. Figure 1 shows four competing reinforcers available at the moment the task is presented: 1) escape from the task, 2) teacher praise, 3) food, and 4) escape from the headache. Within this model, it can be predicted that the most valued reinforcer would most often control which of the available responses (or classes of responses) would be performed. Assume that escape from the task was, for that moment, the most valued of available reinforcers. This would increase the likelihood of a member of the response class that produces task escape (R_1–R_4). In this example, Eric has four responses with a history of leading to task escape (scream/run, throw materials, ask for break, ask for help). However, asking for help or asking for a break often requires negotiation with the teacher. Eric must ask for help or ask for a break several times before he escapes the difficulty of the task. Throwing the material or running away quickly produces the reinforcer (escape from the task), and do not involve protracted interaction with the teacher. These problem behaviors are more "efficient" in terms of the number of responses required and the speed with which the effect is produced (Horner & Day, 1991). Under these conditions, Eric throws his work on the floor, leaves his desk, and moves to an isolated corner of the room. The teacher delivers a request to return to work, but, given that she has other students who are ready to work, she continues the lesson while Eric settles down to a period of isolation he finds rewarding.

At the end of the day, the teacher is heard to comment to her colleagues how "unpredictable" Eric can be. From her perspective, his behavior is very confusing. She presented the same materials, at the same time of day, and in the same way each day. Most of the time Eric started working and was responsive to teacher praise. Today, however, the exact same procedures produced disruptive histrionics. The "unpredictability" in this example exists because the teacher is looking only at those events *immediately* preceding and following Eric's behavior. A more complete analysis that includes the impact of setting events occurring long before the problem behavior both makes Eric's behavior seem more understandable and suggests specific directions for decreasing his problem behaviors.

To better understand the role of setting events, look again at Figure 1, and make the assumption that *food* was the most powerful reinforcer. Consider how the situation might unfold and what behaviors Eric would perform given this assumption and the fact that a special snack had been laid out at the back table for everyone to have after the class period. If the model in Figure 1 is effective, it should help to clarify the array of situations presented in real world settings.

Most teachers and parents are aware that setting events affect the behavior of children. They have not, however, had a way to use that information effectively. The purpose of Figure 1 is to describe at least one specific way in which setting events interact with other events to increase the likelihood of problem behaviors. This model holds value for building strategies that decrease the likelihood of problem behaviors, especially those "unpredictable" problem behaviors and those dreaded "bad days." As with any model, however, it is easier to demonstrate the predicted patterns in a theoretical example than it is in real life. To test if this model has real validity, the authors systematically examined the impact of setting events on the problem behavior of 15 adolescents and adults with long histories of problem behavior. This study is described in some detail on the following pages because it provides an empirical test of the theoretical model in Figure 1.

RESEARCH EXAMPLE OF THE INFLUENCE OF SETTING EVENTS ON PROBLEM BEHAVIOR

Participants

The authors' study involved 15 adolescents and adults with severe intellectual disabilities and long histories of problem behaviors. Direct services staff identified these problem behaviors as being affected by setting events. All data were collected in the homes and communities of the individual participants. Table 1 provides more specific information about each of the participants.

Each participant received an initial functional assessment following the procedures recommended by O'Neill, Horner, Albin, Storey, and Sprague (1990). This assessment identified problem behaviors through interviews with staff and direct observation in the home. In addition, the assessment defined antecedent variables, the presumed function maintaining the problem behaviors, and a listing of setting events associated with increased levels of problem behavior. Table 2 summarizes the outcomes of the functional assessments.

Measurement of Problem Behaviors and Setting Events

Two different outcome variables were monitored for each participant. The first was a measure of problem behaviors. The direct services staff counted the number of problem events in which problem behaviors were observed. Each participant had a specific list of problem behaviors that were identified by his or her staff during the assessment. Each problem event was counted. An event could include many occurrences of the problem behavior (e.g., several head hits) or only one occurrence. A single event could be very brief or last many minutes. A new event was recorded only after there was a 3-minute pause without problem behaviors. This process resulted in an easy method of indexing the general pattern of problem behaviors across long time periods. Data on problem behaviors were collected by home staff continuously during nonwork, nonschool times of the day. In most cases, the data were summarized in 1-hour blocks across 8-hour periods where the participant and staff were together.

The second variable measured was the occurrence of setting events. Each participant had a list of setting events nominated by his or her staff during the assessment. This list was reviewed by each staff member at the

Table 1. Characteristics of the 15 study participants

Participant	Age	Gender	IQ[a]	Other disabilities	AMR[b] level of intensity	Communication
AKY	35	F	Vineland Adaptive Behavior Scales <20	None	Pervasive	Gesture, simple signs, pictures
BTY	31	M	Vineland Adaptive Behavior Scales <20	Blind	Pervasive	Gesture, simple signs
CTA	14	F	Vineland Social Maturity Scale 14 months	None	Pervasive	Gestures
DBI	15	F	Vineland Social Maturity Scale 21 months	Autism	Pervasive	Gestures, simple signs, vocalizations
EBN	15	M	Vineland Social Maturity Scale 20 months	Autism	Pervasive	Gestures, vocalizations
EJN	11	M	Vineland Social Maturity Scale 36 months	Autism	Extensive	Words, phrases
FCY	8	M	Vineland Social Maturity Scale 46 months	None	Extensive	Gestures, vocalizations
GKY	17	F	Vineland Social Maturity Scale 19 months	None	Pervasive	Gestures, vocalizations, simple signs
HSE	28	F	Vineland Adaptive Behavior Scales <20	Autism	Extensive	Short phrases, signs
IRH	40	M	Vineland Adaptive Behavior Scales <20	None	Pervasive	Gestures, pictures
JPP	13	M	Vineland Social Maturity Scale 22 months	Hearing impaired	Pervasive	Sign language, gestures
KKS	21	M	Vineland Adaptive Behavior Scales <20	Autism	Pervasive	Gestures, pictures, simple signs
LKT	23	M	Vineland Adaptive Behavior Scales <20	Autism	Extensive	Short phrases, gestures, pictures, written expression
MJN	37	M	Vineland Adaptive Behavior Scales <20	None	Pervasive	Gestures, vocalizations
NIL	13	M	Vineland Social Maturity Scale 20 months	Autism	Pervasive	Gestures, vocalizations

[a]IQ was determined through the Vineland Adaptive Behavior Scales (VABS) (Sparrow, Balla, & Cicchetti, 1984) and the Vineland Social Maturity Scale (Doll, 1953).
[b]AAMR, American Association on Mental Retardation.

Table 2. Results of functional assessment for each participant

Participant	Antecedent stimuli	Problem behavior	Function of problem behavior	Setting events associated with problem behavior
AKY	Staff demand	Screams, hits others, pulls hair, hits self, eats cigarette butts	Escape	Illness, injury, menses
BTY	Staff demand	Hits face, bites wrist, pulls hair, bites others, scratches, throws objects	Escape	Constipation, illness
CTA	Staff demand	Bites, grabs, pulls hair, throws objects	Escape	Menses, awake at night and left in room
DBI	Staff demand, corrections	Whines/cries, hits/grabs	Escape	Menses, staff change, awake at night
EBN	Staff demand, corrections	Hits others, grabs, bites, hits own face	Escape	Staff change, loud noise
EJN	Staff demand, corrections	Resists, kicks, spits, screams, throws	Escape	Bad day at school, outing denied, staff change
FCY	Corrections, in games—opponent getting ahead	Yells, whines, hits, shows lack of self-restraint	Escape	Schedule change, lost game, staff change
GKY	Staff demand, difficult tasks, corrections	Resists, pulls own hair, hits head, tears clothes, strips	Escape	Menses, fight on bus
HSE	Staff demand, corrections, loss of preferred objects	Pulls hair, scratches, hits, head bangs, bites self, pinches self	Escape	Staff/schedule change, illness
IRH	Staff demand, corrections	Screams, hits others	Escape	Staff/schedule change
JPP	Staff demand, corrections	Pulls away, walks away, throws, tears, breaks	Escape	Agitation, outing denied, bad day at school, staff change
KKS	Staff demand, corrections	Hits others, bites others, tears clothing	Escape	Staff/schedule change
LKT	Staff demand, corrections	Hits others, bites, kicks	Escape	Staff/schedule change, lack of sleep, illness
MJN	Staff demand, corrections	Hits own head, hits face/chin, bites hand	Escape	Staff/schedule change, denied outing, constipation, illness
NIL	Staff demand, repetition of steps in an activity	Whines, pulls hair, screams, cries loudly, hits own face, drops to floor	Escape	Fatigue, agitation

close of his or her shift, and if any setting events had occurred at any time during the shift a check was noted beside that setting event.

Interobserver Agreement A major challenge for this study was the large number of people collecting data and the huge number of hours during which data were collected. Over 45 individuals collected data across 17,712 hours. To assess the accuracy of the data being collected, *agreement observers* went into homes and monitored setting events and problem behaviors during 1-hour blocks. The observers could monitor setting events (e.g., changes in staff, sickness, changes in schedule) by either seeing them occur or by checking permanent products (e.g., staff log, staff absentee report, incident reports). Agreement observers monitored the occurrence of problem behaviors during the 1-hour observations and compared their counts with those recorded by staff for the same hour. Interobserver agreement for problem behaviors was calculated by dividing the number of specific problem behavior events observed by staff by the number observed by the agreement observers and then multiplying by 100%. Similarly, agreement for setting events was determined by dividing the total number of setting events observed by staff (or observers) by the number of agreements (both recorded the same event). The average agreement scores for setting events across participants ranged from 84% to 100% agreement. The average scores for problem behaviors across participants ranged from 78% to 100%. Specific interobserver scores across participants, setting events, and problem behaviors are available from the authors upon request.

Procedures After a functional assessment had been completed for each participant, the staff in each home were trained how to monitor both problem behaviors and setting events. Data were then collected each calendar day (or each school day for some participants) across 121–207 days. No attempt was made to influence the occurrence of setting events or to change the existing behavioral support procedures.

Results

The results focus on two comparisons for each participant. The first comparison was done by taking each nominated setting event and comparing the likelihood of problem behaviors on days *with* the setting event against the likelihood of problem behaviors on days *without* that specific setting event. Given that multiple setting events were monitored for each participant, the authors also compared the likelihood of problem behaviors given a setting event against the likelihood of problem behaviors given that *none* of the identified setting events occurred. Assessment of a targeted setting event was conducted only if at least 15 occurrences of that setting event had been observed. If a setting event occurred at least 15 times across the 100+ days of observation, then the probability of problem behaviors on those setting event days was assessed and compared with the probability of problem behaviors on days when 1) the specific, targeted setting event did *not* occur, and 2) *none* of the identified setting events occurred. Patterns were identified in which the probability of problem behaviors on days *with* the targeted setting events was at least double the likelihood of problem behaviors when the targeted setting event (or no setting events) had not occurred. The results indicated five patterns as follows.

Effects of Pain Four participants provided patterns in which physical discomfort was associated with increased levels of problem behavior. Table 3 indicates the source of the discomfort and the probability that problem behaviors would occur at least once either 1) with the specific setting event, 2) without the specific setting event, or 3) without *any* identified setting events.

Results from these four participants suggest that physical discomfort due to injury, sickness, or menses increased the likelihood of escape-motivated problem behaviors. It is possible that physical discomfort increases the aversiveness of tasks and demands and thus increases the value of escaping from these stimuli. Without the physical discomfort, daily events were associated with problem behaviors 11%–26.5% of observation periods. With physical discomfort, 32%–65.6% of these same shifts were associated with problem behaviors.

Effects of Aversive Events Three participants displayed patterns of problem behavior that were influenced by unique, aversive events (Table 4). For EJN, the aversive event was being denied a planned (presumably preferred) outing. For FCY, the aversive event was losing a board game. For GKY, having a fight on the bus and being reprimanded by the bus driver was the aversive event. When these events *did* occur, an 8-hour shift was likely to include problem behaviors 50%–94% of the time. If these aversive events *did not* occur, the shift was 12.6%–26.8% likely to include problem behavior. The discrepancy was even greater when 8-hour shifts *with* setting events were compared to 8-hour shifts *without any* setting events (5.8%–18.6%).

Effects of Changes in Staff or Schedule Five participants provided results suggesting that changes in staff (new staff or familiar staff working at unfamiliar times) or changes in the typical daily schedule were associated with elevated levels of problem behavior (cf. Table 5). Mornings without *any* setting events were likely to include problem behaviors 5.3%–24.2% of the time. Mornings without staff or schedule changes, but with some other setting events, were similarly likely to include problem behaviors 7.8%–26.1% of the time. However, if the shift included changes in staff or schedule, problem behaviors occurred during 27%–55.6% of the shifts. If staff or schedule changes occurred, problem behaviors were at

Table 3. Likelihood of problem behavior per participant with and without pain (illness, menses, or injury) as the setting event (S^e)

Participant	Observation days	Problem behavior	Specific S^e	Likelihood of problem behavior *with* pain	Likelihood of problem behavior *without* pain	Likelihood of problem behavior *without any* S^e
AKY	134	Aggression	Sick, Injured	61% (22/36)	26.5% (26/98)	27.9% (17/61)
BTY	144	Aggression	Constipation, Sick	65.6% (21/32)	24.1% (27/112)	25% (7/28)
CTA	193	Aggression	Menses	32% (8/25)	19.6% (33/168)	19.8% (27/136)
DBI	203	Whine/Cry	Menses	61.9% (13/21)	11% (20/182)	7.8% (8/102)

Note. Numbers in parentheses indicate the number of days (observation periods) counted (right-hand number) and the number of days with problem behaviors (left-hand number). For example, AKY was observed during 134 mornings. On 36 of these mornings she was sick or injured, and on 22 of these 36 mornings (61%) she performed aggressive behavior.

Table 4. Likelihood of problem behavior per participant with and without an aversive event as the setting event (S^e)

Participant	Observation days	Problem behavior	Specific S^e	Likelihood of problem behavior with aversive event	Likelihood of problem behavior without aversive event	Likelihood of problem behavior without any S^e
EJN	151	Aggression	Denied planned outing	50.0% (10/20)	14.5% (19/131)	5.8% (4/69)
FCY	182	Self-injurious behavior	Lost game	94.4% (17/18)	26.8% (44/164)	18.6% (20/140)
GKY	121	Tantrum	Fight on bus	64.7% (22/34)	12.6% (11/87)	N/A

least twice as likely. To assess if these effects were due to a consistent pattern across weeks (as opposed to many problem events in one short period) the results of these five participants were separated into sequential 30-day blocks (8-hour morning shifts on consecutive 30-day periods). The conditional probability of problem behavior during shifts with and without changes in staff and schedule for each block of 30 days per participant is plotted in Figure 2. These data indicate a stable separation of problem behavior levels when staff or schedule changes had occurred versus those when staff or schedule changes had not occurred.

Effects of Fatigue   One participant, NIL, demonstrated problem behavior that was associated with fatigue. NIL's whining and aggression were associated with nights during which he had no more than 4 hours' sleep. Following a night with minimal sleep, NIL was 82.3% likely to engage in aggression. This contrasts sharply with days following a good night's sleep, only 26.7% of which included aggression.

Stable Rates of Problem Behavior   Two participants (EJN and LKT) did not display dramatic changes in problem behaviors related to setting events. EJN's self-injurious behavior (SIB) occurred on 74% of shifts with the setting event (staff or schedule change), 68% without that setting event, and 56% of shifts with no setting events. LKT's aggression occurred on 36% of shifts with the setting event (staff or schedule change), 25% without staff or schedule changes, and 31% of shifts without any setting events.

Summary of Results   Thirteen of the 15 people studied in this analysis demonstrated patterns in which the likelihood of problem behaviors at least doubled in the presence of setting events. The four patterns we observed are displayed in Table 6. Pain (physical discomfort), reduced predictability (staff or schedule change), aversive events (receiving punishers or having reinforcers removed), and fatigue (sleep deprivation) are but four possible examples of setting events that influence problem behaviors. It is important to note, however, that these results simply show that setting events and problem behaviors covary. A true functional relationship would require more precise experimental control. Carr (1993) has provided evidence of this experimental control in a study of the effects of pain (menses) on problem behavior. Gardner et al. (1986), Kennedy and Itkonen (1993), and Vollmer and Iwata (1991) also have documented examples of setting events being functionally linked to problem behaviors. The impact of the present results, and the growing body of experimental research, is recognition that setting events must assume a larger role in the functional assessment of problem behaviors and in the design of effective behavioral interventions. The next section provides one framework for building practical interventions that respond to the influence of setting events.

Table 5. Likelihood of problem behavior per participant with and without staff change/schedule change as the setting event (S^e)

Participant	Observation days	Problem behavior	Specific S^e	Likelihood of problem behavior with staff/schedule change	Likelihood of problem behavior without staff/schedule change	Likelihood of problem behavior without any S^e
HSE	140	Self-injurious behavior	Staff change, schedule change	47.2% (51/108)	18.75% (6/32)	17.6% (3/17)
IRH	134	Aggression	Staff change, schedule change	33% (16/48)	12.8% (11/86)	10.3% (6/58)
JPP	207	Aggression	Staff change	55.6% (30/54)	26.1% (40/153)	17.9% (17/95)
EBN	134	Self-injurious behavior	Staff change, schedule change	35.1% (20/57)	18.2% (14/77)	24.2% (24/99)
KKS	132	Property destruction	Staff change, schedule change	27% (15/55)	7.8% (6/77)	5.3% (2/38)

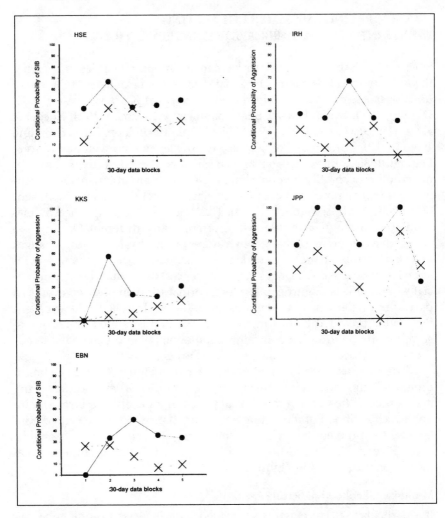

Figure 2.   Conditional probability of problem behaviors per 30-day blocks with and without staff or schedule change for HSE, IRH, KKS, JPP and EBN. (SIB = self-injurious behavior; • = staff change; × = no staff change.)

Table 6.   Four setting event patterns

Setting event	Examples
Pain	Injury, sickness, menses
Reduced predictability	Schedule change, staff change
Aversive events	Fight, loss of privilege
Fatigue	Lack of sleep

INCORPORATING ASSESSMENT OF SETTING
EVENTS INTO CLINICAL BEHAVIORAL INTERVENTIONS

Since the 1980s, behavior analysts have made important strides in applying theory to practical problems. Two major advances have been 1) the use of functional assessment to guide behavioral support (Carr & Carlson, 1993; Durand, 1990; Iwata, Dorsey, Silfer, Baumen, & Richman, 1994; Koegel & Koegel, 1989; Mace & Lalli, 1991; O'Neill et al., 1990; Repp, Felce, & Barton, 1988), and 2) the increased emphasis on multielement interventions (Carr & Durand, 1985; Carr et al., 1994; Meyer & Evans, 1989). Effective behavioral interventions typically involve changing existing environments in a manner that makes problem behaviors irrelevant, ineffective, and inefficient (Horner, O'Neill, & Flannery, 1993). This seldom is accomplished by manipulating a single variable. More often, many different features are changed in concert (e.g., changes in features of the physical setting, changes in task demands, changes in curriculum, changes in pacing, changes in instruction of new skills, changes in consequences) to produce lasting and socially valid effects. Figure 3 provides a format for using setting events as part of multielement interventions. This format builds on the excellent foundation provided by Gardner et al. (1986) and is offered under the assumption that additional clinical manipulations would be needed to address other aspects of a specific problem (Carr et al., 1994).

The basic assumption behind the format in Figure 3 is that a clinical program is in place and is effective except at times when specific setting events occur. The goals of the clinical program typically will be to 1) minimize the likelihood of the setting event and 2) provide strategies for minimizing the problem behavior at times when the setting event has taken place. Five specific suggestions are offered, and the timing of their implementation is depicted in Figure 3.

Minimize Likelihood of Setting Events

If a particular setting event is associated with increased problem behavior, the first effort would be to minimize the likelihood of the setting event. For example, if a poor night's sleep sets the occasion for a long day of problem behavior, a clear effort should be made to ensure that the person has the opportunity to obtain a good night's sleep. Kennedy and Itkonen (1993) found that a specific traffic route to school served as a setting event for tantruming. By avoiding this route they were able to reduce problem behavior. This is a helpful strategy when the setting event is something that can be controlled, but in many cases (e.g., sickness, menses, staff changes) setting events are beyond control. In most clinical contexts, minimizing the occurrence of setting events will be part of, but not all of, the effort to address setting event problems.

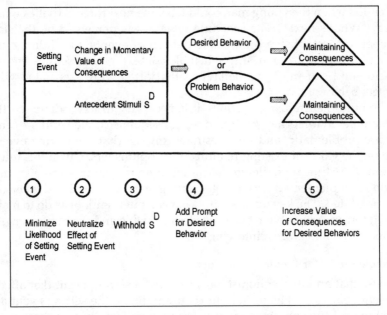

Figure 3.   Five classes of interventions to consider when setting events are identified as influencing problem behaviors.

Neutralize Effect of Setting Events

The most novel strategy is based on an understanding of why setting events affect problem behaviors. If setting events make the reinforcers for problem behavior momentarily more valuable, it should be possible, in some cases, to introduce an activity that neutralizes this effect before the antecedent stimuli (S^D) for problem behaviors are presented. For example, a student who has just had a fight in the playground enters her class in a state of high physiological arousal and is very unresponsive to the variables that typically control academic behaviors. Instead, she is very likely to engage in behaviors that produce escape from academic demands. If, however, the teacher provides the student with a moment to use her trained relaxation routine, the momentary value of escaping instruction may subside, and introduction of academic prompts will lead to instructional behaviors instead of escape behaviors.

An anecdotal example of using neutralizing routines comes from a residential staff member who recently reported that the problem behaviors of a young adult with autism were much greater when his daily schedule was altered. The staff member found, however, that problem behaviors did *not* occur if schedule changes were followed by a brief review of 1) who would be providing support during the day and 2) the next three specific activities that were planned. This review took 2–5 minutes and ended when the young man could label the next three activities when asked, "What's next?" The schedule review was perceived by the staff member to reestablish a predictable pattern of events, to minimize the value of escaping from an unpredictable context, and to reduce the aggression and self-injurious behaviors that often were associated with problem behaviors.

To build neutralizing routines, it is necessary to have identified the problem behaviors, their maintaining consequences, the setting events that are problematic, and the presumed impact that the setting events have on the value of existing reinforcers and punishers. Given this information, the clinical challenge is to define neutralizing strategies that would be implemented *after* a target setting event occurred and *before* the S^D is presented. The key question is: What can interventionists do to make the reinforcers for problem behaviors less valuable and the reinforcers for desired behaviors more reinforcing?

Withhold the S^D for Problem Behaviors

Suppose that an interventionist has identified a setting event that affects problem behaviors. His or her efforts to minimize the setting event are working, but the setting event still occurs occasionally and there is no practical routine that could neutralize the effect of the setting event. A third option is to change the typical routine and withhold those stimuli that are most likely to set the occasion for problem behaviors. This is what Dadson (Dadson & Horner, 1993) did when she identified that, for a young woman with severe disabilities in high school, problem behaviors were influenced by the school bus picking her up late (more than 5 minutes after the scheduled time). If the bus had been late (which occurred about once a week), the student would arrive at school in an agitated state. Her first class was physical education (P.E.), and when she was asked to engaged in aerobic activity (S^D) she would instead perform escape-motivated tantruming. Dadson identified that the bus being late was a setting event that made P.E. activities more aversive than usual. As part of a multielement program, this student would shift from aerobics to stretching exercises (a preferred activity) on days when the bus had been late. The parents would phone the school if the bus was late, and the morning allocation of teaching assistant time (to help with stretching) would be influenced by whether the bus was on time. The result was a substantial reduction in problem behaviors. Instead of first period setting the occasion for a long day of problem behaviors, first period would move from the slower-paced stretching into the regular P.E. program (aerobics) and then into the regular daily schedule. The focused time of the teaching assistant during the first period of the day was typically much less than the amount of staff time that was consumed when the entire day was filled with bouts of intense tantruming. The point of this example is that the S^D for problem behaviors (request to engage in aerobic exercise) was not presented, and the likelihood of problem behaviors decreased.

Add Prompts for Desired Behavior

If the setting event has occured and the S^D is presented, a useful strategy is to supplement the S^D (often a teacher request) with a *precorrection* that defines what the individual *should* do if he or she needs a break or needs assistance (Englemann & Colvin, 1988). If, for example, a teacher anticipates that escape-motivated problem behaviors will follow a teacher direction, then when the direction is given it should be supplemented with the statement, "If you need help doing this, or if you need a break, tell me by. . . ." In some cases it may even be useful to have the student practice the "break" or "help" response before he or she is asked to start the task. The goal is to increase the likelihood that the student will initiate the task or use appropriate communicative alternatives to escape the task, rather than problem behaviors, if the task is too aversive (Carr et al., 1994; Durand, 1990).

Increase the Value of Reinforcers for Desired Behaviors

A fifth strategy is to alter the value of reinforcers available for desired behaviors once setting events have occurred. The logic for this approach is that the setting event has momentarily lowered the value of the reinforcers for desired behavior and increased the value of the reinforcers for problem behavior. To counter this effect, the teacher or parent may momentarily alter the reinforcers for desired behavior. Rather than immediately requiring that the individual begin a task, the teacher or parent might create opportunities for immediate praise, increasing the likelihood that the individual will engage in task-related behaviors. One method of achieving this is through interspersed, easy requests. Horner, Day, Sprague, O'Brien, and Heathfield (1991) presented four participants with difficult tasks such as sorting silverware into the dishwasher, putting on clothing, counting change, computing math problems on a calculator, and so forth. About every three training trials, or at the onset of problem behavior, they interspersed several short, easy requests (e.g., "give me five," "shake my hand"). Horner et al. (1991) found that the participants decreased problem behaviors and increased task attempts when the hard tasks were paired with interspersed requests. In the presence of a setting event, interspersed requests may momentarily alter the value of available reinforcers (i.e., escape from task demand and produce behavior related to following instructions while increasing opportunities for teacher praise).

CONCLUSIONS

Setting events are an important part of all applied settings and a key to the understanding of problem behaviors. As technologies of functional assessment and behavioral support advance, the impact of setting events needs to be included. The recommendations of Pyles and Bailey (1990) provide a strong start toward the examination of physiological setting events. Similarly, work on establishing operations provides a superb example of the directions needed for embedding setting event assessment in the analysis of problem behaviors (Mace, 1994; Mace & Roberts, 1993). The key message is that simple examination of events that occur immediately before and after problem behaviors is a necessary, but insufficient, approach for the analysis of problem behaviors in applied settings. The environment needs to be examined to identify influential events that happen long before the problem behavior occurs.

As setting events are acknowledged in the assessment of problem behavior, it is likely that setting event intervention procedures will become common elements in behavioral support plans. Both research articles (Carr & Carlson, 1993; Dunlap, Kern-Dunlap, Clarke, & Robbins, 1991; Koegel, Valdez-Manchaca, & Koegel, in press) and texts (Carr et al., 1994; Durand, 1990; Meyer & Evans, 1989) are emphasizing the importance of multielement clinical interventions for producing durable, socially valid change in severe problem behaviors. Setting event procedures such as the five proposed here and by Gardner et al. (1986), may prove useful additions to the multielement approach to effective behavioral support.

REFERENCES

Bijou, S., & Baer, D.M. (1961). *Child development: Vol. I. A systematic and empirical theory.* New York: Appleton-Century-Crofts.

Carr, E.G. (1993, May). *The relationship between menses and problem behavior.* Paper presented at the National Conference of the Association for Behavior Analysis, Chicago.

Carr, E.G., & Carlson, J.I. (1993). Reduction of severe behavior problems in the community using a multicomponent treatment approach: Extension into community settings. *Journal of Applied Behavior Analysis, 26,* 157–172.

Carr, E.G., & Durand, V.M. (1985). Reducing behavior problems through functional communication training. *Journal of Applied Behavior Analysis, 18,* 111–126.

Carr, E.G., Levin, L., McConnachie, G., Carlson, J.I., Kemp, D.C., & Smith, C.E. (1994). *Communication-based intervention for problem behavior: A user's guide for producing positive change.* Baltimore: Paul H. Brookes Publishing Co.

Catania, A.C. (1992). *Learning.* Englewood Cliffs, NJ: Prentice Hall.

Dadson, S., & Horner, R.H. (1993). Manipulating setting events to decrease problem behaviors: A case study. *Teaching Exceptional Children, 25,* 53–55.

Doll, E.A. (1953). *The measurement of social competence: A manual for the Vineland Social Maturity Scale*. Minneapolis, MN: Minneapolis Educational Test Bureau, Educational Publishers.

Dunlap, G., Kern-Dunlap, L., Clarke, S., & Robbins, F.R. (1991). Functional assessment, curricular revision, and severe behavior problems. *Journal of Applied Behavior Analysis, 24*(2), 287–397.

Durand, V.M. (1990). *Severe behavior problems: A functional communication training approach*. New York: Guilford Press.

Englemann, S., & Colvin, G.T. (1988). *Generalized compliance training*. Austin, TX: PRO-ED.

Gardner, W.I., Cole, C.L., Davidson, D.P., & Karan, O.C. (1986). Reducing aggression in individuals with developmental disabilities: An expanded stimulus control, assessment, and intervention model. *Education and Training of the Mentally Retarded, 21*, 3–12.

Horner, R.H., & Day, H.M. (1991). The effects of response efficiency on functionally equivalent competing behaviors. *Journal of Applied Behavior Analysis, 24*, 719–732.

Horner, R.H., Day, H.M., Sprague, J.R., O'Brien, M., & Heathfield, L.T. (1991). Interspersed requests: A nonaversive procedure for decreasing aggression and self-injury during instruction. *Journal of Applied Behavior Analysis, 24*(2), 265–278.

Horner, R.H., O'Neill, R.E., & Flannery, K.B. (1993). Building effective behavior support plans from functional assessment information. In M.E. Snell (Ed.), *Systematic instruction of persons with severe handicaps* (4th ed., pp. 184–214). Columbus, OH: Charles E. Merrill.

Iwata, B.A., Dorsey, M.F., Slifer, K.J., Bauman, K.E., & Richman, G.S. (1994). Toward a functional analysis of self-injury. *Journal of Applied Behavior Analysis, 27*, 197–209.

Kantor, J.R. (1959). *Interbehavioral psychology*. Granville, OH: Principia Press.

Kennedy, C., & Itkonen, T. (1993). Effects of setting events on the problem behavior of students with severe disabilities. *Journal of Applied Behavior Analysis, 26*, 321–327.

Koegel, L.K., Valdez-Manchaca, M., & Koegel, R.L. (in press). Autism: Social communication difficulties and related behaviors. In V. Van Hasselt & M. Hersen (Eds.), *Advanced abnormal psychology*. New York: Plenum.

Koegel, R.L., & Koegel, L.K. (1989). Community-referenced research on self-stimulation. In E. Cipani (Ed.), *The treatment of severe behavior disorders: Behavior analysis approaches. Monographs of the American Association on Mental Retardation, 12*, 129–150.

Mace, F.C. (1994, May). *Structural and functional analysis of problem behaviors*. Paper presented at the National Conference of the Association for Behavior Analysis, Atlanta.

Mace, F.C., & Lalli, J.S. (1991). Linking descriptive and experimental analyses in the treatment of bizarre speech. *Journal of Applied Behavior Analysis, 24*, 553–562.

Mace, F.C., & Roberts, M.L. (1993). Factors affecting selection of behavioral interventions. In J. Reichle & D.P. Wacker (Eds.), *Communication and language intervention: Vol. 3. Communicative alternatives to challenging behavior: Integrating functional assessment and intervention strategies* (pp. 113–133). Baltimore: Paul H. Brookes Publishing Co.

Meyer, L.H., & Evans, I.M. (1989). *Nonaversive intervention for behavior problems: A manual for home and community.* Baltimore: Paul H. Brookes Publishing Co.

Michael, J. (1988). Establishing operations and the mand. *Analysis of Verbal Behavior, 6,* 3–9.

Michael, J. (1993). Establishing operations. *The Behavior Analyst, 16,* 191–206.

O'Neill, R.E., Horner, R.H., Albin, R.W., Storey, K., & Sprague, J.R. (1990). *Functional analysis: A practical assessment guide.* Pacific Grove, CA: Brooks/Cole.

Pyles, D.A.M., & Bailey, J.S. (1990). Diagnosing severe behavior problems. In A. Repp & N. Singh (Eds.), *Perspectives on the use of nonaversive and aversive interventions for persons with developmental disabilities* (pp. 381–401). Chicago: Sycamore Press.

Repp, A.C., Felce, D., & Barton, L.E. (1988). Basing the treatment of stereotypic and self-injurious behaviors on hypothesis of their causes. *Journal of Applied Behavior Analysis, 21,* 281–289.

Sparrow, S., Balla, D., & Cicchetti, D. (1984). *Vineland Adaptive Behavior Scales (VABS).* Circle Pines, MN: American Guidance Service.

Vollmer, T.R., & Iwata, B.A. (1991). Establishing operations and reinforcement effects. *Journal of Applied Behavior Analysis, 24,* 279–291.

Wahler, R.G., & Graves, M.B. (1983). Setting events in social networks: Ally or enemy in child behavior therapy. *Behavior Therapy, 14,* 19–36.

17

Contextual Influences on Problem Behavior in People with Developmental Disabilities

Edward G. Carr, Christine E. Reeve, and Darlene Magito-McLaughlin

Preparation of this chapter was supported in part by Grant No. H133G20098 and Cooperative Agreement No. H133B20004 from the U.S. Department of Education.

The authors thank Martin Hamburg, Executive Director, Developmental Disabilities Institute, for his generous support and Sarah Robinson for her helpful criticism.

In one of the earliest models, Skinner created a system of behavior analysis that emphasized the influence of both antecedent and consequent stimuli. Works such as *Schedules of Reinforcement* (Ferster & Skinner, 1957) demonstrated the exquisite control over behavior that could be achieved by manipulating contingencies of reinforcement. Notwithstanding the great interest in and success of these consequence manipulations, there was, from the start of these investigations, a parallel and well-developed theoretical and empirical interest in the role of antecedent variables in the control of behavior (Skinner, 1938).

Based on the above, one might have expected that the application of Skinner's principles (the field of behavior modification) would have produced a research literature that gave equal emphasis to antecedents and consequences. In some areas of study, equal emphasis was apparent. However, in the analysis and treatment of problem behavior, particularly for individuals with developmental disabilities, the overwhelming focus has been on consequences. In an attempt to balance this equation, this chapter addresses the role of antecedent variables as they pertain to problem behavior. Given that behavior is a joint function of immediate stimulus events, context events, and consequences, positive behavioral support necessitates consideration of each of these factors.

ROLE OF CONSEQUENCES IN THE STUDY OF PROBLEM BEHAVIOR

Many people with developmental disabilities exhibit a wide variety of aggressive (e.g., scratching, hitting) and self-injurious (e.g., self-directed head banging and face slapping) behaviors. These behaviors have proven amenable to modification through the manipulation of consequences, so much so that from the early 1960s to the present consequence manipulation has been the dominant motif for work in this area (Carr, 1977; Carr & Durand, 1985a). For example, a pioneering study by Lovaas, Freitag, Gold, and Kassorla (1965) demonstrated that the severe head banging of a young girl diagnosed as schizophrenic became much worse when comforting remarks were made contingent on her self-injury. Contingent social attention was thereby established as an important variable in the control of severe problem behavior, a finding that has received considerable empirical support over the years (Carr & Durand, 1985b; Carr & McDowell, 1980; Lovaas & Simmons, 1969; Martin & Foxx, 1973).

Gaining attention, however, is only one of the many possible reinforcers for problem behavior. For example, some individuals show more problem behavior when they are *given* general attention (i.e., not contingent on problem behavior), suggesting that social avoidance may also be a factor (Taylor & Carr, 1992a, 1992b). Other studies have demonstrated the important role that tangible consequences (e.g., preferred toys, activities, foods) play in influencing the likelihood that problem behavior will occur (Durand & Crimmins, 1988; Edelson, Taubman, & Lovaas, 1983). Still other research has shown that sensory reinforcement in the form of tactile, visual, and gustatory stimuli can alter the probability of self-injury (Favell, McGimsey, & Schell, 1982; Rincover & Devaney, 1982). Biological consequences have also been suggested to play a role in controlling some cases of self-injury (Barrett, Feinstein, & Hole, 1989; Cataldo & Harris, 1982; Thompson, Hackenberg, & Schaal, 1991). Thus, the release of endogenous opiates following self-injurious behavior is thought to reinforce that behavior with the result that self-injury may become self-addicting. When a narcotic antagonist such as naltrexone is administered, the link between behavior and opiate release is broken, and self-injury becomes less likely.

Social attention, social avoidance, tangibles, sensory stimuli, and endogenous opiates all represent consequences that are positive reinforcers. The literature also suggests that negative reinforcers may be implicated in the control of severe problem behavior (Carr & Newsom, 1985; Carr, Newsom, & Binkoff, 1976, 1980; Iwata, 1987; Plummer, Baer, & LeBlanc, 1977; Sailor, Guess, Rutherford, & Baer, 1968; Weeks & Gaylord-Ross, 1981). The prototype for this line of research involves situations in which academic demands are placed on an individual with developmental disabilities. For example, a child may be asked to identify vocabulary cards. The child responds by hitting him- or herself or perhaps by hitting the teacher. The teacher, in turn, responds by removing the vocabulary task (Carr, Taylor, & Robinson, 1991). In this situation, removal of the putatively aversive stimulus (academic demand) is contingent on instances of self-injury or aggression. Thus, these behaviors become more frequent as a result of a negative reinforcement contingency. Academic demands have been among the most common aversive stimuli studied. In clinical work, however, one encounters many other potentially aversive stimuli (e.g., being teased, temperature extremes, high noise level, crowding) whose termination contingent on problem behavior could well serve to maintain and increase the frequency of such behavior in a negative reinforcement paradigm.

Although functional analysis has demonstrated that a wide variety of positive or negative reinforcers can change the likelihood of problem behavior, the most commonly studied consequence for managing problem behavior concerns the contingent application of aversive stimuli, that is, punishment. There is a large literature that demonstrates that the contingent application of a variety of aversives (e.g., electric shock, forced inhalation of ammonia fumes, cold water mist in the face, overcorrection) can produce short-term suppression of severe problem behavior (Axelrod & Apsche, 1983; Foxx & Bechtel, 1983; Guess, Helmstetter, Turnbull, &

Knowlton, 1987; Matson & DiLorenzo, 1984). The application of punishment procedures does not depend on a functional analysis of the variables controlling the problem behavior. That is, a given punisher, such as water mist, might be applied equally to aggression or self-injury that is maintained by attention, escape, or tangible variables. We have argued elsewhere (Carr, Robinson, & Palumbo, 1990) that this nonanalytic approach to intervention lacks the educational focus and systematic prescriptiveness that is the most distinctive feature of conceptual behaviorism. Nonetheless, aversive stimuli have been used and continue to be used as part of consequence-based approaches to the management of problem behavior.

In summary, a variety of consequences involving positive reinforcement, negative reinforcement, and punishment have been the mainstay of the treatment of problem behavior for at least the past three decades. However, as noted earlier, Skinner articulated a critical role for antecedent stimuli as well. Have these variables been underemphasized? Historically, they have; however, this situation has begun to change.

ACCELERATING INTEREST IN THE STUDY OF ANTECEDENT VARIABLES

Background in Stimulus Control Research

The animal literature on operant conditioning is replete with examples of powerful and conceptually interesting demonstrations of stimulus control. Terrace (1963, 1964, 1966), in a series of classic studies, showed that the way in which stimuli are introduced in a discrimination paradigm could strongly influence the number of errors made during acquisition of the discrimination. The *errorless learning* procedures developed by Terrace could be used to shift control from one stimulus class to another and, furthermore, could do so with minimal adverse emotional responding (frustration). These findings have great implications for educational practice because in education one is often confronted with the necessity for shifting control from one stimulus class (e.g., prompts) to another (e.g., specific instructional demands). Terrace's work, as important as it was, is but one part of a large animal learning literature that includes empirical analyses of other topics related to stimulus control, such as *concept formation* (Kelleher, 1958) and *generalization phenomena* (Mostofsky, 1965). Each of these is also relevant to educational practice.

As compelling as these animal demonstrations are, one can always raise the question of whether the principles derived from studies of pigeons and chimpanzees are transferable to humans. Fortunately, operant research on stimulus control has extended beyond the animal laboratory.

For example, the errorless learning procedures developed by Terrace on animal subjects have since been applied and, more important, expanded for use with typical and atypical children. *Stimulus fading* procedures (in which elements of stimuli are changed along some physical dimension such as size or color) and *stimulus shaping* procedures (in which the configuration of a stimulus is altered) have been used to teach a variety of simple and complex discriminations to children diagnosed with mental retardation (Bijou, 1968; Sidman & Stoddard, 1966); variants of these procedures have been used as well with children diagnosed with autism (e.g., Schreibman, 1975). One continuous and programmatic line of research in this area has been carried out by Etzel and her colleagues (Etzel, Bickel, Stella, & LeBlanc, 1982; Etzel & LeBlanc, 1979; Etzel, LeBlanc, Schilmoeller, & Stella, 1981). Their work has highlighted the notion that the use of motivational (reinforcement-based) procedures alone may not always be adequate for solving important educational problems for people with developmental disabilities. More important still, their work demonstrates the utility of creative, stimulus-based procedures in addressing a variety of behavior deficits in the area of discrimination learning. This work, together with Sidman's successful development of the *stimulus equivalence paradigm* for enhancing concept learning (Sidman, 1990), raises the following question: If stimulus-based procedures can have a powerful beneficial influence on the remediation of behavior *deficits*, such as those related to discrimination learning and concept formation, might a greater focus on antecedent variables also be beneficial in remediating behavior *excesses*, such as those related to severe problem behavior?

Stimulus Control and Severe Problem Behavior

Many studies in the literature on severe problem behavior demonstrate the role that discrete antecedent stimuli, such as instructional demands, can have in the control of aggression, self-injury, tantrums, and related disruptive behavior (Carr & Durand, 1985b; Carr et al., 1976, 1980; Carr & Newsom, 1985; Iwata, Dorsey, Slifer, Bauman, & Richman, 1982; Repp, Felce, & Barton, 1988). Figure 1 illustrates a typical example (Carr et al., 1980). For Bob, the demand was simply to "Sit down" in a chair, while for Sam the demand involved a basic self-help skill (buttoning) and the demand was "Button up." As can be seen from the figure, these demands evoked high levels of aggressive behavior (e.g., scratching, kicking, biting) directed at the teacher.

In contrast, the absence of demands was correlated with minimal aggression. This pattern demonstrates tight stimulus control over problem behavior by instructional demands and suggests that the systematic study of antecedent stimuli may be useful in understanding and treating behavioral excesses as well. Closer inspection of Figure 1 also suggests

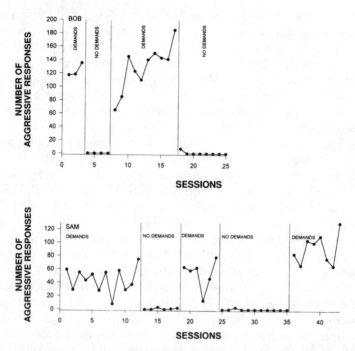

Figure 1.   Number of aggressive responses exhibited by two children with mental retardation during periods in which learning tasks were presented (demands) or withheld (no demands). (From Carr, E.G., Newsom, C.D., & Binkoff, J.A. [1980]. Escape as a factor in the aggressive behavior of two retarded children. *Journal of Applied Behavior Analysis, 13,* 105; reprinted by permission.)

that stimulus control of problem behavior may be a rather complicated phenomenon, in that the same stimulus (demands) evokes different levels of aggressive responding over time. Consider the first "demands" condition for Sam. In Session 8 Sam emitted only 8 aggressive responses during the 10 minutes of instruction, whereas in Session 12 he emitted 77 aggressive responses in the same time period. These data would suggest that there are factors other than instructional demands per se that modulate the effects of the stimuli on the probability of aggression. In this particular case, the teacher reported, prior to Session 8, that Sam was in a "fantastic mood" because there had been a classroom party that day and he had enjoyed it very much. In contrast, the teacher reported, prior to Session 12, that Sam had been in a "dreadful mood" all day because he appeared to have a cold and, furthermore, he had had an altercation with one of the other children a half-hour before and had not yet recovered.

How might one make theoretical sense out of these anecdotal observations? Conceptually, one could hypothesize that the termination of demands contingent on aggression strengthens that behavior in a negative reinforcement (escape) paradigm. Furthermore, demands are made either more or less aversive as a function of the general context in which they occur. The level of aversiveness, in turn, determines the potency of the negative reinforcer and, ultimately, the probability of aggression. In other words, problem behavior is a joint function of a discriminative stimulus (demands) and the context in which that stimulus occurs (ongoing environmental and biological events). Context, or *setting events*, is a topic that has been discussed for some time (Bijou & Baer, 1961; Kantor, 1959). However, only recently have the analytical and intervention implications of this concept been systematically investigated with respect to problem behavior.

Setting Events

The relationships that exist between various classes of discriminative stimuli and responses can be altered by changing the context in which these stimulus–response relationships occur (Bijou & Baer, 1961; Kantor, 1959). Context variables, or setting events (terms that are used interchangeably in this chapter), differ from discriminative stimuli in that the latter events typically have a discrete onset and offset and are temporally proximate and immediately antecedent to the response class that they control. As noted, an instructional demand is a good example of a discriminative stimulus because, for instance, the demand, "Button up," is discrete in nature, immediately precedes the response that it controls (i.e., buttoning), and terminates prior to the initiation of the response itself. In contrast, physical illness (setting event) has none of these characteristics. Illness often has a poorly defined beginning and ending. It may precede, be continuous with, and continue after the buttoning response. In this example, an illness (such as a cold) can influence the response made to the "Button up" command. For a variety of reasons, an individual with a bad cold may show poor compliance as well as problem behavior when presented with the demand, "Button up," but show good compliance and no problem behavior when presented with the same demand while in a state of good health. One possibility, suggested by Michael (1982), is that some setting events alter the reinforcing or aversive properties of stimuli. In this analysis, a cold may greatly exacerbate the aversiveness of the demand stimulus, thereby increasing the likelihood of escape responding and thus, indirectly, minimizing the likelihood of compliance.

Biological contexts (setting events) include not only illness factors but other factors as well, such as drugs, satiation or deprivation conditions, and physiological cycles including sleep and menses (Bijou & Baer, 1978). Context can include characteristics of the purely physical environment such as extreme temperature changes and shifts in the ambient noise level. In addition, context can be sociocultural in nature, as in the case of movement from a classroom to a playground setting and in the effects of the presence versus absence of specific individuals or groups of individuals (Bijou & Baer, 1978). These contexts, and many others, have been noted in the literature for years, but the analysis of their effects has been slow in coming.

Wahler's work with children with problem behavior provides a good example of a systematic analysis of context that has spurred other investigators to look more closely at the issue of setting events (Dumas & Wahler, 1985; Wahler, 1980; Wahler & Fox, 1981; Wahler & Graves, 1983). Specifically, Wahler (1980) demonstrated that mothers whose day-to-day friendly social contacts with other adults were few or primarily aversive in nature were more likely to behave aversively toward their children, and their children, in turn, responded with higher levels of problem behavior. When those same mothers experienced high levels of friendly social contacts, they behaved more positively toward their children, and their children in turn displayed lower levels of problem behavior. In other words, the wider social context that involves other adults outside the immediate family is a setting event that influences child problem behavior.

In the education realm, a prototypical study of context has been reported by Krantz and Risley (1977). Working with kindergarten children, these investigators examined contextual influences on behavior during story time. When story time was scheduled following a period of inactivity, attention was good and disruptive behavior was rare. In contrast, when story time was scheduled following a period of active play, attention was poor and disruptive behavior became frequent. Again, context (in this case, activity sequencing) was a powerful determinant of problem behavior during a given classroom task (story time).

The utility of studying the effects of context is clearly demonstrated in the examples just described. However, both examples involved children not diagnosed with developmental disabilities. The next question, then, is whether the analysis of setting events is also useful with this population.

Setting Events and Problem Behavior

There is an emerging literature on contextual influences in the area of developmental disabilities. Three categories of setting events have been identified: 1) durational events, 2) behavioral histories, and 3) physiological conditions (Gardner, Karan, & Cole, 1984).

Durational Events   This category includes the presence or absence of certain events or objects (e.g., staff members, room configuration). A good example of this category can be seen in a study by Touchette, MacDonald, and Langer (1985). These investigators found that, when a certain staff member was present, the level of self-injury of one individual diagnosed with autism was high. With a different staff member, problem behavior was low. These differences occurred in spite of the fact that the two staff members were implementing the same educational programs. Staff presence represents a continuous, ongoing event; that is, it is contextual in nature rather than discrete. It is not clear from the analysis of Touchette et al. why one staff context was correlated with high levels of problem behavior and another was not. Thus, the controlling variables are not known. Nonetheless, these investigators identified a rather complex stimulus configuration that, at least on the surface, is unlike the kinds of discriminative stimuli that have traditionally been the focus of research in this area.

Crowding is another durational event associated with problem behavior. Specifically, aggression has been observed to occur at much higher levels when people with developmental disabilities live or work in crowded conditions. Aggressive behavior decreases when crowding is alleviated (Boe, 1977; McAfee, 1987). Again, crowding is an ongoing stimulus condition (context) that lacks the discrete properties of discriminative stimuli such as instructional demands.

A third example in the durational event category concerns the use of protective clothing in the treatment of self-injury (Dorsey, Iwata, Reid, & Davis, 1982; Silverman, Watanabe, Marshall, & Baer, 1984). Thus, one may find that placing a padded helmet on the head of an individual who engages in severe self-directed face punching may reduce the frequency of that behavior, even though the helmet does not physically constrain the individual from engaging in this dangerous behavior. Apparently, protective clothing is, in some cases, a stimulus context associated with decreased levels of problem behavior.

Behavioral Histories This category includes the effects of temporally distant stimulus–response relations on responding to current stimuli. One example of this category has been variously referred to in the literature as *interspersal training* (Horner, Day, Sprague, O'Brien, & Heathfield, 1991), *behavioral momentum* (Mace et al., 1988), *pretask requesting* (Singer, Singer, & Horner, 1987), *task variation* (Dunlap, 1984; Dunlap & Koegel, 1980; Winterling, Dunlap, & O'Neill, 1987), and *embedding* (Carr et al., 1976). The essence of these procedures is to present a problematic task (one known to evoke aggression, self-injury, and the like) within the context of stimuli known to be discriminative for nonproblem behavior. To illustrate, if one were to ask a boy diagnosed with mental retardation to clean up his room, he might well respond by becoming aggressive. The "Clean up" request is a discriminative stimulus for problem behavior. However, if one were to present first a series of requests known to be discriminative for compliance (e.g., "Open this can of soda," "Drink it," "Turn on your stereo") and then present the "Clean up" request, one often finds that the formerly problematic request now evokes compliance rather than aggression. The prior series of stimulus–response sequences alters the individual's response to the current discriminative stimulus (i.e., the request to "Clean up").

An example of an even more pervasive event in the behavioral history category involves changing an individual's daily schedule of activities (Brown, 1991). Thus, for some individuals, a schedule that requires the person to perform specific activities at specific times in a specific order may be correlated with problem behavior. In contrast, when schedules are altered so that the individual may choose to perform activities in a different order and at different times across days, problem behavior is minimized. Apparently, activity sequence can be an important historical context for the performance or nonperformance of problem behavior.

Physiological Conditions This category involves the effects of factors such as physical illness, deprivation or satiation, drugs, and other events that have a biological basis. A good example of an event in this category was explored in a study by Podboy and Mallory (1977), who investigated the effects of caffeine level on the aggressive behavior of a group of adults with mental retardation. During baseline, the individuals were permitted to drink their usual amount of caffeinated coffee (4–15 cups per day), and the number of aggressive episodes per day was measured. During intervention, in a double-blind study, decaffeinated coffee was introduced. Aggressive behavior decreased. Apparently, caffeine level may constitute a biological context for problem behavior.

Strenuous physical activity, such as that involved in certain forms of exercise, has a variety of physiological effects as well. Interestingly, exercise may be another contextual variable that influences the likelihood of problem behavior. In one study (Baumeister & MacLean, 1984), two adults who had been diagnosed with severe mental retardation were introduced to a jogging exercise program. Self-injury and stereotypy both decreased from baseline levels as the exercise requirement was increased. Similar results have been reported in several other studies (Kern, Koegel, Dyer, Blew, & Fenton, 1982; Lancioni, Smeets, Ceccarani, Capodaglio, & Campanari, 1984; McGimsey & Favell, 1988).

What Does It All Mean? A number of contextual variables have been discussed that appear to influence problem behavior in people with developmental disabilities. In most of the studies cited, the investigative approach used was macroanalytic in nature. Thus, in the Touchette et al. (1985) study, a correlation existed between the presence versus absence of specific staff and the occurrence of problem behavior. However, because the methodology was macroanalytic, it is not known if the effects were due to setting events per se (e.g., global variables pertaining to staff characteristics such as size, stature, or tone of voice) or to specific discriminative stimuli (e.g., one staff member used many reprimands where another staff member used no reprimands). A fine-grained (microanalytic) approach could help to explore and demonstrate relationships between true setting events and the discriminative stimulus–response relationships that such events frequently modify. To illustrate this process, the following section presents a few examples from our current research program.

Setting Events: Examples from Our Current Research

For several years, we have been investigating the effects of a number of contextual variables including menses, mood, and communicative interpretability. Our investigative strategy has been microanalytic, a strategy designed to identify more directly the impact that setting events per se have on problem behavior.

Menses In collaboration with Christopher Smith and Theresa Giacin, we have been working with several women diagnosed with mental retardation who are currently living in community group homes. Through staff interview, we had learned that these women often exhibited aggressive outbursts in close association with their menses. A number of previous case studies and anecdotal reports also noted exacerbation of problem behavior concurrent with menses (Bailey & Pyles, 1989; Gardner, Cole, Davidson, & Karan, 1986; Kaminer, Feinstein, Barrett, Tylenda, & Hole, 1988). We decided to examine the role of menses systematically and, ultimately, experimentally.

The first phase of our study involved a systematic descriptive analysis. Consider one participant, Kara. Over a period of 9 months, we counted the number of aggressive episodes she had daily during a 2.5-hour time interval each morning. A clear and consistent pattern emerged. For 8 out of the 9 months, aggression was more frequent during premenses and menses than during nonmenses. During nonmenses, the number of aggressive episodes was typically only one to two per morning, whereas during premenses and menses it was typically six episodes or more per morning. Interestingly, for 98% of the episodes of problem behavior, a demand was given prior to the problem episode. Since demands were given at about the same frequency during nonmenses as during premenses and menses, an important question can be asked— namely, is it true that demands are more likely to provoke aggression during premenses and menses? To test this possibility, we carried out an experiment in which demands were manipulated in the presence versus absence of menses.

In the second phase of the study (the experimental phase), there were four conditions:

1. Nonmenses plus demands
2. Nonmenses plus no demands
3. Menses plus demands
4. Menses plus no demands

During no demands, Kara was permitted to relax around the group home and she was not asked to carry out any chores. During demands, Kara was asked to carry out her normal daily routines that included grooming, dressing, straightening up her room, cleaning up after breakfast, and the like. Aggression was high only during the combination of menses plus demands and was negligible in the other three conditions. In other words, demands per se were not sufficient to provoke aggression (e.g., demands plus nonmenses had no effect) and menses per se was not sufficient (e.g., menses plus no demands had no effect). Rather, it was the combination of two variables, menses and demands, that produced the effect. This finding would support a model in which menses constitutes a biological setting event that modulates the response to a discriminative stimulus (in this case, demands to do group-home chores).

We have begun to explore the clinical implications of this dual control model. Because demands were partly at issue, we designed an intervention program in which Kara could choose to reduce the level of demands placed on her when she was not feeling well (much as a person with no disabilities might do in the same situation). We also taught her to request assistance with tasks when she did not feel well. Because menses was partly at issue, we designed an intervention to deal with her physical symptoms as well. That is, we conceptualized menses not as a unique biological event but rather as one of a number of physical conditions associated with pain or discomfort (in this case, bloating, nausea, lower back pain, cramps, and headaches). Thus, we provided, as needed, hot water bottles, exercise regimens, medication, special diets, and massage. The results of intervention were encouraging: 1.5 years after treatment began, Kara was showing near-zero levels of aggression during her menses and she was able to complete most of her group-home chores without difficulty.

Mood In collaboration with Christopher Smith and Theresa Giacobbe-Grieco, we have been working with several individuals diagnosed with mental retardation or autism who are presently living in community group homes. By interviewing group-home staff, we learned that the residents were much more likely to display severe aggression, self-injury, and property destruction in response to demands when they were in a bad mood than when they were in a good mood. Although some investigators (e.g., Gardner et al., 1986; Meyer & Evans, 1989) have suggested that mood may be an important setting event for problem behavior in people with developmental disabilities, no one has yet focused on the role of mood in this population using an experimental paradigm. Therefore, we decided to explore the issue systematically. Because we were interested in studying mood states presumably related to environmental variables, we carefully reviewed the medical records and interviewed relevant staff to rule out the possibility that mood shifts were due to biologically based psychiatric conditions such as bipolar affective disorder or ongoing medical problems such as allergies, gastrointestinal conditions, migraines, and the like.

Next, we had group-home staff rate each resident on a mood scale developed by Dunlap and Koegel (Dunlap, 1984; Dunlap & Koegel, 1980; Koegel & Koegel, 1986). A resident received a score of 0–1 for bad mood (e.g., "Yelling, pouting, tantruming; appears to be irritable, angry, or frustrated; does not appear to be enjoying things"), 2–3 for neutral mood (e.g., "Does not appear to be decidedly happy or unhappy; may smile or frown occasionally"), and 4–5 for good mood (e.g., "Smiles, laughs appropriately; seems to be enjoying things"). After the rating was made, a resident was required to carry out specific group-home chores (demands sessions) or was allowed to engage in various leisure activities (no demands sessions) according to a prearranged schedule. Before any of these sessions were conducted, at least 10 minutes had to have elapsed during which the resident showed no severe problem behavior. This criterion was established to ensure that problem behavior that occurred during a session was not simply a continuation of some ongoing episode.

The experiment proper consisted of six conditions:

1. Bad mood plus demands
2. Bad mood plus no demands
3. Neutral mood plus demands
4. Neutral mood plus no demands
5. Good mood plus demands
6. Good mood plus no demands

The data obtained for one resident, Mary, are typical. One of her chores (demands) consisted of dusting the furniture. Irrespective of her mood, Mary showed no problem behavior in the absence of demands. She also showed no problem behavior during good mood plus demands. She showed a low level of problem behavior during neutral mood plus demands. Most significantly, she showed a high level of problem behavior during bad mood plus demands. In other words, demands per se were not sufficient to evoke problem behavior (e.g., demands plus good mood had no effect) and mood per se was not sufficient (e.g., bad mood plus no demands had no effect). Again, it was the combination of two variables, bad mood and demands, that produced the effect. This finding would support a model in which mood constitutes an environmentally based setting event that modulates the response to a discriminative stimulus, in this case, the demands associated with group-home chores.

We have begun to explore the intervention implications of this dual control model. The implications are twofold. First, attenuate bad mood by identifying and then eliminating the environmental events that lead to bad mood. This strategy is proactive (preventive) in nature. Second, attenuate bad mood by employing strategies for inducing good mood (e.g., the use of humor, noncontingent presentation of strongly preferred stimuli and desired social activities). This strategy is reactive in nature.

Communicative Interpretability A number of studies have demonstrated that teaching specific communicative skills can sometimes be an effective intervention for problem behavior (Bird, Dores, Moniz, & Robinson, 1989; Carr & Durand, 1985b; Day, Rea, Schussler, Larsen, & Johnson, 1988; Horner & Budd, 1985; Wacker et al., 1990). For example, functional analysis may demonstrate that an individual's aggressive behavior is maintained by certain tangible items (e.g., a specific toy); that is, presentation of tangible items regularly follows aggressive outbursts. If the individual is taught to request a toy (e.g., "I want the bear") and the request is honored, aggression decreases. Aggression and requesting are functionally equivalent response classes (Carr, 1988) and strengthening one class (requesting) often makes the other response class (aggression) unnecessary, with the result that the latter behavior becomes much less frequent.

Unfortunately, the situation is not as simple as it might first appear. Among other things, the response of the listener to the communicative act is very important. That is, social context may be a critical determinant of whether problem behavior recurs. As social context is often identified as a setting event (Bijou & Baer, 1978), its analysis with respect to the issue of problem behavior would seem to be worthwhile.

In lay terms, the response of the listener is related to the issue of interpretability. To illustrate, suppose one teaches a young boy to sign or speak the phrase, "I want the (toy) bear," in lieu of repeatedly biting his mother on the leg in the presence of the bear. His mother responds to the request by providing the bear and there is no further difficulty. One night, the babysitter replaces the mother. In poorly articulated speech (or sign), the child makes the request. The babysitter appears puzzled and fails to respond to the request. The child repeats the request a few more times without effect and then begins to aggress. In lay terms, we would say that the babysitter was unable to interpret what the child was trying to communicate. Because the scenario just described comes up frequently in clinical work, we decided to investigate it systematically.

In collaboration with Christine Reeve and Laura Wray Palumbo, we conducted a study in which we identified three children with developmental disabilities whose poorly articulated speech or sign language frequently led adults to fail to respond to their requests, thereby leading to problem behavior episodes. Each child was paired with 10 different adults. In one condition, the adult was told the meaning of the child's gesture (informed condition). In a second condition, the adult was not told the meaning of the child's gesture (uninformed condition). Child and adult interacted in a room filled with a number of toys, only one of which had been predetermined to be preferred by the child. When the child made a request, the adult's task was to try to honor the request by providing the correct reinforcer (toy). Not surprisingly, in the informed condition, the adults were accurate (i.e., they provided the correct toy) 100% of the time. In contrast, in the uninformed condition, the adults were only accurate a quarter to a third of the time. In response to this adult behavior, children often repeated their requests to the adults in the uninformed condition but only rarely to the adults in the informed condition. Adults in the uninformed condition responded with many requests for clarification (e.g., "What do you want?" "Do you want this one or this one?"). Adult behavior in the uninformed condition (i.e., many requests for clarification, offering many incorrect toys) resulted in long delays of reinforcement (i.e., the time elapsed between the initial request and the adult's finally offering the correct reinforcer), whereas delay of reinforcement in the informed condition was very short. Most important, there was a direct correlation between length of delay of reinforcement and level of problem behavior: Children showed no problem behavior in the presence of adults in the informed condition but a great deal of problem behavior in the presence of adults in the uninformed condition.

Social context is thus demonstrated to be an important setting event for problem behavior. When the listener is unable to interpret the child's communication, the child reverts to problem behavior. In operant terms, the explanation probably lies in the concept of *response efficiency* (Horner & Day, 1991; Horner, Sprague, O'Brien, & Heathfield, 1990). Specifically, when the listener fails to respond quickly to the newly taught communicative response, that response is effectively put on extinction; that is, it becomes less efficient. In contrast, problem behavior has a long history of success when caretakers have learned to respond quickly to outbursts as a way of avoiding further escalation. In other words, in the absence of an "informed" audience, ambiguous communicative responses become less efficient than problem behavior and the latter reappears.

Regardless of the explanatory mechanism involved, this study highlights the fact that communicative skills will, by themselves, be unsuccessful unless consideration is given to the social context in which those skills are to be used. Social context is thus a contributing factor to the control of problem behavior.

CONCLUSIONS

Communicative interpretability is but one example of the effects of social context. It is of special interest, however, because the study of communicative interaction is inherently the study of social systems, of people interacting with people, of reciprocal influence. These types of influences are beginning to receive systematic attention in the literature, and the fact that they can be important setting events for problem behavior suggests that it will be worthwhile to expand the analysis of problem behavior to include these variables. Likewise, menses represents but one example of a biological setting event. The number of possible illnesses, physical states, and the like is obviously very great. Given that biological context can influence rates of problem behavior, one could argue strongly for broadening the analysis of problem behavior to include these events as well. Finally, mood, too, is but one example of an environmental setting event. Indeed, mood is simply a summary term for the effects of a large number of environmental events hitherto unanalyzed. Taken together, the three studies of our own that we have described, as well as the small number of studies carried out by other investigators, suggest that problem behavior will not be fully understood until behavior analysts undertake programmatic research on the impact of setting events.

Ultimately, the study of setting events forces investigators to analyze and modify systems whether they be social, physical, or biological in nature. Interestingly, this broader analysis is consistent with the vision articulated by Skinner in *Science and Human Behavior* (1953), a vision that stresses the use of basic principles derived from laboratory studies to account for progressively wider areas of human behavior, including those that are referred to as social and cultural. We are not there yet, but the empirical analysis of context has certainly begun.

REFERENCES

Axelrod, S., & Apsche, J. (Eds.). (1983). *The effects of punishment on human behavior.* New York: Academic Press.

Bailey, J.S., & Pyles, D.A.M. (1989). Behavioral diagnostics. In E. Cipani (Ed.), *The treatment of severe behavior disorders: Monographs of the American Association on Mental Retardation, 12,* 85–107.

Barrett, R.P., Feinstein, C., & Hole, W.T. (1989). Effects of naloxone and naltrexone on self-injury: A double-blind, placebo-controlled analysis. *American Journal on Mental Retardation, 93,* 644–651.

Baumeister, A.A., & MacLean, W.E. (1984). Deceleration of self-injurious and stereotypic responding by exercise. *Applied Research in Mental Retardation, 5,* 385–393.

Bijou, S.W. (1968). Studies in the experimental development of left-right concepts in retarded children using fading techniques. In N.R. Ellis (Ed.), *International review of research in mental retardation* (pp. 65–96). New York: Academic Press.

Bijou, S.W., & Baer, D.M. (1961). *Child development I: A systematic and empirical theory.* Englewood Cliffs, NJ: Prentice Hall.

Bijou, S.W., & Baer, D.M. (1978). *Behavior analysis of child development.* Englewood Cliffs, NJ: Prentice Hall.

Bird, F., Dores, P.A., Moniz, D., & Robinson, J. (1989). Reducing severe aggressive and self-injurious behaviors with functional communication training. *American Journal on Mental Retardation, 94,* 37–48.

Boe, R.B. (1977). Economical procedures for the reduction of aggression in a residential setting. *Mental Retardation, 15,* 25–28.

Brown, F. (1991). Creative daily scheduling: A nonintrusive approach to challenging behaviors in community residences. *Journal of The Association for Persons with Severe Handicaps, 16,* 75–84.

Carr, E.G. (1977). The motivation of self-injurious behavior: A review of some hypotheses. *Psychological Bulletin, 84,* 800–816.

Carr, E.G. (1988). Functional equivalence as a mechanism of response generalization. In R. Horner, R.L. Koegel, & G. Dunlap (Eds.), *Generalization and maintenance: Lifestyle changes in applied settings* (pp. 194–219). Baltimore: Paul H. Brookes Publishing Co.

Carr, E.G., & Durand, V.M. (1985a). The social-communicative basis of severe behavior problems in children. In S. Reiss & R. Bootzin (Eds.), *Theoretical issues in behavior therapy* (pp. 219–254). New York: Academic Press.

Carr, E.G., & Durand, V.M. (1985b). Reducing behavior problems through functional communication training. *Journal of Applied Behavior Analysis, 18,* 111–126.

Carr, E.G., & McDowell, J.J. (1980). Social control of self-injurious behavior of organic etiology. *Behavior Therapy, 11,* 402–409.

Carr, E.G., & Newsom, C.D. (1985). Demand-related tantrums: Conceptualization and treatment. *Behavior Modification, 9,* 403–426.

Carr, E.G., Newsom, C.D., & Binkoff, J.A. (1976). Stimulus control of self-destructive behavior in a psychotic child. *Journal of Abnormal Child Psychology, 4,* 139–153.

Carr, E.G., Newsom, C.D., & Binkoff, J.A. (1980). Escape as a factor in the aggressive behavior of two retarded children. *Journal of Applied Behavior Analysis, 13,* 101–117.

Carr, E.G., Robinson, S., & Palumbo, L.W. (1990). The wrong issue: Aversive versus nonaversive treatment. The right issue: Functional versus nonfunctional treatment. In A. Repp & N. Singh (Eds.), *Perspectives on the use of nonaversive and aversive interventions for persons with developmental disabilities* (pp. 361–379). Sycamore, IL: Sycamore Press.

Carr, E.G., Taylor, J.C., & Robinson, S. (1991). The effects of severe behavior problems in children on the teaching behavior of adults. *Journal of Applied Behavior Analysis, 24,* 523–535.

Cataldo, M.F., & Harris, J. (1982). The biological basis for self-injury in the mentally retarded. *Analysis and Intervention in Developmental Disabilities, 2,* 21–39.

Day, R.M., Rea, J.A., Schussler, N.G., Larsen, S.E., & Johnson, W.L. (1988). A functionally based approach to the treatment of self-injurious behavior. *Behavior Modification, 12,* 565–589.

Dorsey, M.F., Iwata, B.A., Reid, D.H., & Davis, P.A. (1982). Protective equipment: Continuous and contingent application in the treatment of self-injurious behavior. *Journal of Applied Behavior Analysis, 15,* 217–230.

Dumas, J.E., & Wahler, R.G. (1985). Indiscriminate mothering as a contextual factor in aggressive-oppositional child behavior: "Damned if you do and damned if you don't." *Journal of Abnormal Child Psychology, 13,* 1–17.

Dunlap, G. (1984). The influence of task variation and maintenance tasks on the learning and affect of autistic children. *Journal of Experimental Child Psychology, 37,* 41–64.

Dunlap, G., & Koegel, R.L. (1980). Motivating autistic children through stimulus variation. *Journal of Applied Behavior Analysis, 13,* 619–627.

Durand, V.M., & Crimmins, D.B. (1988). Identifying the variables maintaining self-injurious behavior. *Journal of Autism and Developmental Disorders, 18,* 99–117.

Edelson, S.M., Taubman, M.T., & Lovaas, O.I. (1983). Some social contexts of self-destructive behavior. *Journal of Abnormal Child Psychology, 11,* 299–312.

Etzel, B.C., Bickel, W.K., Stella, M.E., & LeBlanc, J.M. (1982). The assessment of problem-solving skills of atypical children. *Analysis and Intervention in Developmental Disabilities, 2,* 187–206.

Etzel, B.C., & LeBlanc, J.M. (1979). The simplest treatment alternative: The law of parsimony applied to choosing appropriate instructional control and errorless-learning procedures for the difficult-to-teach child. *Journal of Autism and Developmental Disorders, 9,* 361–382.

Etzel, B.C., LeBlanc, J.M., Schilmoeller, K.J., & Stella, E.M. (1981). Stimulus control procedures in the education of young children. In S.W. Bijou & R. Ruiz (Eds.), *Contributions of behavior modification to education* (pp. 3–37). Hillsdale, NJ: Lawrence Erlbaum Associates.

Favell, J.E., McGimsey, J.F., & Schell, R.M. (1982). Treatment of self-injury by providing alternate sensory activities. *Analysis and Intervention in Developmental Disabilities, 2,* 83–104.

Ferster, C.B., & Skinner, B.F. (1957). *Schedules of reinforcement.* New York: Appleton-Century-Crofts.

Foxx, R.M., & Bechtel, D.R. (1983). Overcorrection: A review and analysis. In S. Axelrod & J. Apsche (Eds.), *Punishment: Its effects on human behavior* (pp. 133–220). New York: Academic Press.

Gardner, W.I., Cole, C.L., Davidson, D.P., & Karan, O.C. (1986). Reducing aggression in individuals with developmental disabilities: An expanded stimulus control, assessment, and intervention model. *Education and Training of the Mentally Retarded, 21,* 3–12.

Gardner, W.I., Karan, O.C., & Cole, C.L. (1984). Assessment of setting events influencing functional capacities of mentally retarded adults with behavior difficulties. In A.S. Halpern & M.J. Fuhrer (Eds.), *Functional assessment in rehabilitation* (pp. 171–185). Baltimore: Paul H. Brookes Publishing Co.

Guess, D., Helmstetter, E., Turnbull, H.R., III, & Knowlton, S. (1987). Use of aversive procedures with persons who are disabled: An historical review and critical analysis. *Monograph of The Association for Persons with Severe Handicaps, 2*(1).

Horner, R.H., & Budd, C.M. (1985). Acquisition of manual sign use: Collateral reduction of maladaptive behavior, and factors limiting generalization. *Education and Training of the Mentally Retarded, 20,* 39–47.

Horner, R.H., & Day, H.M. (1991). The effects of response efficiency on functionally equivalent competing behavior. *Journal of Applied Behavior Analysis, 24,* 719–732.

Horner, R.H., Day, H.M., Sprague, J.R., O'Brien, M., & Heathfield, L.T. (1991). Interspersed requests: A nonaversive procedure for decreasing aggression and self-injury during instruction. *Journal of Applied Behavior Analysis, 24,* 265–278.

Horner, R.H., Sprague, J.R., O'Brien, M., & Heathfield, L.T. (1990). The role of response efficiency in the reduction of problem behaviors through functional equivalence training: A case study. *Journal of The Association for Persons with Severe Handicaps, 15,* 91–97.

Iwata, B.A. (1987). Negative reinforcement in applied behavior analysis: An emerging technology. *Journal of Applied Behavior Analysis, 20,* 361–378.

Iwata, B.A., Dorsey, M.F., Slifer, K.J., Bauman, K.E., & Richman, G.S. (1982). Toward a functional analysis of self-injury. *Analysis and Intervention in Developmental Disabilities, 2,* 3–20.

Kaminer, Y., Feinstein, C., Barrett, R.P., Tylenda, B., & Hole, W. (1988). Menstrually related mood disorder in developmentally disabled adolescents: Review and current status. *Child Psychiatry and Human Development, 18,* 239–249.

Kantor, J.R. (1959). *Interbehavioral psychology.* Granville, OH: Principia Press.

Kelleher, R.T. (1958). Concept formation in chimpanzees. *Science, 128,* 777–778.

Kern, L., Koegel, R.L., Dyer, K., Blew, P.A., & Fenton, L.R. (1982). The effects of physical exercise on self-stimulation and appropriate responding in autistic children. *Journal of Autism and Developmental Disorders, 12,* 399–419.

Koegel, L.K., & Koegel, R.L. (1986). The effects of interspersed maintenance tasks on academic performance in a severe childhood stroke victim. *Journal of Applied Behavior Analysis, 19,* 425–430.

Krantz, P.J., & Risley, T.R. (1977). Behavioral ecology in the classroom. In K.D. O'Leary & S.G. O'Leary (Eds.), *Classroom management* (pp. 349–366). New York: Pergamon Press.

Lancioni, G.E., Smeets, P.M., Ceccarani, P.S., Capodaglio, L., & Campanari, G. (1984). Effects of gross motor activities on the severe self-injurious tantrums of multihandicapped individuals. *Applied Research in Mental Retardation, 5,* 471–482.

Lovaas, O.I., Freitag, G., Gold, V.J., & Kassorla, I.C. (1965). Experimental studies in childhood schizophrenia: Analysis of self-destructive behavior. *Journal of Experimental Child Psychology, 2,* 67–84.

Lovaas, O.I., & Simmons, J.Q. (1969). Manipulation of self-destruction in three retarded children. *Journal of Applied Behavior Analysis, 2,* 143–157.

Mace, F.C., Hock, M.L., Lalli, J.S., West, B.J., Belfiore, P., Pinter, E., & Brown, D.K. (1988). Behavioral momentum in the treatment of noncompliance. *Journal of Applied Behavior Analysis, 21,* 123–141.

Martin, P.L., & Foxx, R.M. (1973). Victim control of the aggression of an institutionalized retardate. *Journal of Behavior Therapy and Experimental Psychiatry, 4,* 161–165.

Matson, J.L., & DiLorenzo, T.M. (1984). *Punishment and its alternatives: A new perspective for behavior modification.* New York: Springer.

McAfee, J.K. (1987). Classroom density and the aggressive behavior of handicapped children. *Education and Treatment of Children, 10,* 134–145.

McGimsey, J.F., & Favell, J.E. (1988). The effects of increased physical exercise on disruptive behavior in retarded persons. *Journal of Autism and Developmental Disorders, 18,* 167–179.

Meyer, L.H., & Evans, I.M. (1989). *Nonaversive intervention for behavior problems: A manual for home and community.* Baltimore: Paul H. Brookes Publishing Co.

Michael, J. (1982). Distinguishing between discriminant and motivational functions of stimuli. *Journal of the Experimental Analysis of Behavior, 37,* 149–155.

Mostofsky, D.I. (1965). *Stimulus generalization*. Stanford, CA: Stanford University Press.

Plummer, S., Baer, D.M., & LeBlanc, J.M. (1977). Functional considerations in the use of procedural timeout and an effective alternative. *Journal of Applied Behavior Analysis, 10,* 689–706.

Podboy, J.W., & Mallory, W.A. (1977). Caffeine reduction and behavior change in the severely retarded. *Mental Retardation, 15*(6), 40.

Repp, A.C., Felce, D., & Barton, L.E. (1988). Basing the treatment of stereotypic and self-injurious behaviors on hypotheses of their causes. *Journal of Applied Behavior Analysis, 21,* 281–289.

Rincover, A., & Devaney, J. (1982). The application of sensory extinction procedures to self-injury. *Analysis and Intervention in Developmental Disabilities, 2,* 67–81.

Sailor, W., Guess, D., Rutherford, G., & Baer, D.M. (1968). Control of tantrum behavior by operant techniques during experimental verbal training. *Journal of Applied Behavior Analysis, 1,* 237–243.

Schreibman, L. (1975). Effects of within-stimulus and extra-stimulus prompting on discrimination learning in autistic children. *Journal of Applied Behavior Analysis, 8,* 91–112.

Sidman, M. (1990). Equivalence relations: Where do they come from? In D.E. Blackman & H. Lejeune (Eds.), *Behavior analysis in theory and practice: Contributions and controversies* (pp. 93–114). Hillsdale, NJ: Lawrence Erlbaum Associates.

Sidman, M., & Stoddard, L.T. (1966). Programming perception and learning for retarded children. In N.R. Ellis (Ed.), *International review of research in mental retardation* (pp. 151–208). New York: Academic Press.

Silverman, K., Watanabe, K., Marshall, A.M., & Baer, D.M. (1984). Reducing self-injury and corresponding self-restraint through the strategic use of protective clothing. *Journal of Applied Behavior Analysis, 17,* 545–552.

Singer, G.H.S., Singer, J., & Horner, R.H. (1987). Using pretask requests to increase the probability of compliance for students with severe disabilities. *Journal of The Association for Persons with Severe Handicaps, 12,* 287–291.

Skinner, B.F. (1938). *The behavior of organisms*. New York: Appleton-Century-Crofts.

Skinner, B.F. (1953). *Science and human behavior*. New York: The Free Press.

Taylor, J.C., & Carr, E.G. (1992a). Severe problem behaviors related to social interaction. I: Attention seeking and social avoidance. *Behavior Modification, 16,* 305–335.

Taylor, J.C., & Carr, E.G. (1992b). Severe problem behavior related to social interaction. II: A systems analysis. *Behavior Modification, 16,* 336–371.

Terrace, H.S. (1963). Errorless transfer of a discrimination across two continua. *Journal of the Experimental Analysis of Behavior, 6,* 223–232.

Terrace, H.S. (1964). Wavelength generalization after discrimination learning with and without errors. *Science, 144,* 78–80.

Terrace, H.S. (1966). Stimulus control. In W.K. Honig (Ed.), *Operant behavior: Areas of research and application* (pp. 271–344). New York: Appleton-Century-Crofts.

Thompson, T., Hackenberg, T., & Schaal, D. (1991). Pharmacological treatments for behavior problems in developmental disabilities. *Proceedings of the Consensus Conference on the Treatment of Severe Behavior Problems and Developmental Disabilities*. Washington, DC: National Institutes of Health.

Touchette, P.E., MacDonald, R.F., & Langer, S.N. (1985). A scatter plot for identifying stimulus control of problem behavior. *Journal of Applied Behavior Analysis, 18,* 343–351.

Wacker, D.P., Steege, M.W., Northup, J., Sasso, G., Berg, W., Reimers, T., Cooper, L., Cigrand, K., & Donn, L. (1990). A component analysis of functional communication training across three topographies of severe behavior problems. *Journal of Applied Behavior Analysis, 23,* 417–429.

Wahler, R.G. (1980). The insular mother: Her problems in parent-child treatment. *Journal of Applied Behavior Analysis, 13,* 207–219.

Wahler, R.G., & Fox, J.J. (1981). Setting events in applied behavior analysis: Toward a conceptual and methodological expansion. *Journal of Applied Behavior Analysis, 14,* 327–338.

Wahler, R.G., & Graves, M.G. (1983). Setting events in social networks: Ally or enemy in child behavior therapy? *Behavior Therapy, 14,* 19–36.

Weeks, M., & Gaylord-Ross, R. (1981). Task difficulty and aberrant behavior in severely handicapped students. *Journal of Applied Behavior Analysis, 14,* 449–463.

Winterling, V., Dunlap, G., & O'Neill, R.E. (1987). The influence of task variation on the aberrant behaviors of autistic students. *Education and Treatment of Children, 10,* 105–119.

18

Get a Life!

Positive Behavioral Intervention for Challenging Behavior Through Life Arrangement and Life Coaching

Todd Risley

I wish to acknowledge the influence of Judith Favell (Endnote 1), Karen Ward (Endnote 2), John VanDenBerg (Endnote 3), and Mike Renfro (Endnote 4), with whom I collaborated in finding real solutions to big problems and testing the reality of these ideas; of Richard Barth (1986) and Carolyn Schroeder (Schroeder & Gordon, 1991), whose texts have helped me organize and teach these concepts; and of Montrose Wolf, who started it all.

In 1964, the first demonstration of behavioral intervention with a person with challenging behavior was published (Wolf, Risley, & Mees, 1964). Since then, many brave people have taken on the risky task of working with people with challenging behaviors and presenting their work for public scrutiny. As a result, the conceptualization and treatment of challenging behavior have evolved. This chapter presents a personal perspective on what used to be called behavior modification for behavior problems and is now called positive behavioral programming for challenging behaviors. These remarks are addressed to those who are responsible for designing behavioral interventions. It is for those who must live and work with a consumer that a disruptive behavior is a problem. It is for you who are expected to fix it that a problem behavior is a challenge.

CHALLENGING BEHAVIOR AND POSITIVE BEHAVIORAL INTERVENTION

A behavior is called "challenging" because it is seen as dangerous, disgusting, or disruptive by those who live and work with the consumer. What behavioral practitioners know is that people immediately respond, almost without fail, to actions that are dangerous, disgusting, or disruptive. Because consumers who develop challenging behaviors are usually dependent and often considered otherwise unimportant, little else they do is unfailingly responded to by others. Challenging behaviors are therefore inevitably sustained, partially or wholly, by the reactions of the very people for whom they are a problem. This is the first secret of behavioral interventions.

The second secret of behavioral interventions is that one must look away from the challenging behavior and focus instead on teaching new behaviors and on making them noted and important to those who live and work with the consumer. "What should or could or might the consumer be doing instead of the challenging behavior?" and "How can we make those alternate actions be practiced, useful, and acknowledged?" become the focal questions of behavioral intervention. Although the challenging behaviors are taken seriously, they are not the sole or even the primary focus of the intervention. To distinguish it from the "common sense" focus on the punishment of problem behavior, this second secret is called positive behavioral intervention.

LIFE ARRANGEMENT

Behavioral intervention is conducted across very different levels of detail, precision, and time. At all levels of intervention, we have learned to analyze the functions of the challenging behavior and to focus on the positive—to identify, teach, and strengthen prosocial alternatives to challenging behavior.

At the microlevel of *behavior analysis*, we have learned to focus on the positive and construct good habits to replace bad habits through

- Empirical identification of reinforcers
- Precise shaping of new response topographies
- Precise fading of controlling stimuli
- Precise reprogramming of response classes and behavior chains
- Precise contingencies of strong reinforcers

This micromomentary level of intervention requires a degree of sophistication in operant conditioning that very few psychologists or educators (even *behavioral* psychologists or *special* educators) possess.

At the more "common sense" level of *contingency management*, we have learned to focus on the positive and increase the display of prosocial behavior by

- Conceptually analyzing the context and function of challenging behaviors
- Rescheduling to avoid problem contexts
- "Crowding out" the challenging behavior by increasing the level of engagement
- Expanding the display of prosocial alternative behavior by "catching them being good" with social, material, and symbolic consequences more often
- Teaching specific, functionally equivalent social and communicative behaviors that "work" as well as or better than the challenging behavior
- Enhancing the engagement level of "time-in" rather than lengthening time-out

This day-to-day level of intervention can be successfully designed by most behavioral psychologists and some special educators, but still requires ongoing training and supervision to be successfully delivered by most parents, teachers, and staff.

Above the momentary behavior analysis level and the daily contingency management level, there is a third, more global level of intervention. Our focus on the positive and our pursuit of *long-range* outcomes have led us to ask the following:

- How is the person doing *overall* and *over time*?
- Is she or he happy, satisfied, and safe?

- Does the person have a stable home and family and friends on which to base her or his life and future, and after whom to model her or his ways?
- Is she or he practicing independence, productivity, and integration?
- Is the person continuing to develop new interests, new friends, and new skills?

These *quality-of-life* and *general development* issues have been in the applied behavioral literature from the very beginning when "Dicky," without self-injury and with language, was reported to have been "a new source of joy for his family" (Wolf et al., 1964, p. 311). It is reflected in the discussion of *social validity* (Wolf, 1978) and in most descriptions of follow-up outcomes. However, the Oregon group best brought it to clarity with the Neighborhood Living Project (Bellamy, Newton, LeBaron, & Horner, 1990), in which the whole model program was based on quality-of-life tracking measures. The amazing conceptual breakthrough was that *a high quality of life could be mostly achieved by life arrangements—rather than by behavior change.* This third level of intervention is as different from the contingency management level as that level is from the behavior analytic level.

At this level the patterns of the person's weekly and monthly life, and of his or her interactions with the people, places, and things he or she prefers or despises, are the units of consideration. The programming at this level is to arrange for a life reduced in stress, deprivation, and fear; enriched in those things that attract and engage the person's interest and repertoire; and richly responsive to his or her activities—And, I would add, a life that provides the varied and complex experiences over months and years that will produce *development* in the person's reinforcers, repertoire, and fluency. For emphasis, let me label this level of intervention *life arrangement.*

LIFE COACHING

Concurrent with learning to focus on positive programming for people with challenging behavior, we have learned to deliver positive programming where it would do the most good. We have moved from "Train and hope it generalizes" to "Train for generalization (and hope it generalizes)" (e.g., Stokes & Baer, 1977) to "Train and generalize to simulated conditions of use" (e.g., *relapse prevention*) to, finally, recognizing generalization for the powerless explanatory fiction that it is and skipping it by training in the context of use in the first place.

At the behavior analytic level, training in the context of use is called *incidental teaching.* The conceptual evolution from generalization to incidental teaching of language occurred in the following sequence: Risley and Wolf (1964, 1967), Reynolds and Risley (1968), and Hart and Risley (1968, 1974, 1975, 1978, 1980, 1982). Incidental teaching has been employed with minor modifications and many name changes to establish and strengthen prosocial alternatives to challenging behaviors many times since 1982.

The full import of training in the context of use came at the life arrangement level with the supported employment revolution in the 1980s (cf. Kiernan & Stark, 1986). Instead of the traditional practice of *train-and-place* (training general work skills in prevocational sheltered training settings until "ready" and then placing a person in a job), the strategy became *place-and-train* (place the person in an actual job and train her or him while doing that job, day after day, until the person more or less masters it). This has proven such a powerful intervention strategy that we should clearly mark it with a label. Because a job "coach" (Wehman & Melia, 1985) is a label used in supported employment, *life coaching*, I think, is the proper term for the place-and-train strategy wherever it is used. (For clarity, the term *incidental teaching* should be reserved for the micromomentary response to the "teachable moments" that occur "incidentally" in a person's ongoing activities.)

LIFE ARRANGEMENT AND LIFE COACHING STRATEGIES

Getting a life for people and coaching them into it should be considered obligatory features of modern behavioral interventions. Fortunately, just as daily contingency management programming requires less technical precision and specialty training than micromomentary behavior analysis programming, so too do life arrangement and life coaching require less than either. Most people with some experience in caring for others need only a little training to help another person design a good life and help him or her to implement it (professionals may actually need "detraining").

In general, there is a negative correlation between the flexibility of life arrangements available and the technical precision of the behavior programming needed. The wider the latitude available for modifying the life arrangements for a person with challenging behaviors, the less precise and technical the behavior programming needs to be. The opposite is also true in that the less flexible a person's life arrangements are, the *more* technical and precise the behavior programming must be. Most people with challenging behaviors exist in prespecified slots in an array of prefunded services provided by a static service organization with preassigned staff. Within those constraints, technical contingency management or precise behavior analytic programming—to match the person's behaviors to the existing nonoptimal circumstances—is often all that can be done. (Please note, however, that, even when a life can be arranged and coaching provided, competent behavior analysis and contingency management can usefully speed the transition into that life.)

Flexible Funding

Arranging a better life for a person with challenging behaviors requires flexibility and cooperation from funding sources and from other people involved in the person's life. Flexible funding of individually tailored programs is a technological reality. With computers, budgets can be managed with cost and expense centers for each individual. In law and in theory, services have been based on unique individualized education or habilitation plans since the 1970s. That most government funding agencies and local schools and service organizations still find it more familiar and convenient to fund and deliver a small menu of prespecified services to people with challenging behaviors is a temporary state of affairs. As successful examples and successful lawsuits build on one another, flexible funding for real individualized services will rapidly become the norm—especially as the successful examples thus far have cost less than traditional categorical services. Professionals need to learn how to use these new, powerful resources that are becoming available to them. Fortunately, life arrangement and life coaching are low-tech tools. Learning *how* to use them does not take much training—learning *to* use them first and most when dealing with challenging behaviors, however, will take some retraining.

Cooperation from Significant Others

Another issue likely to be difficult for professionals is the need to get all the people who are involved in a consumer's life to cooperate. A person with a history of challenging behaviors usually has many people and many agencies "on his or her case"—the more challenging the behaviors, the more people. All of these people and agencies have some power over some part of the consumer's life, and all have their own definitions of their own responsibilities and of the consumer's best interests. Helping a consumer design a life is not hard—getting everyone else to cooperate is. It takes effort and persistence to get everyone to participate, and time and skilled facilitation to get everyone to agree on a plan, to negotiate their roles in it, and to commit to meeting again whenever anyone thinks the plan needs to be changed.

STEPS TO A MODERN POSITIVE BEHAVIORAL INTERVENTION

With flexible funds available and with the cooperation of the people and agencies important to a consumer's life, modern positive behavioral intervention can proceed. Figure 1 provides a sequence of steps in such an

1. **Enlist the participation**—on a formally established Intervention Team—of all persons who must help or can harm the consumer's program (including, of course, the consumer).

2. **Arrange a long-term living environment** that is *safe* (relative to life threatening behavior) but still conducive to *development* and *intervention*. (Get A Life!, Part 1)

3. **Reduce exposure** to the ecological conditions associated with the problem behavior.
   Maximize exposure to the ecological conditions associated with the person's best functioning.

4. **Use periods of good functioning** to coach skills that are functionally equivalent (or better) to the problem behaviors in producing primary or secondary gains.

5. **After alternative behavior has been established**, eliminate or reduce the primary or secondary gains produced by the problem behavior. (Use penalties, only if necessary.)

6. **Expand reinforcers, repertoire, and fluency** through sampling, observing, and participating in an increasingly varied life with life coaching—to accelerate development. (Get A Life!, Part II)

7. **Plan for postintervention life** through relapse prevention and follow-up, rather than "generalization."

Figure 1. Suggested steps in a modern positive behavioral intervention plan for a person with challenging behavior.

intervention. *The first two steps*, primarily organizational tasks, *are the most important*. Unstinting time and effort should be spent on these at the outset, and these steps should be returned to as often as needed because they represent the source and the solution of most problems.

Step 1: Build a Team

Building a team is not primarily a planning process; it is a *social* process. Its purpose is to negotiate and problem-solve until a public commitment is achieved from everyone who must help or refrain from harming the consumer's program. The most important product is the publicly attested commitment from everyone rather than the written documents of the meetings. The process is not futures planning, nor is it group therapy, although it contains a little of both. It can best be learned from people who conduct organizational strategic planning and team-building retreats.

Step 2: Get a Life

The durably useful part of an intervention for challenging behavior does not even start until the person is facing, with coaching and assistance, circumstances that he or she will be facing later, with less coaching and assistance. Place the consumer into the life circumstances that he or she and the team would choose for the rest of his or her childhood or the next dozen years of adulthood (i.e., the place, the housemates, the neighbors, the job, the transportation, the acquaintances, the chores, the recreation, the helpers, the challenges). Add extra staff for protection, coaching, and reinforcer sampling until they can be faded out. Find *long-term* friends, neighbors, and helpers for the individual, as *people* are the most important part of life.

Step 3: Fine-Tune That Life

This step is somewhat technological as it requires an *environmental analysis* identifying the conditions associated with both problem behaviors and best functioning. (Note that good functioning is not defined by merely the absence of problem behavior, but by being *accessible to the influence of others*.) In a few cases, these conditions will be obscure and require formal quantified assessments (e.g., see Touchette, MacDonald, & Langer, 1985). But, in most cases, informal observation and interviews will suffice and the effort can be allocated where it is needed—to the sensitive readjustments of the person's schedule required to minimize problem incidents and *maximize the time the person is receptive to influence and is practicing prosocial behavior*.

In many cases of challenging behavior, the first three steps are enough. With everyone involved with the person working in concert to arrange a complex and interesting life dominated by prosocial interactions, over time the person will develop new effective skills, discover new reinforcers, and escape the behavioral traps that sustained her or his challenging behavior. If such development is not occurring, one should consider revisiting Steps 2 and 3 and further enhance the individual's quality of life and readjust the time the person spends in different situations.

Steps 4 and 5: Institute Coaching and Contingency Management

Steps 4 and 5 involve familiar coaching and contingency management technology. However, some conceptual sophistication is called for in conducting a *behavior analysis* of the probable functions of the challenging behaviors in both *primary* and *secondary gains*. Primary gains are the immediate and predictable consequences that are likely to serve to reinforce the challenging behavior. Secondary gains are more delayed and probabilistic (but real) effects of the challenging behavior that may or may not function to reinforce it. As an example, violent aggressive outbursts not only get responded to when they occur (primary gains), but also cause the people to attend to the person carefully *at other times* (secondary gains) to monitor his or her moods and anticipate his or her dissatisfaction.

The longer the challenging behaviors have been occurring, the more likely that more delayed and intermittent consequences (secondary gains) contribute to the class of reinforcers that maintain them. Similarly, the more invariant and restricted the person's life has been, the more likely that such secondary gains are functioning as reinforcers for some behaviors. Furthermore, the more verbally skilled the person (e.g., the higher his or her "mental age"), the more likely that secondary gains and their relation to a challenging behavior will have been described verbally and therefore function to maintain the behavior. Secondary gains are usually induced from interviews with the client and others who tend to give them humanistic labels such as "reputation," "role," "importance," "power," and "self-esteem." Labels aside, a complete behavior analysis requires that such real, albeit delayed and probabilistic, consequences of behavior be considered to hold the same importance to the consumer of our services that they hold for us.

Step 6: Accelerate Development

This is the ultimate in positive behavioral programming—to deliberately develop the depth and complexity of the person's knowledge and repertoire by planfully expanding the depth and complexity of his or her life. "The deliberate development of behavior" (cf. Risley & Baer, 1973) is the latent goal of all behavioral interventions. With life coaching in the context of a full life that results in salient experience and practice throughout all the 100+ waking hours of a person's week, development—both deliberate and natural—can actually be expected.

Step 7: Plan for Real Life

The last step is to acknowledge the obvious: If a person already has a decent and durable life, she or he does not "graduate" to another life. People who have had challenging behaviors can best be prepared for infrequent but likely high-risk eventualities by creating them or simulating them in the life context in which they might occur (e.g., see Marlatt & Gordon, 1985). And these people, like all of us, are going to need occasional extra help, and arrangements for making that help available should be planned.

CONCLUSIONS

The strategy of arranging a life for a person and coaching her or him into that life has emerged from the long history of behavioral intervention for challenging behaviors. It appears to be the most powerful, durable, and inexpensive level of behavioral intervention. It requires little technological precision or specialty training and should always be the strategy of choice—leaving sole reliance on the more precise contingency management and the microprecision of behavior analytic strategies for the unfortunate circumstances in which inflexible organizational, funding, and bureaucratic structures do not allow you to get a life for a person with challenging behaviors.

To paraphrase a familiar prayer:

Grant us the power to change those conditions we cannot accept,
the technical skill to work within those conditions we cannot change,

and the wisdom to know the difference.

The difference now is that, while the conditions of life for people with challenging behaviors are often unacceptable, they are going to be increasingly within our power to change. Such changes represent the leading edge of positive behavioral programming.

ENDNOTES

[1]Each year, from 1985 through 1991, Judith Favell and I copresented a workshop at the Association for Advancement of Behavior Therapy meetings. These workshops, which melded her work on treatment of severe behavior disorders and mine on design of living environments, gradually evolved some of the points presented in this chapter. The last workshop (see Favell & Risley, 1991) also contained some of the chapter's organization.

[2]In 1984, I managed to get $500,000 in Alaska State developmental disabilities funds targeted for special programs for the 10 most difficult-to-serve, institutionalized people—to enable us to learn to serve medically and behaviorally challenging people outside our institutions. Only Karen Ward, the director of an Anchorage service organization, was willing and able to take on the challenge. We collaborated on designing and troubleshooting the community programs for these 10 people. We initially failed two of these people, whose sexual behavior posed a risk to their neighbors. Dr. Ward persevered and finally de-

signed an acceptable *relapse prevention* program for them and others with challenging sexual behaviors (see Ward et al., 1992). In 1986, the State of Alaska's Divisions of Vocational Rehabilitation and Mental Health and Developmental Disabilities obtained a supported work "systems change" grant to depopulate our sheltered workshops with job coaching into real work competitive employment, mobile crews, and enclaves. Dr. Ward and I collaborated with Theda Ellis in implementing that grant and in designing a training program on supported work to retread vocational trainers. Dr. Ward further developed the training to be delivered across the state (see Ward & McGlone, 1987; Wilcox, Ward, & Knox, 1992).

[3]In 1987, the Alaska Youth Initiative (AYI) began to bring children and youth, one by one, from out-of-state institutions and "plant" these most difficult and dangerous youngsters in real homes, back in their home communities, with individually tailored wraparound supports and treatment. John VanDenBerg, the State's Child and Adolescent Mental Health Coordinator, designed and implemented this program (see VanDenBerg, 1993). As his graduate adviser and colleague, I consulted on the program development and on some of the more difficult cases. As his boss—when I became Director of the Division of Mental Health and Developmental Disabilities (DMHDD) in 1988—I watched (and worried) as the program matured. By 1990, we were serving 85 of the "most challenging of the challenging" in communities across Alaska with unexpected ease and success at about half the average cost of out-of-state institutionalization (and with no negative political response from their communities!).

[4]In 1988, I took a leave of absence from the University of Alaska and became Director of Alaska's DMHDD—primarily to protect the AYI and explore the use of wraparound services with other populations. The structure of the adult mental health system (particularly the fact that Medicaid categories of reimbursement had "hardened" the services into fixed-price slots of psychotherapy, medication management, and psychosocial rehabilitation) and the ingrained bureaucracy running it prevented much movement toward individualized wraparound services there. It was quite the opposite in the Division of Developmental Disabilities (DD). Retirements had decimated the ranks of DD personnel, and most of the DD community programs were supported by direct appropriations—not Medicaid. Mike Renfro, the newly appointed Coordinator of Developmental Disabilities Services, and I were able to design and implement a system of individualized, wraparound services with every new state dollar that came our way.

After I returned to the university in 1990, Mike Renfro was able to continue to hire and train state DD personnel to be "advocates" (see Renfro, 1994) who know the people and families they serve. He guided the providers and consumers into adopting service principles that, in fact, *required* individualized wraparound services (State of Alaska DMHDD, 1992) and convinced the DD council *and the service provider association* to endorse individualized wraparound services. By 1993, over half of the people receiving state DD support were receiving services "wrapped around" their chosen lives—and those supports cost less (average cost: 1991, $18,400; 1992, $16,858; 1993, $16,442) than the old group home or supervised apartment ($25,000) plus vocational ($10,000) "slots." In the 6 years of individualized wraparound services no one has needed to be admitted to the state DD institution—demonstrating that with individualized wraparound services a DD service system does not need an institution, even for people very difficult to serve. (And, the cost is less. Even the 10 most expensive wraparound service plans average only half the per capita cost of the institution!)

REFERENCES

Barth, R.P. (1986). *Social and cognitive treatment of children and adolescents.* San Francisco: Jossey-Bass.

Bellamy, G.T., Newton, J.S., LeBaron, N., & Horner, R.H. (1990). Quality of life and lifestyle outcomes: A challenge for residential programs. In R. Schalock (Ed.), *Quality of life: Perspectives and issues* (pp. 127–137). Washington, DC: American Association on Mental Retardation.

Favell, J.E., & Risley, T.R. (1991, November). *Treatment of severe behavior disorders in persons with developmental disabilities.* Workshop presented at the annual convention of the Association for Advancement of Behavior Therapy, New York.

Hart, B.M., & Risley, T.R. (1968). Establishing use of descriptive adjectives in the spontaneous speech of disadvantaged preschool children. *Journal of Applied Behavior Analysis, 1,* 253–262.

Hart, B.M., & Risley, T.R. (1974). Using preschool materials to modify the language of disadvantaged children. *Journal of Applied Behavior Analysis, 4,* 243–256.

Hart, B.M., & Risley, T.R. (1975). Incidental teaching of language in the preschool. *Journal of Applied Behavior Analysis, 4,* 411–420.

Hart, B.M., & Risley, T.R. (1978). Promoting productive language through incidental teaching. *Education and Urban Society, 10,* 407–429.

Hart, B.M., & Risley, T.R. (1980). In vivo language intervention: Unanticipated general effects. *Journal of Applied Behavioral Analysis, 13,* 407–432.

Hart, B., & Risley, T.R. (1982). *Incidental teaching of language.* Lawrence, KS: H&H Publishing.

Kiernan, W.E., & Stark, J.A. (Eds.) (1986). *Pathways to employment for adults with developmental disabilities.* Baltimore: Paul H. Brookes Publishing Co.

Marlatt, G.A., & Gordon, J.R. (1985). *Relapse prevention.* New York: Guilford Press.

Renfro, M. (1994). *Advocrat: A bureaucrat who advocates* (DD community services position paper). Juneau, AK: Division of Mental Health and Developmental Disabilities.

Reynolds, N.J., & Risley, T.R. (1968). The role of social and material reinforcers in increasing talking of a disadvantaged preschool child. *Journal of Applied Behavior Analysis, 1,* 253–262.

Risley, T.R., & Baer, D.M. (1973). Operant behavior modification: The deliberate development of behavior. In B. Caldwell & H. Ricciuti (Eds.), *Review of child development research: Vol. 1. Social influence and social action.* Chicago: University of Chicago Press.

Risley, T.R., & Wolf, M.M. (1964). *Experimental manipulation of autistic behaviors and generalization into the home.* Paper presented at the American Psychological Association, Los Angeles. Reprinted in R.E. Ulrich, T. Stachnic, & J. Mabry (Eds.). (1966). *The control of human behavior.* Glenview, IL: Scott Foresman.

Risley, T.R., & Wolf, M.M. (1967). Establishing functional speech in echolalic children. *Behaviour Research and Therapy, 5,* 73–88.

Schroeder, C.S., & Gordon, B.N. (1991). *Assessment and treatment of childhood problems.* New York: Guilford Press.

State of Alaska Division of Mental Health and Developmental Disabilities. (1992). *Alaska Developmental Disabilities service principles.* Juneau, AK: Author.

Stokes, T.F., & Baer, D.M. (1977). An implicit technology of generalization. *Journal of Applied Behavior Analysis, 10,* 349–367.

Touchette, P.E., MacDonald, R.F., & Langer, S.N. (1985). A scatter plot technique for identifying the stimulus control of problem behavior. *Journal of Applied Behavior Analysis, 18,* 343–351.

VanDenBerg, J.E. (1993). Integration of individualized mental health services into the system of care for children and adolescents. *Administration and Policy in Mental Health, 20*(4), 247–257.

Ward, K.M., Heffern, S.J., Wilcox, D.A., McElwee, D., Dowrick, P., Brown, T.D., Jones, M.J., & Johnson, C.L. (1992). *Managing inappropriate sexual behavior: Supporting individuals with developmental disabilities in the community.* Anchorage: University of Alaska Center for Human Development.

Ward, K.M., & McGlone, M. (1987). Supported employment: Transitioning clients and staff from a sheltered workshop environment to integrated community employment. *New Directions, 8*(3), 1–6.

Wehman, P., & Melia, R. (1985). The job coach: Function in transitional and supported employment. *American Rehabilitation, 11*(2), 4–7.

Wilcox, D.A., Ward, K.M., & Knox, C.J. (1992). *Supported employment: Employment specialist manual* and *Supported employment: Master trainer manual.* Anchorage: University of Alaska Center for Human Development.

Wolf, M.M. (1978). The case for subjective measurement or how applied behavior analysis is finding its heart. *Journal of Applied Behavioral Analysis, 11,* 203–214.

Wolf, M.M., Risley, T.R., & Mees, H.I. (1964). Application of operant conditioning procedures to the behavior problems of an autistic child. *Behaviour Research and Therapy, 1,* 305–312.

19

Person-Centered Planning

Don Kincaid

S ince the mid-1980s, people with developmental disabilities, their families, and members of the community have seen substantial changes in how people with disabilities are perceived by others. Along with these changes in the perceptions of and thoughts about disability are many significant changes in how to actually identify and provide the support a person needs and desires. No doubt, words like *inclusion, community, self-advocacy, challenging behavior, lifestyle issues,* and *family support* are found throughout this book and reflect the changes that have occurred in the philosophies and practices regarding the provision of positive behavioral support to individuals and families. One such term, *person-centered planning*, has come to reflect not only a change in the philosophies and values about people with disabilities, but also describes a range of new techniques for identifying and pursuing what a person wants and needs.

Under the umbrella of person-centered planning are a variety of processes that have been developed in the last few years. A few of these include Life Style Planning (O'Brien, 1987; O'Brien & Lyle, 1987), Personal Futures Planning (Mount, 1987; Mount & Zwernick, 1988), The McGill Action Planning System (Forest & Lusthaus, 1987; Vandercook, York, & Forest, 1989), Framework for Accomplishment/Personal Profile (O'Brien, Mount, & O'Brien, 1991), and Essential Lifestyle Planning (Smull & Harrison, 1992).

FIVE ESSENTIAL OUTCOMES OF PERSON-CENTERED PLANNING

These person-centered planning activities share many similarities. Most approaches utilize group graphics (large paper and marker drawings) and facilitation techniques to involve groups in learning more about the person and his or her family and planning for a more positive future. In addition, these approaches share an explicit or implied commitment to seeking five essential goals, outcomes, or valued accomplishments in the individual's life.

1. *Being present and participating in community life.* This accomplishment stresses that the person should not only be present in the same community available to all other citizens but should also have an opportunity to do "regular" things with "regular" people. This goal includes all aspects of living in the community that most people assume to be normal routines and may take for granted. Such things as shopping, going to visit friends, going to church or synagogue, going to a movie, eating in a restaurant, or joining the local health club are just a few of the ways that most individuals participate in their communities.

2. *Gaining and maintaining satisfying relationships.* Many people with disabilities have never been supported in having friends. In fact, some people may never have had a friend who was not actually paid to be there. Similarly, many people with disabilities have never been supported in having a romantic relationship. Families have often been separated from their child with a disability and have not been supported in maintaining family ties. Additionally, people who have cared for the focus person in the past may have lost contact. In person-centered planning, the person with a disability should be supported in healthy interactions with friends and family who provide the person with occasions to give and receive love and affection.

3. *Expressing preferences and making choices in everyday life.* People with disabilities have usually not been allowed to make the choices that they are capable of making. Most human services systems have, in the

past, assumed too much responsibility for the so-called "handicapped" person and have not supported them in learning how to express their preferences. Very few people with mental retardation were allowed to govern their own lives in ways that helped them learn personal responsibility and decision making.

For some people, it is the little things in life that they have been denied power to control: what to eat, when to eat, what to wear, or how to groom their hair. For many more, it has been the big things in life: where to live, who to have as a roommate, where to work, what kind of work to do, or how to spend their money. This goal states not only that the person should have opportunities to express preferences and choices, but that other people should listen and respond appropriately to those expressions. The individual should be supported in making choices in the little and big decisions of life.

4. *Having opportunities to fulfill respected roles and to live with dignity.* This goal is essential to everyone, yet many people with disabilities have not been allowed to gain dignity and respect in the community. Often, people with mental retardation have been kept in living and working situations that prevented them from exercising their abilities or presenting their personal characteristics in a positive way. They have been forced into demeaning roles, been dressed inappropriately, had their hair cut by people who did not care how they looked, crowded together so that their differences were magnified, and not supported in learning the social graces of the community at large.

People with developmental disabilities can make a contribution to the community and find respect and dignity in the process. The person with disabilities should be supported in making a contribution to society, be valued as a person, have self-respect, behave with dignity, and be treated with respect.

5. *Continuing to develop personal competencies.* Competence, for anyone, can be developed through opportunities and support. The first step in developing competence is an attitude that says, "Yes, that is possible. You can do it. I can help you. We can do it together." Each person should be given chances to grow and develop, to take greater advantage of life's opportunities, and to control his or her own life and future. This includes being able to learn new things, to succeed with a minimum of assistance, and to contribute to society.

FACILITATING A PERSONAL
PROFILING AND FUTURES PLANNING SESSION

For several years, the Life Quilters Project has been providing person- and family-centered planning across West Virginia utilizing a process called Personal Profiling and Futures Planning. This approach was initially taught to a number of state representatives by Joseph Patterson in 1989. Since that time, we have modified the approach with additional information gathered from other person-centered approaches and with what we have learned about our own state system and the people whom we support. In fact, each time we facilitate a Personal Profile and Futures Plan, we further revise and adapt the process. Thus, the process as a whole changes over time as we discover new activities that work and revise old activities to be more effective. Also, the uniqueness of each focus person, family, and support community requires significant adaptations each time the process is used.

The first activity, the Personal Profile, utilizes group graphics techniques to develop an overall understanding of the person and his or her environment. The Personal Profile lists who is participating on the team (i.e., the focus person, family members, teachers, members of the community), identifies important people and places in the focus person's life, reviews the focus person's history and health, identifies the person's opportunities for choice making, determines how the person gains or loses respect, identifies strategies that work or do not work, recognizes team members' hopes and fears about the focus person's future, assesses current barriers to and opportunities for attaining desired outcomes, and arrives at overall themes that impact the focus person's life.

The second activity, the Personal Futures Plan, also utilizes group graphics techniques and is built on the information identified in the Personal Profile activity. This activity expands the vision of the group to consider and commit to positive short- and long-term outcomes for the focus person.

Mount (1994) clearly addresses many of the benefits and limits of the Personal Futures Planning process. Benefits of the process include developing a positive view of the person, inspiring motivation in participants, empowering people with disabilities as well as their family and friends, involving and developing community relationships, and producing organizational change. Mount observes that the integrity of the process is challenged if the emphasis moves away from what the *person* needs and wants and centers on what the *system* needs and wants:

> Personal futures planning is least effective when it is used in isolation from other complementary change activities. This fragmentation is most likely to occur if the futures planning process is standardized, implemented on a large scale, or otherwise molded to fit into existing structures of service instead of challenging them. (Mount, 1994, p. 102)

Because the rationale, benefits, and limitations of person-centered planning have been presented by Mount and others, the rest of the chap-

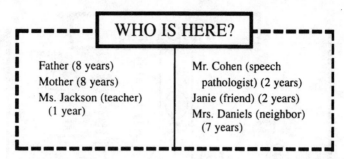

Figure 1. Sample Who Is Here? frame.

ter addresses issues in the practical application of Personal Profiling and Futures Planning techniques. The goal here is that the reader not only become familiar with the process, but also be motivated and comfortable enough with the process to actually apply the techniques her- or himself to facilitate person-centered planning teams.

FRAMES OR QUILT SQUARES

In keeping with the Life Quilters Project's Appalachian heritage and the quilting theme, the individual frames of the Personal Profile and Futures Plan are drawn to resemble quilting squares. Each of the frames is drawn on 2- to 3-foot squares of paper and surrounded by dashed lines; these dashed lines represent the "stitching" that holds the life quilt together. When the frames are all placed on the wall together, they resemble an Appalachian quilt. This life quilt communicates the important information gathered by the team regarding the person's past, present, and future.

The following sections present examples of completed quilt squares from groups that we have facilitated. Each example is accompanied by a description of how to facilitate the frame, what the frame seeks to accomplish, and issues to address at each step in the process.

Frame 1: Who Is Here?

The facilitator begins the process by asking everyone to introduce themselves, identify their role, and make a statement about how they are involved with the focus person. As the participants speak, a volunteer team member writes their names and titles on a *Who Is Here* sheet and indicates the length of time they have known the focus person (Figure 1). This frame allows all of the participants an opportunity to get to know each other and assists with the remembering of names, relationships, and levels of experience with the focus person. After this is accomplished, work on the life quilt frames is ready to begin.

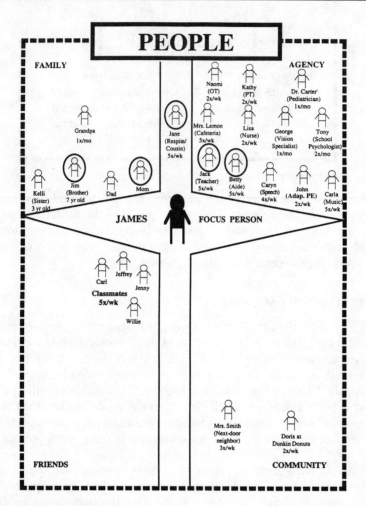

Figure 2. Sample People frame for a child.

Frame 2: People

Human relationships are essential to everyone's happiness and success. However, information involving relationships has traditionally been absent from the records of the lives of people with disabilities. People supported by human services agencies often lost important relationships when family, staff, and friends were separated from them. People with disabilities typically have fewer social relationships than people without disabilities, so the presence or loss of contact with a person has significant effects on a focus person's chances of securing meaningful relationships.

The People frame (Figure 2) indicates with whom the focus person spends time, has the best relationship, and is the most effective. The frame also indicates whether supports provided are natural (family and community) or agency centered. This frame is developed by dividing it into different colored sections for 1) family (blue), 2) agencies (yellow/brown), 3) friends and associates (green), and 4) community (orange). The focus person appears in the center of the frame (purple). The use of color on this frame and throughout the activity is important in maintaining the interest of participants as well as emphasizing aspects of each frame.

The facilitator then asks, "Who are the people who are most important in the focus person's life?" The most important people are drawn closest to the focus person. The team tries to arrive at a consensus if there is a considerable difference of opinion among people concerning their importance in the person's life.

After identifying each person involved with the focus person, the facilitator or other team member writes down how often each has contact with the focus person (total hours per week) and indicates with colored green circles those individuals who are *most* effective with or have the closest ties with the focus person.

Frame 3: Places

The Places frame (Figure 3) allows the team to get a picture of the focus person's current presence and participation in all aspects of community life and requires the facilitator or other participants to

1. Make a picture of all the places that the focus person visits in the course of a month.
2. Include the person's home, work, school, and community environments. Also indicate the type of transportation the person uses and how often it is used.
3. Show activities that occur in the home and community and indicate how often the focus person participates in them.
4. Illustrate what the focus person does while at work or school.
5. Include only the most important friends, housemates, staff, and so forth in this frame. *Do not* reproduce the entire People frame here.

Frame 4: History of Critical Life Experiences

The team should arrange for a person who is familiar with the focus per-

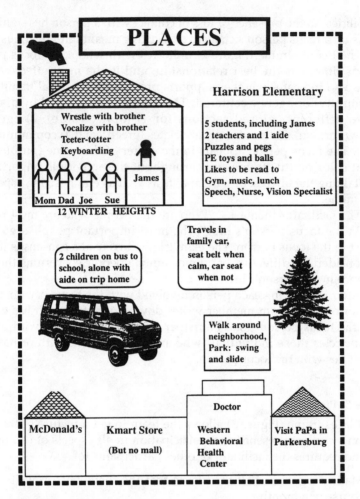

Figure 3. Sample Places frame for a child.

son's history to be present if the focus person is unable to accurately relate the information him- or herself. Review the life of the focus person and note the important events from birth to the present. With young children, there may not be a long history of placements and crises. Yet a history of the parents' or care providers' attempts to seek support and services is no less crucial and important. Therefore, this frame is approached differently based on the age of the focus person.

For an adult, the team illustrates when and where the focus person was born, his or her life with the biological or foster family, institutional placements, hospitalizations, serious illnesses, significant losses of friends

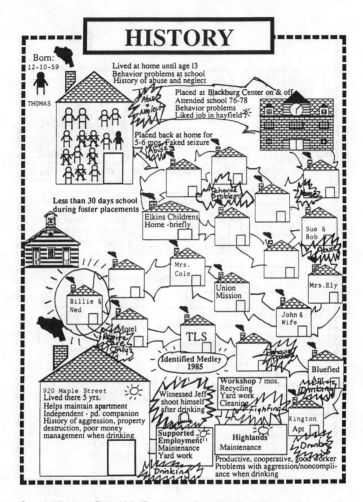

Figure 4a. Sample History of Critical Life Experiences frame for an adult.

and family, and the different places the focus person has lived (Figures 4a and 4b). For a child, however, the team concentrates more on a history of the family's involvement with the service system. As with an adult, the team should illustrate when and where the child was born, the child's life with his or her family, and where the child has lived. However, critical contacts with medical personnel and agency services, accidents, and where supports have continued or were effective and failed to continue or be effective should also be indicated (Figure 5).

The person drawing this frame should write in the dates and people's names at important places. Indicate crises and problems in red. Note

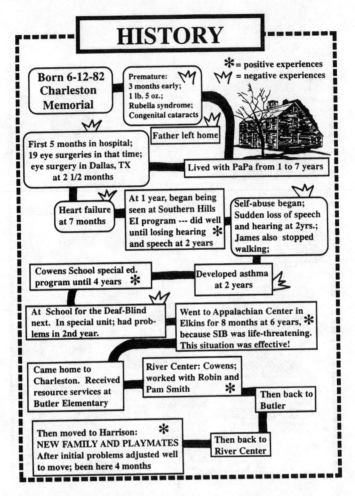

Figure 4b. Sample History of Critical Life Experiences frame for a child.

good times and successes with green. This history should be a sketch. Later, if it is important, the details may be filled in. For now, it is important to get an overview of the person's life up to this point. This frame will stimulate the participants' memories about the focus person and allow them to gain a better understanding of where the focus person has come from and the conditions of his or her life up to the present.

Frame 5: Current Health

In this frame, the team reviews the current health of the person, listing positives (+) in green and negatives (−) in red based on group consensus

Figure 5. Sample Current Health frame for a child.

(Figure 5). A health factor may be both positive and negative. The group notes indicators of good health as well as symptoms or problems of poor health, special care or equipment required, coordination and reflexes, and so forth. Current medications should be noted at the bottom of the frame. The team should be sure to list all behavior-controlling medications. The group should also briefly discuss the positive and negative effects of the medications and list them on the appropriate side of the frame. Discuss whether the current situation is a permanent condition (e.g., visual impairment), a chronic but curable disorder (e.g., ulcers), or an acute transitory situation (e.g., broken arm).

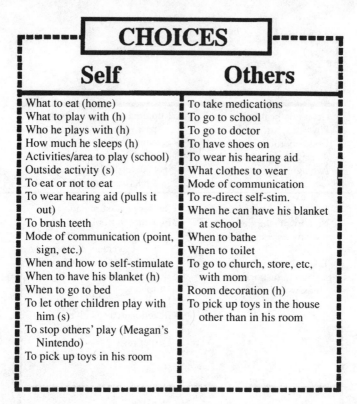

Figure 6.   Sample Choices frame for a child.

For this frame it may be useful or necessary to solicit input from nurses, physicians, or other medical personnel. However, remember this is just a health sketch, illustrating the major aspects of the person's health. Important details can be filled in later. The group should not get distracted by long, detailed discussions of whether this or that illness is, in fact, the "cause" of this person's difficulties.

Frame 6: Choices

The Choices frame is divided into two sections (self and other) and shows how many choices this person makes for him- or herself and how many of this person's choices are made by other people (Figure 6). A discussion of choices will cause participants to begin to see how much control the person has over his or her life and how much control is in the hands of other people. Frame 6 should be completed by indicating how much choice this person has in very important matters (e.g., place of residence, roommates, work opportunities, vacation time, how to spend personal monies, where to keep personal possessions, what kinds of possessions

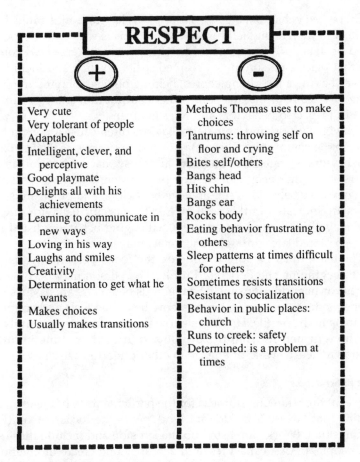

Figure 7. Sample Respect frame for a child.

may be kept, how to spend free or leisure time). This frame also indicates how much choice the person has in issues of everyday personal preferences (e.g., how to decorate his or her room, how to dress, what makeup or jewelry to wear, what food to eat, when to eat, when to go to bed, when to care for personal needs).

Frame 7: Respect

The Respect frame identifies the behaviors that help the focus person gain respect or cause the person to lose respect. The roles this person fills that support respected and dignified behaviors are also indicated. This frame is divided into those behaviors and roles that help the person gain respect (+) and those odd or unusual behaviors that cause the person to lose respect in the community (−) (Figure 7).

Respected behaviors may be as simple as having a nice smile, having a sense of humor, being helpful, and so on. This is where the participants should be asked, "Why do you like this person?" Respected roles are those that place a person in an accepted social position and include such things as having a job, doing chores, helping others, volunteering, participating on a team, or making some other contribution to the group or society. List respected behaviors and roles in green (+).

Conversely, odd and unusual behaviors often cause a person to lose respect in the community. These may include excessive as well as dangerous behaviors. Dangerous behaviors are those that may seriously harm the person or other people or destroy the environment. Excessive behaviors, aggressive behaviors, self-abusive behaviors, and other unusual behaviors are indicated in this section. List the specific behavior (e.g., face slapping, yelling loudly) in red (−). Challenging behaviors listed in red may be explored later through functional analysis activities.

The team must be sure to prepare the focus person for this frame prior to beginning the Personal Profile. The person may become upset when his or her odd, unusual, or dangerous behaviors are discussed. Encourage the focus person to express how he or she feels and continue to participate in the profile. However, allow the person an opportunity to remove him- or herself from the profile activities at anytime in order to calm down, take a break, or engage in other preferred activities.

Frame 8: Strategies

The goal of the Strategies frame is for the participants to brainstorm about anything that "works" or "doesn't work" with the focus person (Figure 8). Things that "Work" are listed on the left side and include those situations, people, places, capacities, and activities that create motivation, interest, and engagement. These are listed in green. Things that "Don't Work" are listed on the right side and include those strategies, conditions, people, places, and activities that create frustration, anxiety, or other problems. These are listed in red.

The Strategies frame should actually be posted and available for revision or additions during the discussions of all the other frames. Frequently, participants will express something that works or does not work with the focus person during the development of the other frames. It should not be assumed that these comments will be remembered later. Immediately add such items to this frame as the discussion of the other frames proceeds. This frame may be addressed directly after the first seven frames, but information may be added to it during any of the other activities.

This frame should list everything participants can offer. There may be some overlap between the settings and times discussed in the other

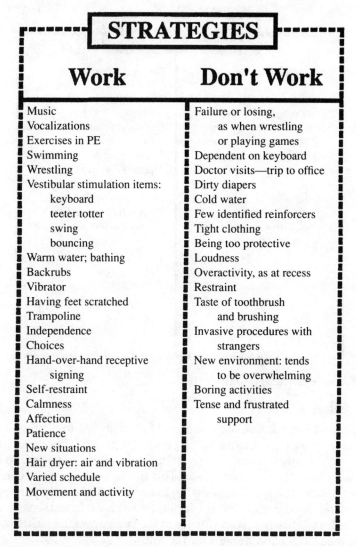

Figure 8. Sample Strategies frame for a child.

frames. All jargon, technical language, and labels should be deciphered so that all participants can understand what is being discussed. Items may fall into both columns at the same time. For example, in some instances a specific strategy may work, but in other instances the same strategy is ineffective. It is important for participants to see that some situations have multiple outcomes. Often people see things differently and see different sides of the same thing. Everyone's point of view is included in this frame.

Figure 9. Sample Hopes and Fears frame for a child.

Frame 9: Hopes and Fears

A Hopes and Fears frame may be useful for the group to express some of its concerns with regard to the focus person (Figure 9). These may involve the person's ability to function in particular situations or the group's ability to meet his or her support needs. This frame has been particularly important in identifying and addressing the concerns of family participants. It is essential for the team and the facilitator to know, from the very beginning, the fears, concerns, and worries of the family and the participants as well as their hopes and dreams for the future.

Frame 10: Barriers and Opportunities

A Barriers and Opportunities frame (Figure 10) gathers essential information prior to engaging in a longer-term consultation. This activity looks at problems within the community or within the agency that may impede the success of the participants' efforts. In addition, this frame looks at what is unique about the community, agency, family, or focus person that can be drawn on to ensure a greater probability of success or opportunities for the focus person.

```
┌─────────────────────────────────────────────┐
│  BARRIERS / OPPORTUNITIES                     │
└─────────────────────────────────────────────┘
```

Board of Education fiscal cuts	Lots to do in community
Assistive technology is expensive	Parents and other students with similar disabilities in county
Grant doesn't pay for equipment	Team and school is supportive
Psychiatrist only consults–not available 24 hours	Fresh start—potential
No physical and occupational therapy	Assistive technology is available
Needs hands on and technical assistance from Kanawha County	Special grant money for training
	Teacher is good and may stay (hopefully)
	Medicaid Waiver funding approved
	Advocate is very active
	Communication between people is very good

Figure 10.   Sample Barriers and Opportunities frame for a child.

The concerns in both the Hopes and Fears and the Barriers and Opportunities frames may be addressed at a later time. It is useful to complete the Hopes and Fears frame immediately before the Personal Futures Plan is developed so that the plan addresses those issues adequately. Immediately after the development of the Futures Plan is a good time to address the *current* Barriers and Opportunities that may impact the pursuing or attaining of the Futures Plan.

Frame 11: Themes from the Personal Profile

This frame (Figure 11) allows the participants to capture some of the most important positive and negative impressions from the profile of the focus person developed in the first 10 frames. Summary statements for Frame 11 might include:

1. From the People frame: "The only relationships Kisha has had are with paid staff and none of those have lasted more than 2 years."
2. From the Places frame: "Gary very seldom goes anywhere in the

```
┌────────┏━━━━━━━━━━━━━━┓────────┐
│        ┃    THEMES    ┃        │
│        ┗━━━━━━━━━━━━━━┛        │
│ Most people interacting with Charles are agency people          │
│ Extended family members have not learned to interact with       │
│     Charles                                                     │
│ Most relationships are with adults                              │
│ Most agency interactions are one-on-one                         │
│ Charles doesn't want to be in an interaction with other kids    │
│     making lots of noise                                        │
│ Charles doesn't go too many places in the community other than  │
│     school and restaurants                                      │
│ He only goes to places he wants to go                           │
│ He likes to go places where he knows he will get something      │
│ He goes out a lot, but to the same places                       │
│ He doesn't like change                                          │
│ Historically, there have been lots of changes with people and places │
│ Health issues occurred from day one                             │
│ There are no conclusions/resolutions for negative health concerns │
│ Sensory problems from birth                                     │
│ History of alternating positive and negative events            │
│ Agency involvement has been positive. There is a team of        │
│     agency folks to support Charles and his family              │
│ Fears are related to safety (self and others), relationships, health │
│     and the future                                              │
│ Charles has lots of choices typical for a 4-year-old            │
│ Main behaviors of concern are aggressive (safety reasons and    │
│     social acceptability)                                       │
│ In general, everyone really seems to like Charles               │
│ Charles is sociable                                             │
│ He has made a lot of progress                                   │
│ His communication skills have expanded recently                 │
│ We know lots of things that work and don't work                 │
│ Charles clearly identifies people, places, etc., that he likes  │
└────────────────────────────────────────────────────────────────┘
```

Figure 11. Sample Themes from the Personal Profile frame for a child.

community and almost never interacts with people who do not have a disability."

3. From the Choices frame: "Julie has very little choice over the large or small decisions in her life."

4. From the Respect frame: "In spite of Charles's challenging behavior he has a great sense of humor and is well liked by his teachers and other students."

5. From the Barriers and Opportunities frame: "There are five different agencies providing support to Miguel's family, and they do not communicate and work well together."

Such summary statements provide guidance in envisioning a more desirable future as well as planning how to implement strategies to achieve the more desirable future. Emphasize the importance of these themes by listing them in purple. Once the Personal Profile activity has been completed, work may begin on the Personal Futures Plan.

PERSONAL FUTURES PLAN

By the time the participants have completed the Personal Profile, they have all begun to realize that this person could live a much better life if he or she could just do more of the things that he or she prefers, live and work with the people he or she likes and who like the person, and be in places that encourage respectable behaviors by providing him or her with roles that facilitate acceptance and respect in the community. Participants also have begun to see that many of the person's difficulties lie in being forced to live and work in situations that are especially unsuitable for that person. They begin to see that the person has been traumatized by being a recipient of human services along with many other physical and emotional frustrations and failures. Most will, by this point, begin to personally identify with the difficulties of this person's life. It is hoped that they will also start to realize why they have been less than optimally successful in helping this person achieve a better life up to this point.

By now, participants have started to say things like, "Wow, if we could just do more of that, he would be a lot happier." Some people will ask questions like, "Why does he have to do that, anyway? You know he hates it! Why make him do it? He would be a lot happier if he could do something else." Other participants are realizing things such as, "Tom will never be happy if he has to keep living in that place," or "We just can't go on until we learn to do things differently ourselves." In fact, the participants may have already begun to see a more positive future. All the facilitator has to do at this point is help the participants shape these ideas into a coherent vision of a real future for the focus person.

With the frames of the Personal Profile placed on the wall for the group to see, the facilitator should briefly review what the group has learned. He or she should read the themes from Frame 11 back to the group. Furthermore, the group should be reminded of the color codes, especially green—for strengths, successes, and positive experiences—and red—for problems, concerns, and crises.

The five focus person outcomes discussed in the first section provide a general framework for envisioning a more positive future. As the group reflects on this person's life, the facilitator can ask questions that will prompt the participants to reflect on how the focus person could realize these lifestyle accomplishments. Recall that the five essential goals include the following:

1. Being present and participating in community life
2. Gaining and maintaining satsifying relationships
3. Expressing preferences and making choices in everyday life
4. Having opportunities to fulfill respected roles and to live with dignity
5. Continuing to develop personal competence

The envisioning of a positive future helps the participants see how the focus person is already telling the group what he or she needs in order to live a more fulfilling life. All the green-coded entries in the Personal Profile tell the group what is working for this person. It is the role of the facilitator to assist the participants in breaking out of the old ways of thinking and envisioning a different future, one that will allow the person to realize his or her goals.

The development of a Personal Futures Plan is not the time to discuss what the group cannot do; rather, it is the time to discuss what can be done if everyone tries very, very hard. However, it may also be necessary to help overly unrealistic "dreamers" ground their dreams in pieces of the reality that have emerged from the Personal Profile. The goal is to assist team members in expanding their vision within the realm of reality.

Figure 12 provides one basic layout of a Personal Futures Plan developed for a child. There may be many variations on the vision, and the facilitator will need to use personal judgment and artistic expression to reflect this vision. One good way to start is to frame the Personal Futures Plan with a few places (home, work, community) and ask the following questions:

1. *Home:* Based upon what we have learned about this person, what kind of home would be best for him or her? Where should this home be in the community? What resources need to be nearby? What about family and friends, how close should they be? What about housemates? A roommate? How much assistance by hired people will this person need? How accessible does the home need to be? What about transportation? What kinds of roles would the person fill?

2. *Work:* Based upon what we have learned about this person, what kind of work, school, or other day program would be best for this person? Specifically, what kind of work? What kind of setting? Where? How far from home? How many other people would work there? How many other people with disabilities? How active or physical would the work be? What special skills does this person already have that would help in this work? Will the work be productive? Is the work respected in the community? How much help will this person need to do this work? What

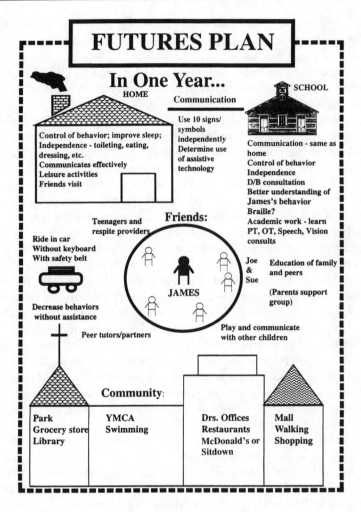

FUTURES PLAN

In One Year...

HOME
Communication
SCHOOL

Control of behavior; improve sleep;
Independence - toileting, eating,
dressing, etc.
Communicates effectively
Leisure activities
Friends visit

Use 10 signs/
symbols
independently
Determine use
of assistive
technology

Communication - same as
home
Control of behavior
Independence
D/B consultation
Better understanding of
James's behavior
Braille?
Academic work - learn
PT, OT, Speech, Vision
consults

Friends:

Teenagers and
respite providers

Ride in car
Without keyboard
With safety belt

JAMES

Joe
&
Sue

Education of family
and peers

(Parents support
group)

Decrease behaviors
without assistance

Peer tutors/partners

Play and communicate
with other children

Community:

Park	YMCA	Drs. Offices	Mall
Grocery store	Swimming	Restaurants	Walking
Library		McDonald's or	Shopping
		Sitdown	

Figure 12. Sample Personal Futures Plan for a child.

about transportation? How much money will the person earn? How will the person be paid? Will there be an opportunity for promotion?

3. *Community:* Based upon what we have learned about this person, what kind of neighborhood and community would be best for him or her? What kind of community would accept and respect this person? Who would be the best kind of neighbors? What about recreation and shopping in this community? What about health resources? Other resources? What about family and friends? What about church? What about accessibility and transportation?

Additional information should address the following areas:

4. *Making choices and exercising competencies:* Based upon what we have learned about this person, where will he or she be able to exercise personal competencies and learn new ones? Where will the person be able to become more independent and empowered to take charge of his or her own life and choose what to do? Where will the person be able to express preferences?

5. *Relationships:* How will this person's network of relationships be expanded and enriched in the future? How will relationships be supported in the community, the home, and at work? What kinds of friends will this person be able to maintain in his or her future?

This activity should be very positive in nature. The team members should talk about the best possible scenario that they can imagine for the person. Then the facilitator should help the team identify goals that are attainable and practical for the focus person. Clarify for the participants that what they are working on will require a significant amount of effort from the focus person, from other team participants, and from the community at large. Therefore, they need to realize that they are committing themselves and their efforts to pursuing a positive future for this person.

With each individual, it is important to identify a time frame for when this positive future might be attained. For some individuals, a time frame of 6 months to a year may be realistic. For others, a time frame of 3–5 years might be more practical. Sometimes there are logical and obvious time frames. For instance, a child transitioning from one program to another program in 1 year may present an ideal time frame. A young adult transitioning from school to employment in 3 years may present another possible time frame.

It is also acceptable to allow differing visions for a positive future for an individual, as long as they are all positive. For instance, a 17-year-old may have a Personal Futures Plan that includes a home environment that consists of an apartment with friends, a supervised apartment, or even continuing to live with his or her family in a supportive and nurturing environment. All of these outcomes may be positive and can be included within the Futures Plan as possible desirable outcomes.

Closing the Session

After the Personal Futures Plan is completed in sufficient detail, the facilitator should ask for any additional reactions from participants. For example, what have they learned from this experience? How did it make them feel? What were some of the positive aspects of the activity, and what were some of the negative aspects of the activity? How might they recommend adapting it? Discuss with them the merits and drawbacks of their suggestions.

Tips for Facilitating a Personal Profile and Futures Plan

1. *Involve the focus person and family as much as possible in Personal Profiling and Futures Planning activities.* This may require altering aspects of the Personal Profiling and Futures Planning situation. For instance, the location of the activity may need to be moved to an area that is more acceptable and accessible to the focus person and family members. The speed at which the information is presented may need to be adjusted so that all participants are able to understand what is being said. The content of the Personal Profile and Futures Plan may need to more clearly emphasize the role of the focus person and family members. It is also important to continually clarify the information, not only for its accuracy but also to make sure that it is communicated to the focus person and family and includes their comments and any additional information. Finally, it is important to consider the possible role that family members and the focus person can take in becoming the leader of their own team. In fact, they may take on responsibilities within the Personal Profiling and Futures Planning activities such as asking questions, drawing in the frames, or directing the team or work group.

2. *Emphasize information from personal knowledge.* This information will come from the focus person, his or her family, and those people who know him or her best. It is critical to realize that professional status does *not* equal personal knowledge of the focus person. Participants and contributors to the team must be individuals who know and care about the focus person to the greatest extent.

3. *Consider and encourage input from everyone on the team.* This requires the facilitator to be knowledgeable about and receptive to social situations and relationship problems that may exist even before the team gathers. For instance, is there an ongoing dispute between agencies? Are there unresolved problems between the family and the agency? Are there personality conflicts among the participants that would impede their ability to work together? If so, these issues may need to be addressed *before* the team begins to pursue a positive future for the focus person.

In addition, it may be necessary to identify reluctant participants and encourage them to participate. The facilitator should give them constructive feedback as well as a tremendous amount of positive reinforcement for all comments. Many team participants may not be used to having their opinions valued and solicited. That will have to change, or the information gathered at team meetings will not be as comprehensive and useful as necessary.

It may also be important to prompt participation from key stakeholders. If there are reluctant participants, it may be important to directly address and involve them with statements such as, "Tom, what do you think about _____?" Sometimes it will work to require all individuals to assist in drawing frames or working at the activity, either putting up sheets of paper or organizing the material.

4. *Get all the facts before solutions are considered.* Personal Profiling and Futures Planning activities are opportunities to gather information and identify strengths and problems, but not an appropriate time to try to solve problems. The team should be directed to provide the information, not to problem-solve or address issues more in depth than is necessary at this stage. Future team activities will begin to look at solutions to the identified challenges.

5. *Explore differences of opinion identified during the Personal Profile and Futures Plan.* Participants may have different ideas on work options, living arrangements, and so forth that the focus person may prefer or enjoy. They may also have different opinions as to what works and what doesn't work for the focus person. A great deal of information about success and failure of efforts in the past can be gathered from exploring *why* there is a difference of opinion. Often, extremely important information can be gathered during this exploration. The team members can come to a consensus later as to the specifics of what they believe and what they feel, but it is important for people to air their differences of opinion during the development of the Personal Profile and Futures Plan.

6. *Carefully assess the demeanor of the team.* At times in a meeting, there are values or responses expressed that are not consistent with the philosophy of person-centered planning. For instance, an individual may refuse to acknowledge the need of the focus person to make choices or may indicate a belief that the focus person is not capable of initiating or maintaining relationships of any sort. These situations pose a problem to the ongoing functioning of the work team. As a facilitator, do you allow expression of those opinions without rebuttal or education? Do you respond to each instance of such statements by team members?

Our approach at the Life Quilters Project has been to carefully assess the demeanor of the work group. Is this an isolated comment, or is it a comment that is persistent and expressed by a number of participants? If it is expressed by a number of participants, it may be necessary to confront them about this philosophy and to engage in some education and values clarification activities. However, there may be times when a general approach of nurturing an individual toward a more person-centered values base may be of benefit.

7. *Be aware of when to redirect attention.* The facilitator must be aware of when to redirect attention of the focus person or team participants back to the scheduled activities and when it is necessary to allow them to explore issues or areas in greater depth. The reasons for this distinction are

obvious. Completing the Personal Profile or Futures Plan can require anywhere from 2 hours to 2 days depending upon whether the work group can consistently remain on-task and address the issues in the structured format presented in this chapter. However, there may be times when important issues arise that need to be addressed at greater length. Sometimes it is beneficial to explore these issues as they come up. At other times, it is more efficient to simply make a note to explore these issues more in-depth in subsequent meetings. An exploration of such issues may be essential to gaining insight and information necessary to support the person effectively.

8. *Observe the team.* It is very important for the facilitator to observe the team adequately. It is recommended that two facilitators work together, one individual drawing or writing on the frames and one person facilitating the discussion. This allows for one person to be aware of visual and verbal cues and issues that may not be strongly or overtly stated by the team members. If the only facilitator is drawing on paper with his or her back to the team, it is difficult for him or her to observe the team's reactions to statements or drawings.

9. *End the Personal Profiling and Futures Planning activities on a positive note.* Personal Profiling activities can sometimes be sobering, shocking, and disturbing to team participants. In fact, some have actually referred to that part of the activity as informative, but "a downer." Occasionally people become very upset and make statements such as, "Oh, I never realized. . . ." Therefore, it is very good to schedule a positive activity following a Personal Profile. The best positive activity is indeed the Futures Plan, which allows the participants to really concentrate on what they can do that is good: How can they motivate themselves and the focus person to "do something about it"?

WHAT'S NEXT?: CONTINUING THE PERSON-CENTERED PLANNING PROCESS

Once the team has an overview of the focus person's past, present, and future, it has the basis for what the planning team or work group is going to pursue. The person and his or her team have a vision of where they want to go; now the team can focus on how to get there. Although the Personal Profile and Futures Plan probably have identified a number of goals and objectives the team can begin to address, there may still be more in-depth information that is necessary to develop a comprehensive support plan that addresses all of the person's quality of life issues. Gathering this additional information and applying it is a continuous process and may include the following additional procedures.

In order to better understand a person's complex challenging behaviors, we frequently conduct a *functional analysis*. Team participants conduct interviews, observe the focus person and his or her environment, and collect data that allow the team to determine why the person's challenging behaviors are occurring.

The team also frequently engages in a *service delivery assessment*, or an in-depth analysis of the focus person's daily activities and the support provided for him or her. This assessment identifies the person's strengths, needs, program goals, and teaching strategies. Issues such as age-appropriateness, functionality, and peer involvement are examined by the team.

Another activity may involve addressing the issue of *community inclusion*. The work group may utilize brainstorming sessions to generate new ideas about how to promote inclusion in neighborhoods, organizations, associations, and other activities available within the community.

All of these activities give deeper and richer insights into how to more effectively support the focus person in the important areas of his or her life. The information can be documented in a *comprehensive work plan* or a *positive behavioral support plan*, which identifies issues to be discussed, actions to be taken, and supports to be implemented. Identifying responsible team members and establishing clear time lines for the completion of the action also assists the team in maintaining its focus on the person and the accomplishment of important goals.

Our person-centered planning process may be summarized as follows: The Personal Profile and Futures Plan initiate the approach, additional information is obtained through various activities, a comprehensive plan is developed, and the team or work group continues to work to accomplish the identified goals. So when is this process complete? *Never.* A person's life and environment are always changing. We are all faced with new challenges, obstacles, and opportunities. Can anyone say that he or she does not feel a daily need for ongoing support from family, friends, colleagues, and the community? People with challenging behaviors or disabilities also face a life of struggles, failures, and successes. With support from their family, friends, and other community members, they may achieve every aspect of their Personal Futures Plan. They may have the home they want. They may have a job they love, one that makes a real contribution to the community. They may be present at and participating in a wide range of community activities. They may have a group of friends who support them and to whom they provide support in return. But life still goes on. As one Personal Futures Plan is attained, a new one is identified and the pursuit continues—good luck to those in pursuit of that positive future.

REFERENCES

Forest, M., & Lusthaus, E. (1987). The kaleidoscope: Challenge to the cascade. In M. Forest (Ed.), *More education/integration* (pp. 1–16). Downsview, Ontario, Canada: G. Allan Roeher Institute.

Mount, B. (1987). *Personal futures planning: Finding directions for change* (Doctoral dissertation, University of Georgia). Ann Arbor, MI: UMI Dissertation Information Service.

Mount, B. (1994). Benefits and limitations of personal futures planning. In V.J. Bradley, J.W. Ashbaugh, & B. Blaney (Eds.), *Creating individual supports for people with developmental disabilities: A mandate for change at many levels* (pp. 97–108). Baltimore: Paul H. Brookes Publishing Co.

Mount, B., & Zwernick, K. (1988). *It's never too early, it's never too late* (Publication No. 421-88-109). St. Paul, MN: Metropolitan Council.

O'Brien, J. (1987). A guide to lifestyle planning: Using The Activities Catalog to integrate services and natural support systems. In B. Wilcox & G.T. Bellamy (Eds.), *A comprehensive guide to The Activities Catalog: An alternative curriculum for youth and adults with severe disabilities* (pp. 175–189). Baltimore: Paul H. Brookes Publishing Co.

O'Brien, J., & Lyle, C. (1987). *Framework for accomplishment*. Decatur, GA: Responsive Systems Associates.

O'Brien, J., Mount, B., & O'Brien, C. (1991). *Framework for accomplishment: Personal profile*. Decatur, GA: Responsive Systems Associates.

Smull, M.W., & Harrison, S.B. (1992). *Supporting people with severe retardation in the community*. Alexandria, VA: National Association of State Mental Retardation Program Directors.

Vandercook, T., York, J., & Forest, M. (1989). The McGill Action Planning System (MAPS): A strategy for building the vision. *Journal of The Association for Persons with Severe Handicaps, 14*, 205–215.

20

A Team Training Model for Building the Capacity to Provide Positive Behavioral Supports in Inclusive Settings

Jacki L. Anderson, Audrey Russo,
Glen Dunlap, and Richard W. Albin

Preparation of this chapter was supported by Cooperative Agreement No. H133B2004 from the U.S. Department of Education, National Institute on Disability and Rehabilitation Research. However, the opinions expressed herein do not necessarily reflect the position of the department, and no official endorsement should be inferred.

The enterprise of behavioral support for individuals with severe disabilities has developed substantially since the 1980s (Carr et al., 1994; Horner et al., 1990). The goals have been broadened beyond simple reductions in problem behaviors. Behavioral support programs are now expected to assist a person in gaining functional competencies, improved relationships, participation in community activities, and access to preferred events. Accordingly, the methods of behavioral support have been expanded to incorporate multiple assessment and intervention strategies. These approaches extend far beyond traditional behavior management procedures. They require consideration of ecological, systemic, and multidisciplinary variables that must be incorporated longitudinally across a diversity of community contexts.

This maturation and expansion of behavioral support presents new demands on service systems that have responsibility for supporting individuals with severe disabilities in local communities. Broadened support goals bring heightened expectations, and with these expectations comes a need to build enhanced capacities at the community level. Thus, in-service training efforts must be elaborated in terms of both the content and the process of training. Training must be comprehensive in nature, addressing the technology of positive behavioral support in ways that facilitate improved quality of life in inclusive school, work, home, community, and recreational settings. To develop local capacities, materials must be useful for a wide range of participants, including teachers and direct service staff, specialized professional staff, families, consumers, and other community members who are involved in the lives of individuals with severe disabilities. The process of training must be longitudinal and include opportunities for supported application of the technology and community-building efforts along with the provision of information.

This chapter provides an example of such training. The example is an in-service team training project designed to address the development of local expertise in the area of positive behavioral support as well as the systems changes and community development necessary to promote the long-term availability of this technology in typical community settings (Anderson, Albin, Mesaros, Dunlap, & Morelli-Robbins, 1993). The team training model was developed as the principal training component of the Rehabilitation Research and Training Center (RRTC) on Positive Behavioral Support (National Institute on Disability and Rehabilitation Research, Cooperative Agreement No. H133B2004). The RRTC on Positive Behavioral Support was established in 1987, and since then the training project has developed interagency state-level training teams in 20 states. The individuals on these teams are providing comprehensive training and technical assistance in a large number of local communities.

This chapter focuses on implementation of the team training model at the local level. It begins with a brief description of the critical features of the training model, including an emphasis on the features that involve training at the local level. In particular, the focus is on the establishment of case study teams that involve application of the training content with focus individuals who are supported by training recipients. The chapter then reviews the basic process and content of the curriculum. This latter part of the chapter is presented by way of a case illustration from one of the states that is participating in the team training project.

Because the chapter focuses on training at the local level, there is much about the national training effort that will not be covered in depth. Readers who are interested in a more detailed discussion of the national training project and its outcomes are referred to Anderson et al. (1993).

GENERAL FEATURES OF THE TEAM TRAINING PROCESS

The approach that we have followed in the national team training project on positive behavioral support is based on a number of critical features. These features include the following:

1. *Adopting a training-of-trainers model:* In this model, initial participants in training serve as trainers for later participants. Numerous reports have shown that this strategy can be effective in disseminating information well beyond initial training efforts (Demchak & Browder, 1990; Jones, Fremouw & Carples, 1977; Page, Iwata & Reid, 1982; Peck, Killen, & Baumgart, 1989). In the project, each state established an interagency state-level team that received comprehensive training from national experts. The state teams were trained as trainers and developed a commitment to working together to replicate the team training approach in local communities throughout their states. Similarly, in many circumstances the training-of-trainers model has been carried out another generation such that some trainees at the local level have been targeted to serve as future trainers of service providers in local communities. This model of dissemination can help to address the ongoing training needs of the local community due, in part, to changing support needs of individuals with challenging behavior and the chronic shortage and attrition of qualified personnel in the fields of education and human services.

2. *Targeting multiple audiences:* The training is provided for audiences who represent a variety of constituencies and agencies, instead of focusing on one specific agency or program, as has been the more traditional practice. Targeting multiple audiences creates a context for comprehensive, coordinated support across the variety of agencies and community and family members who impact various aspects of the lives

of individuals residing in the target community (Dunlap, Robbins, Morelli, & Dollman, 1988).

3. *Utilizing a case study team format:* Much of the training content and process revolve around a focus individual with challenging behavior. Case study teams consist of the people who are involved in aspects of the focus person's life and thus are likely to be included in efforts to deliver comprehensive positive behavioral support. Teams might include parents, teachers, paraprofessionals, related-services staff, inclusion specialists, peers, case managers, co-workers, job coaches, friends, and any other individual who might care for and support the focus person. Each training session might include several case study teams; these members make up the core training participants for their community. The purpose of the case study teams and the process of developing these teams are discussed in more detail in a subsequent section of this chapter.

4. *Interspersing content with supported application:* Following a dynamic training process using in-service and modified coaching approaches allows for the provision of information and supported application of that information to be interspersed throughout the course of the training. With support from the state team, case study team members serve as coaches for one another in understanding and implementing the technology. They work together throughout and beyond the training process to construct, implement, evaluate, and adjust comprehensive positive behavioral support plans for the focus individual, building on support plans as each aspect is presented in the training sessions.

5. *Providing a comprehensive curriculum to address all aspects of positive behavioral support:* The expansion of behavioral support perspectives, including the philosophical and multidisciplinary basis of the endeavor, means that a comprehensive curriculum is necessary for participants to understand the interrelationship of behavioral supports and all other aspects of an individual's life. The curriculum revolves around quality-of-life improvements and includes, but is not limited to, 1) assessment and functional analysis; 2) instructional and curricular modifications; 3) instruction in replacement behaviors, communication skills, and self-regulatory strategies; 4) emergency management strategies; 5) construction of positive behavioral support plans; 6) evaluation of the success of behavioral support packages; and 7) issues in systems change and training strategies.

6. *Facilitating the development of positive behavioral support communities:* Developing an ongoing implementation and expansion of positive behavioral support at the local level is a critical part of each step of the training process. Participants are encouraged to share strategies, issues, and resources across case study teams to create a community of experts working together to ensure positive behavioral support for members of their community. Initially, the focus is on a collaboration to support the

participating focus individuals. As the training progresses, teams are encouraged to identify common needs, resources, and barriers to implementation, along with possible solutions to develop long-term community action plans for the ongoing and expanded provision of positive behavioral supports throughout their community.

7. *Providing ongoing support for state trainers and local communities:* Providing support to state training teams as they conduct their first training efforts promotes fidelity to the content and process in replication trainings throughout the state. State trainers participate in the initial training as case study participants, where the focus is on content and expanding team members' experience with the comprehensive positive behavioral support technology. Then, support from project trainers during the state team's initial replication training allows for focus on the process of conducting the training along with clarification regarding training content and materials.

8. *Providing multiple levels of training:* In addition to these key features, another characteristic of the team training project is that it provides multiple levels of training. Members of the state training team are expected to understand the values, theory, and research underlying the behavioral support perspectives at a sophisticated level in order to train others to implement the technology. At the local level, the expectations range from an ability to participate in the process of developing, implementing, and evaluating a positive behavioral support plan for a focus individual (e.g., family member, friend) to an ability to generalize the application of the technology across individuals (e.g., direct services providers), and, in some cases, to be able to train others to implement this technology (e.g., management or personnel staff).

TEAM TRAINING AT THE LOCAL LEVEL

The remainder of this chapter focuses on training directed at the local community, where case study teams are utilized as a vehicle for supervised application of the training curriculum. As indicated previously, this occurs via the actual development and implementation of positive behavioral support plans. This process is described here and illustrated in a later section with a case description of support plan development and outcomes for a focus individual who participated in the training project.

Case Study Teams

Collaborative teamwork is a primary component of the successful provision of educational and other human services as well as the process through which to improve systems to serve the complex needs of individuals in inclusive communities. The importance of multiple sources of input in determining the needs of individuals with disabilities, and the provision of services to meet those needs, was made apparent by the requirements of the Education for All Handicapped Children Act of 1975 (PL 94-142). This law required that assessment, design, and implementation of individualized education programs (IEPs) be conducted by multidisciplinary teams (*Federal Register*, 1977). Indeed, multidisciplinary, or transdisciplinary, teams operating within the school system have been expanded to include interagency team efforts in the area of individualized transition planning (ITP) for students graduating from school to adult services (Halpern, 1985; Hasazi, 1985; Wehman, Kregel, & Barcus, 1985; Wehman, Moon, Everson, Wood, & Barcus, 1988). The team process is also being used extensively to provide support at the school and class level to facilitate the inclusion of students with disabilities into general education classrooms via school site teams (Chalfant, Pysch, & Moultrie, 1979; Sugai & Horner, 1994), peer support teams (Stainback, & Stainback 1985, 1989; Vandercook & York, 1990), and the student study team process that exists in many general education programs. The increasing use of collaborative teaming is creating the need for changes in personnel training so that professionals and paraprofessionals are better prepared to engage in successful collaborations (Baumgart & Ferguson, 1991; Meyer & Evans, 1989; Racino, 1990; Snell, 1990).

Case Study Team Members

The case study team format creates the structure for the success of the team training model. Supporting quality lives in inclusive settings requires a focus on each individual as a person as well as a holistic view of the person's needs, strengths, and preferences. This is exemplified by selecting the focus individual first, then building the case study team to support that individual. Building case study teams is a multilevel process with the first level comprising people who will provide direct support to the focus individual across the various aspects of her or his life. These people may include parents, teachers, residential or work support staff, child care providers, and others. The next level expands the team with individuals who will have an impact, but in a less direct or less frequent manner (e.g., related-services personnel, school principal, case manager, medical personnel). An additional level of case study team membership can include individuals who have been identified as a priority to receive training, but who may not be directly involved with the focus individual (e.g., agency training staff, administrators, direct service personnel not associated with the focus individuals). These are people who will benefit from the training process, who have responsibilities for supporting other community members who have challenging behaviors, and who have made a commitment to participate on the team throughout the training process. This multilevel framework ensures that each focus individual has the needed support on his or her team and creates a vehicle for all training participants to participate in creating positive behavioral supports as a part of the training process.

Selection of the Focus Individual

Careful selection of the focus individuals and their teams can help address the broader training needs of the community. Typically, three to eight focus individuals and their teams participate in training for a given community. We recommend that enough representatives from a particular program or service agency participate to be able to support one another in helping their program to implement a positive behavioral support model for all individuals who need such supports. For example, the selection of two or more focus individuals from a particular school could result in enough special education teachers and support staff, general educators, family members, related-services staff, and administrators to provide the expertise and commitment to impact the entire school's orientation toward dealing with challenging behavior.

A second consideration in selecting focus individuals is that they represent a range of personal characteristics in order to provide the opportunity for trainers to see the technology applied successfully across ages (children and adults), abilities, and types and severity of challenging behavior. Another consideration relates to the environments in which the individuals spend their time. In order to address the quality-of-life focus of positive behavioral support, it is critical that focus individuals are living, working, or going to school in inclusive settings or settings where there is a clear commitment to inclusion and meaningful interaction with typical peers.

Finally, the focus individuals selected should be those for whom the most comprehensive case study teams can be established to best demonstrate a collaborative team model, to have the greatest potential for impact across the focus individual's life, and to garner a circle of support that will operate well beyond the life of the training project.

Collaborative Working Relationships

The members of each case study team work together throughout the training to implement the positive behavioral support strategies. It should be noted that a collaborative working relationship among all members of the team is not a prerequisite to participation in the training. The focus on step-by-step assessment and intervention for an individual creates the opportunity for positive collaborations to emerge, even in situations where interagency, interdisciplinary, or family–agency interactions have been neutral, nonexistent, or even adversarial. One of the strongest features of the case study team process is that it fosters collaboration and a new level of understanding among community members who are concerned with individuals who have disabilities or challenging behaviors.

The case study teams use a modified coaching approach in which team members serve as coaches for one another. This contrasts with the more traditional dyadic approach described by Joyce and Showers (1980, 1982). Another level of coaching occurs across case study teams as participants provide feedback, support, and resources for other focus individuals not on their particular team. Yet another level of coaching occurs with the state trainers serving a coaching role with case study teams and individual participants. This format offers multiple sources and opportunities for participants to be supported in applying the technology, analyzing the application with nonjudgmental feedback, and adjusting the proposed strategies to meet the needs and preferences of focus individuals. There is consistent emphasis on helping all team members feel positive about themselves and their efforts, particularly during the initial stages of acquiring new skills or shifting attitudes regarding the process and desired outcomes of behavioral intervention. Our experience supports that of Joyce and Showers (1980, 1982), in that the addition of coaching practices to high-quality in-service training results in the transfer of new skills, outlooks, and models into the participants' active repertoires.

Structure of the Team Training Process

Team training at the local level is structured to provide opportunities to apply the cumulative training content throughout the process. The training content is delivered gradually over a 4- to 6-month period. After each training session, case study teams work together to implement the new strategies via field-based assignments in their own programs or homes. The teams then return for the next session of training where they consult with trainers to question, clarify, and receive feedback on their efforts. The next topic of content information is provided, and the process accumulates until full behavioral support plans are designed and implemented by each team. The in-service and coaching components of the training are blended to maximize the knowledge and skills as they are added at each session of the training program. A description of this process of training with the building of positive behavioral support plans is provided in the following sections, along with a case example.

TEAM TRAINING CURRICULUM

This section of the chapter describes the content and sequence of the training curriculum as it is offered at the local level. In particular, the process in which the case study teams engage as they accumulate knowledge about positive behavioral support and their focus individual is related. As the training proceeds over the 4- to 6-month period, support strategies are implemented and a comprehensive behavioral support plan is constructed. Indeed, the process of building a positive behavioral support plan serves as a framework for the presentation of content and the sequence of activities throughout the training.

Table 1 presents an outline of the process in which teams engage over the course of training as they build a comprehensive behavioral support

Table 1. The process of building a positive behavioral support plan

1. Describe the learner and the contexts in which the learner spends his or her time.
   * Begin Personal Futures Planning process.
2. Identify and operationally define the behavior(s) or behavior class(es) of concern.
   * Collect baseline data.
3. Implement behavioral supports as needed while conducting assessments.
   A. Lifestyle Enhancements I
      1. Integration: school, work, living, environment
      2. Enhanced interactions, participation, independence, choice, variety, predictability
   B. Positive Procedures I
      1. Stimulus change
      2. Differential reinforcement of alternative (desirable) behavior(s)
   C. Crisis Prevention and Intervention Procedures I (if necessary)
4. Conduct assessments.
   A. Quality of life (e.g., Resident Lifestyle Inventory [Kennedy, Horner, Newton, & Kanda, 1990]), Person-Centered Assessments (Mount & Zwernick, 1987; O'Brien & Lyle, 1987; Vandercook, York, & Forest, 1989), Social Network Analysis (Kennedy, Horner, & Newton, 1990), Program Quality Indicators Checklist (Meyer, Eichinger, & Park-Lee, 1987), Quality of Life Cue Questions (Anderson, Mesaros, & Neary, 1991)
   B. Ecological environmental systems (e.g., Positive Environment Checklist [Albin, Horner, & O'Neill, 1993], Interaction Observation Form [Albin, Horner, & O'Neill, 1993], Curriculum Activity Profile [Foster-Johnson, Ferro, & Dunlap, 1991])
   C. Functional assessment of target behavior(s) or behavior class(es)
      1. Interviews (e.g., Communication Interview Format [Schuler, Peck, Tomlinson, & Theimer, 1984], Functional Analysis Interview Format [O'Neill, Horner, Albin, Storey, & Sprague, 1990])
      2. Checklists/rating scales (e.g., Motivation Assessment Scale [Durand, 1988])
      3. Direct observation (e.g., A-B-C [S-R-C] Analysis; Functional Analysis Observation Form [O'Neill, Horner, Albin, Storey, & Sprague, 1990], Scatterplots [Touchette, MacDonald, & Langer, 1985], Anecdotal Records, Behavior Maps [Ittelson, Rivlin, & Proschansky, 1976], Communicative Functions Analysis)
   D. Communication repertoire assessment
   E. Learning characteristics assessment
5. Analyze results of assessments.
   A. Generate hypotheses regarding function(s) of behavior(s) or behavior class(es) in reference to:
      1. Ecological variables
      2. Setting events

(continued)

Table 1. (continued)

---

      3. Immediate antecedents and maintaining consequences
      4. Potential competing behavior(s)/functional equivalents
      5. Communication repertoire and communicative functions
      6. Quality of life
   B. Construct a competing behavior analysis
   C. Conduct functional analysis manipulations to test hypotheses (if necessary)
      1. Antecedent/consequence manipulations
6. Articulate new and ongoing questions and strategies for continued assessment.
7. Design hypotheses-driven comprehensive behavioral support plan.
   A. Lifestyle Enhancement II (same categories as I, but specific to assessment/hypotheses)
   B. Setting and immediate antecedent modifications (e.g., alter antecedents/triggers, remove environmental pollutants, alter grouping arrangements)
   C. Changes in curriculum and instruction strategies (e.g., clarify expectations, meaningful tasks, task difficulty, variation, length, predictability, instructional strategies matched to learner characteristics)
   D. Functional equivalence training/instructional programs
   E. Communication, social skills instruction
   F. General skill-building across skill areas
   G. Positive Procedures II (e.g., DRO, DRL, stimulus control)
   H. Self-regulatory strategies
   I. Emergency management procedures
8. Outcomes of support plan implementation and evaluation criteria
   A. Improvements in quality of life
   B. Effectiveness of instruction
      1. Functional equivalents developed or increased
      2. General skills developed or increased
      3. Communication and social skills developed or increased
   C. Basic health and safety improved (e.g., decreases in visits to emergency room, decreases in SIB)
   D. Target behavior(s) reduced or eliminated (and replaced)
9. Establish process and schedule for ongoing positive behavioral support.
   A. Team of friends, co-workers, family members, and service providers
   B. Long-term goals/personal future plans
   C. Evaluation of effects of intervention and subsequent adjustments
   D. Evaluation of lifestyle, social networks, personal preferences, and process for facilitating changes over time
   E. Mechanism for cycling back through the functional assessment intervention process as new behavior, needs, or situations arise

---

From Anderson, J.L., Albin, R.W., Mesaros, R.A., Dunlap, G., & Morelli-Robbins, M. (1993). Issues in providing training to achieve comprehensive behavioral support. In J. Reichle & D.P. Wacker (Eds.), *Communication and language intervention: Vol. 3. Communicative alternatives to challenging behavior: Integrating functional assessment and intervention strategies* (pp. 363–406). Baltimore: Paul H. Brookes Publishing Co.; reprinted by permission.

SIB, self-injurious behavior.

---

plan. The first steps are covered during the first training sessions, and by the end of the 4- to 6-month sequence the full plan has been constructed along with a prescription for maintaining support activities. Depending upon the particular needs and characteristics of the focus individual, there may be overlap and variation in the sequencing. Furthermore, some elements, such as assessment, are ongoing and dynamic aspects of behavioral support. Although the introduction of formal assessment procedures occurs at a particular point in the progression, the general linkage between assessment and intervention is a crucial and continuous feature of optimal support programs. Nevertheless, the general configuration shown in Table 1 has been demonstrated to be a useful and effective approach.

Case Study Team for "Kathy S."

The elaboration of this team training process is aided by describing the case of "Kathy S.," a woman who participated as a focus individual during community training in the state of Virginia (see Case Study 20.1A and 20.1B). Virginia joined the national training project in 1989 and, since then, has conducted thorough training in numerous localities. People with severe disabilities, traumatic brain injury, and challenging behaviors have benefited. The training in Virginia typically spans more than 6 months and is generally presented in four 2-day blocks of lecture, discussion, and practice. These sessions are interspersed with extensive experiential training in typical environments inhabited by the focus individuals. Kathy was one of five focus individuals who participated in positive behavioral support training that was conducted in a typical Virginia community in 1992.

Introductory Training Sessions

The first few sessions of training provide an overview of the broad enterprise of behavioral support, including fundamental values and philosophical perspectives on community living, inclusion, personal dignity, and the expanding options and technologies that are available for behavioral support. Discussion focuses on meaningful outcomes for support recipients (including focus individuals) and how such outcomes must include the achievement of new competencies and improved relationships as well as reductions in challenging behavior (Meyer & Evans, 1993; Meyer & Janney, 1989). The topic of Personal Futures Planning is also addressed (see Chapter 19 for further information).

The case study process begins with a global look at the lives of the focus individuals, the issues they are facing, and the quality of their lives on a day-to-day basis. Instruments and cue questions are provided for teams to begin to examine quality-of-life indicators. The topic of Personal Futures Planning is introduced, and the planning process is initiated.

The trainers then tie the quality-of-life perspective to the area of behavioral intervention, emphasizing that lifestyle enhancement is a major component of the values driving the overall positive behavioral support model (Turnbull & Turnbull, 1990). It is noted that this perspective can indicate specific lifestyle changes that can directly impact the occurrence of challenging behavior. Given this emphasis on overall lifestyle change, the

Case Study 20.1A.   Kathy

Kathy is a middle-age African American woman who volunteers at a nursery and garden store and spends her free time swimming, bowling, and visiting her family and friends. Kathy has lived with the same woman for the past year since she moved out of her mother's home. When positive behavioral support training began, Kathy was 35 years old and had lived with her mother all of her life, except for three separate periods of time. Twice she went to a state institution for persons with developmental disabilities, where she stayed less than 1 year, and once she lived in a state mental health facility for approximately 1 year. She had been diagnosed with severe mental retardation and a history of grand mal seizures, and she had been labeled as a person with challenging behavior for most of her adult life.

Kathy had been the recipient of most community and residential services available. However, most of these services were center based, provided in segregated settings. Available records showed that she completed a special education program in a segregated school at the age of 22 and then attended a prevocational program, only to be dismissed due to "persistent behavioral problems." At the time that she became a participant in the training, Kathy was receiving no services.

Kathy became a focus individual because of her continuing need for behavioral intervention and the lack of support across service systems to include her in community programs. Her case study team comprised her mother, her case manager, a family case coordinator, a member of the respite services agency, and a staff person from a day support program. Some of the participants were individuals who knew Kathy prior to training, and the remaining participants were interested in the replication effort within their own agencies.

Kathy's mother had requested assistance in seeking alternative living arrangements for Kathy. However, she had increasing ambivalence about an out-of-home residence, even though she herself was physically unable to care for Kathy and was becoming more fearful of Kathy's difficult behaviors. She was also afraid if she did not plan for Kathy soon, Kathy would be placed in an institution.

focus narrows to the identification of specific target behaviors of concern and the collection of baseline data.

Initial Assessment and Intervention Activities

Assessment is described to team members as a dynamic process, and beginning strategies for gathering and synthesizing observational data are presented. Initial interventions start shortly after the beginning of training, concurrent with these initial assessment activities. Initial interventions typically occur in the areas of lifestyle enhancement; positive reinforcement; and, where necessary, crisis intervention. Immediate changes to enhance quality of life might include increased time in inclusive settings, supported interactions with typical peers, and increased opportunities for choice and control of one's daily activities. Initial assessment and intervention activities for Kathy S. are described in Case Study 20.1B.

Developing a Comprehensive Behavioral Support Plan

The next several sessions of training are devoted to increasingly systematic assessment procedures and a more specific delineation of intervention strategies. Functional assessment of identified target behaviors is a major topic. Case study team members utilize interview and observation techniques to examine the target behaviors across contexts and to determine the communicative functions(s) and stimulus parameters that govern the behaviors' occurrence. The ecological or environmental systems operating in the contexts where the focus individual is spending his or her time are also examined. Assessment activities are further expanded to evaluate the individual's preferences, strengths, and overall behavioral and communicative repertoire. These assessments are vital for developing effective, comprehensive support plans that include instructional components as well as lifestyle adjustments. Assessment data are analyzed and hypotheses are generated in an ongoing effort to gain understanding of the focus individual and the relationship between the individual's behavior and the environment (Carr, Robinson, & Palumbo, 1990). The hypotheses are tested and modified if necessary (Dunlap & Kern, 1993).

The training proceeds to link assessment results explicitly and logically to available interventions (Horner, O'Neill, & Flannery, 1993). For example, participants learn that the results of a functional analysis should determine the kinds of communicative behaviors to be taught and the circumstances in which to teach them (Carr et al., 1994). Similarly, assessments of preferences and idiosyncratic responding to difficult activities should help support providers create individualized, meaningful curric-

Case Study 20.1B.   Kathy

At the onset of positive behavioral support training, Kathy was not involved in any services provided by the local community services board. Most of the community services systems felt she would not benefit from their programs because of her challenging behaviors. She was not employed, did not have any friends or meaningful social contacts outside of sporadic family visits, and did not participate in any community events or activities. She rarely traveled outside of her home for any reason other than appointments to her physician. She spent her days with her mother, either watching television, doing puzzles, or pacing through the house. The community services staff felt there were no options left for Kathy and that she would run the risk of being placed in an institution if her mother became ill.

Kathy communicated with gestures such as hair pulling, hitting, walking away, and pacing. She did not use her voice, other than to moan or scream. The behaviors that were of concern at the onset of training were hitting others (with a closed or open fist), pacing, refusing to take medications, and bed-wetting. Existing reports provided negligible information regarding these behaviors, and it appeared as if strategies that had been attempted had been short-lived. During Kathy's most distressed periods, she had been hospitalized or terminated from the program in which she was involved.

One of the objectives of the first 2 days of training was to explore and use the strategies of person-centered planning. Using the person-centered planning and quality-of-life assessments, the case study team met with Kathy for over 2 hours. Kathy's mother and her case manager did not think Kathy would remain cooperative through this planning process; however, Kathy stayed in the room during the entire session, and she appeared to be interested and used gestures to indicate her pleasure with the discussion. She consistently nodded in agreement when the team talked with her about moving into another home and developing opportunities to work.

One outcome of this initial planning and evaluation process was to make minor adjustments to Kathy's schedule. For example, Kathy was reluctant to have her hair combed by anyone, including herself. Combing her hair always resulted in Kathy hitting her

(continued)

Case Study 20.1B (*continued*)

mother or anyone else who tried. Her mother avoided this interaction by cutting her hair close to her scalp. The team noted that her hair was unusually short and probably identified her as being different. In addition, they noticed that Kathy spent a lot of time looking in the mirror. The team decided to let Kathy's hair grow out and to use a new, in-home staff person to work on combing her hair. The new staff person began to use conditioner to massage into Kathy's hair. The first few days, Kathy did not allow her hair to be touched. However, within 3 weeks, Kathy was combing her own hair and did not refuse to have her hair washed. At this same early time in the training, another member of the team took Kathy to the mall to purchase new clothes. She spent even more time looking in the mirror wearing her new clothes, and her rate of hitting declined.

A different team member took particular interest in Kathy. Because this team member worked in the capacity of providing services and coordination for adult foster care programs, she wanted to know Kathy better. She took Kathy into the community on a weekly basis. These trips were positive experiences and never included any incidents of hitting or other challenging behaviors. Kathy enjoyed going to the mall, purchasing new clothes (she had never selected her own clothing before), eating in restaurants, and walking in the community.

ula and activity schedules (Dunlap & Kern, 1993). Assessments of relationships and environments are used to identify potential problems and deficiencies in a person's lifestyle. The training illustrates how these data should be tied to alterations in the person's social networks and home and community routines.

The aggregation of thorough assessment data, linked to a growing array of intervention options, comes together in the form of a multi-element, hypothesis-driven comprehensive behavioral support plan for each focus individual. This phase of the training requires considerable lecture and discussion for each of the components noted in Table 1 (and described more completely in Anderson et al., 1993).

Comprehensive behavioral support plans are based on individualized assessment data, and they may or may not include all of the various elements that are presented in training. However, most plans include modifications pertaining to curriculum and instruction in order to create a more positive learning environment. Indeed, a characteristic of effective behavioral support plans is that they focus on skill building (as opposed to behavior reduction). In particular, specific instruction is typically designed to teach replacement skills that are functionally equivalent to target behavior. Self-regulatory techniques and strategies designed to help the focus individual cope with unpredictable and unpleasant events are also important components of many intervention packages. Some plans benefit from explicit descriptions of positive reinforcement techniques, and others necessarily include prescribed steps for managing emergency situations in which the target behavior becomes unacceptably disruptive or dangerous.

Comprehensive behavioral support plans will be inadequate if they do not confront basic quality-of-life concerns. Therefore, the training provides frequent review of these central themes that guide the whole process of behavioral support. In particular, teams are reminded to maintain a focus on the broad, quality-of-life outcomes that are the goals of the process and to direct their support plans toward these essential outcomes. The development of a comprehensive behavioral support plan for Kathy S. is described in Case Study 20.1C.

Producing Meaningful and Durable Change

Although the concluding training sessions have less new content pertaining to behavioral support interventions, they are indispensable for producing meaningful and durable change in the communities and in the lives of the focus individuals. As the various components of the behavioral support plan are defined and implemented, training activities center around evaluating their impact. Teams work together to make data-based modifications and to expand the impact and scope of each aspect of the comprehensive support plan. Evaluation efforts carefully examine the improvements in quality of life for the focus individual and the effectiveness of instruction in developing functionally equivalent behaviors and expanded communication or social skills (Meyer & Evans, 1993). The impact on the reduction or elimination of target behaviors is also examined, with particular attention to improved health and safety for those focus individuals whose target behaviors have resulted in injury to themselves or others.

As the training progresses, increasing emphasis is given to the establishment of a mechanism for the positive behavioral support plans to be implemented over time. A theme running throughout the training process relates to the continuation and expansion of positive behavioral supports well after the end of the formal training process. Case study teams are encouraged to commit to continued, collaborative support of their focus individuals and to establish a mechanism for conducting additional assessments and interventions as the need arises. Personal Futures

Case Study 20.1C.   Kathy

Functional assessments of Kathy's aggression were completed using the Motivational Assessment Scale (Durand, 1988), A-B-C charts, scatterplots (Touchette, MacDonald, & Langer, 1985), and other methods for recording direct observations (see O'Neill, Horner, Albin, Storey, & Sprague, 1990). These efforts revealed a great deal of information and showed that some previous assumptions (e.g., that hitting was performed for attention) were incorrect. The results of these assessments suggested that Kathy resorted to hitting (open palm slapping) after numerous attempts by her to communicate a message had been unsuccessful and when her requests were ignored. Hitting also occurred when she was refusing to participate or when she wished to end an activity. When Kathy wished to escape, she would often get up and leave the area and begin to pace. If participation was then forced, she would hit the person or anyone else within proximity. It was hypothesized that Kathy used these physical means (i.e., pacing, pulling, walking away, hitting) to get her point across because she was nonverbal and had no alternative means of communicating effectively. Her preferences were displayed by being engaged in an event or activity. Boredom or displeasure was communicated by hitting, pacing, and pulling.

These assessment data were tied to intervention in the area of communication. The team quickly designed communication cards based on her known preferences and encouraged her to use these cards to communicate desired objects and activities. In addition, the team began to teach her to sign for "stop" as an alternative to hitting, and prompted her to control her environment with this symbol whenever she was in an unpleasant circumstance.

The time that Kathy had begun to spend in the community provided not only enjoyment and valuable new learning experiences, it also furnished a good deal of information regarding those situations that were associated with positive, as opposed to problematic, behavior. Some of the events and situations that were associated with problems included Kathy's forced participation in activities that she disliked, crowds and noisy environments, and people standing or sitting too close to her. Trips to the mall that occurred early in the day were free of problems because that was when the mall was the

(continued)

Case Study 20.1C (*continued*)

least crowded. However, when the trips occurred later in the day, and significant crowds were present, Kathy engaged in disruptive behavior. It also became clear that Kathy preferred to eat her meals in quieter restaurants as opposed to fast food places. As the team introduced new experiences, data were collected on the circumstances that were associated with successful outcomes and those that were associated with difficulties. In this way, the team gained an improved understanding of antecedent variables and was able to incorporate into Kathy's plan a number of strategies for preventing challenging behavior in public places.

As the team sought reasonable recreational outlets, it learned that Kathy excelled in any form of gross motor activities. She had outstanding athletic abilities, such as running, throwing, and catching balls. However, opportunities for participation in recreational activities had not been available to her due to her history of behavior problems. Since the team discovered she was reluctant to interact in crowded and noisy situations, it felt that Kathy's enrollment in traditional group sporting activities would not be advantageous at this time. Instead the team pursued the development of individual activities that would build her confidence and skills, such as swimming.

As the assessment and intervention strategies were being developed, after approximately 3 months of training, Kathy moved from her mother's home to live with a woman her age in a family care program. Prior to the move, the team worked closely with Kathy and her mother to ensure a smooth transition. At this point, the team had information about effective strategies for preventing the most challenging behaviors. For example, Kathy enjoyed looking at magazines, working on puzzles, listening and dancing to music, riding in the car, and watching reruns of 1950s situation comedies on television. Some successful strategies included watching television shows while combing her hair, brushing her teeth while the radio was playing, and reading a magazine while she was standing in line at a store. Team members also worked with the staff at a day program for supporting individuals in integrated community settings, which Kathy started after 2 months of training, to develop natural opportunities to visit her new home. They involved

(*continued*)

Case Study 20.1C (*continued*)

the woman she would be living with, Leanne, in Kathy's schedule. Part of Leanne's involvement with Kathy would include training in personal care, communication, leisure, safety, and personal living. This training also was incorporated in her day program. All of these programs were developed, implemented, and evaluated as a result of the team process created by the training.

The use of the Positive Environment Checklist (Albin, Horner, & O'Neill, 1993) quickly revealed that Kathy did not have personal belongings that a person her age would have if he or she lived in the same environment. She did not own many items other than ones used for personal hygiene. Most items in the house were "off limits" to her. The team and family members celebrated her move to a new home by taking Kathy shopping to purchase things she would want and need to furnish her new home.

The relationship map (Mount & Zwernick, 1987) added substantial information pertaining to key quality-of-life issues. Among other insights, this tool made it clear that Kathy did not have any friends. The move to a new home and the day support program offered new and natural opportunities to develop friendships. With the team's support, efforts were undertaken to increase community contact with familiar people, to engage in trips to the store, and to make social calls and other outings.

Plans (see Chapter 19 for more information) are revisited and specific long-range goals are identified. Action plans are then developed that include possible strategies for overcoming identified barriers to achieving the goals.

There are often similarities in the goals and barriers encountered by focus individuals, particularly where changes are required in the nature, flexibility, and location of services provided by community, education, and human services agencies. In the latter training sessions, all training participants collaborate to identify common barriers and resources. Additional members of the local communities and agencies from which focus team members were drawn (e.g., agency administrators, politicians, media, representatives from nearby schools and agencies that had not participated in the training) are then invited to the final training session so that they can learn more about successful positive behavioral supports as the teams present their case studies. These community members then partic-

...stems changes that will further increase the capac-
... provide effective positive behavioral support in
...ie outcomes of Kathy S.'s behavioral support plan are
...se Study 20.1D.

Case Study 20.1D. Kathy

At the end of the 9 months of training, Kathy was living in a home
with Leanne, a woman her own age. This living arrangement was
funded through an adult foster care program. Even though Kathy
and Leanne's relationship was formulated as one between a client
and a paid provider, the two women also became good friends.
Leanne began to include Kathy in her family gatherings. Kathy
maintained close contact with her mother and included Leanne in
her regular family visits, to the extent that she and Leanne became a
source of social support for Kathy's mother. The two households
arranged to coordinate their schedules for more joint activities, including dinner at least once each week.

Kathy's hitting was reduced to one incident per month. An additional result from ongoing functional assessments revealed that
some of the behaviors occurred prior to the onset of seizures.
Shortly after the training ended, Kathy was hospitalized for a 24-
hour period because of continuous seizure activity. One concern
that the team continued to address was Kathy's periodic refusal to
take her anticonvulsant medications. A strategy that it investigated
was for the two housemates to take their pills (Kathy, anticonvul-
sants; Leanne, vitamins) simultaneously at meals; however, the resolution was undetermined at the time of this writing.

The communication cards (photographs of household items,
pictures of team members, places Kathy visits, family members,
friends, etc.) that were prepared by the team were used with increasing frequency. Kathy also learned to use signs to express two
requests: "go to the bathroom" and "stop." Within 2 weeks of learning these two signs and the use of the communication pictures,
Kathy was selecting where she wanted to go and whom she wanted
to visit. By the end of the training, Kathy's pacing rarely occurred,
and she had wet the bed only once. For the first time, Kathy began
to make vocalizations that sounded as if she was forming words.

(continued)

Case Study 20.1D *(continued)*

Prior to the team training, the participating agencies and the participants did not have a history of successful collaboration. Kathy's mother had been frustrated with and disappointed in the services. The case manager was not successful in developing training and support opportunities within the existing community services, despite her perseverance and creativity. Kathy's behavior and her reputation were effective at inhibiting the provision of new supports and services in her life. However, over the course of the team training process, this team became cohesive and functional. The team members became so committed in their support of Kathy that, even after the formalized training was completed, they continued to meet and provide support.

At the time of this writing, the team that was created during the training period continues to meet every 3 or 4 months. It has expanded its membership to include Kathy's speech therapist and one of her new neighbors. Most recently, with the team's support, Kathy began work at the corner grocery store for 4 hours each week straightening the shelves.

CONCLUSIONS

The training process described in this chapter has proven to be an effective vehicle for establishing collaborative teamwork and for developing effective, comprehensive behavioral supports for individuals within a community. These supports result in significant improvements in the individual's ability to participate in inclusive environments, along with corresponding improvements in the ability of the community to provide support that is effective and flexible enough to be responsive to individual needs and preferences. In addition, the training results in the local expertise necessary to apply the positive behavioral support technology with these focus individuals over time and to expand to other individuals in the community (Anderson et al., 1993).

REFERENCES

Albin, R.W., Horner, R.H., & O'Neill, R.E. (1993). *Proactive behavioral support: Structuring and assessment environments.* Unpublished manuscript, University of Oregon, Specialized Training Program, Eugene.

V., Mesaros, R.A., Dunlap, G., & Morelli-Robbins, M.
g training to achieve comprehensive behavioral sup-
.r. Wacker (Eds.), *Communicative alternatives to challenging*
functional assessment and intervention strategies (pp. 363–406).
.ı H. Brookes Publishing Co.

.L., Mesaros, R.A., & Neary, T. (1991). *Community referenced nonaversive*
.ɔr management trainers manual (Vol. 1). Washington, DC: National Institute
.ı Disability and Rehabilitation Research.

Baumgart, D., & Ferguson, D. (1991). Personnel preparation: Directions for the next decade. In L.H. Meyer, C.A. Peck, & L. Brown (Eds.), *Critical issues in the lives of people with severe disabilities* (pp. 313–352). Baltimore: Paul H. Brookes Publishing Co.

Carr, E.G., Levin, L., McConnachie, G., Carlson, J.I., Kemp, D.C., & Smith, C.E. (1994). *Communication-based intervention for problem behavior: A user's guide for producing positive change.* Baltimore: Paul H. Brookes Publishing Co.

Carr, E.G., Robinson, S., & Palumbo, L.W. (1990). The wrong issue: Aversive versus nonaversive treatment. The right issue: Functional versus nonfunctional treatment. In A. Repp & N. Singh (Eds.), *Perspectives on the use of nonaversive and aversive interventions for persons with developmental disabilities* (pp. 361–379). Pacific Grove, CA: Brooks/Cole.

Chalfant, J.C., Pysch, M.V., & Moultrie, R. (1979). Teacher assistance teams: A model for within-building problem solving. *Learning Disabilities Quarterly, 2,* 85–96.

Demchak, M.A., & Browder, D.M. (1990). An evaluation of the pyramid model of staff training in group homes for adults with severe handicaps. *Education and Training in Mental Retardation, 25,* 150–163.

Dunlap, G., & Kern, L. (1993). Assessment and intervention for children within the instructional curriculum. In J. Reichle & D.P. Wacker (Eds.), *Communicative alternatives to challenging behavior: Integrating functional assessment and intervention strategies* (pp. 177–203). Baltimore: Paul H. Brookes Publishing Co.

Dunlap, G., Robbins, F.R., Morelli, M.A., & Dollman, C. (1988). Team training for young children with autism: A regional model for service delivery. *Journal of the Division for Early Childhood, 12,* 147–160.

Durand, V.M. (1988). Motivation assessment scale. In M. Herson & A. Bellack (Eds.), *Dictionary of behavioral assessment techniques* (pp. 309–310). Elmsford, NY: Pergamon.

Education for All Handicapped Children Act of 1975, PL 94-142. (August 23, 1977). Title 20, U.S.C. 1401 et seq: *U.S. Statutes at Large, 89,* 773–796.

Federal Register (Vol. 42, pp. 42474-42515). (1977, August 23). Washington, DC: U.S. Government Printing Office.

Foster-Johnson, L., Ferro, J., & Dunlap, G. (1991, November). *Do curricular activities contribute to problem behavior in the classroom?* Paper presented at the 36th Annual Meeting of the Florida Educational Research Association, Clearwater.

Halpern, A.S. (1985). Transition: A look at the foundations. *Exceptional Children, 57,* 479–486.

Hasazi, S.B. (1985). Facilitating transition from high school: Policies and practices. *American Rehabilitation, 11,* 9–16.

Horner, R.H., Dunlap, G., Koegel, R.L., Carr, E.G., Sailor, W., Anderson, J., Albin, R.W., & O'Neill, R.E. (1990). Toward a technology of "nonaversive" behavioral support. *Journal of The Association for Persons with Severe Handicaps, 15,* 125–132.

Horner, R.H., O'Neill, R.E., & Flannery, K.B. (1993). Building effective beh. support plans from functional assessment information. In M. Snell *Instruction of students with severe disabilities* (4th ed., pp. 184–214). Columbus, O. Charles E. Merrill.

Ittelson, W.H., Rivlin, L.G., & Proschansky, H.M. (1976). The use of behavioral maps in environmental psychology. In H.M. Proschansky, W.H. Ittelson, & L.G. Rivlin (Eds.), *Environmental psychology: People and their physical setting*. New York: Holt, Rinehart & Winston.

Jones, F.H., Fremouw, W., & Carples, S. (1977). Pyramid training of elementary school teachers to use a classroom management package. *Journal of Applied Behavior Analysis, 10*, 239–253.

Joyce, B., & Showers, B. (1980). Improving inservice training: The age of research. *Educational Leadership, 37*, 379–385.

Joyce, B., & Showers, B. (1982, November). The coaching of teaching. *Educational Leadership, 4–7*.

Kennedy, C.H., Horner, R.H., & Newton, J.S. (1990). The social networks and activity patterns of adults with severe disabilities: A correctional analysis. *Journal of The Association for Persons with Severe Handicaps, 15*, 86–90.

Kennedy, C.H., Horner, R.H., Newton, J.S., & Kanda, E. (1990). Measuring the activity patterns of adults with severe disabilities using the Resident Lifestyle Inventory. *Journal of The Association for Persons with Severe Handicaps, 15*, 79–85.

Meyer, L.H., Eichinger, J., & Park-Lee, S. (1987). A validation of program quality indicators in educational services for students with severe disabilities. *Journal of The Association for Persons with Severe Handicaps, 12*, 251–263.

Meyer, L.H., & Evans, I.M. (1989). *Nonaversive intervention for behavior problems: A manual for home and community*. Baltimore: Paul H. Brookes Publishing Co.

Meyer, L.H., & Evans, I.M. (1993). Meaningful outcomes in behavioral intervention. In J. Reichle & D.P. Wacker (Eds.), *Communicative alternatives to challenging behavior: Integrating functional assessment and intervention strategies* (pp. 407–428). Baltimore: Paul H. Brookes Publishing Co.

Meyer, L.H., & Janney, R.E. (1989). User-friendly measures of meaningful outcomes: Evaluating behavioral interventions. *Journal of The Association for Persons with Severe Handicaps, 14*, 263–270.

Mount, B., & Zwernick, K. (1987). *It's never too early, it's never too late*. St. Paul, MN: Metropolitan Council.

O'Brien, J., & Lyle, C. (1987). *Framework for accomplishment*. Decatur, GA: Responsive Systems Associates.

O'Neill, R.E., Horner, R.H., Albin, R.W., Storey, K., & Sprague, J.R. (1990). *Functional analysis of problem behavior: A practical assessment guide*. Sycamore, IL: Sycamore Publishing Co.

Page, T.J., Iwata, B.A., & Reid, D.H. (1982). Pyramidal training: A large-scale application with institution staff. *Journal of Applied Behavior Analysis, 15*, 335–351.

Peck, C.A., Killen, C.C., & Baumgart, D. (1989). Increasing implementation of special education instruction in mainstream preschools: Direct and generalized effects of nondirective consultation. *Journal of Applied Behavior Analysis, 22*, 197–210.

Racino, J.A. (1990). Preparing personnel to work in community support services. In A.P. Kaiser & S.M. McWhorter (Eds.), *Preparing personnel to work with persons with severe disabilities (pp. 203–226)*. Baltimore: Paul H. Brookes Publishing Co.

Schuler, A.L., Peck, C.A., Tomlinson, C.D., & Theimer, R.K. (1984). Communication interview. In C.A. Peck, A.L. Schuler, C. Tomlinson, R.K. Theimer, T. Har-

.), *The social competence curriculum project: A guide to* for social and communicative interactions (pp. 43–52). ...ity of California-Santa Barbara.

...uilding our capacity to meet the needs of persons with severe .roblems and proposed solutions. In A.P. Kaiser & C.M. .er (Eds.), *Preparing personnel to work with persons with severe disabilities* —23). Baltimore: Paul H. Brookes Publishing Co.

...nback, S., & Stainback, W. (1985). *Integration of students with severe handicaps into regular schools.* Reston, VA: Council for Exceptional Children.

Stainback, W., & Stainback, S. (1989). Practical organizational strategies. In S. Stainback, W. Stainback, & M. Forest (Eds.), *Educating all students in the mainstream of regular education* (pp. 71–87). Baltimore: Paul H. Brookes Publishing Co.

Sugai, G., & Horner, R.H. (1994). Including students with severe behavior problems in general education settings: Assumptions, challenges, and solutions. In J. Marr, G. Sugai, & G. Tindal (Eds.), *The Oregon Conference Monograph* (Vol. 6) (pp. 102–120). Eugene: University of Oregon.

Touchette, P.E., MacDonald, R.F., & Langer, S.N. (1985). A scatter plot for identifying stimulus control of problem behavior. *Journal of Applied Behavior Analysis, 18*, 343–351.

Turnbull, A.P., & Turnbull, H.R. (1990). A tale about lifestyle changes: Comments on "Toward a technology of 'nonaversive' behavioral support." *Journal of The Association for Persons with Severe Handicaps, 15*, 142–144.

Vandercook, T., & York, J. (1990). A team approach to program development and support. In W. Stainback & S. Stainback (Eds.), *Support networks for inclusive schooling: Interdependent integrated education* (pp. 95–122). Baltimore: Paul H. Brookes Publishing Co.

Vandercook, T., York, J., & Forest, M. (1989). The McGill Action Planning System (MAPS): A strategy for building the vision. *Journal of The Association for Persons with Severe Handicaps, 14*, 202–215.

Wehman, P., Kregel, J., & Barcus, J.M. (1985). From school to work: A vocational transition model for handicapped students. *Exceptional Children, 52*, 25–37.

Wehman, P., Moon, M.S., Everson, J.M., Wood, W., & Barcus, J.M. (1988). *Transition from school to work: New challenges for youth with severe disabilities.* Baltimore: Paul H. Brookes Publishing Co.

Discussion

Gail McGee

As part of my predoctoral internship in a state hospital, I did a rotation on a unit for young men with chronic schizophrenia. They spent their days rocking on the porch, and, although most had town passes, they rarely ventured off hospital grounds. I eagerly set up a behavioral point system to get them moving around in the community, but after several days the defeat was apparent. At a morning group "therapy" session, I confronted the young men on their failure to acquire any community outing points. Their response: "Restaurants, storekeepers, the movie ushers [etc.] don't want us around because we're from the hospital." My response: "So how do they know you're from the hospital?" Somewhat incredulous at my naivete, they pointed to the hospital-issued maroon socks on their feet. This immediate problem was easy to fix by sending a delegation to Woolworth to purchase all different colors of socks. But as proponents of community inclusion have come to find out, lasting solutions to the problem of acceptance for persons with challenging behaviors are much more complex. I wish that these insightful chapters had been available to me at that time, so that I could believe that those now middle-age men are not still rocking on the hospital porch.

An overriding theme of this last collection of chapters is that the goal of community inclusion is to improve the quality of life of persons with challenging behaviors. The implication is that strategies for improving quality of life may more effectively reduce challenging behaviors than the traditional treatment approach of behavior reduction in isolation of lifestyle changes.

Risley (Chapter 18) proposes that behavior analysis has always been concerned with quality of life, and indeed Wolf (1978) gave us an early classic on "how behavior analysis is finding its heart" (p. 203). Perhaps behavior analysis began on the right track, but, if so, the journey has certainly taken a long time. It is true that the field of applied behavior analysis has always had a goal of helping to improve the situation of problem behaviors, but sometimes the "situations" may have been the cause of the problem behaviors. Too often, the real goal has been to make matters better for treatment staff, not the person with disabilities, and the result has been a cycle of problems that continues no matter how fancy the fix.

As investigators have sought to design "quality" living environments for persons with disabilities, there has historically been too little attention paid to *whose* standards are used in establishing these "quality" environments. Presumably, most of us would behave poorly if forced to live in someone else's ideal environment. Throughout each of these chapters, whose focus ranges from the conceptual to the how-to to the technical, there is a fundamental emphasis on the individual. Personal preferences, choices, and hardships are carefully considered in the design of improved lifestyles.

Thankfully, these authors have not thrown out the baby with the bath water. All recognize the key contributions to be played by behavior analysis in obtaining truly improved quality of life for individuals with disabilities. Each acknowledges the sometimes necessary role of functional analysis in reducing problem behaviors. The importance of plans for ongoing support and maintenance is also emphasized in life planning.

The pivotal role of continuing development or learning receives either implicit or explicit attention in each chapter. To be truly honest, proponents of inclusion must acknowledge that some individuals with disabilities do not identify community inclusion as a top preference in their lives. The demands of social interaction may be nonappealing, if not outright aversive, for those with social deficits. However, the prevailing need for an individual to have opportunities for development dictates that inclusive environments be considered in life planning. Moreover, inclusive environments are most conducive to providing other critical features of a high quality of life (choices in activities, scheduling, etc.). Comprehensive, developmental life planning must reconcile those aspects of community living that pose hardships, and these must be dealt with systematically.

Horner and colleagues (Chapter 16) and Carr and colleagues (Chapter 17) address the issue of community inclusion at the technical level, offering new perspectives that go beyond traditional functional analysis of problem behaviors. Horner, Vaughn, Day, and Ard (Chapter 16) introduce the concept of setting events with examples that will translate easily to the experience of teachers and service providers. They articulate a model for integrating setting events into our understanding of problem behaviors, along with clear illustrations that explain why a person may behave in a seemingly "unpredictable" manner. An impressively large-scope study highlights the relationship of setting events (e.g., pain, aversive events, staff or schedule changes, fatigue) to the problem behaviors of 13 of 15 adolescents and adults with disabilities. Most useful, Horner and colleagues outline an innovative model for manipulating setting events as part of multielement interventions for problem behaviors. This chapter should prove helpful to practitioners and life planners, as well as provide an impetus to needed research.

Carr, Reeve, and Magito-McLaughlin (Chapter 17) take an historical perspective on the need to more carefully consider the antecedents of problem behavior, ultimately concluding with experimental analyses that surely would have pleased Skinner. It is proposed that setting events should be examined with respect to biological contexts, physical environment, and sociocultural issues. Also offered is a review of the literature in which setting events have been studied in persons with developmental disabilities. Interesting examples of experimental analyses of the effects of menses, mood, and communicative interpretability are provided to buttress the call for systematic study of contextual influences on problem behavior.

Horner and colleagues and Carr and colleagues give slightly different technical interpretations of setting events, the former placing emphasis on change to the value of reinforcers or punishers, and the latter arguing that context alters the effect of the discriminative stimulus. Further research is needed to isolate the effects of particular setting events, but no doubt both conceptualizations will lead to improved interventions and improved quality of life for persons with behavior problems.

Risley (Chapter 18) outlines a continuum of strategies for dealing with challenging behavior, ranging from the micro-momentary (behavior analysis) to the common sense (contingency management) to the global level (life arrangement). He proposes that, while global lifestyle change may be the most efficacious level at which to intervene, professionals may require retraining to deal effectively at this level. There is a thoughtful acknowledgment of the revolutionary aspects of the laws that dictate individualized programming. The design of truly individualized plans makes it both necessary and possible to rearrange service delivery systems to provide radically new lives for persons with disabilities.

Risley's continuum for life coaching is further detailed by Kincaid in his chapter on person-centered planning (Chapter 19). Following an outline of the values inherent in planning better futures for persons with disabilities, Kincaid describes a very specific process for helping group planning teams arrive at an understanding of the person for whom they are planning, what the person needs and wants, and how to establish short- and long-term goals for the person's future. Practical tips are also offered for keeping the process of planning on track and productive.

Anderson, Russo, Albin, and Dunlap (Chapter 20) provide a description of an in-service team training project that targets system change as well as individual life planning. Assets of the process outlined are that training is comprehensive, multidisciplinary, and longitudinal. A state-of-the-art training curriculum includes the interspersal of information with supported application. Also important, a training of trainers model specifically plans for the spread of this technology across persons with disabilities and their support teams.

Risley, Kincaid, and Anderson and colleagues share agreement that the most crucial step in planning better lives for persons with disabilities involves the establishment of cooperation and collaboration among family members, service providers, participating agencies, and the focal person him- or herself. However, all of the authors recognize that, at least in some cases, more technical precision in dealing with challenging behaviors is indicated.

In sum, these chapters present ideas that are both provocative and practical. Together they suggest that now, at long last, behavior analysis is indeed finding its heart.

REFERENCES

Wolf, M.M. (1978). Social validity: The case for subjective measurement or how behavior analysis is finding its heart. *Journal of Applied Behavior Analysis, 11,* 203–214.

Index

Page numbers followed by "f" or "t" indicate tables or figures, respectively.

evaluation of, 270–274, 281
reform, 171, 193–196, 199
under inclusive education, 194–195
Speech acquisition, 335
Speech capability, language disorder
remediation and, 337
Speech intelligibility
analog training, 345
approaches, 339–340
vs. articulation, 334–335
defined, 334–335
disabilities and, 336–338
as goal of naturalistic language
intervention, 343–344
in inclusive environments, 345–347
as integrated part of language,
335–342
levels of, 334
linguistic components of, 339
vs. logopaedics, 334–335
motor disability components of,
339
naturalistic, 344–345
vs. phonology, 334–335
social skills and, 337
traditional intervention, 338–340
training, 334, 339, 345–347
Speech-language pathologists, 346
Speech-motor approaches, 339–340
Staff changes, problem behavior and,
390
Stereotypy, 413
Stimulus control, 73
adequacy of, 75
research in, 406–407
Stimulus equivalence paradigm, 407
Stimulus fading, 407
Stimulus generalization, 69, 72–76
Stimulus overselectivity, 355, 357–358
Stimulus shaping, 407
Stimulus-response sequences, 412
Stress
behavior support plan selection and,
87–88
parent education programs and, 23
Structural analysis, of problem
behavior, 56
Support environments
current status of, 298
defined, 289
factors affecting, 295

research recommendations, 299–301
social relationships and, 294–298
transitions among, 298
varieties of, 295–298
see also Emotional support;
Environment; Family support
Support groups
parent/school conflict resolution
through, 268–270
social, 44–45
Symbolic play
of children with autism, 358–367
defined, 358–359
language development and, 359
training examples, 362–363
training outcomes, 363
Syntactic complexity, 336
Systematic instruction, 40

Task variation, 412
Teachers
empowerment of, 187–189
in-service training for, 227–256
language intervention effectiveness,
152–155
language intervention training,
155–159
preschool social inclusion levels and,
329
preservice training for, 227–256
preservice training needs, 231–233
standards for, 188–189
Team training
at the local level, 471–474
collaborative approach, 471–474
curriculum, 474–487
member motivation, 247–248
member selection, 472–473
model, 467–487
see also Training
Technical assistance
evaluating, 250–253
fiscal commitment to, 243
involving parent advisory groups in,
249
needs, 230–231, 233–235
on-site, 249–250
team member motivations to
participate, 247–248
team member recruitment, 241–242
team member training, 243–245